# TWO PLANKS AND A PASSION

# Two Planks and a Passion

## *The Dramatic History of Skiing*

Roland Huntford

continuum

Continuum UK, The Tower Building, 11 York Road, London SE1 7NX
Continuum US, 80 Maiden Lane, Suite 704, New York, NY 10038

*www.continuumbooks.com*

First published 2008

British Library Cataloguing-in-Publication Data
A catalogue record for this book is available from the British Library.

ISBN 978-1-84725-236-4

Typeset by Pindar NZ, Auckland, New Zealand

*To my wife, Anita*

# Contents

# Maps and Illustrations

Frontispiece: Poster for the first drag lift in the world, Davos, 1934.

# *Preface*

The origins of this book lie in *Scott and Amundsen*, *Shackleton* and *Nansen*, my cycle of modern polar exploration, which culminated in the victory of Amundsen in the race for the South Pole in 1911. He owed his triumph to the ski and, to dispel the fog of history, I wanted to explain the reasons why.

Books, however, do not always turn out exactly as foreseen. Amundsen was not just a skier. At a deeper level, as a Norwegian, he issued from a culture that happened to include the ski. It was not enough. Other countries beckoned. The distant past loomed over the horizon. One thing led to another. Unexpected topics sprang up; climate change in particular.

These linked the present with the past. Skiers were among the first to sense the latest round of the climatic cycle, for it touched the very existence of their snow. Little Ice Age or global warming, they saw each as a natural phenomenon and adapted to its demands. In the end I found myself immersed in the whole history of skiing. This work is the result.

# Acknowledgements

In the long preparation of this book I have enjoyed much generous assistance. First, I must thank the President and Fellows of Wolfson College, Cambridge, Dr Gordon Johnson in particular. The resources of the University were essential to my work. I am grateful to the University Library, the library of the Faculty of Classics, and the Haddon Library of the Faculty of Archaeology and Anthropology, all inexhaustible scholarly havens in a sympathetic ambience. Even in a digital age, that counts for much. I owe a great deal to many willing helpers of whom I can only pick out a few by name. Mr Charles Aylmer, head of the Chinese section at the University Library, gave indispensable support in translating classical Chinese texts and tracking down arcane sources. Noburu Koyama, head of the Japanese section, was equally helpful in his field. Dr Marsha Levine, of the McDonald Institute for Archaeological Research generously shared her specialized knowledge to help me with the little-known Russian Bronze Age Abashevo culture.

I also wish to thank the long-suffering staff of the British Library in London. Mr Hamish Todd, head of the Japanese section, gave invaluable assistance.

Nick Lewis, Kelly Tyler and Ketil Reitan offered insights into modern polar adventuring. Arnie Wilson lent material on early skiing in America. I must also thank Sir Alistair Horne for continued encouragement. Susie Nixon has kept me on an even keel.

A good editor is an author's best friend, and in that spirit, I wish to thank my agent, Rivers Scott. He devoted much skill and patience to this book.

Norwegian sources were clearly central to my task. The Ski Museum at Holmenkollen in Oslo must be the prime repository of skiing lore, and I spent many a rewarding hour there. I particularly wish to thank Karin Berg, the Director and her assistant, Rune Flaten. They never failed to answer my sometimes frantic calls for help besides spontaneously offering unexpected and recondite material. I am also grateful to Leif Torgersen for generously sharing his knowledge of skiing history and his professional expertise in the physics of snow. To him and Karin Berg I must express my heartfelt thanks for reading through the manuscript and saving me many an egregious blunder thereby. Any faults remaining are my own.

Thanks are also due to the Norwegian National Library in Oslo, always a pleasure to visit. As usual, Oddvar Vasstveit and Sigbjørn Grindheim, of the Manuscript Department, helped beyond the call of duty.

A special vote of thanks goes to Odd Røstvig, formerly of the National Library. Mr Røstvig performed the Sisyphean task of combing the Norwegian press meticulously on my behalf. He turned up much unexpected material. Whole sections of this book depended on his work.

Rottefella A.S., the manufacturers in Oslo of the eponymous cross-country binding, uninhibitedly gave insights into the evolution of their products.

I particularly wish to thank Jan Christensen, my Norwegian translator and a good friend. He drove me round the country to historic skiing sites, and never once complained; even when in a hurry one day he incurred penalty points on his driving licence.

I want to thank Erik Klaveness and Olav and Kajsa Momyr for unstinting hospitality, which made the environs of Oslo a second home. In Oslo, thanks also go to Liv Arnesen, Thor Gotaas, Tor Guttu and Vigdis Ystad.

Next I must thank Elling Alsvik, of the Trøndelag Folkemuseum – the Trøndelag Museum of Cultural History – for great help in probing Russian history, and the Norwegian role in the introduction of skiing to Austria. Professor Helene B. Skjelbred, of the Norsk Folkemuseum – the Norwegian Museum of Cultural History – in Oslo, efficiently linked an episode in modern Norway with ancient Greece. Thanks also go to Steinar Sørensen, of the Glomdal Museum for much scholarly help.

The Norsk skieventyr museum and others in Morgedal cheerfully shared their patriotic devotion to Telemark as a historic source of modern Norwegian skiing.

In Stockholm, Marie-Anne Condé unstintingly shared her research into nineteenth-century and early twentieth-century Swedish skiing. Bertil Flodin was equally generous in helping with the Russo-Finnish Winter War of 1939–40. I thank Dr Michael Stevens, too. The hard-pressed and under-funded staff of the Nordiska Muséet – the Swedish Museum of Cultural History – gave willing and friendly assistance. The Royal Library – the Swedish national library – tracked down obscure but vital early Swedish books.

Also in Stockholm, Lennart and Gunilla Forsling strove to help, not least with earthy humour in moments of despair.

Leena Ruonavaara, of the National Board of Antiquities in Helsinki, patiently dealt with tortuous questions of Finnish archaeology. I much appreciate her help.

I must thank the Museum in Saas-Fee for help with the earliest history of skiing in Switzerland. The monks of St Bernard also did their best. The Glarus museum helped with the origins of skiing in eastern Switzerland; so too did the Schweizerische Maschinen Fabrik in Winterthur. In French-speaking Switzerland, Reuge SA of Ste-Croix in the Jura, took great pains to help with the history of the Kandahar binding.

I am greatly indebted to Dr Timothy Nelson, Director of the Dokumentations-bibliothek Davos. No request was too much trouble and he lightened stern endeavour with much laughter. His collections were essential to an understanding of the origins of Swiss skiing. Likewise, I wish to thank Corina Huber, Director of the Dokumentationsbibliothek St Moritz for much assistance. I also thank the staff of the library and archives of the International Olympic Committee in Lausanne for friendly assistance. In Geneva, Thomas Andréasson was indispensable.

The Director of the Wintersportmuseum in Mürzzuschlag, Hannes Nothnagl, unreservedly opened his archives, an essential resource for the early history of Austrian skiing. I thank him for his cheerful help, and also Barbara Habermann, his colleague. In another part of Austria, I am grateful to Gabriela Köck, of the Turismusverband in St Anton am Arlberg for quick and timely assistance.

I much appreciate the generosity of Nils Larsen in sharing his work on early skiing in the Altai Mountains of Central Asia.

In France, thanks are due to Baroness Nadine de Rothschild for helping with her family's rôle in developing Megève. I must also thank the unnamed official who, many years ago, wittily expounded General de Gaulle's policy for skiing and the Alps.

All this, however, pales before the debt I once more owe my wife, Anita, whom I found all those years ago in Stockholm and to whom this book is dedicated. When needed, she turned herself into an able research assistant, with an eye for the telling document. Without her this book simply could not have been written. Our sons Nicholas and Anthony also played their part.

# Note

Oslo, the capital of Norway, was known as Christiania (sometimes Kristiania) until 1924. The older form is used when the period demands it. Likewise St Petersburg alternates with Leningrad.

To be faithful to the original journals, and preserve the historical resonance, the measure of Polar travel is the nautical mile. This is one sixtieth of a degree, or one minute of latitude, and equivalent to 1 1/7 statute miles or 1.85 kilometres.

In the interests of clarity and simplicity, transliteration of Russian follows the pre-1978 Cambridge University Library system. With the exception of Chinese and Japanese, translations from languages other than English are the author's own.

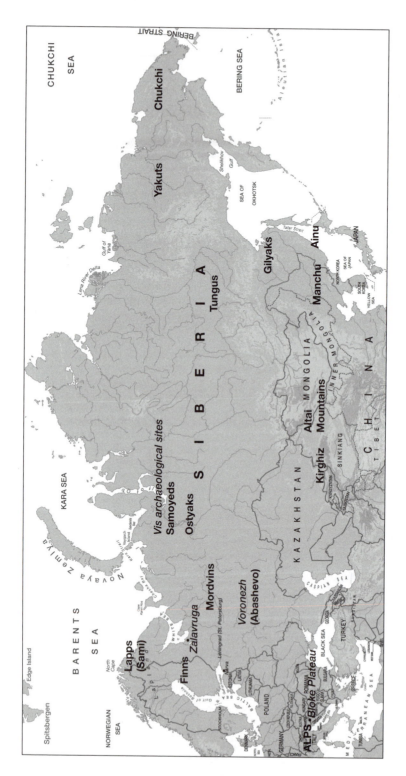

1. Eurasia.

Legend:
* Archeological site
● Place

BARENTS SEA

NORWEGIAN SEA

North Cape

Finnmark
Alta *
Nesseby ●

Tromsø ●

Cape Kanin N

NORWAY

L a p l a n d

Drevja *●
Kvikkjokk ●

SWEDEN

Torne district ●

Salla * ●

WHITE SEA

Kalvträsk *

Oulu ●

Suomussalmi ●

Hoting *●

FINLAND

Trondheim ●

Viitasaari *●

Gulf of Bothnia

Mantta *●

RUSSIA

Heinola *●

Trysil ●
Furnes *●
Bergen ●
Hardangervidda
Oslo(Christiania) ●
Telemark
STOCKHOLM ●
Kristiansand ●

Åland

Helsinki ●

Lake Ladoga

Karelian Isthmus
Leningrad (St. Petersburg)

Gulf of Finland

Narva ●

Skagerrak

Hiiumaa

ESTONIA

Gotland

Saaremaa

G. of Riga

Kattegat

LATVIA

Oland

DENMARK

BALTIC SEA

LITHUANIA

NORTH SEA

Bornholm

G. of Gdansk

RUSSIAN FED.

POLAND

2. Fennoscandia

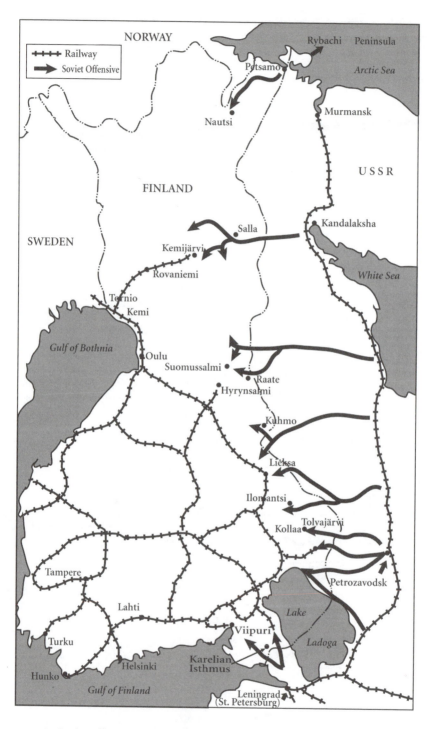

3. Soviet offensives during the Russo-Finnish Winter War of 1939–40.

# *Skiing* Necesse Est

On 14 December 1911, when, accompanied by the muffled scraping of wood on windswept snow, Roald Amundsen reached the South Pole and raised the Norwegian colours, he was careful to record that 'the skiing has been partly good, partly bad'.[1] It took precedence over the fact that he and his four companions had just become the first men to reach 90° south latitude. They saw themselves not as explorers but as skiers. Nor did they feel particularly heroic. They had simply sped over 740 miles and won the longest ski race in the world.

Even now, any Nordic skier will understand. So might others. Three weeks later, Amundsen observed that 'it was a good day for us skiers':[2]

> Loose snow, so that the ski sank about 2 inches: iced and grainy so that the skis glided as if on an oiled surface. But the loose snow was also necessary so the skis could be steered. The one slope steeper than the other. We tore down like a rushing wind. A wonderful sport.

This comes from Amundsen's diary for 6 January 1912. He was recording his descent from the Antarctic plateau on the way home. Within him crackled the spark of the downhill skier.

Man is a travelling animal and skiing began as a means of survival. Amundsen exemplified the tendency of old drudgeries like this to become pastimes, which now and then revert to practical use once more.[3] When he reached the South Pole his English rivals, under Captain Robert Falcon Scott, were still over 300 miles behind. Amundsen had won because he and his companions were the better skiers. The disparity had come about by a simple interplay of men and skis and snow.

Although the great polar explorers were exponents of Nordic skiing, it is the Alpine version that acquired mass appeal. Lifts have abolished the trouble of climbing up and created the illusion of effortlessly running down. As usual, it has come at a cost. Downhill skiing has succumbed to mechanization and has been far removed from its natural origins. Commercialization, climate change, overcrowding and damage to the delicate balance of the mountain world have brought a once simple pastime to the brink of crisis, with reaction setting in.

From a certain point of view this is merely the price exacted by technology but skiing has always been highly technological – from its primitive origins until today. When Amundsen won the race for the South Pole with such devastating superiority he was applying the latest technical advances.

His triumph was wholly appropriate. It was the Norwegians who, as one result of the Enlightenment, invented modern skiing, doggedly developing the techniques that we still use today. To understand this is to understand Amundsen's achievement. To him and his companions, victory at the South Pole was a game, not a serious affair. It was Norwegian polar exploration that finally launched skiing as a universal pursuit.

This in turn had its roots in an ancient tale. Amundsen was heir to those who went before – all the way back to the men in distant epochs among whom the ski arose. They swept in a huge swathe across the Old World. It is a story that began, perhaps, more than 20,000 years ago. The ski is even older than the wheel. Amundsen had inherited a prehistoric device. Together with the hammer, the knife and the axe, the ski is one of the few Stone Age implements handed down to us in their original form. In polar exploration it has changed the course of history. It has done so too elsewhere, in war and peace. The origins of skiing are bound up with the emergence of modern man.

# Ski Tracks in the Milky Way

Among the Ostyak tribe in Siberia, there was a myth of a god who, one day, went hunting an elk on skis.[1] He chased it all over the heavens. In desperation, the creature jumped down to earth. The god followed and eventually caught up. The traces of this hunt can still be seen among the stars. The Milky Way is the god's ski-track in the sky.

The god, called – unfortunately for us – Tunk-Pox, did not have it all his own way. In following the elk to earth he broke a ski so that he had to finish the hunt on just one. To this day you can see this in the converging lanes of the Milky Way, showing the tracks first of the complete pair of skis and then the single one.

It is hardly a surprise to find skiing as the stuff of myth. The invention of the ski and its putative ancestor, the snowshoe, was a revolution for prehistoric northern man. It opened up country impassable in summer, allowing men to escape from their narrow coastal strips and populate the hinterland

Marshes and wetlands, where men would sink, were barriers in the warm season of the year. When frozen, they could bear any weight. Snow evened out the terrain but was still an obstacle to men wading along on foot. It was, however, accessible to the snowshoe or the ski. Snow was the northern highway. Winter became the time for travelling. The snowshoe even had a hand in settling America.

The story goes back to the peak of the last Ice Age, 22,000 years ago. An ice cap a mile high covered Greenland, much of North America, all of Scandinavia, Finland, the Baltic and the rim of Siberia. It spread over Europe, down as far as central France, around Lyon. There, the Palaeolithic Cro-Magnon man hunted the reindeer roaming the tundra that ran up to the line of the ice front. Cave drawings hint that he knew the sledge, the snowshoe and the ski. Climate change, meanwhile, was at work. The world was again becoming warmer. The ice retreated; the reindeer advanced, seeking their natural habitat in what remained of a cold climate, followed by the hunters in their wake.

Ski and snowshoe spread eastwards to the ends of Asia. From Asia, it is generally agreed, the Americas were mostly populated. This took place when the last land bridge was open, approximately between 20,000BC and 10,000BC. It joined eastern Siberia to Alaska and hence Eurasia with the Americas. Its cause was related to the Ice Age and a drop in sea level. With the retreat of the glaciers, the land bridge sank beneath the waters, leaving in its stead the Bering Strait to divide the Old World from the New.

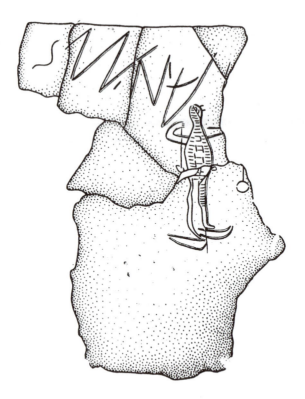

1. Abashevo Bronze age culture, *c.* 1500BC near Voronezh, Russia. Skier with two sticks. After Pryakhin, 1970. *Cambridge University Library*

Across the land bridge came various migrations out of Asia, bringing the snowshoe with them. This enabled people to move along the Arctic corridors between the ice caps still covering North America. By the end of the process, the snowshoe was found over the whole northern hemisphere, from Norway to New England; in Europe all the way down to the mountains of Armenia and in America bounded by a line through northern California and the mid-West, to what is now the north of New York state, with sporadic traces further south.

When the first white colonists arrived in North America, the snowshoe was part of Indian tribal culture. This was first recorded by a sixteenth-century Frenchman, André Thevet. A contemporary of Rabelais, Thevet was a travelled cleric, who had been to the New World, had brought tobacco to France and knew the French explorer of Canada, Jacques Cartier. The Canadian savages, as Thevet put it, 'use a kind of racquet, strung with cords made from the sinews of animals, in the form of a grid … two and a half feet long and one foot wide … They wear them under their feet when it is cold and there is snow.'[2]

This is a succinct description of the main type of North American snowshoe. One variation is the wooden snowshoe. It also survived sporadically in Europe.

It is a simple plank, with a smooth sole. It is presumably the ancestor of the ski. The difference is that the snowshoe is used for walking and the ski for sliding. The transition never took place in America. The ski stopped short at the Bering Strait.

One explanation is the kind of snow. The deep, loose variety of the North American forests and the Great Plains needed the snowshoe. The more compact form that mantled steppe and tundra favoured the ski. In any case, the ski belonged to the Old World alone. It existed where the winters were long and stable, with consistent snow. From Kamschatka and Hokkaido in the East, through Siberia, the Chinese borderlands and northern Russia to Scandinavia in the West, the ski swept in a wide crescent through Central Asia and Europe.

The earliest known traces come from northern Russia, near the White Sea. They were uncovered during the 1960s by Grigoriy Burov, a Ukrainian archaeologist, at a dig called Vis, after an adjoining river. They were in the form of fragments from about 6000BC. Belonging to the Mesolithic, that is between the Old and the New Stone Age, they are among the oldest wooden objects ever found. They predate the invention of the wheel, in south-eastern Europe or Asia Minor, by three-and-a-half millennia.

Although the only tools were of stone, the Vis objects reveal sophisticated workmanship and design, disposing of the misconception that prehistoric man was necessarily crude. One fragment from Vis consists of a ski tip, under which there is a wedge-like protuberance. It is carved in the shape of an elk's head facing towards the rear.[3] It was evidently designed as a brake to prevent slipping backwards – a forerunner of modern waxless cross-country skis. As it happens, it is also an echo of Tunk-Pox and his ski tracks in the Milky Way.

According to the legend, even a god could not overtake an elk on ordinary skis. Consequently Tunk-Pox had made a pair from the wood of a magic tree. It proved, however, so fast that he too found it hard to control. He therefore contrived wedges on the soles of the ski to cut the speed – another neat instance of myth overlaying a kernel of truth.

Some of the Vis finds resemble another Mesolithic discovery several hundred miles to the south west at Heinola, in Finland. This is a sledge runner, dated to about 7600BC. A broad, ski-like device with holes for fixing the superstructure, it is the oldest known complete relic of its kind. It too is technically so advanced, that it might have been made today. It was the precursor, by some 9,000 years, of the ski sledge that revolutionized polar exploration.

Like almost all such finds, the Vis fragments and the Heinola sledge runner came from a peat bog. These are common in the north and luckily preserve certain kinds of wood. About 200 old skis have been unearthed in Sweden, Finland and Norway and an unknown number in Russia. They span the best part of eight millennia. The archaeological record is nonetheless incomplete. Some skis must have been made of birch or other deciduous wood. Almost none have come down to us from the distant past. Most surviving skis were made from conifers, mostly pine. The resin preserves it in the peat bogs, where hardwoods

2. Zalavruga, NW Russia, Rock drawings c. 2000BC. After Ravdonikas, 1936.
*Haddon Library, University of Cambridge*

are destroyed. Nonetheless the broad lines of evolution are clear.

Some ancient skis would have been deliberately immersed. In historic times, this was a way of summer storage. A peat bog kept the skis from drying out, with cracking and warping as a result. It also helped to preserve the upward bend of the tip; painfully produced by coaxing the wood over a fire. Luckily some skis would have been lost, waiting down the years for us to find. Other fragments, like those at Vis, were probably discarded. Refuse is gold for the archaeologist. Tell me what you throw away, and I will tell you what you are.

Excavations are all very well but they need life breathed into them. Contemporary records are best. Such do indeed exist. At Alta and perhaps Rødø in northern Norway there are prehistoric rock drawings of skiers from around 2000BC, and the New Stone Age or Neolithic. Better still is a series of rock drawings from the same period. They are at Zalavruga, in north-west Russia, near Burov's excavations at Vis.[4]

The Zalavruga drawings are carved into the living rock on the bank of a river. At the time, writing already existed elsewhere, notably in Egypt and the Near East. It had not reached anywhere remotely so far north. That is not necessarily a disadvantage. Like most primitive art, Zalavruga gives a glimpse of the psyche that the written word does not convey. The drawings are classics of their kind. They have the quality of animated films. They offer vivid pictures of northern Stone Age life and the ski plays a leading rôle.

The figures are in silhouette. They have a sense of movement. They convey a skier's urgent need of balance. The viewer is somehow drawn into the action, in one picture becoming a spectator at a hunting scene. The sequence of events is plain. There is a ski track that starts off in a straight line, with the marks of the sticks close together, as if skiing uphill. This is followed by a wide curve, with sticks driven in further apart, suggesting a downhill run. At the bottom, three men, after skiing in Indian file, have spread out to attack their quarry, a trio of elks. They all, incidentally, only have a single ski stick. One man, with bow and arrow, is about to shoot. He is skilfully holding ski stick and bow in one hand. Another, leaning on his stick, is in the process of spearing an animal. Ahead of both is the forerunner, very clearly having had to break a trail through fresh snow. He too is an archer and has shot three arrows into his elk. Hunting, archery, skiing, melt into an elegant variation of the everlasting fight for survival.

These images depict events at a time of geological commotion. By about 7500BC, the ice had shrunk to a point where only Greenland was in its grip, as it remains to this day. In Scandinavia, southern Sweden and the coast of Norway were settled. Whence and by whom is still an enigma. The Cro-Magnons may have played a part, bringing the ski with them. The map of northern Europe was still shifting, and not at all what we know now. When men used the skis from Vis, the Baltic was an inland lake. Only in 5000BC, through what is now Denmark, did it find an outlet to the open sea. It was then that Finland was colonized, some five centuries after the interior of Sweden and Norway. Finland was literally rising from the waters. The sheer weight of the ice cap had depressed the earth's crust under Fennoscandia – a term coined (by a Finn in 1904) to mean Finland and the Scandinavian peninsula – and slowly it was moving upwards to relieve the strain and find an equilibrium. The process is not quite finished yet. Even now, the land around Stockholm is still rising at the rate of half a metre a century or more. Fennoscandia is one of the youngest parts of the world to be populated; younger even than the Americas. In its landscape there is, to this day, a beguiling touch of a world still unfinished.

Although the Vis fragments and the Zalavruga drawings come from what is now Russia, they do not lie in the historic Slav homelands. They are in one of the corridors of migration along which northern Norway, Sweden and Finland were supposedly first settled. They therefore properly belong to the ancient past of Fennoscandia.

After Vis, there is a gap in the archaeological record of around 2,000 years to 4000BC. That brings a discovery in Finland; a sledge runner from Lappinlahti.[5] Nearly another millennium passes before the first skis since Vis. These form a group from Kalvträsk[6] in Sweden, Drevja[7] in Norway and Salla in Finland.[8] All three come from the north of their countries. Between them they span the three great Nordic skiing nations. They belong to the new Stone Age settlement of Fennoscandia. Each has been dated to around 3200BC.

In each case, that figure was found by the carbon-14 process. An offshoot of atomic physics, this fixes the age of an object by the decay of carbon-14, a radioactive isotope of carbon that occurs naturally in organic material. It was the first reliable method of dating the distant past. It has revolutionized archaeology.

It has been used on old skis since the 1970s. The Finns in particular, feeling it part of their heritage, have systematically dated all their ancient skis.

To prehistoric northern man, the ski was an instrument of survival. He needed good sliding, preferably without any slip on the kickoff, to overtake his prey. He had to deal with the complexity of snow; almost a fourth state of matter. He had a technical bent and, to cope with the gamut of snow forms, evolved a bewildering variety of skis. It was an object lesson in adaptation to circumstances.

Like snow itself, these early skis can be grouped into two basic forms. The Drevja find represents one; Kalvträsk, the other. The Kalvträsk ski comes from the coastal lowlands of northern Sweden. This is forested and slightly undulating. For most of the winter, the snow is usually loose. This seems to have been true even in the dry, relatively warm climate between the Stone Age and Iron Age. So the difficulty here is to minimize resistance. It is enough to explain the shape of

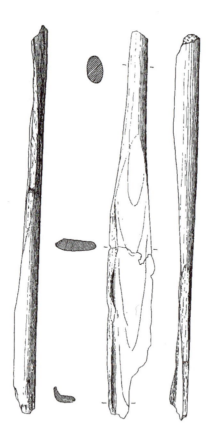

3. Wooden object from Star Carr in Yorkshire, about 8000BC. Excavated by Professor J. G. D. Clark from Cambridge in the 1950s. It is probably the shovel-like top of a prehistoric ski stick. After Clark 1954. *Haddon Library, University of Cambridge*

this generic ski. It is long and relatively narrow. Further to ease a passage, it tapers subtly from front to back, so that the tip, as it were, breaks a trail for the rest. The difficulty is not slipping backwards, but being able to glide at all. For that reason, the sole is completely bare wood, probably untreated. A recent Finnish experiment using the replica of a similar ancient model, proved its efficacy in deep snow.[9]

By contrast with the Kalvträsk ski, the sole of its contemporary from Drevja was almost certainly lined with fur. It comes from a higher and more exposed region, where the wind compacts the snow, turning the surface into crust. Here, smooth wood helplessly slithers about. Adhesion is the crux. Fur is one answer. It also comes to the rescue in a thaw on crust and hard-packed snow. It prevents balling up of the surface slush and thus extends the season by coping with the miseries of spring.

The main reason, however, was to dampen noise. The scrape of wood on the harsh crystalline surface of wind-blown crust, echoes uncannily for miles. This would alarm reindeer and other game with sensitive hearing, attuned to the depredations of man. Fur-lined ski enabled the hunter, with luck, to creep up on his quarry in silence and take it unawares. On that account, this became the native form among the tribes of north-eastern Russia, the Urals and Siberia.

The Drevja ski, like that from Salla, is fragmentary. The Kalvträsk find is not. It is the oldest complete ski yet excavated. Accidentally found by a forestry inspector in 1924, the Kalvträsk ski belonged originally to a pair, together with part of a stick, but one ski crumbled during transport from the peat bog where it was found. Those artefacts reveal an all-too-human touch. One ski had split at heel and tip. Holes had been drilled on each side of the cracks, evidently to repair them by lashings of some sort. Perhaps it was a favourite pair; perhaps the owner shrank from the labour of making a new one with the stone tools at his disposal.

The ski stick from Kalvträsk ends in a broad, rounded shovel. This was a universal implement, the Swiss Army knife of the time, as it were. On the track, the pointed end of the stick gave purchase for the forward lunge, at a pinch serving also as a spear. The shovel was essential in trapping, clearing a campsite, testing the consistency of the snow, and so forth. Until the middle of the nineteenth century this model survived in ancient skiing cultures from one end of Eurasia to the other.

In the Museum of Archaeology and Anthropology in Cambridge there is a narrow shovel-like wooden fragment unearthed from a site known as Star Carr in Yorkshire.[10] At first called a paddle blade, it is in fact identical with the top of the Kalvträsk stick. It dates from around 8000BC. This makes it the oldest known ski relic of any sort. In that case, the skiing crescent swept even further westwards to the British Isles – then linked by a land bridge to the continent – until the conditions withered in some later misty age.

The Kalvträsk ski itself is made of pine, artfully worked and thin. The tip has a high upward sweep. For added strength, the upper surface rises to a longitudinal central ridge along the whole length of the ski, like the keel of a boat. A notorious point of strain, the back is cut off square, bent slightly upwards, and reinforced by subtle thickening, all on sound engineering principles, like a modern ski. The design would not be out of place today – something that could not be said of many prehistoric objects.

Even so, that unknown craftsman had probably been anticipated by the maker of the Vis fragment with the elk's head on the sole. On the upper surface, where the tip flattens out, there is the beginning of a central raised, wavy moulding. Structurally, it would have reinforced the ski in the same way as the keel of the Kalvträsk ski, which extends the life of the basic design to 9,000 years.

Those prehistoric Nordic skiers were as obsessed with bindings as their successors. This is understandable, given the vital function of the link between foot and ski. The boot is also part of the mechanism. We do not exactly know the early Scandinavian forms. They were probably soft soled, resembling moccasins. In any case, bindings are the fertile source of most variation and prehistoric ski are generally classified by their bindings, through the work of Ernst Manker, a Swedish anthropologist.[11]

The Kalvträsk, Salla and Drevja finds make the point. In the centre of the Kalvträski ski there is a low, flattened part for the footrest. This has been pierced by vertical holes for the bindings. By contrast in both the Drevja and Salla relics the footrest is evidently raised and a transverse slot has been cut through it *horizontally*. That principle lasted for 5,000 years.

The binding of the Kalvträsk ski was a single thong threaded vertically through the holes and wrapped around the boot. The Drevja and Salla models would have had a toestrap looped through the transverse slot. A ski found at Mänttä, in southern Finland, has the oldest remnants of this binding – or any other for that matter.[12] It has been dated to the sixth century AD. The toestrap was made of linden bark. In addition, there was a heelstrap of badger skin to hold the boot in place. This system, too, was decidedly long-lived. In Nordic skiing the basic concept still survives.

The Kalvträsk ski is an anomaly. Its length of 204 cm, and relatively narrow width of 15 cm place it among the Western Fennoscandian group of skis. By its vertical binding holes, however, it is an eastern type, once common in Siberia. Like a Stone Age relic, it still exists among Mongolians who have clung to their native skiing tradition in the Altai mountains of Central Asia. If nothing else it is a pointer to early migration. The Kalvträsk ski is the only specimen of its kind in Fennoscandia. There the Drevja and the Salla types prevail.

After Kalvträsk, Drevja and Salla, the archaeological record jumps to the Bronze Age. This brings a curious find from central Russia. On pottery shards dug up near Voronezh, a drawing of a skier has been scratched.[13] He has two sticks. It is the first of its kind when, as the Kalvträsk ski and Zalavruga images reveal, one was still the norm.

The Voronezh find belongs to the Abashevo culture.[14] This is Indo-European with, oddly enough, a resemblance to the Mycenaean civilization on Crete. Its origins therefore lie in a racial and linguistic stock completely different from the tribes in the skiing heartlands to the north. They were still purely hunters, while the Abashevo – belonging to the people who first tamed the horse – were already nomadic agriculturalists. To them, the ski would have been a means of transport, which favoured two sticks, while among the Fennoscandians it was associated with hunting, which needed only one. Around Voronezh at the time there was consistent snow cover for much of the winter. This pushes the ancient skiing lands much further to the south.

The drawing from Voronezh dates from 1500BC. This is the same as a Swedish ski representing another technical advance. It was found at Hoting, in the north of the country.[15] It has remnants of vertical flanges to fix the foot. A whole flange has been preserved on a fragmentary ski from Ärnäs, also in Sweden.[16] It is probably as old as the Hoting find. The flange has been carved from the solid wood. The earliest complete specimen of this type comes from Furnes, in Norway.[17]

This ski dates from around AD100 and the Fennoscandian Iron Age. The footrest is offset from the edge of the ski. This is a sophisticated design feature that lasted for a millennium or two. Its purpose is to protect the boots against snow crust. One of Nature's unadvertised abrasives, this can easily rip soft leather. By raising the footrest and allowing the ski to jut out on either side the threat is held at bay.

The flanges were another ingenious touch. Those on the Furnes ski are low, pierced horizontally for a toestrap. They presaged the metal ears that ruled from the end of the nineteenth century until the advent of the modern safety binding in the 1970s and survive in Nordic skiing still.

A variation of the Furnes binding appears on yet another kind of ski. This has a flat footrest, enclosed by two large vertical flanges, flush with the edges, also carved in one piece out of the solid wood, like a mitre box, enveloping the boot. A toestrap was threaded through horizontal slots. This completes the main repertoire of bindings. Although sporadically found in Fennoscandia, it is in reality a southern type, originating in the Baltic states, Poland and European Russia.

The earliest known example is on a ski found at Viitasaari[18] in south-west Finland. This dates from 400BC but compared with the Mesolithic it is unexpectedly primitive. The ski is short and broad, often wholly flat, without upturned tip and crudely made. One explanation is that it was only used occasionally, for pottering around the homestead for instance, where snow cover was sporadic and rough workmanship would do. It is a curious sidelight that the Stone Age ski makers set the standard. Marks on various relics, experimentally confirmed, indicate the use of efficient, well-worn flint spokeshaves. In the transition to Bronze and Iron Ages, the tools and workmanship of this specialized form of carpentry noticeably decayed.

The Hoting ski and its successors lie in the evolutionary mainstream. This means that the basic structure of ski and bindings as we know them had evolved by the second millennium BC. That, however, is only part of the story. The running surface remains.

On a ski from central Sweden at Färnäs in the province of Dalecarlia, the sole has a low raised flange along each edge.[19] The enclosed space was probably covered with fur. This introduced a refinement. Moving forward, the ski glided on the flanges, while at the kickoff the fur prevented slipping backwards. It dates from AD350 and is the earliest of its kind. It is a transitional type.

Until then, virtually all ski so far found had a completely plane surface without a groove. There are good reasons for this. The purpose of the groove is to give stability on a packed but not unyielding surface, by forcing up a steering ridge of snow. Perhaps the emergence of the groove followed a change of climate, and hence the nature of the snow.

The earliest known grooved ski is the Salla find. In fact, it has not one, but five parallel grooves along the sole. Moreover, there is nothing like it for the best part of three and a half millennia. The next grooved ski come from Liperi and Ikaalis – also in Finland – and dated to around AD400.[20]

Significantly or not, this is the period when racially and linguistically Fennoscandia was assuming its present form. In Scandinavia proper, the ancestral Gothic tribes that had arrived from the south around 1500BC, displacing the aboriginal inhabitants and bringing the horse and the wheel with them, had coalesced into a Germanic population that was in the process of dividing into Swedes, Danes and Norwegians. The ancestors of the modern Finns, meanwhile, were beginning to settle in Finland, having also come from the south.

At any rate the Liperi and Ikaalis ski are the first known ski with the familiar single groove. They embody opposing theories of evolution. The ski from Liperi has a shallow, rounded grove. Now until quite recently, with the invention of ripsaws, the blanks for skis were made by splitting logs. From prehistoric times this was done by driving in wooden wedges: if towards the centre, the result was edge wood, that is with the growth rings perpendicular to the faces; if tangentially, they followed each other to form what is called grain wood. In the pine tree, the growth rings of the heartwood may spontaneously separate, especially in deep cold. When taking out grain wood, this would leave a rounded ridge on the one part and a corresponding, natural groove on the other. At first, it would have seemed a flaw, until someone eventually stumbled on its use.

On the Ikaalis ski, however, the groove is broad, shallow and flat-bottomed with sharp, vertical sides. It has been whittled away by some kind of knife, or even perhaps a chisel – unless the carpenter's plane is older than we think. In any case, here the theory is that the groove evolved from the ski of the Färnäs pattern, with flanges along each edge. In that case, the groove was invented, and not discovered by chance as, supposedly, in the Liperi ski. *Chacun a son goût.*

Whatever its origins, the grooved ski belongs to Fennoscandia. Even there it was not universal. The earliest Norwegian ski with a groove dates from around the ninth century AD, on the verge of the Viking age. It comes from Utrovatn, in the centre of the country. The smooth-soled ski dominated for centuries with interesting consequences.

A groove along the sole is merely one form of specialization. Another appears in a specimen from Anumark in northern Sweden.[21] From around 1000BC, or the late Bronze Age, it is extraordinarily long – nearly 3 metres – and at 18.5 cm it is broad as well. This gives it a large bearing surface. It is also of a widespread type pointed and originally upturned at both ends. It is adapted to deep, loose snow and forested terrain, where the requirements are to avoid sinking down and to prevent the ski from tangling with birch roots and undergrowth. It comes from the coastal area of the Gulf of Bothnia, where those circumstances reign.

Some two thousand years later, around AD 1000, another form of specialization appears in a ski from Arvträsk, again in northern Sweden.[22] It has a convex sole, adapted to harsh wind crust. The same holds for the material. This is so-called compression wood. It is formed in conifers, especially pine trees, growing outwards on a slope. Until quite recently, it has been much prized for making a certain kind of ski. The trees naturally bend upwards towards the light, thus growing to shape for the ski tips. More to the point, the growth rings on the under side, that is away from the sun, are close and compact. This makes the wood tough and hard wearing. It is resistant to the abrasive surface of crust formed both by wind and sun. It can also be highly polished. Its limitation is that in deep cold it becomes brittle.

While growing, the hard compression wood splits away from the main body of the trunk in layers. This may have been the origin of making planks. It is also yet another echo of the unfortunate Tunk-Pox. It was probably the origin of the magic tree out of which he made his ski. According to the legend, that tree had longitudinal cracks that sang when the wind blew. In fact, the fissures in compression wood do creak eerily as the tree bends to the wind.

The association of myth and ski echoes down the years. There is, for example, a latter-day Norwegian fairy tale of a little boy who heard that one could make

4. The Kalvträsk ski, 5,200 years old. This is the oldest known complete ski.

magic ski that move just as fast up as downhill.[23] It was no easy matter to make such ski. They had to be carved on three successive nights at Christmas time. During the procedure utter silence had to reign. What is more, he who carried out the work was not to be scared by anything he saw. Finally, having finished, he was to cut his little finger and let three drops of blood fall on each ski. So, starting at midnight, after diverse supernatural happenings, met with sterling resolve and following the instructions to the letter, the boy got his skis. On first trying them out, he flew over hill and dale as promised. He became involved with a giant whom he outpaced uphill, but not – significantly – running down. Of course it all ended happily when the giant turned to stone at the first chime of a church bell.

This is a local version of a migratory tale about rites of passage. In its home-lands the ski, by its unity with snow, has always been an animistic symbol of the forces of Nature. This does not, of course, detract from its practical use. If there is a moral in this particular folk tale, it is that the artist must let nothing interfere with his art.

# 3

# *The Earliest Written Sources*

The earliest written records of winter travel involve the snowshoe, not the ski. They begin in Greece of the fourth century BC with the *Anabasis* of Xenophon. He wrote about the crossing of the Armenian mountains by the Greek army retreating from Persia; the legendary March of the Ten Thousand from Babylon to the Black Sea. A local inhabitant 'told them how to wrap bags round the hooves of their horses ... when going through the snow, for without these bags, the animals would sink in up to their bellies'.[1] After two millennia, this unlikely device was to be found in the southern Norwegian province of Telemark. During the winter of 1950–1 one farmer was still using it to bring in some hay. It was, he said, 'a bit of an art'.[2] 'You must have at least two bags for each leg. The bag ... closest to the hoof ... must be folded 4 times. On top put one like a sock, folded to double thickness with straps on each corner to fix it.' That widened the hoof and, 'in two metres of ... snow Dobbin [only] sank 15–20 cm'. Xenophon had been right after all.

In the second century AD Arrian, a Greek historian, recorded another march in the mountain snows of Xenophon. The army now was Roman, led by Bruttius, a consul under the Emperor Trajan. 'Since the route seemed impassable', as Arrian put it, Bruttius (like Xenophon)

> conferred with the natives, ordering them to show the way, because they were accustomed to moving about in the winter. Putting rings of withy on their feet, they moved through the snow without danger by pressing on the rings, and it was not difficult for the Romans to follow in their track. In many places the snow was 16 feet deep.[3]

This is the first recognizable description of the primitive 'bearpaw' snowshoe that helped both men and horses all over Eurasia until at least the nineteenth century.

More interesting still is Strabo. He was a Roman of the first century BC, considered the father of modern geography. In the Caucasus, 'because of the snow and ice,' as he says, 'people [climb] by fastening to their feet broad shoes made of ox-hide like drums'.[4] This lends colour to a theory that the snowshoe and the ski evolved from the sandal of primitive tribes. Strabo also observed that in Armenia snowshoes were made of 'wooden discs'. That is the original record of the wooden snowshoe, which was probably a forerunner of the ski.

All this comes from the periphery of the classical world, but at least it is in the realm of fact. The first hints of ski, however, are entangled with the legends masking early knowledge of the North. Among the Greeks, for example, there was the tale of Abaris 'to whom … Apollo gave an arrow on which he rode across … rivers and impassable ground … as if walking on air'.[5] With a little goodwill, this suggests a man on ski.

Abaris was a Hyperborean; literally, 'beyond the North Wind'. The Hyperboreans first appear in Hesiod, the early Greek epic poet of the eighth century BC. They continue a somewhat disreputable existence in Greek literature, followed by Latin literature, for a thousand years. They begin in the twilight world between myth and reality, sometimes as Utopians living in a state of Nature, but ever retreating into the distance as the boundaries of the known world advanced.

Virgil, the great Roman poet of the first century BC, is more realistic. In his *Georgics*, the Hyperboreans are a 'wild race living … under the seven stars of the Great Bear, buffeted by the … Euro [the evil wind from the east that brings famine and pestilence], their bodies clothed in tawny animal furs'.[6] Virgil also mentions the 'Hyperborean ice'; an early glimmering of the Arctic, and the Hyperboreans begin to emerge as a shadowy intimation of northern peoples.

At a certain point, they were linked to another hazy tribe, the Hippopodes. This name, also Greek, means 'horse feet'. The word was first used by Berosus, a priest writing in Greek in Babylon during the third century BC.[7] At about the same time the concept appeared in China too, yet another example of how ancient Chinese and classical Western sources mirror each other. The *Shan Hai Ching*, a strange, semi-mythological work contemporary with Berosus, happens to mention the Ting-Ling, 'people with … horse's hooves'.[8] Later, in the third century AD, another Chinese work, the rather more historical Wei Lio, elaborated: The Ting-Ling 'have the head and body of a man, but below the knee, they are covered in hair, and they have the legs of a horse and horses' hooves. They do not ride horses, but they run faster than a horse.'[9]

About the same time, a Roman author, Solinus, was writing that 'the Hippopodes … are human as far as the soles of their feet, which have the form of horses' hooves'.[10] Hippopodes and Ting-Ling further resemble each other in living somewhere in the north. The *Shan Hai Ching* declares that the Ting-Ling have 'a single arm holding a stick in order to walk'.[11] The location, peculiar gait, stick, distorted feet and hint of superhuman speed dimly begin to suggest skiers as the grain of fact within the myth.

Wholly mythical, the Ting-Ling are not. They have been identified with the Tagar, a Siberian tribe around the River Yenisei. Nor do Hippopodes lack all contact with the real world. In the first century AD, Pliny the Elder – the Roman polymath of Vesuvius fame and the Last Days of Pompeii – firmly puts them in the Baltic. His near contemporary, Pomponius Mela, associates them with what he calls 'Scadinavia'.[12] In other words, Ting-Ling and Hippopodes lie on the periphery of civilization. Between them they define a northern region starting on the frontier of China and ending over in Scandinavia to the West.

These are all misty hints and the breakthrough comes from a Chinese work, the *Bei Shi* or 'Northern History'. It mentions the 'Northern Shiwei',[13] who live around the Tuhe Mountains, where the climate is

> extremely cold ... In winter they go into the mountains and live in earth dugouts ... There is an abundance of river deer, which they hunt with bow and arrow ... When there are large amounts of snow on the ground, fearing lest they fall into crevasses or pitfalls, they ride on wood.

This is the first known direct allusion to ski, anywhere. It dates from the seventh century AD. It is in the realm of the real world. The Tuhe Mountains are now the Lesser Xing'an Range. The Shiwei were the ancestors of the Mongols.

In China, from around the time of the *Bei Shi*, detail starts to unfold. Mu-Ma or 'wooden horses' make their entry.[14] One writer calls them 'footwear ... the head of which is bent upwards'.[15] Another gives the dimensions: 'six inches wide and seven feet long'.[16] Thus in the Mu-Ma lie the first recognizable descriptions of skis, and the ancient Chinese term – itself among the first known of its kind. (Oddly enough, a modern German nickname for skis is *Schnee-Rösslein*, or 'snow ponies'.)

The Chinese dynastic records elaborate on the subject. Thus in the Tang dynasty – AD618 to AD907 – the *Xin Tang Shu*, the *New Tang History*: '[There are] three tribes of Mu-Ma Turks [who] have the custom of riding wooden horses to gallop over the [snow and] ice. Resting their feet on boards and supporting their armpits with crooked sticks, with one stride they travel a hundred paces.'[17] This is the earliest technical description of skiing; cross-country, as it happens.

We owe these and other details to a Chinese passion for meticulously recording their turbulent history. In the late tenth century AD, the *Huan ju ki*, or 'Imperial Geography' of the Sung dynasty, has this to say of the Pa-si-mi, another Central Asian tribe:

> when hunting, they use ... a device attached to the foot called Mu-Ma ... The under side is covered with horse hide in such a way that the hair points backwards, to prevent slipping. The hunter having attached these boards to his feet, and running down a slope, he overtakes the fleeing deer. When he runs over snow-covered plains, he carries a long stick, which he drives into the snow at regular intervals as if pushing a boat forwards, thus even in this case overtaking his quarry. The same stick also serves as a support when climbing up slopes.[18]

As a succinct analysis of a certain kind of skiing, this could hardly be bettered. In a link between epochs, one detail supports archaeology, with its evidence of fur-lined skis, while being confirmed after nearly a millennium by a nineteenth-century traveller in Siberia. Certain tribes, he wrote, 'attach a strip of horsehide to [their skis] by means of reindeer or fish glue so that the hair points backwards'; rather like modern sealskins for mountain touring in fact.[19] To complete the picture, the *Huan ju ki* invokes yet another tribe, the Khirgiz who, 'in deep snow hunt on Mu-Ma, on which the hunter runs both uphill and downhill as if he were flying'.[20]

Around that time, a stray hint of skis appears in a very different quarter. An Armenian traveller in the mountains bordering what is now Iraq described some notably bloodthirsty denizens who, 'due to the weight of the shifting snow, that suddenly falls from the clouds ... have contrived planks which they bind to their feet with straps, like a yoke, and run over the snow as easily as on dry land'.[21]

Despite their contact with skiing tribes, the Chinese did not ski themselves. The climate was against it in the regions of their classical culture. There was no consistent snow cover. Otherwise, the Chinese were gathering military intelligence. The border tribes were a constant threat and it was as well to catalogue their habits.

The chroniclers of the Ming dynasty – 1368–1644 – recorded that another skiing people called the Jurchen

> are accustomed to use dog sleds and mu-ma for lightness and ease of travel. The dog sleds are in the shape of boats, pulled by a score or so of dogs, on which they travel back and forth ... When whipped up to top speed, they can catch up with a galloping horse. Both can only move over ice and snow.[22]

The boat-shaped sledge is clearly the *pulka* or *akkja* used until recently by northern tribes west of the Urals and, in plastic, even has a modern counterpart.

The Jurchen were evidently primitive tribesmen. Chinese records, infused by the national ethos of scorn for all things foreign, characteristically portray them as outcasts from beyond the pale. The Jurchen were 'wild men', either because they had never been civilized or because they had reverted to a state of nature: 'They hunt for food in the mountains ... In summer they live in the open, taking shelter in the winter.'[23]

Sometimes the Jurchen are called Yeti, which suggests the origin of the Abominable Snowman: They are 'wild men' and 'their bodies are very hairy'. Nonetheless they were real enough. They were ironically Tunguses from Manchuria, the probable ancestors of the Manchu who went on to rule China until the beginning of the twentieth century.

Earlier, the Mongols had subjugated China for a time. They also conquered Persia. During their rule, around 1325, a Persian scholar called Rashid-ud-din wrote their history. He mentions a tribe called the Forest Urankhit: 'Since their country has many mountains and much forest, and snow falls in great quantities, they hunt a great deal in winter in the snow, doing so in this way. They make wooden boards which they call *chana*, and stand on them.'[24] (Today the word for 'ski' in Mongolian is *kul tsana*, and *changa* in Kazak.)

Using the same imagery as that applied three hundred years earlier by the Huan ju ki to the Pa-si-Mi, Rashid describes how the Urankhit skiers

> hold a long stick in the hand. They drive this stick into the snow as if they were pushing a vessel through water. Thus they move on the *chana* over steppe and plain so fast both

uphill and downhill that they overtake elk and other game … If an inexperienced person attempts the movement, his legs are pulled apart and dislocated, especially when moving fast or running downhill. Those who have learnt, however, move with the greatest ease. No one believes it until he has seen it.

Reports reached the blessed ears of the Ruler of Islam [Gazan Khan, then Mongol king of Persia] – long may he reign! He therefore ordered a number of people to come to him out of that country, in order to convince himself of the truth of what he had heard. They gave a demonstration, and there was no more doubt. The Ruler ordered another demonstration. These *chana* are known in most parts of Mongolia and Turkestan.

The Urankhit were not in fact Mongolian, but probably Yakuts, a Turkic people. Perhaps before his time, Rashid was intrigued by the noble savage. The Urankhit, so he explained, were nomads, who never left the forest, and dressed only in furs. 'They believe that theirs is the best life, and that no one is as happy as they are.' Reverting to technicalities, Rashid explained the Urankhits' method of transport: 'Alongside the *chana* on which they themselves stand, they drag others attached [to each other] on which they load the felled game.' This is recognizably the sledge with broad, ski-like runners, used by various Siberian tribes.

About the same time, an Arab author, Ibn Battuta, himself considered reaching what he called 'the land of Darkness'.[25] That was in Siberia, around the Urals. The journey, Battuta explained

takes place only by means of small sledges drawn by big dogs … The leader in that land is the dog who has already traversed it repeatedly. He is worth up to 1,000 Dinar … the sledge is attached to his neck, and three other dogs are harnessed together with him. He is the leader, and the other dogs follow him … These dogs do not attack their master … At mealtimes [the master] feeds the dogs before the people, otherwise the [leader] dog loses his temper and runs away, leaving his master to perish.

This is a shrewd insight into the behaviour of sledge dogs and their relation to their masters. A native of Tangiers, Battuta was one of the medieval Arab travellers who, driven by the pilgrimage to Mecca, ranged the Moslem world and, in the process, glimpsed what lay beyond. Some, like Battuta, turned to what is now northern Russia. Before him, in the eleventh century, a Persian called Al Biruni had written about people he called Yura, probably the Ostyaks. They then lived between the Pechora river and the Urals.

5. Abu Hamid of Granada, twelfth century. Diagram of Yakut ski, North Russia.
*Cambridge University Library*

All this, however, depended on hearsay. Someone who avoided the trap of writing at second hand was Abu Hamid, a Spanish Arab from Granada. In the middle of the twelfth century, he went to Russia, reaching Bulgar, the present Bolgya, on the northern reaches of the Volga. There he actually met some Yura and recorded 'the way in which they travel over country continually covered with snow'.[26]

> Walkers attach to their feet specially made planks. Each plank is a fathom [2 m] long and a palm [10 cm] broad, and some of its forward part, as well as the back is raised from the ground. In the middle of the plank there is a place where the traveller puts his foot, consisting of a hole through which a sturdy leather belt runs, which hold the feet.

This is the first known description of a ski binding. 'Both planks, one on each foot,' Abu Hamid continues, 'are attached to each other by a long loop, like the reins of a horse, which the walker holds in his left hand.'

In fact the loop, attached to each ski tip, was found in Russia at least until the beginning of the twentieth century. It was used either to drag the skis or to keep them parallel and turn when running downhill. 'In his right hand', says Abu Hamid, the Yura skier 'holds a stick, as high as a man, to the lower part of which is attached a ball of fabric, stuffed with a great deal of wool, about the size of a human head, and very light in weight.' This is the earliest record of a ski stick and basket.

And then echoing Rashid and the *Huan ju ki*:

> The walker places this stick on the snow, pushing backwards, as if he were rowing a boat … In this way, he moves quickly over the snow; and without this ingenious contrivance, no one could walk at all, because the snow is like sand on the ground, and never gives any support.

Thus by the Middle Ages, oriental savants had amassed a considerable body of information. The West, however, was behind. Knowledge of the remote north had to filter through by other means. With the encroachment of reality, Hyperboreans and Hippopodes give way to Skrithiphinoi. They first authoritatively appear during the sixth century AD in the work of a Byzantine scholar, Procopius of Caesarea, who wrote in Greek. He places them in Thule, the mysterious northern country – Virgil's *Ultima Thule*, 'Furthest Thule'[27] – that had been argued about for 800 years, but which he confidently identifies with what we recognize as northern Scandinavia. A dependable observer, this Procopius was the historian of the Emperor Justinian the lawgiver and was secretary to Belisarius, the great Byzantine general who defeated the Vandals and pioneered amphibious warfare. Procopius calls the Skrithiphinoi 'barbarians'[28] who 'neither wear garments of cloth nor do they walk with shoes on their feet'. It is a curious phrase, which might hint at skis. He checked his references and, in his own words, had actually met 'those who come to us from … Thule'. Living in Constantinople, Procopius probably meant wandering Scandinavian mercenaries, ancestors of the Vikings, who saw in what they called 'The Big City' a lucrative year out soldiering.

The central figure in this story perhaps also gleaned his knowledge from other roving Scandinavians. He was a Lombard monk of the eighth century called Paulus Diaconus. A familiar of Charlemagne, he lived in Italy, probably at Monte Casino, and wrote in (rather vivid) Latin a history of the Lombards. They were a Germanic people, who once ruled Italy but, so Paulus said, originating in Scandinavia. There, he wrote, live a nation called 'Scritobini [who] pursue wild beasts very skilfully by springing and bounding on a piece of wood curved like a bow'.[29]

This is the original Western reference to ski. It dates from the same period as the Chinese description of Mu-Ma in the *Xin Tang Shu*.

Paulus's Scritobini was only one variant of the Skrithiphinoi of Procopius. In different forms, and far apart, the word had been circulating for some time. The Old English poem *Widsith*, for example, probably around AD650, mentions the Scridefinnum, while the sixth-century Gothic historian, Jordanes, called them Screrefennae.[30] Whatever their exact name, they achieved a credibility denied the Hyperboreans or the Hippopodes. They enjoyed even the imprimatur of the Papacy. Around AD850 Pope Gregory IV, and some 300 years later, Innocent II allotted what the one called Scredevindan and the other, Scrideuindie, to the Archbishop of Hamburg, as Primate of Scandinavia.

According to Paulus, his Scritobini 'deduce the etymology of their name from the word for springing in their barbarous tongue'. Now there is an Old Norse word *Skrida*, or 'slide', but which can also mean 'to ski'. To convey this to anyone who had never seen it, 'springing' would do. Scritobini therefore becomes the 'Skiing Bini', and the *Skrithiphinoi* of Procopius, therefore, 'Skiing (or sliding) Phinoi'.

This is at only one remove from reality. Tacitus, the Roman historian of the first century AD, had already written about *Fenni* round the Baltic.[31] In the eleventh century, a scholarly cleric, Adam of Bremen, placed what he called (in Latin) the *Skritefinni* in north Scandinavia 'between Swedes and Norwegians'. Various medieval scholars agreed. This identifies the *Skritefinni* as some other people, probably Finns or Lapps.[32]

Either way, they are set apart, if only by their speech. Both Finnish and Lappish are Finno-Ugric, a branch of the Ural-Altaic family of languages. This takes its name from the Ural and Altai Mountains where its putative origins lie. It sprawls over most of Siberia, much of Central Asia and beyond. It is the generic tongue of people as diverse as Hungarians, Estonians and Ottoman Turks. It is wholly separate from the Indo-European family, to which the Scandinavian languages belong. That spoils Paulus's etymology. Finns and Lapps call themselves respectively Suomalainen and Sami. The name must have been foisted on them by some Old Norse speaker with a gift for words.

In Old Norse (and until recently in Norwegian) the word for Lapp was simply 'Finn'. Among the Swedes, however, it meant the people whom we know under that name. One Swedish scholar defined what he called in his version *Scricfinni* as 'all Finns and Lapps'[33] who used the ski. Most Swedish writers, however, thought that they were only Lapps but the question is not settled yet.

The word 'Lapp' itself has been borrowed from the Finnish. This elegantly completes the circle. The term was coined to mark the difference. Finns and Lapps were separate, regarding each other with mutual suspicion. The Lapps are a distinct people of their own. Today they inhabit northern Sweden, Norway and Finland with a few in adjacent parts of Russia. Ancestral Lapps probably arrived during the second century AD, in the wake of the reindeer, as it moved into north-eastern Europe. They came from an uncertain heartland, perhaps in Central Asia, neighbours of the Mu-Ma Turks and, as Adam of Bremen put it, 'are said to run faster than wild animals'.[34]

# 4

# Old Norse Sagas and the
# Finnish National Epic: Kalevala

These early records had depended on outsiders. It was in Scandinavia that skiing first was woven into the written word by those belonging to a culture of which it was a part. This happened in the medieval Old Norse sagas, a treasury of entertaining stories and delineation of character. The action usually takes place in the tenth and eleventh centuries.

Lapps sometimes top the bill. They are 'so cunning', says one Saga 'that they can follow tracks like dogs, both in thawing snow and on hard crust, and they are so good on skis that nothing can escape them, whether man or beast'.[1] This neatly summarizes ingrained Old Norse attitudes, dichotomous at best. Lapps appear as redoubtable skiers and indeed ski-makers; acknowledged by *Grágás*, a thirteenth-century Icelandic legal code, which wanted banishment for life to last

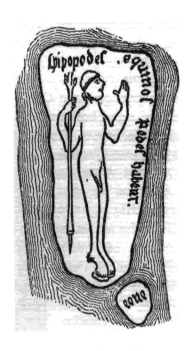

6. Hippopodes, Hereford map, thirteenth century.
*Cambridge University Library*

'as long as … fire burns and the Lapp skis'.[2] Less comfortably, Lapps are portrayed as magicians due no doubt to the shamans who cared for their psychic needs. For their part, the Lapps disparaged the Norsemen as an inferior alien breed.

The Norsemen, naturally, returned the compliment, although their literature guardedly acknowledges the Lapps as the better skiers. To the Lapps, the ski was all-important. They were reindeer hunters and herders and for sheer survival had to keep up with the animals in the snow. The Norsemen were more diversi-fied. They were settled farmers, alternating as mariners, traders and Viking marauders, so to them skiing was not quite so essential and often had an element of play.

Take Harald Hardrade, the eleventh-century King of Norway, for example. He was well travelled, a terror on the battlefield and rounded off his education in Constantinople by serving in the Varangians, the lifeguards of the Byzantine emperor. All this was in the best Norse tradition; so too his pride in the gentlemanly graces. He enumerated them in a scaldic poem beginning 'I am master of eight arts'.[3] They were: writing poetry, being a good horseman, hunting, playing the harp, navigation, swimming, archery – and skiing.

Hardrade was especially proud of his skiing. He brooked no threat to his supremacy. He was so agitated by the existence of an accomplished fellow-Norseman called Heming Aslaksson that – a thought doubtless occurring to others in like circumstances – he decided on liquidation. He commanded

7. Oldest known picture of a Norwegian skier. Hereford map, thirteenth century.
*Cambridge University Library*

Heming to a playoff, as it were. Taking his opponent to a steep narrow slope on the west Norwegian coast, which ended abruptly in a precipice dropping to the sea, Hardrade, according to the Flatey Codex from the fourteenth century,

> said that now you will entertain us with your skiing. Heming answered that it was no place for skis. He said that there was little snow, and it was hard icy and stony. The King replied that it was no test of skill if the going was good. So Heming put on his skis and ran down [with such control] that everyone said that they had never seen anyone ski so well. He went up to the King and said that he wanted to stop now. The King said 'you will do one more run. You will go to the top of the [slope], ski straight down, and stop at the edge of the precipice, if you can.'[4]

Hardrade threatened instant execution should Heming disobey. Heming resignedly clambered to the top of the slope. Hardrade placed himself near the abyss, driving his spear into the snow as a mark. Heming, so the saga continues

> put on his skis, and started from the top of the mountain. He rushed down with such speed that it was a wonder that he did not fall. Nonetheless his skis remained fixed to his feet. He came down to where the King was standing. At the edge of the cliff, he drove his ski stick into the ground, and swung himself into the air. His skis then flew off his feet and went on, and he got a foothold at the very edge of the precipice. However, during his vault, he lost his balance, and to steady himself, clutched at the king's mantle. But the king ducked his head under the mantle and [having already loosened the buckles], slid it off. So Heming fell off the mountain and over the crag. Then the King said: 'Now the dead part company with the living.'

The story, however, was not finished yet. This was the original cliffhanger. Heming was saved by a convenient shrub catching his clothes. Unknown to Hardrade, he escaped and after diverse adventures found himself in England fighting under the English King Harold the Saxon at the Battle of Stamford Bridge in September 1066. The general on the other side was none other than Hardrade. Bringing the Viking Age to a close, he had invaded from the sea in the old fashion. Alone in the English army, Heming could identify the Norwegian king, masked by a helmet as he was. Hardrade was then killed, if the Saga is to be believed, by an arrow from Harold himself. The Norsemen dissolved in defeat, and Heming had his revenge. With typical irony, the saga is rounded off by the Battle of Hastings a few weeks later, when William the Conqueror won, killing Harold the Saxon in his turn, and Heming renounced his skis to become a monk.

Heming was a literary invention, but the tale does make the historical point that Norway was the cradle of skiing as a sport; downhill into the bargain. It is reinforced by another set piece in another saga featuring an earlier King Harald, surnamed Fairhair. One winter's day in Gudbrundsdalen, a valley in central Norway, this King Harald

> was sitting outside watching with a critical eye his followers exercising ... Then he said, 'what is that I see on the mountain? It must either be a whirlwind or a man on ski'. But

the fresh powdery snow was loose, and there was no wind, so it had to be a man. And there were few men able to ski down from the top, it was so steep. When [this man] called Vighardr ... came down, he went to greet the King ... and the King said that he must be a great man.[5]

Vighardr wanted to join Harald's personal entourage and, on the strength of his skiing, Harald gratefully accepted. As well he might. In broken mountainous terrain, when winter was the travelling season, he needed hit men who could ski. The Saga blandly notes two brothers who were 'big, strong, brave, accomplished in ... skiing [but] not generally liked ... The King used them for his errands ... perhaps to execute someone or to confiscate property and so forth.'[6]

This happened around AD900. The ski itself even appears in runes. These are primitive Germanic letters, derived from the Greek, Latin and perhaps Etruscan alphabets. They go back to the second century AD.

Skiers are strewn through the turbulent events and quarrelsome characters of Old Norse literature. In the Saga of St Olav, who reigned in the eleventh century, a man was described as 'an outstanding skier ... well-born and rich' (in that order).[7] From the same Saga comes the tale of one Arnljot Gelline, a bit of

8. Detail from a map in a book about northern Sweden by Peter Högström, 1748.
Probably the first modern picture of a skier with two sticks. *Cambridge University Library*

a brigand and a giant of a man. In company with two others, this Arnljot had to ski from one village to another.

> He put on some skis, which were long and broad, but as soon as he drove his stick into the snow, he found himself far ahead. He waited for the others and when they caught up with him, he said that this would get them nowhere. So he told them to stand on his skis behind him. They did so … Then Arnljot set off as fast as if he had been alone.[8]

Irony leavens this exercise of imagination. The pillion passengers were tax collectors who had been scooping up arrears.

The ski also appears in other, workaday contexts. The earliest surviving Norwegian legal code, from the thirteenth century prescribes that 'No elk may be hunted by men on skis.'[9] In a sad little postscript, 300 years later, when Norway had become subject to Denmark, the local population in a country district petitioned the King in Copenhagen:

> Our lawbook says that elks are protected from those men who run on skis … and there are some who … have asked you for permission to hunt animals on ski, causing great damage to the country … and we beg Your Majesty for God's sake to forbid [this].[10]

The Old Norse lawgivers had understood that an elk, ploughing through deep snow, was at the mercy of hunters on ski, and risked extermination. That in turn raised the spectre of starvation.

9. Tungus tribesman on ski, Siberia, from a German book by Georg Johann Unverzagt, 1727. *Winter Sport Museum, Mürzzuschlag, Austria*

From a different point of view, ski also appear in *The King's Mirror*. This is a Norse didactic work, also from the thirteenth century. The point at issue is that because something is unfamiliar, it need not necessarily be dismissed. The author makes his case by considering foreigners who have never actually seen anyone skiing:

> They must think it is a ... wonder if they are told about people who can tame wooden planks, so that he who is not faster than other people when he has nothing else but shoes on his feet, as soon as he binds planks, eight or nine feet long under his feet, vanquishes a bird in flight or the greyhound in full speed.[11]

This is the closest that Old Norse literature comes to an exposition of skiing. There is however an undertone of something beyond the purely practical. The ski was so anchored in the Norse consciousness that it had a place in their poetic imagery. It was often used as a metaphor for a ship; 'the sea-king's ski', for example. Harald Fairhair was once addressed as 'You who can steer a ship like skis among the skerries.'[12] If nothing else, this indicates how the Norsemen were people of mountains and sea, living in the misty world between.

Fairhair himself talked about practising his *idrott*. This is a peculiar Norse word. It basically means a conspicuous achievement, which can include the arts. In this context, it approximates to 'sport'. In that sense, it survives in the modern Scandinavian languages today; which puts them among the few to have their own word for 'sport'. (Finnish, with its *urheilu*, from a root meaning 'hero' is another.)

In its original form. as Harald Hardrade proved, Norse kings could be quite touchy on the subject of their *idrott*. The Norwegian national icon Olav Trygveson, a tenth-century sea king with echoes of King Arthur, was said to be best in all its variations; skiing most of all, naturally.

*Idrott* meant so much, that it was held to be a divine gift. The Norsemen were said to have learnt it from Odin, the king of the heathen Gods. Odin aside, skiing found its way into the Norse pantheon. 'There was someone called Ull ... Thor's stepson. He was such a good ... skier that no one could equal him',[13] runs a telling passage in the Younger Edda, a medieval Icelandic epic of the old pagan myths, written down in Christian times. Ull was 'the God of skiing' and also, significantly enough, 'the archer's God, the God of hunting, the God of poetry'. He also had a darker side. In an earlier age, he was associated with fertility rites and human sacrifice. Since Thor, the God of thunder is also involved, this points to an atavistic blend of fear and worship of the forces of Nature.

With admirable impartiality, the Edda balances Ull with a female equivalent. Skade was her name. She was married to Njord, a demi-god who 'rules the wind, and calms sea and fire ... Skade wanted to live up among [the] mountains ... but Njord wanted to be near the coast.' They agreed to divide their time between the two.

But when Njord came back from the mountains, he chanted:

> Mountains are my curse …
> It was dreary to hear
> The howl of wolves
> Instead of the song of the swans

Whereupon Skade replied:

> I could not sleep,
> Next to the sea,
> Because of the screech of the birds.

And Skade went up into the mountains [where] she now runs on skis and shoots game with her bow and arrow; she is called the ski Goddess.

The supernatural is linked with skiing in other ways. One tale records a drastic solution to a familiar problem involving what we know as Finns. They 'sacrificed [a Norseman called] Thorri to make sure that snow fell and it was good for skiing'.[14] Amongst other things, this proves that Finns shared the ski with the Norsemen.

Skiing is famously enshrined in the *Kalevala*, the national epos of Finland. In the thirteenth canto, Lemminkäinen, one of the heroes – with the Homeric epithet of 'happy' – demands an enchantress's daughter but is told that first he must catch a magic elk and bring it back alive, moreover doing so on ski. The elk belongs to Hiisi, the playfully sinister forest god.

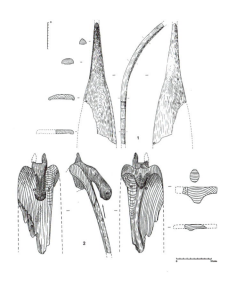

10. Prehistoric ski tips, about 6000BC. The elk's head is to prevent slipping backwards. Vis excavations, north-west Russia. After Burov, 1985.
*Cambridge University Library*

> Hiisi gives orders to his elk …
> Speed ahead, oh Hiisi's elk …
> You must make Lemminkäinen sweat,
> As he vainly skis in hot pursuit!

So:

> From all of Lapland's proving fields,
> Now a fearful din arose –
> Lapland's dogs began to bark,
> Lapland's children loudly cried,
> Lapland's women laughed in scorn,
> Lapland's men in anger growled.

Thus taunted, Lemminkäinen tried a final sprint to overtake the elk, but:

> When he took the first step forward,
> His ski broke off beside the hole,
> Where he threads the toestrap through …
> His spear broke off where the tip was fastened,
> His ski-stick snapped above the basket.[15]

The elk vanished; Lemminkäinen did not get the girl and, as he ruefully reflected, he had broken his whole ski outfit into the bargain. Thus in irony the canto ends.

The *Kalevala* is a compilation of oral epic verse. It was first written down in the nineteenth century by Elias Lönnrot, a fervent patriot, and a founder of the modern Finnish language. By contrast, the earliest surviving Old Norse manuscripts go back to the beginning of the thirteenth century. There are other differences too. Most of the Norse sagas are based on historical events. The *Kalevala* is myth, albeit with some anchorage in reality. The stories probably date from the twelfth century. What both have in common is the place of ski in medieval Nordic society and respect for the Lapps as skiers.

11. Mongolian tribesman skiing downhill, Altai 2005, Sinkiang region of China.
*Dave Waag*

Whether they learned skiing from the Lapps is another question altogether. Despite considerable borrowing between the Lappish, Finnish and Scandinavian tongues, skiing terminology has remained virtually separate.

The word 'ski', for example, is Norwegian. It derives from an Old Norse word for 'split' and originally meant a cloven billet of wood – highly appropriate for the way that skis were made. It has deep Indo-European roots, related to the modern German *scheiden* and ancient Greek *schizo* – as in schizophrenic – both meaning to divide. *Suksi*, however, the Finnish word for 'ski', and *sabek*, a Lappish term, have no known derivation. What is more, the equivalents in other languages are unrelated too. All this sugests that skiing was independently acquired from another source.

To cloud the issue, among the rare loan words in skiing terminology, the Finnish for groove, *olas* and the Lappish, *oales*, are both thought to descend from the Old Norse *áll*.[16] Then the Finnish *suksi*, in its varied forms, is strung out in the related Ural-Altaic languages across the eastern part of the Old World. Among the Mordvins, an ancient Finnish tribe from the Volga, for instance, it is *soks* and yet further eastwards, in Siberia, it is *huk-sille* to the Tungus.

There lies a happy hunting ground for linguists. One school has it that the word and hence the ski originated somewhere in Central Asia, probably the Altai mountains. The implication is that the ski came out of the east. Others argue just as cogently for a western origin, perhaps south of the Baltic, among the Cro-Magnons, whence it spread north and east. Cave drawings discovered in the Sinkiang (Xinjiang) province of North West China, perhaps confirm the prehistoric existence of the ski in Central Asia, but the issue of priority remains uncertain still.

Whatever it was, among the skiing nations, the Norsemen created a literature before the others and so they got their story in first. Nonetheless they were historically upstaged, and had to wait for outside recognition.

12. Sigismund von Herberstein, 1571. Skiers in Russia, near Perm.
*Cambridge University Library*

# 5

# The First Printed Sources

During the Middle Ages, Norse literature was hardly known abroad but misty hints of skiing sometimes did seep out. In England during the thirteenth century, for example, the Hereford map of the world depicted Norway with a man on faggots, like distorted skis.[1] Another vignette went back to the mythic Hippopodes with a naked figure on hooves bashfully clutching what looks like a ski stick.

In fact, after Paulus Diaconus in the eighth century, the ski had long been unrecorded in the West. Authentic reports began arriving with the Renaissance, of which one aspect was a profound curiosity about foreign cultures. The invention of printing in the fifteenth century helped to satisfy that need and, in 1514, the first complete edition of Saxo Grammaticus was published in Paris. Saxo was the twelfth-century chronicler of Denmark who, in the story of a certain Danish King Amlethus, gave Shakespeare the idea of Hamlet. More to the point, Saxo also retold the tale of Harald Hardrade's royal skulduggery on the slopes, but ascribed it to a different King Harald, surnamed *Blåtand* – Blue Tooth. This was the first time that the ski, although not the word, appeared in print. Like most contemporary scholars, Saxo wrote in Latin and therefore had to contrive a term for skis. *Lubricorum stipitum* – 'slippery planks' – was one solution.[2]

The real breakthrough came in 1539, with the publication in Venice of the *Carta Marina*. This was an annotated map of the north. It was the first reasonably true cartographic representation of Scandinavia. Like most contemporary maps, the *Carta Marina* was illustrated. Northern Scandinavia was decorated with vignettes of fierce-looking figures on what the caption calls 'curved strips of wood'.[3] At the same time, extended captions were printed separately, in German and, as *Opera Breve*, in Italian, for the benefit 'of those who at present know neither Greek nor Latin'.

The *Opera Breve* named the figures on the map as the ubiquitous 'Scricfinni' – identified here as Lapps – who

> have on their feet pieces of wood on which they run with great speed over the snow … besides being able to move at breakneck speed on the flying pieces of wood, they also, and this pleases them greatly, go quickly wherever they wish, and have the greatest ability to advance and retreat at will … and with the agility of their bodies and with the aid of these pieces of wood, they attain the greatest skill in attacking and fleeing.

To emphasize the point, there is an illustration, with three skiing figures from the map, each with bow and arrow. One of them, gleaming with fierce intent,

13. Olaus Magnus, *Carta Marina*, 1539. *Cambridge University Library*

has flowing locks and swirling skirts. This, says the caption 'is how the people living near the Pole, both men and women ... pursue wild animals'.[4] It is the first known picture of a woman on skis. 'There are also certain other women', so the text goes on reassuringly, 'who are locked up at home while their husbands are out hunting.'

The author and, indeed, the designer of the map was the seminal figure of a Swede called Olaus Magnus. A scholar, humanist and figure of the later Renaissance, he was the last Catholic Archbishop of Sweden. Olaus kept to the Roman creed and so was driven into exile by the Swedish Reformation. He left the country for good in 1526 to settle in Italy. The *Opera Breve* was only a trailer for what he called 'a more extensive volume'. As all too often, he wrote slowly and someone else got a book in first. That someone was Sigismund von Herberstein, Ambassador of the Habsburg Emperor Maximilian, who, early in the century, had visited Moscow. He was the first known Westerner to do so – on a vain quest, incidentally, to obtain help against the advancing Turks. In 1551, he published his book, in Latin of course, with the snappy title *Rerum Moscoviticarum Commentarii* – 'Notes on Moscow'. Writing of Perm, a province to the north-east, Herberstein observed that 'in winter, they travel here, as in most parts of Russia, almost exclusively on *artach*, which are a kind of oblong wooden sandal, six palms [4 1/2 ft, 135 cm] long, into which they fit their feet, and travel with great speed'.[5]

This was the first published Western description of skiing in Russia, complete with illustrations. It was an early example of travel writing, that product of the Renaissance, then coming into fashion.

When Herberstein came to Moscow, skiing in Russia was already ancient. In

14. Albertus Pictor, fifteenth century, Esau as hunter on skis. Swedish church mural at Österunda, near Uppsala.

a manuscript of the twelfth century, for example, the Metropolitan Nicophor of Kiev, casually wrote to Prince Vladimir Monomakh about travelling on *lyzhi*; the native Russian word for ski.[6] Then an illuminated manuscript from the fifteenth century shows two hunters on ski who have come to worship the princely Russian saints Boris and Gleb.[7]

15. Swedish runic stone (detail), AD1050, at Böksta near Uppsala. This is the oldest known realistic drawing of a skier.

This is one of the first known realistic pictures of men on ski. The other is a contemporary mural in a Swedish church near Uppsala.[8] It too shows a skiing hunter; Esau in this case, complete with bow and arrow. Less realistic, but graphic nonetheless is a rune stone drawing from the eleventh century, also in Sweden, near Uppsala. It is actually the earliest known representation of a skier since prehistoric times. It also depicts a hunt.

Meanwhile in the wake of Herberstein came Alexander Guagnini, an Italian from Verona in Polish military service. He published his book in 1578, naturally in Latin; title, *Sarmatiae Europeae Descriptio – Description of European Sarmatia.* This broadly included Russia, where Guagnini mentioned skiing too.

All this was unadvertised outside Russia. Herberstein's and Guagnini's accounts were too cursory. For his part, Guagnini more or less repeated Herberstein. In addition to Perm, however, he recorded the Cheremiss tribe along the Volga, noting that skis were up to 200 cm long. Moreover, instead of Herberstein's *artach*, Guagnini gives the local name for skis as *narte*.[9] In fact *narta* is the Polish word for ski and in Russian *narte* means 'sledge'. Guagnini was probably the first to use it in print. Otherwise, especially in an illustration, he owed much to Olaus Magnus.

This was understandable. In 1555, between Herberstein and Guagnini, Olaus had published his book at last; in Latin, of course. The title was *Historia de Gentibus Septentrionalibus* – 'An account of the Northern Peoples.' This was one of the formative works of the later Renaissance. It brought the North into the European consciousness. The first book on Scandinavia by a native writer to be published abroad, it was also the first comprehensive description. Over 800 pages long, it was yet no daunting tome but wholly readable, bursting with illustrations and haunted by the spirit of an exile pining for his native land. It was a best seller from the start and quickly translated into Italian.

Much of the writing was done at the Council of Trent. This was the great Church gathering of the Counter-Reformation. Olaus was a delegate, but a wistful one, given the improbability of ever making Sweden Catholic again. Starting in 1545, the Council lasted for eighteen years; Olaus only stayed for the first two. He was outside the charmed circle which, as in any conference in any age, really ran the show. For Olaus, working on his book was an escape from endless tedium. At least the landscape was inspiring; the north Italian city of Trent lies at the foot of the Alps.

Olaus dismissed the notion of the horrors of the frigid zone. He was the first to expound on the charms of the northern winter; the first to offer an authentic disquisition on snow and skiing in print. Scholarly to a fault, Olaus yet was a great observer of the natural world. He had travelled extensively in Sweden and Norway. He had a keen eye for detail. He lovingly described the formation of frost patterns on a window pane. He noted how the Scandinavians incorporated these patterns into their art so that they 'have learned from the beauty of Nature's objects, to no lesser degree than artists elsewhere are influenced by the artifice of skilled masters'.[10] In other words, Olaus praises the Scandinavians for being close to Nature. It is part of his idealized portrait. He was well ahead of his time.

For skiing, Olaus returned to the Scricfinni or Lapps of the *Opera Breve*. Their 'pieces of wood', he now enlarged upon the topic, were 'flat in the form of a bow, the front of which is curved upwards'.[11] Moreover: 'They steer by means of a stick held in the hand, and in this way they run straight up and down, or even obliquely over snow-covered mountains, exactly as they wish.' This is in fact the first description of the use of the ski stick to be published in the West.

> By their skill [Olaus went on], these people can climb mountains which were otherwise completely inaccessible, and also race down into the steepest valleys, especially in the wintertime. In summer, it is not so easy, since even although the snow does not disappear, it is too loose, and collapses under the pressure of the wooden planks. In any case, there is no mountain so steep, that they cannot climb it by some cleverly selected detour. Thus, after leaving the depth of the valley, they will make their way ahead in wide swings round the bases of the crags, and then steer obliquely in short zigzags up the slopes until finally, over precipices and crevasses reach the summit, and the goal they have set themselves. Sometimes they perform such exploits in the heat of the chase, and sometimes in competing with each other, since everyone wishes to appear the best, exactly as, on the running track, one wants to overtake in order to win the prize.

This is the original reference to Nordic skiing as a sport. Olaus goes on to say that even although his patron, Pope Paul III 'refused to believe in such skill and this way of running, nonetheless [it] is exactly as I have described'. Olaus had installed his own printing press in the house of the Swedish Brigittine Order in Rome, so that he could supervise production and save himself from the depredations of uncomprehending editors.

On that account or otherwise, the influence of Olaus was long-lasting and pervasive. He inspired others to follow in his tracks. One of them, at some remove, was Francesco Negri, a modest Italian priest from Padua. In the winter of 1664–5, Negri visited northern Sweden and there he learned to ski. He published the proceedings in a book called *Viaggio settentrionale – Northern Journey*. It appeared, in Padua, in 1700. His masters were naturally the Lapps. 'They have two narrow boards ... six feet [180 cm] long, with the tips somewhat raised so as not to cut into the snow', he explained.[12] 'In a land without roads, there was no other way of travelling.'

To run on the ski, which is what the Swedes call those boards [Negri continued], one never lifts them off the snow with the foot, but lets them glide forward delicately, with the same care as walking over bare ground and it does not make an impression on the snow deeper than the thickness of a finger.

Having disposed of skiing on the flat, Negri then considered running downhill: 'Since it is not possible to run slowly, because once the ski have begun to slide down, they never stop, it is necessary from the start of the descent to adopt a secure position like a statue.' By this, he evidently meant properly balanced, with one foot in front of the other.

> One runs down the mountain in a single sweep, until flat ground is reached, on which one continues to move some distance because of the momentum of the descent. This method is not as reckless as it might seem without trying, because the steepest slopes are not negotiated in this way.

And:

> When I first experienced the perils myself, I fell; then I learned by practice and, taking courage, I stood upright. One must remember to keep the ski pointing straight ahead and parallel, because if the tips approach each other, they form a triangle in the snow with the apex in front, colliding with each other and causing a fall. If the tips move apart somewhat, the same triangle is formed, but the other way about, with the rear ends colliding, which also causes a fall, but no danger ensues, especially if one falls to one side, which mostly happens.
>
> Charitably, the Lapps hurry to raise the fallen runner, because they are able to stop half way down the mountain, or where they wish. This is not done by stopping in the fall line, but by skilfully altering direction to one side or the other, forming a curved line. When one finds oneself turning into the side of the mountain, although the initial momentum makes one run on a little, nonetheless one stops quickly, and the Lapp comes to help up the one who has fallen.

This is the very first detailed technical exposition of skiing anywhere and Negri was the first outsider on record who learned to ski. This is odd, given the spread of printed sources. Somehow they did not inspire to emulation. Negri stood alone. Not even the French and Dutch engineers imported to work the Swedish iron and copper mines seem to have made the attempt.

Negri's power of analysis is striking. So too is the absence of heroics and the

Italian love of *la bella figura*. This says something about the character of the man. Nobody was likely to challenge what he had to say. The journey to northern Scandinavia was as arduous then as crossing the Atlantic. He said that curiosity about the natural world had sent him to Scandinavia. Between the lines another motive lurks. Christina, the ex-Queen of Sweden who, having converted to Catholicism, had abdicated in 1654 and gone into exile, was now living in Rome, surrounded by intrigue. Negri was probably one of various secret agents (vainly) sent to bring Sweden back to the Catholic fold; in his case starting with the Lapps. He certainly knew exactly where to go, visiting the remote Torne district, at the head of the Gulf of Bothnia, bordering on Finland. At any rate, Negri introduced the word 'ski' to the Italian language.

Even Olaus had pedantically stuck to his Latin periphrases. After him in fact, for more than a century and a half, printed records of Scandinavian skiing come predominantely from Sweden. In Norway there were almost none. From the fourteenth century even manuscripts barely mention skis. One reason may be the Black Death, which arrived in 1349. It decimated an already small population. At the same time Norway lost its independence, being absorbed by Denmark with its grossly centralized state and turned into a backwater. It was also the Little Ice Age. This was an interval of global cooling. It began in the thirteenth century, and ebbed out by the middle of the nineteenth century. In Norway it led to the advance of the glaciers, which swallowed outlying farmland. There was periodic crop failure and famine. Heavy snowfall must have made the ski indispensable for winter transport in a sparse population sprinkled along the edge of the habitable world. A glimmering of this appears in a rare contemporary document. 'Our under servant arrived on the second Sunday in Advent with your … letter', the Archbishop of Trondheim – the ancient capital of Norway – wrote to Hans Reff, the Bishop of Oslo on 7 December 1535.[13] 'He had difficult conditions, so that he had to ski over the Dovre mountains and the whole forest to the north.' Trondheim lies in central Norway, and Dovre is a plateau blocking the way to the south, about 1,500 ft. high. 'At this time of year,' the Archbishop continued in a telling aside, 'we cannot call a meeting of the State Council quickly.' Reff had earlier proposed using skiers to maintain the public posts in winter; obviously to no avail.

The word 'ski' first appeared in print some 70 years before Negri, in 1631. Andrea Bureus, another Swede, then published a book about his country, including the now obligatory Lapps and what he called (in Latin) their 'wooden shoes'. These, he explained, were what 'we Swedes call SKIDH'.[14] The more familiar Norwegian 'ski' had to wait for its earliest appearance in print until 1644. Saxo Grammaticus was then reprinted in Denmark, with notes by Stephanius (the Latinized form of Stephen Staphensen, a Professor at Copenhagen University). What Saxo called 'slippery planks' or, in another context, *pandibus trabibus*[15] – 'bent rods' – were in reality, so Stephanius explained, 'oblong soles of wood … called *skidher* by the Swedes and *skiier* by the Norwegians'. The singular would be *skid* and *ski* respectively, as they remain today. He also quoted an Icelander called Magnus Olaus – not to be confused with the Swedish Olaus Magnus – a specialist in interpreting the poems of the Edda. Magnus, said Stephanius, told him that among the old Norsemen skis were also used on 'thin ice, which otherwise would not support the weight of a man. On dry ground, free of snow, [they] also attached wheels to the underside [of the skis], and thus moved three times faster than they would have done without them.'[16]

In other words, roller skis had appeared the best part of a thousand years before they were used by modern cross-country skiers for training on dry ground. So the Norsemen invented dry skiing too.

Stephanius himself possessed a pair of skis. They were 'three ells [2 m] long, and on the underside ... a sealskin is attached. The feet are attached in the middle with fastenings, which fix the soles and, in running do not allow them to sway.' An accompanying illustration was the first reasonably true representation in print of the fur-lined ski, complete with the raised footrest of certain types. Not even Stephanius, however, could resist coining his own word for skis; *xylosoleis*, a Græco-Latin concoction meaning 'wooden soles'.

With the rise of the vernacular, it was nonetheless becoming fashionable to cite local terminology. Three years after Stephanius' edition of Saxo, a German called Adam Olearius published a book about his travels in Russia. He was the first to mention the Samoyeds and their skiing. On his way to Russia, Olearius passed through Narva, in Estonia, then a Swedish province. 'The colonel ... at Narva',[17] he said, 'entertained us by having some Finns run down a long [snow-covered] hill before the city [on] long, broad skates [which] they call *suksi*.'

This is an early reference to the Finnish word for ski. Bureus in 1631 had also mentioned 'suksi'[18], and that was its very first appearance in print. He however wrote in Latin. Olearius used his mother tongue of German, which makes his the first published example of the word in a modern language. Given the historic Finnish rôle in skiing, all this is of more than passing interest.

*Lapponia*, published in 1673, was the first book devoted to the Lapps, linguistic cousins of the Finns. It was a propaganda exercise. It had been commissioned by Magnus Gabriel de la Gardie, the Royal Chancellor of Sweden. The author was Joannis Schefferus, born in Alsace, and now a Professor at the University of Uppsala. Sweden was then one of the Great Powers, with a much-feared army. Her enemies explained away her victories on the battlefield by the magic of the Lapps – who were by now widely regarded as accomplished wizards. This annoyed the Swedes and was definitely not good for policy. The purpose of the *Lapponia* was to erase the myth and show that the Lapps were ordinary mortals. Schefferus tried to do so with a sober ethnographical study.

The Lapps were really of two kinds. Those living in forest and along rivers had settled abodes and were still hunter-gatherers. It was the mountain Lapps who received most of the attention, however. Since the thirteenth century, at least, they had domesticated the reindeer. They were nomads, following their herds. Spread over the northern part of Fennoscandia, they were divided between Denmark-Norway and Sweden but they cheerfully ignored national boundaries.

Their tribal home, mostly above the Arctic Circle, and broadly called Lapland by the Swedes, was still imperfectly delimited. The Swedish Lapps had been laid under the Crown, Christianized and taxed but information had hitherto been scattered. Schefferus now collected it between the covers of one book.

For maximum circulation, *Lapponia* was first published in Frankfurt-am-Main. Although pedantic, it was widely read. As *The History of Lapland*, an English translation was published by the Oxford University Press in 1674, a mere twelvemonth after the Latin original. In winter, Schefferus explained, the Lapps 'slide over the frozen snow, [on] broad planks extremely smooth; the Northern People call them … *Ski* … The way of going in them is this: they have in their hand a long staff … and with this they thrust themselves along very swiftly.[19]

This was the first appearance of the word 'ski' in the English language, and also the first account of skiing. Besides English, *Lapponia* was quickly translated into French, German and Dutch, introducing the word *ski* into each language for the first time. Oddly enough, it was not to be translated into Swedish for nearly three centuries. It was more important to form educated opinion of Lapland and the Lapps in the outside world, and that the book achieved. It more or less disposed

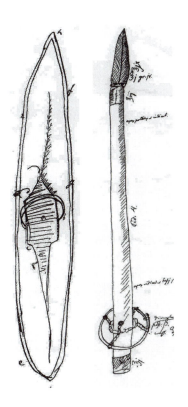

16. Linnæus, 1732. Lapp ski and stick.

of the imputation against the Swedish army, from which it followed that they were the better soldiers, and magic did not come into it.

Schefferus had not visited Lapland himself but had worked largely from unpublished reports that De la Gardie secured from the resident clergy. They were his only trusted agents, of whom a certain Johannis Tornæus was one. Tornæus was enthralled by the symbiosis of the Lapps with the reindeer, and the consequent rôle of the ski. This was needed to follow the domesticated herds in winter, or hunt the wild reindeer, which still continued to exist. The mountain Lapps had by now adopted firearms for the hunt. The forest Lapps still kept to the bow and arrow and they caught Tornæus's imagination:

> Around Lent in winter, when the snow collapses as deep as … six feet … the reindeer must … stay in one place, where they can find food, since they do not have the energy to wade through the deep snow … The Lapps know full well how to seize the opportunity, since the snow [melted] by day in the warmth of the sun, freezes again at night to form a crust that can bear both a dog and a man on skis … At dawn … the Lapps loose their [hunting] dogs and follow … And … when the Lapp hunts the … Reindeer, he uses his bow in his left hand as a [ski] stick … as well as his spear in the right one. At the bottom of bow and spear, a circular device of wood is affixed by crossed leather straps, so that while [skiing] they do not sink into the snow and lower the speed.[20]

This is an early description of the modern ski stick basket. It is also a rare example of using two sticks, when one was still the rule.

'About the [Lapps'] ski', Tornæus continued, 'there is this to be said. They [are made] of the toughest spruce found in the forest … hard as flint … the ski are patterned on top, but underneath as smooth as glass.'

Although Swedish himself, Tornæus was born in the Torne district of Lapland, which had so interested Negri – hence his surname. Tornæus had been a vicar there among the Lapps for more than 30 years when he wrote his report. He spoke Lappish. Mildly deprecating the religious oddities of his parishioners, imperfectly Christianized after a pagan, shamanistic past, he was more interested in their capacity to survive by a mastery of an unforgiving Nature.

So, too, somewhat later was Linnæus, the Swedish founder of modern biological classification. In 1732 he visited Lapland to catalogue the flora but, in between notes of angelica and helleborine, he also recorded the life of the Lapps. He sketched one of their skis; also a stick, amplifying Tornæus's description of the basket: 'A ring of roots, attached through a hole with strips of reindeer hide etc., fixed at the very bottom.'[21] This was the first precise representation of a modern ski stick.

Linnæus also took the opportunity to learn skiing from the Lapps. At the University of Uppsala, where he was a professor, one of his students recorded 'dining with [Linnæus], thereafter we went skiing on Lapp skis in the Academic Gardens, drank coffee, and mightily enjoyed ourselves'.[22] This is the first known instance of university skiing, anywhere.

Their fame as magicians scotched by Schefferus, the Lapps were then seen

17. Finnmark Lapps, Knud Leem, 1767. *Cambridge University Library*

abroad as admirable children of Nature. At home, this had long been the case, although more nuanced. Lapps were 'not noticeably tired by their skiing', one of Schefferus's sources observed.[23] 'I know a Lapp who skied 90 miles in one day. When he arrived in the evening, he downed half a tankard of aquavit, and said that he felt as fresh as when he started.'

The writer, Nicolai Lundii, another clergyman, was himself of Lapp descent, which gives force to his observation. To the clink of pewter goblets, aquavit was a much prized gift of civilization. The Lapps' stamina was not supernatural, after all, but the product of mere earthly refreshment.

In 1659 Johan Ferdinand Körningh, a shady Swedish exile in Rome, appeared incognito in Lapland on a vain quest to reclaim it for Catholicism. On his return to Italy the following year, he wrote a report for the Church authorities in which he dealt not only with theology but also skiing among the Lapps. In particular he noted that

the Lapp fixes a ski about six ells [4 m] long on his left foot, and on the right, a rather shorter one of about three ells [2 m] … Standing with the left foot on the snow, he pushes himself forward with the right foot, and simultaneously with the stick, so fast that he overtakes the swift-footed ... wild reindeer.[24]

This is a record of a singular device. Not only the Lapps, but Norwegians, Swedes and Finns used it too. Technically, the ski meant only the longer, smooth-sliding one of the unequal pair. The shorter one, which gave the kick-off, was called *andor*, with slight variations in the Scandinavian languages. It was usually lined with fur. Today, this is labelled the central Nordic system. It was only found in Fennoscandia. It existed alongside the usual kind of ski with pairs of equal length, as used by Negri. Cervantes, surprisingly, described it. In 1617, he published a fantastical novel called *Los Trabajos de Persiles y Sigismunda – The Travails of Persiles and Sigismunda*. It was set in northern regions. At one point the hero, Persiles, is trapped in the ice off the Norwegian coast, when he observes

> a band of armed people numbering more than four thousand ... They moved on only one foot, in that with the right one, they gave a kick against the left heel, as a result of which they sped along and glided a long way ... and then gave another kick and again glided a long way.[25]

Cervantes had inimitably captured the loping gait of ski and andor. Yet in his day, skiing was unknown in Spain. He may have learned about unequal skis from Olaus Magnus, the first to mention them in print. Arcane sources attested to skiing on a frozen sea, albeit off the shores of Finland. However he knew, the creator of Don Quixote had got it right.

# 6

# Norway – The Cradle of Skiing as a Sport

The central Nordic ski occupied a broad swathe from east to west across Finland, Sweden and Norway. It played a historic rôle. As skis go it was not old, dating from the Middle Ages. It lasted for many hundreds of years and, in remote corners, lingered on until the 1930s. In 1900, it could still be the subject of a book. 'When one puts on a pair of [such] ski for the first time', to quote a telling passage, 'one immediately feels unsteady on one's feet; that the smooth … *ski* wants to run away from under one, while the … andor drags behind, or is completely stuck fast.'[1]

The author was a Swede called Gustaf Schröder. By profession he was an accountant but he was a passionate hunter by choice. His book was a paean to the central Nordic ski. Schröder had grown up in the central Swedish province of Värmland, amongst people who still used it. 'The nature of the terrain', he argued, 'has for the most part determined the form [of ski] … In the same way, the consistency of the snow; its hardness, its graininess, whether coarse or fine, has played its part.'

This neatly expounds the wholly functional process driving the evolution of the ski. 'The running ski and andor', Schröder went on to say, 'have proved to be best suited to the forest and hill dweller … because by using them, he can get through under all conditions even in … loose, fine grained snow … They … are [thus] suited to … the hunter … and those who haul sledges.'

The central Nordic type arose from the lack of proper waxes. In the sense of something that improved glide, waxing had long existed. It took centuries for a substance to emerge that both glides and grips. In the central Nordic system, the functions were separated; the long ski giving the glide and the andor the adhesion. Folklore vindicated Schröder, especially among the Finns. In the *Kalevala*, Lemminkäinen certainly agreed. When preparing to hunt the elk of Hiisi he orders a craftsman to

> Make a *lyly* that runs swiftly,
> Carve for me a well-made *kalhu*[2]

*Lyly* is a special Finnish word for the sliding ski; *kalhu* means the andor. (The corresponding Lappish terms are *kuovta* and *pietsek*.) Finnish also has at least four other words for the andor, besides *suksi*, the ordinary word for 'ski' and *hiihtoh*, which means 'skiing'; all this hints at the richness of its skiing terminology. In parts of Norway, andor has simply been another word for 'ski' and in Old Norse it always meant the same. *Skade*, for example, was called *Ondúrdís*, the andor goddess; it tripped more lightly off the tongue.

The central Nordic ski suited the hunter in his quest for speed and agility. It was adapted to a certain Nordic terrain of dark thick rolling conifer forest and low mountains. It allowed skiing downhill, uphill and on the flat. The andor gave control, and a firm kick-off when hauling trophies of the chase homewards on a sledge.

The ski, narrow and up to 3 m long, was built for sliding. It was generally made of compression wood from fir trees. Its drawback was its weight. The andor, on the other hand, was light, having to be lifted at every step after each kick-off. Shorter than the ski by varying amounts, it was usually made of birch, and lined with fur, the hairs of which sloped backwards, all designed for maximum purchase and kick-off. In parts of Finland, because of the flat terrain and the nature of the snow, the andor too was bare, but gripped just as well. Either way, the upshot was the one-footed skating with a limp recorded by Cervantes – and perhaps the origin of the mythological unipeds, hopping on one leg.

Another difficulty was wet snow. The fur coped well with fine drift snow and the coarse grains of spring. When the fur grew wet, the andor became heavy, and the hairs were scraped off. An overriding advantage of the system, however, was the fact that only one stick could be used, because the technique required a double-handed push on the sliding step, and nothing on the kick-off. To the hunter, this meant flexibility and ease in handling his weapons. With the advent of firearms, the stick became a convenient shooting rest when standing up, and the andor gave an anchorage to absorb the recoil. Above all, ski and andor seemed adapted to the snow of the Little Ice Age.

The pine resin often used to coat the sole of the ski was faster than anything until the advent of modern synthetic materials. In fact, under the right conditions, ski and andor gave a surprising turn of speed. A Norwegian scholar called Hans Barhow made the point:

> A girl in Merager [near Trondheim] ran on ski to Bestaden, a distance of 8 [Norwegian] miles [80 kilometres] and slept with a man. That was 16 miles [160 kilometres] in one night. But … when rivers and everything else are frozen, one can move as the crow flies. [Especially] when it is mostly downhill, with no obstacles.[3]

And: 'The fastest one can run is a Norwegian mile in [40 minutes].' After two-and-a-half centuries, modern cross-country ski racers, with all the benefits of applied technology, have managed to reduce this to 25 minutes. Barhow again:

> [The andor] is made of wood that is bent up, but goes down when one treads on it. Moving on the flat, one just treads on it, and the other knee stiff. Then one pushes a long way. In other words, it was really skating on skis – hence the speed on level ground.

Barhow was writing about 1740. Since early in the century, Norwegian records of skiing had started to flow again after 400 years. To begin with, it was military in the main. Oddly enough, Norwegian ski troops used ski and andor instead of ordinary skis. Their demands, however, were exactly those of the Nordic hunter.

In 1733, a certain Major Jens Henrik Emahusen produced the first formal regulations. They were the first of their kind, anywhere. Compared with the Finns, Swedes and Russians, the Norwegian soldiers were better downhill skiers. Emahusen recognized this. Nonetheless, true to his times and his profession, he reduced everything to a drill movement. Thus for example:

> When the order to [ski down] a mountain, is given, everyone immediately forms up in single file, and moves diagonally across the slope. Each man does his best, observing properly, not to injure anyone else while running. If the mountain is very steep or exposed, then each man will run straight down, but under the following conditions: the guide, who will ski ahead with the advance guard, is to indicate where danger might be found, so that the ski will not be broken.[4]

And on parade:

> At the command, right about turn, the skier will firstly raise his right foot, with straightened knee, so that the ski is standing with the tip pointing upwards, then turn his body halfway round on the left foot, placing the right [ski] against the left one in the opposite direction. Secondly he will raise the left ski a little, and turn his body completely round on the right foot while, in the same movement, bringing the left [ski] back together with the right one.[5]

In other words the kick turn, used by skiers to this day, had its origins on the eighteenth-century parade ground. It could then only be made to the right, because only the shorter andor could be raised vertically, and that was on the right foot. Norwegian military regulations of 1762 also specified the equipment:

> The ski, which must be made of the best pine compression wood, must be [260 cm] long, including the curve of the tip. [It] shall be [7.5 cm] wide, and the front tip must bend so high that it is a good [15 cm] above the ski, and the rear tip must be [3.75 cm] high. When the ski is placed on the ground, it must rise [10 cm] from the snow at the point where the skier's heel is placed, but on the other hand, it must be so soft under the foot, that when the man puts his full weight on it, it must bend so that it is completely flat.[6]

This defines the principles of an all-round ski, which hold to this day. What is wanted is something lively, flexible and suited to the skier's weight. The document continues:

> Along the under side there shall be a groove [3 mm] deep … exactly one third the width of the ski … The … andor shall be of the same width and camber as the ski, but only [180 cm] long including the bend of the tip, and lined underneath with deer, reindeer or elk fur, according to what is available.

The stick was to be made of birch, 160 cm long – above the armpits – with a strap threaded through the top. An iron spike was to be fitted to the bottom. At the joint, to prevent the stick sinking into the snow, there was to be a basket. It consisted of a ring, made of horn, 10 cm in diameter, fixed by two leather thongs forming diameters at right angles. The pattern recognizably still exists.

All this was the first and, for a century-and-a-half, the only recorded specification for ski equipment of any kind, military or civilian. It was a step in the transition of skiing to a modern sport.

The central Nordic technique was difficult. Running straight downhill, for example, required lifting of the andor, and balancing on the ski, with or without the aid of the stick. The same applied to turning. The binding, as ever, was the crux. It was the ancient one of a toestrap let through a transverse hole, and a heelstrap to hold the foot in place. One was made of twisted birch root; the other of leather. Combined with soft boots, however, this was laterally too loose for comfort. Sometimes the only method of control was by twisting the foot across the ski and digging the heel into the snow. Army regulations prescribed that if a recruit 'showed any lack of ability, he must be trained by a practised Non Commissioned Officer in the presence of an Officer [especially] in running straight with the andor'.[7]

Skiing was still deeply embedded in local life. Thus in 1772, a church register noted the marriage of one 'Jon Hansson Rollag, skier and bachelor'[8] to a spinster of the parish. Ability in skiing, so a country priest wrote about this time, was vital for animal husbandry and a necessity of life itself among those living in isolated valleys:

> Therefore they accustom themselves to the use of skis from the tenderest age. It is work to which carefree childhood does not need to be driven with threats! … A little fellow, hardly three years old has both the courage and desire to attach these long shoes to his small feet. He … puts them on and immediately goes to nearby slopes … Then he tries to run down on his ski, unconcerned if he falls head over heels a score of times and is buried in snow … Thus little boys like to spend their leisure hours in winter in this enjoyable pastime … until they have sufficient skill to run down a slope, however long and steep, and know exactly how to bend and turn their bodies, so that they nearly always stay on their feet and arrive at the appointed goal.[9]

In other words, Norwegian countryfolk could swoop downhill with the best, but that was on ordinary skis of equal length, both smooth. It was not easy converting to the other type, with its awkward, limping gait. Somehow the army had to maintain the standard of recruits.

One who was notably concerned was General Carl Schack Rantzau, commander of the Norwegian army. Rantzau was a Dane, which, given that Norway still belonged to Denmark, was only natural. By the easy-going custom of the times, he had once briefly served with the Russian army. More to the point, he had a taste of winter warfare and therefore disapproved when the Norwegian ski regiments were threatened with disbandment. The order came from the Danish-

Norwegian commander-in-chief in Copenhagen. He was in fact a Frenchman, the Comte de St Germain, who had been brought in to carry out a military reform. St Germain knew nothing about skiing but wanted to save money. Sweden was by now in decline and, St Germain thought, it no longer posed a threat, so that the frontier need not be guarded, in winter least of all. Although St Germain was his patron, Rantzau, in the words of a Spanish proverb, decided to 'obey orders but not carry them out'. He saved the Norwegian ski regiments, disguising them as 'grenadiers'.

Ski troops had been called up 15 days a year, and required to practise their skiing during 'church parades … every Sunday before and after the sermon'.[10] Rantzau doubled the annual service. He also managed to appropriate the money to found prizes for regimental ski races. In July 1767 he issued the regulations:

Class 1: 2 prizes of 20 *riksdaler* … for those who, on a reasonable slope, can fire their guns, and are most successfully in hitting certain prescribed targets at a range of 40 to 50 paces.[11]

Class 2: 4 prizes of 10 *riksdaler* … for those who, on a reasonably wooded slope, are best at hurling themselves between the trees without … falling or breaking their skis.

Class 3: 6 prizes of 4 *riksdaler* … for those who, without riding or resting on their stick are best at running down the steepest slope without falling.

Class 4: 8 prizes of 2 *riksdaler* … for those who, on a level space, ski fastest over [2 1/2 kilometres] with full equipment … with gun over the shoulder. In good snow conditions, this shall take place in less than 15 minutes.

Now 5 *riksdaler* bought a good cow in milk; say about £500 at today's values. The comparison is apt. Skiing belonged to the country, not the town. Most skiers were part hunter, part farmer. The ski regiments were raised from the local population. They were strung out along the border with Sweden, south of Trondheim.

Rantzau's four classes of competition define most events as we know them; a century-and-a-half before they appeared in the outside world. Class 1 is the ancestor of a pale shadow of itself, the biathlon – cross-country skiing interspersed with target shooting at rest.

Class 2 is obviously the slalom; except that the word, of Norwegian origin, did not yet exist. The straight downhill race is covered by class 3. Finally, class 4 is a kind of cross-country event. The qualifying time was in itself also a pioneering concept. Nor is the stipulated figure wholly antiquated. It meant 5.5 minutes a kilometre. By comparison, a modern Olympic Nordic racer takes about 2 1/2 minutes, and *he* is unburdened, with the lightest possible equipment, skating on *both* skis.

Rantzau was merely codifying what already existed. He had been preceded two years earlier by an obscure manuscript. The author was one Grüner, identity unknown. He illustrated the various events by a series of naive drawings, with accompanying captions. These anticipate Rantzau's rules. In Grüner, however, the downhill race is timed. This is the first known reference to timing, in any sport. The qualification was '130 paces in less than 1/4 minute'.[12] This is about 20 km an hour. Grüner added that often the speed was so great 'that it could scarcely be measured'.[13] That may have been hyperbole. The stopwatch had been invented almost a century before.

Grüner added the ski-jump, not included in Rantzau's rules. It was done 'when ... a skier is forced to make a jump because of a drop or a hole that he cannot avoid'.[14] It was what we call a terrain jump, incidentally carrying a rifle. This completed the repertoire of skiing events.

Rantzau soon learned the age-old lesson that reforms devour the reformers. In the autumn of 1767, St Germain fell and went home, eventually becoming French Minister of War. Rantzau fell with him, following in his tracks to France. The ski regiments were officially reinstated and Rantzau's competitions abolished. Before then, however, at least one regiment held them in 1768. Thereafter the prize money was abolished and the events reverted to military exercises.

At any rate, Rantzau had published the very first rules for ski racing. He thus atoned for an ability to antagonize anyone within reach. He and Grüner and, before them, Emahusen had documented that the origins of formalized technique and competitive skiing, both Nordic and downhill, lay in the eighteenth-century Norwegian army.

In March 1797, a Dutch naval officer called Cornelius de Jong, happened to be in Trondheim at the right time to witness regimental winter manoeuvres. He

18. A. de Capell Brooke, 1827. Norwegian ski troops. *Cambridge University Library*

recorded the earliest proper, detailed first-hand account of Norwegian skiers in action, particularly running downhill. The Norwegian ski troops, he admiringly wrote, 'flung themselves down [the slope] with a speed that can only be compared with the flight of a bird'.[15] Until the advent of fast railway trains, in the late nineteenth century, a skier was the fastest human being on earth.

'When one runs down a mountain slope,' de Jong observed, 'the knees are bent more, and the body is equally bent, so that one is nearly in a sitting position.' That might have been written today. On the other hand:

> The stick is gripped in both hands, with tensed arms, pointing well backwards, with the iron spike driven into the snow, in order to control the rushing speed somewhat. But the stick also serves more or less like a rudder, since a good skier when running downhill is able to change direction with its help. The most dangerous of all is when one is suddenly faced with a drop ... and one is required instantly to stop. This is done by skilfully moving the stick from the rear and thrusting it between the legs, heaving it upwards with both hands, and simultaneously bending the body backwards. In this way one stops immediately, but it is easy to grasp what a an enormous shock the body has to sustain.

This is a succinct exposition of the downhill technique of the time. Stick riding actually survived here and there until the twentieth century. To De Jong, at least, it was a colourful sight. The Norwegian uniform

> consists of a red serge jacket, lined with sheepskin, and edged with black leather, and with yellow buttons and braid of the same colour. They have light blue waistcoats and trousers, grey gaiters, and red caps with a yellow turned up brim. Besides which the non commissioned officers wear green top coats.

'We all spent the evening uproariously', continued De Jong. 'A number of peasant girls appeared, with whom the skiers danced until the small hours, mostly an extremely tiring dance called the Polish dance [a kind of reel].'

Meanwhile back in the snow:

> The skiers ... went up ... to the top of a steep slope, and started down ... they had built a fairly high mound of wood and snow, over which they jumped as they came down the slope. They shouted as they did so, and when the ski hit the slope again it was with an impact that could be heard from far off ... Even the captain, who was rather advanced in years, took part in everything, while I ... fell the moment [I] put skis on.

The soldiers were sensational in not doing so either. To remain upright, they were practically monoskiing over the jump. If they put any weight on the andor, it would drag behind the slippery ski, with interesting consequences.

A contemporary observer put a figure on de Jong's highly coloured account – about 12 or 15 metres as he said.[16] He happened to be Thomas Malthus, the English inventor of demography. In 1799, Malthus had visited Norway – a land with 'eight months of winter and four months of bad weather', as one citizen, sardonically told him – because the French revolutionary wars were raging, which debarred English travellers from the Continent, but left Scandinavia open.

A quarter of a century later another Englishman, A. de Capell Brooke visited Norway – mainly to hunt – but in the process saw soldiers on skis. 'These machines', as he put it later in the book that he published, 'are by no means easy of use where the ground is precipitous; and it requires no inconsiderable share of dexterity to keep the necessary balance while descending with such extreme velocity.'[17] He also observed that 'the skies [*sic*] are smeared with tar and pitch' – an early reference to what was to become the intricate art of waxing.

Brooke came just in time to see Norwegian soldiers on skis, for this was in the aftermath of the Napoleonic wars. One result had been that, in 1809, Sweden lost Finland to Russia and, as compensation, had Norway transferred to her from Denmark. That happened in 1814, the year before Waterloo. By a bizarre twist of a tumultuous age, the Swedish regent was now a Frenchman: Jean-Baptiste Bernadotte, one of Napoleon's marshals. He had turned against his erstwhile master and became the founder of the present royal family of Sweden. He duly annexed Norway but under surprisingly generous terms. He granted the Norwegians the domestic autonomy, the parliament and the constitution that they craved. After nearly a thousand years, Sweden was no longer a threat and Norway's land border was pacified at last. Bernadotte, however, was taking no risks. In 1826, the Norwegian ski troops were finally disbanded. The post-Napoleonic settlement had left not even the Nordic snows untouched. As a consequence, it was in Norway that the evolution of skiing now had its heart.

# 7

# The Influence of Rousseau

The Norwegian ski regiments had been the ski schools of the age. Their disappearance heralded decay. Under the old order, men from the frontier districts with their garrisons had been better skiers than those elsewhere. Ski troops, drilling on the slopes, set an example. Without the call of duty, incentive withered. To begin with, skiing was no pleasure but an irksome necessity. Skiers became fewer and less able. Better roads reduced the need for skis and hastened the decline. Skiing withdrew to remoter places, where it was still a matter of survival.

The same was true in Sweden, Finland and European Russia. Only in Norway was it a matter of concern. There, the leaders of society saw in it a symptom of degeneration. Even before the union with Sweden they had been worried. In 1812, Napoleon invaded Russia, thus ensuring his own defeat, but he also forestalled a Russian annexation of northern Norway. That was unknown at the time, but the same year, a Norwegian magazine published an appeal for 'Skiing, once so common, and now ... so rare [to be] reintroduced to the country districts, since shooting practice on ski in forest and mountain are of the greatest importance for the defence of the country, and its independence.'[1]

The subject was then aired at the National Assembly of 1814, which framed the present Norwegian constitution. One of the delegates was a Colonel Hegermann, who had been a signatory to the appeal of 1812. He now proposed a kind of junior conscription:

> From their 13th year ... all the sons of Norway, both in town and country are to be trained in gymnastics ... It would be particularly suitable if, in the mountain districts, these exercises took place in winter, in order to practise skiing, that accomplishment which is ... so indispensable for Norway.[2]

The proposal was dropped, but its spirit lived on. It presaged the use of physical exercise for political ends. This was after all the age of nationalism. It appeared in many forms. Here it was waiting on the slopes. Its roots lay in the past.

Under the Danish crown, a Norwegian sense of identity had long been dormant. Since the middle of the eighteenth century, national consciousness had begun to stir. The central figure was a scholar called Gerhard Schøning. Like many educated Norwegians at the time, in search of fame and fortune, he migrated to Denmark. He became Professor of Rhetoric at Sorø Academy, near Copenhagen. In 1771, he began publishing the first modern history of Norway.

He frankly explained that he saw history as propaganda. He used it to mould his own generation in the image of the old Norse Sagas. They were the record of the Golden Age. Their heroes were the examples to be followed; idealized figures of Homeric stature in which contemporary Norwegians could see themselves.

As became a figure of the Enlightenment, however, Schøning was not proposing blind ancestor worship. He deplored the Vikings' spectacular misbehaviour. 'I [would] urge my beloved compatriots to study their forefathers far better than hitherto', he wrote.[3]

> Not for their vices [as he put it]; not for a stiff, unbending and partly unfeeling character … for things that do not suit our age … but … for their cultivation of all kinds of physical exercise … like shooting, swimming, running, throwing a ball … climbing [and] skiing across the snow or on the ice.

All this, said Schøning, 'characterises us as a nation of its own'. Skiing, he added helpfully, 'was counted amongst the greatest arts in olden times.' This is probably the earliest move, anywhere, to use sport as an agent of national identity. Hegermann was simply following in Schøning's wake.

Schøning also broke new ground in abandoning summer as the ideal season. He put winter in its stead. A cold climate produced a vigorous people. What is more, the ancient Norsemen were doubly admirable because they led a simple life, close to Nature. 'The freezing snow was oft their pillow',[4] as Schøning engagingly put it, 'and also the bed on which they lay … An untanned fur [was] their sole defence against the deepest cold, and in which they could run around almost in the nude.'

Schøning was himself a practised skier. He presented skiing as a civic virtue. He also showed the Norwegians to themselves as children of winter, with skiing as the emblem of their national identity.

This was quite unique. It was not even shared by the neighbouring Finns or Swedes. Geography was one explanation. Norway is almost entirely mountainous, and the slopes invade the towns; in Sweden and Finland, forested plains mostly separate the one from the other.

Even in Norway, however, the impetus came from abroad. Yet again, the French Encyclopedists had played the leading rôle. By his own account, Schøning owed much to Rousseau – at least Rousseau's notion of Man being happiest in a state of Nature. This was (unusually) at first hand. Schøning was a linguist, with a mastery of French. He also found in Montesquieu a fitting source of inspiration. In *De l'Esprit des loix*, one of the classics of the Enlightenment, Montesquieu sang the praises of a cold climate. There:

> you have more vigour. The action of the heart and the reaction of the extremities of the [nerve] fibres are more efficient [so that] the heart is stronger. This greater force necessarily has many consequences: for example, more self-confidence, that is to say, more courage; a greater sense of one's own superiority.[5]

Voltaire also chimed in. Nature, he wrote, had given to the harsh Northern climate 'calm skies and pure air'.[6] Besides which: 'The long nights of winter are softened by the aurora and … intensified … by the reflection of the snow covering the ground.'

Indeed Schøning had the best authorities behind him. Contemporary Norwegian poets were affected too. Chief amongst them was Nordahl Brun, Bishop of Bergen. In *Den norske Vintern – The Norwegian Winter*, he wrote that he would 'hardly change it for the spring'.[7]

> Now on ski down mountainsides
> The cheerful valley dweller glides.
> Swiftly as an arrow flies.

Those were among the first lines, anywhere, glorifying winter. They were published in 1786. Brun's Norwegian contemporary, Jens Zetlitz, elaborated on the subject:

> From a lofty mountain, down its slippery side,
> …
> On smooth ski the bold Norwegians glide,
> And smiling follow in their fathers' tracks,
> …
> The rocky crag – where death awaits,
> They avoid with an accomplished turn.[8]

There were more poets of the same or another kind. Pure imagination it was not. Skiing was anchored in the rural population. And not only the male of the species. Thus Zetlitz again:

> On dainty feet, even Norway's daughters bind
> The ski and, proud of heroes' deeds,
> Run from lofty peak to deepest dale
> … and a cloud of snow,
> Runs before the winged heroine,
> Who boldly races with the men,
> And sometimes wrests the prize from them.[9]

In a book published in 1786, a country parson called Hans Jacob Wille was less poetic:

> The higher you go in the mountains [he wrote] the bigger and stronger are the inhabitants … You find extremely few attractive women … They know little of the art of pleasing, but … are the more inured against cold … and hardship. Some can even ski, and have the strength to … overcome … the men.[10]

This was in the province of Telemark, a name to conjure with in after years.

The Lapps, meanwhile played an enigmatic rôle. Whereas Swedes and Finns were competing with them for the same territory the Norwegians, by and large, were not. The Lapps ranged the barren hinterland of arctic Norway, or held the deserted high ground unsuited to cattle further south. They descended only to trade reindeer furs and perhaps skis for necessities like aquavit or, eventually, coffee, to which they became famously addicted. It was a question of live and let live.

What both had in common was an extensive vocabulary for winter travel. To this day, Norwegian and Lappish each have more than 300 expressions for snow and its subtle interplay with the ski. That makes them the richest languages in the field. In Norwegian, for example, ideal skiing is graphically called *silkeføre* – literally 'moving on silk' – when a mantle of dry light powder snow covers a firm underlay deep enough to give steerage to the skis without breaking through to the harsher crystals below. The Lapp equivalent is *jådåt*.[11] Unfortunately, it may be audible, to the point of *gitjerdit*, when ski and sticks creak in deep cold. That alerts the prey, inhibiting the hunt. Best of all, therefore is *linádahka*, when the going is silent, and the hunter can stalk his quarry unawares. More modern, but equally telling, is *Káffabievlla*, which is when the snow has melted enough to bare a piece of ground big enough to light a fire and brew coffee. The term is both a sign of spring, and a measure of travel, a journey defined by the number of *Káffabievlla*, or coffee breaks.

One way or another, the Lapps and especially their skiing had fascinated their neighbours. One such was a contemporary of Schøning called Knud Leem. A Norwegian clergyman working among the Lapps of Finnmark, Leem was a professor of their language to boot. Finnmark is what the Norwegians call their Lapland, a wild region beyond the Arctic Circle in the very north of their country. In 1767 Leem published a book on the subject. The Finnmark Lapps, he wrote

Are ... supple and swift ... They can run and walk quickly over rocks and mountains. With their stick held over their shoulder, and not stuck in the ground for support, they ski down high mountains and slopes at breakneck speed, so that the air whistles in their ears, and their hair streams backward in the wind. Indeed, if you place a cap or something else in their way, they bend down at full speed, and pick it up.[12]

The reference to the sticks is telling. In other words, the Lapps were praised as better skiers than the Norwegians themselves, which is more or less what the Sagas had implied.

Foreign influence, meanwhile, continued to advance. During the latter part of the eighteenth century there was a movement in Germany to cultivate sport and gymnastics. Again it was Rousseau who had sown the seed. Here it was his views on education, as expressed in the form of a novel, *Emile*. He proposed a revolution in the classroom by training the body as well as the mind. As usual, he left others to put his theories into practice; the Germans in this case. A leading disciple was a teacher from Lower Saxony called Johann GutsMuths. He began by opposing the domination of the classics in the schools. He advocated leavening Latin and Greek with modern subjects like geography, but above all counterbalancing pure intellect by sport, gymnastics, music and dancing. This was the way to develop the whole man. His ideas soon made their way to Norway. By about 1800, a follower called Nils Hertzberg, had established a boarding school in Hardanger, in the west of the country. He adapted GutsMuths' principles to local conditions. A former pupil remembered that

> Hertzberg ... had a pair of skis made for each of us. Although we did not achieve any particular ability in this art, and by no means could be compared with the fearless skiers [in Eastern Norway] nonetheless we ran quickly down slopes and hillocks, and, with the aid of our long ski sticks, propelled ourselves at great speed on the flat.[13]

This is revealing. It was, after all, the educated classes, acting on an ideology, who had begun to uphold skiing. That was the precursor of a renaissance. GutsMuths himself was a convert. He published this in *Gymnastik für die Jugend* – *Gymnastics for the Young* – the first textbook in the subject, and a classic of its kind. He was a pioneer of an analytical approach. The aim of gymnastics was to enhance fundamental attributes like strength, co-ordination and suppleness. Skiing promoted balance. It was, said GutsMuths, in the second edition of his book, published in 1804, 'without doubt a healthy exercise, that occupies ... youth ... in idle hours'.[14] He never visited Norway but, in his own words, 'had the opportunity thoroughly to discuss the matter with a Norwegian who was himself a trained skier'. The result was a rare practical exposition of skiing in Norway at the end of the eighteenth ventury. Some of the details are found nowhere else.

The ski were made of ash, pine, spruce or, best of all, birch, which ran quickest of all.

> They are fashioned from green wood, along the grain ... when the wood is fully worked, they must have a suitable camber before they can be used as a ski ... Both are laid together with the soles facing each other, a block of hard wood is placed in the middle, and they are firmly lashed [near back and front]. The tips as well as the heels are then forced apart by inserting pieces of wood, and the whole is then left to dry out completely.

The purpose, GutsMuths went on to declare 'is easy to grasp. The skier stands on an elastic arc; and by forcing it down ... the glide is enhanced, since the vaulted centre presses down on the snow far less than the front and rear parts of the snow, so that the friction is reduced.'

This is in fact the earliest known explanation of the mechanics of the ski. GutsMuths' informant, presumably under skilled cross-examination, had provided the material for this analysis. In his book, GutsMuths even included a drawing, probably the first to illustrate the camber of a ski and hint at the complexity behind an apparently simple device.

In Norway itself, for the first three decades of the nineteenth century, although the ski was embedded in folklore, there were only passing local references in print. Partly it was perhaps evidence of decay. It is also connected with the fact that Norwegian literature then hardly existed. It was still germinating. Its great luminary, Henrik Ibsen, was only born in 1828.

Norwegian literary attention to skiing began in the 1830s. Henrik Wergeland, the first major poet in the modern Norwegian language – a kind of northern Browning – published in 1833 a small, stirring epic about the defeat of some Swedes by Norwegian ski troops during the Napoleonic wars. It includes the lines

> See how in war the landscape,
> Is on the people's side.[15]

This was the murmuring of Norwegian discontent with their – unquestionably tolerant – Swedish overlords. One outcome was the romanticizing of winter to promote national consciousness.

In 1840, a Norwegian folklorist, Jørgen Moe, published a slim volume of poems, one of which was partly set on skis. It concerned the wooing of a girl called Birgit by Knud, a country boy. He offered her a lift on ski to a local dance.

> With a smile she accepted,
> Stood behind on my ski,
> Down we sped like a bird
> Winging along so free.[16]

But alas:

> In the deep, freezing snow.
> Head first like a wild duck I dived,
> And in the snow I lay;
> 'Thanks for the lift!' she giggled,
> And continued on her way.

Lesser poets touched on the same theme. Thus one book of children's verse:

> The snow with a crust is hard indeed,
> On my ski I run at speed.[17]

That was a change of course. Romanticizing winter in general had turned to the romanticization of peasant life. Either way, it brought skiing to a wider world. That was reinforced shortly afterwards in a short story called 'Berte Tuppenhaug's tales'. At a certain point, the narrator is offered a horse to ride home, but casually declares that 'since the route was twice as far, I preferred to go as I had come, in a bee line on ski'.[18] The author was Peder Chistian Asbjørnsen who, together with Moe, eventually published a collection of folk tales that became a cornerstone of Norwegian national consciousness, and one of which, 'The three billy goats Gruff', ended up as a universal childrens' story.

Writing for a childrens' magazine in 1839, Asbjørnsen captured a telling theme. 'On ski the mountain farmers overtake and fell reindeer, elks, wolves and bears that cannot be overtaken on the swiftest horse', he explained, 'and it is only thanks to a pair of such slender strips of wood, that many a hunter is still alive.'[19] To illustrate the point, he quoted someone travelling over the western mountains, who came to a farmhouse 'where an unbelievable number of bear skulls were fixed to the wall'.

> Here, said my father, there lives a man who has shot so many bears, let's go in and talk to him. We went inside and ... under the rafters I saw a pair of long skis, on one of which I noticed some deep gouges that seemed to have been scored with enormous power. I asked the bear hunter, a big, powerful man, somewhat past his prime, how this had happened ... [and] he said ... 'I was hunting a bear just out of hibernation ... As I was skiing down a slope, I shot, but misfired ... enraged with pain, the bear started chasing me, and he was so close, that when I set off downhill as fast as I could, he clawed at my ski, making the marks that you see ... But the slope was so steep that he could not overtake me again. But I didn't intend running away from him, and when I had reloaded my rifle, I turned back, and after a little while met the bear, and killed him with a bullet through the head.'

To anyone living in wild country, the hunter was a heroic, not to say romantic figure. In Norway at the time, he belonged to an elite, because society still had a strong atavistic streak, with the best hunters the symbols of survival. The ski was intertwined with his craft.

Romantic or whimsical stories were all very well but reality, as usual, was more sobering. By the 1830s skiing had not only contracted but had become a middle-aged affair. Young people were now rarely seen on ski. Army officers in particular were deeply concerned. They wanted to restore the skiing regiments. With conscript soldiers this was an efficient way of catching the young and starting a national revival. As it was, however, even among ordinary units, a shortage of ski inhibited winter exercises. There was much talk and, from 1830, the occasional worried article in military journals.

Major General Birch, commander of a brigade in Trondheim, was notably perturbed. In 1831, he petitioned Bernadotte – now King of Sweden-Norway and reigning as Carl XIV Johan, usually called simply Carl Johan – in French, as it happened, because Bernadotte still spoke nothing else. Birch was no fire-eating fanatic. He was highly educated, and a philanthropist to the core. In spite of – or because of – having fought against Carl Johan, he became a personal friend to the point of being a royal adjutant. Nonetheless Birch could not persuade Bernadotte to revive the Norwegian skiing regiments. Birch had however taken another small step in the rise of skiing as a sport, national or otherwise. Schøning's ideas were starting to bear fruit.

# 8

# The Ski in Foreign Literature

Abroad, at about this time, the ski was making its way into literature. Take Balzac, for example, in *Seréphîta*, with its eponymous heroine, part of *La Comédie Humaine*. Set in Scandinavia, this peculiar, mystic novel features a chase on the mountainous coast of Norway with Seréphîta and a companion fleeing wildly from pursuit: 'Were they two creatures, were they two arrows?'[1] They 'whistled over the snow on long planks fixed to their feet, and arrived at the first ridge which chance had arranged on the edge of this abyss'.

Balzac himself had never seen a skier, but he knew a Polish countess who had. In fact, Scandinavia was influencing European thought romantically as the home of unspoiled, uncorrupted people. Since the previous century, it had been an exotic subject of travel writing.

Skiing also appeared elsewhere, less romanticized. In Russia, Pushkin described how a Colonel Bibikov 'sent out his jäger troops who skied over the deep snow and occupied all the commanding heights'.[2] This comes from *The History of Pugachev* – a wayward Cossack who rebelled against Catherine the Great in the belief that he ought to have been on the throne instead of her. With the aid of skis, he was suitably dispatched. Pushkin's work was published in 1833 – about the same time as *Seréphîta* – although the events themselves dated from 1774.

More prosaically, skiing featured elsewhere in the printed word. For at least 200 years, French, German and Dutch travellers had written on the subject, and others too. In 1748 Peter Högström, for instance, a Swedish missionary in Lapland, published a book in German, with a frontispiece depicting a skier with two sticks.[3] It was probably the first of its kind since the Bronze Age Abashevo drawing 3,000 years before. Then a German encyclopaedia, a decade before Högström had, devoted a good scholarly half-column to skis and – 'attached to the feet by [toe] straps of osier'[4] – bindings too.

In 1776, meanwhile, a German savant called Peter Simon Pallas published a book on Siberia, mentioning the Ostyaks – 'timid, superstitious ... but fairly good natured'[5] – and their skis, together with a picture of sorts. He also described the Ostyak tribal hooded garment, called 'parka' – the first recorded occurrence of the word in print.

Pallas had been invited by Catherine the Great to catalogue her eastern possessions. In his footsteps came Alexander von Middendorff, also German speaking, and a doctor, but a Russian subject from St Petersburg who, in the 1840s, explored eastern Siberia. Out of this came an encyclopaedic report in

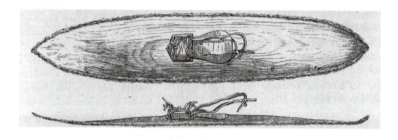

19. Tungus ski and sticks from Siberia, 1844. After Middendorff, 1844.
*Cambridge University Library*

which, amongst many other things, he treated the skis of the various tribes, notably the Tungus.

Their skis, Middendorff explained, were made of Siberian spruce, so skilfully made and so thin that 'they could be used for the resonance box of the finest cello, and just as in the case of the cello, it is a matter of the demands of virtuosity in the exercise of an art, so here it is the even more stringent demands of the daily cares about the hunt'.[6] For here in Siberia, the ski was still an instrument of survival; not only for hunting, but for sheer travel, since the tribesmen were nomads, following the reindeer.

Middendorff described the ski of the Tungus 'to show how exactly they fulfil their purpose', as he put it. Light and flexible, 'everything down to the finest detail … is carefully thought out'. By contrast, he carefully added, to a Siberian, the ski of the Russian settlers, were 'not only clumsy, but unintelligently made'. So much for European technical superiority.

In the historical Siberian mannner, the Tungus ski were lined with reindeer fur for adhesion, but they had a sophisticated flex and camber 'so that every step … was given an elastic push, and when the weight is transferred to the other foot [that push] shakes off snow clinging to the ski'. The footrest was a piece of bark fixed with traditional (and effective) fish glue. 'The purpose was not only to stiffen [the ski]', Middendorff observed, 'but specially to prevent the snow balling up [under the boot], since bark does not absorb water.' Amongst other things, this is an ancient precursor of the modern laminated ski. Also: 'When the snow has a crust in the spring, the Tungus bind a pair of bone plates under their skis, so that they glide better, but do not slip sideways.'

That gave credence to a long-doubted medieval report. In the thirteenth century a Franciscan Friar, William of Rubruck, a contemporary of Marco Polo, went on a secret mission to the Mongol Emperor, and wrote about a northern tribe that 'tie polished bones under their feet and propel themselves over the frozen snow and the ice with such speed that they catch birds and beasts'.[7] So it seems that Friar William was right after all – a lesson perhaps in reading history anew.

Middendorff noted meanwhile that the Tungus ski were short and broad – 150 cm by 33 cm to be exact, so that, as he put it, they 'cause the beginner fatigue and pain by forcing the feet further apart than the breadth of the pelvis … Mongolian nomads, on the other hand, feel the strain less because their pelvis is broader than that of Europeans.'

Middendorff also recorded the downhill technique of the Tungus. The top of their ski stick had a large hook, 'the purpose of which is to clutch at trees when one finds oneself in the grip of too fast a *schuss*'.[8] That was incidentally the first recorded use of the word in skiing. It was connected with the hunt: 'In the mountains, the Tungus follows the high contours and surveys the valley. If he sees game below, or hears it, since the call rises up, he runs down quick as lightning on his skis, and catches the herd before it has time to run ahead.'

Middendorff's contemporary, Leopold von Schrenck, another scholarly German subject of the Tsars, made similar observations among the Gilyak tribe of the Amur region.[9] Neither looked down on the primitive tribes they were observing. Schrenck recorded how skiing was so deeply ingrained in the Gilyak culture that one name for the larch tree was *lakk-char* or 'ski-wood'. Middendorff constantly wondered at 'the inventiveness of Mankind'.

As well he might. The ski that he and others recorded, sophisticated instruments though they may have been, were replicas of their prehistoric antecedents. The Tungus ski were of the Arctic type known to archaeologists. Among the Gilyaks, Schrenck observed a pattern with ridges enclosing the soles, the space between lined with fur: known from the beginning of our era. The design of both had hardly changed for thousands of years. Other contemporary travellers in the Far East published similar accounts. They ranged from Manchuria and Kamschatka and on to the Japanese islands of Sakhalin and Hokkaido.

This was the century of the English traveller and in particular his travel writing. A certain L. Lloyd wrote comprehensively about skiing in his book about the winter of 1828 he spent in Sweden: 'In my novitiate, I … received one or two hundred tumbles in the course of the day; sometimes, besides, I came with such violence against the trees that I used to think I should be dashed to pieces, or that they would be uprooted.'[10]

Lloyd was however not learning to ski for fun. Like many English visitors of the times, all over the globe, he had come to hunt; bears for preference in this case. Here the ski was vital for success.

From Pallas to Middendorff, skiing is still utilitarian. Nonetheless in the late eighteenth century, a Danish author had written about Norwegians using skis 'only for recreation, for running down a slope'; being careful to add that it was only 'those [who are] not particularly practised'.[11] Then in the winter of 1834–5, a Scotsman called Samuel Laing was staying in Levanger, near Trondheim – to study Norwegian agriculture – but noted in *his* book that what he called 'snow skating' was 'going on briskly, at every farm house, with young and old'.[12] These are among the earliest references to the survival of skiing in Norway as a pure pastime.

Spanning its homelands, there was thus by the mid-nineteenth century a body of accessible literature on skiing. For some reason, the ski nonetheless did not spread. This is odd, given the place of snow and ice on the English imagination at least. After all, James Thomson, the eighteenth-century nature poet – no doubt inspired by Schefferus – had written influentially in *The Seasons* of the Lapps who 'love their Mountains and enjoy their storms',[13] while their reindeer

> whirl them swift
> O'er Hill and Dale, heap'd into one Expanse
> Of marbled Snow, as far as Eye can sweep.

Then Mary Shelley's enduring *Frankenstein*, first published in 1818, is largely set in frost and ice, albeit as a gothic horror, with the monster speeding across a frozen world.

Nonetheless skiing remained a curiosity of travellers' tales. It was in Norway that its development now centred.

20a and 20b.  Kick turn as military drill, Grüner, Norway, 1765.
*The Norwegian Armed Forces Museum*

# 9

# Evolution of Skiing as a Sport

On 19 March 1843, a local newspaper in the North Norwegian port of Tromsø carried this historic advertisement:

INVITATION TO A RACE ON SKIS

On Tuesday afternoon the 21st inst., weather and snow conditions permitting, a few people propose to test the speed of their ski and the extent of their powers in a race from the town hall to the well of Herr Ebeltoft's farm on the other side of the island [on which Tromsø lies] and back again to the starting point. The organisers believe that they can finish the course in 40 minutes. We meet in the town square at 3.45 pm. Big and small, ski and andor runners, in short all who are interested in a true Norwegian sport are invited to take part. NB If anyone believes that he can cover the course in a shorter time on andor, he is free to try.[1]

This marked the opening of an age. It was the first ever published announcement of a modern ski race. That is to say it was not military but civilian, open and for fun. Whether it actually took place as advertised is unclear but one race definitely did, on Thursday 30 March. There was another the following Sunday, 2 April. These were the first recorded modern ski races. On 6 April, the same local newspaper – *Tromsø-Tidende*, reported the proceedings. This was the first known press coverage of ski racing in the world; front-page exclusive into the bargain. It was the work of the editor himself, Otto Theodor Krohg, so he too has his place in history. He deserved it. He was one of the skiing pioneers. Tall, massive, ebullient, big-boned, with bulbous features, he whimsically masqueraded under the *nom de plume* of 'Little Theodor'. His report is a period piece of the very finest vintage. Leisurely and conversational, it begins by setting the scene:

Last month ended with a fierce snowstorm which … delayed the [postal] steamship … These April days have by comparison been splendid, and with their fine, calm air, clear skies and good winter conditions, have been frequently used for excursions in the open air, and since November we have not had such good tobogganing conditions as at present. However, it is skis which have been most in evidence during the past few weeks, and given the repeated announcements of ski races in that time, one must say that skiing – although it has never been greatly appreciated here – has now become a true popular recreation … Skiers were particularly numerous last Sunday the 2nd of this month, when a group of eager participants accepted the invitation and appeared at the Town Hall.[2]

21. Otto Theodor Krohg – 'Little Theodor' – the parish priest who organized the first known ski race in 1843.

Having recovered from this passage, 'Little Theodor' got down to business. He was reporting a cross-country race of some 6 km over undulating terrain:

> At a given signal the lightly clad troop started moving, and soon disappeared behind the ridge … Several of the older citizens … stood with watches in hand to decide the fastest runners and take the time to cover the course.

The return was naturally staggered so:

> After the passage of 29 minutes the leader was seen on the crest of the ridge, and at the 30th minute was down in the town. This skier was a boy learning the cobbler's trade, Finnish by birth and, in the Finnish way, had used two sticks

He was ahead of his time; one stick long remained the rule among Norwegians. This was the first documented instance of two sticks appearing in a race outside Finland.

> The public [continued 'Little Theodor',] was not a little amused when someone in full flight down the last slope lost his balance and bathed his tired body in the freezing snow. Nobody was injured by the speed, either the last time or on Thursday [30 March], when a tradesman, a cooper by profession, won the race [on skis and andor.] Although he is an accomplished skier, who is said once, without sticks, to have run down the [steepest local slope] with a child under each arm and one on his head [no doubt the kind of migrating

myth that has been the salvation of many a journalist in need of local colour], on Sunday [2 April] he was only 6th or seventh, since on that occasion only skis were allowed, and not andor, and the art of moving quickly on the former is particularly dependent on the state of the snow and the smoothness of the ski.

So it was in fact that second fixture which turned out to be the first true modern ski race with equipment resembling what we know today. The organizer of both events happened to be 'Little Theodor' himself. This probably made his newspaper the first sponsor of a sporting event anywhere in the world. It was enough for any pioneer but 'Little Theodor' had not finished yet. He had turned the races into a duel between different forms of skis, one with the fur-lined andor and the other without it. He had seen that the andor was doomed. The future belonged to skis of equal length and kind, an all-round model, adaptable to any discipline.

From a certain point of view, Tromsø was an odd place for such historic happenings. Well north of the Arctic Circle, it was then a small, isolated fishing and sealing port. However, it did lie at a crossroads of skiing cultures. Lapps inhabited the hinterland. Finns were part of the population. 'Little Theodor' seemed made for this milieu. Born in 1811 at Alta, facing the Arctic Ocean, near the northernmost tip of Scandinavia, he was a man of the frontier and touched life at many points. Besides being editor and chief reporter, he was the founder and owner of *Tromsø-Tidende*, wrote most of the copy himself and helped in the typesetting too. In holy orders, he was passionately devoted to music as well as skiing, and doubled as a local schoolmaster. 'He both horrified and fascinated me',[3] recalled one former pupil – Jonas Lie, a leading Norwegian novelist. 'How he could wield the cane! And how he could make you laugh! No one could throw snowballs or ski like him.'

On New Year's Eve 1843, 'Little Theodor's editorial review of the year had been another landmark. Its centrepiece was the first published description of a ski tour for pleasure alone:

> There is nothing like a ski tour for inducing a happy mood, when the going is brilliant, skis are smooth and otherwise well maintained and the company is good. Thus to fly in a party of 8, 10 or 12 over the snow-covered ground in the happy certainty that [at the end there] awaits a well-laden board and cheerful badinage, is so uplifting, a healthy digestion so encouraging, that [we] have developed a kind of passion for these afternoon entertainments. As we sailed home in the dark on our trusty ski ... seeing nothing, besides ourselves, except the calm, star-laden sky, hearing nothing but the creak of the ski sticks in the frozen snow, and the ski breaking through the crust; [and] as we raced past each other down the steep slopes, while many a companion, exhausted by the pleasures of the day, suddenly disappeared, enveloped in white-powdered dust ... then we polar inhabitants thought that even these parts gave pleasures which ... many of us would not have changed for the cultivated habits of more southerly places.[4]

In 1866, 'Little Theodor' published a long article called, surprisingly, 'Skiing and theology'.[5] Since 1847, he had been vicar of a remote west Norwegian mountain parish and stayed there for nearly 40 years. The journalist in him was too strong and he had continued to write, although now for the national press. This particular piece was an attack on the Pietistic movement, which then was rife in the Norwegian Lutheran State Church and which, as he put it, represented a 'hysterical theology'

> that only sees the Devil and the fires of hell, and is no longer able to take pleasure in … the many gifts of God in Nature.

'This theology', 'Little Theodor' continued in his earthy way, 'has its origin in an upset stomach.' That in turn was the result of 'a complete neglect of the proper care of the body'. As a cure, he recommended exercise, and especially skiing: 'One strives towards the top … during which effort one … achieves … quick, deep breathing … and the consequent … relief and liveliness of mood and relief in the chest.' But this was 'only the first stage of enjoyment' since 'the top is not the goal of pleasure, but the goal of the beginning of pleasure'.

> One sees at one's feet the long slopes deeply covered with snow … and knows that within a few minutes one will be on the flat below with [little] effort … on … thin planks working in harmony, and that mainly due to one's own skill and strength … The skis seem to take on a life of their own, they hurry, they run, they bend smoothly [and] when the going is really good they will run wildly, out of control, unless their zeal is somewhat checked.

This mirrored a new spirit of the times. More soberly, on 24 February 1849, several hundred miles to the south of Tromsø, a Trondheim newspaper had carried this advertisement: 'Anyone who wishes to participate in a Ski-Tour … on Sunday (weather permitting) should meet in the Market Square at 1 p.m.'[6]

That was also historic in its way. It was the first printed invitation to *organized* ski touring for pleasure. It happened in a town. It centred on the home terrain. It grew steadily until by the beginning of the 1860s, as revealed by the press, it was a regular feature of the local winters.

Trondheim, the ancient capital of Norway, became the cradle of organized ski touring, partly on account of the terrain. Rolling Nordic country, overlaid with conifers, reached almost to the centre of the town. This movement, however, like those in other fields, owed its origins to the burning dedication of one or two zealots.

The first advertisements were anonymous. Behind them, it eventually emerged, lay the bespectacled, unsoldierly figure of Carl Bonaparte Roosen, an engineer captain in the Norwegian army. He it was who single-handed had organized everything. This was symptomatic. Military officers were trailblazers in skiing. It was not merely for the sake of winter warfare. As regulars in a conscript army, they were much concerned with the health of recruits and the behaviour of the rising generation. They were also among a small circle in Norway at the time who were trained to organize.

A newspaper article during the spring of 1863 castigated Roosen because 'Long tours ... drain one's strength without corresponding benefit.'[7] It would have been preferable, so the (anonymous) author declared, if Roosen

> had combined some instruction with his tours [choosing] some convenient slope in the vicinity, suitable both for beginners and experts ... There one enjoys oneself, practises with unity and order, and learns more in a few hours than through repeatedly exhausting oneself.

Roosen quickly answered. He denied that his tours were 'exhausting', and rejected the idea of sticking to one slope.

> This ... becomes somewhat boring and monotonous, and besides is only to be considered entertainment. Ability in a skier does not ... consist of keeping one's balance on a slope, but equally in being able to proceed on the flat, and also in exploiting the terrain, so that, as it were, to be at home everywhere. This can be learned on extended tours, but not by amusing oneself on a slope.[8]

This argument was historic too. It was the first discussion in print about the aims of skiing. It encapsulated two opposing views, especially of yo-yoing up and down a slope. The controversy has persisted to this day.

Up and down the country, skiing as recreation had begun to take root. All that, however, was in the provinces. The capital city lagged behind. Only in February 1860, more than a decade after Trondheim, did *Morgenbladet*, a leading Christiania newspaper and therefore part of the national press, carry the first advertisement for a ski tour.[9] It was probably the start of organized skiing in Christiania. The tour was to Maridalen, on the northern outskirts of the city.

The next known event in Christiania occurred two years later. Again *Morgenbladet* carried a small advertisement.[10] Now the venue was Grorud, to the east of the city, in more attractive terrain. The Press covered the proceedings extensively. That was in itself was something new. What is more, *Illustreret Nyhedsblad*, a weekly picture journal, produced an illustrated feature, the first time that skiing was so honoured, anywhere. It was historic in other ways as well.

The Grorud tour took place on 16 February 1862; a Sunday as it happened. At that point in the climatic cycle, it was midwinter with dependable snow. Some thirty skiers gathered at the Christiania railway station for the short train journey out to Grorud. 'There was some fuss about taking the skis,' so one journalist reported, 'since the management demanded a [shilling] extra [for each]; but we finally departed, and were given a whole coach to ourselves.'[11] That was the first recorded instance of charging for the transport of skis. Also it was the first example of a dedicated railway carriage for a skiing party. Moreover the event was arranged by a local sports club, which made it the first organized skiing excursion with transport included and hence the precursor of the package winter holiday.

The press offered dramatic coverage of a downhill run in three stages down to a frozen river:

> Near the end ... there was [a drop] of 3 feet [90 cm] ... from which, as it were, one fell right down the last part of the slope. It seemed quite dangerous from above ... because it appeared to end in a precipice. It was not really so dangerous, but nonetheless it was quite a respectably long and steep slope that could be a good test of a skier.

The skiers ran down one by one, with a bugler to give the start signal, and eventually to stop the proceedings preparatory to marching off to dinner at a nearby inn. It was unmistakably military, which was hardly surprising as the organizer was again an army officer. The report continued:

> From the bottom of the slope one had a good view of virtually the whole run right to the end, when the skier reached the opposite bank of the river with its contrary slope, and suddenly had to fling himself backwards in order to avoid falling with his nose in the snow.

It was in fact a short continuous downhill run with no relief and no attempt at turning:

> Look at him who has just started off ... there he shoots over the [drop] sweeping through space as if shot from a 24 pounder. 'He's fallen! That was a real somersault', his companions jeered ... Now there's another ... how smoothly and effortlessly he starts off. He barely thinks about his stick, which gently rests in his hands. He has the right posture and balance ... with his body slightly curled, and feet 6 inches [15 cm] apart he runs over the steepest parts, and when, with a quick push he helps the jump over the [drop] and in a flash stops at the opposite river bank, it seems so easy.

That, however, was the exception. The technique on that slope left much to be desired. To quote another newspaper, 'it seems strange that skiing is not practised more in our country, where it can be so useful to the inhabitants'.[12] The writer in the illustrated weekly put it this way:

> When we ourselves were young, 20 or 30 years ago, no little boy was without his skis, and both he and his parents knew how to use them. In reality, skiing is such an invigorating and true old Norwegian sport, that it would be a pity if it fell into oblivion.[13]

The national fervour was still common; so too the lament over decadence. The pundits – as usual – had misread the Zeitgeist. They thought that everything was static and ignored the signs of a renaissance. One stage may conveniently be marked by that first advertised ski tour in 1849. It coincided with profound historical events. The year 1848 saw nationalist uprisings on the continent, the reverberations of which were felt even in Scandinavia. The same year saw an advance in the modernization of Norway. The first merchant bank was then founded. That alleviated the shortage of credit and capital that had hamstrung the modernization of the country. Meanwhile agriculture could no longer support a growing population on its own. Industrialization had started. Coffee was replacing aquavit as the everyday refreshment. The first railway was opened in 1854, the first telegraph the following year. Communications were improving. There was a little more affluence and leisure.

The Grorud ski tour was followed by others in the capital. More to the point, it coincided with the first documented ski race after those at Tromsø in 1843. That was on 22 January 1862 in Trysil. In between, racing continued in different valleys, more or less spontaneously and isolated from each other. This was however the first time since 'Little Theodor's journalism in Tromsø that a skiing fixture was reported in the press. Its crucial advance was to have been organized by a dedicated sporting body. Moreover, unlike the local newspaper of the Tromsø races, Trysil was covered by the national press. It was the first truly modern ski race.

22. Telemark turn. Poster for the first Nordic Games, Stockholm 1901.
They were a precursor of the Winter Olympics.
*Jens Gustafsson, Kungliga Biblioteket, National Library of Sweden*

In a very different part of the country from Tromsø, Trysil lies inland among the rolling landscape of the south-east, with its eskers, the prehistoric moraines, as a reminder of the Ice Age. It had a long skiing tradition. It was the home of a skiing legend in the form of a semi-mythical figure called Trysil-Knud. He was the hero of a poem, the denouement of which was a downhill run somewhere on the west coast. Having previously hung his coat on a handy bush, he plucked it up and put it on without stopping, at full speed, before jumping into a boat at the bottom of the slope and vanishing down the fjord.

Journalism aside, the Trysil race pioneered in other ways. Yet it was also deeply anchored in the native soil. It was part of a traditional winter fair, complete with the timeless traffic jams, horse-drawn in this case. That is what interested the national press, in the shape of *Morgenbladet*. This was a diehard journal, which, incongruously, became virtually the innovative skier's newspaper. Luckily for them, it was an organ of the ultra-conservative governing faction, widely read and influential.

*Morgenbladet* covered the Trysil race on 2 February 1862. For once, an editor recognized a good story. He put it on the front page. It led the paper. The correspondent, in his own words, had stumbled on the event 'by chance'. His report gave a glimpse into a bygone world. 'The snow was pouring down', he began, with the obligatory setting of the scene. 'Each little pine formed a snow cone; every tree trunk had a cap of fresh snow.'[14]

> The track consisted of a long slope, the upper part of which had a gradient of about 35 degrees, below this a flat runout, and thereafter a slope rising on the other side, where judges and spectators were placed. At the bottom of the long slope, that is the real track, snow had been piled up to form an artificial lip with a sudden takeoff which, to a considerable degree, increased the difficulty of an already steep slope. The object was to run down the slope on ski without falling, in addition to which the judges required easy movement and a natural posture.

This was the first reported ski-jumping competition, admittedly combined with a downhill race. As a natural consequence, it introduced the staggered start. Prizes were distributed among those who successfully completed the course three times. It opened a new era in skiing and began the proliferation of modern competitive disciplines. The great innovation was the style judge, copied from gymnastics, with precursors in the military ski races of the eighteenth century. It was part of a campaign to arrest the decadence of skiing.

All this was very different from the Tromsø races, where time was all that counted. 'Little Theodor' wanted to turn skiing from a utilitarian drudgery to a pastime and an all-round sport, with daredevil downhill running merely a part of every cross-country race. In Trysil, however, something more sensational was needed to grip the citizenry, so running downhill, together with jumping, were extracted as a separate event. This ran counter to the Nordic tradition, where stamina was the goal. It meant in part that the formative races of modern skiing were proto-Alpine, as it were. At any rate they enhanced technique, and reached a wider audience by making colourful copy for a passing journalist.

*Morgenbladet's* representative at Trysil certainly revelled in the finer details of jumping. 'The artificial jump at the end of the slope soon proved to be the worst obstacle', he observed.

> With incredible speed, a ski runner would shoot over the jump, and literally soar some distance in the air, but when the ski returned to the ground, they often buried themselves in the snow, and [a] fall was unavoidable ... the tumbling skier always disappeared in a cloud of snow after a number of somersaults.

This was understandable, given that landing was not on the slope, but the flat, with resounding force. Ski and sticks were liberally broken, but luckily no bones. 'Those who overcame the difficulty', continued the reporter, 'did so by daring to jump before they reached the take off, thus preventing the ski taking a direction that would make them dig into the snow.' This is neatly observed. After the best part of a century-and-a half, that remains a concise description of ski-jumping. It is no use letting gravity take its course. You must seize control, actively jump and land with parallel skis. At Trysil, various contestants made the point, as the journalist observed:

> Having negotiated the mauvais pas, the victors shot with irresistible speed over the flat, and far up the opposite slope, executing several accomplished jumps with delirious abandon, as if the difficulties they had overcome were simply bagatelles.

The Trysil winner was one Halvor Dahl. That too made history. He was the first ski champion to be known by name. Hitherto the press had held personal privacy for ordinary mortals to be sacrosanct. Sporting coverage and court proceedings bore a certain resemblance. Skier or burglar, both were steeped in anonymity.

Trysil had yet another breakthrough. The younger boys also took part, albeit on a shorter though equally steep slope. Like the adults, they had to do three runs without falling. One 10 year old overwhelmed press and public by swooping down in great style. This was the first known children's ski race.

The Trysil event began with all the skiers marching in behind a banner and someone blowing an improvised trumpet. In this parody of a military parade lie the glimmerings of the bombastic ceremonial of the modern Winter Olympic games. Echoing the Tromsø newspaper report nineteen years before, the Trysil coverage also emphasized that the skiers were 'to be tested in an accomplishment that is national in a way shown by little else'.

That accurately mirrored the spirit of the times. Norwegian society was then like a man waking up from a long sleep as the country hurried to turn itself into a modern state and resolve a crisis of identity. One aspect of this process was the rise of organized sporting associations. They were introduced in the middle of the century, by German craftsmen on a pattern brought from home. As in Germany, these were originally devoted to gymnastics. Both the German models and their Norwegian offshoots had the same purpose. This was to enhance national feeling and national cohesion. The German gymnastic clubs had much to do with the foundation of the Prussian state.

The Norwegian copies, however, turned out to have more in common with events in another quarter. By a suitable coincidence, away in Prague, within a month of the Trysil race, the Sokol came into being. Sokol – 'falcon' in the Czech language – was a system of mass gymnastics. It was founded by a Bohemian

23. Newspaper advertisement for a ski race, California, 1869. 'Snow shoe' meant ski. 'Dope' is ski wax.

nationalist called Miroslav Tyrs, specifically to promote a sense of national identity. The target was the monarchy in Vienna, where the Emperor Franz-Josef presided over the rambling Habsburg domains.

Skiing and Sokol thus had identical aims. Neither was driven by national aggression; both were concerned with independence. As the Bohemians and Moravians fretted under Austrian rule, so were the Norwegians troubled by relations with Sweden. Since the ski race of 1843, those had taken a turn for the worse, although Norway enjoyed far greater independence under her Swedish overlords than the subject peoples of the absolutist Habsburgs, not to mention the states of the European Union today.

As elsewhere, the 1860s were a turbulent decade. The Poles rebelled against bondage of their Russian masters, and were savagely repressed for their pains, while in Russia itself there was the emancipation of the serfs. Prussia defeated both Austria and Denmark on the battlefield. In the United States, there was the considerably more bloody civil war. Garibaldi marched on Rome, giving impetus to the Italian *Risorgimento*. The modern world was taking shape. Nationalism was on the wing, together with its consequent hungering for freedom. Scandinavia, in its own muted way, was also part of the process. The decade saw the first of many crises between Sweden and Norway. This one was precipitated by a Norwegian demand to abolish the post of Governor General, because of the subservience it implied.

It was in the grip of this conflict that the first wave of sports clubs spread over Norway. Trysil was among them. Tellingly, the word 'rifle' was often in the name, with its connotations of defence. Thus the organizer of the Trysil race was the 'Trysil Rifle and Skiing Club'. It had been formed in 1861, with the aim of holding 'a ski run, with prizes' the next season. That same season of 1862 also saw the founding of the first known dedicated ski club. It was some 200 miles away, north of Trondheim. Its name was *Indreøens skiløberforening* – 'Indreøens Ski Runners' Association'.

Other places followed suit. Not only were there now fixtures every season but they were henceforth sure of newspaper coverage. In fact, this was often what inspired a new race. It was yet another instance of a newspaper not only recording events, but making them as well. The power of the Press! Ski racing had come out of the shadows, and emerged into recorded history. Each race was experimental. Competition was still being formalized. It was in this restless, creative decade of the 1860s that modern skiing finally took shape. The different events were evolving. Although everyday skiing was across somewhat flattish country, downhill, together with jumping, were promoted because they were more spectacular and brought in the crowds.

Trysil led the way again in 1863. That event, too, was historic. A girl wrote asking permission to take part, 'not to win any of the prizes,' as *Morgenbladet* reported,[15] 'because these could only be won by men and boys ... but in a village where skiing is just as vital for women as for men if they are to get out of the house, it might be of interest to see an example of women's accomplishment in the use of skis.'

The organizers agreed. They had chosen a longer, steeper course than the year before, with a maximum gradient of 1 in 2. It was again a downhill run, with a jump included, this time of around 10 m. This was about the limit of contemporary technique. When the girl appeared, 'in her headkerchief and woollen shawl,' to quote the journalist again,

> she quickly worked her way up on skis to the topmost point of the slope, where she stopped a while at the run used for the normal competition. Meanwhile the numerous spectators waited in great excitement to see if she too would dare to start down. Indeed she did start off, and down she flew at lightning speed … over … the jump … and easily, with great assurance stood where many an agile boy had lost his footing before her. And she was given a ringing cheer – the first of the day from the crowd which, during her run, was consumed with anxiety.

The date was 21 January 1863. The girl's name was Ingrid Olsdatter Vestbyen. She was 16 years old. These details are important. Ingrid was the first recorded woman ski racer, and ski-jumper to boot.

After the race there was a festive gathering, with a performance by a local choir and many a high-flown skol. Such proceedings were already entrenched as what became part of ski racing to give it a sense of occasion. In this instance, it generated a spontaneous collection for a gift, in the journalist's words, 'for the lovely girl who skied with such elegance and assurance'.

This was no parochial eccentricity. A month later, after another race, at Aamot, in a different part of the country, the orator at the prizegiving 'recalled the splendid girl at Trysil', as a local newspaper put it,[16] and 'took the opportunity to urge the girls of Aamot to follow her example and not ignore such a useful sport'.

Women, of course, were still encased in long, cumbrous skirts, which made Ingrid's performance all the more remarkable. Male skiers were hardly better off. Special outfits did not exist. They skied in everyday clothes, down to collar and tie, greatcoat and hat where appropriate, which of course intensified the general *schadenfreude* when someone fell.

In 1862, the Trysil event was closely followed by one at Kristiansand on the south coast, facing the Skagerrak. There, a Lieutenant-Colonel Oscar Wergeland, the scion of a literary family and the district military commander, had taken the law into his own hands, and organized a ski race for his troops. 'The city's youth obviously took pleasure in this sport',[17] so a local newspaper declared. 'We wish that skiing could once more be adopted as the national sport; it takes young people away from the fireside and street corners, it is the best winter amusement for everyman, and offends no one except the publicans.'

And then:

> Gymnastics are all very well, but in essence it is too negative, absurd and peculiarly German really to succeed among us … In the bigger towns there are … a large number

of Germans, for whom gymnastics belong to the adjuncts of a dissipated life ... No more gymnastic orders! This cure-all from German chemists has been poured without corking the bottle far too long for our Norwegian stomachs.

At the time, nonetheless, skiing was threatened by a prejudice against all sports, typical of a mid-nineteenth-century mania for keeping up appearances. Even years afterwards, during the boyhood of a champion, as he vividly recalled, when he jumped furthest in a race he at least 'was not forbidden to practise this sport and punished for disobedience. This often happened in narrow-minded homes, and many of my school friends were given a good hiding and kept in "because they flew like maniacs on skis".[18]

An effective deterrent it was not. The pleasure of flying above the snow made any punishment a price worth paying.

Besides, such puritanism was largely urban and only a passing phase. This was neatly illustrated by one newspaper report of a Norwegian ski race in 1863. It took place to the north of Trysil at Haltdal, near Trondheim. To explain the background, the journalist philosophized over a nearby valley called Aunegrenda. In the cold season of the year, it was usually without roads – an efficient snowplough had to wait for mechanical transport. Nonetheless, the inhabitants managed

> because ... both male and female [they] use ski. Not infrequently the Auna farmers and their wives are to be seen on winter Sundays hurtling over the steepest slopes in a cloud of whirling snow down to their church, which lies low down on the banks of the river. Eight or nine year old boys and girls cheerfully ski down with the procession to church, and consider the means of travel the most natural thing in the world.[19]

All in all, skiing was now in its renaissance. Its nature was also subtly changing. Instead of a utilitarian means of transport, or a simple country recreation, it was being appropriated by the official classes for ideological ends. Nationalism was the bait. Together with Sokol, Norwegian skiing was the precursor of sport deliberately used for national prestige. That meant mass participation together with the cultivation of an elite. It involved the development of touring and racing in parallel. For all that, the work remained local for some time. It needed a national focus.

# 10

# The Men of Telemark

These processes and the related pioneering laid the foundations of modern technique. It began with the first ski race in Christiania, the capital, on 15 March 1866. Like others of its kind, it was just another experiment in the search for forms of competition. The provinces were ahead, but Christiania was also liberally provided with skiing terrain. It backed on to a wild upland, the environs dotted with convenient slopes. It was on one of these, opposite the Old Akers Church, a well-known landmark on the outskirts of the city, that the race was run. In another link between the rise of skiing and the birth of popular journalism, a Christiania newspaper called *Aftenbladet* organized the event. 'We live in a sporting age,'[1] so *Aftenbladet* tellingly mused in a long coverage, splashed across two columns.

> Not so long ago, all physical exercises were generally considered a useless waste of time [but] now we have a completely different attitude … It is difficult to say whether our close contact with the English has played a part. But it is certain that the passion for all kinds of sport peculiar to them has also affected us.

It was indeed the time when the English, in the Victorian heyday, at the zenith of their power, were spreading modern games abroad. 'It is a passion that that suits our national taste', the newspaper went on.

> Thanks to that, skiing, that true national sport which, having once been practised … all over the country, then … was falling into disuse … has now re-emerged … as one of the best exercises … and a favourite recreation of men and boys alike.

Christiania was a special case. As late as the 1850s, skiing had been virtually unknown among the native population but the educated classes had begun to take an interest. Skiing was introduced by officials returned from postings to the provinces. The process of revival had been speeded by the university. The only one in Norway, it gathered students from all over the long-stretched land. This planted the seed of a sport that was national both psychologically and as a formal institution.

*Aftenbladet*'s race was run on a slope called Iversløkken. Half-forgotten, forlorn and overgrown today, it commemorates the early days of modern skiing. It had a vertical drop of only 30 m. For contemporary skiers, it was enough. The slope billowed down like the steep front of a wave in a stormy sea. A crowd of 2,000 packed the course – in a city with a population of only 40,000. (That of London was over 3,000,000 at the time.) The arena, to quote the newspaper coverage, 'was seething with ladies and gentlemen who wanted to be spectators at this lively, attractive and genuinely Norwegian spectacle'. They had every incentive because, as one inhabitant put it, otherwise Christiania did not 'offer the interests and amusements of a capital city to any great extent'.[2]

*Aftenbladet* had invited a local champion from Hønefoss, some 90 km to the north in order to show the city dwellers how a real country skier could perform. He was a smallholder called Elling Bækken. A flamboyant figure with green neckerchief and flapping tailcoat, he had won a race a few weeks earlier in his home tract on a steep slope with a sensationally long built-in jump. 'With the speed of lightning', in the words of a local newspaper

> he swept down, came to the jump, which most people believed impossible to survive upright, and soared about [13 m] in the air, landing in proper style, upright on his skis. That which was considered impossible had been proved to be possible.[3]

In Christiania, Bækken was therefore the great attraction. He was supposed merely to give an exhibition. A last-minute call for volunteers turned it into a race. That was manna for the Press. Blanket coverage enlivened leaden columns.

As at Trysil, this was a combined downhill and jumping event; it too decided on the no-fall principle. Usually that meant that the winner emerged from those who kept their balance. This, however, had a new twist. It was a knockout competition. One slip and you retired from the proceedings. The survivors went on to start further up the slope at each following round, 'one after the other turning their legs up towards the sky',[4] as the journalist put it, until they were successively eliminated and only one remained upright. He was the winner. He was not Bækken. He was a Christiania resident called Holmboe. As one newspaper said, 'he had shown that "a man of learning" could also keep his balance'.[5] Like many other challengers, Holmboe was a university student.

The race had begun as a duel between town and country; it ended as one of north and south. The triumphant Holmboe came from 'Little Theodor's' Tromsø, a thousand miles to the north. All in all, the northern skiers had shown themselves better than the southern ones. There was some sympathy for Bækken. A collection for him among the spectators, raised 30 *speciedaler*, the equivalent of some £500 today, as recompense for having taken time off to visit the city for the first time.

Despite florid optimism in the press, Norwegian skiing was still in a state of decay. Style judges repeatedly made the point. The main trouble was the stick. Most skiers still stuck to one and used it as their instrument of control. They rode on it to check their speed. They swung on it to turn. Worst of all, they clung to their massive two-handed staff to keep their balance. The general effect was one of unmitigated clumsiness. Race officials had only themselves to blame. They insisted on one stick, and banned the use of two.

Here too the north of the country was ahead. In late December 1866, at Nesseby, a remote village well above the Arctic Circle, there was a ski race where, shades of 'Little Theodor', two sticks were allowed. That was probably due to the fact that Nesseby lay in the Norwegian province of Finnmark, which on the one hand is Lapp country and, on the other, borders on Finland; each with an ingrained tradition of two sticks.

Nesseby broke new ground in other ways as well. The fixture consisted of a ski-jump, followed by a separate sprint-like cross-country race. This was the first known Nordic combination in the modern sense. A certain Ole Persen – origin unknown – won both first and third prize. One, as the local newspaper reported, was for having 'run down and jumped without sticks in the best style';[6] the other was for 'covering 600 metres on the flat in 3 minutes with two sticks'.

Geographically and culturally isolated, northern Norway was still a world of its own and the practice did not spread. Further south, the tyranny of the single stick prevailed. Climate change also hindered progress. The Little Ice Age had ended. Temperatures were rising. Winters were unreliable, and the limit of dependable snow had begun receding to the heights. One local newspaper also blamed the Sabbatarians, who 'branded as a sin indulging in such an injurious activity as to go skiing on a *Sunday* ... Economic circumstances are no longer so favourable that ... people ... can afford to take much time off work for such activities.'[7]

Around the time of the Christiania race, the first books on skiing started to appear. The decay of skiing was their theme as well. One was by the Lt Col. Wergeland who had organized the military ski race at Kristiansand in 1862. He advocated a law compelling private households to buy skis and keep them ready for use.

More practically, a national sporting body appeared. Its rather cumbrous title was *Centralforeningen for Udbredelse af Legemsøvelser og Vaabenbrug* – 'The Central Association for the promotion of Physical Exercise and the use of Firearms' – generally called *Centralforeningen*. It was founded in 1861, at the same time as the Trysil club. Skiing was on the *Centralforeningen*'s programme. This made it the first national skiing governing body in the world. In fact it was one of the earliest national sporting bodies, anywhere. In England, the Football Association, for example, was only founded in 1863. *Centralforeningen*'s ramifications went beyond sport itself. It was one of the earliest Norwegian national organizations in any field. It played a rôle in fostering national identity. It meant more than politicians in turning a fragmented country into a unified one. It was almost an organ of the State.

*Aftenbladet*'s race cried out for repetition but, though a creature of the Press, it could not count on everlasting sponsorship. *Centralforeningen* took over. The year following the original event, it organized the second documented ski race in Christiania. This took place on the 8th February 1867, again at Iversløkken, and yet again a calculated piece of pioneering.

To begin with, *Centralforeningen* made skiing a true spectator sport. It had to accept climate change in the form of fog and foul going, with icy crust following unseasonable thaws. In those days, long before steel edges, and therefore no grip, running downhill invited mortal danger. Nobody was however seriously hurt. The course had been designed so that the customers could follow all the proceedings and get their money's worth. Similarly, the no-fall rule was dropped so that everyone could complete the course, and thus prolong the spectacle.

The race was no longer pure downhill and jumping. It was designed to test all aspects of the sport. It began as a downhill run down, but then (as at Nesseby) continued on the flat. It ended in a sharp climb with a vertical rise of about 20 m. The course was 400 m long. It had to be completed three times back and forth, making a total of 2.4 kilometres. It included artificial jumps and, most importantly, *sharp turns*.

As Negri had explained, more than a century-and-a-half before, the Lapps had long mastered the art of turning; most Norwegians were defective. Something needed to be done. So far, competition courses had been laid out in a straight line. This was the first to include turning.

There were other innovations. For the first time the competitors – 26 all told – were each identified by a number carried on square pieces of cloth pinned to their clothing. They started singly, the order decided by drawing lots. Strict rules were imposed. One was that skiers had to give way to those overtaking them. Soldiers kept spectators off the course. Policemen were there to keep order. The principles of ski racing were established there. They would be recognizable today.

The aim was to ski as fast as possible but time still was not the only test. Style judging continued, especially in turning, jumping and using the stick. It was manipulated to reward technical ability. It was rough justice but it did encourage technical improvement. It was called for at this stage. A fast run by an awkward exponent was no example. Competition would now drive the development of equipment and technique.

The next advance came in the season of 1868. On the 9 February – despite the Sabbatarians, a Sunday – *Centralforeningen* then organized the third race in Christiania; again on and around the Iversløkken slope. For the first time, the race was deliberately representative. It was in fact, although not in name, the first national championship anywhere. Invitations went out all over the country. Fifty-one answered the call. Some actually skied to take part, perhaps 200 km each way. Norwegian railways were still in their infancy; winter communications poor, and anything but cheap.

One explanation for this event, with its national touch, might have been a reader's letter to a Christiania newspaper the previous year. It came from Sauland, in the province of Telemark, west of the capital, modestly complaining that 'very rarely do you hear anything from us who live so far up in the mountains'[8] and wanting to draw attention to a local ski race. It was a reminder of the half-hidden world in secluded valleys and Telemark in particular. In fact the anonymous author noted another step in the transition to modern skiing. The race was in two parts. One was a simple downhill run, 'long and steep'; the other was a slope with a jump in the middle.

This was the first time that the jump became an event in its own right, instead of merely a hurdle in a downhill race. It was also a return to an older tradition of landing on a slope rather than the flat. That at least was copied in the Christiania race of 1868 and thus founded the modern style of jumping. Otherwise, downhll, jumping and cross-country followed as usual without pause. Starting was at intervals of one-and-a-half minutes to simplify timekeeping. It was the first occasion on which a regular interval was specified and thus the modern system introduced.

Bækken, by now the old dependable, came second and someone from Trysil third. The winner, however, was a newcomer called Sondre Ouversen Nordheim. His time, 18 minutes 55 seconds, was not only the shortest by 27 seconds, but he had the highest style points. The judges gave him a bonus for not riding on his stick to brake. There was, so one journalist enthused

> something so extraordinary about his gait on skis that one might imagine that it was to him some natural, inborn way of moving. With his ski stick carried like a fashionable cane in one hand, and his cap in the other, he set off at a whirlwind speed, and as if it was the most natural thing in the world, made a jump so that the ski did not touch the ground for 2 to 3 ski lengths, and when he landed … there was no trace of unsteadiness …[9]
>
> It is only when one has seen Sondre Ouversen Nordheim, and bears in mind that he is now 43 years old, that one has a proper idea of what a first-rate skier can achieve in his prime.

Nordheim came from Morgedal in Telemark. He was the first among equals. On time alone, there were three Telemark skiers in the first six. It was, however, not their placing that inspired but as that same journalist put it, 'the effortless certainty with which they shot down, without touching the ground with their stick. During the race, they seemed to use this more for show than for anything else.'

The highly charged language answered to the spirit of the age. The search for national identity demanded heroes. They were scarcely to be found among politicians and other pillars of society. Ski champions were the best alternative. Like most Telemark skiers, Nordheim was poor and belonged to the land. He scratched a living as a country carpenter making spare parts for the handlooms that were still a staple of almost every farm. Hardly a model citizen, he yet filled the bill. He was a virtuoso. He had star quality. Insignificant in a crowd, on a pair of skis he came into his own. Among his fellow countrymen, he was a recognizable type. He was a *frikar*; wayward and a wanderer, a bit of an outsider, someone who lived in the half-world between reality and imagination. He resembled the eponymous hero of *Peer Gynt*, the verse drama by Ibsen – himself, too born in Telemark – which had appeared the year before the ski race of 1868. It was a paean to individuality – 'The world behind my brow', runs one memorable line, 'makes me what I am and no one else'[10] – and did much to form the Norwegians' view of themselves. It was at any rate Nordheim to the life. He was one of those figures who appear at the right historic moment. In skiing, the star system devolved from him.

Nordheim was only one example of how the quirky mountainous landscape of Telemark had inhabitants to match. Another was A. O. Vinje, a skier, writer and journalist in that order; an idiosyncratic luminary of the language. As a young man he had skied 400 km in mid-winter to take up a teaching post. Among Telemark skiers, in his own words: 'It was a terrible disgrace to take a tumble, and you weren't allowed to stop until you filled the hole in the snow. He who had too many tumbles could not dance with the girls on Sunday evening, and if he asked them, they merely giggled.'[11]

This dates from 1853, but Vinje was writing of events some 20 years before. Nordheim, born in 1825, was then an impressionable small boy. Vinje was also concerned with national decay:

> It was much more lively then on Sundays than it is now, when people just sit indoors drinking coffee or snaps. You had your Sunday dinner, put on your skis, and ran down the slopes ... and many a bone was broken ... but then they knew how to ski, and not, like now, stick-ride like a witch on a broom. Nonetheless skiing was a popular amusement not long ago, it lasted longest in Morgedal.

That was revealing. Morgedal was the remote valley from which came the triumphant Telemark skiers at the Christiania race. Elegance was their virtue. They, or men of Telemark in general, it was now thought, would cure stick-riding, the bane of contemporary skiing. So fragmented was the nation still, that only now was their reputation beginning to seep out from its native valleys into a wider world.

There had been muted signs before. In the season of 1866, for example, a Telemarking, called Iver Nerissen, was extolled by a journalist for winning a race at Horten, near Christiania, in which a 'Herr Student Bjerke' was the runner-up: 'Nerissen ... did not seem troubled by the little jump that had been arranged ... he ... clapped his hands while he was in the air ... slightly bent his knees and [landed] with ramrod back again.'[12]

This playfulness was a much remarked feature of Telemarkings on ski. Over the years, in scattered fixtures, they had made a considerable impression, but in the provinces alone. It was, however the Christiania race of 1868 that opened the domination of the Telemark school. This was because it was held in the capital, with concomitant press coverage. There were others who in sheer technique might have exerted a comparable influence but the men of Telemark were closest to the capital. There was also something in their character that appealed to the burgeoning romanticizing of the Norwegian country dweller, close to Nature, it was thought, and unspoilt. Above all, because of their steep and twisted home terrain, the Telemark skiers were past masters at downhill and jumping. These provided the drama needed for popularization and not the subtleties of cross-country skiing.

The Telemark skiers were the heroes of the hour. They appealed to journalists. They made good copy. In one way, they were yet another creation of the press. They had a history to match. As late as the eighteenth century, the remote districts of Kvitseid and Seljord around Morgedal were known for fatal brawls with knives and axes. Clergymen needed not so much the milk of human kindness as a good pair of fists to control their parishioners. 'If a good sportsman was not also a good brawler' says one historian, 'he did not enjoy public respect. Folk memory from that time is very bloodstained.'[13] One legendary character was a certain Asgeir Heggtveit. He had acquired merit, as it were, by killing three men. He was also a great skier. Vinje wrote about him skiing down a slope in his native province 'with a little child in his arm, and the child wasn't even woken. With his stick in his right hand and the child in his left, he did three figure eights on the flat',[14] which hinted at a touch of myth. Vinje did however offer circumstantial evidence by identifying the slope, called Flekstveidt skoti, the 'Flekstveidt chute' in the local dialect. 'It is incredible that anyone could ski down [there]', he wrote. 'It is a terrible gully in the meadow from the mountain peak to the [lake]. It is certainly [500 m] long and has a gradient of at least 70 degrees.'

The unstudied exhibitionism of Nordheim and his kind surfaced at another event in 1868, soon after the Christiania race. This was at Hviteseid, on his home ground. Nordheim, 'who must be the most accomplished skier in Telemark,'[15] to quote one press report, took the law into his own hands, and 'climbed even higher up than had been decided, so that the race became even more difficult for him.' In other words, he turned it into a kind of handicap event. 'To everyone's astonishment, he managed the whole run upright [making] a jump of ... about 20 metres. Small wonder that he laughed at the run laid out for him in Christiania, and of course he won the first prize.'

As a matter of fact, the first documented winner of a ski-jumping competition also came from Telemark. He was an army officer, Lieutenant Olav Rye[16] who, at Christmas 1808, jumped 10 m at Eidsberg in eastern Norway. Tradition is older still. A folk song originating there in the (wild) eighteenth century has these lines about the mountain peasants:

> Over the hummock six ells they spring,
> And manage it like anything.[17]

In nineteenth-century Christiania, at all events, the salvation of skiing was quickly seen in Telemark. After the race of 1868, Telemark skiers therefore returned as missionaries. Firstly, on an invitation from the Central Association, they came in 1870 to give a demonstration. On 13 February – as usual now a Sunday – Nordheim and two others performed on the same familiar Iversløkken slope. Again it was a combined cross-country sprint, downhill run and then a jump over which Nordheim once again drove journalists to hyperbole. Nonetheless, he and his companions had little immediate effect. One newspaper was provoked to this outburst: 'Skiing ... in Christiania is still practised in the most incorrect and absurd way. Your little boy, be he never so small, comes along dragging a stick that is twice his height.'[18]

As for the average grown-up:

> he runs down the slope, legs widely straddled, with a stiff, crouching stance, and trunk leaning forward, a ridiculous figure which inevitably rouses the thought that the skier is preoccupied with quite other business than skiing.

And:

> If anyone runs down a slope too steep for him [he] leans backwards on his stick completely stretched out on the snow ... and in that supine state he runs [thirty metres] down onto the flat, where [he] finally begins to rise up, at least if he is still on his skis and his stick is not broken. [Even] the example set by the Telemarkings, who have astonished the public by the straight posture and ability to manage without any aid, has not persuaded local skiers to abandon their all too attractive stick. [Perhaps] the Central Association ... can correct [these] failings by prohibiting the use of the stick in those competitions where speed is not decisive but only remaining on your feet.

The Central Association responded by organizing three more races in Christiania; in 1871, 1875 and then again in 1877. As usual they were a triple combination, with downhill, jumping and cross-country sprints following continuously one after the other. The last two were moved from Iversløkka to a more testing slope on the outskirts called Sandvika. The Telemark skiers won them all.

Whether their example did any good was another matter altogether. There were still local misgivings. 'The essential difference between the Telemark skiers and ... all the others',[19] as one critic put it, 'was that when the Telemark skiers ran down a slope, or over a jump, they depended on their legs and sense of balance, while the other skiers had recourse to their sticks ... Another weakness of the majority', he continued, was that they

> did not understand how to use their skis on the flat. [They] ran off as they normally do when marching quickly, that is they lifted the skis from the snow and stamped them down to the accompaniment of the sound of squelching on the ground. Very few [competitors] had the gliding movement which makes the ski an easy, useful means of transport.

Adults were a lost cause, more or less. Youth was obviously more impressionable. Someone who, as a boy, watched the early Telemark skiers in Christiania, vividly recalled how, when they jumped, they

> soared like a bird far, far, down the slope and, on landing, bent their knees as if it had been some jumping exercise in the gymnasium ... And no sooner had [they] reached the flat, then they leant sideways and swung round so that the snow sprayed high up into the air. That was something quite different from running right down ... to stop the skis.[20]

The writer was Ernst Bjerknes, an engineer, whose elder brother, Vilhelm, was a mathematician and one of the founders of modern meteorology. If the Telemarkings had not exactly invented modern technique, at least they popularized it; or as the younger Bjerknes said:

> To ski 'à la Telemarking' became the motto … of us boys … We abandoned our sticks, and tried to ski with legs close together, jump, and bend our knees on landing. But heavens above, how we tumbled about … It was not so easy to learn the trick of getting our skis to turn. You see we had nobody to teach us.

New stars secured the Telemark domination in the formative years of modern skiing. Nordheim was runner-up in 1871. His last appearance was in 1875. It was a sadly muted farewell. He managed the jump but, now over 50 years old, his joints were stiffening and he was too slow over the cross-country section. He only came sixteenth and won no prize. He was, however, given a modest lifetime award, as it were – a silver trinket and a gold coin worth perhaps £30 today. Technical ability aside, the authorities understood the rôle of his singular personality as an advertisement for skiing.

So having played out his part, Nordheim returned to the obscurity from which he had been plucked, and the rural poverty that was the common lot in the romanticized hinterland. It was as if the educated classes of Christiania were using the Telemark skiers almost as gladiators, of whom Nordheim became an icon to a later generation.

After 1877, the Central Association stopped organizing ski races, sporadic as they were. Climate change with warmer winters meant that skiing in Christiania had faltered during the 1870s. An industrialist called Jørgen Gjerdrum came to the rescue. Gjerdrum was the managing director of a cloth mill at Nydalen, on the northern outskirts of Christiania. He ran a works ski club, through which he brought continuity by running annual races for his employees.

Ahead of his time, Gjerdrum was concerned for their welfare and also wanted to improve their skiing. Rather than importing fashionable Telemark stars, he stuck to local talent. He persuaded Elling Bækken to accept a job at the mill in some unspecified capacity. Bækken's true purpose was to lend lustre by his presence – he was after all an acknowledged champion – and set an example to skiing hopefuls. This was an early example of motivating staff.

A devoted skier himself, Gjerdrum had in fact been a judge at the Christiania race of 1868. He disliked the trend it represented and eulogistic he was not. Skiing, he remarked shortly after the event

> is not an acrobatic performance, in which the participants try to outdo each other in artificial and reckless deeds … It is completely mistaken to suppose that skis are … intended for flying through the air like a bird, any more than a man on skis should be able to … launch himself over every imaginable precipice … He must really be judged not by the length and height of [a] jump … but by speed, stamina, and the ability to move both up and downhill and so on.[21]

Solid, uncompromising, heavy jowelled and stony-faced, Gjerdrum had a taste for the extreme. He had articulated a controversy that is not settled yet. In his support he surprisingly invoked the Telemark skiers of 1868. They were not, he declared, the daredevils of popular belief:

> Even the winner [Nordheim] faltered on landing and steadied himself … with his stick. The other two Telemark skiers also used their sticks quite freely [so] the slope must have been difficult enough. [Such] reckless work ought not to be encouraged, but resisted.

To be fair, in the days before steel edges, the metal spike of the ski stick was the only recourse for control on hard icy snow crust. Thus Gjerdrum perversely credited the Telemark skiers with caution. He did not practise what he preached. At a ski race run by the Nydalen mill in 1872, one newspaper touched on 'the excellent ski slope with built-in jump … Spectators were not wanting … and there was great applause when an intrepid skier managed the jump, and was greeted with a fanfare by the factory workers' own band.'[22]

*Pace* Gjerdrum, this race was not the usual combined event, but ski-jumping alone. There had been ski races at Nydalen for several years, and the same was true of all. These were the first documented examples of a ski-jump held alone as a separate event.

The Central Association presented one of the prizes in 1872 but, as one journalist put it, progress depended on the 'smaller and more private arrangements' because, in a plaintive comment on climate change, 'they can be more easily organised, and thus held annually, while the big ski races, which must give notice far in advance, must often be cancelled because of weather and snow conditions'.

Carl XV, the King of Sweden-Norway once came to watch at Nydalen. This was the first royal appearance at a ski race. It might have been due to the fact that Gjerdrum held a position at Court, but a mere social formality it was not. Norway could boast of few national events and aside from Constitution Day on the 17 May, a ski race was really all that could be found. As Swedes, the sovereigns of the dual kingdom – the Union monarchs as they were called – had to perform an intricate balancing act. In Carl's own rueful words, 'it is not easy to steer between Norwegian pride and Swedish envy'.[23]

Nonetheless, unconventional, witty and genial Carl – nicknamed *Kron-Kalle* ('Crown-Charlie') – was universally popular. He certainly endeared himself to the Norwegian spectators at Nydalen. It was a race for the junior mill hands – which in those days meant from 12 years old. The board of directors turned out on skis in formal dress with frock coats and top hats. The King playfully stood under the lip of the jump and, more than six feet tall, he too surmounted by a top hat, dared one competitor to do his best.[24] The landing was then on the flat so the performance was not without risk for either part. Both survived without a scratch. In recognition thereof, His Majesty presented the skier with a gold coin worth about £40 today.

The next royal appearance was at another Nydalen race, in February 1876. It was also another king: Carl's brother, Oscar II. They were a study in contrasts: Carl rakish and expansive had seemed like a Renaissance prince; Oscar scholarly and very much middle-class. Both were tall, dark with aristocratic features and regal bearing, rather more kingly in fact than most sovereigns of the day and all-in-all a credit to their grandfather, the original Bernadotte who, king as he eventually became, was only the son of a French provincial lawyer from Pau, in Gascony.

Oscar's visit to Nydalen was more formal than that of his brother. Nonetheless he joined in the cheering for the best performers. As well he might. Following the Nydalen custom, it was jumping on its own, with landing now on a slope and many jumps of 10 m or more. Besides the adults, there were junior divisions for the children of the mill hands.

> During an interval [one journalist wrote,] the King himself climbed up to the top of the jump, from which there is an excellent view of Christiania and the fjord. The king's interest ... was particularly aroused by the youngest classes of boys between 7 and 9 years, some of whom moved on ski with truly entertaining dignity. In addition to the first prize ... for the big [adult] jump ... His Majesty also presented five lesser prizes for the very youngest.[25]

Oscar's interest was unfeigned. When young, to please his Norwegian subjects, he and Carl had been introduced to skiing, although at the time it was virtually unknown in Stockholm, where the Union kings had their seat. In the winter of 1840, Major Munch Petersen, who had organized the Christiania race of 1867, sent the young princes, as they then were, several pairs of skis. A Norwegian courtier in Stockholm replied that the skis 'were inaugurated with great glee ... There were very few tumbles considering that it was the first time that the princes had used such machines [sic].'[26]

Royalty or not, the Nydalen races were merely an interregnum. They were, after all, closed and on the periphery. Some other institution had to take over the promotion of the sport. This turned out to be the Christiania Ski Club. It was formed in 1877 by a group of young men from the upper classes. Article 1 of the rules stated that 'the purpose of the club is to practise skiing, and to consider the advantages and drawbacks of the various techniques and forms of ski'.[27]

The club grew out of informal skiing circles. Wholly serious they were not. One playground of these bringers of jollity was a slope known as *Kastelbakken* – 'Castle Hill' outside the western city limits at a farm called Huseby. It was longer and steeper than the other local slopes; besides which, they were being engulfed by rapid urban building. It was at Huseby that the Christiania Ski Club decided to organize the next representative ski race. It proved to be the first of an annual series, which in turn became the first regular national skiing event anywhere. As Huseby, it became a skiing legend.

The previous competition venues in Christiania had been more or less uninspiring nursery slopes. This crossed a threshold to a different order of achievement. Two hundred metres or more in length, the slope was not only longer and steeper than its predecessors were but it had the profile of a modern jumping hill. Half-way up, the slope was intersected by a road. Here on the uphill side, a lip was built as the takeoff by piling up beaten snow. Below the road, there was a naturally contoured outrun with a neat rounded top and a gentle transition at the bottom onto the flat.

That first Huseby race was held on the 12 February 1879. The dismal, shifting climate had relented. The thermometer was happily down to five or six degrees of frost. There was not a cloud within sight. The subtle blue of a winter sky set off the white of the snow and the sombre green of the pine trees, while from the top of the jump, there was a panorama of the city down to the still grey waters of the fjord beyond. It was a suitable background for a historic occasion. This was the transition to something that was recognizably modern skiing.

With the aid of extra railway trains, some 10,000 spectators had gathered – almost one tenth of the city's population. It is in the snow that the Nordic landscape comes to life. This was mirrored somehow in the emotions of the crowd. The move to Norwegian independence from Sweden was gathering pace, and the spectators at Huseby had not only come to watch their ski champions but, consciously or not, as a national demonstration. King Oscar was there, again, but even as the Swedish overlord, he was the target of no ill will and was personally popular. He was, after all, constitutionally the king of Norway as well, generous towards his Norwegian subjects and trying his very best to preserve the Union. Appearing at a ski race was one way of advancing that intention.

Once again, Oscar was placed in a specially built stand opposite the take off, the best place to watch the jump. It had reverted to the combined event of previous years, and the King also had a view over the whole cross-country course. This was also a change to something recognizably modern. It ran up and down some demanding hills, winding in and out of tricky undulating terrain. The distance was about 3,000 metres; again a sprint, but with a concentrated trial of the whole gamut of skiing, and following immediately after the jump, traumatic or not, with no rest allowed, to form a continuous race. The jump was merely one incident along the course. The contestants started at intervals of two minutes, a military bugler ceremonially giving each the half-dreaded signal to begin.

Eleven years earlier, after the pioneering race of 1868, Gjerdrum had warned that at Huseby

> the skier is flung out at a monstrous speed over a distance of [10 to 15 metres] before he reaches the ground again. The hill can occasionally be managed when there is much deep, loose snow, at least by a nimble performer, because the speed and vertical drop are less, but when the going is firm and fast, I consider it impossible.[28]

Now, in 1879, with the slope deliberately tramped down, the going was decidedly 'firm and fast', but impossible it was not. Jumps of over 15 m were the rule. There were none of multiple fractures held up by Gjerdrum as a cautionary tale. It was progress all the way. The jump was naturally the most spectacular part of the race. It was eloquently summarized by the King's guest, the Danish Prince Hans of Glücksburg. He had never seen skiing before. 'They're stark raving mad!'[29] His Royal Highness judiciously observed when the Telemark skiers began jumping. Improved technique was part of the answer but also the contour of the slope.

This allowed critically longer jumps in relative safety. The trajectory was new and proved to be the key. Previously it would drop the skier back to earth like a stone. This one was such that, at touchdown, it was quite tangential to the natural contour of the outrun. That reduced the shock of landing. By the same token, in a fall, it avoided the worst injury to the tumbling unfortunate by modifying the impact and sending him spinning in humiliation but harmlessly on his way. Intentionally or not, this was the first modern ski-jump. It provided the design for all subsequent constructions; an example of art copying nature.

Entrants from all the main skiing districts had been invited. Substantial prizes were the bait. Yet again, the men of Telemark swept the board. They took the first five places. More than their victory, it was once more their jumping style that generated rapture. Although they carried a stick for the cross-country section, they used it not at all in the jump. Hitherto, most skiers had simply allowed gravity to carry them over the jump but, in the words of one journalist, they 'crouched down some 10 to 15 m before taking off, so that at the edge of the jump they could [uncoil and] give themselves extra speed and thus achieve the greatest possible length'.[30]

In other words, a recognizably modern jump. And:

> After having reached the highest point in the air, they stretch out and [land] with a gentle bending of the knees ... whereupon they raise themselves to their full height, and with a military bearing carry on at breathtaking speed.

The real sensation of the day was not however the overall winner, a certain John Hauge. Aside from the adults, there were two junior classes; one for boys under 14, and another under 17. One 16-year-old Telemarking called Olaf Haugan had won the older class, with another, Torjus Hemmestveit runner-up. Both did extra jumps as a demonstration for King Oscar. They

> displayed extraordinary courage and suppleness [the journalist continued]. It was really astonishing to see ... Haugan, the younger of the two, jumped with all the strength of his muscles at least [a metre] above the level of the jump, and then sailed 20 metres down the slope.

This was the longest jump of the day. During practice, Haugan had already jumped 22 m. This was truly historic. He had broken a barrier, for 20 m is the threshold of true ski-jumping as a specialized discipline. It was the breakthrough to modern distances on the first modern jumping hill. Haugan had, as it were, jumped into the future. This was perhaps dimly perceived. He was awarded several extra prizes – including one for swinging his cap in honour of the King while flying through the air in the middle of a jump.

Hemmestveit was overshadowed, but still also given his due reward as a Telemarking. One day his would be a name to be conjured with. His father wrote to thank the Christiania Ski Club 'for the kindness and goodwill you showed my son'.[31]

> The extra prizes and all the good things he was given, surpassed all my expectations, for which I thank you with all my heart.
>
> I have a younger son called Mikkel, who is not behind the eldest [Torjus] in skiing, but we were so short of money for him … that he could not travel, since I have 5 sons, all accomplished skiers, and all have won prizes at ski races in Telemark. I have often thought of visiting the towns with some of them to show their ability to ski in the Telemark way.

Huseby released an eruption of Tele-mania. 'Of all the … skiers', one journalist typically proclaimed, 'the Telemark farmers were the most accomplished, enterprising, controlled; complete masters of their skis, which they treated as if they were skates.'[32]

But also:

> The ski is the poor man's horse … and a good horse at that … when one realises that nine men from Telemark who came to the race at Huseby [on ski] running 100 kilometres in 1 1/2 days, for the most part over wild moorlands, and of that distance 50 kilometres from 8 a.m. to 5 p.m.

The reason was partly poor transport. Besides, skiing to a race meant saving time and money. It had become a habit. The writer also wanted to make another point:

> Skiing is democratic in the best meaning of the word, since nobody is so poor that he cannot acquire a pair of skis … At the same time skiing is a pleasure for the better-off, it expands the chest that has shrunk at the desk. It fills the senses with joy in God's glorious, free natural world. Therefore the ski races which are now being held, enjoy more and more participation.

Indirectly, this records the spread of ski racing, with Huseby simply the most prestigious fixture, or at least the most prestigiously reported. At another level, it is also an early exposition of the romantic Nature-worship that was becoming associated with skiing.

Another piece of journalism pegged to the first Huseby race expatiated on skiing in Telemark. In particular, it repeated others in noting 'the district of Morgedal … where [skiing] artistry has been developed to the point of virtuosity'.[33] Most of the winners at Huseby did indeed come from Morgedal. The author, perhaps because he himself was a Telemarking, impishly declared that for an outsider to assume that mere adoption of the Telemark style – one ski well in front of the other – would make him a Telemark skier, was 'as unreasonable as believing that a lion skin would turn a donkey into a lion'. More soberly, he gave an explanation of Telemark skiing terminology. This arose from the local dialect, a world away from the Danish-Norwegian spoken by the educated classes in the towns. The terms were not known elsewhere:

> The track of … skis in the snow … is called … a 'laam' (plural 'laamir'). A clear distinction is drawn between a race with a jump, and one without. The former is called 'hoppelaam' [literally 'jumping track'] … The other kind of race [is a] 'slalaam'.

That was the first appearance in print of the word which we now know as slalom. This is itself an alternative Norwegian spelling. The exact date was the 8 March 1879. For the record, *Fædrelandet* was the name of the journal.

There was also a third race called variously *vill-låm* or *uvøslåm*; literally 'wild' or 'reckless' track. This was run on a steep slope, usually a swathe cut through a forest for logging, a white band of snow gleaming between the dark conifers, where skiers swept directly down for a few hundred metres in one rush without turning. It was clearly the origin of the modern straight downhill race. Only local daredevils tried this kind of course. It was another contrast to the slalom.

Exactly when that word arose is unclear. So too is the etymology. One favoured explanation is that 'sla' derives from a root meaning 'smooth' or 'even'. In that case, 'slalom' means 'a smooth track.' In any case, the term as it existed in 1879 did not mean exactly the same as the usage of today but the underlying sense of an obstacle course was already there: 'Admittedly a "slalaam" is without a proper jump, but has its own difficulties, which demand just as great skill as the *hoppelaam*. The greatest difficulties arise from the so-called *kneiker*, i.e., short, steep [hummocks,] bends and dips in the terrain.'

By this definition, the cross-country section of the Huseby race was in all but name a *slalaam* as originally defined. Consequently that first Huseby race might also be counted as the first *slalaam* outside its Telemark home. It really had opened modern skiing. Competition, however, was not the whole story.

# 11

# *Development of Technique and Equipment*

'When running [downhill] at speed', someone wrote in a Christiania newspaper on 22 March 1867,

> a skier must [not only] have suppleness and agility [but also] assume a forward crouched position, with knees bent, and such elasticity in rising and lowering, that the body maintains a spring-like power when the slope presents long jumps or obstacles, besides preferably keeping the left leg somewhat in front of the right one, so that, in a way, he mostly rests on it.[1]

This is the first known analysis of skiing technique, downhill in particular. It would hold good today. Unfortunately the author hid behind a pseudonym so he is yet another pioneer who cannot be given his rightful due. Prompted by the second Christiania race of 1867, he was living proof of how competition stimulated an interest in technique. This being Norway, it was polemical and, luckily for us, ventilated in the press.

It was the Christiania race of 1868 that provoked the first argument in print on the technicalities of skiing. It was given at least the same billing as politics, sometimes making the front page, and even led the paper now and then. Luckily the authors were no longer cloaked in anonymity. A country doctor called Nils Thoresen opened the exchange. Given the performance of the Telemarkings downhill, he wrote in *Morgenbladet* on 11 February 1868: 'the difference between good and bad posture is obvious, but nonetheless I believe it would be useful to enunciate the essential rules for proper skiing'.[2]

Dr Thoresen modestly explained that

> Having grown up in Thelemark, and learned to ski there, I naturally applied the rules accepted there for becoming a good skier. These were: Skis close together, so that they made a [single] furrow in loose snow, knees slightly bent and elastic, the one leg in front of the other, straight body, with hands [outstretched] as a balancing aid, always without a stick, unless considered necessary in skiing over trackless and unknown parts, or on long tours.

Thus repeating and disagreeing in one breath with the anonymous expert of the year before, Thoresen had unleashed controversy. His rules, especially the positioning of skis, 'approached those of a tight rope walker's', in the words of one riposte.[3] It came from the Major Munch Petersen who had organized the race in Christiania the year before and established the rules of competition. A very military gentleman, he enunciated as a dictum that 'a soldier on ski does not fall!'[4] Underneath the martinet, however, there were traces of a reasonable soul. Dr Thoresen's principles, he declared, could 'of course be achieved by practice … for what can practice and habit not attain? But obviously it cannot be said to be mechanically correct.'

For lateral stability, Major Petersen advocated skis somewhat apart. Not the metre or so of the awkward incompetent, 'but [15–25 cm], and in difficult circumstances even up to [30 cm], I would find it hard to condemn, even in a good skier'.

Instead of formalism, the Major was suggesting adaptation to circumstances. He was touching on the baleful effect of artificial style on negotiating natural terrain. These were the opening salvos in a debate that has not ended yet. They showed that theorizing, unsurprisingly, was the province of the official classes. As skiing was becoming more organized in form, they were assuming the leadership, and shaping the development. It was such people who quickly followed Thoresen and Petersen in the pages of *Morgenbladet* during February and March 1868.

Under the stern title of 'skiing is not for fun alone', the anonymous author of a newspaper article had already thundered against 'the work of lunatics', because certain races were intended merely to show prowess on 'the so-called jump, not only natural … but also artificial ones … built up … on slopes that are in themselves too steep … of a gradient of 45° or more'.[5]

That would not shame a modern Alpine run. It hints at the sheer ability of the pioneers, unaided by the technical advances that we know. This Jeremiah was however unimpressed. The real goal of skiing was to move across country.

> Therefore you must be able to use your skis to run both up and down … The main point is to develop the muscles in a particular way so that you can keep going on your skis even if you take all day to reach your goal. This ought to be the aim of ski racing, if it is to be of any practical use.

Among those following Dr Thoresen and Major Petersen in the Christiania press of 1868 was someone calling himself 'W' – almost certainly the by now familiar Lt Col. Oscar Wergeland. He declared that proper control downhill 'requires shifting the weight of the body to the inner or outer ski, or evenly distributing it between both, according to whether one wants to hold back, or run unchecked'.[6]

This was the first recorded analysis of the dynamics of skiing. It still holds as a fundamental axiom. It was not, however, the imposition of a theory, but an attempt to codify observation.

In any case 'W' had described the principle of a turn based on sideslipping. Another method was presaged by Dr Thoresen. If, he wrote, 'your legs are kept reasonably close together, the one in front of the other, you can easily drop the hindmost leg so low, that the knee touches the ski'.[7]

That was the foundation of a turn using the balance of centrifugal forces.

This became known as the Telemark, its first appearance in print being in 1893. W's side-slipping method was eventually called the Christiania; the earliest recorded use of which dates from 1902.[8] It was named after the Norwegian capital – commemorated to this day by many a Hotel Christiania in the Alps. Both turns had been used by Telemark skiers at least since the early 1860s. There in the valleys of rural Norway was the cradle of modern downhill skiing.

Technique was all very well but it was intertwined with equipment. The ski itself was obviously the heart of the matter. Concern for design and workmanship culminated in 1863 with a ski-making competition in Trondheim.[9] It was the earliest known example of its kind. The first prize was a heavy calibre bear hunting rifle. This was so valuable that it attracted almost 50 entries. For the record, the winner was a certain Nils Jensen Balstadmo. Who he was, or what his kind of ski was, the records do not say. On the other hand, we know he came from Selbu – a valley in central Norway that was in the heartland of national folklore.

There was then no ski manufacturing industry. It was a local craft. 'Nearly every farm boy in the parish makes ... skis', wrote an eighteenth-century rural vicar. The way to the ski-maker was usually by word of mouth. The earliest known advertisement for skis appeared in a Christiania newspaper in 1820.[10] The ski-maker often worked with beech, because it was light and elastic. Together with pine, spruce, ash, oak and maple, this was a common wood for skis. Occasionally someone might use elm, although even as late as the nineteenth century it was taboo. Elm skis were so smooth and fast that the Devil was popularly thought to be the agent, standing behind the skier, which was bad enough but also, in a kind of homely Faustian compact, anyone who killed himself when swishing down a demon run on such a pair would go straight to eternal damnation.

Superstition aside, ski making was highly specialized. The blanks were cloven out of logs in one piece, then planed and chiselled by hand to give form and camber. The tips were bent by steaming. By tradition skis were often richly decorated on their upper surfaces. They were works of peasant art and repositor-ies of folklore.

Small wonder that the lone ski-maker, deftly shaping wood that had sprung out of the soil into a brilliant instrument of everyday use and pleasure, became a romanticized figure – even the subject of paintings. In practice the workmanship was uneven, and sometimes shoddy. Ski-making competitions probably made for improvement. Quite as important as that pioneering one of 1863, however, were the articles that followed in the local press.

The first one objected to the fact that the competition rules 'stipulated a particular model as the pattern for entries, which certainly has prevented many otherwise qualified entrants from entering their skis'.[11] The author – anonymous yet again – had succinctly attacked the whole prize system. Whether in ski making, literature or art, it meant judgement by committee, with uniformity the outcome. In this case, as usual, it was retrograde. The judges wanted a return to the central Nordic type. In any case, they discouraged innovation by specifying the proportions and details of design. The shape of skis, said Anonymous of

Trondheim, was 'surely a new subject for a newspaper'. It was. He found himself on the front page. As a pioneer he could hardly complain.

Disagreement resurfaced in the newspaper discussion after the Telemarkings' triumph of 1868 in Christiania. The same Captain Roosen who had done so much to promote leisure skiing, now revealed that he was perturbed by variety. He had been anticipated a century earlier by the army regulations of 1762, which issued its specifications for equipment because most 'skis are not of a pure form … and uniformity is required'. Roosen actually wrote a book on those lines, with the subtext of national unity. Now in the columns of the Press in February 1868, he reiterated his idea. He wanted to replace local variations with a single, officially approved, national type of ski.[12]

Someone signing himself simply 'E' objected. 'Because of a proper feeling for the subject,' he wrote, 'skis in the various country districts are adapted to requirements.'[13] In other words, it was the usual conflict between regimentation, or the mealy mouthed 'best practice' on the one hand and free natural development on the other. Roosen would have strangled all advance by diktat. Luckily, he did not succeed.

The variety of skis in the country was staggering. In the seventeen degrees of latitude through which Norway runs, there is a comprehensive selection of climate and terrain. It extends from temperate maritime all the way to sub-Arctic; from lowland forest to mountain plateaux and quasi-Alpine peaks. As a result, a plethora of forms had evolved to cope with a plethora of circumstances. Every district, each village almost, had its own design. This was true even in the middle decades of the nineteenth century. Because of the mountains, and defective communications, Norway was still not exactly a unified state, but a fragmented agglomeration of self-contained fjords and isolated valleys, each preserving its own dialect, culture and hence skiing tradition.

Broadly speaking, skis could be classified in two groups: for ease of running and facility in turning. The variations were endless. At one end of the scale was the central province of Østerdalen. This contained the last bastion of the central Nordic type of ski and andor. There the terrain was largely undulating forest and low mountains; the snow crystalline and dry. Turning was not a considera-tion; ease of running definitely was. So the kind of ski that evolved was both narrow and long – up to 3 m – with a groove along the sole. It automatically ran straight, and thus removed the effort of holding a course. By the same token, it was difficult to turn. It was a model of this sort that Roosen wanted to impose on everybody.

At the other extreme lay the mountainous terrain of western Norway, roughly from Telemark to the Atlantic coast. Here, manoeuvrability was the crux. The outcome was a relatively short ski. The shape was, however, the crux. The eastern type had straight, parallel sides, and the skis were of even width. The western model, however, tapered along its length, broadest at the tip and narrowest at the heel, like a trapezoid.

In the first place, the wide tip breaks loose snow like the bow of a ship, leaving a broad track through which the rest of the ski can slip. Secondly, running downhill, this type is easier to turn. By edging the ski, it automatically deviates from the line of travel, because of the angle of the sides.[14] A ski with parallel sides, by contrast, has to be brought round by main force.

In other words, the western type of ski was the more sophisticated. A complete pair has been retrieved from a shrinking firn glacier near Voss, in Western Norway. It is the oldest specimen of its kind. Its probable date is around AD 1300. It is a respectable antiquity. It lay behind the triumph of the Telemark skiers at the Christiania race of 1868. It grew out of the soil.

Telemark is peculiarly formed. Elsewhere, the valleys are long, even and rounded from their glaciated past, with communication unimpeded. In Telemark, the valleys were short, confused and broken, separated by ridges and low passes, with serpentine gullies and steep forest. Moreover, the nature of farming exploited the landscape with hanging meadows which, in winter, became hair-raising slopes. All this demanded agility and quick turning. The outcome was a highly individual ski. It was relatively short; about 2 m, without a steering groove. That in itself helped manoeuvrability. There also emerged a distinctive local variation of the Western type of ski. This tapered from tip to foot rest and then ran parallel to the heel. Among the victorious Telemarkings of 1868, Nordheim at least used this model.

There was, however, another variation at the time, resembling modern downhill skis. This was widest at each end and narrowest in the middle. It was not as common as the other sort but nonetheless considered by outsiders to be the genuine Telemark ski.

The sides formed a subtle, concave, gentle waisted curve. This shape means that, pivoting at each end, the ski twists to follow the contours, and therefore hugs the snow, giving the necessary control. This is of course vital on a beaten track or crust. Moreover, the weight is concentrated at the ends, so that there is less friction in the middle, which enhances manoeuvrability. Finally, the torsion has the surprising effect of making the centre of the sole slightly convex, which, in consequence, promotes side slipping and hence turning.

One writer in the newspaper exchanges of 1868 graphically made the point:

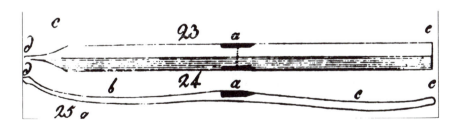

24. Earliest known technical drawing of a Norwegian ski, Telemark style. GutsMuths, 1804.

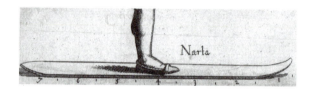

25. Balduinus, *De calceo antiquo*, 1667. Ski with heel strap, as described by a Norwegian.
*Cambridge University Library*

'When one runs down with skis close together and finds oneself leaning to one side, the skis seem to follow by themselves to the same side, like skates, and in this way restore one's balance.'[15]

The first Huseby race of 1879 was a battleground both of men and skis. Most competitors ran on their own local model. There was even a solitary entrant clinging to the central Nordic type with ski and andor. It still survived in a few isolated pockets; and this was its last appearance in a competition. As among the skiers, it was the ski from Telemark that garnered all the praise.

This ski was now recognized as the waisted type. A newspaper article gave the dimensions: about 8 cm wide at the heel, 7 cm in the middle, and 9 cm where the bend started at the tip.[16] It was a subtle shape, naturally evolved, and a kind of unity had set in. At a maximum length of 240 cm, it was short by the standards of the day and also relatively broad. This Telemark ski, as one newspaper put it, 'unquestionably proved to have the advantage over all other types in the jump'.[17] It was also superior in the cross-country course. Because the binding was set well back, with a short distance to the heel, 'it enabled the skier to kick his skis round with remarkable ease and speed, and thus climb diagonally uphill'. What is more, to the chagrin of those who championed other products, a Telemark model won top prize at an exhibition of skis that accompanied the Huseby races. The craftsmen who developed this ski down the ages clearly had an intuitive perception of physical principles and design. It was akin to the great violin makers of the past. It was a classic example of adaptation in a free evolutionary environment.

Whether this waisted type of ski originated in Telemark is another matter altogether. Its existence was documented by GutsMuths in 1804, but merely as 'Norwegian'. It had also been recorded in the middle of the seventeenth century by a Danish scholar called Ole Worm.[18] It is therefore at least 350 years old. What is more, it was mentioned outside Telemark during the revival of the nineteenth century. In the winter of 1863, someone in a Trondheim newspaper praised its qualities, as a local ski. In his view, it even 'served to keep the skis a suitable distance from each other'.[19] In another part of the country, there were models with such a pronounced waist that they foreshadowed modern carving skis.

Whatever its exact origins, the waisted ski was rapidly associated with Telemark. There were variations here and there. Some makers produced a model curved only on the inner edge so that there was a left and a right ski, instead of the usual symmetrical pairs. This, however, was a short-lived idiosyncracy. The normal waisted ski was used by many of the great Telemark skiers who began to emerge from the province. It gave them the technical foundation for their success. At a critical period, skill and equipment combined to give birth to modern skiing.

Skis were only half the story. Bindings were vital too. They are, after all, the link between the skier and his ski. They had a hand in the outcome of the first Christiania race in 1866. Most of the field, including Bækken, used a simple toestrap. Holmboe, the winner, and another successful competitor called Nissen had semi-rigid bindings with heelstraps. This was the custom in northern Norway, where both men had their homes. It probably came from the neighbouring Lapps. Its antecedents went back at least 1,000 years to the Mänttä ski in Finland.

The first occasion that fixed bindings were recorded in a race was three years before the Christiania event. That was near Trondheim in 1863. The course was combined downhill and jumping 'with a gradient of about 1 in 2', so a newspaper reported

> and everybody started with fixed heelstraps, declaring that it was impossible without them … An unforeseen eventuality, a thick, wet snow shower fell at the start – but at the critical moment two wandering musicians appeared, and by squeezing out the most screeching notes one could imagine, they made the momentary depression dissolve in laughter. Soon after, the dark shadow left the heavens and the brows of the organisers.[20]

Shifting moods or not, this race was a technical milestone. Following in its footsteps, and those of Holmboe and Nissen, the Telemark skiers in the race of 1868 also used a binding with some form of heelstrap.

The binding has ever been a fertile source of strife. In the Nordic world, any system has to satisfy two conflicting demands. The foot must move freely up and down and preferably have lateral control as well. Since the Stone Age, all over the skiing crescent from Altai onwards, the first had dominated. This was because moving across country had been uppermost. With the rise in Norway of downhill skiing and jumping, the situation was reversed.

Although the heelstrap had long existed, with the decay of skiing, it fell largely into desuetude. For millennia the simple toestrap had sufficed. It served well on the flat. Downhill, it was an instant safety binding, efficiently decanting the skier in difficulties onto the snow. While technique remained primitive, that meant much. That explained its use by accomplished skiers like Bækken. In fact, the toestrap had long been used on its own in western Norway, with its steep, broken mountainsides. As it was, in 1865, a local newspaper carried the first known report of a broken leg on a ski slope.[21]

There were various devices to prevent the foot slipping out of the simple toestrap. One was a wooden block or an osier ring beneath the instep. Often skiers put their trust in friction on its own. The toestrap was usually of birch root. The heelstrap, where it still existed, was of leather. This, then, was the state of affairs in the middle of the nineteenth century. With the rise of downhill and jumping, lateral control became urgent. A heelstrap was one solution. Leather – as used by the pioneering Holmboe from northern Norway – stretched too easily. To give the necessary support, a type made of twisted birch-root had evolved. Combined with a toestrap of the same material, they firmly held the boot, while allowing some vertical movement – at the cost, alas, of many a blister.

This half-forgotten contrivance explained in part the victory of the Telemark skiers at Christiania in 1868. Sondre Nordheim was supposed to have invented it, as he was supposed to have invented the Telemark ski. This, however, was part of a propaganda exercise to build him up as a national icon, which was unfair to the man himself. As it happened, GutsMuths had already described such a binding in 1804: 'The Norwegians twist tough osier into a cord which, drawn through the [tranverse] hole is wound round the instep, and also behind, above the heel.'[22]

However: 'Beginners must only allow the cord to go round the instep, and under no circumstances round the heel, because the foot must preserve its freedom of movement, when they lose their balance while running.'

In fact this osier heel binding goes back at least to 1667, when a Flemish writer called Balduinus first mentioned it in print.[23] He associated it with the *Scricfinni*, presumably the Lapps. It laid the foundations of most bindings for the next three hundred years. The materials were different, but the mechanical principles remained the same.

Despite the Telemarkings' supremacy, the resuscitated heel binding faced much opposition for nearly two decades, owing to a fear of sprains or broken limbs. Even an advocate of the system observed in a newspaper article that the toestrap 'must not be too big, and the heelstrap so arranged that the foot ... can be freed when one falls'[24] – in other words, a precursor of the safety binding, and a clear definition of its principle.

Much ink was spilled over bindings but little over boots and *they* are the other vital component of the link between the skier and his ski. Until far into the nineteenth century, tradition reigned. What skiing cultures had in common was footwear with a turned-up toe, like high medieval fashion. This was to hook into the toestrap. The Lapps had an ancient sophisticated model made of specialized reindeer fur, from the legs or forehead, for flexibility. With the hair turned inwards, it was known as *komager*; if outwards, the name was *skaller*. The Norwegian word was *Finnesko* – 'Lapp shoe' – whence it made its way into English. It was lined inside with sennegrass, a sedge that is unrivalled for insulation, and absorbing moisture. It was a sophisticated device, supple and following the foot, exactly suited to the circumstances.

Among the Norwegians themselves, there was a version made of untanned leather, called *hudsko* – 'hide boots' – also with the hair turned outwards. Like the Lapp model, it had a soft sole, really an extension of the uppers. This gave perfect flexibility, like a slipper or moccasin. Sometimes it was combined with a so-called toecap. This was a kind of external sock, knitted or crocheted with tough thread, the purpose of which was to protect the leather from damage by rubbing against the toestrap. Roomy, with plenty of space for straw and several pairs of socks, this boot was soft and warm and left the circulation unimpeded. It suited the birch root binding. The heelstrap formed a kind of semi-rigid cage, which gave lateral control but in which the boot could move up and down without blistering the heel because it was protected by the entire filling. For that reason it was highly adapted both to downhill and Nordic terrain. It was universally popular in Telemark.

Ski boots were however evolving in other ways. A transitional type appeared in the so-called *lauparsko*. This was essentially a version of the soft, moccasin-like hide boot but made of tanned leather for strength and easier upkeep. It had a raised heel, and a half sole was eventually added to cope with heelstraps and trying terrain. They were an uneasy compromise.

Outside the skiing world, meanwhile, another solution was waiting in the shape of a Norwegian walking boot, called *beksømstøvler*. This had a stiff, welt-sewn leather sole and soft uppers. It was a different answer to the skier's rising need for lateral stability. By transferring that from binding to boot, it not only permitted a firm heelstrap, but also functioned with a simple toestrap for those who condemned any form of fixed device. It was in use by the time of the Christiania race of 1868. It showed the beginnings of the modern ski boot.

# 12

# The First Nordic Marathon

The climate, meanwhile was playing its little tricks. In 1880, there was a drought of snow. The Huseby races were cancelled. The following winter reverted to another age. Temperatures sank and, in January 1881, a violent blizzard swept over western Europe. Paris was smothered in snowdrifts. In England, the *Daily News* resignedly commented, 'we are utterly unprepared for … a large snowfall … The … country [presents] the picture of a general blockade.'[1]

It was a suitable opening for the decade that shaped the modern world. In the sciences, it saw fundamental discoveries like that of radio waves by the German physicist, Heinrich Hertz. In the arts, Ibsen and Strindberg, for example, revolutionized the theatre. Skiing also shared the surge of innovation. In Norway of the 1880s skiing finally found its modern form.

Skiing had faltered in the uncertain winters of the 1870s. It was revived by the glut of snow and frost in 1881. All over the country there were more races and more competitors; perhaps 3,000 in all. It was a kind of turning point. In Christiania itself, after the enforced gap of a year, the second Huseby competition was finally run; on 7 February, as it happened.

Superficially, it seemed much the same as the first. Again it was a continuous jumping and cross-country race, now of about 3,000 m. Again the crowds streamed up to watch. Again the pistol crack of skis landing after a jump shattered the winter air. Again, apprehensive or not, competitors waited one by one at the top of the jumping hill for the sound of the bugle from the depths below, which would call them to their fate. And again Telemarkings swept the field, taking the first five places.

Skiers from elsewhere, however, were now creeping up behind. Improved technique helped; so too did style judging. As before, races were decided by points allotted in three equal parts; to jumping and turning, to style and bearing, and finally to time. With two-thirds of the marking subjective, favouritism could be judiciously masked.

Nonetheless, the method of counting time is of more than passing interest. It was taken as the total from the start of the jump to the finish of the cross-country, points being given according to time difference. Marking was by penalty, so that least was best. At Huseby in 1881 the scale was 1 point to the fastest skier, with a penalty of 0.1 point for each 15 seconds slower. That was the origin of the modern system for deciding combined events. To this day, the principle remains the same.

The year 1881 also saw the foundation of the first Norwegian sports journal, *Norsk Idrætsbladet* – 'The Norwegian Sporting Newspaper' more or less. Based on English models like *The Field*, it was in fact one of the first of its kind outside the British Isles. It gave *skiing* exhaustive coverage and a forum for debate during the critical years of evolution.

Thus at Huseby in 1881, *Idrætsbladet* – as it was usually called – could report that, surprisingly, the Telemarkings objected to the jump because the end sloped perilously downwards. Flinching at the sight, 'their legs trembled' on the approach run. 'But does the honourable public know the cause of this trembling? Well the Telemarking cuts the speed of his skis by twisting them so that they dig into the snow with the inner edges; hence the trembling.'[2]

That was the first documented use of the snowplough.[3] For another thing, the organizers printed a map of the course; the first of its kind, anywhere. The Huseby races had become a skiing laboratory in which innovations were tested, and from which the country took its lead.

At Huseby in 1881, there was another advance in technique. *Idrætsbladet* praised a certain Telemarking in the cross-country stage for his 'supple and powerful gliding over the even surface of the snow'.[4] This is the first record in print of a true modern Nordic style. It explained the supremacy of the Telemarkings. They had learned how to use their thigh muscles to give a kick off the back foot and generate a slide on the flat. It distinguished them from other racers, who got away with 'sprinting' or 'tramping,' with or without sticks. Form, as usual, followed function.

In Christiania, at least, the Telemarkings were now seen as paragons of style so, after the Huseby races of 1881, some of them turned that to account with skiing courses before going home. The nucleus was the Hemmestveit family; the father, his son Torjus and his other son, Mikkel, who could not afford to run in the previous Huseby event. The courses lasted between one and three weeks. Men and women were accepted. The syllabus was running downhill on various slopes round the city, together with instruction in the two turns, which later became known as the Telemark and the Christiania.

Even discounting military ski instruction in the eighteenth century, this was not the first ski school. Every Sunday, a local newspaper had reported from Trondheim in March 1866, 'with the generous assistance of the accomplished skiers of our district, arrangements were made to give boys instruction'.[5] Nonetheless, that in Christiania 1881 was the first ski school in the modern sense. It was commercialized with continuous graded courses, and agreed prices. It was also the first formal instruction in the Telemark style and hence the start of modern skiing, not to mention a precursor of fashion in the way we are taught to ski. As a result of the Telemarkings' example, their ski classes, or the abundant snow, or a combination of all three, 'a few days afterwards',[6] so one journal reported, 'there was hardly a decent pair of skis obtainable in the whole town, while there was a glut before the race'.

This was all very gratifying but an argument on the aims of skiing had now erupted. One school of thought held that the cross-country event was the essence of skiing. The great proponent was Axel Huitfeldt, a Christiania lawyer, an uninhibited polemicist with many an acerbic column inch to his credit. He opened the confrontation in *Idrætsbladet* soon after the Huseby races of 1881.

He was contradicted by the same Dr Thoresen who had promoted the Telemark school in the debate on skiing technique 13 years before. The doctor now disparaged the cross-country event because it had turned skiing from 'a test of skill'[7] into a mere 'test of heart and lungs'. Moreover, in 'deep cold and heavy snowfall, such effort is not without risk, [because] under such conditions one is particular prone to pneumonia'. He was ridiculed in the press, notably by someone masquerading under the initials 'bg':

> The cross-country event ... is a ... test of strength and stamina [which] should be the deciding factor, and not simply acrobatic performance.[8]
> Anybody who participates in rowing, horse racing or in a ski race must train.

This was the first time that the word 'train' was applied to skiing. It was also an early appearance outside the English language, which was its origin, and from which it has been widely borrowed. To train, in the words of this author, meant:

> that through daily exercise, diet, and a regular way of life, one hardens oneself for the fight. This is something that is the abc for any sportsman; just look at the University boat race in England, for example. It will be held this year on the 9th April, and both boats have been in action since the middle of February. At first, practice took place this year under great difficulties because of heavy frost. Clothing is very light [and] the Herr Doktor [Thoresen] may be sure that the English weather in February was not far short of the Norwegian in severity. What does the sports-loving Englishman do under such circumstances? He simply keeps moving until he can change. This simple but practical method is recommended for participants in a ski race.

In essence, 'bg' was agitating for less mollycoddling. He also revealed something about the society out of which skiing evolved. On the one hand were the peasants, where fitness followed naturally from their life and work; on the other, the townsfolk, who had to achieve it by conscious effort and who had yet to see the point. It was an emerging dilemma of urbanization everywhere. Axel Huitfeldt took up the theme in an article when, percipiently, he hoped that the Telemark domination might persuade the Christiania skiers to

> grasp the significance of training. Note how seriously this is taken in preparation for rowing; but where a ski race is concerned, people still believe that they can come straight from the whisky glass and cigar and even think of taking up cudgels with the best skiers in the country.[9]

For his part, 'bg' did remember to say: 'There is something about skiing that is specifically Norwegian, that gives it a particular stamp above all other sports.'[10]

This was not quite a repetition of the old nationalistic war cry. The contemporary spread of sport usually meant borrowing from the British. Here were the Norwegians with something all their own. It even distinguished them from Swedes and Finns, amongst whom

> skiing is also known ... but if [it] is to attain any significance as a sport, it must be practised in a country with undulating terrain, and in that respect, Norway is ahead. To work oneself ahead on skis over endless marshes and frozen lakes is truly no pleasure. No; the 'charm' of skiing lies in variation, now slowly up, now flying down.

From another point of view, skiing was cheap, so that 'both rich and poor can participate. While the moneyed classes cultivate it for pleasure and the sake of sport itself, it is practised by our countryfolk to travel over field and forest in winter.'

That was a succinct exposition of the unifying ideal and the parallel course of skiing. Moreover, 'Skiing is also a sport that suits the fair sex.' There was an ulterior motive behind this honourable utterance: 'It is mothers who have the greatest influence on the spirit of the child ... and we want to open womens' eyes to the advantage of sport, so that children can be ... encouraged to take part from an early age ... their boys must be brought up as men, and not as hothouse plants.'

This was all very well, but nobody yet understood the consequences of extreme effort in deep cold. The Boat Race was hardly a suitable guide. Nor were Scandinavian hunters and their like because they were not racing, but doing things at their own comfortable speed. From a certain point of view, the Huseby races had become a cautious, protracted experiment to see how far the human organism could be safely stretched and the cross-country discipline extended.

A doctor had informally observed the proceedings in 1881 and decided there was no obvious risk to health. Two doctors were officially appointed to the next Huseby race. That was only in 1883; since the previous year, the climatic cycle, with abysmal weather and no snow, had once more forced cancellation. Now these doctors presented a report. 'Our attention [they wrote], was directed to the effects of great effort during the [cross-country] race, like excessive sweating, flushed face, heavy gleaming eyes, sagging posture, slow, hesitant speech, heavy breathing, as appeared from observation without causing offence.'[11]

About 60 per cent passed these tests. Of the remainder, the report went on

> most were the youngest participants, and we were left with the distinct impression that the younger ones were generally inferior in stamina ...
>
> In a future ski race, we propose that attention be given to fixing a lower age limit of 20 years for *participation in a cross country race*. Human beings are not fully developed until the age of 25 ... In addition there is the easily aroused ambition of the young, with their poor experience in balancing ability and willpower.

This being unique in its way, the authors deserve to be identified. They were

Professor Heiberg and Dr Irgens. They were the first doctors officially to supervise a ski race, and provide a medical report. It was an early example in any sport, and a precursor of sports medicine.

One thing, however, remained almost depressingly familiar. Telemarkings dominated yet again. They took the first seven places overall. The winner and runner-up were the Hemmestveit brothers, Torjus and Mikkel, who became living legends in their time and whose father had quietly proclaimed their talent in 1879.

They were not, incidentally, the blond giants or latter-day Vikings of popular legend. On the contrary, they were of medium build, dark-haired and springy in step. Much the same held for others of their kind. They were also good at the polka and other dances of the national rustic sort; dancing and skiing, using the same kind of balance, often go together.

That third Huseby fixture of 1883 brought other innovations. Instead of following continuously on the jump, the cross-country section was run separately, although still on the same day. It was now an event in its own right. The results were still combined by the usual points system to give overall placings but it was another step towards modern skiing.

The organization had also changed. The races had grown too big for the exclusive membership of the Christiania Ski Club. Early in 1883, to take over the event, they founded the Foreningen til Ski-Idrættens Fremme – The Association for the Promotion of Skiing, generally known as Skiforeningen. A popular movement, it was also de facto a dedicated national ruling body, the first of its kind in skiing.

As in other fields, the decade was one of experimentation. In 1884, because of an unseasonal thaw, the cross-country event at Huseby was dropped, leaving the jump alone. The historic outcome was the breaking of the Telemark hegemony. The winner was one Richard Blichfeld, an art student from Christiania. The best Telemarking was Mikkel Hemmestveit, runner-up. The pupils were overtaking their masters. More to the point, the results showed that the Telemarkings' domination had owed much to superiority in the cross-country discipline. They probably regretted their complaints over what they called the 'sprint', which partially led to its removal from the programme. After a furious argument, the experiment was not repeated.

Huseby served as a national arena and, being in the capital, appeared to be the focus of skiing in the country. This had much to do with the fact that businessmen and the official classes had more or less taken over the leadership of skiing and its ideology too. However, skiing was obviously widespread. New ideas appeared elsewhere and not only in Telemark but also, for instance, in Trondheim, which, with its province of Trøndelag, was historically a centre of innovation. It was now the scene of a crucial advance.

On 10 February 1884, a cross-country race in Trondheim was decided as a separate event on time alone.[12] All style judging was abolished. One precursor had obviously been 'Little Theodor's' Tromsø event 40 years earlier; another an earlier race in Trondheim in 1864. The Trondheim fixture of 1884 was, however, the breakthrough. The next year, Huseby followed suit by reinstating the cross-country event and counting only time.

In other words, the standard of skiing had spectacularly risen. Style judging had fulfilled its aims. It was now superfluous, in the cross-country event at least. It survived only in ski-jumping, where it remains to this day, albeit touched by controversy.

The Trondheim race broke new ground in other ways. There was no jumping. This presaged the separation of events or, put differently, reverted to the Tromsø race of 1843. Also the course was increased to 8 km, approaching a real test of stamina. This persuaded the organizers of Huseby to raise their cross-country event modestly from 3 km to 4 km in 1885 but still combined with the jump for general placings. The ideal of the all-rounder was however on the wane and specialization loomed. In the cross-country event, success was supposed to be its own reward. The big prizes were reserved for the jump, combined with a test of turning. This was to attract the star performers from the countryside. Ski racing offered an escape from the serfdom of forest and field. The Telemarkings resumed their hegemony, taking the first three places in the cross-country race and first and third in the jump.

At least the crowds were acquiescent. The Huseby fixture of 1885 was only the fifth, but already it seemed like a tradition, to the point of an unofficial national day, like the Palio in Siena. A stand was temporarily erected round the flat outrun of the jump for customers of means. 'Anyone who can get away from work,' as one journalist exuberantly put it

> makes their way out by train, sledge, on foot, horseback or skis. The city's cab ranks are empty, no cab owner has a single horse left … Huseby presents a beauiful and lively sight … the stand is teeming with ladies and gentlemen … Lining the slope are soldiers on ski to control the swarming crowd. On the top, the skiers are ready … Down below it is crawling with [sledges]. Horses are whinnying, bells tinkling and harnesses gleaming, and coachmen … enjoy the festival from the sledges abandoned by their masters … Perched up on the trees, little boys loudly drop cheeky remarks … safe on their elevated perches.[13]

King Oscar was there again. By custom, this had already become a royal occasion. The King continued to do what he could to please his Norwegian subjects. The flags flying round the jumping hill, however, hinted that for all the good-natured cheering of the royal party, this was a national demonstration. The spectators were participating in the sense that in one way they had come almost as a patriotic duty. The drive to independence was gathering pace. There had been a recent crisis leading to parliamentary government against the royal veto and this was a polite way of making the point. Nobody round the slopes felt any personal resentment towards the King, and the other way about. Ski-jumpers were preferable to agitators; they could hurt nobody but themselves.

By the same token, it was the individual that counted. Clubs were proliferating but they were really administrative constructs. Likewise, territorial attachment played little part. The Nordic skier is the ultimate lone wolf and what mattered was performance and personality. 'The ladies are particularly keen on fortune favouring the ... boys from Christiania,'[14] one journalist observed of the 1885 Huseby, 'but otherwise commendable impartiality reigns. Whoever falls, is greeted with a gale of laughter, and the applause is equally heartfelt, whoever masters [the jump].'

The experience from the point of view of a not-so-heroic participant was described by the same Ernst Bjerknes who has already appeared in this story. The Huseby competition of 1885 was his first attempt, at the age of 19. 'I had only gone out to watch the cross-country', as he told the tale. He was among the knot of spectators at the distribution of the numbers and, in the informal manner of the age: 'At the end a few ... were left over. We were asked if anybody wanted to take part. Nobody volunteered, but after much persuasion, I drummed up the courage to do so. I borrowed a *krone* [about £10 today] to pay the entrance fee, and was given number 69.'[15]

He did respectably in the cross-country, finishing in the first half of the field, but

> the jump was worse. Brave I was not, and it did not help when I arrived at the top of the jumping hill ... I had never tried this one before ... I nearly fainted ... I could not see further than the edge of the jump. It seemed for all the world as if one would fall immediately right down to the flat, far, far below [where] thousands of spectators were standing ... A long drawn out bugle blast sounds from below ... The first man [starts] He takes off, soars in the air, and disappears under the lip of the jump. The seconds pass. Will he never reappear down there on the flat? Yes, Yes, there he is, and Heavens above, he managed upright ... Again the bugle call, and one after the other they set off ... The waiting is long ... expressed by gallows humour ... Shall I withdraw ... At last [the call] Number 69 ready. Now it's too late ... I summon up all my courage and move to the edge of the [in-run. Then the order] No. 69 go. Ye Gods, I did not feel particularly confident, but I set off at full speed, and stretched up like a candle lit at both ends. I heard the murmur of applause, but before I reached the take off, I lost consciousness. I have no idea how I issued from the jump but was told later that I took off in the normal way.
>
> At first I dreamt that I was at home in bed. But then I had snow in my face, and felt how arms and legs were being slung here and there, and when the tumbling was finished at the foot of the outrun, I had regained consciousness. I rose up, and shook off the snow. My arms were still in one piece, and so were my legs and skis.

In his own words, Bjerknes felt like a friend who suffered the same fate, looked up at the jump and said to himself: 'You can't make a silk purse out of a sow's ear.'

It was about this time that the Telemark ski-jumpers had finished changing their style. Hitherto, they would crouch down in flight, with legs drawn up, the so-called *optræk*. With the use of sticks penalized in the jump, they adopted an upright stance. This was what Bjerknes had tried to copy. It was the beginning of modern technique.

Also at this period, terminology evolved; two words in particular. *Langrend* first appeared, finally to be translated into German as *langlauf*, the term for cross-country racing. The other newcomer was *løipe*, a Nordic ski track, which eventually made its way into the French and German languages.

At the next Huseby meeting in 1886, the cross-country race was increased to 11 km. This was the first true test of stamina in a major event. Again it was a Telemark victory, the old familiars Mikkel and Torjus Hemmestveit coming first and second.

This event of 1886 was a watershed. The *Skiforeningen* declared that 'skiing is best and most naturally advanced by the cross-country discipline'.[16] That more or less settled the fulminating argument. It was also an acceptance of reality. With lengths now of 20 m or more, the ski-jump was moving beyond the reach of the ordinary skier and even that of many a gifted cross-country racer, as Ernst Bjerknes had so graphically confessed. Ski-jumping, exclusive, aesthetic and sensational, remained the great attraction but it was the cross-country star with whom any Nordic skier could identify. That helped popularize skiing.

Numbers had been rising over the years. Already in 1874, the police banned skiing in the streets of Christiania, on the grounds of horses being startled by madcap skiers. The regulation was never strictly enforced but remained a serious annoyance to any skier of spirit for nearly a generation before it was repealed. Then to satisfy the demand for skis, new sports shops appeared, a dozen or more in Christiania during the early 1880s alone.

The 1886 Huseby showed modernizing flair all round. With longer cross-country distances, it was becoming difficult to squeeze everything into one session. So the programme was spread over two days; the cross-country on Sunday 31 January, followed the next day by the jumping. There was also a new discipline called the 'turning-race'. This was run on the slope next to the jump. The course was marked by two pennants, round which the competitors had to turn in an S-bend. It was set by one of the skiing pioneers called Fritz Huitfeldt, brother of Axel, who appears prominently in this story again. With the artificial obstacles, this race was the first of its kind. It was in all but name a kind of slalom.

A few weeks later, towards the end of February 1886, another race was explicitly called by that name. It was run in Telemark, at a place called Siljord. It was, however, used closer to its original meaning, not yet widely known outside its native Telemark dialect. 'As far as is known,' in the words of one journal, 'a slalom ... means a race in uneven, difficult terrain, which ... requires the avoidance of natural obstacles. Quick reactions are needed in order to get out of a tight corner.'[17]

This was the second occurrence of the word 'slalom' in print.[18] It was also the second published report of such a race. One of the rare outside competitors was Edvard Lillehagen, another name to conjure with. He recorded the race in detail:

The run, called Raukleiv, was a cleared timber path, quite narrow at the top, and wider below, and 5 to 600 metres long. The uppermost 150 to 200 metres were fairly steep … Everyone gathers at the top of the slope, and is sent off one by one when the trumpet … sounds. The runners can brake and choose what speed they want, but they must not cross the finishing line. The finish is marked with small pennants in the middle of the lower part of the slope. Points are given for style and courage and mastery of their skis. The competitors can do what they like, stopping to right or left, but in any case they must stop before the marks. [This] was the so-called slalom, which I had not known previously.[19]

In other words, this slalom was a race round natural obstacles in natural snow. Sometimes narrow gateways in a wooden fence lay across the course. It was a way of testing mastery of skiing away from the beaten track. It seems to have originally been the event combined with the ski-jump to decide competitions. Huitfeldt's 'turning race', with its artificial obstacles, was the prototype of the modern slalom. He had visited Telemark a few years previously, and evidently adapted what he saw. At the tenth Huseby races in 1890, the word 'slalom' was finally used in print to describe the event. A Christiania newspaper offered the first known coverage of a slalom in this sense under that name. The historic date was 23 February 1890.

Seventeen degrees of frost overnight meant that early in the morning skis flew horribly fast, so at the last moment the slalom … had to be changed, because the speed was absolutely terrible. The fact is that at such overwhelming speed, the tiniest twig or dip in the snow is often enough to make the skier lose his balance, which means a tumble so violent that one does not really know what has happened. I had the opportunity of seeing a couple of such somersaults the day before the race, but I cannot imagine anything more helpless than the skiers on that occasion. One of them tumbled some way down the slope so that arms, legs, skis and sticks bristled like needles in crochet work. [On the day however] the westerly wind did its work, so that … by the time the first runners [started] the slalom had completely lost its character, and did not turn out to be the intended touchstone. The speed was miserable downhill, and everyone except for three skiers stayed upright. That was regrettable, but there was nothing to be done about it.[20]

Thus, unheroically, a contrived discipline had evolved from a test of skiing in natural terrain, but made history nonetheless.

Meanwhile, at Huseby in 1886, a doctor had once more been on duty and written the second known medical report on a ski race. Again it concerned the cross-country event. 'Not one of the skiers', he categorically declared, 'showed any signs of *over-exertion, exhaustion*, or having suffered *organic injury* as a result of the considerable exertion.'[21] In other words, racing 10 or 11 km had been shown to be safe.

The following year, after some discussion, the distance was increased to 20 km. A changing climate played another joke, with fog, rain, a monumental thaw and a coarse-grained messy water-ridden slushlike porridge that passed for snow.

The organizers, perhaps still living in the past, with the stable winters of their youth, let the proceedings go ahead. Skis hardly slid and moving demanded sheer brute force against the clinging underfoot. To add insult to injury, there was a massed start, with its chaos and ill will – an experiment not to be repeated for over a century. All in all, it was an uncovenanted test of the human organism and human spirit but the competitors did not unduly suffer. Heart and lungs had been shown to stand the strain.

Despite various prophets of doom, this led in 1888 to the first 50 km race – the skiers' marathon. It was part of the Huseby programme that season. The race was run on 7 February. The declared aim was 'to encourage young people to train sensibly, and to have a proper understanding of the benefits of skiing'.[22] It also enhanced the prestige of the annual event. 'There was a very poor attendance at the Stock Exchange', one newspaper reported. 'Even there, the Huseby races exerted its power of attraction.'[23]

Predictably, Torjus Hemmestveit won, so the prize was yet again to Telemark. It was not as simple as it sounded. His time was nearly four-and-a-half hours; twice that of victors over the distance after a century. It meant prolonging the mental agony. With sequential starts, there was constant fear of the unseen enemy behind among the trees, his only herald the distant eerie low-pitched squeak of ski sticks straining in the snow.

The significance of that 50 km race was that it was separate, with prizes of its own, divorced from jumping, and decided exclusively on time. There was another 25 km event for the Nordic combination of jumping and cross-country. For long, it remained the elite event, the first prize being a floating trophy presented by King Oscar; called inevitably the King's Cup.

This programme accomplished the final separation of cross-country and jumping disciplines. That in turn paved the way for the proliferation of events and its corollary, the specialist. Also for the first time, the ski-jumping was decided over two rounds, instead of one. There had been agitation to that effect for years, to reduce the element of chance.

Another innovation at those Huseby races of 1888 was the appearance of various competitors 'thinly clad in knitwear jerseys and ditto trousers', to quote one reporter.[24] This was obviously copied from speed skaters; another locally favoured spectacle. It was the first recorded use of a specialized outfit for ski racing – and a precursor of modern synthetic skin-tight aerodynamic clothing. Hitherto, heavy ordinary working clothes had been in vogue. If nothing else, it brought a touch of style to the track.

Most important of all, was the example of Ernst Bjerknes, who atoned for his little embarrassment on the jumping hill by sensationally coming fourth in the 50 km race. Moreover, as the journalist also observed, he 'used two sticks, and he used them so that it was a pleasure to watch. Others did the same, and they all liked it a great deal … Two sticks will … soon be … usual.'[25]

Two sticks first appeared in a major event at Huseby in 1887. Until then they had been banned. Racers had either poled themselves along with a single stick, as the old Chinese had described, or just stumped along as if on snowshoes. Elegant it was not and the cross-country racer seemed clumsy compared to the ski-jumper. With the arrival of two sticks – borrowed from the Finns – all that changed. The action became smoother, balanced and more varied.

The acceptance of two sticks finally gave skiing its modern form. To complete the picture, at Huseby in 1889, there was a short straight downhill run. Thus during the 1880s, all events, Nordic and Alpine had emerged on a modest slope in the Norwegian capital.

# 13

# The Conquest of the Mountain World

While ski-racing evolved, the Norwegians began to explore their own mountains in winter and thus invented ski touring. Like most recreation, it grew out of necessity.

Hunters and trappers had always skied far over the uplands to search for game. In the Little Ice Age it was a matter of survival. Moreover, winter travel sometimes required mountain crossings. None of this seemed extraordinary. Perhaps on that account, records were sparse. Occasionally an obscure newspaper paragraph might report that so-and-so never reached his destination. Some of the more gruesome or whimsical events left their traces in folk memory.

There was, for example, the story, apocryphal or not, of two merchants who set off to ski some 50 km across a certain massif.[1] This was before the days of ready-made bindings so, before starting, one of the men took the precaution of obtaining three withies as spares. The other thought that it would suffice for both. Halfway across, one of his bindings broke, and so he asked for one of the withies. His companion demanded 10 *daler* [about £50 today] which, under the circumstances, he could not refuse. However he demanded and actually obtained all three. Soon after the deal was done, one of the first man's bindings broke. He in his turn now needed a spare, only to find that the cost had doubled, and he had to pay the asking price, thus giving another twist to the law of supply and demand.

Better documented was another event with a touch of history. In January 1850, the first Norwegian national theatre was to open in Bergen, on the west coast. The prime mover was a violin virtuoso called Ole Bull. A patriot to the core, he was an exponent of national romanticism in music and one of the first Norwegians to become known abroad. Bull had never forgotten what he owed to a self-taught country fiddler of genius whose real name was Torgeir Augundsson but, his father being a miller, was only ever called the Miller's Boy.[2] Bull wanted him to play at the opening of the theatre. The Miller's Boy, however, lived inland. Bull had only made up his mind at the last minute. Between them lay 240 km of mountainous terrain. Roads were poor, nor had railway or telegraph yet appeared. It was midwinter, and the snows blocked the direct route overland. So at Christmas 1849, Bull sent a skiing messenger post-haste, and eventually one Bergen newspaper was tersely able to report that 'the Miller's Boy [arrived] on the 1st January [1850]. As soon as he received Ole Bull's invitation, he set off, and crossed the mountains on ski.'

This bland paragraph hid a little saga of its own. The Miller's Boy was thin, undersized, poor, malnourished and drank more than was good for him. On the other hand, he came from Haukelid, in Telemark and, as a Telemarking, was more or less born with skis on his feet. However, he and Ole Bull's messenger had chosen to cross Hardangervidda, the Hardanger plateau; high, barren and exposed, its weather more unpredictable than that of the Antarctic. The Miller's Boy and his companion were overtaken by a blizzard.[3] They were forced to stop and sleep in the snow without tent or sleeping bag. They were drifted over by the unrelenting storm. They saved themselves from suffocation by pushing their ski sticks through the snow, wind-packed above them. The Miller's Boy – and his violin – apparently none the worse, gave his recital.

The unknown messenger had made the first recorded crossing of Hardangervidda on skis and, together with the Miller's Boy, the first from east to west. Historically, it meant a geographic goal. Its true significance is that it was taken as a matter of course, which implies many an unrecorded crossing down the years. Even beyond his ski tour, the Miller's Boy deserves to be remembered. Some of his compositions still survive in the wider world through piano arrangements by Edvard Grieg.

The skiing adventure of the Miller's Boy was rooted in necessity. A quarter of a century earlier, Captain George Prahl, a Norwegian army officer, did something similar for fun. That was the first known mountain ski tour in the modern sense.

Prahl was posted to Bergen but happened to be in Christiania. It was midwinter when the order came. Some 350 km of mountain and fjord intervened. There was a recognized winter route, using post-horses, sledges and boats. Prahl preferred to ski. So one day in January 1824 he set off.

To avoid Hardangervidda, Prahl chose a more southerly route than the Miller's Boy. He still faced a trying journey over frozen lakes and across low but treacherous mountains from one valley to the next. He needed guides here and there but, as he told the tale in later years, 'tourist was then nearly an unknown word. When a so-called educated man hoisted a knapsack on his back to make a long journey it caused a stir.'[4]

The first crisis came when Prahl had to make a mountain crossing of some 50 km from a place called Børte in Telemark to the valley of Setersdal. It was a Sunday, and he faced much of the local population who had come to stare at 'the overdressed townee', as he put it.

> I sought a guide among the crowd … but in vain … they all took the view that this stranger might well say that he could ski, but when he was well on his way, he would become overtired through lack of practice, and both the guide and the stranger would risk … being caught on the mountain track, surrounded by miles of snowbound desert.

Prahl could not afford any delay. He had to arrive by a certain date, or risk fourteen days' confinement to barracks:

When the populace had satisfied their curiosity, men and women began to race on skis. The ... steep slopes and brilliant snow conditions were so inviting that I also put on my skis ... and I kept up well. When they saw this, it was no longer difficult to find a guide. Many offered their services, and therefore the cost was low.

The villagers' reservations were well founded. Prahl was led up a ridge but, as he recalled: 'Heavens how bitterly cold it was, and how difficult – several times I was on the point of turning back ... and when we finally reached the top, I was so tired that I do not have the words to express my fatigue.'

After a short rest, Prahl and his guide continued, but their trials were not over yet. Crossing the next pass, a matter of 30 km, like the Miller's Boy, they were overtaken by a blizzard:

The guide was not without resource. We had just stopped next to a hard snowdrift ... and he said, here we will find shelter for the night. He made an opening in the drift with a ski, and dug out so much ... that there was plenty of space for 2 men. Then we covered the opening with snow, and we sat sheltered in our little room of snow.

Again like the Miller's Boy, they made

ventilation holes with a ski stick, and there, under the circumstances we were quite comfortable. Sleep came unbidden, and the rest gave strength. Next morning towards 8 o'clock, we left our snow cave. The weather was good, we [skied] quickly, and arrived [at our destination] in Suldal at a reasonable hour.

Eventually they reached the Hardanger Fjord and Prahl finished his journey by boat. Rock and water; ships and skis were still a peculiar Norwegian amalgam.

Prahl was a transitional figure. He combined within himself a utilitarian attitude and the idea of mountain skiing for pleasure. This derived from the national romantic movement that was taking hold of the country, and of which one aspect was an embryonic Nature worship.

After Prahl's exploit – escapade perhaps – the record was almost silent for decades. It was only in 1876, 50 years later, that the first full contemporary article on mountain skiing was published. Over three pages in a popular magazine, the anonymous author elaborated on a blizzard he had survived. Whoever he was, he had a feeling for the natural world:

I have carried out boat journeys in harsh waters along the [Norwegian] coast, and sometimes been overtaken by menacing seas, when you have to sail for dear life to save yourself from the ocean, and yet found myself in a pleasant position compared to that with which we were now confronted. He who has not faced a snowstorm in the mountains, has no concept of what it is like. Beyond the pure physical suffering caused by the cold, there is something so confusing to the senses, so awful about the complete lack of visibility in this game of blind-man's-buff that makes the circumstances horrible.[5]

There is a gusto in this which is quite new. It suggests an appreciation of Nature in all her moods. The events it describes were in the frontier mountains between Sweden and Norway. They were not even the wildest part of the country.

Some half-a-century earlier, there appeared in a journal of popular science an article entitled 'Some information about a hitherto unknown part of [southern] Norway.'[6] It was unknown, that is, to all but the few hunters, fishermen and herdsmen from the contiguous valleys. It was unmarked on any map. Covering an area of some 3,500 square kilometres between Christiania and the western fjords it was, as the author said, 'a mountainous region, which undoubtedly is the wildest and perhaps the highest in Norway ... but the central part is filled with true Alps in the sense that [they are] of the same configuration as the Swiss Alps ... with cone-formed, pyramid forms, sharp horns and summits'.

It was a contrast to the usual rounded contours of Scandinavian mountains, shaped by glaciation of the Baltic shield. It had been formed by folding in the earth's crust, like the Alps or Himalayas. It had never been surveyed and did indeed contain the highest peaks in the whole of Scandinavia. They were only around 2,000 m high, half that of the crest of the Alps, but their latitude, isolation and exposure to the North Atlantic storms made them appreciably harsher.

The author was a Norwegian geologist called Baltazar Keilhau. He was writing about a journey which, together with one companion, he had made in the summer of 1820. This was the first coherent exploration and Keilhau's article the first published account. Except on the outskirts, the region was *terra incognita*. It was as yet unnamed. Keilhau called it 'Jotunfjeldene' – 'The Giant Mountains', a direct translation of the German 'Riesengebirge' in Bohemia. In 1862, the same A.O. Vinje, who had written so entertainingly about skiing in Telemark, now invented the more romantic 'Jotunheimen' – 'The Home of the Giants' – and that was the name that stuck.[7]

Soon after Keilhau's discovery, another Norwegian wrote of these 'mountainous regions ... of Norway ... which are rarely trodden by human feet, where one can go on journeys of exploration with the same success as in ... the most unknown countries in the world'.[8] The author was a physicist called Christopher Hansteen who, a few years later, made an extraordinary journey through Siberia and central Asia to measure the magnetic field of the earth. Together with the great German scientist, Alexander von Humboldt, he was one of the founders of geomagnetism. As Hansteen had put it, the Norwegians were distinguished among Europeans by living with exploration on their doorstep.

It was, however, only in the 1860s that they began seriously to explore Jotunheimen. Vinje and another patriotic zealot, Professor Ernest Sars, were among the first. Again, the impulse was national romanticism, those wild dark grey massifs of wayward strata, it was thought, reflecting the Norwegian character.

There were sporadic skiers, notably a legendary character called Jo Gjende. He was a semi-recluse who, during the middle decades of the century, lived much of the time in a primitive isolated stone hut on the banks of the forlorn Gjendin lake. In season, the scrape of his ski on the crust was heard coming home from the chase. With a home-made flintlock gun he was frenetically devoted to hunting the reindeer. Half-wild in appearance, in a typical Norwegian contradiction, he was nonetheless well read, with a taste for Voltaire. He was one of the models for Henrik Ibsen's Peer Gynt. He had been driven to this outcast's life, so it was said, because he could not marry the girl he loved, her father forbidding the banns.

For another generation, however, Jotunheimen remained a summer playground. English climbers and German ramblers dominated the clientele. Ordinary ski touring was unknown. Meanwhile in 1868, the year of the seminal ski race in Christiania, Den Norske Turistforeningen – 'The Norwegian Touring Association' – was formed to open up the mountains and persuade the Norwegians to explore their own country. It still exists, the oldest of its kind anywhere. It may or may not have been the impetus for the first real ski tour into Jotunheimen, with the skiing an end in itself.

At Christmas 1882, a Christiania chemist called Ludvig Schmelck who, in his own words, 'had long had the intention of visiting Jotunheimen in the wintertime',[9] made an approach from Gudbrundsdalen in the east. He stayed at various *sæter*, or alpages, in the foothills, where a sprinkling of hunters and hill farmers clung on to primitive shelter through the cold season of the year. They for their part had never seen a winter tourist before. This unfamiliar being is said to have survived in folk memory as someone who appeared sane, but in reality was touched; an eccentric apparition in close-fitting ski clothes and a long red cap, reaching to his waist.

Schmelck returned the compliment; only *his* recollection was preserved in print. He wrote for *Morgenbladet* where, as so often in the case of skiing, this story made the front page too. He echoed the point made by Prahl and Hansteen, that exploration here so close to home was not only of landscape but of people. In their way they were as exotic or miserable as any in remoter parts.

Schmelck also described the eerie fall of darkness at one particular *sæter*:

> To be faced with this cold, lifeless Nature, where everywhere the same pale monotony of snow and moonlight met the eye, was almost to be overcome by dread. One felt so homeless in these unfamiliar surroundings, as if one were removed to some place up near the North Pole.

That accurately conveyed the mood that dogged this pioneer. By his own account, Schmelck was only on a 'reconnaissance'. Like so many of its kind, it too ended in a sort of failure. Schmelck was heading for Jo Gjende's Lake Gjendin. This was the gateway to the crest of Jotunheimen. He had to turn before he reached his goal. The reason was apparently lack of time. He had to be home by New Year's Eve. Technical deficiencies, however, lay at the heart of the matter.

Schmelck was used to lowland snow in the forest. The forms above the treeline in the mountains took him by surprise. He was faced with flint-hard crust and drifted fields like quicksand. He often slithered, sank or stumped along. There were as yet no commercial waxes to slide and grip and help him on his way. He was learning that there was no bad snow, only bad equipment.

For instance, he only had one stick, without a basket, so it often sank deep into the snow without support. Moreover, steel edges were still decades in the future. That in turn implied that skis could not bite on crust and give control. Schmelck graphically recorded the consequences. On the way back, he had to run down a steep slope and:

> hardly had my skis pointed down, before they attained a huge speed on the hard crust, where a pair of skates would have been a better means of transport. It was an unpleasant run ... The wave-like formation of the snow made it impossible to keep the skis together, while they made jump after jump over the small sastrugi, hard as flint, that lay strewn across my downward path.
>
> Balance was soon at a premium ... unexpectedly I received the coup de grâce at a short passage in soft snow ... after a few seconds, the saga ended with a grand somersault.

And apropos of an as yet undecided controversy: 'Here I was glad to have skis fixed with heelstraps, because if they had slid away, I might have spared myself the effort of looking for them.'

Finally, Schmelck had used Telemark ski. However, he felt that

> [although] adapted to snow conditions and terrain round Christiania, they are not suited to mountain tours, where they do not float on the snow, and slither too much on the crust. Under these conditions, when sharp turns are rarely needed, one would be better served by a pair of really long ski, preferably with a groove underneath in order to glide more securely on the crust.

The first skiing traverse of Jotunheimen had to wait until New Year 1887. Three Christiania army officers, Thomas Heftye, Louis Bentzen and Niels Slaalien, crossed the whole massif from west to east. They were led by a well-known mountain guide called Knud Vole. He lived in Bøverdalen, at the western foot of the range. His main clients were English mountaineers who came in summer, drawn by new routes and unclimbed peaks in Jotunheimen, as yet uncrowded. Their example popularized the range among the Norwegians themselves. 'As you know,' Vole wrote to a Christiania newspaper, 'we travelled through some of [Jotunheimen's] grandest and most beautiful parts. The weather was still brilliant, and ditto the skiing. What a lovely run on ski it was over the snow-covered mountains!'[10]

The following season, on Christmas day 1887, Vole led the first ascent on skis of Galdhopiggen, the summit of Jotunheimen and the highest peak in Scandinavia. This was the first ski ascent, anywhere, of a major summit. It was the birth of ski mountaineering.

Climbers from other countries probably bridle at the thought. The participants could ski unconstrained up and down. But most Norwegians did not hanker for the summits or court the thrills of suicidal rock faces. They preferred them as stupendous backdrops while they skied along the valleys. Tellingly, even Vole felt that he had to defend his actions. 'A question that I … had to answer [was]: "Isn't it dangerous to climb Galdhopiggen at this season. Is there no danger of avalanches"', he wrote in a Christiania newspaper.[11]

> I answered … that … why had I not seen traces in summer, as in other places, where there are avalanches. I always came to the conclusion that it couldn't be dangerous.
>
> We reached [the summit of] Galdhopiggen safe and sound. The snow was good and firm, and we had a lovely view. We sped like arrows on the descent.

Jotunheimen was not the only stage. In January 1887, three medical students from Trondheim had decided to ski from the valley of Østerdalen to Gudbrundsdalen on their way back to university in Christiania. This was the first known ski tour in that region. Philosophically, it was of great intrinsic interest.

For the record, the names of these pioneers were Oscar Semb and the brothers Peter and Alexander Holst. Peter wrote about their tour in a Trondheim newspaper – again a front-page story. 'None of us', he declared, 'had seen real mountains above the treeline in winter dress before.'[12] Their experiences were the by now familiar blend of pleasure and setback dictated by the elements, the traverse achieved with little discomfort. What was new was the attitude evinced. 'It was with melancholy that I thought that I had said goodbye to the mountains for the winter', Peter Holst said, looking back on events.

> While I sat hunched over my books, all the sunlit days would pass before my eyes, all the wonderful beautiful pale moonlit nights in the uplands; henceforth the light in which I would see all this would be in the halo of memory. No, I would rather indulge in daydreams of my next mountain tour.

This was an early expression of the forces beginning to drive skiers to the mountains. It had been captured in the 1870s by Henrik Ibsen in a haunting poem called *På viddene – On the Heights*. The theme is the age-old flight from the common lot. It is the story of a man who abandons everyday existence for a life in the mountain world. 'Now I am steeled, I hear the call/the uplands to roam and rove' runs one verse,[13] and the poem ends with the revealing lines:

> Up here on the heights, God and freedom reign,
> Down below the others flounder on.

More prosaically, Peter Holst said in his own foretaste of the stress of urban living, that 'as time passes such ski tours will become just as common as walking tours, and I cannot finish without recommending them most warmly to every skier'. In fact the ski tour even then was spreading. Partly it was due to the advance of modern communications. Railways were opening up the mountains. Another explanation lay in the features written by the pioneering skiers – and above all the sane editorial policy that gave them appropriate display.

奥地夷圖其二

26. Ainu hunter on skis, Japanese print, Mamiya Rinso, 1855.

Two months after Semb and the Holsts, other pioneers crossed some mountains south of Trondheim. They wanted to test equipment for ski touring. They were the first known to have done so. Starting on the 26 March 1887, they were also among the first to try mountain skiing in the spring.

Their names were E. A. Tønseth, and an army lieutenant, Oluf Dietrichson. Their route ran northwards across a range near the Swedish border, from one railhead at Røros, to another one at Meråker, some 100 km away. The country in between was not yet fully mapped. That was quite usual for the times, so also the crossing itself, featuring a bivouac in a draughty, snowed-up dry-stone hut along the way and, at the end, the startled peasants who, in Tønseth's words, thought them 'two drunken tramps that came staggering', as they appeared from the heights.[14]

What lifted their tour out of the ordinary was the playful devilry of spring snow, now powder, now wet and clinging or crust hard as flint. They were among the first ski tourers to undergo these conditions because almost everyone else still stuck to midwinter.

Above all, they stood out by their experimentation. Dietrichson had Telemark skis and stiff-soled boots; Tønseth, long and grooved Leksvik skis and soft Lappish *finnesko*. Both had heel bindings made of cane. They agreed that the Telemark ski came out best, because it was easy to steer, and superior 'in climbing and running down in tangled downhill runs and forest', as Tønseth put it. He also reviled the *finnesko* because it allowed the cane binding 'to gnaw into the feet'. Provisioning was also instructive. They blithely took a bottle of cognac to drink, that being common in midwinter as an antidote to cold. Springtime caught them unawares:

> the powerful … sun and intense sweating produced by effort, caused an unbearable thirst. Brandy now proved to be the worst fluid … on such a tour, because instead of slaking thirst, it burns the throat and seems enervating. Cold tea or milk would have been infinitely better … Spirits are poison during exertion.

There were more lessons of the same or a different kind: 'Use a compass constantly in poor visibility, otherwise you will go round in circles', and so on and so forth. Those pioneers were the first to enunciate the principles of ski touring – the preserve of an elite, which was about to be changed by faraway events.

# 14

# Fridtjof Nansen and the first crossing of Greenland

Having proved its worth at home, the ski ought to have been a natural tool of polar exploration. Like much else, however, it had to wait on its pioneer. He was Baron Nils Adolf Erik Nordenskiöld, the illustrious Finnish-born Swede. This was ironic in a way. Nordenskiöld was a mineralogist who invented the polar expedition as research into the natural sciences rather than pure geographical discovery. Beginning with Spitsbergen in 1858 at the age of 26, he made 12 Arctic forays during the next quarter of a century and for most of the time remained oblivious to the ski. He seems first to have realized its potential on the expedition that made him a hero of his times.

This was the voyage of the *Vega*, in 1878–9. Nordenskiöld then became the first man known to have navigated the legendary North-East Passage from the Atlantic to the Pacific and the first to circumnavigate the Old World. While wintering on the Arctic coast of eastern Siberia he came into contact with the Chukchi tribe. In his own words, an 'implement for travelling over snow was offered by a [Chukchi] who drove past the [*Vega*] in the beginning of February [1879]. It consisted of a pair of immensely wide skis of thin wood, covered with seal-skin, and raised at both sides.'[1]

That was Nordenskiöld's first encounter with the Arctic ski. 'I had difficulty in understanding how these broad shapeless devices could be used', he went on, 'until I learned from [a certain] drawing.' It depicted an Ainu on broad skis ski-joring behind a reindeer.

The Ainu are an ancient skiing tribe found on Hokkaido, the northernmost main island of Japan and also on Sakhalin. They are non-Japanese and semi-outcasts. Nordenskiöld nonetheless found his picture of the ski-joring Ainu in a Japanese book, *Henyō Buskei Zukō*, about travels on Sakhalin. On the way home, the *Vega* put in at Yokohama and Nordenskiöld seized the chance to form the nucleus of a Japanese library, by purchasing some thousand books, amongst which was this particular work.

Nordenskiöld then decided to try skis on his next expedition. This was an attempt to make the first crossing of Greenland in 1883. Although a competent distance skater on sea ice, Nordenskiöld could not ski himself, so he took two Swedish Lapps to do so in his stead. Even in his day there was a historic reverence of Lapps as the repository of skiing lore. This was coupled with its virtual absence from Swedes outside the northern provinces.

On 22 July 1883, after various setbacks, Nordenskiöld reached a point on the

Greenland ice cap some 100 km in from the West Coast at Egedesminde, in Disko Bay. There he decided that he had to turn. Hauling sledges by plodding through wet snow on foot had sapped his strength. So there he stopped, together with his seven Scandinavian followers. He sent the Lapps out on their own eastwards on skis across the ice cap on a reconnaissance. In their tribal dress of long jerkins, known as *kolt* in Lappish, incongruously matched with wide-brimmed European hats, they set off at 2.30 in the morning.

Their names were Pava Lars Nilson Tuorda and Anders Pavasson Rossa; the one so tall, the other so short. Tuorda was 35, Rassa, 38 years old. Both came from Jokkmokk, in the flat, forested terrain of southern Swedish Lapland. In the Lapp fashion, they had two ski sticks. As his left-hand stick, however, Tuorda carried a spear, with which he had killed several bears at home and, vainly as it turned out, now hoped to bag a polar bear as well. At any rate both he and Rossa possessed stamina. Mobility was their weapon. They had neither sledge nor rucksack, carrying the barest minimum of food in the pouch of their *kolt*. Once over the horizon, they vanished for two days. They returned to Nordenskiöld around noon on 24 July. They had been absent for 57 hours. During that time, they claimed to have reached a point 230 km to the East, skiing 460 km all told. The snow ran on as far as the eye could see without the slightest hint of land. They had had to shelter against a gale in the snow for four hours but had not slept for two days and nights. They needed a rest but were not noticeably exhausted.

'The skiing was of the best kind', so Nordenskiöld reported.[2] Tuorda 'had never before seen such smooth ski terrain. The skis ran with utmost ease.' Such was the first journey into the interior of Greenland. This was how Nordenskiöld presented his main achievement:

> For the first time, the polar explorer had had revealed to him a new means of transport [skis], which ought to ease his task fantastically, enabling him to force his way, where otherwise he could not, and the use of which the Scandinavian, by his use of skiing from childhood, almost has a monopoly.[3]

Ainu and Lapp; the two tribes at the extremities of the historic crescent of skiing peoples, had finally opened Nordenskiöld's eyes. With the fervour of a convert, he believed Tuorda's and Rossa's assertion. Others were not so trusting. To settle the matter, Nordenskiöld proposed a ski race. It was financed by Baron Oscar Dickson, a Swedish philanthropist (of Scottish descent) who had paid for most of Nordenskiöld's expeditions. Local officials, headed by the provincial governor, a certain Widmark, organized the event.

The course ran between Purkijaur and Kvikkjokk in the yet almost untouched, eerie, forested Lappish heartland of northern Sweden. It followed a chain of frozen lakes, to simulate the flat surface of the Greenland ice cap. The distance was 110 km, to be covered back and forth, so the total was 220 km. The terrain was north of the Arctic Circle. This meant that at the proper season of the year, it was light around the clock. This was important, so that the race could be run at one stretch. The date was chosen with that in view.

The race began on 3 April 1884. Sixteen skiers started. Tuorda was one but not Rossa. Most were Lapps, or of Lapp extraction. At their request, it was a massed start, instead of the customary sequential. The participants were drawn up in two lines, one behind the other. Their skis were of a Lapp type, long and narrow, mostly of birch but one or two of pine compression wood. Bindings were either simple toestraps, or combined with equally simple leather thongs round the heel.

Because of snowfall and a rise in temperature with resultant sticky going, the start was delayed. There was still no wax to combat Nature then. It was only 6 p.m. when the starting signal finally came. The local police chief, one E. A. Vesterlund, was an ambulant referee, following the competitors on horseback. 'It might just happen,' as someone drily said, 'that someone or other – familiar with the conditions along the big lakes – might for example have a reindeer or a horse in readiness behind some promontory to save a mile or two.'[4]

That was within the bounds of possibility. Honour was not in it, nor even sporting glory. The contestants were reindeer herders or hunters, men of the wilds, used to skiing long distances and inured to the elements. Ski racing was no relief, but merely an extension of workaday, and hence devoid of interest. The bait was mercenary.

This was personified by one entrant in particular. His name was Apmut Andersson Arrman. Small, sinewy and stocky, he presented a pathetic figure, known to be poor, and therefore the butt of much jeering along the way when he skied the 90 km to the start. He was a Lapp settler from a family that had forsaken the nomadic life following the reindeer to begin farming instead. In that harsh climate, he found that a little fishing was his only income. Here was his last chance to escape destitution. Money prizes were on offer. The winner was to get the equivalent of £600 today. It was a fortune at that time in wild country still being settled, on the edge of the habitable world.

Tuorda wanted that first prize. A clergyman acting as an official at a control post, was supposed to have said that, as Tuorda sped past him, skis scraping on the harsh, early morning crust, with his long black hair flapping the back of his neck, that 'he looked more like a wild animal than a human being'.[5] And also: 'I saw that he would rather risk his life than let Per Olof hold his lead – that lead so cunningly, not to say unpleasantly won.'

This Per Olof, surnamed Ländta, was versed in the local byways of human ingenuity. At the turning point in Kvikkjokk, he and Tuorda were equal first. Together with Arrhman, they were ahead of the field. They agreed to stop and rest and eat and then turn back together. It was now 4 a.m. on 4 April. They had skied 110 km through the springtime polar night with no rest and only coffee and a quid of tobacco fed to them along the course. While Arrhman and Tuorda were making their way to the local farm for a meal, they looked back to find that Ländta had slipped off. Arrhman recalled that 'he was a kilometre away … he cheated us; he didn't keep his word … then we ate for a bit … When we came out, I asked [Tuorda] if we should catch up with [Ländta] and he said we'll try.'[6]

In fact they overtook the ingenious Ländta after 20 km. For the remaining 90 km the race was a triangular combat between them. Now the cool of the Arctic night was replaced by the Arctic day with its unrelenting sun and burning reflection from the snow. Heat is the true enemy of a skier in the polar regions, not cold. In the florid words of a contemporary:

> more and more profusely bathed in sweat, they began to be forced to exhaust their strength … If only this unbearable thirst did not plague them! In vain, they threw themselves down and tore at the crust with their teeth, gulping the cold snow … In vain! Despite all effort, the stronger and stronger morning sun, which thawed the night-time crystals to soft, clinging little particles of snow, which stick to the skis, makes them almost feel as if they are standing still.[7]

Arrhman himself had a highly personal slant. About 50 km from the finishing line, the going improved but he was still lying third. A damaged ski handicapped him. A piece had been ripped out of the sole and the snow balled up in the resultant cavity. This made the going harder for him than for his rivals. He had been given a bottle of aquavit and, in his own words, echoing those Swedish chroniclers of the seventeenth century:

> I thought I would take a drink, and I would revive. So I drank a little, but it went to my legs, and then I became sleepy, and hadn't any strength and I left my companions and sat and slept a little, because my sweat had stopped, the snaps went into the pores, and I was absolutely finished. But then I woke and thought of my companions behind me, and must get up so they don't overtake me. I lost the five minutes I had gained … I had to be satisfied with third prize.[8]

Which was exactly how the race ended. Tuorda was first, Ländta 5 seconds behind, followed by Arrhman after another 11 minutes. They arrived back at Purkijaur between 3pm and 4pm on the afternoon of 4 April. Of the original 16, only 11 finished. Such was the first long-distance ski race on record. It remains the longest ever run.

Money aside, Arrhman had the satisfaction of confounding his tormentors. His trials, however, were not over yet. Returning home, he was berated by his wife for an untimely absence. A bear had ravaged their few remaining cattle. So without pause, Arrhman put on his skis again, raced 50 km up into the mountains, found the bear, killed it – with a shotgun – and hence acquired the equivalent of £150 in prize money. Together with the £250 for his third place, this was an uncovenanted little flood of capital. It gave him the new start for which he had been longing. It enabled him to live comfortably for the rest of his life. From his point of view, the Nordenskiöld race, as it came to be known, had meant salvation.

In the wider world, the race had historic repercussions. Tuorda's winning time was 21 hours 22 minutes, including rests. He had not slept at all. Nor was he exhausted. Given the 220 km he had covered this gave at least a sheen of plausibility to his claim up on Greenland Ice Cap.

The race also stimulated the popularization of skiing and the advent of ski racing in Sweden and Finland. It had reverberations elsewhere. In Norway at the time, cross-country events were still cautiously approaching 10 km. The Nordenskiöld race showed what skiers really could sustain and probably speeded the arrival of the first 50 km race in 1888. Also, together with the Baron's expedition, it was what finally goaded a certain Fridtjof Nansen to attempt the first crossing of Greenland himself, and to do so on skis.

Nordenskiöld had proved that skis could indeed be used in the Arctic, but Nansen, being Norwegian, was the first polar explorer from a skiing culture. Born in 1861, and a pioneering mountain skier himself, he was doubly qualified. His crossing from Bergen to Christiania at Christmas 1882 was one of the earliest ski tours in the modern sense. Nansen was driven to that exploit because his work as a marine biologist in Bergen had condemned him to a rainy, maritime climate and he was suffering the pangs of a skier without snow.

Among the pioneers of mountain skiing, Nansen was one of those set apart by being an accomplished competition skier too. In 1881, he ran at Huseby. As one of the Telemarkings, Mikkel Hemmestveit, recalled, he

27.  Fridtjof Nansen, the first crossing of Greenland, 1888. On the Inland Ice.
*Author's Collection*

was a hard and temperamental skier. He jumped and ran for dear life. I once overtook Nansen ... He blocked the track ahead for a long time. [Which strictly ought to have entailed disqualification, the rule being that in a Nordic race, you must give way to the faster skier.] But then I skied past him. When I turned my head and looked at him, he had stopped, tongue hanging out – and two men overtook him.[9]

Style judging allowed Nansen to make up leeway in the jump and he came seventh overall. He belonged to the generation now starting to overtake the Telemarkings and in that race he beat ten of them. He was in fact the best skier from Christiania. Nonetheless, years later, he wrote in a children's' magazine:

It was the first time that I saw Telemarkings ski, and I understood that I was nothing compared to ... the Telemarkings ... They used no sticks; they flew over the jump, depending on nothing except their muscular strength and the firm and supple posture of their bodies. I understood that this was the only proper way.[10]

All very admirable after the event, but at the time his chagrin may have been at least partly due to the fact that, as one reporter put it, 'The outcome would have been different if ... F. Nansen, having managed the turn [during the cross-country section] had not inadvertently sprawled horizontally in a hollow made by someone who had fallen, which he did not notice.'[11] Nansen did, however, sincerely hold the Telemarkings in high regard. As he put it in another article for children:

they are undoubtedly the best skiers in our country, and I may safely say without exaggeration, the best in the whole world. They have taught the city boys a completely new way of running, and have thereby raised skiing to what it has become in recent years.[12]

Nansen was however no slavish romantic. After his success at Huseby in 1881, 19 years old, and about to start university, he was already worried about the future of skiing. It was, he wrote

like every sport [in that] its purpose is to strengthen and develop the body. [It] is far superior to other sports in developing presence of mind and courage ... It is [fundamentally] a means of travel ... One thing is certain, the aesthetic enjoyment, and the noble and uplifting spirit of skiing disappear if it is confined to everlastingly going up and down the same slope to perform a jump.[13]

This comes from an unpublished article. It encapsulated the controversy then raging over the purpose of skiing. When, in 1884, Nansen skied across the western mountains from Bergen to Christiania for the second time, he was shadowed by another influential pioneer sharing the same doubts; a shorter, thinner looking-glass version of himself.

Henrik Angell, born in 1861, was an eccentric army lieutenant, whose hero was the Swedish warrior king, Charles XII. If Nansen, by his own account, was a man of the forest, Angell belonged to the mountains and sea. He came from Luster, beneath precipices dropping down to an inner arm of the Sogne Fjord, the longest of the west Norwegian fjords, with all that meant for an eccentric, highly individualistic and obstinate personality. As a boy, he moved to Bergen, where his father was prison governor and where, allowing for the infrequent snow that had plagued Nansen, he became a pioneering skier.

Early in January 1884, Angell skied from Bergen to Kongsberg, in the hinterland of Christiania. Unlike Nansen, who stuck to his old route over the mountains abutting the Sogne Fjord, Angell chose to travel via the Hardanger Fjord to the south. He started his journey by boat to a place called Odda. He went in full uniform dragging, as he himself put it, a 'big military cape ... which became heavier and heavier in ... rain and sleet'.[14] Even up in the mountains, unseasonal temperatures were then intruding.

Angell's story appeared in *Morgenbladet* on 10 March 1884. Yet again it was a front-page spread. It extended the interest beyond landscape and skiing to the inhabitants. It helped to establish this as a necessary ingredient of such writing. The newspaper story of a ski tour was becoming a genre of its own. In a certain isolated valley, Angell observed that it was about 90 km to the nearest doctor, but he

> was not needed up there ... The population are so thoroughly hale and hearty, which can best be seen by the great age reached, in spite of heavy, exhausting work ... It is surprising to see how long people keep healthy and nimble ... Thus I saw ... an old woman, a great-grandmother in fact, come sweeping down a slope on skis, and splendidly she ran, shrunk and bent as she was.

And also: 'The higher one climbs up into the mountains, the pleasanter and more hospitable are the inhabitants.'

This expressed a growing romanticization of the unspoiled peasant. Angell was realistic enough to record peasant vices, particularly dirt and mulishness, which irked him most. Therein lay a contradiction. While the educated classes were seeking the simplicity of natural surroundings, peasant skiers were moving in the opposite direction to the city, enticed by money prizes, to profit by their skill.

A few weeks after Angell's article, *Aftenposten*, a rival Christiania newspaper, began printing Nansen's story of *his* ski tour This was more fulsome. 'Storms had raged for many weeks and packed the snow firmly together', ran one typical passage.

> Mild weather had laid a weak crust on top, and on top of that a thin layer of loose snow, whereupon you have the finest conditions that a skier can imagine. My skis barely made tracks along the way, and almost ran by themselves on the flat, driven only by the wind blowing on my back.[15]

This is probably the earliest description in print of the Nordic skier's ideal natural snow.

'My smooth skis simply flew', Nansen went on, continuing in a different vein: 'But now I crossed some tracks – what was this? Wolves! Three wolves! … The tracks continued far into the terrain … Later I also passed tracks of lynx and wolverine. There you have the reindeer's three worst enemies after human beings.'[16]

Although so different, Nansen cut a curiously similar figure to Angell. No soldier, but a scientist, *he* was dressed with equal heterodoxy in the skin-tight woollen garments of Dr Jaeger's Patent Sanitary Clothing. Both had skirted Hardangervidda; Angell to the south and Nansen to the north. Each saw his journey as an end in itself, but nursed ulterior motives just the same.

Angell cultivated skiing as a way of building the soldierly qualities; Nansen, as his outfit revealed, saw it from an athlete's point of view. However, Angell had to return to the military academy in Christiania. Nansen, for his part, was on his way to run in the Huseby races of 1884, where he came a respectable ninth – ironically, given his opinions, the one year when the cross-country event was cancelled and only the jump remained.

Nansen's life was episodic. Now in 1884, at the age of 23, he felt that he had fulfilled his promise as a ski racer. Within a few years, he felt the same about his research in marine biology which, embodied in his doctoral thesis, became part of the foundation of modern neurology. By the spring of 1888, he was able to return from the microscope to the ski. It was time for the crossing of Greenland.

Nansen was not exactly a polar explorer; he was a skier who happened to turn to polar exploration. He saw the crossing of Greenland as simply another ski tour and an extension of his home terrain. With his gift for circumventing difficulty, he conjured up the money for his enterprise and overcame various difficulties along the way. Sailing on a Norwegian sealer called, appropriately for an explorer, *Jason*, Nansen finally went ashore on 10 August at a place called Umivik, on the east coast of Greenland.

It was *terra incognita* in more ways than one. No human foot was thought to have trodden the dome of the ice cap gently glinting up above through the eerie wolf's-tooth skyline of the coastal mountains. Nansen's whole approach was untried. By reversing all previous attempts, which ran from west to east, Nansen invoked the instinct of self-preservation to drive him on instead of dragging him back, like his predecessors, since the west coast was inhabited, but the east coast was not. He was also exploiting the mentality of the skier, hypnotized by the finishing line ahead or the hut at the end of the tour.

Here the great unknowns were men on the one hand and, on the other, snow and skis. Hitherto, Nansen's efforts had all been solitary; now he had to cope with a group and that was the real enigma. Nansen wanted good skiers, of whom there were enough, but they were curiously reluctant to join him. Suitable companions were even more difficult to find. As if to prove the point, the first applicant was Henrik Angell, about whose skiing there could be no doubt. Nansen however was not sure he wished to share his destiny with Angell. For one thing, Angell's letter of application was too highly charged for his liking. 'If you are afraid of having a straggler along the way,' ran one telling passage, 'I give you permission to make an end of me.'[17] A thirst for martyrdom was hardly a recommendation and Angell had other oddities. Recently he had ridden from Christiania across the Alps to Nice, then North Africa and back again on a penny-farthing; 5,000 km on one of the most impractical, unstable, bone-shaking contraptions devised by man for man and a record of some kind. He considered the journey, however, not so much a test of stamina as penance for what he saw as a sinful crisis of self-doubt. More openly, Angell told Nansen that he had wanted to run in the 'Nordenskiöld race' in 1884 but that the army had refused to give him leave.

Nansen ended up with an odd human assortment. Himself an academic, he first chose an authentic Norwegian type from a very different milieu: a ship's captain, part seaman, part farmer, part skier called Otto Sverdrup. Next came an army officer; not Angell, but the same captain Oluf Dietrichson who had been experimenting with ski equipment. Angell went off to pursue a career rarely far from skiing.

Dietrichson came not from Nansen's favoured Telemark but that other skiing province, Trøndelag. So too did the fourth Norwegian, Kristian Kristiansen Trana, a forestry worker with few words and illimitable stamina. Sverdrup was from Trøndelag too, although born in Northern Norway.

Finally, like Nordenskiöld four years earlier, and on his advice, Nansen took two Lapps; Samuel Johannesen Balto and Ole Nielsen Ravna, both from the north Norwegian province of Finnmark. In one way this was bizarre. Unlike Nordenskiöld, Nansen had no need of the Lapps' skiing powers. Different in background, mother-tongue and culture, however, they did bring with them yet another division in this fragmented company.

At least Lapp or Norwegian, they all had skiing in the blood. In any case Nansen, not being well versed in the byways of human nature, was more at home in technical matters. The great riddle was how snow and skis would function at those latitudes, at different heights, and these particular atmospheric conditions at that season of the year.

Science could hardly come to Nansen's aid. Little was known of the behaviour of the substance on which the ski depended; still less about the mechanics of sliding. He was thrown back on his own experience and intuition. Nordenskiöld's Lapps hardly gave dependable guidance because they had been 2,000 metres above sea level almost three weeks earlier and much further north.

With standardization far off, the skis themselves were naturally a matter of experiment. Nansen, always the restless innovator, was not attracted by the proliferation of existing types, least of all the Telemark racing ski. Short, without a steering groove, and flat, without camber, it was easy to turn, but hardly adapted to holding a course in unfamiliar snow. That was also the view of experienced skiers who charitably offered unsolicited advice. Two in particular were concerned about the difficulties of climbing. Both recommended the use of animal fur to secure adhesion on a slope. One suggested the andor, still surviving in odd corners amongst country dwellers and North Norwegian Lapps. The other was dead against it. An engineer called Einar Isachsen, he was another pioneer, having skied for 40 years, and experimented with skis for almost as long. Because these Lappish ski were completely covered in sealskin, he explained, 'they run sluggishly, and besides are unsteady and wobble downhill'.[18] Instead, he proposed an obscure variation devised by another engineer called Dahl from Trondheim. This model had a strip of sealskin, hairs pointing backwards, let into a broad groove in the sole. They were fastened by threads running through holes drilled upward through the skis. Because of the groove, Isachsen explained:

> These skis steer well, and can also be used on hard crust, and run much more easily than ... Lappish skis ... [And] they have *the immense advantage* that one can climb *straight up any slope* ... up to a gradient of 1 in 1, without the use of sticks ... Moreover [in] conditions where you need to move more quickly, it is a simple matter to remove the skins ... and later, if you want, to sew them on again.

That anticipated a sophisticated modern system by a hundred years. For some of his ski, Nansen chose this pattern with modifications. He designed a ski, made of birch, the sole of which, like the runners of his sledge, was lined with thin steel plates. Instead of sealskin, a strip of elk fur was fixed in a slot cut through the steel lining in the middle section of the ski. The purpose of the steel was to cope with wet, grainy snow on which a wooden ski did not glide and for which no wax yet existed.

The start was unpromising because, from Umivik, there was a long, embattled plod up a tongue of the ice cap in the frontier zone between skiing, polar travel and mountaineering. Nansen and all his men were out of their element with a gloomy mood to match.

After an upwards grind of nearly 150 km, the promised ski tour began at last on 2 September. Nansen then, having struggled on foot or Canadian snowshoes brought in reserve, finally got onto his skis. The gradient had slackened. What was recognizably skiable snow ran westwards to the horizon. It was like coming home.

Nansen had brought two kinds of ski. There were seven pairs of the Dahl birch pattern shod with steel and elk fur, but also two made of oak. These had bare soles that, by contrast, had three rounded grooves. Their shape was of an ancient west Norwegian kind. They were 230 cm long – nearing a jumping ski today – and 9.2 cm at the bend of the tip, narrowing to 8 cm in the middle and thence parallel to the heel. Nansen used one of these pairs. There turned out to be little difference in the behaviour of either kind. There was none of the wet, grainy slush for which Nansen had prepared. Instead he was faced with thick crust lined with a layer of small, sharp, needle-like flakes. At least this gave plenty of purchase, and luckily so.

Unlikely to have draught animals, Nansen knew he would have to haul his own supplies. With a creative dip into folk wisdom, he adopted the ancient sledge with broad, ski-like runners, found in Scandinavia and Siberia. His innovation was to give the runners a proper camber and have a light superstructure, all lashed with leather thongs to ensure flexibility so that the sledge followed the contours of the terrain, to ease the strain of hauling. The only metal was in thin false runners of steel. Having tested a prototype before departure on yet another crossing of the mountains between Bergen and Christiania, Nansen proved that he could haul his new sledge on skis. Once up on the ice cap, however, he was faced with unexpectedly heavy going.

Against that, the party's clothing performed as intended. In their design, Nansen was also a pioneer. It was not enough, like other explorers before him, simply to guard against wind and cold. The essence of skiing is mobility and he had to design an outfit that would not impede the distinctive movement of men on skis. He began with the layer principle – probably the first to do so – and a devotion to the virtues of wool. Undergarments were of thin woollen material. Outer clothing was made of a robust Norwegian wool fabric called vadmel. There was a simple jacket with a large overlap buttoned across the chest to keep out the cold and arms cut so as to allow full freedom. This was combined with not-too-wide-cut knee breeches and finished off with leggings of vadmel too. Nansen had in fact devised the first specialized skiing garb on modern principles. It all gave a sporting touch, which torpedoed the heroic ideal of garments for the great outdoors. The only trace of that was in the outer garments for bad weather. These were made of a kind of thin canvas, the jacket of which was modelled on the anorak of the Eskimos, or the parka of the Siberian tribes, with a deep hood covering the face.

The sober grey and brown, utilitarian appearance of the Norwegians made a contrast with the dun-coloured reindeer fur of the Lapps' exotic winter *kolt*, to which they held. Each in his own way had worked out how to cope with the surroundings. The controversy about one or two sticks in racing had been left behind. Hauling on a sledge, two sticks were vital to secure purchase and balance. The sticks towered above head height, without baskets, one of each pair topped by a miniature ice-axe head.

The party settled down to an unchanging pattern, one day much like another, with a run of 10 km to 20 km. Only a storm broke the monotony. Easy it was not. Because of low temperatures and the devilry of drift snow, the skis continued to run grudgingly. The general gait was a sluggish slide. Also, hauling the sledges was enervating. Although technically it worked, the ski was not meant for pulling, as one of Nansen's friends had warned. It destroyed the rhythm that is the heart of skiing. Hauling 50 kg a man was a trial; even on the long, billowing, wind-packed waves, like the swell of a frozen sea, on the dome of the ice cap summit. Sometimes Nansen, at least, was dispirited. He acquired a deep aversion to man-hauling.

Nonetheless, their attitude, as Nansen had foreseen, was not that that of an explorer in alien surroundings but that of a ski tourer in familiar terrain, rather easier in some respects than mountain routes at home. The past is, however, another country and it is hard to gauge exactly what Nansen and his companions were going through. In 1988, to mark the centenary, a group of Norwegians under Stein Aasheim, a practised mountain skier, repeated the journey, using replicas of the original equipment. It was all heavier than anything today. 'The sheer drudgery was worse than we had imagined', as Aasheim put it. 'Apart from a fantastic sunrise, it was all an inferno.'[19] He graphically showed the impossibility of reproducing the mental experience of those pioneers in their isolation, lost to the outside world. 'The West Coast or death, said [Nansen] … The West Coast or 122.5 MHz on our emergency transponder said we.'[20]

In another telling remark, Aasheim said that if he were to repeat the journey, it would be with modern equipment – except for the boots and bindings.[21] Even the latest alloy and plastic devices could not compare in comfort with the warmth and freedom of movement of Nansen's system.

Nansen had eschewed the first patented bindings then just coming onto the market, especially those of cane. In his own words, 'they are absolutely not suited to moving over great expanses'.[22] Because the Greenland ice cap was gently domed, with no need to run down steeply or turn, they 'were not necessary for [lateral] control of the skis, and … a stiff … binding … tires and impedes the foot'. What he chose was an old military pattern of a leather toestrap, and a soft

28. Ski-jumper landing at Huseby, Christiania [Oslo] 1883, having cleared 20 m.
*Ski Museum, Holmenkollen, Oslo*

heelstrap, also of leather. 'It is my experience that the less one feels the binding, the longer one keeps going in the great open spaces.' For the same reason, he abandoned Norwegian ski boots, and resorted to soft Lapp *finneskoe*, with their supple, light reindeer fur, and turned-up toes.

That gave Balto and Ravna wry satisfaction. They were victors in a clash of cultures. By their nature, they patronized the Norwegians as inferior skiers but they also wished to please. They submitted to Nansen's ukase on equipment, with heelstraps, while they were used to simple toestraps.

As a skier, Nansen could enjoy the success of his elaborate experiment. He had proved that even at the highest point, some 2,800 m above sea level, snow behaved much as it did lower down. Skis still moved in a familiar way, and therefore the mechanism of sliding, as yet not understood, still functioned at high altitude. That alone was a discovery worth the effort.

Arduous as man-hauling was, Nansen also proved another point. Because skiing was economical in terms of energy, he and his companions were sometimes tired but never overtaxed. They kept within the limits of the human organism. They began each day refreshed. That alone distinguished them from most of their predecessors, who drove themselves to exhaustion.

Around 16 September, they reached the summit of the ice cap. It levelled out and then began gradually to slope down. A fortnight later, and 150 km further on, the gradient was such that Nansen rigged sails on the sledges to run before an easterly wind that sprang up. Then it was a matter not of hauling but steering the sledges like ships, albeit on a choppy sea. 'The whole day passed and we had no time even to eat. It was such fun to ski', as Balto artlessly put it.[23] They covered 70 km; nearly five times their average daily run so far. This anticipated the wind-powered parachutes of latter-day skiing adventurers. Almost casually, Nansen and his men had demythologized the polar environment and revolutionized polar exploration.

The first crossing of Greenland came to an end on 21 September 1888. Then the snow finally gave out, exposing the harsh bare blue surface of the ice cap, dome debouching in a broken, congealed cataract down to the Ameralik fjord on the west coast below. Nansen and his men had come 400 km from Umivik. Of that, they had skied 250 km continuously in 19 days. The whole journey had taken just under six weeks.

What remained was an undignified scramble down. Early in October, the whole party was in Godthaab, the Danish outpost that served as the capital of Greenland. Having missed the last boat of the season and without cable connection, they were caught for the winter, still isolated from the outside world.

Nansen returned home in the summer of 1889 to a tumultuous reception. He had achieved one of the last of the geographic goals. More to the point, he had invented the skier as polar explorer. He had sensationally glorified the skier and his ski. In victory there are no questions asked. All reluctance gone, Nansen's compatriots saw in him a gilded image of themselves. He looked the part. Tall, big-boned, blonde, handsome in a Nordic way, with blue eyes aglint with stern purpose and a personality to match, he was everybody's idea of the Viking.

Not everyone joined in the chorus of acclaim; especially when it was suggested that Nansen had been in the service of science. This particularly irritated Knut Hamsun, the future world-famous Norwegian novelist, early exponent of the stream of consciousness as a literary device, winner of the Nobel Prize for Literature and no mean skier himself. Never afraid to express an opinion, Hamsun now wrote in a newspaper that Nansen

> did a ski tour, which required personal courage, before which anyone with a knowledge of sport is willing to genuflect. However, the world decided that Nansen came back from a scientific expedition – on Greenland! ... Nansen has constantly declared this to be wrong. He came back from a ski tour.[24]

'In the Greenland expedition,' as one Christiania newspaper baldly put it, 'skiing has celebrated its greatest triumph.'[25] Nansen himself said: 'Without skis, this expedition would have been an absolute impossibility ... we would ... never have returned alive.'[26] He meant that the speed and economy of effort they conferred, saved him from overrunning his supplies.

In London, the *Spectator* wrote that 'we are spared ... the painful interest that attaches to many Arctic narratives, – the mournful uncertainty that enshrouds a vanished name, or the horrible details of a timely or just-too-late relief'.[27]

That went to the heart of the matter. Despite all the hero worship and his heroic appearance, Nansen was essentially an anti-hero. That was the nature of the skier, with his admiration for quiet mastery and a distaste for heroic struggle. Even when faced with setback, Nansen's emotions and language were that of a skier, not of a suffering explorer. He had cast off the debilitating mantle of heroic pretensions. As a skier, he was at ease on snow. The interior of Greenland had turned out simply to be an extension of his home terrain after all. By the application of skis and the psychology of the skier, he had demythologized the polar environment. That was one result of this ski tour, for a simple ski tour, after all, this expedition had turned out to be.

It was Nansen's message when he came to write his book about the expedition; in the original Norwegian *Paa Ski over Grønland* – literally *On Skis Across Greenland*. It was widely translated – into English as *The First Crossing of Greenland*. Engagingly if discursively written, it was a eulogy on skiing – 'the most national of all Norwegian sports, and a wonderful sport it is'.[28]

Nansen had set out to prove that skis could be used in the polar regions. He had dramatically done so, but it was in the obverse that his reputation fully flowered. It was as a skier, not an explorer that Nansen had acquired instant fame. On the one hand he had turned polar exploration into a branch of sport; on the other, through polar exploration, he had taken skiing out of northern mists and revealed it to the outside world. It was a seminal achievement. This was not Nansen's original purpose but he too had to live with the law of unintended consequences.

# 15

# The Nordic Olympia

Before skiing could spread abroad it had first to be consolidated in its heartlands. Even Nansen, in a toast at a banquet after his return, hoped for 'the advancement of skiing in Norway'.[1] The rôle of propagandist had been thrust upon him. Unwittingly he had inspired the country. People did not, however, grovel from afar; they identified with him. Every skier felt that, with a little bit of luck, he could have done the same. Children on their skis acted out the crossing of Greenland. Commercially there was a Nansen craze. He had effortlessly popularized skiing to a degree – even as a spectator sport – where ardent evangelists had failed.

Climate change meanwhile was inexorably marching on. In Christiania, poor winters forced the annual ski races to move from Huseby higher up to a place called Holmenkollen. At an altitude of some 300 m, it was thought to offer certain snow. Also, nestling under an escarpment of the massif behind Christiania, Holmenkollen provided a bigger, natural jump. In 1892, Huseby was abandoned and the fixture transferred.

The timing was appropriate. It was the 1890s, the decade of change, with fateful cross-currents in every field. That held for skiing too. Huseby symbolized one stage; Holmenkollen, the beginning of the next. For one thing, Huseby was down on the outskirts of Christiania; Holmenkollen lay up on the heights, in a natural arena. The outrun ended on a convenient frozen tarn – *Besserudtjern* – for competitors more or less gracefully to stop.

One journalist appropriately waxed lyrical: 'The new ski-jump' he wrote, 'stretched like a giant web on a field of bleach up through the dark pine forest … and … to the south there were a few glimpses of the Christiania Fjord.'[2] And more in the same vein.

Nature of course intervened with yet another mordant joke. Despite the altitude, when that first Holmenkollen event opened on 30 January 1892 with the cross-country race it was greeted with westerly winds, a thaw and deep wet sticky snow balling up under every ski. 'Such conditions', as one newspaper blandly put it, 'were not the kind in which to ski a long-distance course.'[3] There is no record of what the competitors felt. Over a distance of about 15 km the winner's time was 1 hour 58 minutes and 30 seconds – about half an hour longer than a 30 km race now.

The jumping event, the next day, was marginally better off. The wind backed north; the temperature fell just below freezing. Nonetheless the snow was soft and treacherous. There were three rounds but of some 114 individuals who started, only about half-a-dozen managed every one and nobody jumped further than about 20 m. 'We have never seen skiers set off so reluctantly', one journalist reported:

> They tumbled … like ninepins … so that it was horrible to see, and only came to a halt at the foot of the slope … in a cloud of snow … in the most varied contortions … Skis snapped like matchsticks, but no one was injured.

Nor were the spectators immune. On the tarn, in a horseshoe, stands had been erected. The snow, however, was wet and water, trapped by the underlying ice, began seeping around one of the stands so that the front row had to be evacuated. Despite the thread of low comedy, there was a sense of occasion. Ten thousand people had made their way to the new hill. Christiania was like a ghost town while the jumping was taking place. Perhaps the new name played a part. Huseby was prosaic; Holmenkollen had a certain ring and not only to Norwegian ears.

The winner of this first Holmenkollen was yet another Telemarking – Svein Sollid from Morgedal. So on the surface not much seemed to have changed. In fact, it only eased the process of transition. The Telemark domination was coming to an end. Huseby, then Holmenkollen, served as informal national championships, and mirrored advancement all over the country. In Trondheim, for instance, early in March 1892, someone jumped 30 m, 10 m more than anyone else before.

All this was significant at home but the influence of Holmenkollen spread abroad from its start in 1892. A Swedish army officer, Captain Viktor Balck, was among the spectators. A fierce and very military-looking gentleman, with the welfare of his country at heart, he was a pioneer of physical education in Sweden, especially that of women. He had come to see what he could learn. Holmenkollen, as the successor to Huseby, so Balck wrote in a Stockholm newspaper on his return, was a 'unique sporting event … in its grandeur it had no equivalent anywhere in the world, and I would even go so as to assert that in Scandinavia there is no sporting event of such great national significance as these annual ski races'.[4]

As a Swede among Norwegians hoping to break loose from his country, Balck was showing admirable impartiality. The 1890s were a decade of nationalism resurgent. In Norway, national feeling was intensifying. Skiing, as usual, led the way as a channel for that particular emotion. This was ahead of its times. Sport was still far from being a general agent of national identity – armies and navies still held the stage. The nearest equivalents to skiing in Norway were Sokol in Bohemia, rugby in South Africa and cricket in Australia.

From the start Holmenkollen, with its evocative Nordic overtones, became a focus of the drive to Norwegian independence. Both for competitors and spectators, presence at the event was in part a patriotic demonstration. The strife between Sweden and Norway was now approaching its culmination. The first Holmenkollen coincided with yet another political crisis, more serious than before. As a half-way house to independence, in 1892 the Norwegian parliament proposed the establishment of a separate Norwegian consular service. The outcome was a humiliating retreat and skiing became a kind of compensation.

As a military man, Balck scorned politics and politicians. He went out of his way to emphasize the friendliness with which he was personally received in Christiania. In any case, he was only interested in the purely sporting aspect. His newspaper articles were rare published accounts of the first Holmenkollen by an outsider. 'In spite of the different social standing of the competitors, representing ordinary people, academe, working class, businessmen and army', Balck admiringly continued, 'there was an absolute feeling of equality and camaradarie.'[5]

> The greater part of the spectators make their way ... on skis ... The wooded slopes on the way to the arena teem with skiers [who] run down the slopes with a speed and self-confidence which compel admiration. [Someone] has calculated that around 35,000 pairs of skis are in use [here] this winter. Poor people save their pennies in order to ... buy a good pair ... for the great [Holmenkollen] race day [when] some 5000 skiers are on the move; it was a parade of young Christiania on skis.[6]

'It is a strange, picturesque scene on Saturday evenings to see whole crowds of skiers ... running down the nearly 10 kilometre slope from [Holmenkollen] at high speed holding flaming torches', Balck went on in romantic vein.

> Even the authorities encourage skiing ... for example when some [people] complained that horses were frightened by the sheer number of skiers swarming along certain roads ... all traffic was forbidden [there] on Sundays and holidays so as to avoid clashing with young people on skis ... Skiing ... exercises a sound influence on coming generations, especially since both men and women participate ... The young skiing ladies' rosy cheeks and shining eyes bear witness to health and joy of life.

At Holmenkollen itself, meanwhile, Balck dispassionately reported the cross-country event in terms recognizable today:

> The race began at 10am ... Starting was one at a time, at intervals of a minute. Consequently it took about an hour before everyone was on his way. On the map, the course was about 15 kilometres. [It] was marked with red ribbons on the trees or pennants tuck in the snow. In addition, officials were posted at important points. The track had been prepared by a number of skiers before the race so that the first runners would not find it easier than those who followed.
>
> The crowds of spectators ... moved out into the terrain to watch the runners along the course ... Soon after midday the first competitor was glimpsed as he arrived at the finish [followed] by one after another. When someone arrived early bearing a high number, meaning that he had started late, he was greeted with cheering ... At the half-way point a peeled orange was served out for the runners to slake their thirst, and at the finish, chilled

beer or boiled milk was provided. (The origin of the colourful modern Nordic feeding station along the track, with its intensely marketed popular drinks and accompanying logos. Racers have to keep up their strength and, above all, avoid dehydration.)

Balck was trying to import the egalitarian spirit of Holmenkollen to the hierarchical society of Sweden. He also wanted a model for a ski race that he was helping to organize in Stockholm at the end of February. This was to be an international event although the rules declared that it was open only to 'Scandinavians and Finns'. Norway and Sweden, although different countries, were united in one kingdom. Finland, on the other hand, then belonged to Russia, so the fixture was international by any definition.

As Balck's event followed the first Holmenkollen in 1892, its precursor, also in Stockholm, was held soon after the first Huseby competition in 1879. This was the first modern Swedish ski race. Norwegians also competed. They swept the board.

Their presence was due to the even-handed policy of the Union kings. In Stockholm, they stationed both a Swedish and a Norwegian life guard regiment. Winter after winter the Norwegian guardsmen had got out their skis in the Stockholm parks, to the amazement of the citizens. They were lucky. One of the rare Swedish skiers in Stockholm at the time, from the north of the country, bitterly explained how 'before 1879 extremely few [locals] practised skiing in Stockholm and its surroundings'.[7] He and a northern Swedish friend had been 'almost the only ones ... we were subject to the jeering and insults of the population, and even came to blows'.

Norwegians from the life guards changed all that. They popularized skiing in Stockholm and more or less gave impetus to the country. It was a pattern eventually repeated in the wider world outside. The Stockholm race of 1879 – called Bellevue after the locality – was the manifest breakthrough.

The Bellevue race was by no means as spectacular as that of Huseby. Their forms were different, because Stockholm was different from Christiania. Christiania lay in broken mountainous terrain, on the verge of only half-tamed land, still with a touch of the frontier town. Stockholm was at heart still the capital of a once great power, an elegant spired city of granite and water in low, undulating forested country, straddling an archipelago between the Baltic and an inland lake. This race was run on the northern outskirts, at the edge of a royal park, the creation of the Francophile eighteenth-century King Gustav III

Gustav's romantic park was a splendid backdrop for the Bellevue races. There was no jump but there were two other events instead. One consisted of a short cross-country course. It comprised a short loop starting and finishing on land and running on the flat over the ice of a frozen waterway. It was barely 700 m long, and there were two laps. Again the changing climate bedevilled the proceedings. 'The thaw of the last few days',[8] to quote *Aftonbladet*, a leading Stockholm newspaper, 'meant that the going was not [of the] best, which was clearly indicated by the difficulty with which otherwise so speedy [skiers] moved over the soft layer of snow covering the ice.' Few things are so dismal as wet snow on a sodden underlayer. And also, on the slope leading down to the ice 'some skiers ... pitched head first into a snowdrift, to the cheers of the surrounding crowds. Unfortunately one skier was seriously injured in these circumstances when a broken ski stick ... pierced his cheek immediately below his left eye.'

This kind of injury was an accepted hazard in the days of a single ski stick made of solid wood. The accident occurred during the second event. This was a kind of downhill race. It was run on a gravel mound, quarried by the city for roads and building work. To that extent, this makes it the first known artificial ski slope. The race consisted of seeing how far each skier could reach on the flat using only the momentum of the downhill run. For the record, the winner of the cross-country run was a Private Enger. His time was 12 minutes 15 seconds. The thaw had taken its toll. This is equivalent to two hours over a 15 km course – which takes barely 50 minutes today.

Huseby had had King Oscar; Bellevue had to make do with his sons. Nonetheless, Bellevue was in the vanguard. For one thing, the outcome was decided on objective performance alone; time for the cross-country event, distance for the downhill; for another, allowing for political niceties, Bellevue becomes the precursor of international ski racing.

Balck' s Stockholm event of 1892 remains the first true international fixture. It was also more sophisticated. There was now ski-jumping and a cross-country race, held on separate days. The event had moved to the romantic, more dramatic surroundings of the royal park of Djurgården and there, on a proper slope at a residence called Sirishov, a ski-jump had been installed. A wooden superstructure had been built on top to extend the in-run. It was probably the first artificial ski-jump in the world.

The races opened on 28 February 1892 with the ski-jumping, accompanied by fanfares and another large, distinguished crowd. The Norwegians, as expected, won overwhelmingly. They took the first 12 places, with jumps of around 15 m.

Next day, the cross-country event was another story altogether. The Norwegians were trounced. International skiing had opened with a thoroughgoing upset. Finns took the first three prizes. As a matter of historical justice, their names must be recorded. The winner was a 21 year old called Juho Ritola, followed by Juho Räihä and F. Liljeberg.

The distance was 30 km; the winner's time about 2 hours 20 minutes, quarter-of-an-hour less than the first Norwegian, in fourth place. The temperature was –15°C but, as a local reporter put it, 'superfluous clothing was thrown off, and in spite of the biting frost, several skiers ran in only long underpants which was not at all unbecoming'.[9]

There were rational explanations for the outcome. For one thing, because Stockholm lacked proper ski terrain, the course was laid out on the low islands and frozen channels intersecting the city, so it was level almost all the way. The Norwegians were not used to flat going; the Finns were. They usually raced on their numerous frozen lakes. The Finns also had more experience than the Norwegians in long-distance skiing. At least since the mid-1880s they had regularly competed over 30 km or more.

That was not all. The Finns had evolved skis to suit the terrain. They were long, narrow, light and impregnated with pine tar to ensure good glide. The skis of the Norwegians, by contrast, mostly of the Telemark pattern and its variations, were shorter, heavier and more robust to cope with their own very different landscape; violently undulating and broken. It was the glimmering of specialization in skis. There was also another difference, adumbrated by a Norwegian journalist:

> The Finns ... used a technique adapted to saving energy and promoting physical stamina. Whereas [the Norwegians] use their sticks evenly in time with their legs, the Finns ski in a different manner. They take a step with legs only to get up speed, then push forward with both sticks, take another step with legs alone, push again with the sticks, and so on. In this way, the legs rest while the arms work, and the other way about.[10]

This technique was unknown to the Norwegians, who now thought that it would be worth trying. On the other hand

> the Finns' long, light, tarred and slippery skis, which had proved superior to the Norwegians' on flat terrain without obstacles ... absolutely could not be used in the [broken] Norwegian terrain, where their length would prevent proper manoeuvrability, and their slenderness meant that they would break at the slightest obstacle.

Finally, unlike the Norwegians, the Finns used a simple toestrap binding. It gave them the greatest flexibility. They needed no heel fixture on their flat courses. At the rare incline, they often slipped out of their ski, and tripped lightly up the slope before quickly re-engaging the toestraps and continuing on their way.

For all the cheering and the crowds, the Stockholm races were not the popular festival for which Balck had hoped. Nor did ski racing quickly become a national sport either in Finland or Sweden, as its advocates intended. Despite their reverse, the Norwegians remained the exemplars.

They returned in 1892 with various lessons to apply. In Stockholm, the jumping and cross-country events were separated. Holmenkollen, and hence Norway, took time to follow suit. For the rest of the 1890s, the Nordic combination of jumping and cross-country – about 18 km – remained the only recognized event, as the accepted ideal. At last, from 1900 there was also a separate cross-country race of 30 km to begin with and then, starting in 1902, of 50 km. It was the first since the isolated precursor in 1888. The doctors had maintained their fear of extreme effort. The example of Swedes and Finns eventually forced them to recant. Also Finnish skis and the Finnish double-stick heave forced the Norwegians to rethink their equipment and technique.

In any case, it was at Holmenkollen that the various disciplines took on their modern shape. The reform of 1902 set the pattern until the early 1930s. Oddly enough, the jump continued as a temporary pile of snow, rebuilt every season for more than a decade. Only in 1904 was a permanent lip constructed out of stone. In 1895 and 1906, a slalom was also run but these were aberrations. The event dropped into desuetude. For long, Holmenkollen remained exclusively Nordic.

As the years passed, Holmenkollen Sunday, when the jump took place, turned into a second national day. The whole event achieved an almost mythic significance in the national psyche. Holmenkollen had virtually become a second Olympia. Like athletics to the ancient Greeks, skiing became sacrosanct to the Norwegians. That also was to mean much for the wider world. To begin with, Holmenkollen was restricted to Norwegians but in 1903 it was opened to outsiders. That year the first foreign competitors appeared. Suitably enough, they were all Swedes.

# 16

# The Waisted Telemark Ski

Holmenkollen also became the stage for technological advance. 'Many ... bindings broke', so one reporter noted at the first event in 1892.[1] 'It was the patent clips that failed.' In other words, technique had outstripped equipment on the jumping hill. Skiing was profoundly technological. Ski-jumping, with the most critical dependence of all disciplines on speed and balance, was a forcing-house. Once again it showed how competitive sport drove the evolution of marketing and design.

Since the Telemark pioneers of the 1860s, bindings had been troublesome. This was unfortunate because they were the link between the skier and his ski. The old pattern of twisted osier persisted.[2] Each skier had to wind his own. It was an involved little craft, illustrated by these contemporary instructions:

> The ... osier ... must first be soaked [in water] until it is quite soft ... You put on your skiing footware, and start work.
>
> The thoroughly soaked osier is fixed [at one end] at the front part of the [transverse] binding hole ... You then twist the osier thoroughly (it is always twisted clockwise), thread the thin end through the hole from the opposite side, pull tight, and run it over the toe ... and tighten it ... Then you twist the osier again, thread it once more through, and repeat the procedure.

Industrialization was still some way off. Twisting osier was second nature to country dwellers. It was said to be used as a test by some fathers of suitors for their daughters. It might partly explain the superiority of skiers from the provinces. How to make bindings was part of the instruction offered by Telemarkings at their ski school in Christiania. Racers usually arrived with extra osiers hanging round their necks for quick repairs. Although flexible and versatile, the osier often broke. Cane about the thickness of a little finger made its appearance.

Homemade bindings were irksome. Rising numbers of skiers created a demand for the ready-made article. The first commercially produced binding appeared on the market in 1884. It was the invention of a cobbler called Fossum. It consisted of a leather toestrap with a heelstrap made of a double loop of cane enclosed in sealskin, with the hair facing outwards, fixed to the side of the ski with screws. This was the first commercial binding to grip the boot properly – at the cost, alas, of many a blister. It found its niche amongst ski-jumpers.

In 1889 another binding appeared. Here the heelstrap was made of a spiral spring enclosed in leather. It was designed by a Christiania gunsmith called Gunerius Schou. Fossum had tried to patent his device but was rejected on the grounds that sporting equipment was unworthy of protection. Schou was luckier. His was the first patent ever granted in the field of skiing. With its sprung heelstrap and adjustable length, Schou's binding paved the way for modernization. As so often is the case with critical inventions, it was ahead of its time and the inventor hardly became a millionaire.

The 1890s were a period of rapid technical development; so also in ski bindings. However, they were linked to footwear, which lagged behind and thus served as a constraint. Schou's heelstrap foundered on soft-soled boots unsuited to longitudinal pressure. His springs were abandoned in favour of cane, about the thickness of a little finger. Around 1890 a clutch of cane bindings were patented. The basic principle was an adjustable heelstrap, fixed to the top of the ski, forming a cage in which the boot could move vertically, but was supported sideways.

None of these bindings gave true lateral rigidity. They foundered on the persistence of traditional soft footwear. Its drawbacks, meanwhile, led to the gradual advance of ski boots with strong welted soles that could withstand pressure. That in turn paved the way for the great modernist revolution in bindings. It was the brainchild of the same Fritz Huitfeldt who had introduced the precursor of the modern slalom. It is an object lesson in the process of invention.

The story began in 1881. Huitfeldt had just started working for a gunsmith called Larsen, who ran the leading Christiania sports shop. An unusual pair of skis was delivered for repair. The toestrap, instead of being threaded through the ordinary lateral slot, was attached to two square iron links, the ends of which were serrated, bent at right angles and hammered into each side of the ski. The purpose was to avoid weakening the ski with a lateral slot, and to simplify changing the toestrap. The device was typical blacksmith's work. It came from Telemark, although similar models had appeared in other parts of the country over the past 50 years. Huitfeldt, as he put it in retrospect,

> brooded over this manifestation, and for many years, I could not get those 2 clamps out of my mind. Something told me that [they] contained the germ of an idea which could be used to form the basis of a possible ski binding; but as I say, footwear was the stumbling block.[3]
>
> But meanwhile as footwear changed and ... finally ... was provided with a [proper] sole and heel; then and only then was the ground ripe for reflection ... over how ... those ... iron clamps could be used.
>
> So one fine day – it was in 1893 – the scales fell from my eyes, and the whole principle was so obvious ... that I could not understand that no one else, not to mention I myself had not discovered [it] before ...

Huitfeldt ordered some iron clamps from a gunsmith – early ski equipment owed much to gunsmiths. These clamps were like open squares, with a hole drilled at each end. They were attached to both sides of a pair of skis by means of bolts running through these holes and the lateral slot of the ski, and secured by substantial nuts. The clamp was then hammered to fit the front of the sole. A leather toestrap and heelstrap threaded through the clamps held the boot in place. 'rather a primitive arrangement', as Huitfeldt himself put it, 'but the binding … gave better control than any others that we had used before.'

This was in fact the very first binding to grip the boot, exploiting a stiff sole to give proper lateral support and make the skier at one with his skis. It was the original modern binding with fixed metal ears. Gone were the blisters and frostbite of yesteryear. It was the start of a new epoch. For the record, the new binding was patented on 18 September 1894.

It was far from ideal. Made of wrought iron, the clamps often broke in deep cold. They were also difficult to fit to the boot. Huitfeldt immediately began rectifying the defects. He devised a new model consisting of a single thick rectangular mild steel plate, stamped out, with slots for heel and toe straps. The plate was pushed through the lateral slot, which was standard on most skis, then bent vertically upwards and hammered to fit the boot. It was patented on 2 November 1897. Under the name of the Huitfeldt binding, it 'gradually won approval', in the inventor's own words, 'and spread more and more, not only in this country, but all over the world where climate and conditions allowed skiing'.

In fact when the new device first appeared on the market, the customers held back. The workshop that actually did the manufacturing, grudgingly took a first order of 500 and feared the worst. Sales finally soared when a few leading Norwegian skiers won their events while using the new binding. Huitfeldt had persuaded them to do so by supplying it free. This was the first known case of product placement in skiing.

Huitfeldt's invention – although he was unlikely to have known it at the time – went back to the Bronze Age. His binding, with its fixed metal ears, had been presaged by the carved wooden flanges on the ancient Hoting, Ärnäs and Furnes skis. So from a certain point of view, this first modern binding descended from three-and-a-half millennia of evolution.

Huitfeldt's design suffered from one drawback. The boot could not easily be fixed because of a defective heelstrap. The wife of a Christiania industrialist called Sigurd Høyer-Ellefsen found the solution. After a ski tour one winter's day at the turn of the century Høyer-Ellefsen, so the story goes, found himself drawn into yet another interminable discussion about ski bindings.[4] His wife was present, and quickly grasped that the failing of Huitfeldt's product was the lack of an efficient tensioning device on the heelstrap. Ordinary buckles, as used, clearly would not do. She happened to be closing an old-fashioned mineral water bottle with a patent stopper pressed home by a fixed lever device with eccentric mountings. Could this, she asked, be applied to a heel strap?

Like the sensible husband that Høyer-Ellefsen no doubt was, he listened to his wife. With the stopper as a model he invented the first lever tensioning clasp.

His original patent was dated 4 July 1904. The principle survives to this day in downhill ski boots and certain specialized Nordic bindings.

More to the point, this was the breakthrough that Huitfeldt needed to perfect his invention. His toe irons with the Høyer-Ellefsen heelstrap became the first modern ski binding. It was a legendary piece of industrial design, holding its own against all competitors to become the standard product everywhere, for the next quarter of a century.

As became a pioneer in a nation devoted to the cult of the individual, yet faced with powerful forces of conformity, Huitfeldt was a man of strong character and inner tension. Opinionated, obstinate and an indefatigable polemicist, he often took things to extremes. His appearance conformed to these traits. Of middling height, sinewy, moustachioed, dark-haired, he had fierce eyes with a penetrating stare. He was a sportsman to his fingertips; he rowed, hunted and fished. He had the gift of managing dogs, which at least could not answer back. His great passion was skiing; not so much as a performer, but as an innovator. At the same time, he was surprisingly retrograde. He clung to the outmoded practice of one ski stick. He was a university dropout, spent his whole career in the manufacture and marketing of ski equipment. His was a household name yet, in his own wistful words, 'I ... have not had *any pecuniary benefit whatsoever* from this binding of mine.' He was a brilliant innovator, but a financial genius he was not.[5]

In 1896, Huitfeldt published one of the early skiing handbooks. Of bindings, he wrote that 'hardly any subject ... has caused so much brain-racking'.[6]

> Almost every skier has his own improved binding ... It has become a business to put a new 'improved binding' on the market every year, the purpose of which is simply to extract money from the pockets of gullible people ... Things have gone so far that people who have never put on a pair of skis ... make bindings for us.

This emotional outburst was symptomatic. In a country where skiing had become a way of life, all kinds of people, goaded by bitter experience, were experimenting with equipment. Huitfeldt and Høyer-Ellefsen represented in their different ways the most creative milieu; the professional and artisan classes of Christiania.

Høyer-Ellefsen, a trained engineer, also had a fertile mind but his approach was more technical. Long before his tensioning clasp, in 1890, he had already patented one of the more popular cane bindings. In fact it survived sporadically well into the Huitfeldt era. In 1895, he invented the first adjustable metal binding with fixed ears, attached to the top of the ski. It was another device too far ahead of its time. The principle only came into its own after some three decades.

The Huitfeldt system opened the way for the popularization of skiing and the rapid development of technique. It was the original all-round binding. Its lateral stability promoted both jumping and downhill skiing. At the same time, by allowing the heel to move up and down, it suited moving across country too. It was particularly adapted to undulating terrain.

With all the flurry of attention to bindings, the question of the ski itself had been comparatively neglected. There was no system. It was here that Huitfeldt caused another revolution.

It originated in a classic shift from craftsman and customer to middlemen, manufacturing and trade. On 3 February 1820, the first known newspaper advertisement of skis for sale appeared in Christiania's *Morgenbladet*. In rising quantity, skis began appearing in markets and urban shops. The Telemark pioneers benefited in their own way. Some were also ski makers, and their products had begun circulating in Christiania during the 1860s. In a precursor of merchandising, ordinary skiers wanted the same implements as the champions, and this promoted the spread of the Telemark ski. The quality, however, was uneven.

The demand was growing too much for the craftsman at his bench. In 1882, a ski maker called Simen Rustad opened the first ski factory in the world. At Fåberg, near Lillehammer, in central Norway, he dammed a stream and drove some machinery with a water turbine. Other enterprising ski makers followed suit. Rustad had founded a whole new industry.

His enterprise coincided with the advent of hickory. This was the first new material in ski making for centuries. It originally came to Norway in 1882 on a vessel belonging to Thomas Fearnley, a big Norwegian shipowner and a skiing pioneer in his own right. To promote experiment, he gave this first cargo of hickory to skiers and ski makers around Christiania. A close-grained wood from the Southern states of America, hickory proved to have a combination of hardness, flexibility and resistance to wear, unrivalled in ski making. Against this, it was heavy and difficult to work; notably because of sand embedded in

29. Studio photograph of (l. to r.) Laurentius Urdahl, Roald Amundsen and Vilhelm Holst, preparatory to Amundsen's first mountain tour, Christmas–New Year, 1893–4.
*Ski Museum, Holmenkollen, Oslo*

the bark from the soil in which it grew, playing havoc with saws and other tools. The advantages, however, outweighed the drawbacks. Solid hickory extended the capacity of skis. It could be polished as smooth as glass, and at low temperatures slid faster than almost any other kind of wood. It became a favourite of ski-jumpers, where speed was all, and weight, no handicap. Because of its strength, virtually eliminating breakage, hickory was also used for skis in rough terrain. It played a vital rôle in the advance of mountain touring.

Meanwhile, in the winter of 1896, Skiforeningen held the first ski exhibition in Christiania since 1884. Creeping industrialization was begetting an insidious and sterile uniformity, which the organizers were trying to combat. As one of them put it, the trouble lay in 'bad copies of the models pouring out of Christiania all over the country, so that even the farmers had stopped making their own skis, so that all originality disappears'.[7]

Huitfeldt entered a pair of skis to his own design. It won a gold medal. Following the law of unintended consequences, it had the opposite effect on the organizers' stated aim of encouraging variety.

Huitfeldt based his ski on a Telemark model. It had gently waisted sides. It was 235 cm long, 9.4 cm wide at the base of the tip, 7.5 cm in the middle and 8.6 cm at the heel. Huitfeldt stood over the craftsman making the ski, insisting that the dimensions were kept to the millimetre. He diverged from the ordinary Telemark ski by putting a narrow steering groove in the sole instead of leaving it flat. The reason was to make it function on crust as well as soft snow. Another innovation was to give the tip a deep and gentle upward bend as a kind of shock absorber in broken terrain. There was little camber and the ski was soft. It was made of either pine or ash. In a characteristic touch, the tip finished with a small protuberance, like a piece of lump sugar.

Fortified by his gold medal, Huitfeldt started manufacturing his ski. To standardize production he had templates made for cutting out the blanks. This model was inspired. Adapted to jumping, turning, running downhill, or across country, it turned out to be a brilliant all-round concept. It swept the market to replace local variations with its single uniform design. It was the origin of the modern ski, both Alpine and Nordic. Although materials have changed, for its purpose, no subsequent technology has managed to improve upon the shape. The present-day steel and plastic devices are its direct descendants. It was dubbed the Telemark ski, although historically that was a misnomer. It was a modern construct, which ought by rights to have been called after its inventor, but 'Telemark' was unarguably a better brand name. In any case, it is to Fritz Huitfeldt that we owe the first modern ski, the first modern binding and the birth of mass production in ski making. He was one of the architects of skiing as we know it.

# 17

# The Rise of Ski Touring and the Misadventures of Roald Amundsen

While equipment advanced, ski touring, inspired by Nansen, did so too. His crossing of Greenland triggered its popularization. This began in Nordmarka, the as-yet unspoiled skiing hinterland of Christiania. The size of an English county Nordmarka, with its high, protected, rolling terrain, running down to the city, meant touring on the doorstep. It had long attracted pioneers; it was now interleaved with an urban population in a way found nowhere else outside Scandinavia. Here was the cradle of modern Nordic skiing, with its blend of man-made infrastructure and contact with the natural world.

It owed much to the Ernst Bjerknes who had so notably recorded an early ski-jumper's lot. In 1887, at the age of 22 he qualified as an engineer and found himself unemployed. 'To have something with which to occupy myself', as he put it, 'I decided to produce a map of Nordmarka, on which I would mark all known ski tracks.'[1]

Nordmarka was many things. It was part mountain farmland, part untamed heath, part undulating woodland dotted with lakes. Within living memory wolves had padded between the trees. It was no conifer jungle but rather a working forest. With undergrowth cleared and managed space, it was a natural skiing nursery. Ski tracks sometimes followed logging roads, paths and cattle runs. Nothing, however, was signposted; everything was stored in memory and tradition. Skiing had grown out of the landscape. In his own words, Bjerknes

> went on a journey of exploration in Nordmarka. I carried on all summer and long into the autumn. [I went] through undergrowth and bogs, after all it was winter tracks that I was looking for. I asked about ski tracks [everywhere], and gradually I drew the red lines on the map.

It came on the market in the winter of 1889 as Nansen fever broke out – and luckily so. Bjerknes had to publish the map himself, and sold it on subscription. The customers flocked round. Without Nansen, the map might not have appeared.

Like most things, it had a precursor. The oldest known example of its kind in fact dates from 1761. It was drawn by Captain C. W. Klüwer for Norwegian ski troops in the province of Trøndelag. Bjerknes's skiing map, however, was the first in the modern sense. His innovation was to grade difficulty. In the violently undulating terrain of a homely *terra incognita*, skiers would not know what perils the next downhill run might hold. The Bjerknes map – with luck – gave the answer. Menacing turns and schusses were shaded red. Really steep slopes were picked out with three thick transverse red bars, gentler ones with two. This is the origin of the colour coding of ski runs today.

In Nansen's wake, Bjerknes typified the skiing popularizer that followed the generation of pioneers. His father, Jakob Bjerknes the elder, was a university professor and, in his own field of theoretical physics, a pioneer too. Nansen had an aristocratic lineage. Thomas Heftye, one of those who made the first skiing traverse of Jotunheimen, had inherited a bank. In a word, they belonged to officialdom, the professional classes and the mercantile patricians of the cities, with leisure or money, or both – and they still constituted an elite.

The same held, more or less, for the first wave of skiers to spill over Nordmarka. They were mostly middle class. They lived closest to the skiing grounds, in the fashionable western districts of Christiania, which led some wit to dub their progress 'How the West was won.' One goad was the ever-present search for independence from Sweden, and an inchoate fear of strife. This encouraged activities related to defence. Rifle practice was one; skiing was another. So ski touring could thank the threat of war for some of its advance.

In the end, however, that depended on a few single-minded zealots. One such now appeared. He was Laurentius Urdahl, the prophet of mountain touring. Born in 1865, he was dark-haired, of medium height, articulate and stern of aspect but hiding a droll sense of humour. He was in one way a romantic. He personified the urge to flee from expanding cities that led to the cult of the great outdoors.

From another point of view, Urdahl was severely practical. After leaving school he then became a journalist. In 1885, at the age of 20, he helped to found the first football club in Norway. Sport and the open air were his great interests. He was a determined cyclist. Skiing, however, was his ruling passion. He was a sufficiently good ski racer to run at Huseby in 1888, coming nineteenth in the 25 km cross-country event. He also ran for Norway in the 30 km race at the first international event in Stockholm in 1892. Nonetheless, his true vocation was mountain touring in unfrequented paths.

His nursery was Nordmarka. Where other pioneers stayed in farms and huts, Urdahl would sleep out in any amount of frost. Equipment was his obsession. Nothing was ready-made. He had to try things out himself. Polar explorers, even Nansen, gave only partial guidance because they had helpers and hauled sledges with their loads. Urdahl, as became a skier, wanted speed, rhythm and unencumbered gait at almost any cost. That meant carrying everything on his back. The frame rucksack had not yet been invented and lightweight, down-filled cold-weather gear was still unknown.

Urdahl took the polar explorer's sleeping bag of reindeer fur, which, slung over his shoulder, with food and equipment rolled up inside, also served as a rucksack. Reindeer fur was warm and relatively light, but it was bulky so that Urdahl with his awkward load looked like a snail with a cylindrical shell. That silhouette became his hallmark. He never took a tent, or bothered about digging himself in but simply spread out his sleeping bag on the surface of the snow. He did the same when he graduated from Nordmarka to the wilder surroundings of the western mountains. He was a pioneer of classic ski touring, carrying everything on his back. It was the extreme skiing of the age.

On that account, Urdahl had difficulty finding companions. He was reduced to advertising for one and sometimes had to go alone, although he recognized the risks. The ski resort was as yet unknown. In Norway, even the approach to the mountains for the city dweller was still a little enterprise and, once there, he was something like an explorer, having to manage on his own. Urdahl eventually found a kindred spirit in a medical student called Bredo Berg and together they pioneered various skiing routes. One was the first winter ascent of Gausta, the highest mountain in southern Norway. Its altitude was only 2,000 m, insignificant by Alpine standards but latitude more than compensated – these mountains were 700 miles nearer the North Pole. 'We felt what winter weather really meant', as Urdahl characteristically put it, 'and how powerless a human insect is when faced with the overwhelming forces of Nature.'[2]

That was in 1889, during the second bid to climb Gausta, the first having been made the year before. Urdahl and Berg finally succeeded at the third attempt, on 28 December 1890. Climbing the approaches, they met some ptarmigan hunters on skis tending their traps. 'If we were surprised at this unexpected encounter', said Urdahl, the hunters

> were not less so – And we did look strange! – Grey skiing clothes with scarf and cap hiding nearly our whole faces to keep out the bitter cold; and in addition there was our huge reindeer fur sleeping bag ... so it did not surprise me in the least that the poor hunters doubtless considered us supernatural or infernal; they never imagined that they would meet city dwellers in the deserted mountain fastness at dawn during Christmas, miles from the nearest habitation.[3]

So rare was a mountain skier still, and such the residual force of myth lurking in isolated countryfolk. More rationally, they considered city dwellers who skied in the mountains for pleasure as insane. Urdahl's hunters 'scattered to the four winds', as he put it

> and hastily disappeared down the mountainside ... We followed, and managed to overtake two of them, a young boy and his father, who could not get away fast enough. They looked terrified when the 'demons' caught up with them, but we were soon able to reassure them and show that we were Christian people after all.[4]

Climbing Gausta was only the hors d'oeuvre, as it were. Thereafter, Urdahl and Berg skied northwards, dipping in and out of valleys, to Jotunheimen, which, with various little setbacks such as bitter cold and playful thaws, they proceeded to traverse. They finally returned to Christiania on 20 January 1891, having been absent for a month and covered nearly 1,000 km. It was another pioneering effort, but for Urdahl it was not enough. At heart a crusader, his mission was to turn skiing into a safe popular sport. He found Nansen's influence dichotomous. On the one hand, the crossing of Greenland enticed people into the snows without understanding the risks; on the other, it was a catalyst for technical development. Single-handedly, Urdahl set out to deal with both.

Television lay several generations in the future, so he could not reach his audience with a neat little open-air production. Public meetings were the only medium of instant impact. In December 1890, Urdahl organized his first one, at a Christiania hotel. Experts were on the bill. Entrance was free. An audience of nearly 200 had assembled. They were a good proportion of the mountain skiers in Christiania at the time.

Urdahl was concerned that most skiers went touring between Christmas and New Year. In the deserted uplands, this was the cruellest time, as he had every reason to know. Daylight was short – six hours at most – with much frost and capricious weather and snow. The opening speaker, Dr Oscar Nissen, another pioneer, proposed February or March instead. This was however, the era before statutory holidays, and skiers could only take time off in midwinter. Given that, they had to be taught how to take care of themselves.

Nissen advocated good equipment, an axe in particular. This was, as he blandly put it, 'for hacking away the ice in front of the doors when one wants to spend the night in uninhabited huts'.[5] This was a delicate way of hinting that one had to be prepared to break into shelters open only in summer. The winter season did not yet exist. Early ski touring from hut to hut was based on the felony of breaking in, as Nissen, in everyday life a highly respectable citizen, a prominent Christiania gynaecologist and zealous teetotaller to boot, was happy to admit. To be fair, miscreants like him usually sought the owners afterwards and paid the bill.

Urdahl lectured on skis and bindings and gave a neat summary of contemporary equipment. Skis were still made out of solid wood and those intended for the rough conditions of mountain touring had to be stronger than normal ones. Pine skis wore out too quickly. Hickory, being most resistant to wear, was occasionally tried, but it was still scarce, and skiers stuck to the familiar ash.

Cold-weather clothing also concerned Urdahl. He advocated fur outer garments. At a second meeting soon after, Nansen appeared, and begged to differ. Furs, he said, were too warm. That conveyed the dilemma of the Nordic skier. When he stood still he froze but, while actually moving, such was his exertion that overheating was the problem – not cold.

Urdahl continued his soirées for a year or two. Mountain huts belonging to the Norwegian Tourist Association were now being legally opened in winter. The spread of mountain skiing from an elite had begun. On 13 December 1892, for the third successive year, there was another meeting in Christiania with another packed house. The star turn was the seminal figure of Nansen himself. Even more than the earlier ones, this meeting was not so much a seminar but an evangelical rally. Skiing was turning into a way of life.[6] It was a metaphor of escape. The drive to get out was part of the national psyche. It was epitomized by the mountain skier as he hurried off from his urban alienation on his own internal flight from workaday reality.

Nansen began by repenting the sins of his youth. 'Skiing was turning into an acrobatic exercise', declared that old ski-jumper. 'He who did the greatest aerial leap was best.' The real accomplishment was moving over natural terrain as quickly as possible. Despite having used the Telemark form of ski on the crossing of Greenland, he now turned against it. It suited ski-jumpers, beginners and children, but definitely not the mountain skier or the explorer. Its short length and smooth sole meant that it yawed from side to side on hard snow. For mountain touring and polar exploration, Nansen advocated the longer Selbu model with a deep, broad groove and parallel sides. It was harder to turn but, in his own words 'the purpose of the ski was not to turn, and up in the mountains, there was less need.' The skier ... ought not to arrange his route so that turning was everlastingly required.'

Nansen, as usual, was swimming against the tide. The polemics flowed and he brought down the wrath of other skiers on his head. What particularly enraged his opponents, was Nansen's high-flown praise for the Finnish form of ski. By contrast with the Telemark model, this had parallel sides, like the Selbu type, or was even broadest in the middle, with a narrow tip and always had a groove. Nansen hardly mollified his compatriots when citing as proof of his contention the Norwegian defeat by the Finns the previous winter in Stockholm. His point was that standardization, whether round the Telemark or any other form meant compromise, and compromise, as everyone knew, was an abomination. It was best to use different ski for different circumstances.

Urdahl had by now bowed out of organizing the event, leaving it in other hands. For one thing, this kind of forum had served its purpose by spreading technical knowledge to an influential circle. Urdahl was now concerned with the invasion of what he called 'sporting madness'.[8] Foreign countries, he wrote in an impassioned article about this time, 'are setting us a bad example'. He wanted to 'issue a serious warning before unhappy effects arise, and not only bring ... sport into disrepute, but act in a personally destructive way on many of its devotees'.

He cited a string of examples, from a hill race in Bayonne, in France, to a horse race from Vienna to Berlin; exemplifying cruelty to men in the one case and animals in the other.

Records must be broken, and big prizes won ... The competitive mania of youth is fired by the thought of ... gold medals and clinking coins that await them at the finishing line. Newspapers run column after column about their virtues, and the prospect of breaking world records and becoming champion has unbalanced more than one sportsman. Something nervous and unnatural has appeared; everything depends on tenths of a second.

Skiing, so far, had been least affected. Even there, however, Urdahl detected signs of 'sporting mania', whether it was trying to break records in ski-jumping, setting dangerous courses in cross-country racing, or taking mountain tours to extremes.

> We must specially take care of skiing, which has such great significance for our people, not only as a practical accomplishment, but as strengthening and uplifting both for body and soul ... let us therefore agree to banish the sporting fever which is in the process of pouring over us from abroad. It is bringing us nothing beneficial.

In this purism, the example of Nansen could be detected. At any rate, Urdahl found all these baneful impulses a distraction from his own mountain skiing. On 15 December 1892, just after the Christiania meeting, he set off alone to ski across the deserted winter upland of Hardangervidda. It was his first attempt and, unlike others, he succeeded; starting from east to west and then back again. His published account, featuring the usual hazards of a deserted landscape swept by snowstorm and frost, was becoming familiar in the genre. One day he was battling against a temperature of −30°C. and a biting wind when

> the steel plate by which the toestrap is attached to the ski broke – I don't use a [transverse] hole for the strap so as to strengthen the ski in the middle. Probably this was due to the cold (if it was not because at the skiers' meeting I had praised my bindings for their exceptional strength.) I was not prepared for such an accident, and had not taken a spare plate. Therefore I could not fix the ski to the foot, and it was hard going.[9]

This had a bearing on Nansen's talk at the meeting in Christiania a few days earlier. Nansen had then also touched on bindings. He stated the obvious by distinguishing between those for jumping and others for long tours. He reiterated his opposition to the new-fangled devices streaming on to the market. He wanted unrestricted freedom of movement. He stuck to his old idea of the simple unadulterated device of leather toestrap and heelstrap; with this difference that now he had adopted the Lapps' custom of using untanned hide, because it was weather-proof. 'Iron and steel on a ski are a monstrosity', Nansen proclaimed.[10] 'Screws should quite simply not exist on skis.' That also brought the fury of critics down on his head.

Fritz Huitfeldt was even then close to launching his revolutionary system, of which Urdahl's device was clearly another predecessor. In this instance Nansen was turning his back on the fertile innovation that characterized the age. By his sweeping generalization, he seemed to show once more how the fractured personality could combine great originality in one sphere with retrogression in another.

Things were not so simple, however. Urdahl's experience gave force to Nansen's reservations. New technology was all every well but it had to be thoroughly tried out before it could be trusted away from civilization, when mechanical failure could be a matter of life and death. At the very least, metallurgy had been shown still to be defective at low temperatures. For the moment, sticking to ancient, proven ways best ensured survival.

When Nansen talked about equipment, it was *ex cathedra*, as the man who had first skied across Greenland. By a neat little irony, he dealt with the Christiania firm in which Fritz Huitfeldt was one of the partners. Besides his binding, Huitfeldt was even then developing what became the standard Telemark ski. Consumed with opinionated verve as he was, he knew when to hold his tongue and did so now. For all his prejudice, Nansen was the colossus that had sparked the advance of skiing. He had profoundly affected the milieu of Nordmarka, from which he, as a skier, had sprung.

Despite Nansen's example, although numbers had increased, ski touring was still the pursuit of a minority. Railway building had stagnated, so the mountains remained closed to the crowds. From railhead and quayside, the mountain skier had to make the approach by horse-drawn transport or on foot.

In summer, as a refuge from the first ripples of mass tourism, Norway attracted to its fjords and hinterland a fairly select kind of visitor, from the very Kaiser Wilhelm II of Germany, to upper-class English anglers fishing the salmon rivers, and august members of that very English institution, the Alpine Club. In winter, a domestic Norwegian skiing elite took over. Sturdy yet lithe figures in coarse-cloth knee breeches, they had the uplands to themselves. Urdahl was one of the better known.

At least with ski touring now fixed in the public consciousness, no longer did he have to advertise for companions. Indeed he now had thrust upon him the rôle of individual mentor. His acolyte was a certain medical student called Roald Amundsen.

Amundsen, like others, had played Nansen crossing Greenland on the ski tracks near his home but at some point crossed the line between make-believe and reality. Such men are dangerous because they have the gift of acting out their dreams. Amundsen had decided to become a polar explorer himself. To him, the ski was obviously the key to success. He had to begin, therefore by training as a mountain skier, because that was like a nursery of polar exploration. Urdahl seemed the answer. He had written about his own mountain tours in the Press. His articles were full of journalistic bravura. They were given the front-page spread of climbs on Everest or polar expeditions in another epoch. Under the circumstances, they were after all tales of discovery too. One passage, from Urdahl's second attempt on Gausta in 1889, would have struck a chord:

> Last year we had an extremely exhausting [ski] tour ... It might seem strange to many people that despite the difficulties one is compelled to undergo on a mountain ski tour, we started off again ...
>
> And yet the mountains exert such a force of attraction, that we have no peace at home. As winter approaches, the longing becomes stronger and stronger, we can see the mountains before in their wild, white costume, all the familiar summits wave to us ... greetings arrive with the first snowfall, with frost and aurora, until one fine day we make our preparations, and we flee to the unsullied, white regions where we feel so much at ease. Only when we are up on the heights can we breathe freely, and feel the blood course more swiftly in our veins ... Emotions that we do not understand rise in our breast ... Nonetheless it is not this alone that irresistibly attracts us. We also have other motives

for our mountain tours in winter. Skiing seems to us the best and most uplifting of all sports. Is there any more dashing sight than a fast skier flying down a slope fearlessly, and with erect posture, lithely ... overcoming hummocks and dips.[11]

Urdahl received many requests to follow him on his ski tours. All were politely declined, until Amundsen appeared. *He* had connections. They were related by marriage. Urdahl agreed to take him on his next excursion so that, as he said, Amundsen 'would be initiated into the mysteries of the high mountains in midwinter'.[12]

It was now the autumn of 1893. As his experience hitherto in Nordmarka had shown, Amundsen was not a particularly good skier. Surrounded by many better ones, he felt humiliated. This was one of the factors goading him on his way.

Amundsen, born in 1872, was 21. Urdahl was seven years older and felt responsible for the younger man. He had just been appointed editor of a newspaper in Ålesund on the west coast of Norway. He was to take up the post early in January 1894. Because travel overland was still backward, most connections were by coastal steamer, so he decided to sail from Bergen, which he would reach by crossing Hardangervidda once more on skis. This was the training enterprise that Amundsen was to share.

To make up the numbers, Urdahl took a third companion. He was another relative, a medical student called Vilhelm Holst. Like Amundsen, he too was a novice in mountain skiing. Urdahl saw the proceedings as low comedy. That at least was what emerged from the reportage he published in his newspaper soon after ascending the editorial chair. Holst appeared as 'The Doctor'; Amundsen tellingly as 'Goliath'. He was the tallest of them by far; he also had a huge parrot-like nose, and a temperament which earned the sobriquet.

They left Christiania by train on Christmas Day 1893, reaching the railhead at Krøderen, at the entrance to the valley of Hallingdal, the road to Hardangervidda, in the afternoon. They immediately began skiing, weighed down by the usual bulky reindeer sleeping bag topped with other impedimenta. Among the special clothes to fight the wind and cold, said Urdahl, 'we particularly put our trust in an Anorak (Greenland jacket) of waterproof material'.[13] Applied to skiing, this is one of the earliest examples of the word in print.

Despite their burdens, Urdahl and his companions now skied 16 km westwards and mildly uphill in three hours to a place called Sigdal. There they were hospitably entertained to a seasonal dinner, and the next morning began the first proper climb. 'After the previous ... days' heavy Christmas fare,' wrote Urdahl

we had visibly increased in volume. Now our rounded forms shrank hour by hour and, with great interest ... through his gold-rimmed spectacles, 'The Doctor' observed 'Goliath' who, in the end looked like a bundle of crumpled, wet clothes hanging on a long pole. Thus the poor man struggled to climb up the slopes on his hitherto untested skis. They proved to have bindings that were too big and loose, so that he constantly tumbled head over heels in the snow.

Poor fellow, he had a hard job before winning through to the heights![14]

All three presented a curious aspect with heavy sticks and skis with huge deep curved tips pointing vertically upwards at least a foot above the surface of the snow. From one point of view this suggested the prow of Viking ships; from another a dangerous weapon that could and did injure someone falling forward. Eventually, Urdahl and his companions were faced with a steep descent into the valley of Numedal, glimpsed menacingly between their skis and far below:

> All 'Goliath's' courage justifiably deserted him. As we were setting off, the wind came blowing through the juniper scrub, one of his skis became attached to a branch, and suddenly the poor devil was hanging from the top of a juniper tree the height of a man, and making a fearful fuss as he tried to free himself. He did not succeed, until 'The Doctor' and I had plucked him and all his belongings down, like Christmas presents from the evergreen tree.[15]

That, however 'was not the end of all our troubles', Urdahl went on:

> A little further down the slope, the ski cut through the crust and stopped dead. Neither 'Goliath' nor his sleeping bag were prepared for this. The latter gave a violent lurch and instantly landed on the top of his head, upon which all balance was lost. 'Goliath' performed a magnificent somersault, and disappeared head first into the depths of the snow, leaving only legs and skis visible.
>
> 'The Doctor' and I were frightened to death. We could not know whether our poor friend had killed himself on the spot, or whether there still was a spark of life in him deep down below the surface of the earth. Quite horrified we rushed over, and started digging him out. But then his legs began to wave. His skis were still fixed to his feet, and now flapped like the vanes of a windmill, so that we were afraid that he would decapitate us. Luckily 'The Doctor' did not lose his head. He grabbed the giant's flailing legs and held them still, while I dug him out. When he emerged once more into the light of day, it turned out that he had not lost his head either; only his nose had lost a few pieces of skin. 'The Doctor' immediately covered it with sticking plaster.

And so it went on, with Amundsen somehow always the hero of some ludicrous mishap. Urdahl, by his own account, had overestimated Amundsen's ability. Also he admitted that the route he had chosen, with steep climbs and downhill runs 'was not exactly ... for beginners'.[16]

In the background, demonic winter weather raged over wild terrain, with the usual blizzards, unpredictable skiing, forced bivouacs and wildly fluctuating temperature from thirty degrees of frost to arbitrary thaws. In fact, the going was so poor and the delays so great that Urdahl finally had to turn back and go to Ålesund by another route so that he could start his new job in time. Holst and Amundsen were left to carry on alone but they could not prevail against the elements. They too had to turn round and head for home without crossing Hardangervidda. Holst took the result with equanimity; Amundsen less so.

At the time, Amundsen did not himself see the humour of his predicament, like a Don Quixote of the snows, with Holst his Sancho Panza. However, he forgave Urdahl because of a certain even-handedness. Thus at a wooded slope, Urdahl described how

> the forest was thick ... 'The Doctor' was very short-sighted, and before he knew what was happening, he ran straight into a little pine tree with a leg on each side, and flung his arms affectionately round it, while his cap fell off. The pine tree trembled only a little at this unexpected embrace, and discharged a whole cascade of snow down on to the poor man's reverentially bared head ... We other two laughed until we had tears in our eyes.[17]

That at least was also a joke in retrospect. Amundsen showed his appreciation by spontaneously writing Urdahl a long letter about his next ski tour. It was two years later. Amundsen's companion was now his elder brother Leon. Urdahl, meanwhile had left Ålesund, and was now the editor of a provincial newspaper in Frederikstad, a town south of Christiania on the east side of the Christiania Fjord. Amundsen had hoped to accomplish the now legendary winter crossing of Hardangervidda, which had defeated him in 1894. He and Leon left Christiania on 3 January 1896. Urdahl published his letter unedited and uncut. It was spread over six generous instalments. It was one more addition to the now established genre of the ski tour as a newspaper feature.

It was rather different from the first clownish antics with Urdahl; at least in the telling. Amundsen faltered, but did not repeat old mistakes. He detailed his meticulous planning which, except for '10 [stamped] penny post cards'[18] read like a minor polar expedition. Hardangervidda was a fitting simulacrum of Arctic and Antarctic. At an altitude of 600 m, it was naked and exposed, its only vegetation being scrub and lichen and subarctic plants. Visited in summer by both hunters and tourists, in winter the plateau was still uninhabited. Without natural protection it was prey to the weather driving in from the North Atlantic. Wind-gouged hummocks told the tale of blizzards sweeping over the treeless expanses of unrelieved snow with a fickleness worse than the polar regions, compounded by the eerie sense of human habitation since prehistoric times, when the first men visited the heights from the coastal strips where they were clinging to existence.

Amundsen allowed himself a purple passage or two. Thus after one of the storms that dogged him along the way, 'We saw a sunrise, so beautiful that we will not forget it for a long time', he wrote to Urdahl.

> The plateau lay calm and quietly. It was resting after the effort of yesterday, and gathered new strength for another attack.
>
> How fantastically beautiful is ... Nature, even if it only consists of snow and ice! The sun rose up in purple-red tints, and coloured the tops of the endless hillocks gold. It was a wild landscape that lay before us, but you would have to search far and wide for one that was more beautiful.

This is a typical specimen of the deistic nature-worship that informed the early ski tourers, and survives among their Scandinavian descendants still. It was written in the glow of retrospection. Whether such philosophy actually helped at the time was another matter altogether. Amundsen and his brother found themselves aimlessly wandering about the plateau, unable to reconcile compass with map, sleeping out in the snow, battered by cold and storms. Amundsen detailed the classic pitfalls of skiing over unknown territory in poor light:

> We had to run down a short, gentle slope – as it seemed to us, at any rate – when [Leon], a few ski's lengths ahead of me [suddenly] disappeared.
>
> I stopped immediately. [Leon] had gone over a cliff about 60 ft. high. That he had not smashed arms, legs, ski and sticks was surprising. How ever, he had landed on his sleeping bag, and that was what had broken the fall.

And the next worst thing that can happen to a skier – a sudden unexpected thaw: 'It is heavy going in dry drift snow [said Amundsen], but my goodness wet, sticky snow is worse. You have a mass of snow balling up under the skis, which you avoid in drift snow.'

Amundsen and his brother never finished the crossing. They had to turn back and go home. In an editorial footnote, Urdahl praised Amundsen's 'usual unpretentious style':

> They were lost in the storm-swept mountains for 8 1/2 days, and for 3 1/2 days they were completely without food, whilst at the same time they had to cope with great exertion.
>
> To those who read the report, it seems as if the tour has been a trifle for Herr Amundsen. He does not even mention the ugly frostbite which he and his brother sustained ... and which threatened amputation of fingers for weeks afterwards. But Amundsen is a great figure, with a little of the old Norwegian Viking ... next winter, if we are not mistaken, he proposes to make another attempt to cross Hardangervidda.

In fact, Amundsen never did so. Hardangervidda remained for him the demon that he could not overcome but only circumvent. In later years, Urdahl wrote that 'at home [Amundsen] had already learned what blizzard and frost meant'. Less crassly, Amundsen had committed his beginner's follies where they would not be fatal.

Urdahl could take some of the credit. He was the born pioneer, the forerunner fated to live in the shadow of great men. He was unconcerned. Amundsen's misadventures advanced his ambition, to propagate ski touring. Urdahl was after all by nature a propagandist. In 1893 he published a textbook, *Haandbog i Skiløbning – Handbook of Skiing*. This was the first modern Norwegian work of its kind, although not the first Nordic one. A Finnish equivalent, *Hiihtourheilu Suomessa – Skiing in Finland –* by Hugh Rich. Sandberg, preceded it in 1891. Even earlier was a section on skiing by E. Collinder, another pioneer, in a Swedish sporting encyclopaedia that appeared in 1888. Collinder had written the first skiing instructional text and Sandberg the first manual in the world.

All three pointed to the advance of skiing as a sport in Fennoscandia. Both Collinder and Sandberg, despite their common ancient heritage, held up Norway as the example. 'Certainly men have not acquired the means of flying as soon as they put skis under their feet', so Sandberg waspishly wrote.[19] 'But neither ought we to display fear when running downhill, since manliness is one of the Finn's natural gifts.'

Then followed an uplifting tale. Sandberg was in northern Finland during Lent, the great local skiing season, when he came upon a lonely farm in the endless pine forest.

> what do I glimpse among the trees? … children skiing down a slope … An emaciated little boy in the brood … stood, sunk deep in the snow, awaiting his turn [for] the family's common skis, since there were only two [pairs] while the simple dwelling was full of children. [When] it was finally his turn, and he waded out of the snowdrift on to the skis, I immediately saw that he had bare feet … This insignificant detail … did not seem to bother him much. He quickly arranged his skis, and sped down the slope, laughing … Afterwards he climbed back up the slope on his skis, and quickly ran home, happy with his speed.

As in Norway, skiing here was used to promote a national virtue. In this case it was *sisu*, an untranslatable word, meaning roughly illimitable stamina from the inner being, held to be the great Finnish quality.

The Swedish and Finnish titles were adequate surveys of contemporary skiing. So was Urdahl's book; but something more as well. It was both historical and didactic. It was an attempt at a primer for beginners, and the first of its kind. Those who do things naturally, however, are not necessarily good teachers. Norwegians simply expected pupils to copy their masters by the light of Nature. Urdahl saw the difficulty, and tried to rectify the situation. Unfortunately dispassionate analysis was not his strong point. He wrote with verve. Unashamed propaganda was more his style. 'Skiing [is] our most wonderful and spirited winter sport', as he put it.[20]

> Can one imagine anything more wonderful than speeding through a forest decked out with snow on a cold, clear winter's day? … There's the real winter for you! – Something for all ages and both sexes … Father is up in the mountains with his lively sons, and sometimes Mother is out on the slopes with her daughters. That particularly skiing has made such enormous headway among young ladies, is of greater significance than most people suspect.

Urdahl himself was in part the cause.

# 18

# As Important as the Plays of Ibsen

In 1891, Urdahl invited women to run in the annual championships of the Asker Ski Club on the western outskirts of Christiania. This was almost to have broken a taboo, for ski racing was still virtually a male preserve. Urdahl was an impenitent reformer. Besides, he was both chairman and founder of the club.

It was the breakthrough of women's ski racing. The date was 1 March 1891. The winner was a local girl called Hanna Aars. Her recollection of that day was still vivid after 40 years:

> Ladies' ski races were then something new, and my parents were not quite sure that such a public appearance could be reconciled with 'real womanliness'. But I managed to wheedle permission, and one brilliant winter's day skied off five kilometres to the race.
>
> It was terribly exciting to stand at the top of the slope with a number on my breast and wait for the starting signal. Everywhere it was full of spectators, and amongst them was Prince Carl himself. Luckily I managed all three runs.[1]

The course was the outrun of the men's jump, so it was a kind of downhill race. Prince Carl was a younger son of King Oscar; affable and a skier, he enhanced the tradition of skiing as a royal sport. 'The prizegiving took place immediately after the race', continued Hanna:

> and the Prince stood there, tall and handsome, and presented the prizes with his own hands. I was not a little proud when I had to go forward on my skis to receive my 1st prize – a lovely brooch in gold with the prince's name. I had a smile and a handshake into the bargain, and curtsied as well as I could on my skis.
>
> And so I wended my way homeward. Naturally there was great pleasure and excitement. And I was teased for a long time afterwards because I did not wash my right hand for 8 days in order to preserve the prince's handshake as long as possible.

As well she might. It was a historic occasion, and young Hanna Aars was a historic figure. There had naturally been precursors. The first documented ski race in the world *officially* open to women was run at Skedsmo, near Christiania on 27 February 1870. The course was also a short downhill run. None of the entrants were deemed worthy of a prize. The next recorded event was in 1879 at the Bellevue races in Stockholm, where what one journalist dismissed as 'a pair of females' also took part.[2] In both cases, anonymity ruled. Hanna Aars was the first named women's champion.

The Asker race was distinguished in several ways. For one thing, entries were invited from other districts too. It was the first representative women's ski race. The women ran in a separate class. It became an annual fixture, with imitators soon following in its path. That event of 1891 was the origin of modern women's ski racing as we know it.

The distinction between male and female skiers is comparatively recent. After all, in the eighteenth century men and women were still considered equal in the snow. Even in the early nineteenth century, when the roads were impassable, both men and women travelled on skis, mothers often with their unweaned babies on their backs. So in the country at any rate, there was hardly sex discrimination in the snow. Ski racing did continue as the prerogative of men, although in the self-effacing Ingrid Vestbyen, Hanna Aars had a forerunner almost 30 years before. Prejudice belonged to the later nineteenth century and was mainly urban. The enemies of women on skis were not men, but women themselves. Urdahl put it in these words:

> While both men and women practised skiing in olden times … when the sport was revived in the towns, it turned out that … with few exceptions it was only men and boys who practised skiing. Mothers decided that it was unwomanly for their daughters to practise that wonderful sport; it was suited only to men.[3]

Skating, on the other hand, was permitted. It was thought to be ladylike. What Urdahl – one of the feminists' male accomplices – called the 'high-handed viewpoint' of Christiania matrons 'was soon rejected'.[4]

> Certain younger ladies and little girls practised skiing in secret, and one fine winter's day, in the surroundings of Christiania, a whole crowd of woman skiers could be observed, smartly running down the slopes. Rosy cheeks, shining eyes, health and strength were the reward for their breach of 'refinement', as many a prim, narrow-minded mother called it.

The significance of all this went far beyond the slopes. Skiing belonged to the armoury of female emancipation. When Norwegian women achieved the suffrage in 1913, among the first in the world, it was arguably due to the ski that it happened so painlessly and so soon.

None of this, of course was happening in a vacuum. The year 1879, that of the first Huseby races, also saw the international breakthrough of another famous Telemarking, Henrik Ibsen, with the first performance – in Copenhagen – of *A Doll's House*. Its central character Nora, the disillusioned wife who leaves husband and children to start a new life, became the first modern female rôle, much sought after by great actresses. The shock waves decisively advanced the cause of female emancipation.

In Norway, skiing also played a part. It did at least as much as the plays of Ibsen – where there are few heroes, but often heroines. The ski track was the one refuge for women to break away from their menfolk, do something on their own and play Nora for an afternoon.

By the same token, skiing gave an innocuous outlet for family rebellion. The forests and open country lapping at the outskirts of the towns hid daughters doing their worst against parental disapproval on skis, which thereby became a metaphor of liberation.

One result was that women's ski clubs began to appear. In the face of family displeasure, they led an ephemeral and clandestine existence. The earliest documented example was in 1886, in Trondheim. It featured in a talk by a certain Antonie Løchen. She was a campaigner for women's rights, showing more concern, however, for female prudery than male domination. 'When [the] ski club was formed', Mrs Løchen said

> I heard a young lady mention it. She shook her head. I could clearly discern that it struck her as a little unwomanly ... Everything that one is used to seeing women do is called womanly, and everything new, that they are not accustomed to doing, is called unwomanly until – one has grown used to it ... Let us see how long it will take before skiing is just as womanly a sport as skating.[5]

It was not long. The first all-woman ski club to come out of the shadows and openly declare its existence was founded in March 1889 at Steinkjær, at the head of the austere fjord north of Trondheim. This was the first of its kind in the world. The club was an outgrowth of a highly respectable sewing circle. The members made their own colourful, skiing costumes – probably the first known specialized ski wear. They wanted to call their club Skade, after the old Norse goddess of skiing. One maiden lady, with humour, unconscious or otherwise, objected on the grounds that Skade's reputation 'was by no means unblemished. She was married to Njord, but nonetheless had a son with Odin, and even if it was a great honour in [my] opinion the story [is] indelicate.'[6] The objection was thrown out and Skade it remained. The purpose of the club was social as much as anything else. A hive of virulent feminism it was not. Disarmingly, it held night-time forest ski tours with spluttering torches, to which gentlemen of the place were invited.

Skade appeared in the heady, liberating aftermath of Nansen's crossing of Greenland. That same year, for the first time a man's ski club admitted women as members. This was in the capital; the club was Christiania Skiløberforening or 'Christiania Skiers' Association'. Asker followed in due course. Even there it stood out by being the first ski club with a woman official. She was the treasurer, who happened to be Urdahl's sister, Emma. She struck a whimsical blow for equality by extracting money from the gentlemen to buy a Ladies' Cup for the men's race and, *mutatis mutandis*, a Gentlemen's Cup for the women.

Towards the end of the 1880s, women had started ski touring. The first on record was probably in 1888, when two ladies crossed from Steinkjær to Namsos, in central Norway, a good 60 km.[7] Around Christiania, as Urdahl himself observed, they were skiing through Nordmarka in force. In December 1889, that well-known dogmatist, Axel Huitfeldt, reproved the monstrous regiment. 'A long and penetrating scream runs through you to the marrow of your bones', he wrote in a magazine article:[8]

> An accident … to the rescue! But the next instant, the scream is interrupted by shrill laughter, then a couple of squeals, and when you arrive, you find a couple of ladies lying helplessly in the snow in the last spasms of laughter and screech … Good Heavens, ladies, why must you howl and scream and whine and cackle with laughter if you tumble on a ski slope … If you only realised how disagreeable and unwomanly it seems, and how you tear asunder the harmony of Nature.

Huitfeldt was not complaining about women on the ski track *in principle*. He only wanted to save them from their excesses. He was actually writing in a feminist journal called *Nylænde*. He had sage advice on dress: 'petticoats may reach a little below the knee, but not much longer … wide-waisted dress. If it is made of thick material, no jacket is required. [Underneath] a pair of trousers made of thick woollen material.' Above all: 'Away with corset and bustle. Is there anything as ridiculous as a lady on skis with a thick bundle on one side a little below the back, because I have never seen any lady on skis with one in the middle.'

The appeal to throw the corset overboard was another sign of the times. It showed that Huitfeldt's heart was in the right place. To those working for women's liberation, the corset, with its tight lacing and suffocating stays, in the pursuit of an artificial figure as a feminine ideal, was an instrument of subjection. There was a crusade against it that cut across the sexes. Huitfeldt, in his idiosyncratic way, was simply following the trend; or perhaps he preferred a natural figure in his womenfolk.

Urdahl joined the campaign. In his textbook, he warned his female readers that 'if you wear this "means of stiffening", you will not benefit from any of your skiing'.[9] One of the illustrations shows a man sternly climbing up a slope, and looking back with envy overlying a flicker of lust at a girl whizzing down, as Nature made her, definitely uncorseted, skirts cut conventionally well below the knees, but billowing untrammelled in the rush of air to reveal glimpses of her ankles veiled by snow kicked up by her skis, and on her face an inscrutable expression.

The corset was only one aspect of a campaign for female dress reform in the 1890s. Skiing accelerated it, demanding, as it did, untrammelled movement. Inspiration came partly from Victorian Englishwomen who visited Norway in summer to climb or fish and characteristically flouted convention, once safely abroad. For their part, Norwegian women originally skied in everyday clothes, with long skirts and voluminous petticoats. Trousers were obviously the ideal but that needed a revolution of sorts.

In 1893, Huitfeldt returned to the attack. His complaint was now the popularization of skiing around Christiania. It had turned into a fad. It had meant overcrowding of a few wide forest tracks with skiers slavishly following each other across country like a teeming horde of ants. This happened also in the dark which, so Huitfeldt wrote in a Christiania newspaper:

> combined with the well developed café life is what seems to have attracted a great number of our skiing ladies … Not infrequently one meets [them] with hip flasks, and personally I have repeatedly heard young ladies at Holmenkollen [restaurant] order 'wee drams'. Indeed I have even observed many skiing ladies who were not quite steady on their feet, and whose behaviour could only be explained in this way … something must be done to stop both the nocturnal canoodling and this tendency to 'wee drams' which our skiing 'ladies' are now exhibiting. [They] bring the sport into disrepute.[10]

Someone else, by contrast, had written earlier about seeing

> a male figure with a torch held high, and 3 ladies in his tracks. In the dark of the night (it was 10 o'clock) they had skied down … the steepest runs with the sharpest turns that the undulating terrain round Christiania can offer … At night, they had run down a track where one of my friends … one of the best skiers … had refused to follow me a few hours earlier because 'he had crashed there once before, and did not want a repetition'.[11]

The party was asked into a nearby hut and, it was also admiringly recorded, 'the dashing ladies … did not refuse a class of beer after the troublesome climb and not less exhausting run down'. Which was the moment of conversion remains unclear, but:

> I had always believed that women on skis were simply a matter of fashion, but now I have completely changed my opinion. I see that they can reach a standard, if not as high as our outstanding ski-jumpers … at least on a level with good male skiers. I now understand that our womenfolk also regard skiing with true affection and practise it seriously.

Someone else published a riposte to Huitfeldt, notably his allegation that some women skied with legs far apart, instead of close together, with unsteadiness as a result. 'It is the snowplough that sends the straddlers falling head over heels', he charitably wrote:[12]

> The army of women that now go skiing are a militia, which has sprung out of the earth almost instantaneously. You cannot expect to find troops among them that are models of style and posture, but they possess an assurance, freshness and strength which many older skiers perhaps had not expected to find in that camp.

All three were simply observing the same phenomenon from different points of view. Huitfeldt had triggered an awkward controversy. As a matter of fact his main concern was the technical decay of skiing in Christiania. This was due to the absence of Telemarkings from the later Huseby, and now the Holmenkollen races. These were not only a sporting fixture but a demonstration of good technique. Since the ski school was hardly known, nor was teaching codified, it was almost the only way to learn. As long as the Telemarkings dominated, standards were more or less assured. However, with the decline in prize money, they abandoned the races in the capital. Their absence meant that few remained with the power to inspire by example. Technique regressed. Straddling once more invaded the slopes. The awkward scrape of stick riding once more disturbed the air.

Huitfeldt's grousing reflected a vein of public opinion. He began his next article by quoting from the classified columns of the Christiania press:

> 'A beautiful, lively lady seeks a cultivated, bold [gentleman] skier of good appearance as escort for sports tours …'
> 'YOUNG SPORTING LADIES A businessman, 21 years old, seeks a cultivated young lady for skiing. Photograph and note …'[13]

Lonely Hearts, or Meeting Place, were well known everywhere, but it was in Norway that the ski slopes first became the stage. Once more Huitfeldt showed understanding. 'For generations,' he wrote, women had 'cultivated corsets, dancing, delicate constitutions and anaemia, and then suddenly a complete reversal:'

> Away with the corset! [he repeated.] Undoubtedly that is all to the good, but then such immediate ferocity … Ladies on skis! To me, they are as welcome as flowers in May … but … they are acting with tearaway speed.
> But such is always the case when one has suffered oppression [as] the ladies – Woman – [have]. They cannot be reproached for wishing to make up for lost time. That is really their due, as long as it does not affect themselves … and the coming generations.

This generation was in the first flush of emancipation. In Christiania, it was largely being played out in the snows. Girls were ostentatiously smoking cigarettes on the ski tracks, or the restaurants and huts dotting Nordmarka as an exhibitionist show of independence.

As Huitfeldt had delicately hinted, the winter forest was also a background to sexual liberation. Christiania was still a small provincial town of perhaps 70,000 inhabitants. It had a difficult climate, and when the clammy fog rolled in from the fjord, the clean air of Nordmarka was a nearby means of escape from the dull damp claustrophobic streets. Even the *demi-monde* followed their clients up into the heights. In another piece of pioneering, the ladies of the night had taken to their skis.

Mostly this was concentrated round Christiania, with its charged *fin de siècle* atmosphere of bohemian life and intellectual ferment. Outside the capital, the trends were less extreme. Someone signing herself 'a country skier' wrote to the press in February 1893, echoing Huitfeldt's opinions. She urged 'Christiania's skiing ladies' to replace aquavit with coffee in their hip flasks.[14] She also told them to practise so as to master

> all the temperamental whimsy of skis. You use muscles and tendons you have never strained before … I know how a woman skis, and what she can achieve. I [can] see

immediately why, whether practised or not, she appears on a pair of skis; whether for the sport itself … or to be seen and make gentleman acquaintances.

And: 'You must not scream and screech as much as before. Use … your lungs more sensibly. We look half crazy in our outfits as it is, without making it worse by our behaviour.'

That was a *cri de coeur*. Special skiing outfits were now starting to come on to the market but, given the limitations, were still 'half crazy' as she said. Woman skiers had been liberated from the corset and wore trousers, as authoritatively recommended, but were still required to cover them with a skirt of ankle length. Someone remembered how it 'often had a broad hard frozen edge which lashed us about our legs'.[15] On that account, or otherwise, Eva Nansen, Fridtof Nansen's wife, was one who dared to flout convention.

Like her husband, Eva was a skiing pioneer. In 1892, at Easter, they had crossed Hardangervidda together. Eva was probably the first woman skier to do that particular route. Together they were among the pioneering ski tourers who turned Easter into the great popular festival of spring skiing that it remains in Norway to this day. The first known Easter ski tourers had gone out from Bergen in 1884.

Eva had been skiing since the age of 16. She was born in 1858, and therefore came from the first generation of women skiers to break their bonds. She ignored all convention by skiing through adolescence and into adulthood as the scion of a well-known family. Her father, Michael Sars, was an internationally known marine biologist. Eva herself was a trained concert singer; a mezzo-soprano who had given the first performance of some works by her contemporary, Edvard Grieg.

Music and skiing were Eva's ruling passions, but it was skiing that fixed the direction of her life. Independent to the core, she flouted yet another rule by skiing

30. Norwegian lady skier, 1880s. Probably Eva Nansen. *Author's collection*

in Nordmarka alone, in the dark if need be. She was technically accomplished. Nansen claimed that she was one of the best skiers in Norway.

They had actually met on the ski track. Love in the snow was a new phenomenon. It was yet another aspect of the conjunction of the sexes that was bothering the critics. This was one version of the romantic glow that was beginning to colour the rise of skiing. Marriages were made on the ski track. What the contracting parties turned out to be in the drab light of everyday existence was another matter altogether.

At any rate, for her crossing of Hardangervidda in 1892, Eva audaciously wore a revolutionary skiing outfit. It consisted of a pair of loose trousers, worn under a kind of doublet, like a Lapp women's garment, with a short skirt reaching below the knee. It made skiing easier. Its real defiance was to expose a recognizable portion of the legs. In fact, it was Nansen who, putting his impress on skiing even at one remove, had designed the ensemble. Eva, a willing accomplice, had made it with her own hands out of thick grey wadmel. She would have preferred trousers undisguised but, independent as she was, submitted to a proper pace of change.

On her first public trial of the outfit in Nordmarka, she wrote to Nansen in February 1892, one of their friends 'was quite taken aback at the sight of my immoral skiing costume. He thought that I was a martyr for a good cause and believed that in ten years the ladies would follow my example.'[16]

It took until the 1920s, although the first known woman on skis with trousers

31. Norwegian mountain skier and hunter, 1880s. Evidently Fridtjof Nansen.
*Author's collection*

unadorned actually appeared in 1896. She deserves to be remembered. A 23-year-old Christiania inhabitant called Kristine Drolsum, she was inspired by a lecture on dress reform to sew herself a dark blue skiing outfit of long trousers, with the revolutionary complement of a jacket *above* the knee. It was edged with astrakhan which, hinting at position in society, was perhaps the one unanswerable argument.

Kristine was a private individual and a lone harbinger. It was Eva Nansen who had the public standing to make her opinions heard. In more than one way, Eva was ahead of her times. Physically, she was not the contemporary ideal of the massive feminine voluptuary. Small, neat and dark-haired, she was the forerunner of another age. She had a cool and forbidding exterior, which gave her the attributes of a later fashion model. She thus had the figure and temperament to carry off her husband's creation and make it known to the point of allowing herself to be widely pictured.

As the wife of a world-famous figure, Eva also exploited her position to refute the critics of women skiers in print. Skiing as a new way of life was her theme. 'When I think back' she wrote now in 1893 at the age of 35:

> the many healthgiving tours in ... winter form the brightest and happiest memories that life has given me. They hold the unadulterated beauty of all life and Nature in a lovely indelible image, which has exercised a purifying influence on my spirit, and will continue to do so, and I remember them with gratitude for all the health they have given body and soul.[17]

This is one of the most convincing latter-day professions of faith to come out of the Romantic Nature-worship at the heart of early skiing. 'When I think of this, as I often do,' Eva went on, 'I always have a feeling of happiness at the realisation of how fortunate our young girls are in that respect, and how freely they can now move over forest and field, unhindered by the many prejudices that we had to defy.'

Then came the real attack:

> Can anyone seriously maintain that women become more immoral by skiing, even if together with men? Does anyone believe that the dance halls, streets and cafés of Christiania are morally healthier places for young girls than the forests and open spaces around Christiania? ...
>
> Now that many thousands of women are skiing, it is asking too much that there should not be a number of loose living ones among them. Skiing in particular cannot be expected to be clinically free of such people ... It is just not possible to keep the Demi-Monde away.

Finally, where drinking was concerned, Eva mordantly pointed out that the critics had the cure in their own hands: 'withdrawal of licences' from the restaurants round the popular resorts of Holmenkollen and Frognersæteren.

Eva was reviling double standards. Her name and reputation, together with her arguments – perhaps those of her husband? – abruptly stopped the whole Press debate. Women had more or less acquired equality in skiing, as they were doing in other fields. There was now a feeling that perhaps they were getting the upper hand. Humorists took up the theme. In 1894, a satirical journal printed cartoons of a downtrodden male, forced by his fiancée to ski, although he himself had never done so in his life. 'He was most unfortunate,' ran the caption, and 'so embittered that he immediately broke off his engagement, and from that day onwards, has regarded all skiing ladies with a burning hatred.'[18]

Then in 1896, Asker ski club organized the first national championship for women in name as well as in fact. It followed a men's race and, in the words of one newspaper, was 'of much greater interest'.[19] The men ran a Nordic combined event of a 12 km cross-country race and a jump. The women's fixture was decided on the outrun of the ski-jump, with a small hummock, ending in a reverse slope. It was therefore again a downhill race, to which, it was thought, women were best suited. The field was divided into those who had been confirmed and those who had not. The best in either class were allowed to try the jump as a demonstration. The day was marred by the kind of unseasonal thaw that, in a time of climate change, was becoming all too common.

For the record, the winner, and hence the first women's national champion in the world was Ingeborg Tandberg, and for those not yet confirmed, a certain Solveig Amundsen. As the journalist wrote, the women 'performed to everybody's satisfaction accompanied by roars of applause'. However: 'Ladies ... a piece of advice. Either learn not to fall on your stomach or start wearing "divided scirts" [sic].' They had first appeared in America:

> We are all at heart quite respectable, and we are sometimes disturbed to find a woman on her head with her skirts covering her far up. A pair of fetching legs in grey woollen underpants or tasteful tricot is undoubtedly a splendid sight ... but we believe that the ladies themselves would be better served by saving themselves the fruitless effort of keeping their skirts down, while they sail down a slope. They can avoid all this with 'divided scirts'.

That was a step too far for this skiing milieu. Even Laurentius Urdahl, to whom the championship owed its existence, would probably have been unable to help. Besides, driven by his restless nature, he had already moved on, with the acceptance of women's ski racing already something in his past.

# 19

# The Spread of Skiing on the Continent

Skiing, meanwhile, was long limited to its heartlands. When at last it began to spread, the agents were itinerant Norwegians. This was understandable. Circumstances were driving them out into the world, as in the Viking Age.

Germany was the first country in which the Norwegians demonstrably implanted skiing. There was a prelude with the publication in 1767 of odes to skating by Friedrich Gottlieb Klopstock, a founder of modern German poetry. One passage refers to the 'Norsemen's sky [*sic*]'.[1] 'Sky', Klopstock explained in a footnote, were 'skates, on which one runs on hard snow. They are completely different from those on ice.' The passage runs:

> Von des Normanns Sky. Ihm kleidet die leichte Rinde des Seehund,
> Gebogen steht er darauf und shießt mid der Blitzes Eil
> Die Gebirge herab;
> Arbeidet dann langsam und wieder herauf am Schneefelsen.
> Die blutige Jagd trieft ihm an der Schulter. Allein des Schwung,
> Die Freude, den Tanz der Lehrlinge Tialfs kennet er nicht!
> Ofte schleudert ein Orkan sie, als in Schwindel vor sich her,
> Am vorüberfliegenden Felsgestad' hinab.
> Schnell, wie der Gedanke, schweben sie in weitauskreisenden Wendungen fort,
> Wie im Meere die Riesenschlange sich wälzt.

> With the light pelts of seal, the Norsemen's ski is clad.
> He crouches on it and down the mountainside shoots
> With lightning speed.
> He then walks slowly up again on snow-clad slopes,
> On his shoulder bearing the bloodstained quarry. Only the turn,
> The joy, the dance of Tialf's apprentice he does not know.
> Oft does the storm fling him, giddy, off his feet,
> And down, over the rocky place he flies,
> Quick as a thought, they soar in wide turns,
> As the sea-serpent in the ocean wallows.

The books on old Norse history and literature that were now in circulation must have partly inspired Klopstock. His skiers are hunters and their ski fur lined. With poetic licence, he makes Tialf, Thor's assistant, the god of skiing and of skating too. Nonetheless, questions remain. Where did Klopstock get his intimate knowledge of skiing turns, not to mention the proper 'egg' position when running downhill?

In practice, the German forerunner was GutsMuths. The records of the school at Schnepfenthal, in Thuringia, where he worked, have this entry for 28 January 1795:

> A little while ago Herr GutsMuths received from a stranger a precise description of a kind of snowshoe, generally used by the Norwegian farmers in winter. With this information, he had a pair of such snowshoes made; 6–8 feet long. He made some attempts to walk on them, which were quite successful.[2]

This makes GutsMuths probably the first German to ski. The school's 'stranger' was in all likelihood the same mysterious Norwegian that he mentioned in his book of 1804. The Norwegian influence, however, began in earnest after the Napoleonic wars, with the transfer of Norway to Sweden from Denmark in 1814. One consequence was a flood of Norwegians studying on the continent. It resulted from the same national renaissance of which skiing was a manifestation, combined with want of opportunity at home.

Partly due to the German intellectual and scientific dominance of the age, Germany was the first choice of Norwegians studying abroad. They naturally wanted to ski where they were. The first known instance was someone called H. Müller. In 1851 or 1852, he spent a winter in Danzig, then a Prussian city. In a book published some time later, he surprisingly concluded that the flat strandline of this Baltic port offered good skiing terrain. The prehistoric moraine ridges round Danzig, he wrote, 'sometimes slope gently upwards from the plain, sometimes rise more steeply … or here and there form takeoffs, allowing for the finest jumps'.[3]

The only imponderable was snow of course. This particular winter happened to be a good one, the Baltic obliging with stable weather so that 'all February and some of March were very cold. The snow was deep up on the heights, and the going was splendid.'

> The slopes were enticing. I simply had to have a pair of skis. But where were they to be found in Danzig? I found a carpenter, made drawings, gave him instructions, and stood by him while he worked.

Together they waxed the skis in the traditional way with hot Stockholm tar. A reasonable pair soon emerged and with the practice thus gained a second, better pair was also on the way. Müller took the first pair to try out the snow. 'I dared not carry them myself through the city,' so he said, 'but let someone go ahead with them, and great was the astonishment that the strange objects aroused in all the passers-by.' Outside the city, he put on his skis and, to the open-mouthed amazement of the porter, swept over the snow into the forest. After a pleasant tour, he found an inn up on a hill, deposited his skis, returned to Danzig by road and the following day came out again on the second, improved pair. The innkeeper gleefully had a tale to tell. A local forester had followed the ski tracks with growing puzzlement so that upon arrival 'he had to have two *schnapps*':

> The innkeeper … was much amused by [the forester's] mystification, and did what he could to make it even greater. [The tracks] could not belong to a human being who had dragged something behind, because there were no footprints. It had to be an animal … but what kind? … The innkeeper [suggested] that it must be the tracks of a snake … a sea serpent perhaps [but that] did not pass muster. The whole thing remained a mystery, until finally the innkeeper announced that it really was an animal, that he had caught it, and had it locked up in his shed … The forester was told to observe the greatest care and silence, they approached the [shed] on tiptoe … until finally the innkeeper flung open the door … My first pair of skis … turned out to be the only inhabitants of the shed.

The innkeeper, meanwhile, was intrigued by this strange pastime, and wanted to try it himself. Müller lent him a pair of skis, and he turned out to have an aptitude. 'He quickly advanced to the point where he could run down fairly steep slopes … partly on his skis, partly [leaning] on his stick. For some time he accompanied me on all my ski tours.'

It all ended abruptly when, after a thaw, on an icy slope, the innkeeper fell and dislocated his shoulder. 'Thereafter he stayed behind his counter', as Müller put it, 'and each time I entered, he received me with a most strange expression, half friendly, half annoyed'.

Thus Müller may be said to have brought the modern ski onto continental Europe, with Danzig the improbable venue. The tale is emblematic of how skiing was introduced to Germany.

The process was slow and imperfectly recorded. The next known example was in 1884, when a Norwegian student – hiding behind the initial 'G.' – wrote to a Christiania journal about his skiing in Germany. That was far south of Danzig, at Gera in Thuringia, near Bavaria. In the intervening 30 years not much had changed. G. sent for his skis from Christiania, instead of having them made locally, but at the customs he learned nonetheless 'that skis were an apparatus which had hitherto not been seen in Gera. I had a long conference with the gentlemen before I was allowed to heave my beloved property on my shoulders and toddle home.'[4]

Outside the town he found a reasonable slope, built a jump and impressed the citizenry, who cheered him to the echo. On the other hand, when he struck out into the Thuringian countryside, the peasantry, in his own words, looked at him 'with a an expression that clearly indicated that I was considered … half insane'.

The following year, another part of Germany featured in the published adventures of yet another Norwegian student. Now it was the Harz mountains, near Hanover. 'A keen skier ought always to take his skiing outfit when … staying in North Germany', he wrote.[5] 'A normal winter … offers a Norwegian great opportunities to limber up with that sport which is dearest to him because it is his own.' A pattern was emerging. Again there was the problem of undesired attention:

> Unfortunately I had to drag my overcoat with me … to cover my skiing outfit: light grey trousers, striped woollen shirt, blue jersey jacket with matching mittens, light grey cap with my ski club's badge, not to mention *finnesko* – a costume that would certainly have attracted close attention in the villages down here.

Again there was the enervating climb up deep snow along unprepared tracks – this time redolent of literary associations. The goal was Brocken; the setting for the witches' chorus on Walpurgis night in Goethe's *Faust*. Appropriately or not, this skier – hiding behind the initials 'A. S.' – was rewarded for his climb with a downhill run of fully 10 minutes. Thereafter A. S. went up and down a short slope with an audience of foresters: 'Then I lent [them] my skis, they being very eager to try them. As you might suppose, things turned out unimpressively, the one fall worse than the other, and my skis were returned to me, luckily undamaged.'

Such scenes were played out near many centres of learning and industry. Some Germans had already had their first glimpse of a ski in 1881 at an exhibition of hunting equipment at Cleves. The Norwegian stand included a collection of skis on the principle that the ski was the most national of exportable artefacts.

Around the time of G.'s and A. S.'s promenades, various Germans were independently acquiring skis. Either they imported them from Norway or, more often, had them made by local carpenters. Mostly their purpose was utilitarian. It was among foresters and hunters that skiing first spread in Germany. As a pastime it still hinged on resident Norwegians.

One way or another, skiing was imperceptibly taking root. As in his homeland, Nansen's crossing of Greenland was the turning point. Whereas among his fellow countrymen it was the deed itself, abroad it was his book about the expedition. In 1891, the German translation was published as *Auf Schneeschuhe durch Grönland*. It was not so much the crossing of Greenland itself that had the power to inspire as the chapters on skiing and its history. It was in fact deliberate propaganda, summarized in this well-known passage:

> Is there anything cleaner and healthier than to put on one's skis one fine winter's day, and go off into the forest? Is there anything finer and nobler than our Nordic landscape, when the snow lies feet deep, sprinkled soft and white over mountain and forest? Is there anything more liberating and exciting, than when one shoots down the tree-lined slopes, fast as a bird in flight, while the winter air and pine branches rush past one's cheeks, and eyes, brain and muscles are on the alert, ready to avoid each unexpected obstacle that can appear at any moment? It is as if all civilisation is immediately washed away, and left with the city air, far behind: one somehow grows together with one's ski and the surroundings. It is something that develops not only the body, but the soul as well; it has a deeper significance for a nation than most people realise.[6]

It is enough to explain the stimulus exerted by the book, especially in the German-speaking countries, to which rhetoric of this kind appeals. The development of skiing, notably the founding of clubs, followed the Norwegian model. To their credit, the Germans never denied their historical debt. They freely admitted that it was from Norway that they received the ski and it was to Norway they looked for an example.

This was related to a romantic obsession with the Nordic world, and the old Norse myths as the repository of the Germanic soul, exemplified in the Ring operas of Wagner. On a different plane, German travellers in Norway were not so much concerned with salmon fishing and field sports, like their Victorian English counterparts, as with excogitation on the landscape. For example this passage on Jotunheimen in the 1820s:

> Terrible steep rocky summits ... sweep out ... from the domed covering of snow and ice far below and their dark grey makes a stark contrast to the blazing white beneath them and the clear cerulean blue above, they appear to strive heavenward in unshakeable calm, defying the approaching northern storms, like giant monuments of a buried world.[7]

There was similar effusion in the first German skiing instruction book: 'Sharpening of the senses, promotion of presence of mind, changing the whole nature of a person, whether a polished city dweller or a son of the mountains; all this and much more is due to the [ski]!'[8] The author was Theodor Neumayer, from Munich. The title, in translation, reads 'Practical hints on how to learn snowshoe (ski) running.' This was in fact the first textbook on skiing to be published outside Norway. It appeared in 1893, the same year as Laurentius Urdahl's manual, so they share the palm for the earliest publications of their kind.

Neumayer followed the Norwegian example in concentrating on Nordic skiing. The fact is, most of the terrain in northern and central Germany, with low, rolling hills, mirrored that of Norway round the centres of population. It was simply an extension of familiar country and favoured the domination of Nordic technique.

Consequently the first ski race in Germany, albeit among the foothills of the Alps in Bavaria, was also a Nordic event. It took place at Taubenberg on 25 February 1894. Norwegian students in Munich lay behind the organization and dominated the results. For the record, someone called Birger Kielland won the cross-country race. He also came third in the jump, with a certain Wilhelm Scheel second, and a well-known pioneer, Otto Wium, the winner, to make a clean sweep for the Norwegians.

Another historical pattern was emerging. On the Nordic model, Norwegian students were founding German ski racing. Besides winning, some also acted as instructors. They included some prominent academics. One of them, Johan Kiær, became a palaeontologist of repute.

Norwegians also swept the board in the first German district and national championships; the one in the Harz mountains, the other on the Feldberg in the Black Forest. As a curiosity, the fourth man in the jump at the former event was a

South African, E. Cronin from Pretoria. With a length of 13.24 metres (How did they measure with such accuracy?), he was only 1 metre behind the champion, one Ludvig Manskow. All the prizewinners, however, fell gloriously. The only jumper to remain on his feet was a certain Hans Halvorsen, with a jump of 13.21 metres, which normally would have made him the winner. Either way, it was a Norwegian triumph.

It was, however, not the same easygoing Germany that the early pioneers knew. Since Müller in Danzig, Bismarck had won his 'three lucky wars', including that against France in 1870–1, and had unified the country. It was now the German empire, with Kaiser Wilhelm II on the throne. The fixation with the Nordic world persisted. Norwegians were still admired. The Kaiser took his holidays on his yacht *Hohenzollern* in the Norwegian fjords. A strident nationalism, however, had supervened. It touched everything, however trivial. According to a Christiania newspaper report on the Harz district championship

> As … one trophy after the other made its way into Norwegian hands … the patriotic feeling that we Norwegians were better than the Germans in something reached such a pitch, that the Germans themselves made remarks about excluding Norwegians from the next event.[9]

Before the first race in Bavaria, Otto Wium described another conflict that bedevilled skiing:

> To start with, we had a miserable existence … and everywhere met animosity, because the Bavarian landed gentry were extremely conservative and against anything modern. In the middle of the [eighteen] nineties I led a [ski] tour to Krottenkopf at Christmas together with some Bavarian friends. When we returned to Garmisch-Partenkirchen … we entered an inn near the station, where we were placed next to a table with 'mountain guides', who heaped insults over our heads, and challenged us to fisticuffs. For a long time mountaineering was dominant and deeply antagonistic towards skis.[10]

*Pace* the Harz race most German skiing pioneers, on the other hand, were above petty animosities. In self-defence, they used Norwegian examples. Thus one of them recorded how Bjarne Nilssen (an engineering student in Darmstadt, and later a prominent Norwegian industrialist) won the first German skiing championships:

> and for the first time showed us what skiing really was, whether in cross-country, downhill running, jumping technique and turning.
> I … remember our astonishment when we were awaiting the cross-country racers, and saw a man [skiing] down with some peculiar movements. Nilssen increased his speed by … skating steps … heaving [on his sticks] … a technique that we had not yet seen.[11]

One reason was that while Nilssen, like most Norwegians, now used two sticks, Germans skied with one. This was largely due to the enormous influence of Nansen. Nearly a decade after the event, his book on the crossing of Greenland was still a kind of skiing Bible in Germany. It was often used as a prize at races. Although on the actual crossing of the ice cap, Nansen used two sticks, in the extensive chapter on skiing in Norway, he featured only one. That represented his unshakeable opinion. Like many a pioneer, Nansen hid a core of retrogression. To the end of his days he stuck to a single stick.

Slavish imitators, however, the Germans were not. Some experimented with the long, narrow running skis of the Swedes and Finns, but the Norwegian pattern was found to be best suited to the local terrain. Importing skis from Norway turned out to be expensive, so early in the eighteen nineties, the Germans started manufacturing their own.

The process more or less began with a Norwegian student in Dresden. Some German friends wanted to acquire skis, so he wrote for advice to a relative who happened to be Einar Isachsen, the same mountain skiing pioneer who had given Nansen technical advice for the crossing of Greenland. In a long letter dated 22 September 1890, Uncle Einar answered with drawings and meticulous instructions for making skis. His ski was waisted, and therefore what later became known as the Telemark type. They were however asymmetrical, curved slightly inwards from the centre, so that the forward part of the outer edge was convex. He had learned this from some hunter up in the mountains, who explained that 'that they were much more stable … and in loose snow did not slip sideways so easily'.[12]

Isachsen found this to be the case. Furthermore he diverged from the classical Telemark ski by abandoning the smooth sole, and making a substantial groove, also in the interests of stability. His skis were around 2.5 m long, with an elegant camber to turn a dead billet of wood into a live, responsive instrument (Isachsen was an amateur violin maker too). The details give a fascinating insight into the transition from ancient lore to modern manufacture. Thus 'Birch bark is [fixed] under the foot [to] prevent snow sticking to the ski' – the same device known to primitive Siberian tribes. The tips were bent 'after softening [the skis] in boiling water'. The problem in those days, before laminated construction and modern industrial methods, was to prevent flattening out, so Isachsen 'always kept [the skis] bent after use'. He did so by means of a rod forcing the tips apart, with two clamps holding the skis together, front and rear, at the natural points where the camber allowed the skis to touch. Spruce, fir, willow, rowan, birch, oak, ash and even maple, could all be used to make skis.

This and other advice the early German manufacturers took to heart. They did, however, add their own technical ingenuity. In 1891, for example, a precursor of the modern cross-country binding appeared. It consisted of a plate strapped to the boot, hinged at the toe, and fixed to the ski by a lever mechanism that allowed it to be fixed or removed at will. The aim was to give absolute freedom of movement. It was far ahead of its time.

During the first decades of its existence, German skiing as a sport was more or less the preserve of academics and the professional classes. As a practical aid, foresters and border guards quickly adopted it. In 1892, the ski was first put to military use at Goslar by the 82nd Infantry Regiment. About the same time, country postmen in East Prussia started using skis. All this, and much else like it, was noticed by the press. Indeed, the spread of skiing owed much to newspaper coverage. The underlying philosophy was strangely utilitarian: to stop winter being the dead season of the year and to help build a healthy population, no doubt with recruits for the huge German conscript army in mind.

Still throughout the 1890s and beyond, German skiing remained Nordic in character. This was dictated by geography. Only along the southern border of Bavaria was there Alpine terrain. Even here, resident Norwegians were the masters. Because of the varied landscape at home they were the ultimate all-round skiers. 'They displayed a fantastic elegance', in the words of one German pioneer:

> and they finished a downhill run with a Telemark turn, not with a jerk, but in an elegant curve … How amazed we were when we saw how they negotiated steep forested slopes with astonishing speed using a short [Christiania] turn, while we ran down slowly with stem turns.[13]

All in all, the Norwegians showed courage and polish. They were poor examples to follow, however. Their way was to negotiate steep mountainsides in a succession of straight downhill rushes, stopping when the speed was too foolhardy even for them. It made a good spectacle but it was the outcome of a particular temperament combined with having skied since childhood. It was hardly conceived for relative beginners with another kind of personality. Nor was it adapted to an Alpine landscape. The German downhill pioneers, schooled in lowland Nordic skiing, had to feel their way in finding a new technique to cope with steeper slopes.

The key transitional figure was a retired German army officer called Hauptmann (Captain) Vorwerg. He was the first proper German all-round skier, the first mountain tourer and the first with a proper technique. Originally he saw skis on a summer climbing trip to northern Norway during the 1880s. He wanted to try them in his home tracts of the Riesengebirge, the mountain range on the south-eastern border of Germany. He imported skis from Norway and, after an autodidact's embarrassing disasters, met two Norwegian engineers – a far-flung breed that did much to spread skiing. 'The real central European ski terrain is in the mountains', he wrote in a textbook, one of the earliest of its kind, published in 1894.[14] 'As time passes', he went on, 'winter will be just as lively [in the mountains] as in the summer.' Also, he cogently remarked, 'skiing in central Europe is far from achieving the significance in everyday life that it has in Norway'. In other words he was prophesying that it would mostly be a recreation; as indeed the difference has turned out to be.

In the late winter of 1893, Vorwerg made the first skiing ascent of the Schneekoppe, a peak in the Riesengebirge. 'Between the Alps and the Carpathians, and the highest parts of Norway,' he explained in an article on his ski tour, 'the

Schneekoppe is the highest mountain.'[15] Besides which the difference in height from base to summit was about 1,000 m over a distance of 7 km, a run 'which is not available for skis everywhere'.

> I like skiing in a blizzard [he continued]. One has to coordinate thoughts and observation in order to survive. This blocks all other [troublesome] thoughts that occasionally pursue one … In other words, spiritual repose. The matter also has an ethical side, even its physical charm, apart from the movement. You are always exposed to the risk of freezing your nose, ears, etc, which are entirely different troubles from those which one can have down below in a warm room, and variety, as we all know, is the spice of life … Besides which you become aware of things that would never attract your attention in clear weather.

Whether this is an accurate representation of feelings at the time or philosophizing after the event, Vorwerg was trying to convey the experience of a *föhn* storm that afflicted almost the whole of his tour. However, he reached his stated goal, so he had succeeded. Success has to be paid for one way or another, and Vorwerg's penalty was warm sticky snow that made him puff and pant like a steam engine on the way down.

At any rate, his was the first recorded mountain tour in Germany, and also one of the first in Alpine-like terrain anywhere on the continent. It was an early step towards adapting the Norwegian system of skiing to another landscape.

Vorwerg had been moving in border country. The Riesengebirge straddle what was then Germany and, on the other side, the Austro-Hungarian empire. There, in the polyglot domains of the Habsburg monarchy, events followed another course.

# 20

# Norwegians bring Skiing to Austria-Hungary and Montenegro

The Habsburg empire harboured pockets of indigenous skiing unconnected with Norwegians. One such was to be found in the Riesengebirge. The Austro-Hungarian side rose in what is today the Czech Republic, but was then the province of Bohemia. Some of the inhabitants used ski that they called *Lyzsche*. This is not Czech but Russian. Apparently a Russian forester working for Prince Schwarzenberg, a magnate of the Habsburg monarchy, introduced those ski around the middle of the nineteenth century.

A much older skiing tradition had survived in a very different corner of the Empire. This was among the Alps of Slovenia, near Ljubliana, in what was then the Duchy of Crain. The skiing there was first recorded in a book called *Die Ehre des Herzogthums Crain – The Honour of the Duchy of Crain*. It appeared in 1689. The author was a Count Valvasor, himself from Crain. 'The peasants of Crain', he wrote

> possess a strange invention, which I have never seen in any [other] country. In winter, when there is snow [they] take two wooden planks, about a quarter of an inch thick, half a workman's shoe wide, and about five … long … bent upwards at the front. In the middle is affixed a leather strap in which you put your foot … In addition, the peasant also carries in his hand a stout stick, held under the shoulder [and] leaning on it … and pushing himself down the steepest mountains … they all know how to avoid any obstacle that appears in their way … on such a downhill course they twist and turn like a snake. But if the road is clear … they glide directly down … leaning backwards on the stick.[1]

Valvasor's seventeenth-century 'peasants of Crain' thus become the oldest known central European skiers, and the first of the Alpine downhill breed. Although by his own account Valvasor had never seen skiing elsewhere, he knew about its existence in Scandinavia through the literature from Paulus Diaconus onwards.

The ski of the Riesengebirge were short, broad and aways fur lined. They evidently came from Siberia and belonged to the eastern type. The origin of the Crain skis is not at all so clear cut. They were unlined and, according to Valvasor, found only on what is now known as the Bloke plateau. His description, and existing specimens, suggest that the Bloke skis belonged to the Southern type. They were around 1 m 50 cm long with stubby tips. They resemble the skis that feature both in Herberstein's and Guagnini's books, published at least a century before Valvasor. This hints that Herberstein, who himself also came from the Crain, might have brought them in.

Slovenian patriots would like them to be older. What is certain is that Bloke skiing had its own terminology and survived at least until the 1930s like some living fossil from another age. Even now, in Slovenia, ski are known by the native word *smuci*; derivation uncertain at best. The Bloke plateau is a place of hard winters and the ski was a necessity. That, together with isolation explains why native skiing never spread. Nonetheless it might indirectly have influenced what eventually followed.

When the Norwegian ski finally invaded the Habsburg lands it did so without the help of resident Norwegians. Its first known appearance was at the Universal Exhibition of 1873 in Vienna. Meanwhile knowledge of its existence was filtering through. The occasional traveller had visited Scandinavia and seen skis in action. Newspapers also played their part. At least since the 1880s, a Scandinavian form of skiing was found in parts of the Habsburg empire. A Prague firm had imported ski from Norway in 1889 and ski were adopted professionally by foresters and gamekeepers.

Unlike Germany, when pleasure skiing finally appeared in the Habsburg Empire, the early pioneers were lone domestic acolytes; shadowy figures who left few lasting traces. Again, Nansen's first crossing of Greenland in 1888 was the catalyst. From him proceeded the breakthrough. Again he acquired an almost mythic status.

It was in Austria that advancement now centred. For one thing, it was the German-speaking overlord of the Dual Monarchy and the seat of the Imperial capital at Vienna. More to the point, Austria held the Alpine hinterland, ebbing out in Vienna itself. By 1890 there were some local Viennese pleasure skiers. In October 1891, the Vienna Ski Club was founded; shadowy, exclusive, short-lived but the first of its kind in central Europe. Viennese were avid in copying things foreign. Unlike Germany, not many Norwegians stayed in Austria but nonetheless it was the opportune appearance of a few that gave skiing its local impetus.

In January 1893, the same Captain Henrik Angell who had made the pioneer crossing of the Norwegian Western Mountains, found himself in Vienna, complete with skis. 'I arrived in a blizzard, the like of which I had never seen, even in Norway', he said. 'All ... traffic had stopped ... I skied right across Vienna, over the Danube, and up to Kahlenberg, and had a splendid tour ... My skis immediately brought me a number of acquaintances among [army] officers in the wonderful imperial city.'[2]

Angell was only passing through. He was heading out of the Habsburg lands on his way to Montenegro. Towards the end of the month, he finally reached his destination. He had brought his ski because he expected snow in the mountainous Balkan principality. 'Skis could already be used from the first village after the [Croatian] frontier', he happily recorded. 'Big stones, detached boulders, everything had disappeared under a firm, white mantle. I have rarely seen better skiing ... unless it be high in the [Norwegian] mountains, when the snow has been compacted by the wind.'[3]

Angell was in Montenegro through a romantic admiration of its people. They were bloodthirsty warriors who had held their own against overwhelming odds through centuries of Turkish onslaught. Their history was violent. Individualistic and ferocious, they were natural guerrillas. They were the only Balkan nation not to be swept into the Ottoman empire. Squeezed in between the Ottomans and the Habsburgs, they had kept their independence. They were, Angell thought, a model for his own fellow countrymen in their drive for separation from Sweden.[4]

Although Montenegro – literally 'black mountain' – was said to be full of brigands, Angell wafted over the snow unscathed. His singular, quixotic form, like someone touched, sheltered him from superstitious tribesmen. In his own words, as he crossed a pass to the capital, Cetine:

> There were the most wonderful slopes, and here and there it was quite lively. A shepherd, who had seen a dark man from a distance sweeping down a mountainside … almost … faster … than a bird could fly … later … explained that he had seen the devil himself.

On that account or otherwise, Angell's skis secured him the entrée to the Court at Cetine. Capital in name, in reality it was a modest little town nestling among the peaks. On the adjoining slopes, Angell demonstrated skiing to Nikola I, the reigning Prince. Nikola was an enlightened despot. Educated in France and Italy, he was trying to modernize his backward people. Angell was simply another of the foreign experts brought in to that end, except that he had unexpectedtly dropped in. The Prince saw sport in general and now skiing in particular as one agent of advance. He asked Angell to start a ski school and Angell immediately telegraphed both home to Norway and to Vienna for some skis.

Angell was impressed by the fact that at a royal banquet

> even the waiters [were] armed … All the Montenegrans sitting round the table had not borne their revolvers … in vain. They [had] all … distinguished themselves in the latest wars … They are tough men with grim faces … in which … one can read [that] they would fall heaped one upon another, rather than lose liberty and independence.[5]

'If you come to them as a guest … you are given the heartiest welcome', Angell admiringly went on.

> Many an evening after lively instruction … in skiing, have I sat by the fires in their dark, soot-stained huts and enjoyed their hospitality to the full … Finally we all wish each other goodnight, the host puts his revolver aside in front of his guest, you wrap yoursef in plaids and blanket … and sleep the sound, dreamless sleep of the sportsman [everywhere].

Angell stayed for most of the winter to implant skiing. Prince Nikola led the way by putting himself and the whole royal family, men and women, through Angell's ski school. On 5 February, Angell wrote home with quiet pride, the first ski club was founded in Cetine. Both school and club were among the earliest of their kind on the continent.

Thus Angell, the accidental missionary, brought skiing to Montenegro and, eventually the Balkans. To this day, in Montenegro, he remains a local hero. He offered yet another proof of the law of unintended consequences.

In one way, that also applied in Vienna, on the way down. When Angell skied through the city, he merely wanted a quick ski tour and there was some convenient snow. As it turned out, he helped to bring skiing to Austria. He was not of course the first to ski in the Habsburg capital but through him, the ski made its ceremonial entrance. Angell's military bearing and strange, forceful personality made sure of that.

Earlier that same winter, two other Norwegians, unknown to Angell were also skiing through the streets of Vienna. Their names were William Bismarck Samson and Georg Wedel-Jarlsberg. They were on their way to teach a select class of *aficionados*. Unlike Angell their conscious aim was to spread skiing in the city on the Danube.

That story began the previous winter of 1892. Both Samson and Wedel-Jarlsberg had recently arrived. They went to Pötzleinsdorf, a park in the Vienna Woods, on the north-eastern outskirts of the capital. There, they marched into a restaurant, collared the owner, one Ludwig Strasser, lectured him on the virtues of skiing and then, before a certain audience, gave a demonstration. In Wedel Jarlsberg's own words:

> When we left Pötzleinsdorf, Strasser had become a ski enthusiast, and that afternoon skiing acquired many inspired adherents ... Articles about the two Norwegians and their 'skis' often appeared in the newspapers ... One morning two gentlemen appeared in my office, and presented themselves as Baron Wangenheim and E. Bratmann. The purpose of their visit was to invite us to the founding of a ski association, and to secure us as instructors.[6]

Wangenheim, elderly and no active sportsman himself, had that same year published the first book on skiing by a central European. He was under the intoxicating influence of Nansen's *First Crossing of Greenland*. He was advocating what he called 'the naturalisation of skis in suitable regions of other countries'.[7] On 26 November 1892, in Vienna, the Niederösterreichischer Ski-Verein (The Lower Austrian Ski Association) was founded, soon to be called Österreichischer Ski-Verein (The Austrian Ski Association), the first national organization of its kind outside Scandinavia. Samson and Wedel Jarlsberg were only too happy to act as instructors. They began by organizing a little demonstration, on 19 January 1893, again at Pötzleinsdorf. 'The astonishment of the spectators', as one of their number put it

> rose to amazement as Samson ran down the mountain in wonderful manoeuvres, first slowly, then quick as lightning. At his request, some workmen quickly piled up snow in an improvised ski-jump. And when Samson made jumps of 10–12 metres on this primitive installation the audience, which had never seen such a breath-taking display of human accomplishment, broke into frenzied applause.[8]

The 'primitive installation' was a snow-covered pile of manure. Thus a dung-heap had the honour of being the first ski-jump in Austria. To the flighty Viennese, in the last days of the Habsburgs, under the bitter-sweet rule of the Emperor Franz-Josef, it might have been just one more of the many ironic jokes they characteristically told against themselves.

Samson, 21 years old, was a journeyman baker working for a pastry-cook to learn the legendary art of Viennese confectionery. He was typical of the few Norwegians who came to Austria. Those who went to Germany, did so to become scientists and engineers; their compatriots in Austria were more concerned with food.

Samson's trade earned him the respect of the sybaritic, expansive Viennese, which redounded to the benefit of his skiing. For different, but equally characteristic reasons, Wedell-Jarlsberg also shone. He worked in the Swedish-Norwegian Legation, albeit in the consular division so he was, broadly speaking, a diplomat. He also belonged to the only remaining Norwegian titled family and could call himself 'Baron' – although not in Norway. In the exclusive, aristocratic preserves of Viennese society, where quarterings were counted, this last was indispensable.

So every Sunday, and sometimes on weekday afternoons too, the baker and the Baron dispensed skiing instruction. Their pupils were mainly aristocratic, with servants to carry their skis up the slope after running down. To satisfy the demand, at least a hundred pairs had been imported quickly from Norway; notably from the Christiania firm in which Fritz Huitfeldt was a partner. Probably Wedel-Jarlsberg had paid; perhaps too Prince Hohenlohe, later a passable ski-jumper, or perhaps even the banker, Baron Rothschild, whose two sons eventually became accomplished skiers.

'We were fêted, and invited home to the best families', Samson said of himself and Wedel-Jarlsberg.[9] Exclusive the Viennese aristocracy might have been but they too hungered for celebrities, and suspended rigid rules to admit them to their salons. In the ennui of the last days of the Habsburgs there was a desire to escape from an airless claustrophobia that, amongst other things, affected the young Sigmund Freud as he was conceiving his psychological theories. Samson and Wedel-Jarlsberg swept in like a gale with the mystique of the North. Samson's ski-jumping was like an antidote to a jaded world.

Vienna was the grand illustration of how skiing for pleasure first took hold in the cities. As in Norway, the upper reaches of society were the first exponents. In Vienna, this meant aristocrats and academics Only they had the means and it was they, too, who had the psychological need. Unlike the peasant, still anchored to the soil, they sought escape from the growing artificiality of urban life.

Even before the breakthrough in Vienna, pioneers had been at work in other places. They mostly came and went without immediate consequences. It was one of these lone wolves, however, who finally brought skiing to the Austrian Alps. As he told the tale, he owed nothing to the frivolous world of Vienna. He came from Graz, a city of a different stamp lying, not on the Danube plain, but among the Alps in the adjoining province of Styria, to the south-west. His name was Max Kleinoscheg.

Born in 1862 Kleinoscheg, an unremarkable figure, was an accomplished mountaineer, with first ascents to his credit in the Alps, the Pyrenees and the Caucasus. Early in November 1890, he took a party climbing the Hochschwab, a minor Alpine peak of some 2,000 m, in northern Styria. The first snows had already fallen and in the cold of early morning the ascent was a smooth progression on solid crust. Going down was another matter altogether. The sun had thawed the surface and the party broke through sometimes chest deep. What had begun as a light-hearted excursion ended as a nightmare. A descent that ought to have taken one hour, now dragged out at least to four. 'We ... reached the valley ... completely exhausted', as Kleinoscheg himself put it. 'In addition, we were in mortal danger, while we no longer had enough moral strength; our physical powers were nearly at an end.'[10]

This was Kleinoscheg's road to Damascus:

> It was there that the thought first struck me: If we had only had a sledge with broad runners, or something similar, that could have brought us quickly over the few kilometres to the valley floor over this horrible crusted yet fragile snow.

Returning to Graz by train in the small hours, Kleinoscheg went into a café and there he found an English illustrated newspaper, that some tourist doubtless had left behind. 'And what did I see? A skier sweeping down a slope, with the caption "Sport in Norway!" ... *That was it!*'[11]

Now Kleinoscheg was a stamp collector. As a result, he had made contact with a Norwegian businessman, Nikolay Noodt, in Trondheim. On 28 November, Kleinoscheg wrote to Noodt, asking about skis. 'Skiing is better than anything else! [Noodt replied]. If you have enough snow, i.e ... at least 1 foot, I would advise you to obtain skis and start immediately. Here in Norway you can see children of 3 and 4 years on skis.'[12]

Noodt went on to offer considered advice for a beginner:

> I cannot hold out much hope for the first winter, since it takes several years to become a good runner. Hillocks, undulating terrain – preferably with forest or scrub, are the usual skiing grounds here – the steeper the better, and the faster you run down, the better you ski.

In the event, Noodt presented Kleinoscheg with his first pair of skis, together with detailed instructions They arrived around New Year 1891. Kleinoscheg tried them out immediately; first on a lawn in Graz; then on a mountain slope outside the city. His slithering humiliation was observed by various acquaintances who, in his own words, 'laughed to scorn my idea of introducing a winter sport on these unwieldy boards!'[13]

The following Sunday, after another hapless failure, Kleinoscheg went to show off his skis to a friend called Toni Schruf, who plays a leading rôle in this story.

Schruf lived at Mürzzuschlag, a small, semi-industrial Alpine town on the railway between Graz and Vienna. They went down to a sloping meadow and there, after yet more demeaning falls, Kleinoscheg let Schruf try instead. At his first attempt Schruf, never having seen a ski before, 'ran down perfectly', as Kleinoscheg put it. 'I left the skis with [him] and returned the next Sunday. He was already running perfectly.'

Kleinoscheg ordered several more pairs of ski from Trondheim, and Schruf determinedly continued practising. He did have Noodt's instructions but they were unclear, not to say misleading – especially about leaning too far back – and in essence he was self-taught. From the start, he had a constant companion on the slopes, a certain Ludwig Chlupatys. Chlupatys recorded their early travail:

> Practice was confined to … dragging the planks [instant local slang for skis] up the steep meadow, putting them on at the top, and then tearing down where they wanted, because there was no question of control. Naturally these downhill runs often led one into unpleasant predicaments …[14]
>
> A lot of practice nonetheless resulted in some success. Gradually one became confident in running down. One invoked the help of the 2 metre long [ski stick], in that one could brake by putting it between one's feet, and pressing on it with the weight of one's body. Thus one now had the ability to run where one wished … Naturally this gave us more pleasure and encouragement.

A slope had to end in a flat outrun. It was the only way then known of stopping. Downhill skiing consisted of mad rushes interspersed with horizontal checks. This, more or less, is what Schruf and Chlupatys were fumbling towards. After some time, as Chlupatys said, 'Kleinoscheg returned, [and] we were already far ahead of him in skill and, because of much running, also had more confidence.'

Kleinoscheg and Schruf were very different characters. Kleinoscheg was well known as an athlete but little more. Schruf, tall, bespectacled, urbane, always with the shadow of a smile, owned the Hotel Post in Mürzzuschlag; the main hotel in the town. He had learned his trade in Vienna and worked in other countries, notably Switzerland, England and Egypt. He was a born hotelier, which meant that he had a way with people. He was also well read with wide interests beyond his occupation.

While still taking his first steps on skis, Schruf grasped their business potential. Winter in the Alps was the dead season of the year. Only spring and summer brought the visitors. The ski might entice them up into the snows and become the salvation of many an hotelier. Schruf was a pioneer of skiing as an agent of winter tourism. He was a forerunner in commercializing the slopes. First of his kind, he wanted to turn Mürzzuschlag into a ski resort. Together with Kleinoscheg, he started a campaign to bring skiing to the Styrian Alps.

Schruf's *métier* was the spoken word. He addressed public meetings and argued persuasively with influential acquaintances. Kleinoscheg, on the other hand, wrote for the Press. He published articles as far afield as a German-language newspaper in mountain-ringed Sarajevo; for Bosnia-Herzogovina, although nominally still Turkish, was now an Austrian protectorate, divided between two ramshackle empires.

Kleinoscheg's motives were slightly different from those of Schruf. In his own words, he wanted to use the ski 'as a means of carrying out mountain tours in the winter': 'but also to introduce it as a sport that could be practised during those months when cycle touring was impossible. I considered that skiing would keep the body fit until road racing could recommence.'[15]

Kleinoscheg and Schruf were both dedicated cyclists. It was their point of contact. Kleinoscheg was a well-known racer, having won various road events. He recognized that skiing, in the quasi-Nordic form that was being introduced, bore a relation to cycling. Both were tests of endurance; both meant climbing up and running downhill in a certain rhythm; each required management of cadence, and exercised the same muscles in the thigh. They also shared something else. Both as a recreation and a sport, cycling was then blossoming in Austria as elsewhere. It was one of the phenomena of the age. Advancing industrialization was constricting freedom. In *Voici des ailes*, a novel about cycling, the French author, Maurice Leblanc, makes one character say that nothing

> evokes the idea of speed more than two wheels ... with spokes, slender and vibrating like nerves ... Man has now been given all powers. Steam and electricity [merely serve] his well-being: the bicycle perfects his very body ... it offers a faster pair of legs ... It is not a man and a machine, it is a man with greater speed.[16]

In plain figures, it was four times faster than walking. Man was no longer bound by the narrow formalization of city life. The bicycle was a symbol of escape.

All this could be transferred to skiing, as it was taking root in the Alps. It differed from Norway by lacking the elements of romantic Nature worship and national identity. Stern gymnasts, both in Austria and Germany, wanted to ban it because it was 'un-German'; a neat reversal of the Norwegian gibe, 30 years previously, that it 'was skiing that was their own, and gymnastics were "too German" for their tastes.'

In fact it was among cyclists that Kleinoscheg made the first converts to his cause. He placed much of his propaganda in cycling magazines. Yet again, Nansen was the deus ex machina. The appearance of the German edition of his *First Crossing of Greenland* in 1891, coincided with the critical formative years. Its phenomenal success, helped by more or less fanciful press reports of the miraculous filaments of wood, created the wave of enthusiasm that the pioneers wanted. In one sense, Kleinoscheg and Schruf were merely following in Nansen's wake. They soon had proselytes enough.

They themselves practised hard and untutored. Autodidacts as they were, in their second season, *pace* Noodt, they had advanced enough to make a winter ascent of the Stuhleck on skis. They had a third companion in the person of Walter Wenderich, a postman from Brück-an-der-Mur, a town nearby, whose first season this was. As Alpine peaks go, the Stuhleck was not much. It was only about 1,700 m above sea level, one of the picturesque but undemanding mountain tops with wooded flanks encircling Mürzzuschlag. Nonetheless Schruf and his companions ensured it a place in history. This was the first climb of a mountain on skis in Austria. It took place on 2 February 1892.

Mainly thanks to Nansen's book, skiers were now beginning to appear in appreciable numbers along the Austrian Alps from the modest escarpment in the Vienna Woods all the way to the Swiss border. Mürzzuschlag, however, was the centre of technical advance for the next decade. A small provincial town and no tourist haven, without grand scenery, it was an unlikely setting for a cradle of winter sports. On the other hand, nestling on a river in a valley, it had the landscape and ambience to attract Brahms for two summers in the 1880s and there he wrote his haunting Fourth Symphony. That may or may not be connected with the fact that it also attracted the skiing pioneers. At least it had the prealpine terrain suited to the capabilities of the age.

On 13 October 1892 a Norwegian ski manufacturer called Ydal told Nansen that they were about to send their 'first consignment of skis abroad, namely Styria in Austria'.[17] Private orders had been trickling in to various firms for some years. This was earlier than the order from Vienna and probably the first commercial Norwegian export to the Alps. It went on sale in Graz. It already faced local competition. In Mürzzuschlag, a certain Josef Bachman, 'Ski-maker, saddler and upholsterer',[18] as he called himself, was offering his products to 'the honoured friends of skiing', given the 'continually rising demand'. He was almost certainly the first Austrian ski manufacturer. He was typical in coming from existing crafts. With a fresh eye, he had even modified the original Norwegian cane binding. He added a loop round the ankle to stop the heelstrap slipping and causing blisters.

Bachman's enterprise was only a mirror of pioneering in other ways. On reaching the summit of the Stuhleck, Kleinoscheg, Schruf and Wenderich, by their own account, were so elated that they then and there decided 'to gather all Styrian skiers, as well as their sporting counterparts in the other Alpine provinces in a single association'.[19] The outcome was the Verband Steirischer Skiläufer – The Association of Styrian Skiers – which, mirroring events in Vienna, was formed in the autumn of 1892. Its first act was to arrange, on 2 February 1893, a competition at Mürzzuschlag. It was the first ski race in the Alps and only a year younger than Holmenkollen. It was also the first downhill event in the modern sense.

The race was run on a sloping meadow along a water conduit outside the town. The course was about 600 m long, with an average gradient of 9.5°, including 'a right-angled leftwards turn, and finally a flat finish of 20 metres'.[20] Sticks were allowed but no baskets, here called 'braking disks'. That much was clear. The organizers, on the other hand, were uncertain how to run the race. They had seen nothing like it before, they knew nothing of the Scandinavian systems, and they had to feel their way. What the Norwegians had been grappling with since the 1840s, the Austrians were now repeating half a century later. Since they were mostly cyclists, they applied the rules of cycling. There was to be a massed standing start. With 20 entrants there had to be eliminating heats. Five were run, each with four competitors, the winner of each to go on to the final, which would decide the race. In case of a dead heat, the race would be rerun. The cycling origins were clear in the obligatory dress. Coloured jerseys replaced identifying numbers.

The participants came chiefly from Styria and Vienna; the spectators, some 2,000, from all over the Habsburg empire. They were led, broadly speaking, by high society. There were landowners from Styria, nobility from here and there. Perhaps they sensed history in the making; perhaps they were merely hungering for novelty. Whatever it was, they packed the course and paid high prices for a seat in an improvised stand. Special trains brought in the customers. William Samson was the attraction; he having been inveigled to take part, so that there would be a real Norwegian on the slopes. He had an exalted fan club as, back in Christiania, a sporting journal waspishly reported. Two weeks earlier, he made

> the Viennese, represented by their greatest aristocracy from the Prince and Princess of Lichtenstein, down to small fry like major generals, swoon in astonishment at his performance in ski-jumping ... our mutual friend ... will be impossible when he comes home again.[21]

At Mürzzuschlag, a local reporter took a similar view. Samson was expected to be the star performer; not least by himself. He was drawn in the third heat of the downhill run.

> In his manifest confidence of victory, he nearly lost to the best representative of Vienna, Viktor Ramschak. In the second half of the course, the Viennese suddenly attacked, surprised the carefree Norwegian, and left him standing, but only to within a few metres from the finish, where unfortunately he fell, and had to concede victory to Samson. The incident elicited a frantic storm of cheering from the assembled crowd.[22]

Some of this was due to Samson's skill in stopping and turning quickly. At a mild dip along the course, ash had been strewn on the snow to check the speed. This was soon churned up into a sodden sooty mire, from which anyone who fell rose black as a chimney sweep from top to toe. That enhanced the spirits of an already lively crowd.

The final was an anticlimax. Samson had learned his lesson. He broke away at the start to win by an insulting margin. No time, unfortunately, was recorded. His crushing superiority was partly explained by a judicious use of two sticks. The spectators loved it.

There was also, incidentally, a womens' event, which makes this the very first women's Alpine race. For the record, the winner, in the swirling skirts of the age, was Fräulein Mitzi Angerer, from Langenwang, a small town some 20 miles away. She deserves her little place in history.

To round off the event, Samson obliged with an exhibition of ski-jumping. The jump was built up – again – with manure and the gradient was too slack, so that he could only manage about 6 m. Nonetheless, as Schruf remembered in after years, it 'caused more amazement at the time than the familiar achievements of ski-jumpers today'.[23] Samson also gave an impromptu master class in turning. He left a small group trying for hours to copy what they had seen.

Above all, journalists were there in force; especially from Vienna. The coverage was fulsome. Skiing was brought to the notice of many who had never heard of it before. Sporting spectacle aside, as a means of generating publicity, which was Schruf's prime intention, the event was an unmitigated success.

That winter was historic in more ways than one. In March 1893, Franz Reisch made the first ascent of the Kitzbüeler Horn on skis. At nearly 2,000 m, this was one of the first truly Alpine peaks thus to be climbed. Reisch was both a dedicated climber and Mayor of Kitzbühel, then a small, unknown Alpine town. He was the father of skiing in the Tyrol. He was also a pioneer of Alpine ski touring.

He, too, was inspired by Nansen's *First Crossing of Greenland*. He claimed to have taken his first steps on skis only a month or two before his ascent in January 1893. In his own words, however,

> Running on the flat, or small hummocks soon gave me too little variation, so I made attempts in the mountainous terrain. The whole region of the Kitzbühel Alps is made for it, since the summits generally fall precipitously only on the North side, while in the other direction, there are sloping Alpine meadows ...
>
> Skiing is justifiably called the sport of sports. This holds only in high mountains [with] grandiose ... swooping downhill runs ... The instant reactions in rushing through uneven terrain tax presence of mind to a high degree. The pleasure in looking back on a long course [you have] covered in a few moments, neither the horseman nor the cyclist knows.[24]

In lapidary form, this evokes the spirit of skiing downhill; it could hardly be bettered even now. Reisch, however, was an anomaly. So too was another, less articulate precursor. Wilhelm von Arlt, born in Prague – another Austro-Hungarian city – in 1855, went to university in Vienna and then settled in Salzburg. There, already a passionate mountaineer, he took to skiing in the early 1890s. The ski had been brought to this province not by the customary Norwegian but for once by a Swede; an engineer surnamed Åberg.

On 5 February 1894, Von Arlt climbed the Sonnblick. This was the first ascent on skis of a *dreitauzender*; a mountain over the mystic threshold of 3,000 m altitude and another milepost in the evolution of ski mountaineering. He then did a downhill run with a vertical drop of 1,500 m in 32 minutes, repeated the following year in half the time. Brute force was his style. He had no technique beyond a single heavy stick with which, like the primitive tribesmen of the Chinese annals, he used to turn, stop or check his speed. According to one story he would often cycle to his ski tours and he was so strong that, when necessary, he would carry his cycle on his back up the mountain and then down again. What is certain is that in June and July 1896, he skied on the Pasterze, in the Gross Glockner region, and thus became the original pioneer of summer skiing.

Thus at the turn of the century and in the last days of the Habsburgs, skiing was taking root in Austria. However, there were few individuals like Reisch and Arlt. The resorts that later became so famous played little part in the pioneering days. Even Kitzbühel had to wait its turn. Vienna and Mürzzuschlag remained the centres of advance. There the Norwegian influence prevailed. Despite the example of men like Reisch and Arlt the high Alps were thought unsuitable for skiing. Its proper field, as in Germany, was considered to be lower down in the foothills, as a mirror of Scandinavian terrain. This was the Nordic era of Alpine skiing. Ski-jumping and cross-country racing were transplanted as the proper ambitions of the true skier.

So in 1894, when Toni Schruf decided to repeat the fixture of the previous year at Mürzzuschlag, it was predominantly Nordic. There was again a small downhill run but the main events were ski-jumping and a cross-country race of about 12 km. Schruf wanted Norwegians again, to inspire the halting steps of the locals and to bring in the crowds. Samson had gone home but Wedel-Jarlsberg was still consul and he arranged for resident Norwegians to run, including another baker's journeyman from Vienna.

For publicity, however, Schruf also wanted someone straight from Norway. With local help, he secured one of the best skiers in the country, Jonas Holmen. Holmen was not yet of age, so he needed his father's permission to travel. Holmen *père* thought that his son's place was at home, and refused point blank at first. Appeals to his patriotism finally made him relent. Jonas thus became the first Norwegian skier officially sent to race on the continent. By the same token, he was also the first true international skier in the Alps.

His appearance at Mürzzuschlag helped to bring in a record crowd of some 3,000. As an extra attraction, Schruf had also organized a winter sports exhibition to coincide with the races. Here, too, he broke new ground. At least since the 1860s there had been similar events in Scandinavia. They had been confined to skis, however. The Mürzzuschlag exhibition covered winter sports in the broadest sense. It was the first of its kind anywhere. Held in the assembly rooms of the local river bathing establishment, draped in green for the occasion, it included skis, skates, sledges, clothing and even the few existing works of skiing literature, headed naturally by Nansen's *First Crossing of Greenland*. A Viennese sculptor had sent a statue of a skier; arguably the first of its kind. The centrepiece was of course the skis themselves. There were Austrian products but they were outnumbered by the exhibits of Norwegian, Swedish and Finnish manufacturers.

Out in the snow, meanwhile, the Norwegians scooped up all medals in all events, both Nordic and Alpine. Holmen was supposed to be the star attraction. Because of his father's intransigence, he only arrived the night before the races opened on 5 January with the ski-jump. He had also lost his skis along the way, so had to perform on borrowed ones. His jumping ended in disgrace.

Next day, he redeemed himself by winning the cross-country event in style, partly because the Austrians, ironically enough, were poor downhill runners. The course was difficult, having a total of 600 m vertical difference in height, with long climbs, and steep descents, often through narrow forest paths where most time was gained. Although Holmen started last, he overtook everyone else, and arrived first of all; so soon, in fact, as to be totally unexpected. 'When I approached the finishing line', in his own words, 'there was no one to be seen at the timekeepers' table.'[25] This was placed, by design, next to a convenient *gasthof*.

> Those who were responsible sat [inside] drinking beer and enjoying themselves. When they heard someone shouting that one of the Norwegians had arrived ... They rushed out with watches in hand, and they must have been clever timekeepers, because I had mine to within one tenth of a second: 55 minutes 53.6 seconds.

Nordic races now became fairly regular in Austria. One in Vienna, in January 1896, was symptomatic. It was run in the Vienna Woods at the now familiar Pötzleinsdorf Park. There was ski-jumping and a cross-country race, whimsically dubbed the 'Vienna Derby'. First-class Norwegians were brought in to compete. In the words of one journalist:

> their art ... overwhelmed everyone like a revelation ... In the course of this event ... Lieutenant [Karl] Roll, who won the Derby of 12 kilometres ... in the fanstastic time of 52 minutes, demonstrated his control during the home straight. A gust of wind blew off his cap, and quick as lightning he changed course, caught his headgear in mid air, a [turn] brought his skis back into the prescribed course and, after a telemark that sprayed snow head-high, Lieutenant Roll came to a halt before the astounded spectators ... More than 500 pairs of skis were sold in Vienna immediately after the race, which turned out to be a fantastic advertisement for skiing.[26]

It was so fantastic that one slope was lit for night-time skiing. This was the first ski track in the world with artificial illumination.

Karl Roll had been the runner-up at the first Holmenkollen race in 1892. He became one of the founders of modern skiing. His performance in Vienna was the kind of play acting that made the Norwegians the heroes of the pioneer Alpine generation. He appealed to the Viennese.

Those virtuosi on their strips of wood, however, were unexpectedly subversive figures. Sweden-Norway was the other dual kingdom, mirroring Austria-Hungary. As the Norwegians, children of the zeitgeist, personified the surge to independence from their Swedish overlords, so too were they examples to Czechs, and the other subject peoples chafing with nationalistic undercurrents that were tearing the absolutist empire of the Habsburgs apart.

# 21

# Skiing Comes to Switzerland

Circumstances were different across the border in Switzerland. Excepting France, it was then the only European republic. For centuries it had been the emblem of the Alpine world. Nonetheless, at first the Swiss trod a familiar path. The ski came to them from Norway but they too had precursors of their own.

On 20 December 1849, Johann Josef Imseng skied down from Saas-Fee, high up in the Pennine Alps in the canton of Valais, to the neighbouring village of Saas-Grund on short crude skis that he had improvised himself.[1] It was the first recorded ski run in Switzerland, and the first in all the Alps outside Bloke and the Crain.

Imseng was a singular character. The priest of the Saas valley, he wanted to serve his parishioners even in heavy winter snow with all other means of transport blocked. It was after all the waning of the Little Ice Age. At some point Imseng began experimenting with skis.

32. Olaf Kjelsberg, the Norwegian-born engineer, a pioneer of the electric locomotive, who brought modern skiing to Switzerland, late 1880s.

The snowshoe would have been more natural. It had long been known in Switzerland. It was mentioned by Josias Simmler, a Professor at Zürich University, in *De Alpibus Commentarius – Notes on the Alps* – which, published in 1574, was the first printed book devoted to mountains. Imseng nonetheless sought out the ski. He could have learned about it from a respectable number of printed sources. GutsMuths was one; a German encyclopaedia of physical education – Gerhard Vieth's *Versuch einer Encyklopädie der Leibesübungen*, published in 1794 – was another. There were other descriptions in the ever more popular genre of travel writing from the seventeenth century onwards.

Imseng lived in the Swiss Enlightenment, one luminary of which was his contemporary, Louis Agassiz, the man who first discovered the existence of ice ages. In his own way, Imseng was following the spirit of his times. The Swiss Enlightenment also helps to explain the direction taken originally by skiing in Switzerland. Instead of a competitive sport, it started as a means of exploring the mountains in winter, not so much from Nature worship as a spirit of rational enquiry. Mountaineering was a product of the original Enlightenment and Imseng, besides being a parish priest, was a mountain guide as well, with a profitable sideline of accommodating clients in his vicarage.

After Imseng, the next precursor appeared at the other end of the country, in the easternmost canton of the Grisons, in the high, enclosed valley of the Engadine. In 1860, at Sils-Maria, near St Moritz, a carpenter called Samuel Hnateck produced an implement for sliding on snow. It was made of pine wood, 170 cm long by 14 cm wide, pointed back and front, so it looked like a ski, down to a leather toestrap in the middle. However, it was flat, so it was difficult to use. After some experiment another model, of larch, with some kind of primitive raised tip was made and used by some villagers, including Hnateck himself.

No more than Imseng is Hnateck likely to have reinvented the ski. Hnateck actually came from Berlin. His name, however, implies Croatian or Slovenian descent. That in turn suggests some acquaintance with the Bloke ski, which his handiwork resembled.

From around the same period, comes another shadowy figure. In 1868, a certain Konrad Wild from the canton of Glarus in eastern Switzerland, was said to have owned a pair of Norwegian skis.

These were the forerunners. In Switzerland, as in other countries, Nansen became the spiritual father of skiing. The stimulus was once more the translation into German of *The First Crossing of Greenland*. However, as a Swiss author blandly put it, Nansen's exploit 'did not automatically, and of itself touch the hearts of the Swiss who, from time immemorial have been known for not being very receptive to innovation'.[2]

So when Nansen arrived on the scene, there was no rush of native Swiss disciples but one such did appear. His name was Christoph Iselin. He came from Konrad Wild's canton of Glarus. This is very different from the Valais of Josef Imseng. Imseng's home in Saas-Fee was dwarfed by the overpowering ice-hung massif of the Dom-Mitschabel, on the crest of the Alps. Iselin lived in the lower and gentler terrain of eastern Switzerland, among the Prealps, away from the everlasting snows. There, geological metamorphosis had produced long, wide sympathetic runs, awaiting the advent of the ski.

Glarus became the cradle of skiing in Switzerland and Iselin its pioneer. What distinguished him was a certain gift of turning ideas into action. Of medium height, thin, dark-haired, he radiated an aura of intensity. He was then 22 years old, about to enter the Swiss conscript citizen army as a regular officer. He ended up as a colonel, its highest rank in peace. A morally brave man, he had to fight the jeering of his compatriots before anything new. As he himself told the tale, characteristically referring to himself in the third person:

> It was in the winter of 1891 that [the writer of these lines], spurred and inspired by Nansen's *First Crossing of Greenland*, himself produced a pair of 'original', extremely primitive [skis], and made trial runs only in darkest night or blizzards. For woe betide him who then presumed to practise on such peculiar implements. He would inevitably become the target of general ridicule ... He would risk either being held up as an idiot, or exposed in the Shrovetide carnival newspaper. That's what it was like in the year of Our Lord 1891.[3]

Iselin eventually found two other acolytes. On their improvised skis, however, and trying to teach themselves, their attempts dissolved into a caricature of the heroic manoeuvres portrayed in Nansen's book. The obvious solution was to be taught by a real Norwegian. In the course of 1892, Iselin opportunely found one. He was Olaf Kjelsberg, living in Winterthur, near Zürich, barely 80 km away. Kjelsberg had been in the country for more than a decade and was about to take Swiss citizenship. To Iselin, until then, however, Kjelsberg had remained unknown. Iselin had made the contact through his acquaintance with a Dr Eduard Naef from Winterthur, whose climbing friend Kjelsberg happened to be.

An engineer at the Schweizerische Locomotiv-und Maschinenfabrik in Winterthur, Kjelsberg was a pioneer also of the modern electric locomotive. Tall and powerfully built, he had been an accomplished skier in his youth. He was born in 1857 at Lodingen, in the Lofoten Islands, in northern Norway, above the Arctic Circle. The jagged, unglaciated mountain peaks running, like wolf's fangs down the sombre mainland coast, presaged the Alps. Understandably when, in 1881, having finished his professional training in Norway and Germany, he came to Switzerland, he felt at home. He was already a devoted skier; he now became a passionate climber too.

Kjelsberg's presence on Swiss soil coincided with happenings in the Valais, on the other side of the country, apocryphal or not. The Augustinian monks of the St Bernard hospice on the Great St Bernard Pass between Switzerland and Italy, are best known for breeding the dogs that bear their name and once helped them to bring succour to travellers in distress. They had lived at an altitude of 2,000 m since the twelfth century, through the Little Ice Age, regularly marooned by snow, without, apparently any aids to winter travel until the early 1880s. At that point they are said to have acquired skis, presented by a visiting Norwegian. What is certain is that contemporary photographs show them skiing in 1890. This puts them among the forerunners.

In 1890 Kjelsberg also climbed the Bachtel on skis. The Bachtel is a modest mountain near Zürich, with an altitude of no more than 1,100 m. Kjelsberg had nonetheless made the first known ski ascent of an Alpine peak. Before then, he went through a process of experimentation. In Norway, he had skied on Østerdal skis, 3 m long, and adapted to the local, undulating terrain but not, as he quickly discovered, to the steeper Alpine slopes. He changed to the Telemark model, 2 m 30 cm or so in length, and found that, being easier to turn, they functioned well. So by the time that he met Iselin, in September 1892, he was technically attuned to the surroundings. He was more than the true pioneer of skiing in Switzerland; he was an early link between the Nordic and the Alpine world.

From Blichfeld & Huitfeldt, Fritz Huitfeld's firm in Christiania, Kjelsberg ordered three authentic pairs of Norwegian skis for Iselin and his companions. They continued ignominiously to somersault until, on Sunday 11 December 1892 Kjelsberg appeared in Glarus, with another Norwegian called Ulrik Krefting. A few inches of powder snow had freshly fallen and, in perfect conditions, they demonstrated their repertoire. The audience comprised Iselin, his friend Jacques Jenny and Friedrich Iselin, 11 years old, all from Glarus, together with Dr Naef, who had come over from Winterthur for the occasion. They were all agog, never having seen proper skiers before – even Dr Naef.

Style is the man. To make a point, Kjelsberg and Krefting unashamedly showed off. In one number, they shot straight downhill and grandly swept to a stop, with perfect control, amidst snow spraying up like a geyser. Krefting, 'an agile sportsman, tall as a lamp-post' in Iselin's words, notably impressed by jumping over a wall 60 cm high, and landing at least 8 m further down.[4]

When Christoph Iselin tried to spread the good news, he was met with compact disbelief – especially Krefting's jump. Thus mortified, Iselin embarked on a crusade to prove what skis could really do. He chose the crossing of the Pragel pass, between the cantons of Glarus and Schwyz. It took place on 29 January 1893, another Sunday. Iselin was joined by Kjelsberg. The party was completed by Alexander von Steiger, from Glarus and Dr Naef. Kjelsberg, Iselin and Steiger were on skis, but Dr Naef was armed with *schneereif*, the native Swiss mountain snowshoe. The aim was to test the one against the other.

In a newspaper article, Dr Naef wrote how the three skiers rushed over the snow 'with astonishing speed'.[5] When they came to the climb, however, he nearly overhauled them because they had to zig-zag, while he simply plodded straight up. After a short rest, they started the descent on the other side and Dr Naef, in his own words

> had hardly moved 200 metres from our resting place before my companions were sweeping down ... a fairly steep slope which dropped away ... into the depths ... Clouds of whirling snow revealed their path, and they soon disappeared far beneath into the forest.

> With long, swift steps I struggled after them, but the snowshoes allowed no sliding movements. For the distance that they had covered in minutes, indeed seconds, I needed infinitely more time …
>
> I reached [our agreed rendezvous] in an hour and a quarter; the skiers had run down here in 20 minutes. They had thus attained a lead of nearly an hour.

They also happened to have made the first crossing of an Alpine pass on skis. That was no concern of Dr Naef's. He wanted to 'answer the question posed about the practical usability of the ski in the Alpine regions'. That was the race within a race and the skiers had won. The doctor was impressed by the fact that in a metre of loose powder snow, the skis sank only 2 or 3 cm. 'That is not to say', Dr Naef judiciously remarked, 'that the same Norwegian [skis] are suited to all kinds of snow and mountains.' They were of little use, he decided, on hard crust. Under the circumstances, he had a point. Steel edges were a quarter of a century in the future and wooden skis could not grip steep icy Alpine slopes. Even Kjelsberg agreed that skis 'could only be adapted slowly to the real high Alpine mountains'.[6] He allowed that 'walking on snowshoes does not have to be learned; skiing, on the other hand, is an art that needs assiduous practice'.

Despite the caveats, the ski had given the snowshoe the *coup de grâce*. In spite of himself, Dr Naef had made the case for skis. He originally published his article in the *Winterthurer Tagblatt*, his local newspaper. It was reprinted in practically the whole Swiss press. 'What more could we wish for?' asked Iselin, the exultant evangelist.[7] 'Now the mountains were open to us.' This being Switzerland, however, the process continued at a measured pace. Glarus remained the centre for years to come. On 22 November 1893, the Glarus Ski Club was founded, the first ski club in Switzerland. Here too, Christoph Iselin was the prime mover, and first president, with Olaf Kjelsberg a founder member.

The club's aim, to quote its first rule, was 'the promotion and advancement' of skiing.[8] The club was really a subdivision of the Tödi branch of the Swiss Alpine Club in Glarus. Only existing members of the SAC were admitted. One reason was to exclude frivolous beginners and select only those who were seriously interested in the mountain world. Another was a far-seeing desire to avoid the conflict between climbing traditionalists and skiing upstarts that eventually plagued other countries. As a consequence, the Glarus Ski Club pioneered Swiss ski mountaineering. For the next decade, its members made most of the first ascents of Alpine peaks on skis.

The year 1893 also saw in Glarus the founding of the first dedicated ski factory in Switzerland and indeed on the continent. The owner was a carpenter called Melchior Jakober, but the moving spirit was a member of the Glarus Ski Club called Philipp Mercier. Being Swiss, they had a talent for importing technology, then refining it and adding a quality of workmanship of their own. They wanted to produce authentic Norwegian skis but improve them along the way. Kjelsberg designed two models for production. One was basically the Norwegian Telemark ski for jumping and cross-country. The other was something new. It was shorter and broader, 180 cm to 200 cm in length and 10 cm to 12 cm wide. Kjelsberg had grasped that the steep, often constricted Alpine slopes needed a relatively short ski to make turning easier. This was in fact the first specifically designed Alpine ski. With Kjelsberg's designs, Jakober built up an international reputation. He was the precursor of the modern Alpine ski industry.

Meanwhile, the ski was spreading westwards across Switzerland from canton to canton, often with the help of resident Norwegians. Every Norwegian was now expected to be 'born on skis' – a saying of continental origin. This was asking too much. Take, for example, Julius Andersen who, in the winter of 1897–8, was at the watchmaking school at Le Locle, a French-speaking town in the Jura. This is the ancient, low forested mountain range that has given its name to the Jurassic geological system of limestone rocks. The first skis had reached Le Locle from Glarus around 1893 but made little impact. Andersen's Swiss friends rediscovered skiing for themselves by reading about its practice in Norway. They wanted genuine Norwegian skis and applied to him for help. In his own words: 'They absolutely would not believe that I could not ski properly.'[9] Nor could he convince them that Stavanger, his home town, on the south-western coast of Norway, exposed to the Gulf Stream, was virtually free of snow, while the surroundings of Le Locle had a metre or more.

However, in the country of the blind, so to say, a one-eyed man is king. Good patriot that he was, Andersen ordered skis from a factory in Telemark and one fine winter Sunday organized a ski tour. Three ladies wanted to come along. In Andersen's own words, they

> had to work hard to persuade their respective mothers to allow their daughters to go skiing, because they considered it unseemly for ladies. They would probably land upside down in the snow ... and reveal themselves to the gentlemen.
>
> I suggested that they put on their dark gymnastic suits, and then they were given permission.

This was the first time that women skiers are known to have appeared in trousers, unadorned, which put them ahead of the Norwegian pioneers. There was another diversion in an eccentric pharmacist who turned up in opera hat, bow tie and galoshes. Andersen led his party to La Chaux-de-Fonds (Le Corbusier's birthplace), a town a few kilometres distant. The Jura was pure Nordic in its contours but with its large, southern conifers and distinctive population it possessed another ambience. Julius Andersen brought his gaggle of beginners 'slowly but surely' over the gently undulating terrain to their destination. 'The homeward journey was dramatic,' he said. 'We stayed too long in La Chaux-de-Fonds' – due either to skiers well established there, or to the mellowed charm of the white wine of Neuchâtel, or both.

> Darkness and fog began to fall. I myself nearly fell into a railway cutting on the main line [from] Paris ... We only arrived back at our pension at 1.30 in the morning ...

> In subsequent practice, it was a pleasure to see the energy with which everyone, both men and women, applied themselves to skiing, and they soon became quite good. We founded a ski club, which eventually had several hundred members ... A few [cross-country] ski races were organised while I was there, but no ski-jumping. The ladies also became quite good at skiing, but it took some time before their mothers thought that it was ladylike to ski in the vicinity of the town.

Andersen's semi-comical experience illustrated why Norwegians were so much in demand. It was not only because of a certain affinity between themselves and Switzerland. A little snobbery was involved. There was status in having someone from the home of the ski. It was also for a very practical reason. Even now there was no systematic analysis of skiing technique and hence no teaching method. Textbooks were still few and unsatisfactory to a degree. The only way of learning was by mimicry.

Not every tyro could find an expert to lead the way. There were dedicated souls who tried to work out the elements of technique for themselves. In 1890, for some reason, a Louis Dufour from Les Avants, in the canton of Vaud ordered a pair of skis from Christiania. He tried his best under the delusion that they could only be used on hard snow crust. It was only on meeting a certain Monsieur Thudichum from Geneva some years later that, for the first time, he saw anyone ski properly.

This Thudichum was an influential autodidact. He came to skiing through one of the newspaper reports of Iselin's crossing of the Pragel Pass. He ordered a pair of skis from Jakober, and first used them in 1894. In the gentle terrain of the Jura, the sober northern backdrop to Geneva, he taught himself to ski. On 31 January 1896 he had advanced far enough to make the first recorded ski ascent of the Dôle – a summit that has given its name to an esoteric, pleasing red wine.

Like most skiing pioneers in Switzerland, Thudichum belonged to the Swiss Alpine Club. In 1896, he published two articles in *L'Écho des Alpes*, the journal of its French-speaking members. Being a Swiss institution, the club respected the delicate balance of a polyglot population living crammed up against each other in mutual toleration by publishing, even-handedly, in the three national languages of French, German and Italian.

Thudichum's two articles were in effect a manual of skiing. Philosophically, he was much influenced by Nansen, whose book on the crossing of Greenland had first been published in French as *A travers le Grönland* in 1893. Practically, Thudichum's method was all his own. His articles remained the only manual in French for many years. They also happened to be the clearest instructions yet published in any language – and that included the books of Urdahl and Huitfeldt in Norway. Having had to learn by experience, bitter or not, might be one explanation. Another could be the proverbial logic of the French mind, with mania for analysis. Also, as a Genevois, Thudichum would have spoken a kind of French that had not changed much since the eighteenth century and the Age of Reason. Whatever it was, Thudichum had arrived at the correct axioms. Thus: 'If you lose control, and observe some obstacle over which you fear to hurl yourself, you must instantly crouch down and fall *sideways* into the snow, where you will make a hole, and where you will stop.'[10] And: 'This ... is absolutely innocuous and most comical for the gallery. Your friends will shower you with compliments. However, if you fall backwards, you will simply sit on your skis, and the speed of descent will hardly be reduced.'

The beginning of wisdom on the slopes really is learning how to fall. Thudichum had rediscovered – or learned about – a fundamental rule. He dearly wanted to spread skiing among all mountaineers, French-speaking Swiss in particular, but for some reason only gathered round himself a small coterie. Awkward in manner, perhaps, he did not have the power to persuade. He was one more of the unhappy breed of forerunners, who only pave the way for others to succeed.

In 1900, a Norwegian engineer called Ole Houm came to work in Geneva. Knowing that besides being the city of Calvin and Rousseau, it lay among mountains under the Jura and at the foot of the Alps, he naturally brought his skis. For a season or so he explored the surrounding terrain in winter, with never a ski track to see and always on his own. He understood the risks of solitary skiing, especially in steep, unknown country on a kind of snow he did not fully understand but, *pace* Thudichum, he knew no other skiers. In 1902, he advertised for companions. He had exactly one reply. It was from a Dr Léon Weber, according to whom the following exchange took place:

'Why is it that in a country with such wonderful snow, you don't ski?'

'Oh, I ski all right, but I don't know how to do it.'[11]

It happened to be true. The winter before, Weber had been working at Leysin, in the Alps of the French-speaking Canton of Vaud. In the window of a local souvenir shop, stranded among the music boxes, painted wooden plates and cuckoo clocks, he saw some mysterious objects, ornately decorated with pokerwork. The proprietor thought that they were what he called 'snow skates' from the Black Forest; in other words a pair of skis. On an impulse, Weber bought them, and tried them out 'audaciously', in his own words, 'straight downhill': 'Naturally I fell, I got up, I slid backwards, I fell again. Nonetheless, an eager autodidact, helped by instinct, I managed to make a few runs in front of [a crowd of] astonished [spectators].'

Anyway, Houm took Weber up into the Jura and taught him how to ski, including the Telemark and Christiania turns, the latter name just coming into use. It was still naturally Nordic skiing, across country, coping with natural obstacles. Quite soon, they had a flourishing group frequenting the nearby pass of La Givrine in the Jura, on the border with France. It was under the aegis of the local section of the Swiss Alpine Club and only then did Weber learn about Thudichum.

Houm and Weber were not quite the ordinary pioneers. Both had a technical bent and proceeded to improve their equipment. Before starting to teach Weber, Houm fitted his skis with the Huitfeldt binding. The heelstrap remained the weakest link as the Høyer-Ellefsen tensioning clip was still not on the market. Weber invented and produced a device that all but anticipated it. So did Houm. His solution was more radical. Using the Huitfeldt metal ears, instead of a tensioning lever on the heelstrap, he placed it *in front* of the binding.

By a neat coincidence, this application of technology marked the end of an era. Skiing had now spread all over Switzerland from Glarus in the east to its western extremity in Geneva. Thudichum summed it up in this way: 'The ski has turned the snow which, hitherto has only been a prison, into a superb means of communication.'[12] The Swiss Alpine Club, however, did not supply firewood to heat their winter huts because as one member put it, they 'scarcely sought to encourage winter excursions, veritable tours de force, undertaken for pure notoriety'.

There is a simple explanation for the evolution of Alpine skiing in the last two decades of the nineteenth century. The classic age of mountaineering ended around 1870, by when the great summits had been climbed. The ski offered something new. It removed the last vestige of fear from the mountain world. It completed a historical cycle that goes back to Ancient Egypt. From the New Kingdom around 1200BC comes this prayer by Nofer-Abu, a 'repentant sinner' as the hieroglyphics say, to the goddess 'Mersegert, Mistress of the Heavens ... whose fair name is "the mountain summit of the West"':[13]

> [I am] an ignorant man, with no understanding ... I prayed to the all-powerful mountain-top, and to every god and goddess: ... 'Look, I say to great and small ... "show humility to the mountain top"' ... Verily, hear all ye that have ears, that live on the earth: show humility to the mountain tops of the West.

Geneva was wholly suitable to give such awe a modern cast. In the background to the South, on French soil, hovering above the lesser ranges like a mirage, loomed Mont Blanc – in clear weather – the famous sight, emblematic of the city, the summit of the Alps, its ice dome set off by the dulled silver waters of Lake Geneva. Appropriately, a Geneva citizen, Horace de Saussure, financed its first ascent in 1786. A more famous Genevois, Jean-Jacques Rousseau, recommended mountain air because 'in rising above the habitation of men, one leaves behind all low and earthbound emotions'.[14]

Houm and Weber were the heirs of Saussure, Rousseau and all who went before. Swiss skiing now had a place in the exploration of the Alps. The protagonists, however, for the most part came from the cities. In the mountains, a parallel development was under way.

With more than a century of tourism behind them, the Swiss had catered to the visitors who had come variously to gaze at the high Alps or climb its peaks. They had colonized the upland valleys with hotels. Historically, their season was confined to spring and summer. Economics dictated that it be prolonged. The ski came to the rescue. It led to the Swiss invention of the winter sports resort. That in turn meant that skiing had a divergent evolution. On the one hand were the foreign visitors; on the other, the native pioneers. It was a dichotomy peculiar to Switzerland. Driven by self-preservation Alpine villages were turning into cosmopolitan ski resorts, Davos being arguably the first.

# 22

# Davos: The cradle of the Ski Resort

Davos epitomizes the Swiss form of skiing. By a trick of topography it has a distinctive air of isolation. The cities lie in the plain between the Jura and the Alps. The snows are up in the mountains, often far away. Lying in the canton of the Grisons, at the eastern edge of Switzerland, Davos seems particularly remote. Its origins as a resort lie in a search for health. Its founder was Alexander Spengler. He was one of those men who, somehow, personify the age.

A German from the Rhineland, Alexander Spengler was born in Mannheim, on 20 March 1827. In due course he entered the University of Heidelberg. There he lived the life of a student of his type and class. He fought the obligatory *mensur*, fencing with sharpened weapons, the aim of which is to draw a little blood, leaving facial scars as a badge of entry into a conventional elite. Surprisingly, the year of revolt in 1848 found him not on the side of the ruling establishment but

33. Tobias Branger, pioneer of skiing at Davos. Snapshot by Arthur Conan Doyle, 1894.
*Dokumentationsbibliothek Davos*

as an officer with the revolutionaries in the Grand Duchy of Baden. With the defeat of the uprising, Spengler fled over the border into Switzerland. He was condemned to death in absentia.

This was the man, with his contradictory nature, who fathered the modern ski resort. How he arrived in Davos is a story in itself. It begins with the Swiss confederal system. Political asylum was the business, not of the central government in Berne, the capital, but the individual Cantons. Luckily for Spengler, he knew three Swiss, Hans Hold, Gaudenz von Salis-Seewis and Caspar Latour, who had been fellow students of his at Heidelberg. They were well connected and came from the Grisons. Somehow they persuaded the cantonal authorities – on payment of a cautionary deposit against becoming a charge on the public purse – to admit Spengler as a stateless refugee.

That was in 1851. The previous year, meanwhile, he had resumed his studies at the University of Zürich. There, he was befriended by a fellow-German, Carl Friedrich Wilhelm Ludwig, Professor of Anatomy and Physiology, who also had liberal sympathies and found it convenient to leave his homeland. At Heidelberg, Spengler had read law but now, at Ludwig's urging, he changed to medicine. He qualified in 1853, whereupon his friends from the Grisons suggested that he practice in Davos. To be a country doctor was not exactly what Spengler had in mind. However, he felt that he owed a debt of gratitude to the friends who had helped him when in need. Moreover, his safety was involved. His political asylum was temporary, and could be revoked at any time. He had long since abandoned

34. Dr. Alexander Spengler, who began it all, strolling down Promenade, the main street of Davos, in 1897. He is the bearded figure in the foreground. The Kurhaus, an early sanatorium is on the left. This was the original ski resort. The winter visitors of those days did not yearn for the quaint alpine village. They wanted Piccadilly, or the Faubourg St. Honoré in the Alps. *Photosammlung Bruno Gerber, Davos*

politics but, stateless still, he needed a nationality and a passport. Davos held out the prospect of both. It had lacked a doctor of its own for five years. Spengler would acquire legitimacy through doing work that Swiss nationals avoided – a phenomenon that has lasted to this day. He accepted the post of district doctor in Davos.

He took up his appointment on 8 November 1853, after a long ride on a horse-drawn wagon up the valley of the Prättigau. He had been there before but still he was homesick and melancholy as he arrived. What hove into view was a bleak, scattered mountain village, cut off from the world; a place that time had forgotten. It had the eerie feeling of ancient habitation. The Romans had been there and, long before, unknown prehistoric tribes of the Bronze Age. Heathens had worshipped at the hot springs of Spina down the valley.

Accustomed to urban pleasures, the company of prominent men and lively conversation round the *stammtisch* of the émigré community at the Café Littéraire in Zürich, Spengler, now faced with mountain peasants, felt as if he had been driven again into exile. There were compensations, of course. Less than two years later, he married a local girl, Elisabeth Ambühl, sister of his first landlady in Davos. A month before, through the intercession of Hans Hold, he had received the Grisons citizenship and hence Swiss nationality. Nonetheless, to the inhabitants of Davos, Dr Spengler was still a refugee, for which his wife had to bear unspoken disapproval. Spengler himself long felt an outsider. In a moment of despair, whatever the consequences, he thought of returning home to Mannheim. The German authorities were still persecuting former revolutionaries. 'How do you know that in the worst case you will only be sent to prison for two years?' Hold wrote in answer to an agonized letter:

> And even if that is the case, you will be wasting too many of your best years, not to attain a great goal, but for *nothing* … what could you not do in that time, not only for yourself, but for your fellow-men? This duty to yourself, this sacred duty to your fellow-men weighs more than all the reasons that make you want to go to prison.[1]

Hold managed to dissuade Spengler from his quixotic undertaking. In the end he remained in Davos for good. Tuberculosis was the explanation.

This was the scourge of the times. Almost by chance, two cases, following hard upon each other, caused Spengler to undergo a mental revolution. There was at the time in Davos a Protestant pastor called Christian Forchhammer, of Danish origin. He contracted tuberculosis. Spengler followed conventional treatment. This saw mountain air as injurious and required a mild southern climate. In 1858, Forchhammer was sent down to the lowland and died the following year. In the meanwhile, he had been replaced by one Ernst Schrenk from Bâle.

Schrenk was himself an invalid. He arrived in March 1858, the valley covered in snow and therefore, by reigning ideas, the worst season of the year. Spengler made him sleep in a cowshed. This was not the usual treatment but belonged to folk medicine. As a comment on Spengler, this was interesting enough. The idea was that the ammonia produced by cattle was curative, although repulsive. Despite this experience, Schrenk sensationally recovered.

Tuberculosis was not his trouble but something to do with the nerves. Nevertheless, this gave Spengler pause for thought. Luckily he was at heart a physiologist. He was influenced by Ludwig, who in fact happened to be the founder of modern physiology. Spengler had the streak of originality to see his patients not so much as individuals but as specimens through whom he could observe disease in the round.

Schrenk and Forchhammer were only two cases, but Davos was a unique clinical laboratory in which to pursue the matter. Its population of some 1,500 provided a manageable sample. Spengler was struck by their robust good health and longevity but above all by an almost complete absence of pulmonary tuberculosis. He also noticed that inhabitants who went abroad into the lowlands and the cities, often contracted tuberculosis but on return were spontaneously cured.

It was an age when the humblest physician, unfettered by medical bureaucrats, could still make ground-breaking discoveries. Spengler, like others, was now tryng to find a cure for tuberculosis. In Davos he thought that, perhaps, he had found the key. It lay, he decided, in the altitude.

Others had noticed that Davos was a health-giving place. It was 1,600 m above sea level. Moreover it was dry. The valley in which it lay ran roughly between north and south so that it was protected from the prevailing winds. The valley being wide and the mountains set back, there was plenty of sunshine. To Spengler, however, altitude counted most. He was the first to see it as a cure for tuberculosis. Moreover, he was the first to give a rational explanation.

In this he was following Karl Ludwig's lead. Ludwig's great innovation had been to apply the physical sciences to physiology. Spengler followed his lead in working out the effects of rarefied air on the organism, notably the amount of oxygen in the blood and the effect on breathing. He was the first to touch on the subject. Most of his reasoning has stood the test of time. He was the founder of high altitude physiology.

He put it to therapeutic use. He began treating tuberculotics by bringing them to Davos. He was pioneering the concept of high altitude in the treatment of tuberculosis. He had turned conventional medical wisdom on its head. He had to fight the medical establishment.

When Spengler first arrived in Davos in 1853, it had no travellers to speak of. Isolated in a cul de sac, without sensational romantic scenery and great peaks, it was off the tourist and climbing itinerary. Nonetheless rumours of Dr Spengler's new treatment began filtering through. Davos had been opened up in 1858, when the railway from Zürich reached Landquart, at the mouth of the Prättigau valley in which Davos lies. Patients were coming with the trains.

They were attracted not only by Dr Spengler's medical skill, but his personality, curative in itself. Hotels were beginning to appear to house his patients. The first in Davos-Platz opened in 1860 followed, the next year, by the Hotel

35. Downhill technique, Switzerland (Davos) 1890s.

Strela, a more accommodating establishment. The metamorphosis from village to resort had begun.

Davos was strictly a district strung out along the valley. Davos-Platz was one village – the capital, as it were; Davos-Dorf another and there were more. Spengler, like most men of substance, lived in Davos-Platz.

The cause of tuberculosis was only found when the German doctor, Robert Koch, discovered the tuberculin bacillus in 1882. In Spengler's day, the disease was considered to be due to a faulty metabolism. It was not thought to be contagious so there was no call for isolation.

Spengler, however, had no illusions about the state of knowledge. He believed in some unknown factor. He eschewed medicines, most of which he despised as quackery. His treatment was based on initial rest, then plenty of brisk walking in the fresh air, early bedtime, and a fortifying diet. He advocated dairy food and, in moderation, Veltliner, the red wine of the mountains, which he felt was a cure in itself. Even today, his regime would make good sense. He was treating the organism, not the symptoms, promoting a sense of well-being and, as we would say, building up the immune system. Surprisingly, he ordered cold, early morning showers. He did not believe in constant supervision but made it clear that the patients had to depend on their own self-discipline. Psychologically, this all made good sense.

Spengler was at last beginning to feel at home in Davos. However, he had one more battle still to fight. His patients, like other visitors, only came in summer. In the face of prejudice, he insisted that, however cold the air, winter was the healing season too. For years he made no headway. The turning point came on 8 February 1865, when two Germans drove up unannounced in a horse-drawn sledge. One was a bookseller called Hugo Richter, from Königsberg in Prussia; the other, Friedrich Unger, a doctor from Leipzig.

They were not exactly welcome. Under protest they were admitted to the Hotel Strela. It had a few heated rooms, but was only prepared for summer guests. That the new arrivals had come in the off season was unheard of, and made them objects of suspicion. They were thought to be German revolutionaries hiding in Davos to plot an insurrection and were reported to the police who, however declared them innocuous. Richter, in fact, could hardly walk. Both he and Unger were supposed to be in the last stages of tuberculosis. Having failed elsewhere, they were desperate for help. Dr Spengler was their only hope. Such were the first known winter guests in Davos.

They were, however, not the first of their kind. They were preceded by a certain Herr Mayr, a Swiss from Arbon on Lake Constance. He spent the winter of 1834–5 in Samedan, over the mountains near St Moritz. He was what was then called asthmatic and hoped to find a cure.

In Davos, Spengler at least was delighted with his unexpected patients. Glassed-in verandas were unheard of. Spengler improvised deck-chairs from hay sledges covered with boards, on which, weather permitting, Richter and Unger lay out in the fresh air. They made sensational recoveries. Afraid of tempting fate by returning to the lowlands, like Spengler, they settled permanently in Davos. They became the nucleus of a resident colony in search of health. They played a leading rôle in the emergence of the resort. Richter, like Spengler, quickly married a local girl, Magdalena Michel. He took over the management of the Hotel Strela and eventually started a bookshop, publishers and printing works. Dr Unger set up a medical practice. They were soon joined by a band of patients; mostly from Switzerland, Germany and Holland, with a few from Russia. In those days, by definition, all were well off. They brought investment and business acumen to Davos. Hotels sprang up, one beside the other. The transient population had begun overtaking the indigenous one. Thus Davos became the first organized Alpine winter spa.

The process affected the whole district. The inhabitants had historically been subsistence farmers. Poverty had driven many out to find work. Now the reigning diet for tuberculotics, based on fresh dairy products, ensured a profitable local demand. Moreover, the visitors wanted attention. Shops were opening to cater to their needs. This in turn meant that jobs were appearing on the doorstep. When local youths went out into the world now it was not so much from dire necessity as to garner experience of foreign cultures and foreign languages, to serve a cosmopolitan clientele on their return. A threshold had been passed in the change from village to resort. An unintended consequence of all this was to slow the drift to the cities with rising industrialization and eventually to halt depopulation of the upland valleys. It was a pattern that eventually shaped the Alps. With a little oversimplification, Alexander Spengler could be called the father of it all.

In 1873, a visitor presented him with a pair of skis. They were, unusually, of the central Nordic type, unequal in length, and came from Scandinavia, probably

Sweden. Dr Spengler tried them briefly by walking in his garden; so did Carl, his elder son. Apart from the mysterious visitor, they thus became the first people known to have used skis in Davos. It was a decade before anyone seems to have followed suit. In the autumn of 1883, a local newspaper reported that

> this winter it is proposed to try the Norwegian sport of ski-running in Davos. Skis are, as is well known, a sort of snow shoe more than a metre long, with which one can move quickly over soft snow, and go uphill as well as downhill. Why should skis not replace the inconvenient snow shoes which are so common in this country?[2]

From several points of view, this is of great interest. Firstly, the journal, *Davoser Blätter* was aimed at foreign visitors. It was the first newspaper in Davos. It had been founded by Hugo Richter in 1874. He wrote much of the copy. To his obvious displeasure, snowshoes were clearly well established. In fact, during the winter of 1875, *Davoser Blätter* had already reported that 'some courageous visitors taking the cure [for tuberculosis] have climbed up to the Schatzalp and Strela Pass with the help of snowshoes ... We would advise the enterprising mountain climber to take some wine or brandy on an excursion up there,' the journal helpfully went on, 'because the restaurant ... is closed during the winter.'[3]

At least winter sports had started to take root, albeit among supposed invalids; itself a telling detail. The snow shoe was a kind of half-way house. The implication of *Davoser Blätter*'s report in 1883 is that knowledge of the ski was becoming general, at least among the educated classes. The peg for the piece was even more intriguing.

The attempt to ski was to be made by an 11-year-old German schoolboy called Wilhelm Paulcke. His father was a well-off pharmacist from Leipzig who had been living in Davos for some years on account of his wife's health. Wilhelm was also supposed to be sickly. He attended the Fridericianum, a school for children of the foreign colony. His behaviour was a catalogue of naughtiness, which hinted at a sound constitution after all. The ski he was to try were a Christmas present from his father. As he himself told the tale in after years:

> My fondest wish, to possess such miraculous boards, was fulfilled! ... Our wonderful governess, much loved by us children, a big blond Norwegian, Agnes Duborgh, had told us about the Telemarkings who came to Christiania and astounded the city dwellers with their skill in skiing. And skis [like theirs] now belonged to me![4]

Paulcke's father had ordered skis from Christiania through Agnes. Thus a Norwegian governess and a naughty German schoolboy reintroduced skiing to Davos. They were also indirectly responsible for its first appearance in another resort. There was a friend of Paulcke's father, Dr Otto Herwig, practising in the village of Arosa, in the next valley. When he heard of Wilhelm's forthcoming pair of skis at Christmas 1883, he wanted one too. Agnes arranged the matter in Christiania, as she had done for Paulcke. Dr Herwig tried the skis but, without instruction, merely somersaulted about in the snow. He quickly gave up, condemning the terrain as unsuitable for skiing.

Wilhelm was made of sterner stuff. For one thing, he had Agnes by his side. Her home in Christiania was actually within sight of Huseby; she would have seen the Telemarkings as a child at Iversløkken and elsewhere. Presumably she could ski herself but could not teach the art, so she wrote to *Norsk Idrætsblad* in Christiania for advice. 'You are asking the … impossible when you want us to teach … skiing by correspondence',[5] came the reprimand in print. Nonetheless: 'We will try to formulate a few concise rules.' Downhill for example: 'Keep the skis close together, the right … ski 10 to 15 centimetres in front. If you meet unevenness in the terrain, move [it] even further forwards' and so on. 'The art of skiing' came the conclusion: 'is quite simple. Beyond the above mentioned rules, there is only this to observe: Never afraid! – voilà tout! You must not throw yourself down when you begin gathering speed, just "let it go, out of the way!"'

Judging by results, Agnes successfully transmitted this unexceptional advice. In Paulcke's own words:

> The new Norwegian devices aroused great enthusiasm in the Fridericianum. [They] were taken to a Davos cartwright, who made copies for some of my school friends. And then the first blissful runs on the long planks began on the secluded and hitherto untouched slopes of Davos, from the Oberwiese down to the [River] Landwasser; better runs were on the Ditschma slope.

These are quite demanding runs, even for beginners today. There were technical reasons for Dr Herwig's failure and Wilhelm Paulcke's success. Bindings were the cause. The first Norwegian patent was still six years in the future. What arrived in Davos and Arosa were simple toe loops of cane, without any heelstraps. Dr Herwig simply took what he was given, which is enough to explain his tumbles in the snow. Young Wilhelm, on the other hand, realized that he could not

> begin with such primitive fastenings. I went to my workbench and the tool cupboard [and] cut two planks of wood a little over a foot long and exactly the width of the skis. [I] made a hole in each of these planks for the heel of the boot, and attached them in front to the skis with hinges. The foot was secured to these childish 'sole bindings' with a toestrap in front, and, behind by a strap round the instep – like skates used to be.

For an 11 year old, Wilhelm Paulcke showed perspicacity. Skating was then well established in Davos and he had seen how to transfer technology. A precocious innovator, he had anticipated an invention by a decade at least. More to the point, he had devised a way of securing lateral control, essential to downhill running. Also he and his companions really earned their pleasure. Ski lifts were a thing of the future and every inch of running down had to be paid for with a corresponding climb.

All in all, young Wilhelm – and his much-loved Norwegian governess – were among the pioneers of skiing in the Alps. They must be classed with Olav Kjelsberg and, perhaps, the monks of St Bernard.

If Wilhelm's father had intended those first skis as a bribe he had achieved his aim. Having invented his binding, Wilhelm became a reformed character. He turned into a model pupil at the Fridericianum. This continued when, after a year or so, the family went back to Germany. More to the point, as he recorded, since the stay in Davos, 'I have been faithful to the ski and became its dedicated apostle.' He ended as a university professor and a pioneer both in the study of snow and of ski mountaineering.

Skiing lapsed in Davos after the departure of the Paulckes, as it did in Arosa after Dr Herwig's gawky trial. The *Davoser Blätter*, still the champion of the ski, was driven to deplore the fact after eight years had passed. The explanation, so the journal uncomprehendingly declared in January 1891, was that

> for years tobogganing and skating have been the favourite pastimes of the many companions of the chest patients in Davos. In fact the English have developed tobogganing to such a pitch that many of them spend the winter in Davos or the Engadine [St Moritz] mainly on that account, because they can indulge in the sport here as nowhere else.[6]

The reference to the English is revealing. After the arrival of Unger and Richter in 1865, Germans dominated the foreign colony. Then from 1873 to 1879, an economic crisis in Germany drastically reduced their numbers. The Davos hotels had recklessly expanded, and could not fill their rooms. The British came to the rescue and took the Germans' place. Solid late Victorians, they put their stamp on Davos and thus, in the end, superimposed on Spengler's pioneering, gave the Alpine winter sports resort its final form. Its essence was a stupendous mountain backdrop, furnished with civilized amenities.

# 23

# The English Skiing at Davos

The first Englishman known to have wintered in Davos was a certain Arthur William Waters. Arriving in the summer of 1869, he was the advance guard of the English invasion. Mrs MacMorland, an Edinburgh Scot, followed him in 1871. Both were invalids drawn by Spengler's growing reputation. Both became pioneers of winter sports. Waters, born in 1847, had been a tuberculotic since childhood; exactly what ailed Mrs MacMorland is unclear. She was said to be 'delicate', which usually meant the nebulous psychosomatic afflictions of Victorian women, deployed now and then for tactical advantage. At any rate, Davos turned her into a bundle of energy and she lived to a ripe old age. She became part of Alpine history. In 1855, together with her parents, she had visited St Moritz. They were the first British family to do so.

Plain and indomitable, Mrs MacMorland was born Elizabeth Macdonald Bradshaw-Smith in 1839, of a wealthy land-owning father and a Lockhart mother. Somewhere along the way she acquired as husband the spectral John MacMorland, a Church of Scotland minister. Hers was the first British family to settle in Davos.

Waters left in 1871, after two winters, apparently cured. He returned in 1881 after a relapse, and stayed for the next 24 years. Mrs MacMorland, by contrast, settled down at once. She appeared with her mother and daughter, followed eventually by her husband. Meeting an expatriate German entrepreneur called Johann Carl Coester, they bewailed the absence in Davos of a hotel specially run for the English, as in other Swiss summer resorts. This meant chiefly solid food and enhanced hygiene in the form of hot baths and flushing lavatories. For his own health, Coester also wanted to stay in Davos. He spoke English. He saw his chance. He built a hotel for British guests. It was called the Belvedere. It broods over Davos still. It opened on 17 July 1875. The MacMorland family moved in and stayed for 13 years. They were the progenitors of the English winter sports hotel, from which foreigners were tacitly outlawed.

Invalid or not, Mrs MacMorland had sporting attributes. In the winter of 1876–7, she opened a skating rink. The first one in Davos had been built by Waters, the pioneer six years before, but this was the first permanent installation. Mrs MacMorland arranged to tap the Landwasser, the river running through Davos, and flood an artificial rink. That same season she helped to organize a toboggan race; the first of its kind in the Alps. She was one founder of Davos as a winter sports resort. The other was a very different character.

John Addington Symonds, Harrow and Balliol, the son of a Bristol doctor, was an aesthete, something of which Elizabeth MacMorland could never be accused. Symonds arrived in Davos in August 1877, two months before his thirty-seventh birthday. A slight figure at best, he was now ravaged physically by tuberculosis and mentally by an insatiable homosexual drive. Davos treated both in its own fashion. Symonds was actually married. Together with his embittered but complaisant wife and four daughters, he went to live at the Hotel Belvedere. He romanticized the sturdy mountain peasants and quickly formed an attachment to Christian Buol, the notably handsome scion of a local family. Having found his refuge, Symonds built himself a large chalet at Davos-Platz called Am Hof, after the meadow in which it stood. He moved in on 25 September 1881. In honour of the day, a Union Jack was hoisted on a lightning conductor.

Symonds was of independent means and soon after leaving Oxford had devoted himself to the literary life. He was a prolific author and, regrettably, a versifier too. He made his name with the *Renaissance in Italy*, in seven volumes, which did much to form the English view of the subject. Most of his major works were written in Davos. He started the literary associations of the place.

He did more. Surprisingly, like Mrs MacMorland, he harboured sporting instincts and, like her, he was drawn to tobogganing. In 1883, he organized the first international race in the Alps, drawn from visitors to Davos. It became a regular event. Two years later, he presented the Symonds Cup as a floating trophy. This was one of the earliest winter sports prizes in the Alps.

Naively or not, Mrs MacMorland and Symonds publicized Davos in England. She wrote a whole book: *Davos Platz: A New Alpine Resort for Sick and Sound in Summer and Winter. By One Who Knows It Well.* This appeared in 1878. The same year, *The Fortnightly Review*, a solid literary journal, published an essay by Symonds, *Davos in Winter*. 'The Alps, in their winter robe of snow, offer a spectacle which ... is unsurpassed', Symonds wrote:

> Sledging is an excellent amusement, and ... skating can be reckoned on ... But in spite of this, life is monotonous. The mechanic pacings to and fro, which are a condition of the cure, become irksome ... Then it cannot be denied that a great deal of snow falls in winter ... Snow fall is, however, no interruption to exercise ... On the contrary, I had the exhilarating consciousness that I could ... advance steadily under conditions which in England would have been hopeless.[1]

This and other publications, medical or not, began drawing the English to Davos. Among them was the unlikely figure of Robert Louis Stevenson. Yet another tuberculotic, he arrived in November 1880, searching for a cure, and stayed – naturally – at the Belvedere. With him was his American wife Fanny, and stepson, Lloyd Osbourne. They remained for two winters, Stevenson and Symonds becoming friends. It was a surprising constellation: the one a commonplace Bohemian, the other so prim and academic. Stevenson's passion was playing with lead soldiers but, unexpectedly, like Symonds (and Mrs MacMorland) he liked tobogganing too; albeit with a highly personal twist. 'The true way to toboggan is alone and at night' he wrote in one of several newspaper articles from Davos.[2]

> You push off; the toboggan fetches away; she begins to feel the hill, to glide, to swim, to gallop. In a breath you are out from under the pine tree, and a whole heavenful of stars reels and flashes overhead ... in an atmosphere tingling with forty degrees of frost ... and adds a new excitement to the life of man upon his planet.

However: 'A mountain valley has, at the best, a certain prison-like effect on the imagination', Stevenson also wrote about the same time.[3] In other words Stevenson, as yet unfulfilled, cordially loathed Davos. Nonetheless, it was there that he completed *Treasure Island* and in the fractured personality of Symonds very likely found the germ of *The Strange Case of Dr Jekyll and Mr Hyde*, which goes to show that stimulation does not necessarily come from liking where you are.

Stevenson also touched on something else:

> [Davos] is half English ... but it still remains half German; and hence we have a band which is able to play and a company of actors able ... to act ... Meantime in the English hotels home-played farces ... enliven the evenings; a charity bazaar sheds genial consternation ... and from time to time the young folks carol and revolve untunefully ... through the figures of a singing quadrille.[4]

The English at Davos were never in the majority but, in the age of Empire, they did colonize the place. They formed their own hermetically sealed community. They congregated in the space between Davos Platz and Dorf. It was dubbed The English Quarter. Symonds and Mrs MacMorland were exceptional in speaking German and observing the life of the local Swiss. Otherwise, the English brought their own brand of awkward self-conscious insularity but nonetheless moulded the surroundings.

Not only English invalids came to Davos. Their more or less healthy companions came as well. To satisfy their demands, shops, hotels, tea rooms, even a theatre attached to the Hotel Belvedere sprang up. By the 1890s the proto-winter sports resort, as an English product, had arrived. Ribbon development swamped the original high Alpine villages with the undistinguished aspect of a Victorian seaside town, complete with Anglican church. Davos Platz and Dorf grew into one, strung out along Promenade, the main thoroughfare, and among the longest of shopping streets. Davos had taken on its present form. Pretty it was not, but this was the forerunner of the purpose-built resort.

It was properly opened up in 1890, with the arrival of the Rhätische Bahn, the Rhaetian railway, the narrow-gauge branch line from Landquart – but only just. This being Switzerland, a referendum was called and the project was almost quashed by worried inhabitants of the Prättigau. The line joined Davos to the railhead and obviated the long approach by carriage or horse-drawn sledge.

At first it hardly affected traffic. In 1891, the *Davoser Blätter* used a review of the German translation of *The First Crossing of Greenland* to complain that since Wilhelm Paulcke, 'skiing has never been regularly practised in Davos ... Will this noble art never be adopted here?'[5] To the writer's disbelief, skating and tobogganing still ruled. 'Our article', so the *Davoser Blätter* bewailed after nearly two years

> has had no effect. Admittedly we have seen some young men dragging themselves painfully over the snow-covered valley floor on skis, as was the case in previous years. In fact we have even seen skis displayed in a shop, but that is all.[6]

This unwittingly covered the start of a local skiing renaissance. The journal soon gracefully admitted that those awkward-looking figures included 'Herr Tobias Branger who with ... resident foreigners [is] fervently interested in skis. We also understand that it is due to him that the ski has been introduced here.'[7]

This Tobias Branger, solemn, tall, dark and athletic, was a local businessman. He had invented the Davos sledge, the plaything of generations of children. He had another claim to distinction. He owned the shop with skis. He is said to have first seen a pair in the Swedish-Norwegian pavilion at the Paris international exhibition of 1889, when, incidentally the Eiffel Tower was inaugurated and Nansen, having just returned from Greenland, was the hero of the hour. As a consequence or otherwise, Branger ordered skis from Norway. He received them in the autumn of that year, initially to hire out. He was probably the first to do so, and thus founded a whole specialized industry. He was a pioneer in more ways than one.

Tobias soon began trying his skis himself. He had an example near to hand. During the winter of 1889–90, an English visitor, Colonel Napier, came to Davos, bringing in his entourage a Norwegian manservant called Nils Nilsen. Napier had found him at Suldal, in Western Norway, when salmon fishing. Nilsen brought his skis to Davos. He only stayed for one season. He became the stuff of legend. He was said to have skied from a hotel with a tea-tray for his employer.

It was all very well for foreigners to indulge in blatant eccentricity but, like other Swiss pioneers, Iselin, for example, Tobias Branger was the object of mockery when observed. Nonetheless, his family and certain audacious friends, joined him, preferring to do so at night. Without guidance they taught themselves an outlandish technique, depending heavily on straddling their single stick to brake and clinging to it sideways, while leaning absurdly backwards to control speed.

In the meantime, *Davoser Blätter*'s review of *The First Crossing of Greenland* had stimulated the interest of Tobias Branger's brother, Johann. Nansen, as it were, persuaded him to join the coterie. Early in the winter of 1893, Tobias and Johann Branger, and two friends made a trial ascent to Schatzalp, on the southern slopes above Davos. In Johann's words:

> This climb was certainly more drudgery than enjoyment, but convinced most of us that

it might be easier to learn [to ski] than [we] had supposed. Going up, only Tobias ... was on skis, we others walked, dragging them behind.[8]

Soon afterwards, Johann and a friend climbed the Strela Pass 'more easily and with more pleasure, returning on skis'.

Tobias, meanwhile had started a ski school on the valley floor for foreign visitors and residents. This makes him the first professional ski instructor for tourists in the Alps and secures for him another niche in history.

On 23 March 1894, Johann Branger noted that he, his brother and 'an Englishman, Dr Doyle ... did a major ski tour over the Mayenfelder Furka Pass to Arosa'. This Doctor Doyle was in fact Arthur Conan Doyle, the creator of Sherlock Holmes. To the Brangers, however, he was just another foreign client.

Conan Doyle had appeared during the autumn of 1893. He had come on account of his wife, yet another tuberculotic in search of a cure. Davos was no longer what it was in Spengler's genial heyday. He had been supplanted by Karl Turban, another German doctor, but of a different kind. Rigid and authoritative, Turban enforced a quasi-military discipline of diet, rest and exercise. He had arrived in 1889 as the director of the first sanatorium to be built in Davos. Since then the place had become the colony of hotels and sanatoria; of invalids and sportsmen that created its peculiar character. Spengler died in 1901, commemorated to this day by the Spengler Cup, awarded to the winner of an annual ice hockey tournament in Davos. Hardly anyone remembers Turban.

In his novel *The Magic Mountain*, the most substantial piece of literature to emerge from Davos, Thomas Mann described how the tuberculotics, oppressed by the claustrophobia of their regime, 'enjoyed the activities of the healthy people ... also the sporting events that they proposed to watch although it was strictly forbidden [by the doctors]'.[9] In this community, Conan Doyle neatly played his part.

He himself was in good health. He arrived with an interest in skiing. Nansen, as so often, was again the spark. Conan Doyle had read *The First Crossing of Greenland*. At home he was a passable cricketer, and practised other sports. After crossing the Mayenfelder Furka, he claimed to be 'the first save only two Switzers to do any mountain work ... on show-shoes'.[10]

A year earlier to the day, however, the Brangers, with another Davoser, Paul Kaiser, had already skied over the Mayenfelder Furka pass. A bare two months before, on the Pragel, Iselin and Kjelsberg had made the first known crossing of an Alpine pass on skis. Kaiser and the Brangers had made the second. At an altitude of some 2,500 m, it was also the highest so far, besides which, a few days later, on 26 March 1893, Dr Stäubli, from Basle had climbed the Aroser Rothorn, the first ascent of a major Alpine summit on skis. Even without Kjelsberg's climb of the Bachtel in 1890 and the various early Austrian and Swiss pioneers, at best this makes Conan Doyle perhaps redolent of the self-proclaimed Irish within him.

The first known English mountain skier was Cecil Slingsby. One of the great Victorian climbers, he fled the over-popular Alps to pioneer mountaineering in the uncrowded expanses of Norway, and in 1880 he briefly tried skiing in Jotunheimen. Conan Doyle was not even the first Briton to ski in Davos. Tobias Branger had several in his classes from 1891 or thereabouts. It is bizarre that none had appeared earlier. For over a decade skiing in Norway had been covered by the *Field*. It called itself 'The Country Gentleman's Newspaper', and therefore aimed at the kind of Englishman in the Alps. Already during the winter of 1879, the *Field* covered the first of the Huseby races. This was the first report of skiing in the English press. To ski, said the *Field*, was 'to run down … at a rate of speed that [a railway] engine can hardly equal'.[11] Speed was the thing. A skier was still the fastest human being on earth. Soaring in his jump, he was as yet the closest that Man had come to flying. Coverage went on year by year. In 1888, the *Field* ran an illustrated feature, the first of its kind, with pictures of Norwegian skiers performing what recognizably came to be known as the Christiania turn.

Conan Doyle may or may not have read this but nonetheless when he arrived in Davos he found a small band of initiates already established. At any rate, he could claim to be the first *English* Alpine ski mountaineer. His crossing of the Mayenfelder Furka was historic in another sense: since he had the Brangers to show him the way, this was the first guided ski tour in the Alps, with Conan Doyle the first client.

It is notable for something else too. Under the headline of 'An Alpine Pass on Ski', Conan Doyle wrote about it in the *Strand Magazine*, where Sherlock Holmes originally appeared. This was the first printed account of Alpine skiing in England. Conan Doyle conformed to the gentlemanly ideal by hinting that as the inspired amateur he had taught himself to ski. Tobias Branger had in fact been teaching him all season. The technique was idiosyncratic. Having touched on an early start at 4.30am and elaborated on the protracted crossing of the pass, this was how Conan Doyle described the run down the last steep slopes before Arosa:

> The brothers Branger agreed that the place was too difficult to attempt with the 'ski' upon our feet. To me it seemed as if a parachute was the only instrument for which we had any use, but I did as I saw my companions do. They undid their 'ski', lashed the straps together, and turned them into a clumsy toboggan. Sitting on these, with our heels dug into the snow, and our sticks pressed hard behind us, we began to move down the precipitous face of the pass … I dug my heels hard in, which shot me off backwards, and in an instant my two 'skis' … flew away like an arrow from a bow, whizzed past the two Brangers, and vanished over the next slope, leaving their owner squatting in the deep snow … I made my way down in my own fashion [and] save that [Johann] Branger … sprained his ankle badly all went well with us, and we entered Arosa at half-past eleven, having taken exactly seven hours over our journey.[12]

Steel edges being still a thing of the future, hard crust was the cause of their distress. Johann Branger's injury was in the name of progress. He had ordered a new binding from Christiania. This was the latest of the ephemeral patents

## SKATING.

### SKATING AT CHRISTIANIA.—TEN MILE CHAMPIONSHIP RACE.

ON March 4 Harald Hagen succeeded in wresting from his former master, Axel Paulsen, the title of champion skater. The race, which was one of the best that has ever taken place, came off in bright, cold weather; and the ice was, with the exception of a comparatively small stretch, in exceedingly good condition. The course was roped off on the "Frogner Kile," that picturesque arm of the fjord running between the Drammen Road and the Island Bysdö, past the graceful towers of the Royal château "Oscar's Hall," and was surrounded by at least ten thousand spectators, while thousands more crowded the rocks along the shore. At four o'clock the skaters appeared—Paulsen in a suit of dark-blue tricot, Hagen in white, and both looking in splendid condition and full of confidence. Paulsen, it was said, was in matchless form, and could not any of his records up to and including ten miles, while Hagen, who has the advantage of some twelve years, and is, moreover, as much above the average height as Paulsen is below, had also good reason to hope that he would prove himself the better man.

The start took place at some distance from the judge's box, for the course measured 3ft. from the inner side, 1027 metres, and the distance to be run was 16,030 metres, or 342 less than sixteen times round. Paulsen got well away, and maintained a slight lead for about a round and a half, when Hagen, who kept almost in the centre of the course the whole time,

NORWEGIAN SKI.—No. 3. THE SKING.

drew level and gradually got ahead. Paulsen seemed at first inclined to keep close in Hagen's wake, but he soon returned to his inner track, and so they continued until eight rounds, or about five miles (half the distance), had been covered. Then Paulsen had to bring his arms into requisition, and clearly had to do all he knew in order not to let the gap of three or four yards widen. The expectant crowd, accustomed to see Paulsen waiting on his men and beating them as he pleased, thought they were going to see their favourite rush past and teach the presumptive youth that he would "have to eat a little more pudding" before he could become

36. First known illustrated coverage of skiing in the English press. *The Field. The Country Gentleman's Newspaper*, 24 March 1888.

streaming onto the market. Produced by Larsen's Vaabenforretning, Fritz Huit-feld's employer, it was another forerunner of the toe binding. It consisted of a special boot, to the sole of which a steel plate was fixed. This was attached to the ski by a clamp opened and closed by a single large screw. In this way, as Branger at first put it, the skis were 'easier to steer, and more comfortable'. The binding, however, had one defect: 'Because of the screw thread, [my] skis were fixed too firmly to my feet for undulating terrain.' Another innovation was more successful. Branger had also imported the ancient device of sealskins, and found, naturally that they eased the climb. This was probably their first use in the Alps.

Conan Doyle touched on none of this. Doctor as he was, and creator of the ultimate scientific detective, in real life he seemed oblivious to technology. What he did bring to skiing were the English concepts of holidaymaking on the one hand and sports and games on the other. He also transferred the English mountaineers' ethos of the amateur depending on the professional guide. He continued their invention of the Alps as the Playground of Europe. He launched the popularization of the sport. As he put it in 'An Alpine Pass on Ski', 'I am convinced that the time will come when hundreds of Englishmen will come to Switzerland for the 'ski'-ing ... I will not by many a thousand be the last.'[13]

Conan Doyle stayed for the winter of 1895, guided still by Tobias Branger. Meanwhile, on 12 March, two Englishmen, surnamed Steele and Danday, set out to repeat his crossing to Arosa, guideless. That in itself was the first of its kind. After countless tumbles and an unplanned night in an empty hut, they skied down next morning, frozen and exhausted, and finally reached habitation. Only it was not Arosa, but the village of Küblis in the Prättigau. They had spectacularly lost their way. They were given a hero's welcome nonetheless. They had stumbled on the Parsenn, the first of the classic Alpine ski runs to be found and still widely considered the finest of them all. At 15 km it is, at any rate, one of the longest.

Further advance, however, remained in the hands of native pioneers. When, on 5 January 1896, the Oberalpstock, in central Switzerland, became the first Swiss peak over 3,000 m to be climbed on skis, the participants, numbering four, were Swiss and German, without guides. The leader was Wilhelm Paulcke. When the time came, he went to the University of Freiburg, convenient for skiing in the Black Forest. 'All participants returned safe and sound' he wrote about the ascent of the Oberalpstock.[14] 'The tour ... demonstrated that skis are of much wider application than generally assumed. They are also called on to play a rewarding and vital rôle in winter climbs.' And also, in a sage aside: 'A skier must be used to managing without a stick, so that, in case it is lost, he is not left helpless, like a cripple without his crutches.'

Paulcke, in fact, became the great pioneer of ski mountaineering, with Switzerland his stage. In January 1897, also without guides, he did the first traverse of the Berner Oberland, the first high-altitude ski tour. A year later, on Monte Rosa above Zermatt, in the Valais, Paulcke and a Swiss companion, Robert Helbling, became the first skiers to climb above 4,000 m.

The British, meanwhile, generally stuck to recreational skiing on the lower slopes, always following professional guides and concentrated in Davos, which had become the cradle of skiing as the British knew it. During the 1890s they dominated the slopes. Among them, at the start, was the active figure of Katherine, one of John Addington Symonds' daughters.

The first Englishwomen to have skied were probably the mid-Victorian Lady Di Beauclerk and her mother. They spent the winter of 1867–8 in Norway and in Christiania. As Lady Di recorded:

> On the 2nd of January 1868, I find myself and my mother appearing in snow-shoes, and enjoying ourselves immensely. [In February] we went to many Carnival parties, which consist in making up a large party, and sledging miles away into the country to some rural inn, where, after passing several hours in ... going across the country on snow-shoes (two or three yards long), you return to your inn, eat the best of dinners, dance or play cards, and return by moonlight.[15]

A quarter of a century after Lady Di and her mother, Katherine Symonds was perhaps the next Englishwoman to ski. Beskirted and more solemn than Lady Di, there were many like Miss Symonds on the slopes of Davos.

These late Victorian skiers were of the middle classes and well off. They put their own stamp on Davos. Dedicated sports shops followed Tobias Branger as the forerunner to offer skis to these pioneering winter tourists. Tobias found a profitable sideline in skis for local children. In any case, these shops were the first of their kind. Together with Conan Doyle, they completed the metamorphosis of Davos into the prototype of the ski resort. Slowly the concept began spreading along the Alps.

In the meantime, the Brangers continued their work as pioneering ski teachers and guides. Together with other Davos skiers, they were concerned at their backward, self-taught method. In 1893, a plan was mooted either to send someone to Norway on a course or, better still, to bring a Norwegian skier as an instructor to Davos. This foundered for lack of funds. In January 1895, a Norwegian appeared at one of the speed skating races for which Davos was becoming famous. In Johann Branger's words, he was persuaded 'to remain an extra day ... and demonstrate skiing in his way. [He] certainly ran considerably better than any of us and ... demonstrated rather tight turns and stops.'[16]

It was however the new century and the end of the Victorian era before the next demonstration appeared. In the winter of 1902, as Tobias Branger told the tale:

> there appeared ... two powerful tall gentlemen 'armed' with ski. They made swings and turns to right and left, just like skaters on the ice. We realised ... that we knew nothing about ski-running! ... We tried to find out who they were, who could thus outshine us in our self-taught art. We thought they must certainly be Norwegians, but discovered that they were Englishmen, brothers named Richardson, who had brought the true Norwegian ski technique to Davos.[17]

They were E. C. and C. W. Richardson. As Cambridge undergraduates, in the winters of 1895–6 and 1896–7, they had been to Christiania and learned to ski. To a certain extent, they absorbed the Telemark, and what later was called the Christiania turn. They were the first Englishmen in the Alps with a reasonable technique. They began imparting what they had learned and may be called the fathers of British skiing.

In 1903, they started the Davos English Ski Club, supposedly the first of its kind in the Alps. The first English ski club was however the Yukki ski club in Russia. It was founded in 1881 by John Baddeley, the St Petersburg correspondent of the London *Standard*, with members from the British colony. The name derived from the clubhouse, a dilapidated old forester's hut at Yukki, a hamlet north of St Petersburg, in the flat forested marshlands of the Karelian Isthmus, near the Finnish border. The name is not Russian, but Ingrian, a relative of Finnish. It was the language of the original inhabitants, before the Russians conquered the province in the eighteenth century. 'The Yukki Club', said Baddeley, had 'three rules, and three only ... Rule No. 1: *In this club there are no rules* ... Rule No. 172 ... *Ask for nothing, help yourself* and, finally, rule 365: *Never go out alone.*'[18]

This last was only common sense. Baddeley had absorbed local skiing. It was obviously Nordic, in semi-wild country, where wolves and bears still lurked. By comparison, the Alps were culturally tame. Civilization lapped the flanks of the highest peaks, and nowhere was human settlement remote. Geology told the tale. The classic skiing terrain of eastern Norway evolved by erosion and glaciation of the granite outflow of the Baltic rock shield. The Alps, on the other hand, are great folds in the earth's crust. They were caused by the tectonic collision of Europe and Africa. As a result, in Scandinavia the terrain is gentler, rolling and continuous. The Alpine contours are sharper, with longer, steeper slopes, but disjointed. The consequence for skiing was the necessity of finding an appropriate technique. There was no pool of instinctive native skiers to help. The Richardson brothers saw one solution in applying the Norwegian system. The Brangers, meanwhile, had followed another path. Since the end of the century they had been interested in Mathias Zdarsky and thus had become onlookers at a feud.

# 24

# *Mathias Zdarsky*

Mathias Zdarsky was the true father of Alpine skiing. Another unsettled subject of the patchwork Habsburg empire, he came from a German-speaking enclave in Moravia, now part of the Czech Republic. The tenth child of a miller, he studied painting and sculpture in Munich, before training as an engineer at the Polytechnicum in Zürich. He was an accomplished gymnast, and claimed to be 'familiar with most sports'.[1] In 1889, at the age of 33, he withdrew to Habernreith, a farm he had acquired at Lilienfeld, at the edge of the Alps near Vienna; 'to my mountain isolation', as he put it, 'to live according to my scientific [and] artistic ideas undisturbed'. He certainly looked the part. Tall, thin, ramrod-straight and unsmiling, a hermit with no domestic help, he was thought to be a crank. In a childhood accident, he had lost the sight of his left eye and through the other, like one-eyed Wotan, he stared out bleakly upon the world.

When the German translation of Nansen's book on the crossing of Greenland appeared in 1891 Zdarsky, like so many others, admitted that 'Nansen fever gripped me too',[2] although in his case the outcome was perverse. With plenty of snow at Lilienfeld, he ordered a pair of skis from Norway. When they arrived, he put them on immediately outside the post office. He had never seen a ski before. On the flat, he managed more or less but as soon as he started climbing to Habernreith, understandably he floundered. Habernreith, in Zdarsky's own words, 'had very steep difficult terrain with gradients of up to 58 degrees (measured by surveying instruments)'. It was hardly suited to these skis. They were not of the Telemark model. Nearly 3 m long, they resembled rather a Swedish or Finnish type adapted to flat terrain. Turning was out of the question.

After this fiasco, Zdarsky instantly damned Norwegian skiing as useless in the Alps. He decided to invent a new system of his own. His sole aim was mastery of a true Alpine slope – more than 35° to the horizontal. Behind this lay his personal philosophy. 'The enjoyment of Nature in her wintry garb', he declared, 'is a source ... of recreation, strength, and health-giving for body and soul.'[3] He wanted this not only for an elite, but everyone, 'whether man or woman, young or old, rich or poor'.[4]

The obstacle was what Zdarsky called 'the ... evil of the modern Norwegian skiing technique'.

It needs a long time to learn. "One must ski from childhood if one wants to attain

37. Mathias Zdarsky, idiosyncratic prophet, and founder of Alpine skiing.
*Zdarsky-Ski-Museum, Lilienfeld, Austria*

mastery!" This [is a] drawback ... Top performance can never be the common property of all the people.[5]

There was in this a grain of truth. The Norwegians still felt that instinct and example were the best instructors. They had no system for teaching beginners. Zdarsky proposed to change all this. He began by experimenting with the ski. He arrived at a short model, 180 cm long, without a groove. The aim was ease in turning. That also demanded absolute lateral control, which in turn meant another binding. The original pattern on the ski from Norway was a crude device of cane in which the boot wildly yawed. If Zdarsky is to be believed, he made over 200 experiments before finding a solution. It was a metal plate, to which the boot was strapped, and which was fixed to the ski by a hinge at the front.

Finally, from first principles with his knowledge of physics, anatomy and gymnastics, or so he said, Zdarsky devised a new technique. It was based exclusively on what he called the 'stem'; that is, with the ski tips close together and the heels wide apart, like a 'V'. This was for turning and controlling speed. Integral to the system was a long solid single stick, without a basket but ending like a spear in a fearsome barb, designed to harpoon the snow and act as the pivot round which to turn.

All this seems like reinventing the wheel. The shorter ski for turning was embodied in the Telemark pattern, which had long since made its breakthrough. Zdarsky's binding had been anticipated a decade earlier by the adolescent Wilhelm Paulcke, while a similar German product had appeared on the market in 1891. An Austrian called Schollmayer had written about the stem in 1893. Zdarsky's originality lay in combining these elements into something new. He had produced the first system for turning continuously in linked turns on the steepest slopes. That was the origin of Alpine skiing, as we understand it.

Zdarsky, however, refused to acknowledge that he owed anything to his predecessors. 'I worked through six winters … six years of completely secluded work', so he claimed.

> After [thus] satisfying my skiing hunger, I was curious to see how other skiers mastered their skis. I made some short journeys and, to my great surprise, proved to myself that I ran quite differently, that is I had created something new in my hermitage.

In other words, Zdarsky saw himself as a visionary who had gone into the wilderness, and emerged to preach a new gospel. It was hard going to begin with. At his first public appearance, in a ski race near Vienna, he was outclassed and found himself and his equipment the object of derision. With difficulty, he persuaded a few doubters to ski with him in high Alpine terrain, to which his method was adapted. There he proved that he had succeeded, where others had failed, and taught himself to move safely, if awkwardly over the steepest slopes. There, as a result, he made his first converts. His original rebuff, however, left him with an abiding bitterness. He was goaded into expounding his ideas in a book.

It was published in 1897. It was called, revealingly: *Lilienfelder Skilauf-Technik. Eine Anleitung für jedermann, den Ski in kurzer Zeit vollkommen zu beherrschen – Lilienfelder Skiing Technique. A Guide for Everyman to Master the Ski Completely in a Short Time.* Despite or because of the evangelistic style, and the author's cultivation of himself in the image of a prophet, it was a pioneering work.

This was the first true skiing textbook. It was the first to analyse the dynamics of skiing and simplify it in a small number of distinct movements that a beginner could understand. It was also the first work that used photography to illustrate the different phases of technique. That the pictures were posed, with Zdarsky himself as the model, is irrelevant. He enunciated one revolutionary principle. In turning, 'the weight of the body is to be moved forwards as far as possible … The more confidently and markedly one carries out this … "*Vorlegen* [forward leaning]" … the more elegantly and securely one runs.'[6]

That was the original definition of the *vorlage*, or forward-leaning posture, the basic tenet of downhill running. Zdarsky had made it possible with his binding. By a spring-loaded mechanism, it held the heel down.

Zdarsky spread his method by personal instruction, mostly in the environs of Lilienfeld. He did so out of idealism, charging not a penny for his work. Like most idealists, he was fanatical, dictatorial and ambiguous. He belonged to the sinister breed of great simplifiers. His legacy was far reaching. It is with us still. He promised his acolytes the earth. 'Anyone who follows my instructions precisely', he wrote, 'will master … the ski … in from two to six days.' His whole system was designed for the rapid inculcation of minimum technique. This was the origin of ski schools as we know them. Zdarsky was a proselytizer, attracting people with no natural inclination. He planted the seed of mass winter tourism. The teeming pistes of today can be traced back to him.

One facet of the Norwegian school that Zdarsky particularly despised was a doctrine that over-steep slopes were 'not skiing terrain'. It is true that Norwegians at that time preferred a mountainside that they could negotiate in a series of straight *schusses* interspersed by occasional, isolated turns into the slope. Zdarsky, on the other hand, abhorred speed. He liked control instead. He sought out the steepest slopes for his pupils. This forced them to snowplough in continuous turns, zigzagging right down to the end. This was the origin of mastering long steep slopes, and the birth of downhill skiing. The shadow side was that turning became an end in itself. This is the root of the obsession with mechanistic technique that became the hallmark of the Alpine school.

Zdarsky's power centred on Austria and Germany. He was implacably opposed to the 'Norwegians', which meant anyone who skied in the Norwegian style. He caused a bitter strife that lasted for more than a decade. He was even threatened with a duel. The challenger was Captain (later Colonel) Georg Bilgeri, an Austrian army officer. It was Zdarsky's peculiar stiff-necked brand of malice that turned the aristocratic-looking Bilgeri to thoughts of sabre and pistol. Bilgeri was a leading exponent of the Norwegian method. He published its first systematic instruction manual, as a highly effective riposte to Zdarsky's book.

Zdarsky is said to have taught 20,000 pupils in the course of a career spanning two decades. His followers congealed into a kind of enclosed sect. The Lilienfelders, as they were called, conducted a bitter feud with the 'Norwegians', in the broadest sense.

For all their infelicities of style, the Lilienfelders were the first to practise a dedicated Alpine technique. Their influence gradually increased, and was at its strongest during the early years of the twentieth century. Their method, however, was stagnant from the start. This was due to Zdarsky's personality. He had something within him of the biblical evangelist. Illogically, he decried all racing. He believed that he alone knew the way to salvation on the slopes. He admitted of no possible improvement to his method. His was the ultimate revelation.

By now the two opposing schools were hardly on speaking terms. It was threatening the future of Alpine skiing. At stake was what equipment and what technique was best suited to the terrain. Zdarsky wanted to compare systems in the field. The Austrian 'Norwegians' boycotted the Lilienfelders. They branded them as charlatan and mercenary. To settle matters, Zdarsky issued a challenge to a skiing duel, albeit strictly on his terms. The local 'Norwegians' declined.

This left Zdarsky unhappily in limbo. Then one of his devoted followers, a German called Willy Rickmer Rickmers, wealthy and eccentric, proposed a solution. He suggested inviting a genuine Norwegian competitor and offered to pay all expenses. The challenge was duly issued. Zdarsky's reputation, however, had filtered through to Norway. The Skiforeningen, as the responsible authority, were unenthusiastic. After some negotiation, including the visit of an emissary from Zdarsky to Christiania in December 1904, they agreed at last to send a representative. He was an accomplished all-round skier called Hasse Horn, an engineer by profession. He belonged to *Skuld*, a prominent Christiania ski club. He was not supposed actually to compete but simply to demonstrate the Norwegian style. This suited Zdarsky for, behind his polemics, he craved recognition. He was also harbouring yet another resentment. A Norwegian journal had called him a 'skiing clown'. It was an insult he never quite forgave.

Horn's real mission was to spy on the Lilienfelders because, in his own prophetic words, 'We Norwegians ... should carefully follow [what] is happening abroad. If we don't look out, one fine day we might ... be outstripped.'[7] Thus on 4 January 1905, he arrived at Puchberg, a mountain village near Vienna, to join a gathering of Lilienfelders. As a foreigner, above local squabbles, he was welcomed 'with open arms' as he said. This was how Zdarsky appeared to him:

> I had a vivid impression of this man's overwhelming power and influence among alpinists. The most incredible questions were addressed to him; everyone hung on his lips, and his least bidding was instantly obeyed ... The image I had formed of him in advance did not correspond ... with the reality. I was ... surprised to find a cultivated ... man with knowledge ... of astonishingly many subjects. He is a great eccentric ... He cannot tolerate opposition; that makes him flare up like a thunderstorm, but if he is treated gently, it soon blows over, and he is once more the soul of kindness.

Such was the person with whom Horn was now to try conclusions. Early next morning, 5 January, they set out, together with a few dozen of Zdarsky's acolytes. Originally this was to have been the challenge race against the 'Norwegians', but following their refusal, Zdarsky had arranged a private competition among his Lilienfelders instead. Horn was now in the absurd position of running as an observer, while Zdarsky could exploit him to his own ends.

The slopes were on the Schneeberg, above Puchberg and, at 2,100 m above sea level the highest mountain in the province of Lower Austria. The weather was what was becoming common, with rain in the valley but a snowstorm further up. For 6 km they marched over bare ground, the Austrians 'burly types', as Horn said, dressed in 'kneebreeches, checked stockings, heavy, iron-shod boots, hat or cap with a feather, and finally a colossal rucksack [with] Lilienfeld skis slung by a strap over the shoulder like a rifle.' Soon after the climb began, snow appeared, and with it the first distinction between Lilienfelder and Norwegian.

'It was horribly steep through the forest,' said Horn, 'but with the help of my two sticks I gradually dragged myself past the others, and soon took the lead.' He had quickly proved that at least in climbing the lower slopes the now usual Norwegian custom of two sticks eclipsed the Lilienfelder's single one.

Emerging from the forest onto the steep bare upper slopes it was a different story. The snow was hard and covered with wind crust. The gradient was around 40° to the horizontal. Here, in Horn's own words:

> the Lilienfelders apparently had a substantial advantage in their thick, solid stick, which they held horizontally against the mountain as a support while shifting weight from one foot to the other ... On the other hand, I had little joy of my double sticks now ... there was no other way out but to put them together and warp myself along like the others. But the baskets were in the way, and I was often desperately clawing so as not to shoot down helplessly.

The trouble here was yet again the inability of wooden skis to bite while traversing steep slopes on hard snow. That was still the great gap in Alpine equipment. In any case, the snow conditions on that day were so poor that Zdarsky cancelled his plans. Horn was disappointed at not seeing 'this ski race of the Alpine type'. It would have been something wholly new to him. The aim was 'to demonstrate ... ability in moving down a steep mountainside on skis in a controlled manner. Any other consideration, like speed ... style and so forth, would not be taken into account.' It was not really a race, but more of a test. As things turned out, they made do with skiing down, in Horn's words, for 'a bit of fun'.

> Zdarsky went first ... in semi [stem] position diagonally to the left, then with a swift forward leaning of the body, in a tight turn down the incline, and so on to right and left in an unbroken snaking line ... He used his stick competently, although not more than could be reasonably expected in such steep terrain and such snow.
>
> It was immediately obvious to me that there was nothing new at all in Zdarsky's method of skiing. His 'stemming ...' is only [a] variation of our 'snowplough' [documented in Norway for at least a quarter of a century].
>
> But I must admit that I have never seen anyone manage these manoeuvres so steadily and with such control as he in such terrain and such snow ... but that is about all that can be said about his skiing ability.

The rest of the party began moving. So as not to be left behind, Horn threw himself straight down the slope.

> My skis, being longer, were faster than the others. It was all I could do to preserve a dignified posture, and I was relieved to reach the treeline without disgrace, safe and sound, but with aching ankles and cramp in my legs.
>
> On the slopes above, the herd was on its way down. They went slowly and carefully

in short bursts of regular, finicky curves and flourishes, but they did come safely down, which is not to be despised.

In the forest, among the pines, it was steep and broken but, to a Norwegian, more homelike. Horn's ski, in his own words:

> evidently thought so too, for they set off without a care in the world at breakneck speed … in and out among dense trees and undergrowth so that twigs danced before my eyes. Here I was soon at ease, and when, after a short while, I was down on the flat, and heaved along with my two sticks along the ditch at the side of the road, which was now snowed up, my faith in Norwegian skis had revived.
>
> How the others managed, I have no idea. I only saw them again towards evening among the fleshpots of [the hotel], and then I heard that most of them had left their skis at the foot of the mountain.

Horn skied with Zdarsky for four days in all. He described how on the last run of his stay he began by following Zdarsky's every twist and turn.

> But then Nature overcame upbringing. I shot past him straight down so that the snow sprayed round me like a cloud. I rushed along with rising speed, which gradually reached an alarming level. I had then arrived at the hotel, and prepared for a stylish turn, but my skis caught an edge, and I performed an impressive somersault. [On arrival] Zdarsky remarked drily that 'the young man is foolhardy', glancing smugly at his children, on whom not a single snowflake was to be seen.

Trying to be fair, Horn admitted that Zdarsky had managed to teach his pupils enough technique in a short time to manage difficult slopes. The Lilienfeld

DR. CONAN DOYLE ON "SKI."

38. Arthur Conan Doyle, the creator of Sherlock Holmes, and his sister, Lottie, at Davos. *Strand Magazine*, London, 1894. *Cambridge University Library*

system was undoubtely suited to the terrain for which it was designed. Horn's overriding impression, however was of

> the stiff, solemn way in which [Lilienfeld] skiing is conducted. Everything seems to proceed according to accepted rules and predetermined orders ... And behind everything there is Zdarsky, the revered model, whom everyone tries to copy down to the tiniest detail ... It seems odd to an outsider. There is obviously great danger for the healthy development of skiing in that the individual opinion can easily be completely crushed.

This is enough to explain how the domination of the Alpine ski schools began, with their formalism, artificiality, cultivation of fashion and automaton-like products. Zdarsky has much to answer for. Horn compared Norwegian and Lilienfelder in this way:

> If the question was somewhat undecided on the worst parts, I definitely had the advantage as soon as the slope eased enough for me to ski straight down. That also held for deep snow, running on the flat or in broken terrain – and of course the Lilienfeld skis are completely useless for jumping.

Summing up, Horn had the distinct feeling that

> during our short encounter, even the Alpine skiers had to admit that they have developed things somewhat one-sidedly. They have clearly concentrated on steep slopes to the exclusion of all else, as a result of which they have neglected the cultivation of the all-round ability which we [Norwegians] demand of an accomplished skier.

On the other hand, he concluded: 'This can be ... corrected, and we Norwegians can help, if only we approach the [Lilienfelders] with understanding. Very possibly this could be of mutual benefit.'

Zdarsky begged to disagree. He considered the clash on the Puchberg as a draw. He pursued the thought of victory. Later that season, he organized another race. It was held on 19 March 1905 at Lilienfeld, on a local mountain called the Muckenkogel. In Alpine skiing, date and place are historic.

As usual, Zdarsky was starter, course setter, judge and jury. Over a distance of perhaps 3,000 m, he fixed pairs of flags to form numbered gates. They were arranged in a highly serpentine pattern to force sharp, continual turning. Zdarsky had arranged the course, as he imagined, to favour his system.

Of the 24 competitors, all but one were Lilienfelders. The exception was an Austrian 'Norwegian' called Josef Wallner. A natural athlete, his status was ambivalent, and foreshadowed a protracted controversy. He was one of the first ski instructors, and therefore clouded as a professional, not to associate in competition with the amateurs. It was his employers, the newly formed Österreischischer Wintersportclub, who had naughtily sent him to the Muckenkogel. This is Wallner's own record of the race:

There were about 200 … gates, through which I easily ran with broad-gauge Christianias or Telemarks. As I was in the hollow before the [finish], I saw Zdarsky, and he said 'Ha – he's missed a gate; disqualified from the run.' I looked up and, quite right, there was a gate far to the left, nearly at the same height as the previous one about 50 metres higher on the steep slope. I said 'That's nothing', tramped in deep snow up to the gate before the one I'd missed, and ran the section once more. I still crossed the finishing line 4 minutes ahead of the best Lilienfelder. I won the 1st prize.[8]

Wallner had cut through all the argumentation. For the first time, at a blow, he had proved that Norwegian technique could be adapted to downhill racing. The event on the Muckenkogel was historic for another reason. Zdarsky dubbed it a *Torlauf* – a 'gate run'. It was in all but name the first modern slalom. The original term survives to this day in *riesentorlauf*, the German for giant slalom.

Zdarsky performed other services to skiing. He helped to introduce the ski to the Austrian army. This led him to pioneer the study of avalanches as they affected the skier. He was caught in one during the Great War, on the Italian front. That left him a semi-cripple, the sad eccentric, founder of Alpine skiing, a prophet in spite of himself.

Wallner had removed the whole justification of his approach. It lingered on long enough for another edition or two of his instruction book. There, with characteristic self-delusion, Zdarsky could still write in 1908 that 'for Alpine skiers … the Telemark turn and the Christiania turn … are only good for entertainment on the practice slopes'.[9] In fact, he and his supporters carefully suppressed all reference to their defeat by Wallner. The Lilienfeld system, however, was doomed. Although it spread as far afield as Japan, by the early 1920s it had disappeared.

Zdarsky had pioneered Alpine skiing, but his technique was retrograde. He lapsed into obscurity. His great disservice had been the limitation of his method. He was obsessed with running downhill. He opened the schism between Nordic and Alpine skiing that has lasted to this day. In any case, the Lilienfeld school had been overtaken by Norwegian technology. The Huitfeldt binding was making inroads into the Alps. Its steel ears together, after 1904, with the Høyer-Ellefsen tensioning clasp on the heelstrap, provided firm fixture, lateral stability and, above all, robust construction together with light weight and simplicity. By comparison, the Zdarsky pattern was heavy, intricate and easily breakable. The Huitfeldt binding ousted Zdarsky's pattern and for a quarter of a century was destined to rule. And in the end, Huitfeldt's 'Telemark' ski proved highly adaptable to the Alps.

There was in this a hidden irony. Although issuing from opposing schools, Huitfeldt and Zdarsky had much in common. Each had a profound sense of his own infallibility. Both had great force of character. They were all-round sportsmen, each devoted to his version of skiing. They were near contemporaries, with a taste for swimming against the tide. Both clung to the use of a single stick, long after two had taken over. Once more, a touch of the fanatic was needed for the propagation of an idea; once more, the radicals of yesteryear turned into the reactionaries of today.

The Lilienfeld system had been a necessary aberration. Wallner was the beginning of the end for Zdarsky and marked the final ascendancy of the Norwegian school.

# 25

# St Moritz

Meanwhile Switzerland, as usual, took another course. The number of Swiss skiers had risen since Christoph Iselin's pioneering but their quality lagged behind. This exposed them to the baleful influence of Zdarsky, as evinced by the Brangers of Davos. In a counter-attack, Norwegians were brought in before it was too late. Switzerland being the cradle of modern winter tourism, this is of more than passing interest.

The movement started, appropriately, with the original Swiss ski club in Glarus. On 26 January 1902 the club held the first ski race in Switzerland. It was more than a decade since Iselin had made his first halting steps. Touring was the original object of the Swiss. The natural world was their goal. Competition was not really in the blood; it had to be imported.

The Glarus race, as usual then, was Nordic. It presaged things to come. For the first time, a Norwegian did not win the cross-country event. A Swiss, surnamed Müller, came first, with Norwegians second and third. Iselin was deeply chagrined. Patriotism was hardly his concern. He had organized the race and he wanted to show off 'his' Norwegians. They had been invited for the occasion from Zürich, where they were studying. Nor was there a jumping competition to offset the undesired result. The following winter, Iselin rectified the situation. For the second Glarus fixture, in January 1903, he included a ski-jump and brought in two competent Norwegians. It was, he said 'a historic day for Swiss skiing'.[1]

It was not so much that the Norwegians had duly won, as the publicity they created. For the record, they were engineering students from Darmstadt, in Germany. Their names were Thorvald Heyerdahl and Anders Holte. Holte came first in the jump, with Heyerdahl runner-up. Heyerdahl, *hors de concours*, set a Swiss record of 24 m. Under a bright winter sky, a crowd of 6,000 was deeply enthused. 'Everybody', in Iselin's words, 'wanted to see the jump with their own eyes … Heyerdahl and … Holte became … famous … overnight.'[2] They were the stuff of journalism, as this far-flung newspaper coverage from Lausanne revealed:

> Norwegian [ski] jumping is to be recommended to the devotees of exciting sports. It is difficult to imagine a more extraordinary spectacle … Starting from the top of … a very steep piste [an early use of the word – French for 'track' in skiing]… the jumper begins by running down at a giddying speed on his long wooden laths; then suddenly he is hurled into space in an immense parabola …[3]

This was written nine months before the Wright Brothers made their first heavier-than-air flight at Kittihawke. A ski-jumper was still the nearest thing to flying. By accident almost, Iselin had discovered the value of jumping as propaganda. It was the embodiment of elegance and courage. It had an aesthetic force. Like the ballet, it had the power to inspire, without necessarily a wish to emulate. It has meant much for skiing in all its forms.

For example, a German-born skiing pioneer and Alpinist called Victor de Beauclair – later killed on the Matterhorn – decided to exploit the Glarus sensation by asking Heyerdahl to return the next winter as an instructor.

Heyerdahl brought along a fellow-Norwegian called Trygve Smith, then studying in Dresden. Glarus was rightly thought to be off the beaten track. Instead, they held classes at Lenzerheide, in the Grisons. They had 70 pupils. There had been at least one earlier course run by members of the Swiss Alpine Club but this was the first given by native-born Norwegians. They outshone all that had gone before. Nothing could have been farther from the dogged earnestness of the Zdarsky school. Heyerdahl and Smith had the cheerful flamboyance that makes converts too. They showed that Nordic and Alpine skiing were different only in degree and that the qualities needed for the one held also for the other. They proved that jumping, arms spread like a bird on the wing in the manner of the day, demanded the same flair as an Alpine slope. The steep outrun was simply a *schuss* by another name.

At St Moritz, the Alpina Ski Club, then only a few weeks old, was organizing the first major ski race in the resort. It was a two-day meeting. Heyerdahl and Smith were asked to take part. They interrupted their classes at Lenzerheide, to hurry over for the fixture in January 1904. That they could do so at all was due to the recent opening of the Albula tunnel. This was one of the engineering wonders of the age. It brought the railway into the Engadine. Trains now reached the outskirts of St Moritz

So the two Norwegians arrived in comfort, and proceeded to change the face of skiing in the valley of the Engadine. The first event, on 18 January, a Tuesday as it happened, was a race from the post office in St Moritz up to the summit of Piz Nair and back again. This involved a climb of some 750 m. The total course was 11 km. Heyerdahl won in 1 hour, 20 minutes and 55 seconds, followed in second place by Smith some 7 minutes behind, both well ahead of the field. On the Wednesday, they amused themselves with a duet in the ski-jump, both clearing over 16 m simultaneously. 'Nothing like this had been seen … before', as a local newspaper admiringly put it.

> We were amazed and entranced: such elegance and self-confidence was really amazing. Both soared out [and] returned to solid earth with agility, and continued with tearaway speed for a while without losing balance or complete mastery of their skis.[4]

Again it was not the result that counted, but the example that they set. 'The short time that they spent in St Moritz', the journalist continued was enough … to give an idea of what real skiing is, and this is of the greatest significance for the future development of this sport … What was clear to all spectators was the great difference between the posture of the Norwegians … and most of the [other] competitors … The contrast lies in a complete difference in the use of the sticks. [Here] the stick is a means of braking [unlike] the Norwegians, who use it much more for acceleration. To this end, they do not use a single heavy stick, but two small, light sticks … Their free, supple, proud posture contrasts greatly with the fearful, hideous leaning backwards on the stick that is so common among us.

In other words, Heyerdahl and Smith were a sufficient antidote to Zdarsky. They had helped to consolidate the Norwegian school among the Swiss. They had also popularized skiing in the environs. Hitherto it had trailed behind other winter sports, notably skating, and bob-sledging, with its suicidal tinge on icy runs. The fatalities there were likened to a colonial war. Skiing was now seen to be relatively harmless and quickly dominated the slopes of St Moritz. This was critical for the further spread of skiing in the Alps and, in particular, for the final shape of the winter sports resort.

Iselin, meanwhile, wanted to extend the Norwegian influence. For the season of 1905, as an added selling point, so to speak, he obtained two Norwegian skiers direct from Norway. They toured Switzerland, giving lessons in eight centres from Lenzerheide in the east of the country to Les Avants, above Montreux, on Lake Geneva, over to the west. They were Leif Berg and Thorleif Bjørnstad – names to remember. Watching them, in the words of one pupil, 'almost drove me to despair!'[5]

If only I were 15 years younger! I have learned much from both … Bjørnstad … seemed to be a better teacher than Berg who, on the other hand, surpassed him in skill, elegance and courage. On that account he did not need to talk much, as long as one kept one's eyes open.

That was a lapidary definition of true teaching. In fact, neither Norwegian was a trained ski instructor, which Berg, for one, cheerfully accepted. At Engelberg, in Central Switzerland, 'a pretty daughter of Eve, completely encased in snow', as he put it, 'Came and begged me so demurely to help her and asked what she ought to do so as not to fall. That was a difficult question, and I thought for a while before answering. At last I answered – the only way is to remain standing on your feet.'[6]

Whatever their lack of formalized teaching method, at 19 years old, both Norwegians had the fire of youth. Both came fresh from the Christiania racing milieu. Each had run at Holmenkollen. Berg was a specialized jumper who, in 1903, had won the junior class. The same year, Bjørnstad had come third in the junior division of the Nordic combination of jumping and cross-country. The aura of Holmenkollen as a kind of skiing Olympus was filtering abroad. On that account or otherwise, Iselin was now dubbed 'the Norwegian importer' – a sly

39. Katherine Symonds, probably the first Englishwoman to ski in Switzerland, about 1889. Photograph taken in Davos, 1905. *Dokumentationsbibliothek Davos*

dig at his native canton of Glarus, centre of the Swiss textile industry, and thus an exporter of note.

On 21 and 22 January 1905, again in Glarus, Major Iselin, as he now was, helped to organize, de facto, the first Swiss national ski championships. He inveigled Bjørnstad and Berg to run *hors de concours*. In the cross-country event, Berg trounced the opposition by more than a quarter of an hour. The conditions were tailor-made for Scandinavians; bitterly cold, with powder snow and the same structure from start to finish. In the jumping event, like Heyerdahl and Holte the year before in Lenzerheide, he and Bjørnstad did a double jump for fun. They reached 25 m. Berg alone then sensationally set a record of 27 m. This was 10 m more than the best of the rest – although their style was noticeably improving. A crowd of 10,000 had come to watch – a record of sorts for Switzerland. It was, said Iselin, a touch hyperbolically, 'the mightiest impulse [for] Swiss skiing ... A new era dawned. Gone were the reservations about the new elegant technique. Gone for ever was the old "cumbersome" method. The stick as a brake moved into the museum!'[7]

Together with Heyerdahl and Smith, Bjørnstad and Berg were the vanguard of a latter-day Viking raid. Norwegians started drifting down to Switzerland as itinerant teachers. They were driven by national pride, more perhaps by an urge to escape from a provincial environment. They were attracted by the chance of fame and modest fortune. It was not among the native Swiss, however, that they found their *métier*, but the burgeoning winter visitors. They were among the founders of modern commercialized skiing, in the interests of which they cheerfully exploited their nationality.

Bjørnstad stayed in Switzerland, settling in Bern. Meanwhile, Trygve Smith returned to the country with his brother Harald. They came from a peculiar milieu in Christiania. This consisted of small, selective ski clubs formed by teenagers, often with their own little huts and names tellingly derived from old Norse mythology. The Smiths belonged to the Verdande club. Verdande was one of the three Norns who controlled the fates of gods and men. She was concerned with the future. It was quite a percipient choice for the dozen or so schoolboys who started the club in 1894. Trygve and Harald Smith did respectably at Holmenkollen and in the early winter of 1906 both appeared in St Moritz, there to teach, to show off and generally lend lustre by their presence. Another Holmenkollen runner, Bjarne Nilssen, joined them. Norwegians in Switzerland were repeating the rôle of the Telemarkings in Norway 30 years earlier. They were the exemplars of a proper style

When Nilssen reached St Moritz, in January 1906, there were some 1,500 visitors, mostly English. They brought with them a touch of sturdy opulence. It was, after all, the high noon of the Edwardian era, with its fevered thirst for entertainment before Armageddon. Nilssen recorded that even in midwinter, when the sun was shining, 'it was too much for certain extravagantly dressed Englishwomen, in that one not infrequently met specimens in short-sleeved dresses, straw hats and parasols strolling in the snow!'[8] He was not exactly impressed by the passing parade. In his student days at Darmstadt, during the 1890s he had been a model for rising German skiers. Returning home after a month in St Moritz, he published some embittered articles, the burden of which was that in Switzerland (but by implication not elsewhere), skiing was considered 'exclusively for commercial reasons'.[9] The Swiss, he said, 'do not miss a chance to earn money, and in skis they had found a new chance'. He warned his compatriots not to follow suit and

> in working to attract a stream of tourists ... lose the distinctiveness of our national character, as in those parts of Switzerland most ravaged by the swarms of tourists. We must also hope that in order to ... earn a few paltry pence we do not destroy our own mountains ... with monstrous hotels ... and with railways to [various] summits. (The latest fashion in Switzerland, if you please, is to climb mountains by lift.)

And more to the same effect; notably that Norwegians were being exploited to promote Swiss winter tourism.

News of Nilssen's philippic made its way back to St Moritz, where it provoked annoyance in a local newspaper. Nonetheless, in his own mordant way he had discerned the truth. Skiing was being commercialized in the Alps. Some Swiss themselves were uneasy. There was a growing dichotomy between serious local skiers and the tourist trade.

To be fair, Nilssen did understand the complex relation between men and mountains. He implicitly conceded that in a country with no natural resources, any way of earning money was justified. Nonetheless, as a purist he saw it as an affront to an ideal. To him, skiing was not a business but part of the culture into which he was born. Its function as an agent of national identity loomed large. Norway had finally attained its independence from Sweden a few months earlier, on 7 June 1905. This partly explains Nilssen's discontent. But he also saw a philosophical threat to purity of purpose. Skiing to him, as to Laurentius Urdahl and many other pioneers, was not sport but almost a religion. Commercialization would corrupt it.

Nilssen spoke for a whole school of thought, not only among his fellow-countrymen. He wanted to preserve his snows undefiled. He returned to his work as an electrical engineer, nevermore to visit the Swiss Alps. He became a director of the plant at Rjukan, in Telemark, later celebrated for producing the heavy water that might perhaps have given Hitler the atomic bomb.

Nilssen was a prophetic voice from the genesis of the modern ski resort. The Smith brothers did not share his resentment. This may be because they had come of their own accord to teach privately. Nilssen, on the other hand, had been officially invited by St Moritz. This made him feel as if he had been used. However, he was dispassionate enough to identify other, awkward historic trends. 'It will not be long', he remarked, 'before we [Norwegians] find dangerous rivals amongst the Swiss [and] they will take the palm from us both in jumping and cross-country.'[10] And in a clear-sighted barb at his compatriots:

> Where ... ski equipment is concerned, the Swiss have come far in their efforts at manufacture. To begin with, almost all orders went to Norway but ... the equipment they received was not at all satisfactory ... The Swiss soon came to the conclusion that if they could not obtain better things from Norway, they might just as well make skis themselves. Now in Switzerland there are several big ski factories ... Not many [Norwegian skis] are exported ... compared to what might have been ... if our ski manufacturers had not underestimated foreigners' ability to judge skis.[11]

Less critical, the Smith brothers unreservedly enjoyed themselves at St Moritz; as well they might. Davos had pioneered the modern ski resort but St Moritz brought it to perfection. Davos was, so to say, bourgeois; St Moritz a cut above it. Besides, St Moritz did not have the historical leveller of disease; it was devoted to the pursuit of pleasure.

Nilssen's taunt of 'monstrous hotels' was unfair. He was perversely succumbing to the power of architecture. Admittedly St Moritz, like Davos had become a colony of hotels, but of a different kind. In the Engadine, a distinctive style had emerged. It was a branch of the luxury establishment that had sprung up during the Belle Epoque under the generic name of Palace. This was a mass of masonry with hundreds of rooms and a façade that evoked a baroque ducal chateau. The purpose was to create an illusory aristocratic ambience as the ideal of the new moneyed classes.

It became notably popular in Switzerland. This was ironic because, as a republic, the country lacked royalty and an aristocracy. On the other hand, it was the Swiss who adapted this kind of architecture to the holiday without a goal, as distinct from health seeking in the spas, or commerce in the cities. It reached its apogee in the Engadine, of which the prime example was Badrutt's Palace Hotel at St Moritz. With its crenellations and spires, it looked like a castle on the hill. More to the point, although the rooms were relatively modest, the public spaces were grand. The luxurious surroundings were redolent of wealth and doing nothing gracefully. As one Swiss writer put it, this was a deliberate architectural trick 'where the holidaymaker was waited on and liberated from any kind of work. This … consideration is not only of historical interest. In the hotel of the nineteenth century the needs and concepts were minted, which to this day largely shape everyman's holiday dreams.'[12]

In other words, St Moritz became the quintessential Alpine resort. Cut off from the outside by a ring of mountains, it was in a little world of its own, dictated by geology. It lay in what is called the Engadine Window, where the ancient underlying strata break through the sedimentary overlay to form the peculiar jagged peaks that dictate the landscape and offer a romantic, not too intimidating view. There was a lake, regularly frozen in winter and snow-covered. The town, with a picturesque old centre lies up on a south-facing escarpment to give the pleasing perspective of the middle view. Skiing was merely one more extra pastime. Here it was finally divorced from its Scandinavian roots.

Such were the circumstances that Nilssen and the Smith brothers so differently interpreted in St Moritz. Harald found the place so agreeable that he quickly settled there. He established himself as a ski maker and ski teacher. He became a formative figure in the Alps. With his brother, for example, he amused the throngs of foreign visitors one day at Christmas 1905 by careering on skis behind a pair of sorry nags between St Moritz and the neighbouring village of Champfer. This was how ski-joring – of Swedish origin – arrived in St Moritz. With more respectable horses, the Smiths turned it into a serious competition on the lake. There, on a circular course of some 1.5 km, they raced round, fighting without quarter for the inside curve in entertaining mimicry of a Roman chariot race. This soon led to normal horse racing on the lake, even now part of the season.

In February 1906, meanwhile, Harald Smith found himself at Sous d'Oulx, in the Italian Alps, running ski classes. Skiing had arrived in Italy around the turn of the century, but it lagged behind its neighbours, notably Switzerland and Austria. This was the period when skiing was spreading on the Continent. Norwegians were much in demand a teachers and competitors. While Harald Smith busied himself in St Moritz, his fellow-countrymen were implanting the ski in the entire sweep of mountains from the Carpathians in Hungary, through the Alps, over to Spain in the West. As part of this process, in 1909, Smith broke the world record by jumping 43 m at Bardonecchia, in Italy, raising it to 45 m a little later at Davos. His great service, however, lay in another direction altogether.

Switzerland had invented the commercialization of skiing. It was bound to spread. St Moritz had laid down the pattern of the ski resort for others to follow in its wake. There, too, Harald Smith played a part.

# 26

## *Skiing in France*

St Moritz had become a haunt of the beau monde, amongst whom was Baroness Noémie de Rothschild, of the French branch of the banking family, with Harald Smith her private ski teacher. When the Great War broke out in August 1914, the Baroness turned her home in Paris into a military hospital. In 1916 she returned for a little recreation to St Moritz. There, Switzerland being neutral, she found the place crowded with Germans, which quickly drove her back to Paris in distaste. She asked Smith to find her somewhere in France for her to ski instead. He finished his survey in 1919, the guns having fallen silent the year before. He had two proposals for the Baroness. One was Val d'Isère, of later repute, high up in the Savoy Alps, snow certain and eminently skiable, but austere and remote. The other was Megève, lower and less certain of snow but more accessible and an appealing Savoyard village into the bargain. Smith's compatriot Ole Houm, together with Dr Weber, had pioneered skiing there at the turn of the century.

Baroness Noémie decided on Megève. She built the first hotel there at Mont d'Arbois. In the image of St Moritz, the Baroness had devised the first modern French ski resort and thus founded the winter sports industry in France. She brought her Parisian set with her. In its train followed her own characteristic genial touch of elevated chic, a cousin, so to say, of the turf in France (in which her family was also involved, as in the allied field of grandiose chateau wines). At Megève, the Baroness had given skiing the touch of exclusiveness and *snobisme* that tinged it between the wars and, in certain circles, strangely lingers still. Her fashionable fringe was simply one branch of a movement that pioneered French skiing.

The first man to ski in France was probably Henri Duhamel, from the region of Grenoble. He was born in 1853. Like Tobias Branger in Davos, he first saw a ski in the Swedish-Norwegian pavilion at one of the Paris international exhibitions; in his case that of 1878. Somehow Duhamel cadged a pair, and returned to Grenoble to make his first attempts.

Duhamel loved the mountains. Unusually for the times, he did so in winter too. Having private means, he could indulge his passion to his heart's content. He certainly needed all the leisure he could get. So far, in winter, his transport had been a kind of local snowshoe. Its use was more or less instinctive. Skiing was a different matter altogether. He had no instructor, so like the other Alpine pioneers, he had to teach himself, and bear the derision of the populace. For a decade, his progress was sluggish, complicated by the fact that he had no proper bindings. His informant at the exhibition had airily explained that a pair of straps would do. At last in 1889, Dumamel met a Finnish diplomat, who gave the necessary explanations, photographs and even an instructional booklet in French, written by a Finn. What is more, Duhamel now obtained 14 pairs of skis with proper bindings, which he distributed among a group of friends.

Still they were thrown on their own devices. Skiing on the level or uphill was beyond them. Somehow they did manage running downhill. Their technique included hugging trees to stop. Unlike other Alpine pioneers, they were without the help of handy Norwegian students. These were concentrated in Switzerland, Germany and Austria-Hungary. Those who did come to France congregated in Paris, far from the Alps. In good winters, a few did ski in the Jardin du Luxembourg, or perhaps it was the Bois de Boulogne. Like Duhamel and his companions in the Dauphiné, however, they formed a closed coterie, with no permanent effect.

Nor did Nansen influence the outcome as he had done elsewhere. The French translation of *The First Crossing of Greenland* – *A travers le Grönland* – appeared in 1893, to widespread applause but without immediate consequences for the spread of skiing in France. There were other sporadic attempts, notably at Chamonix during the 1890s, but they were all isolated. France was years behind the other Alpine countries. In the end, it was the French army that popularized the ski. This revolved round the figure of a Captain Henri Clerc.

In 1900 Captain Clerc was transferred to the 159th Alpine Infantry regiment. It was quartered at Briançon, a small isolated town, which, in Clerc's plaintive words, suffered from 'an absolute lack of intellectual pursuits'.[1] Given the boredom of French garrison life that was sapping the army's morale, those were strong words. Then one day, on a visit to Geneva, where skiing already had a foothold, the captain's wife bought a pair of skis as a distraction for her husband. He tried them out. He was instantly enthused.

He found a precursor in Lieutenant Auguste Monnier, who had been with the 159th since the middle of the 1890s. Monnier somehow taught himself to ski. He proposed in a report to the General Staff that all mountain troops learn to ski as well. Down the chain of command came a refusal. Skis were thought to be difficult to master, dangerous for beginners and impossible to use in mountainous terrain. Captain Clerc, however, saw the point and in him Monnier now had a fervent successor.

The 159th was on frontier duty. It kept watch on the Italian border. This ran along the crest of the Alps from Mont Dolent, at the junction of Italy, Switzerland and France, all the way to the sea. Like other French troops of its kind, the Alpine snows confounded the regiment.

Where Monnier – now a second-lieutenant in the reserve – had failed, Clerc was permitted to experiment with skis on some of his soldiers. He did so in the winters of 1900–1 and 1901–2. He invoked military necessity. Every day, Italian frontier guards could be seen skiing. They had been doing so since 1896. Italian Alpine troops already had a ski school. Scouts were being trained to ski. It was a worrying advantage. Briançon lay in the Hautes-Alpes, well to the south on a historic invasion route and Italy was a legitimate object of suspicion. She was part of the Triple Alliance, together with the French ancestral foes, Austria-Hungary and Germany. Both were also well advanced in the military use of skis.

A born staff officer, Clerc was a model of systematic preparation. He began by reading Nansen. He also read the works of Lt Col. Oreste Zavattari, commander of the Third Italian Alpine regiment, and the pioneer of military skiing in Italy. Clerc acquired skis from Norway, Germany and Russia, for comparison. He had some made locally, by an armament factory near Lyon, with a version of the cane binding. At the end of his two seasons of trials, in 1902 he produced a meticulous report.

Like others before him, Clerc began by comparing skis and snowshoes, the latter already used by the regiment. The ski, he also proved, was superior: 'The area supporting the foot is increased, so that a man [on skis] sinks into the snow ten times less than [one] on snowshoes. Besides which instead of being compelled to lift his foot at each step, glides like nothing else.'[2]

One way or another Clerc taught his men. He demonstrated that the ski could indeed be used in winter warfare. However, he grasped that instruction by practised skiers was now required. He advocated the founding of a military ski school in Briançon. This was the first ski school in France. It would begin by training instructors.

40. French postcard, about 1907, with W. Durban-Hansen, a leading Norwegian skier, in the Savoy Alps. A scholarly Francophile, he was also a specialist in seventeenth century French literature. The French regarded him as their skiing prophet.

*Ski Museum, Holmenkollen, Oslo*

252 TWO PLANKS AND A PASSION

The natural thing would have been to copy the neighbouring Italians. As among the French, however, skiing in Italy was still confined to a narrow coterie. It was also derivative. The ski had come to Italy via Switzerland. The forerunner was Adolf Kind, an industrialist from the Grisons who had settled in Turin, and skied in the nearby Alps since about 1895. Clerc went to source instead. Like others of his kind, he wanted missionaries from Norway. In November 1902, one such providentially dropped in.

He was a very junior Norwegian army lieutenant from Christiania, called Herman Schultz. A gifted ski-jumper, he wanted to visit France as a ski instructor in order to get out into the wider world and simultaneously learn French. He corresponded on the subject with Captain Thomas Heftye, the military attaché at the Swedish-Norwegian Embassy in Paris. Heftye told him simply to come down to Paris and bring his skis along. Obtaining leave, Schultz took him at his word, and was promptly sent on to Briançon. Clerc, assuming no doubt that Heftye was working *le système 'D'* – the time-honoured French device for wriggling round officaldom – greeted Schultz with open arms.

In so doing, Clerc – and Heftye – became the unwitting cause of an imbroglio. Schultz had come in a highly unofficial capacity, but on this occasion the authorities were touchy. Channels had to be respected. In December 1902, after a typical bureaucratic wrangle, the French General Staff sent an *official* invitation to the Swedish-Norwegian Embassy in Paris. Two officers were thereupon – officially – rushed from Norway to Briançon. One was Lieutenant Finn Quale, later a prominent international skiing administrator. The other was the same Captain Henrik Angell who, 10 years earlier, had brought skiing to Montenegro. They arrived on 26 February 1903, late in a notably poor season for snow. Schultz was there to welcome them. During the little crisis, he had tactfully removed himself, sampled the fleshpots of Nice, and showed off his jumping in the Alpes Maritimes, at Peïra-Cava, a future ski resort. He was quickly back in Briançon, co-opted into the ski school. *Le système 'D'* had triumphed after all.

It was an oddly assorted trio now dispensing instruction. Shultz was a carefree youth; Angell even more the florid, eccentric Francophile. Quale was the most dispassionate observer. Before going to Briançon, he had doubted stories of the legendary marching ability of the French soldiers. He changed his mind 'after having seen what the soldiers at the ski school could accomplish … when, untrained and unpractised as they were … they marched up to 50 or 60 km a day on skis without really being worn out.

'The soldiers' red trousers, blue jackets and dark berets', he went on blandly, 'showed up well against the snow.'[3] That at least was what he wrote for publication. More privately, he remembered, with disapproval, that Clerc wanted long, record marches, so that his men were often exhausted. By a horrible irony, Clerc fell on the day that the First World War broke out in August 1914.

The long marches at Briançon were not only a matter of drill. The town itself was starved of snow. Skiable slopes lay some way off and up in the heights. This sometimes meant starting from the barracks at 4 a.m., not returning until eight or nine at night. The Norwegians taught the rudiments of all-round skiing, on the flat, uphill and turning and stopping downhill with the stem. They were hampered because 'the skis and bindings [of the French] were thoroughly bad', as Quale put it. 'They came from factories in Germany, Italy, *none from Norway*', he added with distaste. Worse still, the outfit included a retrogressive single stick.

To add to all their woes, the pupils were required to ski with full military pack. This weighed a good 20 kg. Worse still, it was carried awkwardly, in the French army style that went back to Napoleon, high up over the shoulders, surmounted by a rifle.

Top-heavy, it disturbed the balance in a way that would have worried a practised skier. As Angell recorded of these tyros:

> When they came swishing down the steep slopes with their horrible loads ... their skis ... often stuck suddenly in a snowdrift – and then the skier shot like a cannon ball head first into the snow ... Worst of all was when ... they were so miserably top heavy [that] in addition they suffered a blow from the rifle barrel when they fell ... the Frenchmen ... mumbled something unchristian deep in the pile of snow, but when we went up and asked how they were, they always answered with a smile: 'Ça va bien, mon capitaine!' ... And with the same good humour the skier padded on.
>
> You cannot help liking such fellows.[4]

Schultz and Quale agreed – with reservations. The company was made up of volunteers; some 30 officers and men, all embryonic instructors, so there was no failure of will, and they were eager to learn. On the other hand, the Norwegians were supposed to lead this ski school but in practice found themselves under the orders of Captain Clerc. He considered – rightly – that they ought to teach, not by precept but example. He also thought that they were capable of anything. The Norwegians themselves were not so sure. One incident stuck in Quale's mind as typical of their stay:

> We marched up 1,000 metres [above] Briançon and when we reached the top, there was an equally steep [slope] on the other side. At that point we had been climbing for 4 hours. 'Now the Norwegians will run down here', said [Clerc]. First we must have some food, we said, for we don't want to cross into eternity on an empty stomach. After we had eaten a little, we ran down in wide turns, and far down we saw the Frenchmen like tiny flies up on the mountain. [They] were moving almost horizontally back and forth. If one of them went too fast, he deliberately fell. It was nearly 2 hours before they all came down.[5]

One run, he noted, was 'so long and tiring that even we Norwegians had to lie down 3 or 4 times to catch our breath, because our legs would no longer bear us'.[6] In almost the same breath he admitted that the scenery 'outshines our own mountains in grandeur and wildness', and 'we also had runs, the like of which I have never previously seen'.

Nonetheless, Quale decided that 'The terrain in the Alps is not as favourable for skiing as, for example in our own [Norwegian] forest lands, since it is too steep and … uneven.'[7] And, tellingly, 'something that I missed was our mountain expanses which with their long, even, slopes, instil a certain feeling of peace and quiet which is absolutely lacking in these parts'.

In other words, he was uncomfortable when technique became an end in itself. That embodied the Nordic skier's dilemma, and the future clash with the growing Alpine school. Temperamentally, Quale and his kind were not suited to the surroundings; any more than they were born to analyse and expound. It was what Clerc already sensed. He wanted his Norwegians not so much to convey technique as to inspire by their presence.

The ski school was so exhausting, both for teachers and the taught, that it only ran from Monday to Thursday, with the rest of the week free; for the French soldiery at any rate. On Friday and Saturday, the Norwegians were expected to teach the regimental officers and on Sundays, their wives. The Colonel's lady, as befitted a senior officer's consort, was particularly keen. Quale described how he and Schultz would support her on each side. One Sunday the nursery slope was overlaid with fragile crust. Quale advised against skiing. However, perhaps because he was only a lieutenant, she demurred:

> Snow conditions were as much double Dutch to her as skiing. Anyway we skied down. She was wearing a hat and veil! … Suddenly her skis broke through [the crust], and we ran on, but in confusion. It was not a dignified regimental commander's wife who got to her feet, covered in blood, with hat awry and tattered veil. Afternoon tea with her was cancelled. We didn't see her for 14 days.

It was a scene worthy of Rabelais or Voltaire. It may have helped to spread the ski among a population averse to authority. Sometimes Angell travelled round the valleys, complete with heavy magic lantern to give slide shows in his fluent and idiosyncratic French. To highly appreciative audiences, Schultz and Quale jumped; the one clearing over 20 metres, to the other's 16 or so. The spread of skiing as usual owed much to the jump, in its elegant conquest of space. As in the swoop of a falcon, it had the power to inspire.

There was much propaganda in the marching of the ski school through the mountain villages on the way to the slopes. The Norwegian officers, tall, erect, in field grey and, where Schultz and Angell were concerned, with flamboyant manner, were the exotic attraction. At each stop, locals would examine their skis and take careful measurement. Village urchins mimicked them with sticks lashed to their feet. The local branch of the French Alpine Club was also captivated. Thus the ski was spread out from the military cantonments.

In any case, when the ski school closed at the end of March, the Norwegian mission had inculcated the elements of downhill skiing, notably the stem, Telemark and Christiania turns. They had done much more. They had brought Norwegian skis to demonstrate. These were Huitfeldt's Telemark model. Clerc reported that they were 'infinitely superior' to the wider, shorter skis used by the Swiss and Italians. 'They never break, and are much easier to manipulate.' There was more in similar vein. This was another link in the rise of what became the Alpine ski.

As a reward for their work, Clerc took Quale and Angell off to Chamonix for the first known attempt to climb Mont Blanc on skis. Angell, more than ever a northern Don Quixote, wanted to plant the Norwegian flag on the summit at any cost. His companions had some difficulty persuading him to turn when avalanches and dangerous snow argued for retreat. They all came down safely in the end.

Failed or not, the Norwegians' reputation was undimmed. 'Everywhere ... we encountered the greatest kindness', said Quale. 'My service at the ski school in Briançon ... and all the hospitality we enjoyed, will always remain one of [my] most wonderful memories.' He returned home, like Angell, a confirmed Francophile. 'In Chamonix ... after a stay of several days [living] like princes ... the kind and unassuming [hotelier] declined ... all payment ... the knowledge that we had nothing to complain about, was enough'.

It was not perhaps the ordinary behaviour of the Chamonix inhabitants. On the other hand, Quale and Angell were not ordinary visitors. Between them they, together with Schultz, had planted a seed. Clerc himself had reasons for his work beyond the immediately technical. He was worried by what he called 'this degeneration of the race'[8] of which, in the Alps, 'one is sadly aware'.

> It is enough to observe that of 6 male births ... hardly one man of 20 years is produced for [military] service. [This] is due, not to alcholism ... but to the way of life ... during the winter. As soon as the cold arrives, and the snow covers the ground, the inhabitants abandon the upper floors of their houses, to live higgledy-piggledy with their livestock in the stables in the cellar ... Excepting a few ... hunters, poachers and smugglers, the inhabitants, hindered by the thick cover of snow ... go out as little as possible [and] become tubercular.

This fear of degeneration was part of the malaise of the West. The form varied, but the background was the same. In England, the puniness of the man in the street was the concern. In Germany, it was a matter of maintaining robust health. The French, by their own account, were in dire straits. They were still suffering from the ravages of the Napoleonic wars, and the war with Germany of 1870–1. Much of their soldiery was undersized. The Norwegian skiers were admired not only for their mastery of snow, but also for their towering physique.

They were, thought Clerc, an example to his compatriots, amongst whom 'skis might ... in the long run, improve the race by changing habits'. This trust in physical exercise as a nostrum was also typical of the age. By an experience of his own with the ski school, Clerc made the point:

> In December 1902, when we arrived in the course of our marches at the village of Valloire, the inhabitants could not believe that we had crossed the Rochilles pass on our skis ... When we returned at the end of March 1903, we were astonished to find a small group

of skiers, led by a civilian doctor, and composed of young people from 18 to 20 years. They already [skied] very well.

Clerc drew up plans for a military ski school, which the General Staff broadly accepted. By now, they had begun to consider skiing as more than a technical aid to winter warfare. They saw it also as a means of regeneration and hence of supplying healthy recruits. Among the Alpine nations, they were not alone. Like their looming enemy, the Germans, the French army became the chief sponsors of the ski. The military presence on the tracks was never far away.

One way or another, Clerc felt that he had begun to popularize the ski. He was not, of course, alone. There were other scattered examples, in the French Jura, for example, and particularly at Chamonix. Quale noted that the guides who were with him on Mont Blanc used skis with sealskins. In fact, before Quale had even arrived in Briançon, a Chamonix doctor called Michel Payot had already pioneered what is still arguably the great classic ski tour in the Alps. This is the Haute Route, between Chamonix and Zermatt; from Mont Blanc to that other legendary peak, the Matterhorn. There was fresh snow; conditions were wholly favourable. Four guides accompanied Payot. They did the traverse between 17 and 22 January 1903.

Born in 1869, Payot first started skiing in 1896. It was around that time that the first skis appeared in Chamonix, probably brought from Scandinavia. Winter still swathed the valley under Mont Blanc in snow, and paralysed travel. Like Imseng at Saas-Fee half a century before, Payot was originally driven by a sense of duty. He wanted to visit his patients in all weather and the ski was the answer that he sought. Besides the Haute Route, he pioneered now famous local ski tours like the Vallée Blanche, along the Mer de Glace. Each winter, bearded, wide-eyed and anything but athletic-looking, he made his way on skis to probe the sprawling lower reaches of Mont Blanc for yet another route, or do his doctor's rounds.

Nonetheless, skiing did not spread as quickly as Clerc, for one, had hoped. This was partly due to a clash between mountain climbers and skiers. The climber felt that he was the aristocrat of the hills, and custodian of the pure approach. The skier threatened to invade his preserves with the *canaille*, bringing pollution in their train. This was of course far-sighted. The Club Alpine Française (CAF) – the French Alpine club – by contrast, saw danger in exclusivity. As an antidote, on 11 February 1907, the Briançon section organized ski races at the nearby mountain village of Montgenèvre.

From several points of view, this was a historic occasion. It was the first proper skiing event in France and the first recognized international competition, anywhere on the Continent. It was also the first international military ski race in that French and Italian Alpine troops were competing against each other. That too was extraordinary. In the disbelieving words of one Frenchwoman among the spectators: 'The officers were fraternising … Observing such sincere cordiality, one feels more than a thoughtless prejudice dissolve … each one of us, at this moment, is tempted to declare himself, with Socrates "citizen of the world!"'[9]

A little high-flown perhaps, but that these particular countries should have met on the ski track would have been unthinkable a year or so before. All this reflected a change in the shifting alliances of the age.

As it happened, the French were narrowly beaten. Nonetheless, as an act of propaganda, the consequences were formidable. There was persuasive coverage in the press. This was the event that launched the ski in France. It was largely due to the French soldiers in the tracks. Although the CAF was the nominal organizer, this was really a military occasion. In France, that meant much. The army was the pillar of the State, above Parliament and judiciary. It was the guardian of the national soul, the keeper of the Napoleonic flame. What the army wanted, the army got. Since the army was now seen to have endorsed the ski, it had an irresistible power of advance.

At Montgenèvre, as the Press happily noted, French senior officers were in evidence. Chief among them, wrapped in greatcoat, with kepi much gilded, was General Galliéni, the shambling unmilitary figure with a touch of genius who, a few years later, in 1914, was be the victor of the Battle of the Marne, which wrecked the German plan and, at the start, decided the outcome of the First World War.

The Montgenèvre competition was, however not all military. Two of the ubiquitous Norwegians brought their usual touch of class to the event. They demonstrated the jump, hors de concours, 'showing a mastery which brought the crowd to transports of wild enthusiasm',[10] to quote the CAF journal. In plain figures, the Norwegians jumped about 30 m. By now, powered flight was an accomplished fact, but the ski-jump could still enthral. One of the Norwegians was a Holmenkollen performer called Harald Durban-Hansen. The CAF had invited him as an instructor. His chance companion was Harald Smith, who had made one of his periodical forays from St Moritz into Italy, and found himself in Turin at the time. Together with a party of civilian skiers from that city at the foot of the Alps, he appeared at Montgenèvre. He and Durban-Hansen did much for the propagation of skiing in France.

Besides the Italians, there were ordinary French participants. They were watched by some 3,000 spectators, who had defied the dismal communications to come from Paris and Grenoble. The races themselves were all cross-country and jumping. In other words, despite the Alpine surroundings, the occasion was purely Nordic.

So too was the second French international ski festival, in early January 1908. Again, the main event was military. Now there were official teams from Switzerland and the Royal Guards in Norway. Through the intervention of Dr Payot, the event had been moved from Montgenèvre to Chamonix. It was sponsored by the Chemin de fer de Paris à Lyon et à la Méditerranée (PLM) railway, which happened to serve Chamonix, and marketed the place as a tourist resort with its dramatic view of Mont Blanc This neatly illustrates the blend of motives for the enterprise. Payot was the local patriot. The CAF wanted grander scenery and hence more prospective skiers. The Army's concern was national defence. For their part, the PLM saw money in a winter season and more passengers. It was an early fusion of Mammon and Olympus.

Overpowering the wooded valley, and mundane Chamonix, the stupendous ice falls of Mont Blanc were an appropriate backdrop to proceedings. The military patrol race, on 3 January 1908, was from Argentière to the Col de Balme, and back to Chamonix. That meant a distance of 30 km with a total difference of height of 1,200 m.

The Norwegians were not at ease, because the climb and succeeding run down were all at one stretch, and not broken up as in their native terrain. What is more they had been catapulted into the event without training or acclimatization. The Swiss, in the words of Lt K. Vilhelm Amundsen, the Norwegian team leader, 'were all highly respectable skiers. They ran in a completely Norwegian style, with good posture and use of the skis.'[11] The Norwegians kept them at bay by dint of skiing better downhill in breakable crust, and won by 3 hours 35 minutes and 30 seconds to 3 hours 55 minutes and 12 seconds. To avoid publicly embarrassing their hosts, Norwegians and Swiss had agreed to run *hors de concours*. As it was, the first French team trailed by an hour. There was an ironic touch in the CAF motto above the finish line: *Pour la Patrie, par la Montagne*.

This wry outcome, however, masked progress. For one thing, an embryonic French ski industry was gestating. This was due to the military pioneers in the now celebrated 159th Regiment at Briançon. In the words of Captain Rivas, who had succeeded Captain Clerc as head of the ski school, a

> group of propagandists were to teach young people how to ski. But the results would be zero ... because one would run up against that enormous difficulty: *the high cost of skis* ... It is only ... the price which is preventing the sport becoming democratic.[12]

So in the winter of 1907, Rivas had arranged a course in ski making at the workshops of the 159th for selected craftsmen from different regions. He wanted thereby to secure cheap skis by establishing a cottage industry. It seemed to have worked. From the Vosges to the Pyrenees, 'the ski is recruiting adherents just about everywhere', *Le Figaro* could report in covering the Chamonix races of 1908.[13] And also: 'Women having decided to rival men in all sports, it was hardly surprising to see [them] launching themselves ... valiantly onto the snow-covered slopes with long skates attached to their shoes.'

In plain language, there was also a women's cross-country race. Beskirted, and some behatted, nine skiers, all from the vale of Chamonix, ran over an undulating course of 3 km. *Le Figaro* again:

> The snow was thin and hard. The falls were ... many. None of the competitors were able to finish the course without tumbling in the snow several times ... The French lady skiers have still much to do before they can equal their Norwegian sisters.

From a Norwegian point of view, Lt Amundsen thought that

> many of the ... fair Chamonix ladies ... were very competent. [They] seemed in good

form at the finish, fresh, lively and laughing, although their faces were naturally rather flushed, and coiffure not in the best state ...

Well, striving and sweating ladies in a cross-country race are not exactly the kind of female skiing which is aesthetically appealing to us [in Norway]. I believe that the French will also turn away from demanding trials of strength from the fair sex to ... skill in pure running downhill, where style and posture are the criteria.[14]

Be that as it may, those girls from Chamonix were pioneers. There had been women's cross-country races before, notably in Sweden, Finland and even at Nome, in Alaska in 1901, but this was the first of its kind in the Alps. It was the precursor of what was to come. What is more, they were technically more advanced than the men. Probably coached by Durban-Hansen, now seasonally resident, they used two sticks, where the French military teams were still retrogressively keeping to a single one. It was one explanation of their rout.

Nonetheless, the events in Chamonix inspired a popular weekly, *L'Illustration* to expatiate:

Winter sports do not belong to those which one is content to watch; it is necessary to take part. No summer sport is their equal in a perfect and healthy pleasure. It cannot be analysed: it is an abundance of joy, movement, exaltation and health. It is the death of neurosis and dark thoughts; it is the ruin of the doctors, it is the crash of patent medicines; it is strength, it is a flowering, it is happiness.[15]

This revealed the proverbial French hypochondria, and the forebodings of the age. It was also prompted by the Norwegians at Chamonix. The victors of the military patrol race were impressive enough. The real trigger of high-flown prose was, as usual, the ski-jumping. On two days, led by Durban-Hansen, the Norwegians gave a demonstration, reported by *Le Figaro* in these words:

The Norwegian skiers launched themselves ... into the air, to land after a distance of thirty metres with a superb mastery. They were to be seen in the middle of space, arms along their trouser seams, [their] skis glued to each other in parallel, and they regained the snow without ever falling. With breathtaking speed, they then descended the slope onto which they had been projected, and ran with truly extraordinary control down to the valley, where they stopped ... the most illustrious, M. Durban-Hansen, both lawyer and ski manufacturer, jumped a distance of 34 metres [which] was much applauded.[16]

Significantly, the French were then leaders in aviation, and it would only be another eighteen months before Louis Blériot made an early breakthrough and became the first to fly the English Channel. Still a ski-jumper was faster than manned flight. In other words, it was Nordic skiing that still induced general rapture, and remained the power in propagating the sport.

On that account, an annual fixture was now envisaged; by the Army in particular. The Chamonix event was repeated in 1909, but more elaborately. Yet again, a Norwegian military team had been invited. Its leader was the same Finn

Quale, now Major, who had taught the French soldiers to ski at Briançon six years before. To advance the spread of skiing, the races were extended to cover the widely scattered venues of Morez in the Jura and, in the Alps, Albertville and Grenoble. During January 1909, a caravan of officials, journalists, skiers and hangers-on, sped from one to the other by railway and horse-drawn sledge. In the background, perhaps, lurked the example of the early Tour de France, which had been running since 1903.

Chamonix still remained the prime arena in 1909. On this occasion, the Norwegians were better prepared. They trained at home before departing. What is more, they were better organized. Since February 1908, the Norwegian Skiing Federation – Norges Skiforbund (NSF) – had been in existence, so now, belatedly there was a national skiing body.

The French at Chamonix had correspondingly improved. Gone were the heavy single sticks of 1908; two were now the norm. Also strips of fur under the skis to help in climbing, but were a drag elsewhere, had been discarded. Both were thanks to Harald Durban-Hansen. He was the force behind an almost exponential rise in skill. He had some choice words in print. 'The sport of skiing, not the sport of the stick, that is the point', he wrote in the CAF journal:

> He who *leans back* on his stick, in the hope that his skis will find the right path, does not ski … I have noticed that this poor method is very common among the French. At the top, before departing, they carefully arrange their skis parallel, in the desired direction. Thereafter, they no longer care about their skis, and lean heavily on their stick. As soon as the speed becomes troublesome, and the skis move in the wrong direction, they simply fall down.[17]

In the snow, Durban-Hansen was helped by various compatriots. One was the ubiquitous Harald Smith. Already France had a ski champion in the modern guise of a celebrity. He was Alfred Couttet, from Chamonix, the first of a famous skiing clan. He outclassed his compatriots both in jumping and cross-country. He was good enough to be invited to run at Holmenkollen that winter of 1909. He was the first Frenchman to do so. At the age of 20, he came 11th in the junior division of the Nordic combination. He beat eight of the best Norwegians.

At Chamonix, meanwhile, there was other proof of progress. The women cross-country racers had dumped their skirts and, on the ski track, now wore trousers alone. That made them truly pioneers. They were probably the first women ski racers so to appear in public.

When the Norwegians left Chamonix, on 29 January it was, in the words of *Le Figaro*, 'a grand occasion':

> a regimental band at the head, generals, the Prefect, the Mayor, *tout Chamonix* … accompanying them to the railway station. When the train started, and it was the moment of the last farewell, after the last embraces, for a few seconds everyone felt an inexpressible emotion.[18]

It would be hard to discern that this was not the celebration of a victory, but acknowledgement of a lesson learnt. Nationalist as they are, the French paradoxically have never shrunk from paying their historical debts.

These Norwegians, *Le Figaro* continued, had been

> the pleasantest companions of the caravan, but they also have the right to our recognition as Frenchmen ... It is they who have revealed the ski to us ...
>
> In that there is something inconceivable. Consider that the ski, which has existed in Norway since time immemorial, was only introduced into France some three or four years ago, and also that sport was needed in order to discover a means of locomotion which has given to the valleys, hitherto immobilised by snow, the life and bustle of a more clement season.
>
> The ski has been a revolution; a revolution analogous to that of the bicycle, if not more significant ... The montagnards are now skiing. Even the ragamuffins of the mountains have become enthusiasts. Finally the villages, which in days gone by were isolated by snow from the rest of France, are now in communication; since the postman collects and distributes the mail on skis.

All this was inspired by the usual ski-jumping, but also by the military cross-country event the day before. The distance was 18 km. The Norwegian team was a quartet and they took the first four places. It was an intensely emotional experience. A Nordic ski race, with its sequential starting, is a matter of art imitating life. The first across the finishing line is not necessarily the winner. Along the way, there are two competing strains: the strategic, or one's overall standing, which is not evident, and the tactical, which is. Here it is a question of overtaking or being overtaken, which may or may not have a bearing on the final result.

One of the Norwegians was worth more than a second glance. His name was Olav Olavson Bjaaland. He was at Chamonix in his capacity of private in the reserve. He came from Telemark; indeed from Morgedal, which had been so prominent in the gestation of modern skiing. Born in 1873, Bjaaland belonged to the second generation of pioneers. He almost personified the birth of modern skiing. He was probably the finest all-round skier of his generation. Small, wiry, compact, dark-haired, with oval face, he hardly looked the Viking on a raid; but a marauding skier he was. He had twice won the Nordic combination at Holmenkollen; in 1894 and 1902, besides a succession of good placings. For recreation, he tore down the wild downhill runs around his home. A farmer by occupation, he was also a skilled carpenter and ski maker, besides being highly musical with a dry sense of humour into the bargain. Before the age of specialization, he was also good at the 50 km ski event. There, he had crowned his career in 1908, at the age of 35, by being runner-up at Holmenkollen. Nonetheless, in his own words, Chamonix 'was my hardest race'.[19]

He started last, at number 92. In a Nordic event, that is the place of privilege because the later you start, the better your overview of the proceedings. 'Thorvald Hansen from Christiania was just ahead', as Bjaaland recalled in after years. Before

41. Olav Bjaaland, Chamonix, January 1909. *Author's collection*

Hansen came the other two Norwegians, and in front of them 88 Frenchmen:

> That was a sprint to remember [as Bjaaland put it.] About the half-way mark I caught
> up with Hansen. He was the best skier in Christiania at the time, and a tough man in
> cross-country. I dogged his footsteps, overtook one Frenchman after the other, and finally
> I was first in the track. I was winning uphill, but on the flat, Hansen drew ahead. It was
> hard going. So I said to Hansen, who was in front: There's no point in killing ourselves,
> let's take it easy, we've got such a lead.

Bjaaland very sensibly believed in not driving himself to the utmost. It was not
worth jeopardizing one's health simply to win a race. That is incidentally a good
rule for avoiding heart disease. But principles succumbed to the instinct of the
chase:

> Hansen wouldn't listen. He simply charged ahead, and wanted to make up the half
> minute that I had gained on him. Now I understood that this wasn't only a fight between
> Norway and France, but it had also become a fight between Christiania and Telemark.
> And so I hurled myself forward, and shouted: 'You can run as fast as you like, Hansen,
> but you won't get away from me.'

And so it was neck and neck right to the end, changing places again and again. But I crossed the finishing line first – And then for once wasn't I worn out.

His time was 1 hour 31 minutes 17 seconds. The best French skier was 40 minutes behind. That was one reason for the emotional parting at Chamonix.

Bjaaland had another historic claim to distinction. On the train between Christiania and Hamburg, while travelling down to Chamonix, he had met Roald Amundsen. Amundsen thereupon asked him to join the polar expedition that he was in the midst of organizing.

# 27

# Polar Exploration

The approach to Bjaaland was yet another sign that the ski was revolutionizing polar exploration. Nansen and Nordenskiöld were the honoured pioneers, but they had an early predecessor. Jens Munk was another Norwegian who, in 1619 sailed out in search of the North West Passage. This was the fabled short seaway to the splendours of the East through channels in the Arctic outlands of America. In Hudson's Bay Munk, with his two ships, was frozen in and forced to winter near the mouth of what is now the Churchill River. Scurvy and cold killed most of his companions. Somehow he, with two others, survived and managed to escape in one of the ships, eventually returning home. In the book that he published, Munk soberly observed: 'If we had skis, which are common in Norway, and people who knew how to use them, it is possible that we could have found [help] otherwise it is impossible to move in such places in winter.'[1]

Munk proposed another expedition to the Danish King Christian IV – Norway then belonging to Denmark – but now with practised skiers. The King declined and that was the end of the matter.

Apart from rare proof that skiing was indeed still common in Norway at the time, this was the first known advocacy of skis in polar exploration. As it turned out, William Parry, an English naval captain, was the first man known to have tried putting it into practice. In 1827 Parry, commanding HMS *Hecla*, a naval sloop, sailed out to reach the North Pole. On the way, he put in to Hammerfest, in northern Norway. There he bought skis, which he called 'snow-shoes' and, as he put it, 'we practised our people in the manner of walking on them in deep snow, which afforded them fine exercise and amusement'.[2] Off the coast of Spitsbergen at midsummer, however, preparing to leave the ship, and travel over the pack ice, 'it appeared highly improbable, from what we had seen of [its] very rugged nature ... that ... the snow shoes ... would prove of any service ... I gave up the idea of taking them.'

Thanks to the ski, Nansen of course had brought it all to fruition on his crossing of Greenland in 1888. Skis did not, however, at first loom large on the next expedition, his audacious attempt to reach the North Pole by deliberately freezing a specially built ship, the legendary *Fram* ('Forwards') into the pack ice, and moving with the drift. At first, when he left, in the summer of 1893, he took skis as a precaution in case of disaster, so that he could retreat to safety over the ice. They soon became his only hope when, after a few months beset north of Siberia, it was clear the drift would not take him anywhere near 90° north latitude.

He could only attain his goal by a long journey over the pack and there, to anyone with his upbringing, skis were indispensable.

On Greenland Nansen had been forced to man-haul. He devoutly hoped never to suffer that pestilence again. Consequently, on *Fram*, he had brought dogs and was soon learning to drive them pulling a sledge. On 18 February 1894, he was out practising on the snow-covered ice next to *Fram*. He was riding on the sledge, while three of his companions were accompanying him on skis. One of them, Sigurd Scott Hansen, recorded in his diary: 'We can say that skiers and dog sledge kept up with each other.'[3]

This was the record of a historic discovery. The natural speed of a cross-country skier was the same as that of dogs pulling a load. For the second time, Nansen had revolutionized snow travel, the application of the ski being the first. He was about to exploit the interplay of skis and dogs. This was the foundation of the Norwegian school of polar exploration. It meant higher useful loads drawn by the dogs, freed from the parasitic burdens of their masters.

All this had been presaged by Eyvind Astrup. He too a product of the Nordmarka skiing milieu, Astrup was born in Christiania in 1871. For whatever reason, he never raced but skied wildly over unfrequented terrain. That was merely one facet of a constitutional restlessness. In 1891, his family sent him to an elder brother in Philadelphia, in the hope that America would give him a sense of direction. It did so, but not exactly as foreseen.

Soon after arriving in Philadelphia Astrup, as he later recalled, was reading a local newspaper:

> Strikes, murders, and bank-robberies ... filled the columns ... I wished nothing more than to get away from the civilised world [and] suddenly my eye caught a small paragraph ... 'Robert E. Peary, engineer at the Naval Dockyard, is now engaged in fitting out his expedition to North Greenland' ... the very quarter for Norwegian enterprise ... I determined to offer myself as a member of the Expedition.[4]

Astrup was immediately accepted, and within a few months found himself in Greenland with Peary. They made a telling contrast. At the age of 35, Peary was gripped by the obsession of being the first man at the North Pole, for which this journey was a preparation. His only Arctic experience so far had been a few short weeks in 1886, on an attempt to make the first crossing of Greenland. He nursed a lifelong resentment at having been forestalled by Nansen. Peary's aim was now to cross the northern part of the ice cap, a longer journey than Nansen's, and thus redeem his disgrace. Astrup, although much the younger, had rather more experience of snow travel.

On that account, Astrup became the teacher, and Peary willingly the pupil when, on 25 May 1892, after wintering at their base in McCormick Bay on the north-west coast of Greenland, they found themselves alone up on the ice cap, together with 14 sledge dogs, about to start the crossing.

Astrup naturally ran on skis. He had made them himself out of ash, some two and a half metres long, with leather bindings of his own construction.

Peary started on North American snowshoes. He had been introduced to skis on his first expedition in 1886 by a Danish official in Greenland called Christian Maigaard. Now, however, with Astrup, for the first time, Peary saw how skis were properly used. He began using them tentatively himself. He recorded the outcome in his diary:

> The hard surfaces, the hummock slopes, and the strong cross wind have made the 'ski' worry and tire me very much. Frequent falls. Yet they are superior to snow shoes ... Note [the] alternating stroke of ski in good going, like motions of connecting rods of locomotive, also crisp swish, swish on the snow like steam escape from cylinders. God grant these ski may keep up their stroke to Greenland's *ultima Thule*.[5]

Peary meant the northernmost point of Greenland. That was the real goal of his endeavour. With his new-found, almost mystic faith, he now saw in skis the magic key to success. He and Astrup completed the crossing of the ice cap and, at land's end, they found an airy bluff dropping sheer down between their legs to the waters below. Peary called it Navy Cliff. The fjord it overlooked, he dubbed Independence Bay, in honour of the day, 4 July. On 8 July Peary and Astrup started on the return and, on 5 August, reached winter quarters. They had been travelling for 97 days, and covered some 3,000 km. It was the longest skiing journey yet, and skis saved their lives. Peary had cut supplies to the bone, dogs had to be slaughtered for want of food and only musk oxen shot near Navy Cliff saved them from starvation. Time was their enemy and the skis gave Peary and Astrup the extra turn of speed they needed for survival.

On his return to Christiania in 1892, Astrup lectured on the expedition. He took the virtue of skis for granted and concentrated on the Eskimos, fascinated as he was by their adaptation to a hostile environment. He sketched out a fusion of their primitive lore and modern technique that anticipated a new method of polar travel. He had also taken the first steps in the momentous discovery of an interplay between the ski – unknown to the Eskimos – and the sledge dog.

Having accepted the ski, Peary talked Astrup into joining his next expedition to Greenland. This was to start in the summer of 1893, as Nansen was sailing north in *Fram*. In particular, Peary asked Astrup to obtain 'say twelve of the very best ski that the Norwegian makers and your own experience can devise. I think that half of these ski, at least, should be not less than nine and perhaps not less than ten feet in length.'[6]

So with those skis, Astrup had vanished into the Arctic beyond human ken. He came home in 1895 a disappointed man. The enterprise was an unhappy failure. Peary lost faith in skis, and so passes out of this part of the story. At Christmas 1895, Astrup started off on a lone ski tour in the Dovre Mountains and was never seen again alive. He was found dead in the snow near his starting point, apparently having committed suicide. No satisfactory reason ever emerged but he was somehow broken, perhaps by Peary's bullying. What remained was an engaging book about Greenland and the hidden influence behind more famous men. He was after all Peary's mentor and the forerunner of Nansen learning to combine dogs and skis on the floes around his ship.

Nansen had retained his innovative sledge from Greenland with broad ski-like runners. At least it was straightforward in one respect. It merely had to slide. The ski had both to slide forward and adhere for the kick-off from the back foot. Like other skiers back in civilization, here in the wilderness, Nansen was experimenting with the ski itself. He continued to dismiss the Telemark model as the toy of 'acrobats'. It could hardly suit the untouched snow fields of the Arctic, so he thought. Instead, he had brought along some 50 pairs of different types. He turned to his old favourite, the Finnish pattern, which he had so brazenly advocated to his reluctant fellow-countrymen. This ran best on the flat, and ought therefore to suite the polar ice. Light and supple, it followed the contours underfoot, and hence ran with extra ease. Unfortunately it broke too easily. While there was still time, Nansen learnt the danger of the Nordic skier's obsessive pursuit of lightness in weight at almost any cost. Chastened, he now decided on a heavier but stronger ski. It was a modified Østerdal type, about 2.5 m long, with a substantial groove. That meant that it would hold its course with an economy of effort. That might mean the difference between coming home or not.

The shape of the ski was only part of the problem. The material was just as perplexing. Solid wood was still the rule. Nansen finally settled for maple and hickory. Being close-grained, they did not easily soak up water. By the same token, they were difficult to wax and waxless skis were far in the future. Untreated wood worked well at the low temperatures and dry snow of midwinter but was prone to wear and tear. The soles of the skis had to be protected. The only known method, dating back to the Stone Age, was impregnation under heat of some witches' brew based on pine tar. Nansen chose tallow and candle wax as his own extra ingredients. The process had to be repeated many times thoroughly to force the mixture into the wood, so that it would last the expected months of constant use in all kinds of snow. It was arduous work, carried out over the ship's forge by Hjalmar Johansen, the single companion whom Nansen had chosen for the polar journey.

Short and compactly built, Johansen was an all-round sportsman and a versatile skier. Appropriately he too came from Telemark. Johansen was also a skilled handyman as any skier had to be in those days before industrialization of the sport. Besides the chore of waxing, the skis of that era demanded everlasting upkeep. There was no composite structure to maintain shape. The camber had to be maintained with blocks in the middle, the ends held together to force the skis apart. The tips also needed attention. Bent by heat and steam, they had an irritating tendency to straighten out.

When Nansen and Johansen finally set off for the North Pole on 14 March 1895, they ran on maple skis. Between them they had three sledges on which there were spare skis of different wood, including birch. It was the only available method of coping with different kinds of snow. The odd heaving lope of the two skiers speeding over the polar ice, betrayed the single stick to which Nansen was fiercely devoted. On the binding, he was still dogmatic too. Here in the Arctic, it was the same vexed question of lower latitudes. The binding was, after all, the critical link between the skier and his ski. Now it was not a matter of pleasure, but survival. Nansen stuck to his axiom that 'iron and steel on a ski are a monstrosity'. It sounded retrograde but he did in fact have a point. Comfort and ease of movement were vital. The awkward contraptions of cane and steel then in vogue guaranteed neither. Nansen reverted to the Lappish type that he had already used in Greenland. It consisted of leather thongs wound over the toe and round the heel. Now he even abandoned the buckles he had previously used. This was a little more than purism. The device was simple, light and supple, allowing heels to lift unhindered, giving unrestricted movement and hence saving of energy. It was also easy to repair. A simple knot sufficed.

Also in footwear, Nansen reverted to ancient lore. He used the Lapp *finneskoe*, made of reindeer fur and lined with sennegrass. They were soft as slippers, not entirely suited to a heelstrap. They were however warm, and as yet there were no stiff-soled boots to cope with heavy frost. *Finneskoe*, however were adapted to dry cold, and were destroyed by damp. For the wet snow of summer, Nansen took traditional Norwegian ski boots of untanned hide waterproofed with pine tar.

Thus equipped Nansen and Johansen, followed at the start by 28 sledge dogs, skied across the shifting plain of ice swirling on the polar sea. On 8 April 1895, after three weeks on the march, they reached 86°14' north latitude, before extreme cold and ever more broken ice persuaded them to turn. They were 350 miles short of their goal and they had left *Fram* at 84° north latitude. At least they had set a new record for the furthest north. On 8 April 1895, three weeks after starting, they turned and headed homewards. For 147 days, they wandered over ever-changing

42. At a depot on Amundsen's journey to the South Pole 1911–12. Skis stuck in the snow, centre stage. Note the bindings slung over the skis, to saved them from being eaten by the dogs. *Author's collection*

snow and ice, covering 750 miles, before they had to winter alone on the northern edge of the Franz Josef Land archipelago in an improvised stone hut.

Most of the time in violently changeable conditions, Nansen and Johansen were able to ski at the same speed as the dogs. Frequently they had to ski using only toestraps so as to be able to get on and off their skis quickly as rotting summer snow demanded. As time passed, they killed their dogs one by one, feeding them to the others. They had kayaks for crossing open leads and when confronted with a wide channel before reaching land they were forced to kill the last of the dogs and thereafter haul their sledges themselves.

Skis had been their salvation. Their speed at the start of the homeward run had brought them within range of safety. The ski relieved the drudgery of travel. It saved vital energy. By spreading the weight of the skier, it allowed him to pass safely over the treacherous thawing ice of summer, otherwise a death-trap, with dark icy water gaping a few inches below.

Their race for survival had a happy ending. On 17 June 1896, at the South-western corner of Franz Josef Land Nansen, by sheer chance, met the English polar explorer, Frederick Jackson. He too was trying to reach the North Pole – with even less success than Nansen, as it turned out. Nansen had left *Fram* with no very clear idea of how exactly he was to return to civilization. Now a kind Fate let him do so in Jackson's expedition ship. When he landed back in Norway in August 1896, for the second time he achieved instant fame, and he did so as a skier above all.

Without their skis, Nansen and Johansen would not have returned alive. The ski had filled a psychological need as vital as its practical advantage. The sense of contact with the snow that the ski confers, removed a nagging fear. That alone might have helped to save their lives. All this appeared in the obligatory book of the expedition, which Nansen wrote. It became an international sensation. When, as *Farthest North*, the English edition appeared in 1897, it was received, at one level, as a heroic tale although Nansen, as a skier, was the anti-hero. He and Johansen were not intruders in a hostile environment, but skiers in their element. Nansen's book was propaganda for the ski. The other way about, it consolidated the revolution that had started on the crossing of Greenland. It confirmed the case for skis in polar exploration.

The process continued with the next Norwegian polar enterprise. This was also in *Fram*; albeit after a refit in which the half-deck was covered. It has gone down in history as the second *Fram* expedition. It lasted from 1898 to 1902. The leader was Otto Sverdrup, who had been captain of the ship under Nansen. He had with him 15 companions. In the channels of the Canadian Arctic near Jones Sound, he discovered 250,000 square kilometres of new territory. Until the advent of aircraft, it was the greatest single geographical discovery in the polar regions.

'Adventures', according to one saying, 'are a mark of incompetence.'[7] By that standard, Sverdrup was notably efficient. He had hardly an adventure to show. He gave the reason in his own lapidary fashion:

Polar exploration has two naturally defined necessities: *skis* and *dogs* ... to achieve the best results, we must learn from the two primitive peoples who, through centuries of experience, have understood how to exploit these necessities: *Lapps* and *Eskimos* ... I am inclined to believe that an adaptation of the Lapp kind of ski is the most useful type of polar ski, and the Eskimo dog an ideal companion on a polar expedition.[8]

Sverdrup picked up his Eskimo dogs from Greenland on the way. His Lapp-like skis, long, narrow, with a marked groove, he had brought from Norway. It is part of this story that he came from the northern Trøndelag province, where the southern Lapps then lived. *Fram* was mostly ice-bound, and exploration was on sledge journeys away from the ship. With 35 dogs to start with, Sverdrup travelled some 4,000 nautical miles over frozen sea ice. In so doing, he perfected the combination of running sledge dogs and men on skis. In his own words: 'Whatever the snow conditions, we skied by the side of the sledges, and that meant quite another speed. Out on the bare ice, we wet ourselves, as you might expect, but we used our skis just the same.'[9] *That* was the real outcome of the whole expedition.

As a by-product, Sverdrup also invented the double tent, with an insulating layer of air in between to prevent the formation of rime frost inside. Another novelty was the banishment of masochism. That followed from having skiers as the backbone of the expedition. Sverdrup did have a word of caution. One of his crew was a zoologist called Edvard Bay. He was Danish, and therefore unused to skis. As a consequence, on one sledge journey:

he struggled horribly [because] he could not use [skis] ... It was extraordinary that Bay managed to follow me, but the struggle told on him ... one day he fainted twice from over-exertion. From this one can understand the enormous advantage of knowing really how to use skis.[10]

In other words, the ski might have revolutionized polar travel but it needed practice. Beginners were potentially a fatal burden. It was a warning not lightly to be ignored.

Sverdrup never had the popular recognition that was his due. This is a pity, because it was he who systematized the whole Norwegian method of running dogs with men on skis that Nansen had stumbled on among the floes, and thus launched the classic school of polar travel.

It was not only a question of matching the speed of dogs and skiers. Sverdrup knew that men and dogs thrived best with routine. So on the march he insisted on regular rests and regular meals. Above all, he banished the epic self-punishment that had blighted polar exploration and of which even Nansen was sometimes guilty. As a skier, Sverdrup abhorred approaching the limits of endurance. He let men and dogs work well within their powers. As a result, those long journeys with ski and sledge passed without noticeable strain.

Sverdrup's successor was Roald Amundsen. In June 1903, he left Christiania to sail through the North West Passage. Since Jens Munk's day, its existence had been

43. Roald Amundsen arriving at Eagle City, Alaska, 5 December 1905, after skiing 800 km
from Herschel Island to telegraph the news of having completed the
North-West Passage. *Author's collection*

proved but never yet navigated on one and the same keel. That is what Amundsen
was setting out to do. By now the North West Passage had lost any practical
purpose and had acquired the aura of one of the romantic geographical goals
that symbolized the end of the era of terrestrial discovery. With six companions
in a tiny West Norwegian sloop called *Gjøa*, 47 gross registered tonnage, and a
derisory 70 ft overall, Amundsen achieved his stated aim when, on 30 August
1906, he emerged from the Bering Strait, having indeed brought his vessel from
the Atlantic to the Pacific as intended.

Paradoxically, however, that was a sideshow. The true outcome lay in the fact
that Amundsen had taken another step in the use of the ski in polar exploration.
For two years, *Gjøa* stayed at the same anchorage on the south coast of King

William Land in the Canadian Arctic. It is known as Gjøa Haven now. Amundsen made various journeys using skis and sledge dogs, incidentally becoming the second man in history to reach the North Magnetic Pole. Even Amundsen saw that as a sideshow. More to the point, he had learned about snow in the New World. From a certain point of view, here in the open, treeless expanses of Arctic America, it seemed familiar, as this diary entry suggests: 'We used skis, and did so much better than on foot, since the snow freezes in the evening, and provides brilliant skiing.'[11]

The real ski tour of that expedition had nothing to do with the Magnetic Pole. In late 1905, *Gjøa* was trapped for the winter in the ice off King Point, off the Yukon coast of Arctic Canada having passed through the operative part of the North West Passage. To get the news through, Amundsen needed a telegraph station. There was one in Eagle City, Alaska, 800 km away. So with local Eskimos, and an American whaling captain stranded on the coast, he skied over the coastal mountains down the Yukon to Eagle City and, in different company, back again to *Gjøa* at King Point.

Once across the mountains on the outward journey, Amundsen left the tundra and had to learn about skiing in the north American forest, with loose snow of a strange consistency, hitherto reserved for the Canadian snowshoe. Not even Sverdrup had done that. It was an awkward lesson, but nothing compared to Amundsen's skiing misadventures in his home tracts They had prepared him for almost anything. From his diary on the way to Eagle around the middle of November 1905: 'How good it is to have skis, which are superior to snowshoes as long as one can avoid working with the toboggans. Otherwise I think that snowshoes are much better in these parts.'[12]

In this way Amundsen discovered the limitation of skis; so also of the Arctic sledge with ski-like runners, which sank in the loose forest snow. His party had changed to toboggans because, with their large bearing surface, they floated on top – a precursor of the modern *pulka* or boat-like sledge.

Meanwhile, from Netsilik Eskimos at Gjøa Haven, Amundsen had learned how to dress in deep cold. He adopted their system of fur clothing, especially the anorak, or parka. In his own words:

> Both inner and outer anorak hang loosely outside the trousers and the air has free access all the way up the body ... I find it excellent, and the only way to wear fur clothes, if one is to avoid sweating. Now I can move as I want to. Am always warm, without sweating.[13]

To a skier, with his astronomical expenditure of energy and heat, this was the most valuable discovery of all. It laid the foundation of properly designed ski clothing. Humidity destroys insulation. Dampness and heat are the real enemies of the skier in a cold climate.

Amundsen had also been a skiing pioneer in the south. In 1897, a year after his attempt on Hardangervidda, he was on his way to the Antarctic as an officer on *Belgica*, the ship of a Belgian expedition under Adrien de Gerlache. *Belgica* was caught in the pack ice of Western Antarctica, so that this became the first expedition known to have wintered in the Antarctic.

In August, during the southern winter of 1898, Amundsen was skiing experimentally on the frozen sea around the ship. 'Skis of ash would not slide on the freshly-fallen snow', he noted one day in his diary. 'My oak skis slid splendidly.'[14] And also: 'If you break a bamboo ski stick, you can't repair it. If you break a wooden stick, you can easily fix it.'[15] Thus Amundsen succinctly defined the limitations and strengths of natural materials. He showed heroic detachment. He was recording the behaviour of skis in unfamiliar circumstances, while all around him his companions were ravaged by scurvy, and unhinged by darkness, cold, isolation, together with fear of the unknown.

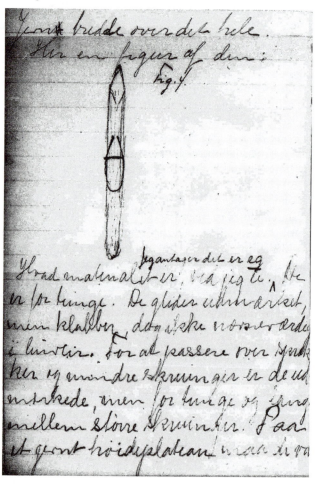

44. The first ski to be used on Antarctic terra firma. From Amundsen's diary on *Belgica*, 5 August 1898. *The National Library of Norway*

Meanwhile, in the previous southern summer, on 26 January 1898, off Graham Land, Amundsen had written in his diary: 'I went ashore on the island [called] "Two Hummocks", and tried my skis. It went well, but I had to turn back on account of thick fog.'[16]

This is the laconic record of the first time that the skis were used on Antarctic terra firma. Amundsen was, however, not exactly the first to ski in the Antarctic. A compatriot had preceded him. Carl Anton Larsen was a whaling skipper from the district of Larvik, on the south coast of Norway. In the southern summer of 1893–4 he went into the Weddell Sea to prospect for a whale fishery. His ship was the same *Jason* that had taken Nansen to Greenland for the crossing of the ice cap. There were, of course, skis on board. On 11 December, *Jason* was near Christensen's Island, off the eastern coast of Graham Land. As Larsen wrote in his diary:

> The First Mate and I put on our skis [and] moved off in the direction of Christensen's Island. There was a route of about 4 miles from the edge of the [pack] ice to the island. It was very heavy going and difficult to make headway, because the snow was deep and wet, so that it clung to the skis.[17]

They never actually reached land, but that unpropitious little tour was the very first time that skis had been used in the Antarctic.

Larsen was an unsung pioneer; so too was his fellow-countryman Carsten Egeberg Borchgrevink. Sailing under British colours, Borchgrevink landed at Cape Adare, at the entrance to the Ross Sea, in February 1899 with 10 companions and 90 dogs to become the first man known to have wintered on the Antarctic continent. On 31 July 1899 he became the first to ski on the continental Antarctic mainland. He did more. On 17 February 1900, he was landed at an inlet in what was then called the great Ice Barrier and there he made a little excursion to the south with 12 dogs, two sledges and two companions, like himself on skis. Having covered 15 nautical miles, he reached a latitude of 78°50'. This was a record for the furthest south and the start of the race for the South Pole. More importantly, Borchgrevink had shown the way ahead by importing Nansen's (and later Sverdrup's) method of running dogs and skiers to Antarctica.

Another unsung pioneer was Frederick Jackson, whom Nansen had providentially met on Franz Josef Land after his Arctic crossing. After Parry's attempt, Jackson was the first English polar explorer to use skis. He had bought them through Nansen's brother in Christiania and saved himself many an enervating plod thereby.

Jackson started his expedition in 1894. He returned to England in 1897, the same year that Sir Martin Conway went to Spitsbergen. Sir Martin – a future Professor of Fine Art at Cambridge University – was one of the great mountaineers of his generation. By chance he became an instant convert to skis. In 1896, he had made the first crossing of Spitsbergen without them; now he was returning to rectify the omission. He published a book – *With Ski and Sledge over Arctic Glaciers* – that was an unashamed paean to the ski. Without the ski, 'progress in any direction would have involved intolerable discomfort', ran one passage, which became the *leitmotif*.[18] The ski, declared Sir Martin, contradicting received wisdom outside Scandinavia, was equally useful in loose snow and hard: 'The actual motion was pleasant: ski and sledges often ran of themselves.'[19] About ease of running, he also said that explorers 'should be freed as much as possible from the mere mechanical labour of making the way. Every foot-pound of energy put into sledge-hauling ... precludes more important mental activities.'[20]

This was a lucid textbook on the ski in polar exploration. It was the first of its kind in English. In fact it was the first book on skiing written by an Englishman. Typically, it had no discernible effect on the first all-British expedition to explore the Antarctic mainland. Led by a certain Royal Naval officer, Commander Robert Falcon Scott in his specially built ship, *Discovery*, the expedition left England in the summer of 1901. Scott had never skied; in fact he had an almost pathological aversion both to skis and advice but, in the words of his own second-in-command, 'prefers to learn by the experience of [his own] mistakes'.[21] The upshot was an enterprise teetering between farce and tragedy, with the farce prevailing – then. Its centrepiece was a journey led by Scott in the southern summer of 1902–3 which set a new record of 82°17' for the furthest south. It set a record of another kind with men *dragging* their skis behind them on a sledge.

Three years after the return of the *Discovery* in 1904, the next expedition sailed under Ernest Shackleton. The attainment of the South Pole had become a global obsession and he badly wanted to be first. He had been with Scott on his furthest south in 1902. Shackleton perpetuated Scott's irrational dislike of skis, probably because he too lacked the patience to learn their use. He tried to *walk* to the Pole. On the 9 January 1909, he reached 88°23'S – by dead reckoning – before turning back. It was a new record, but it was not the Pole. Other things aside, by wasting time and energy, his rejection of the ski was sufficient cause of failure. It was symptomatic of British pole-seeking in the south.

The quest had a new urgency. In September 1909, the American explorers Frederick Cook and Robert Peary returned to civilization, both claiming to have reached the North Pole. Only the South Pole was now left. In a famous turnabout Roald Amundsen who, having attained the North West Passage, was organizing an attempt on the North Pole, secretly turned south instead because it was the only world left for him to conquer. Soon after deciding to do so, he found himself with a rival on his hands.

The same Robert Falcon Scott of the *Discovery* – now promoted to Captain – announced that he too was going to make an attempt on the South Pole. For his part, Amundsen was relieved to be going south. Antarctic terra firma promised better skiing than the grinding Arctic pack. Early in the game he understood the importance of morale. That was why he asked Bjaaland to join him. Bjaaland was after all, the equivalent of an Olympic gold medallist today. He also came from Telemark, which then had a semi-mythic ring. His presence among a party of Norwegian skiers was an inspiration, even before he knew that he was going south. When Amundsen – having concealed his change of plan even from his men – dramatically revealed the truth, at Madeira, on 9 September 1910, during the voyage to Antarctica, Bjaaland reportedly said: 'Hurrah! That means we'll get there first!' The appearance of Scott had turned the attainment of the South Pole from a ski tour into a ski race.

Either way, Amundsen's whole approach revolved round the ski. As he told the tale, he had read in *The Voyage of the* Discovery, Scott's book on the eponymous expedition, that 'our skis … have been of little value'.[22]

> What on earth did the author mean? [wrote Amundsen.] I … read the statement carefully … again – I might perhaps have [misunderstood].
>
> But no, it would not have helped if I had re-read it a hundred more times … There must have been some misunderstanding.
>
> The author had just [clearly] described the [Great Ice] Barrier's appearance. From this it followed that the barrier was a flat, even glacial structure … ideal … for the use of skis.

It was Scott's opinion, as Amundsen also would have read, that 'in the Antarctic Regions there is nothing to equal the honest and customary use of one's own legs'.[23]

Nonetheless Scott had a sudden, late conversion to skis. This had happened at Fefor, in Central Norway, during March 1910. Scott had gone there for trials of a motor sledge, which he believed would be the secret of success. Fefor was one of the earliest Norwegian ski resorts in the modern sense. Foreign visitors, especially English, had started to appear. That may have affected Scott. He was to sail in a few months, and would have to practise in the field.

In all this, Bjaaland had a vital rôle to play. Like many of the pioneers, he was not only a brilliant skier but an accomplished ski maker. The ski, to anyone steeped in a skiing culture, was no sterile plank, but a complex, living structure that needed maintenance. As ski-racer and ski-carer, Bjaaland filled the bill.

Amundsen proposed winning the race by his own adaptation of the Nansen-Sverdrup method of skis and dogs. His fate depended on them both. They took priority over the men. Each was pampered to a degree. In an unbroken voyage of four months, over 100 dogs and a large stock of skis had to be got safely through the Tropics with violent changes of humidity and temperature. The ship was Nansen's and Sverdrup's *Fram*, refitted and rerigged yet again. Of his skis, Amundsen wrote that 'we had to share our own accommodation with them; they were all placed under the deck of the fore saloon, We could not offer anything better.'[24] And later: 'I might say that we loved our skis. Because on infinitely many occasions we saw how helpless we would have been without them.'

> We really patted and fondled them each time we put them on – each time we took them off.

Eventually, on 14 January 1911, after 14,000 nautical miles non-stop from

Madeira, *Fram* lay to at the Bay of Whales on the Great Ice Barrier in Antarctica, and Amundsen could put his equipment to the test. His skis were of his own design. He had settled on a model that was very long, about 2.4 m and relatively narrow. The length was to bridge crevasses. On the other hand, the bearing surface was great. This reduced the risk of breaking through snow bridges or sinking in loose snow of mysterious consistency. The proportions made it easy to hold a course and save energy. One innovation was an unusually narrow waist and a deep flared tip to ride up over drifts. It was a variation of Huitfeldt's Telemark pattern, and a forerunner of the modern carving ski, although the antecedents of both went back several centuries to western Norway. Amundsen ordered 20 pairs made of what he called 'the most carefully chosen [solid] hickory'.[25] Heavy, but strong and flexible and, more important for the likely circumstances, hickory slid better at low temperatures than most other kinds of wood. In the event, Amundsen was vindicated. On a preliminary run to put out depots in March 1911, he reported −46°C and good going.

Of course Amundsen faced setbacks but he had the moral and material reserves to overcome them. He had learned his elementary lessons in his home mountains long before. Besides, compared to the caprice of Hardangervidda that had nearly done for him in 1896, the predictable dry cold snow of Antarctica was child's play.

It was the skier's everlasting plague of boots and bindings, that caused Amundsen more trouble than anything else. He defined the problem in this way:

> I had always [favoured] bindings that were fixed loosely on the foot.
>
> The fact is, I have always been afraid of frostbitten feet through using stiff bindings.
>
> But this time I … discovered that with … loose bindings … the foot [makes] many unnecessary lateral movements … I decided that this unnecessary waste of energy [now] had to be avoided at any cost. It was a long way to the Pole, and if we were to … reach it, every possible factor had to be taken into account.[26]

And so:

> On a long tour like that in prospect … one must have a ski that is fixed absolutely firmly. I know nothing more tiring than when … the foot can move [sideways]. I want the skis to be a part of oneself, so that one always has complete control over them … I decided … to try a combination of stiff and soft footwear, so that we could use the … Huitfeldt-Høyer-Ellefsen binding.[27]

This was what he adopted. It was modified with extra straps round the instep to keep the boots anchored under all conditions. The true hurdle was the boots. With soft footwear, it was easier to avoid freezing. The Huitfeldt-Høyer-Ellefsen binding needed a stiff sole, but this risked impeding the circulation and causing frostbite, which might well have fatal consequence. These conflicting demands had to be reconciled.

In other words, Amundsen proposed to develop a stiff-soled boot to give lateral rigidity, but which could be used in low temperatures. It had never been tried before. He designed a model and had it made up for the expedition before sailing from Norway. In the field, it turned out to have various drawbacks. It took two years to perfect. The final reconstruction only followed at the last moment, after wholesale frostbite of the feet on a false start for the South in September 1911. The trouble was threefold. The boots were not big enough. It was difficult to adjust the precise stiffness of the sole to give lateral rigidity, while allowing the heel to rise, and not interfere with blood circulation. Also boot leather as a substance was too stiff. Amundsen experimented by successively modifying the sole and enlarging the whole boot. In the end, leather was confined to the soles and toe caps, while the uppers were made of soft canvas, with plenty of room for seven layers of socks, insoles and other insulation. The principle was exactly that of cross-country racing boots today, nearly a century ahead of its time.

When, on 20 October 1911, Amundsen finally set off in earnest, the dogs numbered 52 and the men, five, of whom Bjaaland was naturally one. He and Amundsen were complemental archetypes. Amundsen was the mountain skier; Bjaaland, the born competitor. He was arguably the most important of them all. To him, this was just another race; longer than anything he had known, but still a race. The psychology of this group was exactly that of a Nordic contest. Bjaaland intimately understood the isolation of the staggered start, where the world is reduced to the snow around your skis and you have nothing but self-reliance, running your own race. It is comfortingly impersonal because your opponent is the clock.

This was enough to explain the sense of relief that swept over the polar party as soon as they were on the way. By now the temperature had risen to more human values of around −30°, with consequently better going. Amundsen was not to know that even before he started, he had already won. Apart from the fact that his base was nearly 60 miles closer to the Pole than that of Scott, out of sight far to the west at McMurdo Sound, Scott only set off on 1 November. By then, Amundsen was 200 miles in front, and drawing ahead at the rate of 3 miles a day. Scott's much vaunted motor sledges had failed. His conversion to skis had faltered.

Meanwhile, in the *Field*, Nansen obliquely commented on Scott's predicament. Writing about skis in polar exploration Nansen, in an echo of Sverdrup remarked:

> You ought to be accustomed to them ... The beginner ... who puts on ski to use them on a sledge expedition ... will ... be more tired than if he went on without them. [He] will feel as if his ski were always in his way ... and he will strain muscles which take some time to become fully developed.[28]

Simple figures made the point. Amundsen and his companions had at least a hundred years of skiing between them; Scott and the four others of his polar party could barely muster three. They struggled with a beginner's awkward plod, squandering time and energy, as Nansen had foreseen. For most of the way Scott and his companions, like Shackleton before them, man-hauled every step. Even now, in he midst of action they bizarrely pursued an everlasting argument about the merits of the ski. On the 6 January 1912, up on the ice cap, 3,000 m above sea level, meeting difficult, hummocked terrain, Scott dumped all skis and shambled doggedly along, only returning after more discussion to put them on again. Incomprehensibly, before then, he had already ordered Henry Bowers, the fifth man of his party, to leave his skis behind. So four men ineptly struggled forward on their skis, stamping as if they were on snowshoes, while Bowers stumped along on foot, sinking into the snow at every step. A skier, and not only a skier, might regard this as evidence of mild insanity in Scott.

Amundsen, meanwhile was floating over the snow with a fluent Nordic skier's glide. He was running where no one had been before, and therefore pioneering a new route all the 700 miles to 90° south. He had to find his own way up to the ice cap with no precursor to guide him, while Scott was retracing a road surveyed to within 100 miles of the Pole.

Largely due to defective skiing technique, Scott was always on the brink of exhaustion. Amundsen, by contrast was intent on conserving strength so as to avoid mutiny on the part of men and dogs. Neither had a taste for self-punishment. Bjaaland, as the ultimate skier, maintained his old prejudice against risking his well-being merely to win a race. He had no hankering for martyrdom.

It was as skiers, rather than explorers, that Bjaaland and the rest found a way up from the Ice Barrier to the Polar Plateau, a steep climb of nearly 3,000 m over territory never trodden by men before. Without steel edges on their skis, they had to negotiate the steep crevassed Axel Heiberg Glacier waiting, like a silent monster, for them to fall into its maws.

By sheer mastery of technique, they overcame this trap and other little tricks of a playful Fate such as sluggish snow, like sand, before cantering on skis up to what Bjaaland called 'the goal of our desires'[29] at 90° south latitude on 14 December 1911. When Scott finally arrived at the same point, 34 days later, he had fallen behind by 23 days since the start. Amundsen's average speed was about 15 miles a day to Scott's 10.5 or so. If this had been a mile race, Scott would have been lapped just before the bell. The return was equally crushing. Amundsen took 39 days, at an average of 17.5 miles a day. Bjaaland, incidentally, had brought a spare pair of light racing skis for his greater enjoyment when the going was good.

Once down from the heights on the Ice Barrier again, Amundsen simply ordered a sprint for home, so that even Bjaaland, swooping over the snow with his characteristic swing, had his work cut out to keep ahead. No longer driving dogs, he had been made forerunner for the whole way back and strongly objected to any man or dog getting a nose ahead. It resembled the last lap of a ski race, with the swing of sticks and the familiar sough of skis in loose snow, or scrape on crust, casually picking up depots along the way like drinks at feeding stations at a long-distance event.

The whole Norwegian party, man and dog, reached their base on 26 January,

10 days earlier than expected, healthier and fatter than when they had started out on their journey of 1,440 miles 99 days before. Scott was still at 88° south latitude, 600 miles behind and Amundsen had increased his lead by some 400 miles since starting for the Pole.

Scott of course never got through alive. Under obscure circumstances he and all his companions, struggling like a routed army in retreat, perished on the way back. The three who survived longest ran out of food within 11 miles of the next depot. Other explanations aside, unpractised skiing was good and sufficient reason. Wobbly improvised bindings that wasted energy and reduced speed would alone have sealed their fate.

45. The triumph of dogs and skis. One of Amundsen's companions, Oscar Wisting, at the South Pole, 14th December 1911.

Many have pandered to Scott's complaint that he was caught by unseasonable weather and unexpected cold. Amundsen knew, what every skier knows, but Scott evidently did not, that there is no bad weather, only bad clothing. In the end, skiing tipped the scales. Scott was a beginner who, in Bjaaland, faced a world champion.

By contrast Amundsen and his men were the best of their kind and, even in a nation of skiers, one would have been hard put to find anyone better. They were a virtuoso team. The fight for the South Pole *had*, after all simply been a ski race writ large. Without skis, as Amundsen quaintly said, it 'would have had to wait many years more for our visit'.[30] Even in the last place on earth, exposed to the force of Nature, they were at home. Bjaaland, the old Holmenkollen winner, and the one Telemarking among them, inimitably spoke for them all when, on reaching the Pole, he observed that 'Here it's as flat as the lake at Morgedal, and the skiing is good.'[31] It was not so very different from his feelings on outclassing the French at Chamonix two years earlier, because after all it was only another ski race. Having led all the way home for 740 miles, he chose to sum up the whole polar journey with the Nordic ski racer's usual complaint on starting first: 'It was a damned hard job being forerunner.'[32]

# 28

# The Inventions that Founded Modern Skiing

Scott's morbid rout obscured the real lesson of the race. This was the triumph of technical superiority, centred round the ski, and Amundsen's book about his victory – *The South Pole* – was read in this light, at least by open minds. He had brought the era of terrestrial exploration to a close and rounded off the rôle that the ski had played. He was the last of the great skiing pioneers, although to him the ski was simply a means to an end. It was an age of rapid technical advance, which Amundsen had channelled to polar exploration, in particular the ski. This was the period, between 1912 and 1939 – interrupted by the Great War of 1914–18, when the evolution of skiing concentrated on the advance in equipment. The technical impulse that eventually gave skiing its modern form can be traced back to Amundsen.

For instance, Amundsen replaced the tight garments of yesteryear with the roomy Eskimo anorak or parka. For moderate temperature, he had one outfit made on that pattern, not in fur but Burberry cloth, then the most advanced weatherproof material. This was the clothing with which, in the historic photograph, he and his men were pictured at the Pole. In the ski boots that took him there, he made an even bigger advance. He had laid the foundation of subsequent design with his principle of firm soles combined with soft uppers, not entirely obvious before.

The great technical deficiency persisted in the running edges of the ski. On steep slopes in hard conditions, wood quite simply could not bite. Amundsen – and Bjaaland – had been lucky with loose spring snow on their run down the Axel Heiberg Glacier in January 1912. Their touch of entertainment masked a descent that would try even a modern Alpine skier.

Did they but know it, their own countrymen had long since arrived at a solution. In 1887, when Nansen was preparing to cross Greenland, someone wrote to tell him that the inhabitants of Eidfjord, a notably harsh district with steep, quasi-Alpine slopes among the fjords of western Norway

> have invented a method of preserving the edges of their skis. By means of screws, they fix [a strip of] galvanised hoop iron [19 mm] wide to both sides of their skis, so that the skis bite firmly on snow crust and frozen earth, something that they consider absolutely essential here.[1]

Bone edges appeared on skis from Transylvania recorded in the early 1920s. The letter to Nansen, however, is the earliest recorded metal edge. It was the forerunner. For reasons of terrain, most Norwegians did not urgently feel the need but Alpine skiers did.

The first known experiments date from 1917. They were carried out by an Austrian climber and mountain skier called Rudolf Lettner. He came from Hallein, near Salzburg. He started production in 1926. His system was a refinement of that described to Nansen. It consisted of a metal strip 8 mm × 1 mm, fitted into a rebate in the sole, so as not to interfere with the running surface, and attached by vertical countersunk screws at intervals of about 50 mm. In the interests of flexibility, the edge was divided into separate sections, each moving independently. Various metals were tried but mild steel proved best.

So far, technical advances had all come from Norway. Lettner's steel edge was the first that did not. He had broken the Norwegian hegemony. He had many imitators, all more elaborate. His remained the simplest and it was therefore the pattern that prevailed. It was an object lesson in design. With various improvements, notably the reduction of the sections from 30 cm to 15 cm, it lasted as long as the wooden ski. It dominated the field for the best part of half a century.

Bindings also changed the face of skiing. In the race for the South Pole Amundsen, or at least Bjaaland, devised one material improvement. On the march, the dogs had begun wolfing the leather heelstraps as hors d'oeuvre, so Bjaaland fitted metal hooks to make them easily detachable and moved to safety when required.

It had another effect. Hitherto the straps were permanently fixed to the metal ears. This meant constant bending at one point with material fatigue and persistent breakage as a result. Bjaaland's device eliminated this by allowing free movement between the hook and the ring to which it was attached. In all the

46. The Huitfeldt steel toe iron binding, patented 1897, with the Høyer-Ellefsen tensioning heel clip, patented in 1904. This was the first modern all-round binding, both nordic and alpine. *Ski Museum, Holmenkollen, Oslo*

1,500 miles to the Pole and back, not a single heelstrap broke. Unintentionally, Bjaaland had cured a fault of the Huitfeldt-Høyer-Ellefsen system, and invented the first quick-release binding into the bargain.

What Amundsen whimsically called the 'Huitfeldt-Høyer-Ellefsen-Bjaaland patent'[2] – with other advances – continued to lead the field for another two decades. This was despite a fundamental defect. The lateral slot needed for fixing brought structural weakness in its train. It caused many a broken ski although luckily not when Amundsen was on the way to the Pole. The solution was obviously to fix the metal ears on top of the ski.

The first known design, or at least patent, appeared in 1895. It was also the work of Høyer-Ellefsen. This was a compromise because a lateral hole was still needed for the toestrap. It made little impact, perhaps because of poor marketing. Nor did similar attempts succeed. The breakthrough finally came in 1924, with the invention of a well-known Norwegian ski racer, Marius Eriksen. It obviated the need for a lateral hole, by dispensing with the toestrap. Instead, the boot was held down by lugs pressing against the welt. What is more, the ears could be adjusted to the boot instead of hammered to shape. This was achieved by toothed bits and slots meshing with each other and fixed by screws driven into the ski. The Marius Eriksen binding presaged the end of the Huitfeldt hegemony and, paradoxically, Norwegian domination in the field as well.

The story begins with a Swiss manufacturer of music boxes at the French-speaking village of Ste-Croix in the Jura mountains, near Neuchâtel. It was a family business called Reuge. It exists to this day. In the late 1920s, like other companies, it fell on hard times. A grandson of the founder, Guido Reuge, was faced with the problem of saving the concern. Born in 1904, he had qualified as an engineer at the Eidgenossische Technische Hochschule, the Swiss technical

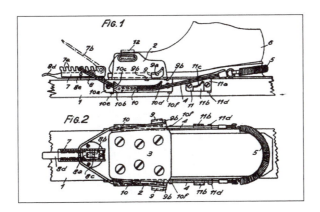

47. Guido Reuge, drawing for patent application for Kandahar binding, Ste-Croix, Switzerland, 1929. *Reuge SA, Ste-Croix, Switzerland*

university in Zürich. Due mainly to the advent of the gramophone, the demand for music boxes had slumped. Reuge felt that his only hope lay in diversifying.

Now he happened to be a passionate skier. He saw the need of a proper downhill binding. In 1929 he invented it. Like the Marius Eriksen binding – which he may or may not have known – Reuge's model was based on adjustable pressed steel ears mounted on the top of the ski. Then Reuge shifted the tightening lever from the side of the boot to the front of the ski and out of the way. That, too, had a forerunner in Ola Houm's binding a generation earlier. So also did Reuge's replacement of the leather heelstrap with a steel cable. A manufacturer called Sessely-Richardson, in Geneva, had anticipated this. Most inventions have a paternity.

Reuge's real innovation lay in the tensioning device. This was a powerful coiled spring, attached to the cable and fitted round the heel of the boot. Reuge quickly started to manufacture his design. It revolutionized skiing. It was the technical advance that made downhill skiing possible as we know it. Reuge had found the classic gap in the market. His binding swept the world, and became a legend in its own right. It was in fact the first piece of proper industrial design in ski equipment, and the first that lent itself to mass production. It opened an era. As such it has a place in history. Almost incidentally, it saved the Reuge business. Guido Reuge called it the Kandahar binding, after an exotically named Alpine race. It was an inspired choice. It rolls off the tongue, and probably was part of the success.

The great advantage of the Kandahar binding was that the new cable system introduced parallel tension. What is more, by a system of hooks on the ears and

48.  Guido Reuge, inventor of the Kandahar binding. *Reuge SA, Ste-Croix, Switzerland*

the side of the skis, the heel could be left free, or fixed down, with varying stages in between, according to requirements. For nearly 40 years, until the advent of the safety binding, the Kandahar held sway.

There were various modifications, notably the replacement of a toestrap with lugs, like the Marius Eriksen binding, to fix the boot by gripping the welt. The number of fixing screws was reduced from six to four and the mechanism of the forward tensioning lever refined. But the basic concept remained the same. The latest model could be recognized from the original drawings. It was a tribute to an inspired piece of engineering – or artistry. Guido Reuge was a bit of an artist and after the Kandahar he returned to music boxes, specializing in elaborate designs for rich customers, like a modern Fabergé. But it was the Kandahar that allowed the company to survive.

For all its versatility, the Kandahar failed in one respect. It did not suit real Nordic skiing. It was too heavy and the cable inhibited heel movement. What was needed was a pure toe binding. For various reasons this was an exclusively Norwegian affair.

From Haukeli in Telemark comes the earliest known attempt. It dates from the middle of the nineteenth century. It consisted of simple hinged iron toebands that clamped the boots, with two nails in front to prevent them moving forward and leather strips under the arch to lock them in place. It was devised for hard crust and never spread outside the valley of its invention.

The first commercial product appeared in 1892. A Christiania shoemaker called Hans A. Solberg then patented a kind of clip with two pins that meshed with corresponding holes in the welt in front of the toes. This was even more advanced than appears at first sight. Special boots were required, with the front of the sole lengthened to make space for the mechanism. It was in fact the first system of boot and binding designed as a whole. It was too far ahead of its time. Leather was unsuited to this particular kind of point strain. The concept had to wait for modern synthetic materials, and the Solberg binding quickly lapsed.

Meanwhile, the dearth of proper toe bindings led to stagnation in technique. The breakthrough had to wait until 1913. It was then that the first practicable toe binding appeared. The inventor was Olaf Selmer. In the first place he came from Lillehammer, in Gudbrundsdalen, and therefore outside the traditional skiing provinces. More to the point, he was a gunsmith. That meant he had the appropriate talent for functional design and his product betrayed the fact.

It consisted of two loose arms hinged to an angle plate screwed to the top of the ski. The arms each had a short serrated lug, which gripped the welt when they were tightened with a leather strap across the top of the boot. When pressure was thus applied, spikes on the binding plate also gripped the underside of the sole.

This was the first successful toe binding to go into production. It sold for more than 30 years. The marketing was as innovative as the design. Known as the Bergendahl binding, is was named after Lauritz Bergendahl, a well-known Norwegian competition skier. It was the first skiing product named after a performer.

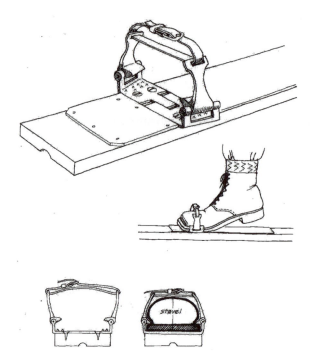

49. The first free heel toe binding to go into production. Selmer's 'Bergendahl' binding, Norway 1913. *Karin Berg, Oslo*

The implications went further. This was also the first manifestation of the star system. Bergendahl was the first skiing star, Nordic or Alpine, anywhere. He was called simply the 'ski king'. Between 1910 and 1915, he won the 50 km race at Holmenkollen five times. Born in 1888, he was nearly lost to skiing through religious revivalism, but his other vocation was too strong. His stardom arose from the lack of national heroes in the aftermath of independence and the poor calibre of politicians. Bergendahl was probably the first sporting figure, anywhere, *faut de mieux*, to do duty as a national icon. Today's footballers, for example, can trace their roots back to him. He atoned for this in other, more productive ways. He was the first skier to train methodically. He systematically developed both speed and stamina. He was a pioneer of tempo training. He also analytically evolved technique. In particular, he was interested in coordination of sticks and skis. He was a pioneer in adapting the Finnish double heave on the sticks as part of an innovative tactical adjustment of technique to terrain. He was the founder of modern Nordic skiing, and the analytical system of coaching. By trade he was a forester, like most of the early Nordic skiers, mainly because of the strength and suppleness developed in wielding axe and saw. Selmer showed acumen when he named his binding after Bergendahl.

The next stage was a prime example of how technology evolves. There was a Norwegian ski racer called Bror With. He disliked the Bergendahl binding because it destroyed his boots. On the eve of a ski race near Oslo – as it now was* – in 1927, he finally did something about it. He took out the steel frame of an old bicycle saddle, and hammered it into the shape of a bail mounted in holes that he drilled in the ears of a pair of Marius Eriksen bindings. He finished off with some pins in the base of each binding to hold the boots. The lever, anchored by a leather strap, pressed the boots down and kept them in place.

On the way to the start, so the story goes, the then Crown Prince Olav of Norway met him and asked about the unfamiliar device, whereupon With is supposed to have answered that it was only a *rottefella*, a rat trap. Indeed the resemblance was close. When manufacture started in 1928 it was dubbed the Rottefella binding. It became proverbial among skiers and a classic piece of industrial design. The principle of a sprung lever holding down with modest pressure a supple boot, kept in place by pins engaging with holes let into the sole, has never changed. On the other hand, the design constantly evolved with new materials, new skiing technique and, above all, new colours and appearance to follow public taste. For 50 years or so the system dominated the ski tracks of the world. It virtually monopolized Nordic racing and lowland touring. It was never licensed; all production was concentrated in a factory near Oslo. Competitors were held at bay by systemic adaptation. Even now the Rottefella continues in wilderness Nordic touring and the Telemark renaissance.

Meanwhile, by coincidence or not, 1929, when Reuge was inventing the Kandahar binding, and a year after the Rottefella went into production, the German chemical giant, I. G.-Farben, launched the first synthetic resin adhesive. It was called Kaurit. It was a two-part preparation, which gave the ultimate control in use through timing activation by mixing the components. Apart from anything else, that eliminated wastage and simplified production. This was the breakthrough that led to the modern ski.

The ski that took Amundsen to the South Pole were primitive implements. They had not changed in essence since their prehistoric origins. Whoever made the Kalvträsk ski 5,000 years ago would have instantly seen the resemblance. Amundsen's skis were made from a single block of solid wood, exactly like their stone age forerunners.

This continued for another two decades. Skis were hand crafted, albeit with some mechanical assistance, and manufacture was a glorified cottage industry. It could not cope with an incipient mass market. Specialized workmen were in short supply. Quality was uncertain. The real trouble, however was a shortage of raw material.

Norwegian ash had become a favourite wood. It combined lightness of weight

---

* Having been changed from Christiania in 1925. Oslo was the Old Norse name, and reverting to it was a manifestation of independence. It marked the tercentenary of renaming Christiania after the Danish King Christian IV, a somewhat warlike gentleman.

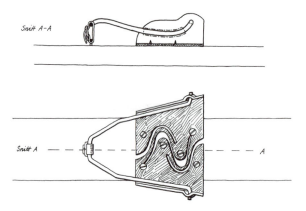

50. The original Rottefella ('Rat trap') toe clip cross-country binding, Bror With patent, Norway, 1927. The snaky pattern in the middle is to fit the binding to the boot by squeezing. *Karin Berg, Oslo*

with good sliding properties and, above all, resistance to wear. The popularization of skiing raised domestic needs, and rising exports made the situation worse. Slow growing and anything but plentiful, the supply of high quality ash could not keep pace with the demand.

The problem was already exercising an earlier generation. In December 1891, at one of the meetings of pioneering skiers in Christiania, Amundsen's old mentor, Laurentius Urdahl had this to say: 'Nowadays there is talk of making ski [with] different kinds of wood [glued together]. If the promise is fulfilled, this will be of great significance for the development of skiing.'[3]

Urdahl was thinking of laminated skis even then being produced in Christiania. They were the first ones in the world. H.M. Christiansen, who made Nansen's sledges, was the innovative pioneer. He was followed by a clutch of imitators all over the country. The shortage of ash was the primary incentive. It was only needed for the running surface, so laminated construction, by using other wood for the body of the ski would eke out supplies.

The manufacturers soon found other advantages. Combining different kinds of wood improved the product. It could avoid points of weakness, for example, by limiting the effect of natural faults like knots. As usual, competitive sport started driving technology. Racers wanted faster, lighter, stronger skis. Willow and alder were often used for the upper layer. Laminated skis were about 40 per cent stronger than their solid counterparts. Many Norwegian ski racers used them to great affect. They were, however, no advertisement, because they preferred to keep the secret of their success to themselves. Hopes of mass production faded. Manufacture all but ceased by about 1910, although a small specialized output continued sporadically until the early 1920s.

BRUKES OVER HELE VER-
DEN AV DE MEST FREM-
RAGENDE SKILØPERE

ANERKJENT SOM DEN
IDEELLE TUR- OG LANG-
RENNSBINDING

Efter et års patentforbud her i
landet er den nu atter fri for salg

*Fabrikanter:* **With & Wessel A/S**
Rådhusgt. 12, Oslo

BROR WITH'S SKIBINDING ("Rottefella")

51. Early advertisement, c.1930, for the Rottefella, the first practical cross-country toe binding. *Karin Berg, Oslo*

These skis suffered from inherent faults. There were only two layers, which meant frequent distortion. The main difficulty, however, lay in the adhesive. Ski makers only had traditional carpenter's glue, based on natural materials. It was not waterproof, nor could it tolerate sudden impact or undue strain. Skis came apart spontaneously. These forerunners, in workshops and on the ski track, were ahead of their time. It was the appearance of Kaurit that brought their pioneering at last to fruition.

The agent of this revolution was a quiet Norwegian called Bjørn Ullevoldsæter. He invented the modern ski. Born in 1891 Ullevoldsæter, an elegant figure, grew up in a place of that name in Nordmarka. He therefore sprang from the classic skiing milieu of Oslo. With a childhood spent in a working forest, he also grew up with a feeling for wood. Instinct served him well. He was apprenticed to the ski-making firm of Thorvald Hansen, which made some of the early laminated models. About 1920, Ullevoldsæter started his own ski factory at Nittedal, on the eastern edge of Nordmarka. Down in the valley among the granite and the trees, it lay on the main railway line running north out of Oslo. Appropriately or not, dynamite and matches were made there too.

Ullevoldsæter began with solid skis, of hickory for strength, heavy and stiff as usual. In the early 1930s, after the arrival of Kaurit, he started experimenting with laminated construction. He was, of course, not alone. A few others, including one from Germany, also tried. They all merely perpetuated old sins. Skis still warped and started splitting at the everlasting weak point of the heels. It was the consequence of flat horizontal laminations cut along the grain, as before. Ullevoldsæter showed most originality. He used three laminations instead of the usual two. The intermediary layer, thickest in the middle and tapering to each end, gave the ski its longitudinal profile. It was patented in 1932. Ullevoldsæter had achieved something lighter and stronger, but not exactly what he wanted. He also had fallen into the familiar trap of using a new technology in an old way.

Then on 21 October 1935 Ullevoldsæter patented a radical new design. Instead of simple horizontal laminations, the ski was built up of vertical elements, eight in all, standing on their edges like miniature beams. They were of different kinds of wood, with the grain angled against each other to balance out the strain. The upper surface of the new model was covered by a thin layer of hard, flexible wood to secure the underlying structure. This was the first reliable composite ski in the world. The principle of the bonded element underlies every model made since then, of whatever material.

The idea probably came from the furniture industry. It resembled a certain kind of reinforced veneer. Because of advances in technology, this was a time of rapid change in woodworking production. Ullevoldsæter had grasped, what other ski makers had not – that the new adhesive, being so powerful, worked on a much smaller area than before, overturning all reigning concepts. That was the key to his innovation.

When Ullevoldsæter started manufacturing his new ski, he also presaged modern production methods. He mechanized the process, and standardized production. Skilled workers were eliminated. Instead, machine operators were needed to cut, assemble and glue. It was the end of the traditional ski maker.

On the other hand, the new method revolutionized design. The camber and bend of the tip were fixed by the glue, eliminating most of the constant old maintenance with cumbersome blocks and clamps. Quality was now even. Warping was virtually eliminated. For the first time, the ski became an inherently stable product. Because the elements were narrow, the need for wide logs was

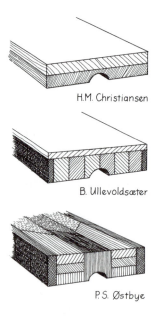

H.M. Christiansen

B. Ullevoldsæter

P.S. Østbye

52. Genesis of the laminated wooden ski, the basis of all subsequent composite models. Cross-sections from top to bottom: Christiansen, 1891, was the first known to have made laminated skis. Ullevoldsæter's ground-breaking design of multiple elements was patented in 1935. Østbye perfected Ullevoldsæter's invention by making the elements themselves composite, using different kinds of wood.

*Karin Berg, Oslo*

eliminated, thus economizing on timber. Above all, because the structure could be precisely adjusted, the characteristics of the individual ski could accurately follow specification; notably whether hard or soft, according to the skier's taste and weight or the kind of snow.

Ullevoldsæter's invention shifted the skill from the worker to the designer and the engineer. This is the essence of mechanization. Ullevoldsæter had paved the way for mass production. He also coined the first trade name for a ski: 'Streamline', thinking of exports no doubt. It was a catchword of the thirties, derived from the new cult of speed on land and in the air that was a characteristic of the age. He was the Henry Ford of the ski industry, as it were.

As usual, it was the market that decided. Ullevoldsæter answered a looming demand. Skiing had turned into a mass recreation. It was a product of the railway. In 1907, the Oslo-Bergen line was completed. This opened up the mountains, saving time on the approach for the crowds released by the advent of statutory paid holidays. Resorts like Geilo and Finse catered to the new customers. Private huts meant a whole reservoir of skiers. Mountain huts maintained by various tourist associations along established, marked wilderness routes popularized hut-to-hut touring. The Easter influx in search of spring skiing became a Norwegian institution. All in all, skiers were numbered in their hundreds of thousands. In other words, this meant the rise of a mass market for the ski. That in turn inflated the demand for raw materials. There was serious concern for the supply of proper wood. By limiting the use of rarer species, like mountain ash, to where it was needed, and thus a fraction of the whole, Ullevoldsæter's composite ski appeared at the right time to eke out the reserves.

Ullevoldsæter was however at heart an innovator and not an entrepreneur. He was quite content with the rustic ambience of Nittedal. Nor did he have capital. Another pioneering compatriot, however, not only had the wherewithal but also business flair. His name was Peter Østbye. Twice he licensed Ullevoldsæter's patents; first the original one in 1933 and then again the Streamline model – for the equivalent of about £50,000 today. Østbye altered the original design by making the elements themselves composite, with three layers each. This further increased strength and flexibility of design. He took out a patent on 9 October 1937. He called his product *Splitkein*.

The word was derived from the English Splitcane, a kind of fishing rod made of bamboo strips glued together, analogous in design and intention to the ski. Splitkein conquered the snows, its legendary small circular red and gold trademark with a Viking head picked out on each ski tip. Østbye licensed his product from the start. Under the Splitkein brand or not, similar ski were produced all over the world. Authier and Attenhofer in Switzerland; Rossignol in France were famous Alpine examples in their day. There was, of course, piracy but also a host of new patents, some dubious, some not, all based on Østbye's and hence Ullevoldsæter's invention. They almost all shared the same composition: Hickory, with its hardness, close grain and resistance to humidity and wear, for the sole, ash or some other tough wood veneer for top and sides, and a plethora of species in between. Even the once-despised pine found a place for its elasticity and light weight.

Splitkein had the mass market; it was never a monopoly. It lived side by side with many small manufacturers, each with its own characteristic; each filling its own niche. The age of mass uniformity was still in the future.

The versatility of the Splitkein revolution was its strength. It applied equally to any form of ski. It triggered a rash of variation. At one extreme was the light, narrow, supple cross-country racing ski which, gradually becoming wider, evolved into a bewildering variety of Nordic touring skis imperceptibly merging with broad, stiff, heavy downhill models and, at the other end of the scale, jumping skis, longest and widest of all. Splitkein, with the Rottefella binding on cross-country racing tracks, or various Nordic touring bindings out in the terrain, or the Kandahar on Alpine slopes, defined an era that lasted nearly 40 years.

When the Lettner edge first made its way to Norway, it was shunned in the Nordic disciplines because it deadened the ski and, with its 150 screws, added at least a kilo to the weight. In jumping, it was a death trap because it could disastrously catch the snow and obliterate control, like the landing gear of an aircraft sheering off at touchdown. This illustrated the abyss opening between Nordic and Alpine skiing.

However, even in Nordic touring, edges that kept reasonably sharp were desirable. In the words of Ullevoldsæter's original patent, the outer layers 'or their lower parts, can be made of a hard material appropriate for a protective edge, so that this edge is integral to the construction of the ski, and thus is securely attached.'[4] Eventually, Splitkein (and others) added an edge of Lignostone; a trade name concocted from *lignum*, a Latin word for wood. Made of compressed wood and synthetic resin, the product was undeniably hard-wearing. The Lignostone edge was in one piece, and bonded with the ski; another precursor of modern methods. Except to the purist, it did not materially stiffen the ski, and served most Nordic terrain in most conditions. Also, despite all prejudice, the steel edge did encourage Scandinavian mountain touring in the spring, through the mastery it gave on heavy abrasive snow crust. It also, eventually, promoted downhill skiing.

The Kandahar binding also had its part to play. It, too, appeared in Norway, where it was quickly produced under licence. This was because of its adaptability. Although invented for Alpine skiing, it was ideal for ski-jumping as well. It was the breakthrough that made possible long jumps of 70 m or more and ski-flying, with the first jumps of over 100 m in the 1930s. The Kandahar binding also turned out to be wholly suited to Scandinavian mountain touring because it allowed the heel to move, while being laterally strong and safe under any conceivable strain. Together with the Lettner steel edge, it completed the technique of skiing down steep slopes by giving the necessary lateral control to exploit side slipping when required. Splitkein, Lettner and Kandahar defined a whole era.

The ski stick completed the picture. Gone were the single staff and heavy old implements of solid wood. Instead the bamboo stick, light and flexible, now reigned. A particular strong species was imported from Tonkin, in what was then French Indo-China. Straightened in a fire, varnished, with leather wrist straps and large baskets of cane, it added to a little world still based on natural materials.

One consequence of the Kandahar and its various imitators was the evolution of heavier boots with thicker, stiffer soles to sustain the pressure of the cable spring, with all that implied for technique and leg fractures. Likewise, in Nordic skiing, the Rottefella led to specialized boots with wide welts and soles reinforced at the toes to sustain the pressure of the clamps, but broken bones, because of free, untrammelled heels, were virtually unknown.

Østbye was a pioneer in more ways than one. At his ski factory in Oslo, he created an apparatus of sponsorship. He gathered round him a group of talented cross-country racers. Times were hard; the Depression was felt here as well. Most ski racers were still forestry workers, more or less poverty-stricken. Østbye gave them jobs, spurious or not. This enabled them to devote themselves to their sport, and circumvent the amateur rules, which were then in full flower. For his part, Østbye thereby had a circle of guinea pigs that helped him to develop new skis. He was among the first manufacturers in any sport, anywhere, to keep a stable of competitors. Partly he was an idealist but he was also thus assured of publicity, by discreetly making known that particular individuals used Splitkein when winning this jumping competition or that cross-country race. He was in the vanguard of celebrity marketing.

Peter Østbye had another claim to distinction. He established the first systematic production of ski waxing. But this story has a prelude in America.

# 29

# *The New World*

Skiing in America – as indeed later in Australia and New Zealand – was introduced quite late from the Old World to the New as a result of colonization. The story of American skiing begins in Russia during the glittering reign of Catherine the Great. With all Siberia in her hands, and wishing to increased the empire of the Romanovs, she had designs yet further across the Bering Strait on America. In 1783, at the apogee of her power, a group of her subjects founded a settlement on Kodiak Island, off the Pacific coast of Alaska. They were the first to use skis in the new continent.

Rough, tough, resolute, ruthless and cunning, these settlers were mainly Russian fur traders, trappers and hunters from eastern Siberia. By their piratical adventuring they had already colonized that territory for the Tsars. They thought to repeat the process in Alaska. That involved penetrating the wild hinterland, in winter if need be. One of their number whose name and record have come down to us was a certain Vasilii Ivanov, who in the early 1790s skied up country and reached the River Yukon.[1] Another Russian document observes that 'in the winter of 1796 the settler Tarchanov went on skis from Yakutat Bay to ... the [Copper River].'[2] These are the earliest known references to skiing in the New World.

The Russian colonists had absorbed their skiing from the native Siberian tribes, Yakuts, Ostyaks and Gilyaks in particular. On that account, the skis they used in Alaska were of the Siberian type: short, broad and probably lined with fur. There were others like Ivanov and Tarchanov, and for the next three-quarters of a century they traded and hunted in Alaska, on skis where possible. They found winter travel on snow easier than on the underlying swamp and rock in the warmer seasons of the year. Frequently they killed, or were killed by, local tribesmen.

This unusual colonial enterprise soon failed. Through overhunting, the fur trade had catastrophically declined. Mineral wealth was undreamed of. The place seemed a dead loss. At home, too, the Tsar, Alexander II, was having his own troubles. Best known for emancipating the serfs, this emperor should also be remembered for selling his Alaskan territory to the United States. The year was 1867. The price? Two cents an acre.

As the actors in this isolated episode departed, another wave of immigration was sweeping in. On 10 March 1866 a local newspaper in central Norway carried an advertisement headed 'Ski Race', followed immediately by another inviting

'Emigrants to America'.[3] In fact, there had been a steady trickle since the 1820s, but this was the start of a flood tide of mass migration. Over the next half century nearly 700,000 Norwegians, in their own times of trouble, were driven across the Atlantic by rural poverty, land hunger and unemployment, linked to a wholly characteristic urge to see the larger world outside. As a result, America became the first country to which they brought their own kind of skiing.

Few sports have been so completely dominated by one nation as skiing by the Norwegians. Even football, that quintessential English invention, had little direct English influence in its propagation. It was quickly naturalized, often introduced by native acolytes who had seen the game elsewhere, perhaps in England itself. Such was not the case with skiing. The Norwegians were roving missionaries, intentional or otherwise. In the United States, besides dominating the practice and teaching of the sport, as they were eventually to do in Europe, they also took charge of its administration.

The Norwegian immigrants in America included some of the pioneering skiers, notably from Telemark, especially Morgedal. For all of these, hard times had been made doubly bitter by a sense of abandonment. After the victory and applause at the races in Christiania, they often had to ski home for lack of money for travel expenses and then were forced to sell their trophies for want of money. Thus in 1884 Sondre Nordheim joined the hordes on one of the emigrant ships heading over the Atlantic to the Promised Land in the West. At the age of 59, he was still looking for his own farm and a better life.

Some Norwegians, with their skis, made their way to Canada. They might have been forestalled by Lord Frederic Hamilton, a British diplomat who had learned to ski in Russia. 'In January 1887 I brought over to Canada the very first pair of ski ever seen in America', so he claimed:

> I used to coast down the toboggan slides at Ottawa on them, amidst universal derision. I was told that, however useful ski might be in Russia, they were quite unsuited to Canadian conditions, and would never be popular there, as the old-fashioned 'raquettes' were infinitely superior.[4]

The reaction sounds all too authentic; otherwise, as Talleyrand said, 'it is a question of dates'. In 1879, a Canadian newspaper reported that a Norwegian had skied from Montreal to Quebec.[5] This is the first reliable dating. A few years earlier, perhaps, Norwegians were skiing in Rossland, a mining town in British Columbia. Skiing, however, did not really take hold in Canada until the first decade of the twentieth century.

The explanation is that Canada attracted few Norwegians. *Their* El Dorado was the United States. Even there they had certain predilections. Some did stray to New England and the east coast, but mostly they congregated in Minnesota and Wisconsin. These attracted Scandinavians because of a familiar landscape and climate. Nordheim began his new life in Minnesota and ended in North Dakota, finally with his own plot of virgin soil but still the unfulfilled outsider. He died in

1897, at the age of 71, unhappy as a mountain dweller in the alien surroundings of the Great Plains; poor and restless to the last.

The Hemmestveit brothers shared a happier fate. Mikkel emigrated in 1886, having just won the classic Huseby Nordic combination for the second time, followed in 1888 by his elder brother Torjus, who had done the same and, in addition, had won the 50 km event. They found skiing and ski clubs well established in the Norwegian settlements of Minnesota and Wisconsin. It was like a little Norway overseas – a feeling exactly like that experienced by the English when they brought cricket and fox hunting into the outlandish corners of Empire. In the Alps, meanwhile, the first stirrings of skiing had only just begun. Torjus Hemmestveit arrived in America the same year that Nansen crossed Greenland, and Kleinoscheg had not yet brought the ski to Austria.

The Norwegian settlers in America were well informed about events at home. Consequently, among their expatriate fellow countrymen the Hemmestveits arrived as local heroes. Profiting by this, they made their own ski and travelled round competing, or giving exhibitions. They confined themselves to ski-jumping, for this, with its touch of sensationalism, was what brought in the crowds, exactly as it eventually did in Europe and elsewhere. At least now, with decent prize money in the uninhibited vistas of America, they had all the incentive to perform. They did more. They raised the standards among their fellow-countrymen and, by a twist of personality, gave the sport a new cachet. For nearly a generation skiing remained the preserve of Norwegian-Americans but the Hemmestveit brothers prepared the breakthrough to the rest of the country.

Of course the new environment had its effect. Style counted for little; numbers were all. In 1891, at Red Wing, Minnesota, Mikkel Hemmestveit set a world record with a jump of 31 m. Torjus broke it two years later at the same place by jumping 40 m.

So far, ski-jumping had been limited to natural slopes. An outrun, where the jumper landed, could generally be found. The problem lay in the approach, which provided the speed and the correct levelling at the end for the takeoff. At Ishpeming, Michigan, in 1903, that was solved. Some Norwegians built an artificial approach in the form of a wooden scaffolding. This was the first of its kind. In a familiar historical process, it made its way back across the Atlantic to its origins. The modern reinforced concrete structures, breaking the skyline and ornamenting mountain slopes everywhere, all descend from it.

The man who finally brought American skiing out of its pale of settlement in the Mid-West was another immigrant from Norway. His name was Karl Hovelsen. Born in 1877, he came from Bærum, on the outskirts of Christiania. A stone-mason by trade, he was a skier of no little talent. He won the combined jumping at Holmenkollen in 1903, and the 50 km both in that year and in 1902.

In 1905 he also emigrated to America. On the way, in Hamburg, he received a telegram from the Skiforeningen in Christiania asking him to go to Austria instead of Hasse Horn, and take up the challenge issued by Zdarsky. Because of the impossible stipulations by Zdarsky, the invitation was quickly cancelled, with who knows what consequences. Hovelsen was by far the better skier, and he had a character to match. He would certainly have overpowered Zdarsky, thus sealing the triumph of the Norwegian school earlier than was the case. Instead, he continued on his way to America.

In 1907 he was to be found in Barnum & Bailey's Circus ('Greatest Show on Earth'), billed as the Flying Norseman. Starting on an artificial jump, greased with Vaseline, he performed what was called 'ski sailing' in thin air over elephants and other assorted animals before landing on a platform that rose out of the depths after a distance of 25 m. Being chiefly a question of ballistics, the risk was more apparent than real, but he was paid $200 a week (about $2,000 in present-day terms) and attracted hordes of sensation seekers, especially at Madison Square Gardens in New York. By an interesting coincidence, other Norwegians were then giving similar exhibitions of indoor ski-jumping in London, at the Crystal Palace. For all their commercialism, they were effective propagandists for the ski. In sheer numbers, however, Hovelsen was far ahead. With a total audience estimated at several hundred thousand, he did more than anyone else to bring skiing to public attention. Nonetheless, when Henrik Angell, having helped to establish skiing in France, visited America in 1909, he could still write that

> Some Americans are said to be very interested in [skiing], and support it in many ways. Otherwise it is supported exclusively by Norwegians or Norwegian-Americans ... In all sports shops from Minneapolis in the south to Canada in the north, one sees skis in the windows, ski clubs ... are springing up, ski tournaments are held one after the other.[6]

In any case Hovelsen was not exactly enamoured of his fellow-Norwegians abroad. He went out West. Around 1912 he appeared in Steamboat Springs. He was the pioneer of skiing in Colorado. *Pace* Henrik Angell, the sport was now beginning to spread.

Elsewhere, skiing had sprung up in a different, unconnected guise. It began with the Californian Gold Rush of 1849. This followed the discovery of alluvial deposits north of San Francisco, in the foothills of the Sierra Nevada.

Gold is the only metal that occurs naturally, pure and uncombined. 'Like fire flaming at night', to quote Pindar, the ancient Greek poet of the Olympic Games, it 'gleams more brightly than all lordly wealth'.[7] The nodules of the surface lode in California enticed with the prospect of plucking treasure like pebbles from a beach.

Among the polyglot horde of fortune hunters that swarmed in from the four corners of the globe were the ubiquitous wandering Norwegians. It is enough to explain the appearance, early in the 1850s, of what were called Norwegian snow-shoes; skis in all but name.

It was a matter of necessity. To begin with, the mining season was in summer. A few prospectors were trapped by winter, or stayed of their own accord. They found a harsh climate with heavy snowfalls that settled for months on end, with isolation or worse as its consequence. At first, men unused to snow floundered

53. 'Longboard' racing among the miners, California 1874. Skis being 'doped' or waxed, bottom right.

in the drifts on foot, or awkwardly plodded on snow-shoes improvised from pieces of wood. Indian snow-shoes appeared with miners familiar with them from Canada or those states where they were indigenous.

They were all swept aside by the ski. The fact that skis ran faster was explanation enough. Their introduction was an object lesson in adaptation to circumstances. The snow in the Sierra Nevada was loose and powdery, unlike the more compact variety of Scandinavia. So the skis had to be long and broad to give sufficient bearing surface. With a length of 3 m or more, they were distinct from most types then emerging in Norway. They were made on the spot, out of Douglas fir, the only appropriate local wood. Their shape was symptomatic. They tapered evenly from tip to heel. This identifies them as western Norwegian, probably Telemark. It discounts other origins, in Scandinavia or elsewhere. At any rate, the introduction of the ski allowed the early miners to remain in the diggings all year round and hence paved the way for the settlement of the mountains.

Among the cosmopolitan transients, in some unspecified capacity, was a Swiss called Giocondo Dotto. He learned skiing from a Norwegian gold miner. Dotto came from Airolo, in the Italian-speaking canton of the Tessin, at the foot of the Alps. Clearly the Norwegian and his skis made a deep impression. When Dotto returned home, some time in the 1860s, he had a pair of skis made, and became one of the earliest Swiss skiers. Thus California had a hand in transmitting the ski to Switzerland.

Dotto's instructor may have been one of the pioneering Norwegian skiers in California who were originally sailors, but had deserted their ships and headed for the hills; others, like most of the early gold diggers, came overland. One of the overlanders eventually acquired a semi-mythical status.

He was born Jon Thoresen Rue, or Jon Torsteinsson, on a farm at Tinn, in Telemark, in 1827. Emigrating to America as a boy in 1837, his name was Anglicized to John A. Thompson. With or without his family he shuttled between Illinois, Missouri and Iowa, before heading West in 1851 to the Californian gold fields. By then, the first fruits had been scoured and there were no more easy pickings. Thompson belonged to the great majority that had been lured out West by a mirage. Like many of his kind, he stayed to become one of the early Californian settlers, farming near Sacramento.

In the winter of 1855–6 Carson Valley, an enclave across the State border in what was then Utah territory (now Genoa in Nevada,) found itself isolated. The only contact with the outside world lay across the Sierra Nevada to California. The range was more heavily encrusted with snow than usual. Thompson volunteered to carry the mails on skis.

He did the first crossing in January 1856. His route ran from Placerville, a small town in the region of Sacramento, over the Sierras, down to the southern end of Lake Tahoe, and across the State border to Carson Valley. The distance was about 100 km, most of which was through snow of one kind or another. Thompson took three days for the outward journey and two for the return. Regularly thereafter, for three seasons, skiing back and forth, he was the Carson Valley winter postman, which meant doing these gruelling journeys four or five months each year.

It was a heroic, not to say a quixotic gesture. After all, Carson Valley lay over the mountains and far away. Perhaps Thompson was a frontiersman at heart, and the rhythm of farming meant ennui to him. Perhaps he had retained enough of his Norwegian upbringing to nurse a love of conspicuous achievement, besides seeing the chance of a ski tour where others saw only superhuman obstacles. As well he knew, the mail carrier on skis was now a familiar figure in the Sierras and it would have been only human to prove himself the best of them all. Perhaps too he wanted to prove that skis were better than Indian snow-shoes. Others had sporadically tried using these to carry the Carson Valley mail but they gave up when he arrived.

At any rate, he was the stuff of legend and he had the appearance to match. Brooding eyes stared out over high cheekbones. He did not actually have the typical skier's compact and unimpressive build. On a tall, big-boned frame had been grafted the powerful musculature and massive body of the New World. He had the attributes of a giant. He carried – or so it was said – up to 80 lb on his back.

With all this, from his bout of ski touring, he emerged with the nickname of Snow-shoe Thompson. He became part of the mythology of the West, embodying both its high points and its disappointments. He probably did the job to earn money in the dead season of the year but he was never properly paid. Years afterward he went to Washington to claim arrears from the federal authorities but got nowhere. He had been naive enough to do the mail run without securing a contract.

He was a symbol of a romantic era already on the wane. Roads were being built, the railway arrived and the mountains were opened up. The local postman on skis remained but the need for a long-distance skiing mail carrier was obviated. Snow-shoe Thompson moved with his wife to a ranch near Carson Valley and there he lapsed into obscurity.

Nonetheless his deed lived on. Snow-shoe Thompson was a true pioneer, one of those who introduced the ski to North America. He made his own skis out of oak. They were heavy, but adjusted to his massive frame. He was a consummate mountain skier; whether through childhood training or otherwise. Crossing the Sierras meant quasi-Alpine touring, with hard climbs and steep descents. At first his claims of mastery in both were met with disbelief. One massive ski stick was then the rule, in the Sierras as elsewhere. Punting along on the flat, skiers resembled the Ting-Ling of the ancient Chinese *Shan Hai Ching*. Stick riding was the only downhill technique known to the locals who had adopted the ski. To convince the doubters, before he started on his first mail run, Snow-shoe Thompson demonstrated his downhill skiing. He also used only one stick, but it was lighter than those generally in use. One of the spectators afterwards described how

> he flew down the mountainside. He … held … his [stick] horizontally after the manner of a tightrope walker. His appearance was graceful, swaying his [stick] to one side and the other in the manner that a soaring eagle dips its wings.[8]

Hyperbolic no doubt, but the description of the early Telemark style is authentic. In the light of other developments it is of great intrinsic interest.

This being frontier country, evolution was telescoped, and skiing quickly turned from utility to play. In 1863 a competition was recorded at a place called Onion Valley. It was a form of downhill racing. The terrain was broken with short, steep slopes. The races were run over 1,000 m or less. The course was in a straight line with no turning whatsoever. This was reasonable, because it avoided the boring business of learning technique. Only balance and temerity were needed – by definition quick to apply. At 4 m or so, the skis were almost comically long; which inhibited turning in any case. The critical point, as usual, was the binding. Only simple toestraps were ever used. Lateral control was weak. Any attempt to turn would mean disaster.

Since the Norwegian military competitions of the eighteenth century these were the first known downhill races in the modern sense. They had certain peculiarities. For one thing, starting was simultaneous; for another, speed was all. There was no variation of terrain and no testing of technique. The course finished on the flat and, once past the winning post, the racers awkwardly stopped by braking with their sticks or relying on the natural decrease of momentum.

It was not so much downhill racing as we know it, as akin to the modern flying kilometre. This is a short, specialized precipitous slope with a flying start – hence the name – made to set speed records and nothing else.

Until the appearance, in the 1930s, of the flying kilometre, what might be called the Sierra form of ski racing was only found in California and, oddly enough, Australia. There too it was associated with a gold rush; at Kiandra, north-west of Sydney, in New South Wales. There too Norwegians were involved.

Some of them, having failed to strike it rich in California, moved on early in the 1850s to try their luck in the Australian gold fields and, incidentally, bring skiing to the island continent. Others brought it to South America. In 1887, two Norwegian engineers, surnamed Hermundsen and Rosenquist, began investigating a winter route for the Transandean railway from Chile to the Argentine. They naturally used skis, and in the process became the first to do so at what became the Chilean resort of Portillo at the summit of the line. Between them, these pioneers brought skiing to the Southern Hemisphere.

One of the few early Norwegian gold prospectors in Australia to be known by name was Carl Christian Torstensen Bjerknes. Born in Modum, near Christiania, he was an uncle of the Bjerknes brothers – Ernst the skiing pioneer in Norway, and Vilhelm the mathematician. Carl Christian went to California in 1849, going on to Australia in 1851 and finally to New Zealand in 1855, before returning home to Norway without much gold in his pocket. However, he could – and did – brag about skiing in the Antipodes.

At any rate, the similarity of ski racing in California and Australia hints at a common origin. It points to the *uvyrdslåm* of Telemark. In the ambience of the mining camps, and then mining towns that sprang up in the Sierras, it naturally took on a character of its own. Of some interest is the appearance, in the American townships especially, of local terminology. The skis were called 'longboards', the competitions 'stake racing'. This was graphic and said all. These ski races were professional, with money prizes; up to $1,000, and monumental betting. The distinction of amateur and professional was unheard of. Clubs sprang up in the 1860s, with names like Alturas, Onion Valley, Table Rock, Port Wine, Poker Flat – all redolent of the West.

Being the American West, there was a shootout from time to time. One is said to have happened during a race at La Porte, in the mid-1860s. In California there was no prejudice against women on the slopes and a female figure won, aided, it was said, by a wind blowing on her skirts. She turned out to be a man, whose name has come down to us as Jim Wilkinham. Why he appeared in drag has never been explained, but the exploit cost him dear. He was shot dead at the finish, with the traditional Colt, by a certain Chadwick, the local gambling magnate, who justified himself by saying (and if it is not authentic it ought to have been): 'Bin a givin' a dern skunk his deserts. No dang dead-beat can ever get any of my money by such a fraud upon the community as this one. I go for all sich, every time, you bet!'[9] But Chadwick too received summary justice. He was hanged on the spot.

Better documented is the murder that occurred in 1868, at a mining camp called Saw Pit Flat. One longboard racer, Robert Francis, shot down another, Robert Oliver, because he had once started in a stake race before the 'tap of the drum', which was the usual starting signal. After due process of law, Francis was found to have suffered grievous provocation, as a result of which he was convicted only of second class murder and sentenced to 15 years penal servitude. Then, in the manner of the early Golden State, he was pardoned after three years and set free.

On the whole, however, longboard racing was a civilizing influence, channelling aggression into an innocuous form. It waned with the decay of mining and the drift of population. The railway played its part. This was the route of the transcontinental line from coast to coast. It crossed the Sierras at Donner Pass and joined the Union Pacific at Promontory Point, Utah, on 10 May 1869. Already in 1867, the Central Pacific Railroad was running excursions to the snow for Californians.

The railways brought the more orthodox kind of skiing introduced by the Norwegians further to the east. It culminated, by the 1930s with the first Western ski resorts, at Truckee in the Sierras. Longboard racing petered out and the last race was run in 1911.

In the winter of 1938, there was a revealing epilogue. At Jamison Ridge, on the eastern slope of the Sierras, some old surviving longboard racers ran against modern skiers in a recreation of a short stake-racing sprint. The old longboarders trounced the skiers. This was interesting. The skiers had the latest Splitkein, or Splitkein-like, composite skis, with Kandahar bindings. The longboard was a historical relic. It was still made of solid wood. In 80 years since its original appearance it had not changed in any way. The binding was the same old simple toestrap. Since there was no turning, it was a matter of technology, not skill. Victory was due not so much to the skier, as to the running characteristics of the ski, notably the behaviour of the sole.

The explanation had been succinctly offered by an advertisement for the races of the Alturas Snow Shoe Club 1869. 'Dope is king' it proclaimed.[10] 'Dope' meant ski wax. 'Hi snow-shoer, how's your dope?' is said (in retrospect) to have been a customary greeting.

In fact, the longboard racers had soon grasped that winning depended exclusively on lowering friction. Dope specialists sprang up. Like their modern counterparts, the ski-waxing experts, they appeared at races secretively with mysterious boxes jealously guarded from prying eyes. They split the purse evenly with the racer. Early in the game, they had shown a sophisticated understanding of the shifting complexities of snow and its relation to the atmospheric conditions. 'There is one dope for cold snow and one for warm or damp snow' as one old longboard racer put it:

There is another for dry snow and one for wet; one for hard and one for soft; one for forenoon and one for afternoon; one for extreme cold or frozen snow. Some go as far as to have a different kind for every hour of the day. For moist snow the dope is soft. It is made harder for an increase in temperature, up to the frozen, when a hard dope is required.[11]

This could hardly have been bettered by a waxing specialist today. The preparation of the skis for the dope hints at its origins. Stockholm tar was melted in and the soles polished to a mirror-like finish. This suggests Scandinavian influence. More to the point, in the 1860s, the Sierra Nevada dope specialists were already making and selling what amounted to commercial preparations nearly 40 years before they appeared in Scandinavia. Being isolated, like the whole of early American skiing, they apparently had no influence on skiing elsewhere.

The Scandinavian miners kept contact with home and tales of this miraculous waxing from the Wild West would have filtered through. However, early Nordic mixtures did not even vaguely resemble their Californian precursors. This is well illustrated by a generic recipe from the Sierra Nevada; 'Frank Steward's Old Black Dope', which ran: 'oz spermacetti, 1 tablespoon balsam fir, 1/4 oz pine pitch, 1 tablespoon oil of spruce, 1/8 oz camphor'.

This concoction certainly won many races and, despite all advances in technology, modern firms might like to know just how it was made. But the actual manufacturing process remains a secret to this day.

# 30

# The Study of Snow Structure

All the Californians' expertise could not solve a fundamental problem: what, precisely is snow, apart from being the raw material of skiing and the fickle substance which all waxes have been designed to tame? This is not as simple as it seems. In fact the whole question is so complex that an answer only appeared with the advent of modern science. Before then, the curious had to content themselves with the *forms* of snowflakes, which are only part of the story.

The earliest of such savants on record was a Chinese called Han Ying, about 135 BC. 'Flowers of plants are generally five-pointed', he wrote, 'but those of snow … are always six-pointed.'[1] This is the first documented observation of snow structure. It became almost a Chinese literary convention. Take these lines, for instance, from a Chinese poem of the sixth century AD:

> The ruddy clouds float in the four corners of the caerulean sky
> And the white snow-flakes show forth their six-petalled flowers.[2]

Recorded European study began in the thirteenth century with the learned German scholastic and bishop (and sometime tutor of St Thomas Aquinas incidentally), called Albertus Magnus. He considered snowflakes star-shaped. Olaus Magnus came next, in the sixteenth century, and he was more informative. 'Especially in the Scandinavian countries,' as he put it, 'there are many opportunities of observing a manifold variety in the wonderful forms and images of snow.'[3]

> The closer one approaches the North Pole, the more does the snow seem to vary in quantity and structure. Not infrequently, in fact, during a single day, 15 or 20 and sometimes even more different forms may be observed.

This is the earliest recorded observation that snow structure varies. It was truly historic, although in detail, as his illustrations show, Olaus was uncertain, the fate of many a forerunner, alas.

It was only with Johann Kepler in the seventeenth century that the first true insight came. Kepler was the great German astronomer who discovered the laws of planetary motion. His interests were eclectic; heavenly bodies and earthly phenomena were all the same to him. As he told the story, in 1609 he was crossing the Charles Bridge in Prague when by a happy chance water-vapour was condensed by the cold into snow, and specks of down fell here and there on my coat, all with six corners and feathered radii. 'Pon my word, here was something smaller than any drop, yet with a pattern ... the very thing for a mathematician.'[4]

This was apparently the inspiration for an outstanding little treatise by Kepler, in Latin, *De Nive Sexangula*, 'On the Six-Cornered Snowflake'. It was the first exposition of the regular hexagonal structure of snow. It was also the first published presentation of the ideas of regularity and close packing in the building of matter.

Descartes, a few years later, pursued this line of thought. In the age of enquiry, snow and ice were becoming regular objects of study, almost like another state of matter. Advances rapidly followed. Robert Hooke, the pioneering English physicist and chemist – best known for the law of elasticity that bears his name – published, in 1665, what were almost certainly the first pictures of snowflakes seen through the microscope. This was followed soon after by the first documented evidence of the metamorphosis of snow according to atmospheric conditions. This broke new ground. It was the work of an extraordinary German naturalist called Friderich Martens who, in 1671, went on a whaling ship to the Arctic:

> When it is moderately cold and rainy [he recorded], snow falls as little rose thorns and tiny grains. When the cold moderates, snow falls like stars with many points like ferns ... In severe cold, without wind, snow falls like stars in clusters, because they are not separated by wind.[5]

The critical insight came in 1681, with the publication of *La Figura della Neve* – *The Forms of Snow* – by Donato Rossetti, an Italian priest and mathematician from Leghorn. He called snow 'crystalline ice'.[6] This is the original declaration that snow is made up of crystals.

The essence of a crystal is that it is replicated, with plane surfaces, and a capacity for growing and variation. Rossetti also made the first attempt to classify the forms of snow. But his great service was to enunciate its crystalline structure.

Crystallography, the study of crystals, became a science of its own. Nonetheless, it was 250 years after Rossetti that sliding on snow at last received a plausible explanation. This was due to that distinguished polymath, Fridtjof Nansen. Besides polar exploration, neuroscience and skiing, he was a pioneer in, amongst other things, oceanography and the study of climate change. Where the behaviour of snow was concerned, on his two Arctic expeditions, he had had ample time to ruminate. In 1929, he became the first to propose the now generally accepted principle that sliding on snow depends on the lubricating effect of a film of water. The uncertainty lay in how it arose. Nansen thought that 'the tops of the snow crystals are pulped'.[7] He was not far wrong but, as he himself admitted, 'the sliding of skis ... on snow ... is an immensely difficult subject'. It had not been 'scientifically investigated to any great extent'. Nor was it to be for several years still.

Eventually two mechanisms were identified. One was simply the melting caused by pressure. The other was rather more subtle. Within the snow crystals, there was found to be a thin layer of a water-like substance, naturally occurring. Unlike water in its ordinary state, this did not freeze at the normal temperature, but kept its liquid properties far down into deep cold. The phenomenon had first been glimpsed by Michael Faraday, the pioneering English physicist in 1842.

It was not until the arrival of the electron microscope during the 1950s that proof was forthcoming. In any crystal, the molecules are arranged regularly in a lattice. In the case of snow this breaks down at the surface. The forces holding the structure together are unbalanced and free molecules escape. The amount depends on the flow to or from the surrounding atmosphere, according to its state. This neatly explains the effect of weather on the behaviour of the snow. The upshot is a quasi-liquid layer of molecular thickness covering the snow crystals. This mechanism fails at about −80°C, when all sliding stops.

The situation is complicated by other factors. From the moment of falling, snow is not static but prey to the weather, constantly changing as it settles. At low temperatures, the crystals grow extra pointed branches, which, for the skier, mean hard going. When it is warmer, the crystals degenerate, losing branches, becoming in the end a grainy mass, coarsening with a rise in temperature, until it turns into squelchy globules, which also vilely raise friction. Here the culprit is liquid drag. Nature, however, is not always obligingly simple. This ignores, amongst other things, humidity, wind, barometric pressure, the amount of trapped air, the frost or otherwise of the underlying ground and cloud cover, which affects both ablation, or evaporation from the solid state, and the sun's radiation, all of which interact subtly on the unstable structure of the snow and hence the way it acts.

Olaus Magnus had glimpsed the truth centuries before, but none of this was known to the skiing pioneers. On the other hand, observation and instinct had taught them that snow behaved in a fiendishly complex way, varying with time, place and outward circumstances. The longboarders of the Sierra Nevada had quickly grasped this and turned waxing into an empirical science. This was quite logical. With their roots in mining, they had a working knowledge of geology and snow bears a resemblance to certain kinds of rock. Both are the outcome of liquid crystallizing; on the one had water; on the other, magma from the molten mantle of the earth.

Although there were trained scientists among the early Norwegian skiers, they too were thrown back on a kind of homespun alchemy. Even Nansen, after all, had resorted to tradition. As long as winters were cold and stable, neither he nor anyone else had the incentive to produce sophisticated waxes. Their kind of skiing was rooted in cross-country. It needed a compromise between adhesion and gliding to ensure a kick off the back foot when moving on the level or uphill and yet running freely even on a modest slope.

In favourable circumstances, Nature was happy to oblige. At the reigning winter temperature of the age; say between about −4°C − the ideal value for sliding – and –15°C, the snow behaved itself. That is to say the crystal points were strong enough to grip the ski when weighed down but weak enough to break off when the pressure was released and sliding began. In both states, they supported the ski, so that only a tiny part of the bearing surface was actually used, and friction correspondingly decreased. At appreciably lower temperatures, the crystalline structure would be strong enough to hold back the ski and, when warmer, weakened to the point where most of the sole was needed, and surface drag increase, yet further complicating the mechanics of sliding on snow.

Of course the snow itself was only half the story; the other was the running surface of the ski. Before the age of plastics, that meant wood and wood is a living material which, amongst other things, subtly interacts with snow. To this day, no synthetic material can match its sensitivity. It still has, for example, no parallel in conveying the sensation of what in Norwegian is graphically called *silkeføre* – literally 'silk-going' – a light coating of fine, dry, powder snow on top of hard crust. In principle, wood needed no wax in midwinter conditions. Within a certain range, different kinds of wood could cope unaided with different circumstances. Thus, as Amundsen knew, hickory was best in deep cold. Higher temperatures called for ash or pine.

The great drawback of wood, however, is that it absorbs moisture. This greatly impedes its running qualities. Its fibres must be protected against water rising from the snow. Waxes are mostly essential.

The earliest record of waxing comes from the Swedish clergyman in Lapland, Johan Tornæus, in 1672. The Lapps, as he put it, 'waxed … their skis … over a fire, so that the snow crust does not break through and wear down the ski'.[8] This explained one reason for waxing, which was to protect the running surface. Tornæus does not say what kind of wax, but in *Lapponia* his contemporary, Schefferus, noted pine pitch and resin.[9] Published in 1673, this is the first printed reference to waxing skis. Schefferus omitted the means of application but he and Tornæus between them defined waxing for the next 300 years. Melting the wax on of course still holds.

Pine pitch was the first ski wax, going back to the Stone Age. Dark and viscous, it is extracted from the roots of conifers. Alongside resin, it was the basic ingredient of most ski waxes until well into the twentieth century. The lingering acrid aroma of pine pitch was eerily redolent of winters in the snow.

In 1779 Nikolay Jonge, a Danish author, wrote that Norwegian skis were sometimes

> covered with tallow, so that ice or snow will not stick, which otherwise would hinder movement.[10] Such skis are no use in climbing a slope, since there is nothing to grip, as a result of which they will slide backwards. By contrast, they serve on level ground, as well as down a slope.

This neatly defines the main function of waxing and, for long, its dilemma. To combine sliding and climbing in one preparation seemed unattainable. An eighteenth-century Norwegian author recorded one solution: if a skier 'wants to go up a mountain or a slope [he] must take his [skis] off his feet and carry them in his hand'.[11]

The only answer to adhesion on a steep incline remained fur-lined soles: hence, in particular districts, and in the Norwegian army, the persistence of the central Nordic ski. Even so, speed downhill and on the flat was vital. Thus army regulations of 1804 ordered recruits 'to burn in their skis with pine pitch'.[12]

When this appeared, the Little Ice Age was ebbing out, but the winters were still obligingly cold. In everyday life, on the flat or in gently undulating terrain, pine pitch or other simple nostrums would do. In Scandinavia, away from the Atlantic coast, the snow was such that for all practical purposes waxing could be ignored. Less than a 100 years later, that was no longer true. The last decades of the nineteenth century brought warmer, more capricious winters. It was not a matter of temperature alone. Solar radiation was increasing, with subtle effects on snow. The pioneers were forced seriously to consider waxing. In other words, skiers were among the first consciously to grapple with climate change.

In his campaign for mountain skiing during the 1890s Laurentius Urdahl had graphically expatiated on the subject:

> In a thaw, as everyone knows, it is extremely difficult to ski, especially on freshly fallen snow. At every step, it is as if the skis are stuck in tar, and very soon one is literally walking on stilts, because monstrous heavy lumps of snow cling under the skis along their whole length, so that one is exhausted very soon.[13]

Competition skiers, as usual, were ahead of the game. For the best part of a decade, races had been victims of the weather. The Huseby competition of 1884, in which Nansen had distinguished himself, brought a turning point. The date was 4 February. Midwinter as it was, the weather once more failed, with the thermometer well above freezing, a copiously thawing slope and hence poor natural glide.

Hitherto, skiing events had been cancelled under like conditions. On this occasion, the jump was held as planned. In the words of one newspaper, it was

> the first time that a ski race was held in the country at a temperature of 6 degrees above zero. Yet there were just as many elegant jumps as the year before; in fact, I believe there were *more*.[14]
>
> The explanation was that the skiers carefully 'waxed' or 'tallowed' their skis before starting down. Perhaps we will never again see a ski race postponed on account of 'poor conditions'.

This is the first recorded instance outside America of waxing in a competition. There were still no products on the market. Each man contrived his own. Urdahl once listed the homely nostrums of pine pitch, linseed oil, soft soap, 'salt herring, pickled pork and other fatty substances'.[15] More conventionally there was paraffin

wax 'simply rubbing [it] in', or better still 'ironing it in with a hot domestic iron …
in such a way that the wax can penetrate all the pores, so that water is prevented
from seeping into the ski, and snow from sticking in thick layers'. There is a story,
apocryphal or not, that the organizers of that pioneering race in 1884 provided
a block of cheese for waxing, but that some competitors preferred to eat their
ration instead of wasting it on the soles of their skis.

It was a classic case of demand waiting for supply. Eventually a product did
appear. Manufactured by a certain O. Thrane, a Christiania businessman, it
was launched in 1888. That was a good three decades after the Californian gold
miners began peddling their 'dope', but it was the first commercially produced
ski wax on this side of the Atlantic. Although it was said to work in sticky snow,
for some reason it soon vanished from the market.

There was no successor for nearly a decade until the first patent in the world
for ski wax. It was granted in 1897 to Emil Selmer, a Christiania littérateur. He
had long been experimenting, and finally put his formula into production. He
was the second known manufacturer and a revolutionary one at that. He broke
with the traditional ingredients like pine pitch. Instead he used metal powder,
normally bronze, suspended in varnish. It was by far the most effective product
in preventing wet snow sticking to the ski and ensuring good glide even in
malevolent slush. It was marketed, regrettably, as *Fart* which, in Norwegian,
happens to mean 'speed', and thereby hangs a tale.

When Henrik Angell and his companions arrived in Briançon in 1903 to teach
French Alpine troops to ski they brought Selmer's product and fortunately so. In
an unexpected thaw, it made the slopes skiable. Through the soldiery, the trade
name was absorbed into the French language as the word for ski wax. From it
*farter*, to wax, was derived. Both noun and verb still exist to this day. They are
among the few Norwegian words in French, and a classic example of a proprietary
name becoming a generic term.

Metallic powders resurfaced sporadically in wet snow waxes until the 1950s
and 1960s but the original product disappeared around 1905. Selmer was too
far ahead of his time and duly paid the price. The market wanted traditional
ingredients – and that is what the market got.

# Skiløbere

anbefales **Thranes Skismørelse**, der gjør
Skiene glatte og holdbare.    Ingen Ski burde
sættes væk Sommeren over, uden at være
overstrøget med denne Smørelse.
(28)          **Larsens Vaabenforretning**.

54.  The first known advertisement for a commercially produced ski wax: A Norwegian
product, *Thranes Skismørelse, Norsk Idrætsblad* 10 March 1888.
*Ski Museum, Holmenkollen, Oslo*

After Selmer, manufacturers of ski wax began springing up. In 1900, a Finn called William Sandberg patented a new product. It was notable for its exotic ingredients: ambergris, graphite, oil of bergamot, talc and petroleum jelly. It was the first wax that was easy to apply; simply spread on, and not too messy into the bargain. Marketed as *Blixt-skidsmörelse* – 'lightning ski wax' – it prevented snow clinging to the ski, and bid fair to succeed. For some reason, it soon disappeared; the fate of many a product.

Despite Sandberg, wax manufacture, for obvious reasons, was centred on Norway. It was a cottage industry, typified by a legendary product called Record. The inventor was a Christiania ski maker called Theodor Hansen. The ingredients included paraffin wax, tallow, coal tar and pine tar. They were melted in a small cauldron and stirred by hand. It was too much like cooking for a man, so Hansen's two daughters-in-law did the work. Production started in 1902 and, for traditionalists, continued until 1977, in the same small wooden house at the edge of the forest, on the outskirts of the city, dark brown, aromatic and handmade until the last. It was packaged in green metal cylinders with artless, black lettering that never changed.

In its heyday, Record was the classic ski wax, not only in its homeland. A stable compound, with the nostalgic whiff of pine-pitch, it produced good glide 'for slalom and jumping' as the packaging baldly said – slalom then being the Norwegian term for downhill. The two were after all related. Record made its way to the Alps, even winning an award in 1925 at an exhibition in Grenoble. It led to a rash of imitations, both at home and abroad, Germany in particular; most with an ephemeral existence.

For the first decade of the twentieth century, the problem besetting both Nordic and Alpine skiing was the same. Somehow glide had to be induced in deteriorating conditions. For ski-jumpers and downhill skiers the problem was simple; not so for cross-country racers and hence Nordic tourers. Glide was all very well, but in unfavourable circumstances it also meant slipping backwards, with no purchase for the kickoff. This sometimes involved dragging oneself round a course, up to 50 km, by main force with arms and sticks.

This was not confined to an elite. Cross-country racing in Norway was then the national sport. Every winter weekend there were local fixtures around the country, with their queues waiting to start, and timekeepers, with their chronometers ticking, stolidly sending them off one by one. The participants ran into tens of thousands. Changing climate meant that the irritating conditions around freezing point and above were becoming commonplace. As technique improved, it was becoming more difficult to separate competitors. That was the impulse that drove the evolution of ski waxes.

The original quest was for the philosopher's stone that produced both glide downhill and grip *uphill*. There were then no laboratories developing new products. There was instead a rash of home-made preparation. Any racer with self-respect mixed his own concoction. Perhaps this mirrored a naughtier national taste for illicitly home-brewed spirits. Here was a still softly bubbling;

there a pot simmering with compounds for some skis, each surreptitious in its way. 'Womenfolk can tell hair-raising stories of how every week the family's skiing hopeful drove the kitchen's rightful owner out of the door with his fanatical waxing alchemy', wrote one disbelieving race organizer.[16]

> Everybody knows the [ingredients] but it is the preparation that is the key to success ...
> The start of a race is a nerve-racking chaos. Skis and waxing devices are jumbled up, and since most preparations require heat to apply to the skis, the start is soon ... enveloped in an atmosphere that is [an insult] to the sense of smell.

Ears were also assailed by the nostalgic roar of many a Primus blowlamp – first produced in 1895. Part of skiing ritual, it was used not only to apply the final wax but also to prepare the wooden ski with pine pitch, both as waterproofing and a base to which the outer layers could adhere. It required fine judgement to pass the blue tipped flame up and down to keep the preparation simmering without scorching the sole.

Out of the amateur brewing emerged a branch of the chemical industry, which in the end benefited Alpine skiing too. Yet again advance was due to the subtle demands of the Nordic disciplines. Alpine tourers simply put on sealskins for a climb; their Nordic counterparts wanted speed and continuity both uphill and down.

From the horde of homely experimenters there emerged, around 1908 a clutch of innovators who solved the problem. The solution was simple but, because each skier shrouded his own formula in closely guarded secrecy, it had to be discovered and rediscovered.

The key figure here was a 19-year-old cross-country racer from Christiania called Birger Hansen. He listened to his mother. She told him that when she was a girl at home in the mountainous district of Hallingdal, the local skiers used pine resin for steep climbs and proposed that he do so too. So he went into the adjoining forest one night and, like a sorcerer preparing a spell, secretly tapped a supply from the gnarled bark of pines. He added it to his own confidential witches' brew of pine tar, paraffin and other inflammable substances stirred over an open fire. He survived. What is more, in 1913 he ran in the 50 km event at Holmenkollen and outclassed even the stars uphill.

Hansen now became an early victim of industrial espionage. A master at that game was a certain Sverre Østbye. He was the brother of Peter Østbye who, a quarter of a century later patented the Splitkein ski. Sverre, as was his wont, prowled around the skis strewn around the finish and, not so secretly, scraped off a sample of Hansen's wax. In what was probably the first intrusion of science into skiing, he and Peter had it analysed. As a consequence, on twentieth December that same year of 1913, Peter was granted a patent, of which the operative passage ran:

> known ski waxes ... have the drawback of being too slippery uphill ... By adding ... a
> suitable amount of pine resin ... or other adhesive material ... I have produced a ski wax

which, besides giving a glide, possesses ... the new attribute of also providing adhesion when going uphill.[17]

Hansen may have provided the impulse, but this was the principle behind all the pioneers' work. Peter actually listed all ingredients that he suspected skiers of using. He missed two of the more ingenious: old gramophone records and rubber from the inner tubes of bicycle tyres. Rubber, in fact, made its way into niche products, much appreciated, for instance by a celebrated Norwegian skier called Thorleif Haug. At any rate, Østbye quickly put his new wax into production.

This was the original *klister*. The word simply means 'glue' and was coined by a journalist in 1915. Østbye himself did not use the term until 1923, perhaps because it was redolent of the product's sticky mess, with contamination guaranteed. At least it avoided the gruesome black stain of pine pitch. The main ingredients being turpentine, beeswax and pine resin, its hallmark was a characteristic yellowish tint. It was the first commercial product to cope with the wet, thawing, granular, slippery, but turgid snow that was becoming ever more the rule. It was a classic case both of patenting traditional lore and filling a gap in the market. It helped many a star to win. It became a staple in every skier's armoury. In 1920, it was first packaged in tubes, like toothpaste, as its descendant products still are to this day.

After *klister*, around 1919, Østbye brought out dry waxes, each designed for varying forms of snow at different temperatures. He thus contrived the first waxing system. The fundamentals still remain in use. He quickly ran into competition. The 1920s and 1930s saw a proliferation of manufacturers. A bewildering array of waxes streamed onto the market; the original *klister* soon had many imitators. A few producers sprang up in Sweden and Finland and, in 1933, the Swiss firm of Toko entered the market, having made shoe polish before. Symptomatically or not, it outlived all its contemporaries, existing to this day. Despite these and other examples in various countries, technical advance was still concentrated in Norway, and its products – even the messiest – dominated the market.

Nonetheless, making waxes remained a cottage industry. A producer was often one man and his cauldron. Retired ski racers entered the business, if only to lend their name. It was a little niche in which to beat the Depression of the 1930s. For most of the decade, however, the field remained empirical and instinctive.

The first glimmerings of a scientific approach appeared in the winter of 1937. Lars Brandstrup, a Danish industrialist working in Norway, then retreated to the western mountains in Hallingdal, on the Oslo-Bergen railway, to carry out systematic experiments on waxing. He was prompted to do so by one of the worst seasons on record, with snow of the most volatile kind. He took with him on his retreat three prominent ski racers. More to the point, he also had two meteorologists. For the record, their names were Arnfinn Refsdal and Elias Grytøyr. In their own way, they were historic figures. They were the first scientists to work in this field.

The upshot was this. In 1938, Brandstrup launched a new range of four waxes, sold under the trade name 'Tyri'. In itself, this was unremarkable. Brandstrup, however used a new snow classification. He also colour coded the packaging. That was his great innovation. For the record, green meant dry, cold snow down to −30°C.; yellow, old grainy snow just under freezing point. Red indicated wet snow above +2°C, and blue, a klister, was intended for hard snow crust at all temperatures. All this broke new ground.

Brandstrup, however, still used natural ingredients. Something else was still required. That story begins with a Swedish industrialist called Börje Gabrielsson. He was the managing director of Astra, a big pharmaceutical concern with headquarters at Södertälje, near Stockholm.

Gabrielsson was a devoted skier. To him, like other Nordic skiers, waxing was the bane of his life. Existing products were clearly imperfect. A determined character, he eventually induced the Astra board to finance a search for something better. He needed all his powers of persuasion. A new ski wax obviously belonged to the chemical industry but had little to do with medicines, although both added to the sum total of human happiness. This was especially so since, at the same time Astra was preparing to launch a revolutionary local anaesthetic called Xylocaine. Together with Gabrielsson's idea, this belonged to the last wave of inventions that lay behind the historic, but now stagnating Swedish affluence. Gabrielsson's enticement was the waiting market. Not only were Norway and Finland just across the border but, in Sweden itself, skiing had by now become a national pastime. Exaggerating just a little, there were half a million potential customers in the Nordic area alone.

Gabrielsson proceeded to give an object lesson in developing a new product. He avoided preconceived ideas. He engaged scientists to start with fundamentals. Almost as importantly, he employed a ski racer called Martin Matsbo to act the guinea pig.

Matsbo was an unusual figure. One of the Swedes who had broken the Norwegian hegemony in cross-country racing, he was thoughtful and a rare example of an elite performer with a feeling for technology. He had himself tried manufacturing ski waxes. In his day, he was an elegant stylist. He came from a little town in Dalecarlia, the classic skiing province; the Telemark of Sweden, as it were.

Matsbo was said indirectly to have spurred Gabrielsson to act. He had won the 18 km event at Holmenkollen in 1937, one of the first foreigners to defeat the Norwegians on home ground. Gabrielsson liked skiing in Norway, probably for the ambience and on that account was present. He also skied himself in the surrounding terrain, only to be trapped by the much feared transitional state hovering around freezing point. With snow alternately freezing and thawing at every turn, it was enough to induce mild hysteria even in the most phlegmatic souls. Slipping or sticking, but never sliding forward, Gabrielsson did not enjoy himself. His Norwegian companions said that such snow was impossible to deal with. 'Impossible', so the story went, was not in Gabrielsson's vocabulary. Thus it was that finally he launched what had become his pet project under Astra's more or less willing aegis.

The year was 1943. It was the middle of the war. Sandwiched between Norway and Finland, each in is own way among the belligerents, Sweden was neutral and isolated. International sport was obviously in abeyance. Gabrielsson could work discreetly. At the time, the mechanism of sliding on snow, especially the rôle of friction, and heat conduction of the bearing surface of the ski, was still sketchily understood. This project therefore began with basic theoretical and practical research; notably by physicists at the Royal Technical University in Stockholm, using a low-temperature laboratory. It was a complex problem with a high mathematical content.

This was rapidly translated into applied experimentation at Astra. Natural materials were abandoned, mainly on the grounds that pine pitch and resin were not homogeneous, and therefore difficult to manage. Instead, synthetic products were tried. These were new hydrocarbons beginning to appear. Ofshoots of the new plastics, usually by-products of the petrochemical industry, they had long molecules, and could be precisely controlled. Copious experiments were discreetly carried out in Astra's laboratories and field trials conducted with strange machines far from prying eyes in remote corners of the Swedish mountain world. The results were applied to skis by Matsbo, endlessly tramping and sliding and climbing in all kinds of snow.

Finally, in 1946, after barely four years' work from scratch, Astra launched their new products, under the trade name of Swix. It was a technical revolution and a break with the past. These were the first synthetic ski waxes. Products would thenceforth be designed for particular circumstances, and quality controlled. They were a harbinger of the technology that was to envelop skiing.

Astra had learned from their predecessors by presenting a system. Their first wave included three dry waxes and two klisters. They were designed to cope with most kinds of snow, including the dreaded transitional state. They too were colour coded but the waxes themselves, being colourless, were tinted as well. Not so the klisters. It was a selling point that they obviated the messiness of their forerunners; they only gave carefully unadvertised sticky fingers.

Swix was the first skiing product to which modern marketing was applied; although it was emphatically not to be the last. The pioneer here was the head of the Astra group, K. A. Wegerfelt himself, another passionate skier like Gabrielsson. He saw to it that the packaging was properly designed to be eye-catching and form repeat patterns when displayed en masse in the shops. The colour coding: green for very cold, blue for moderate frost, and red for anything above zero, were psychologically correct and good for display.

Nonetheless, the product had a slow start. For one thing skis, still being made of wood, needed base preparation to hold the new waxes. That meant applying old-fashioned pine-pitch preparations with heat or, at best, coating with some creosote-like compound. Besides, skiers showed a depressing reluctance to abandon traditional methods. Worst of all was compact resistance in Norway.

This was partly due to another manifestation of the historical rivalry with Sweden; more to a feeling that Norwegians knew all that there was to be known about skis and skiing and that there was something sacrosanct about it, with no foreign intrusion wanted, thank you very much. The fact that Wegerfelt launched the new waxes simultaneously in Norway and Sweden, to the extent of having local Norwegian production, made hardly any difference at all.

Eventually, these new synthetic waxes made their own way by dint of superior performance. In fact Swix rapidly ended up with a complete range of downhill waxes that swept the Alps and elsewhere. The complexities of snow had finally been mastered.

It was yet another example of how Alpine advances started in the Nordic world. For one thing, Nordic skiing makes subtler demands; for another, snow conditions in Scandinavia are more temperamental. Low-lying snowfields exposed to air streams from Arctic and Atlantic make skiers the prisoners of place. In the Alps, snow is more even and predictable. It is also much easier to flee to another climatic belt by a quick trip up a mountainside. By contrast, in Scandinavia, it may be necessary to travel hundreds of miles for the same effect. Besides, steep slopes and high speed mask the complexities of snow. Also, paradoxically, the atmosphere at or near sea level is much more changeable, so that the snow may change bewilderingly in the course of a few miles or so. All this meant that the snows of Scandinavia offered a natural laboratory and an incentive to find drastic solutions more urgently than elsewhere.

As it was, before Astra had a breakthrough with their product, they needed some dramatic promotion. This came in the fifth Winter Olympics at St Moritz in 1948. The Swedes won all the cross-country events, with a clean sweep in the 18 km race. They had all somehow been persuaded to use Swix. In another advertising coup, this quickly filtered down to the ordinary skiers, reluctantly in Norway too, so Astra had their market after all. For the first time in winter sports, the Olympic cachet had shown its business worth. That was another advance of sorts, and it embodied a neat historical irony.

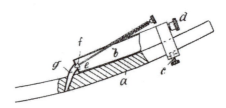

55. A century ahead of its time. Norwegian patent from 1907 for 'automatic waxing device on skis'. A container (b) is fixed to the top of of the ski or, as illustrated, where the tip bends upward. The outlet (g) feeds a distribution channel so that the wax flows along the gliding surface as required. The inventor was a certain Olaf Berg, from Steinkjer in central Norway.

# 31

## The First Winter Olympics at Chamonix

Skiing was long excluded from the Olympic Games. This was the work of Pierre Frêdy, Baron de Coubertin himself, the man who restored the Games after a lapse of 1,500 years. His great ally was Viktor Balck, the Swedish army captain who had promoted the Stockholm ski races in 1892. In March 1914 Coubertin, a genuine French aristocrat of proper quarterings, published an article headed 'The decadence of winter sports':

> The number of those participating [he wrote] has greatly increased … but the quality has fallen … The fault … lies with … the hoteliers who outbid each other [from] solely pecuniary interest, and hence the new clientele they have thus produced … Noisy and intrusive … idlers … sports humbugs … poseurs with leggings and jerseys [who] ask nothing more than to have been born [and] residences worthy of their *snobisme*.[1]

This onslaught was aimed at Switzerland but Coubertin had all the Alps in mind and that, to him, made winter sports unworthy of Olympic recognition. He was echoing the gloomy forebodings of Bjarne Nilssen in 1906. Like Nilssen, Coubertin and Balck distinguished between Alpine commercialization and the Nordic snowfields, idealized and undefiled; the schism that lingers still.

In February 1901, Balck, lieutenant colonel as he now was, organized the first Nordic Games in Stockholm. They encompassed winter sports. They were the brainchild of a Swedish eye specialist and national romantic, Professor Johan Widmark. Coubertin called them the 'Boreal Olympics'.[2] In fact they were designed as anti-Olympics. Balck believed that the Olympic Games should be confined to summer sports. Winter belonged to the Nordic world. He wanted to keep it that way.

He and Coubertin were an oddly assorted coalition. Tall, athletic, erect, fiercely moustachio'd, stern of eye and in uniform, with high gold-braided Prussian collar, Balck was martial to behold. Coubertin was short of stature, thin, wide-eyed, with shrill voice, his dark moustache adroop and seemed somehow effete. They were, however, both lifelong Anglophiles, both correctly regarding England as the home of modern sport. Each went to see for himself, with widely differing consequences.

An accomplished fencer and gymnast, Balck visited England in 1880 at the head of a group to demonstrate what came to be known as Swedish drill. Hitherto he had subscribed to the gymnast's creed of mass participation with the individual submerged in the group. What he saw in England overturned that view. He was fired with the Anglo-Saxon worship of individual prowess and the virtues of competitive sport. He launched a crusade to remould his fellow-countrymen in that image. He had the position to do so. He was not only an army officer but a gymnastic teacher as well. He taught at the Gymnastiska Centralinstitutet, the Swedish national college of physical education, the first of its kind in the world. From 1887, he was its principal. He has been called – amongst other things – the father of Swedish sport.

Coubertin was a man of a different stamp. He first visited England in 1883 to study the place of sport in education. This meant Oxford and Cambridge but, above all, the public schools. He was barely 20 years old. He happened to have read *Tom Brown's Schooldays*. By his own account, he was entranced. It was this classic piece of schoolboy fiction by Thomas Hughes, set at Rugby in the 1830s under the great reforming headmaster, Dr Arnold, which was Coubertin's guiding influence. He arrived in England with romanticized opinions. He made a pilgrimage to Rugby, especially to meditate at Dr Arnold's grave in the school chapel. Rugby under Arnold, with its emphasis on the care of the whole man, and with sport an integral part of school life, became fixed as Coubertin's ideal. The schools in France distressed him because they only trained the mind and ignored the body. He proposed reforming the whole French educational system along the lines of the English public schools, with each lycée a Gallic Rugby, as it were, leavening the tyranny of the intellect, with a regime of compulsory games.

Unlike Balck, Coubertin lacked official standing. Originally he wanted to be a writer and enter the French literary pantheon. There he failed, as he did in the sports that he tried. He took no university degree; he entered no profession. He was mistakenly seen as a dilettante. In fact he was goaded by the melancholy fate of ambition exceeding talent.

A good athlete he could not be, a bad one he would not be, so he became a sporting crusader instead and he turned out to have a gift for that. He was a prolific author, pouring out his tracts. Behind his frail appearance he hid a mastery of dissimulation. He had an elaborate coterie of influential friends. A private citizen, he turned himself into a public figure by judiciously organizing committees that, through the conscription of celebrities and politicians, acquired quasi-official status. He even persuaded the French government to send him officially over the Atlantic in 1889 – at his own expense – to investigate sport in America. Eventually, he saw his proposals for sport in French schools half-heartedly adopted, and watered down. It was a quixotic campaign, mired in bureaucracy and doomed from the start, but Coubertin was not finished yet.

On 25 November 1892, he delivered a speech, of which the operative passage was a call to help him in his 'grand and beneficent work, the restoration of the Olympic Games'.[3] This was Coubertin's public pronouncement of what was to be his life's obsession. His cover was an innocuous conference on the history of sport; his carefully chosen stage the grand university aula of the Sorbonne in Paris.

Coubertin was not exactly the first to make the proposal. Since the late

Renaissance in the sixteenth century, others had done so too. They included some Frenchmen, notably Ferdinand de Lesseps, the builder of the Suez Canal, in 1885. There had even been parochial attempts at revival from Greece itself to the village of Much Wenlock in England. Coubertin, however, was the agent of realizing the grand idea. He had found the one cause that would give meaning to existence.

Single-handed, during the summer of 1894, Coubertin arranged an international conference in Paris 'to propose in all seriousness', as *The Times* characteristically reported, 'a revival of the Greek Olympic games'.[4] Indeed, in all seriousness, Coubertin cajoled prominent delegates from Europe and America. He had to face polite scepticism and indifference. He spent his own fortune on ceremonial banquets and entertainments, so that the participants were overcome by a gastronomic and cultural stupor, which made them as putty in his hands. Again he held the proceedings in the Sorbonne to exalt his rhetoric and invoke, as he himself remarked, 'every splendour which enhances the mighty working of a symbol'.[5] The upshot was that on 19 June – presumably a date to remember – the conference voted unanimously to revive the ancient Greek Olympic Games, suitably adapted to modernity. Like the Greek original, they were to be held every four years but, unlike them, they would move between different locations. On 24 June, to control the Games, the International Olympic Committee was founded as the self-perpetuating body that it remains to this day. It was modelled on the Académie française and, like that autocratic body, had a thirst for imposing rules.

Coubertin himself filled the Committee with his own placemen. Victor Balck was one. Thus he could work from the inside to achieve his aim of keeping winter sports out of the Olympic grasp. He was the perfect Trojan horse. On the other hand, at the outset, he put in Sweden's claim to hold the summer Olympics. Earlier than most he foresaw the financial and political advantages that might ensue.

Olympicism was in the air. For one thing, this was the era of international exhibitions, which fostered global thoughts. Balck probably owed his place as a founder member of the IOC to his first meeting with Coubertin at the Paris Exhibition of 1889, when he led a Swedish national gymnastic team.

It was then that Coubertin's own Olympic passion was born. It was kindled by German excavations in Greece, which uncovered the site of the ancient Olympic Games and featured at the Paris exhibition. Coubertin was, after all, characteristically of the late nineteenth century, a fervent neo-Classicist. So too was Balck; he was also affected by those same excavations. Both would have known Pindar, the Greek poet of the Olympics in the fifth century BC, especially perhaps the lines about 'the choicest prize of deeds of prowess ... exalting thy city'[6] and 'let us not think to praise a place of festival more glorious than Olympia'.[7]

Coubertin's true accomplishment was not so much the revival of antiquity as the internationalization of sport. Outside the British empire, international sport hardly existed before the advent of the modern Olympics. The change was in the spirit of the times. Coubertin gave it shape by a vision of bringing the whole world together in peace with sport a panacea for strife.

Balck, by contrast, admired the original Olympics for having 'the power … to gather the most advanced people in the world to a national sporting festival'.[8] This exclusiveness was closer to ancient Greek ideas than Coubertin's misty thoughts of universal brotherhood. Balck considered the new Olympics as an arena in which to fortify patriotic fervour, uniting all classes to that end. Coubertin, however, regarded the athlete as an aristocrat subscribing to a lofty ideal, excluding the hoi polloi.

Balck juggled his Olympic and his Nordic rôles with skill. In the one he fought for Swedish national interests; in the other, he parried the creeping intrusion that was threatening the first. Always he subordinated the Olympian to the Nordic. Winter sports originated in Scandinavia. They had purity of purpose and were closer to Nature. They were not so much recreation as part of national identity, with a quasi-religious, pagan streak. They had to be shielded against contamination. When all was said and done, Balck preferred Valhalla to Olympia.

Born in 1844, and thus 20 years older than Coubertin, Balck was another of those figures who somehow personify the age. He dominated international skiing. For nearly a quarter of a century he saved it from Olympic encroachment. He was devoted to the wellbeing of the nation, the means of which he saw in physical exercise. It would, he thought, ensure moral fibre, the only proper aim. Every inch the patriotic orator, he once said of himself that he was the 'trumpet' of the Fatherland.[9] This was how he enunciated his purpose in arranging the Nordic Games:

> Given the development of sport … during the past few decades, we have … the resources to produce something genuinely Swedish …[10]
>
> Besides the fostering of a strong race, the innermost significance of the Nordic Games has been a *gathering* of Swedes round something truly national. For a long time it has been a weakness of ours that we have not had anything attractively national which could unite the whole people. On that basis, when we strove to find a subject for a national festival, we thought that its kernel might lie in sporting … competition.

It would be too simple to call Balck a nationalist. These games were also intended as

> something characteristically Nordic [and] unique …
>
> That the Nordic Games have been held in winter has a natural explanation … in that only winter sports can be called *Nordic Games*, and they are more characterstic of us … than those of the summer … It was in the wintertime that we in Scandinavia could realise a sports week like no other people in Europe.

Balck was a pan-Scandinavianist. That too was in the spirit of the times. He saw the Scandinavians as a breed apart, united by language, history, religion, culture and descent. Yet they were ridden by strife. The union of Sweden and Norway was near breaking point. Finland which, since 1809, had enjoyed an easy relation with its Russian overlords, was now troubled by the Slavophile and nationalistic Tsar Nicholas II, the last of the Romanovs. Balck saw in his Nordic Games a method of using sport for political purposes by drawing the Scandinavians together and comforting the Finns. The word 'Nordic' had in fact been coined to make them honorary Scandinavians, although most of them, by language at least, were outside the family.

Balck's pan-Scandinavianism belonged to the amalgam of nationalism and the Gothic Revival sweeping over the north. There was a late Romantic cultivation of the old Norsemen and their deeds; in Finland, of the national epos *Kalevala* and its semi-mythical heroes. It was to be found in many forms; from the High Norse Style in the decorative arts down to a popular revival of the old Norse Christian names. The first Nordic Games bore witness to all this. The pageantry ranged from medieval heralds parading the streets of Stockholm to a historical gala at the opera house that featured the Vikings in Constantinople.

Meanwhile, there had already been two Olympics. The first, in 1896, had been awarded to Athens in recognition of Greece as the homeland of the ancient Olympics. The second modern Olympics took place in Paris in 1900. Both had been tainted with confusion. The Stockholm event was well organized, as became the Swedes. A proper winter gave a suitable backdrop. Like some icebound Venice in its lagoon, the heavily frozen waterways of Stockholm on its islands between landlocked lake and Baltic sea, bathed in a low red February sun. Snow mantled the city and its environs, with green conifer forest and grey granite outcrops intertwined.

One facet of Coubertin's attainment was once more to bring different sports together at one gathering. In modern times this had disappeared. It is the hallmark of the Olympics, both ancient and modern. Balck's Nordic Games followed suit. This was the first event to unite varying winter disciplines.

Running for a week in mid-February, the programme stretched the definition of Nordic to the limit. It almost seemed a kind of quasi-Olympics that happened to be held in winter. There was skiing, of course, besides speed and figure skating. Fencing also found a place. So did various forms of horse racing on snow and ice. Indeed equestrian disciplines abounded, in particular across country, reflecting a deep military interest among army officers. One had wider implications. This was *skidkjörning* or being pulled on skis by a horse. Originally it was intended for communications in winter warfare. At the Nordic Games, two handsome Stockholm girls – 'Heroines' and 'Amazons' as they were dubbed by a ladies' magazine[11] – won prizes for daredevil performances. One of them, Anna Ouchterlony, was descended from the old Pictish kings of Scotland. On that account or otherwise, this was the inspiration for 'ski-joring' in the Alps.

Skiing was the kernel of these games. It brought one innovation. This was a relay race that started at Falun, a town in the province of Dalecarlia, historically redolent of skiing, and ended on the outskirts of Stockholm. The distance was 250 km, run in three equal stages over two days, with a rest in between. It was a cross between an ordinary relay race and a long-distance cycling event like the Tour de France. It grew out of an ancient method of sending urgent messages. For the record, the winning time, by a Swedish club, was 19 hours 38 minutes and 32 seconds. It was the precursor of the cross-country skiing relay race, not to be internationally accepted for more than 30 years.

The outcome of the normal skiing was a repetition of the 1892 event. The Finns dominated the cross-country disciplines. Again it was due to their technique, with powerful double-stick heaves and long, light skis, suited to the flat courses. There were 30 km and 60 km races, laid out largely on the snow-covered ice of the Stockholm archipelago in the Baltic Sea. The Norwegians, as before, made a clean sweep of the ski-jumping – with objections just the same. At home they were used to being marked for style alone but the Swedish organizers also took account of length. This was the first time it was done, although eventually the practice was to prevail.

Just as important was what happened away from the competitions. The arrangement was invested with nationalistic symbolism. There was royal patronage, and a social round for distinguished visitors and the Stockholm *gratin*, fortunately leavened by aristocratic glitter but mystifying to foreigners with elaborate meals and heavy ritual drinking. On the ski tracks themselves, the main events took place in a new Stockholm garden suburb called Saltsjöbaden, complete with its own railway line. This was the work of a legendary Stockholm banker, Knut Wallenberg. A sponsor of the games, he used them to publicize his property development. The games were also used to promote Swedish winter tourism although, as one local journal waspishly admitted, 'to compare … Stockholm … with Davos or St Moritz would be nonsensical'.[12] A substantial foreign press corps offered a captive audience – or so the organizers hoped. It was all a precursor of a future Olympic Winter Games. It had set the pattern.

One immediate result was emulation, notably at Mürzzuschlag, the fount of Austrian skiing. In 1904 Mürzzuschlag held its own Nordische Spiel – Nordic Games. In France, the ski races at Montgenèvre in 1907 and Chamonix in 1908 and 1909 also trace their origins to the Stockholm of Viktor Balck.

Mirroring the Olympics but as a bulwark against them, Balck wanted his Nordic Games repeated every four years, always in Stockholm. He had his way but, unfortunately for him, the second event, in 1905, coincided with the last of the recurrent crises that had been bedevilling the Swedish-Norwegian Union. It led to the independence of Norway, on 7 June. Because of mutual ill will the Norwegians stayed away from those games and were excluded from the next in 1909 by the Swedish hosts.

The Norwegians, meanwhile, yet more hostile to intrusion on their own preserves, were promoting Holmenkollen as *their* alternative to any winter Olympics. Perhaps because of the ring of the name, or its emblematic power as the cradle of modern skiing, the event had acquired a certain cachet abroad. A fixed forum in a mountain amphitheatre with ritual and tradition, it had more in common with the ancient Olympics than their modern imitation. Holmenkollen had been opened to foreigners and entrants from Nordic and Alpine countries; besides America were appearing by the winter of 1912.

That same year, the fifth Olympic Games were to be held in Stockholm. In May 1911, at the IOC session in Budapest, the Italian representative, Count Brunetta d'Usseaux, asked whether winter games were being considered too. This was aimed at Balck. Besides his membership of the IOC, he was also chairman of the Swedish organizing committee. He tersely answered that the idea was impossible because of the Nordic Games in 1913. Brunetta thereupon proposed that they be 'annexed' by the Olympics. This was of course anathema to Balck. By sheer force of character he had it quashed. It was not the first time the issue had been raised but never with so little tact. As it was, Balck had already lost one skirmish. The London Olympic Games of 1908, with an artificial indoor rink at its disposal, had appropriated figure skating, which thus became the first Olympic winter sport.

Brunetta's intervention was one hint that the Alpine countries were growing restive. Balck stuck to his belief that only the Nordic countries had the moral right and practical ability to organize winter sports. Perhaps the full force of the threat that confronted skiing was brought home by the Stockholm Olympics. This was the first truly modern Olympic Games. It was an extravaganza with all the familiar trappings of building dedicated amenities, in this case a stadium of dull brown brick, redolent of Nordic imagery and stern resolve, unhurriedly completed in two years and still in use. Perhaps Balck saw the creeping strength of the Olympic movement, with the corruption and lordly lust for meddling inherent in supranational bodies, ruled by autocrats brimming with ideals and an appetite for power, although which was worse must still remain a moot point.

Whatever their differences, the Nordic skiing leaders were at one with Balck in stopping Olympic encroachment. At least Nordic skiers now had a voice, Sweden, Norway and Finland each having founded a national ski federation in 1908. As the collective homeland of skiing, it was rather late. Russia, Bohemia, Switzerland, Austria, Germany and the USA, had, oddly all preceded them.

In June 1914, at an IOC Congress in Paris, the Norwegians turned a complete somersault and agreed to winter games under the Olympic aegis. This took the whole assembly by surprise. The Nordic countries felt betrayed, because they too had been kept utterly in the dark. The Norwegians did have various excuses. For one thing, climate change and warmer, greyer winters were eroding Stockholm as a reliable venue. Somehow, in sleet and rain, it was proving difficult to recapture the spirit of those cold, snowy days in 1901. Crowds dwindled. The games were ineluctably declining. Also the Nordic region started to feel provincial. The Norwegians, from a small, newly independent nation, and historically outward looking, wanted to make their mark on the wider world. They had already done so with Amundsen's skiing victory in the race for the South Pole in 1911.

That was something with which any competition skier could identify. It was enough to turn the scales when the Norwegians faced the IOC and scented lesser snows of conquest. The Germans were caught off guard. They had the Olympics of 1916 and hurriedly had to improvise a winter event in the Black Forest. It was, of course, all academic. A month after the IOC congress – once more in the Sorbonne – the Great War broke out.

Three years after the Armistice in 1918, the Olympic movement finally picked up the threads. In June 1921, yet another IOC Congress debated the question of winter games. Things were no longer quite the same. The venue was Lausanne, with a view across Lake Geneva to the Alps beyond, which gave immediacy to the deliberations. Also, like everything else, Olympic matters were affected by the great upheaval. For one thing, Finland had fought her way free of Russia after the Bolshevik *coup d'état* in 1917 – the 'October Revolution' – and was now independent for the first time in her history. For another, the League of Nations had been formed and the era of international organizations had begun. This gave the IOC a whiff of authority, which in turn affected the proceedings in Lausanne.

In another volte-face, the Norwegians resumed their opposition to the whole idea of Olympic Winter Games. Again they joined a united Nordic front. They faced, however, a different IOC. The duumvirate of Balck and Coubertin had cracked. Like many a pioneer Coubertin, called the 'renewer', was reduced to a figurehead. The power passed to two compatriots: Count Justinian de Clary and the Marquis Melchior de Polignac, of Pommery Champagne. Both were men of presence. Idealists they might have been but they were unquestionably politicians to their finger tips. Faced with the Nordic recalcitrants, they sprang a trap.

This was a preliminary consultative session on winter sports suitably rigged. On the one hand were Sweden and Norway; on the other, France, Switzerland and Canada. The Scandinavians insisted on their monopoly of arranging winter sports. With angst they saw it threatened. Through the fiery rhetoric of Clary, their opponents protested that they were just as capable. Outvoted and outmanoeuvred, the Scandinavians were hauled unwillingly into the official sessions of the IOC. The main business was the 1924 Olympic Games in Paris. The French organizing committee wanted to run a winter event in Chamonix. By half-heartedly threatening a boycott, the Nordic countries averted the Olympic label. A face-saving formula was devised of a winter sports week linked to the forthcoming summer games in Paris, under the auspices of the French Olympic Committee. It was the only crumb of comfort. Coubertin somehow came to terms with his Waterloo. Balck himself could not stomach the defeat, and forthwith resigned from the IOC.

Although his Nordic games were to continue for some years they were doomed. They lived on as the forerunner of the Chamonix event. When that opened, on 25 January 1924, they were the model on which the organization was based, down to a purely Nordic programme in the skiing events.

There were other similarities. The Nordic Games had been prophetic in the strains of incompatible sports. The introspective Nordic skier on the one hand, for example, and bob runners and ice hockey players, on the other, regarded each other with mutual incomprehension. Then tourism was also promoted, although on a grander scale than Stockholm. Yet again Chemin de fer de Paris à Lyon et à la Méditerranée – PLM – railway wholeheartedly ran a publicity campaign for Chamonix – in its own interest, of course, because it still controlled the railway communications, as at the previous events before the war. The French State obliged by investing in a new outdoor skating rink, a ski-jump and a bob run beneath the Aiguilles du Midi.

One of the skiers at Chamonix was a Swede called Ernst Alm; sixth in the 50 km race. He represented an innovation to match the Olympics, without their troublesome overtones. In 1922, at home in Sweden, Alm had won the first *Vasalopp*, literally 'Vasa Race', but never known by any other name. Run in the province of Dalecarlia, it was a cross-country ski race to commemorate the quatercentenary of an exploit involving Gustav Vasa, a notable Swedish king.

In the way of strong leaders, Gustav did not enjoy the undiluted admiration of his fellow-countrymen. At New Year 1521, while still pretender to the throne, he found it expedient to escape to Norway. With one companion, he set out discreetly to cross the border across the snow. He was popularly supposed to have gone on ski. In fact, being no skier, he actually used snowshoes instead, which was just as well. At the last moment, the men of Dalecarlia, the Swedish frontier province through which Gustav was hurrying, had decided that they would rather like him to lead them after all. So two skiers, known only as Lars and Engelbrekt, set off from the town of Mora to fetch Gustav back. It was a close-run thing. They finally overtook him at Sälen, on the border, after a chase of over 80 km. Gustav, turned, took command, quickly became king, and liberated his country from the Danes. He founded modern Sweden and renewed the onslaught upon Russia. He also instituted the Swedish Reformation, with profound consequences for the rest of Europe.

The Vasalopp was the idea of a provincial newspaper editor called Anders Pers. It would, he wrote, be 'a real test of manliness', as well it might. It honoured the feat of Lars and Engelbrelet, although in the opposite direction. The distance was 85 km, from Sälen, where Gustav Vasa turned back to Mora, with the squabble of a massed start into the bargain. This race was unique in its historic association. It was distinctive in other ways: it was the longest ski race in the world and a test of endurance that anyone could enter. It became an annual event, existing to this day. The first Vasalopp had 136 entrants; it grew eventually to nearly 20,000. It spawned imitations across the world. Most had no historical associations. All, it must be said, lack the unique spirit of the Vasalopp. It was the original mass sporting event. It contained the seed of the London Marathon and its like. Most importantly, the Vasalopp was independent from the start. It was free of outside interference, the Olympic movement in particular. For long, it was a bastion against creeping bureaucratic intrusion. More than the Olympics, the Vasalopp, and its offshoots, applied Coubertin's apocryphal dictum that 'the important thing is not to win but to have taken part'. At any rate it gives ordinary skiers the chance to race in the same track as the stars.

It was Coubertin who gave the closing oration at Chamonix in 1924. 'Winter sports are among those of the greatest purity', he said, disingenuously, overturning his original resistance to appropriate the credit.[13] 'I have always wanted to see them take their place among the Olympic events.' And in the end the IOC had the last laugh. At their congress in Prague the following year, they retroactively declared the Chamonix fixture the first Olympic Winter Games. These were to be regular and autonomous, awarded independently of the summer Olympics but following the same four-year cycle. The next event was to be at St Moritz in 1928. The Winter Olympics had been established. The Nordic countries felt comprehensively betrayed.

That same year Coubertin retired from the IOC after 30 years, the last 28 as President. For all his idealism, the Olympics cast a blight on the surroundings that has only increased with the years. It was particularly noticeable at Chamonix, the flat valley of which is uninspiring at best. The embryonic opening and closing ceremonial was vaguely embarrassing. The atmosphere affected the participants. 'The curse is also dogging me on skis down here', a Norwegian called Johan Grøttumsbråten, one of the great Nordic ski racers, was writing to his fiancée on 30 January.[14] He had just run in the 50 km cross-country event. He had the Nordic skier's nightmare of a low start number – 'the worst you could possibly imagine.'

> I soon overtook the two who started before me and then I ran ahead the whole time … The track, which ran up into the heights [under Mont Blanc], was drifted over at certain points, because a blizzard was raging up in the mountains during the whole race. So you can see that it was not easy to ski first [and break the trail].

His self-disgust arose characteristically, in that order, from not having enjoyed himself and only coming third. The fact that his fellow-countrymen took the first four places, consoled him not at all. As he rounded off his lament: 'All the boys are now out training, only I'm at home [in the hotel], because I don't give a damn now about training, there's no point when your luck's out.'

In the end, the Norwegians won all the skiing medals, both jumping and cross-country, except for a single bronze in the 18 km event – and that went to a Finn. A Swedish journalist described how Jakob Thullin Thams, having won the special ski-jumping,

> attacked the record for the hill. [He] rose unbelievably into space, soared alongside the treetops, and then one's heart stopped for fear of something dreadful. When the heavy eagle-like flyer landed with a crashing sound, and slithered on but remained standing, then every breathless heart began beating again … And a wild screech of mad enjoyment echoed in the long, broad, swathe of snow

All this was ironical, given the long Nordic fight against the Olympics. At home, the Norwegians indulged in an orgy of self-congratulation. It was understandable, since the country had only been independent for 19 years.[15]

Overall, Norway won those first games, with Finland runner-up. It was a prelude on a modest, not to say human scale. Seventeen nations participated with about 300 entrants and 100 officials, watched by a total of 10,000 spectators.

Great Britain was the surprise of these games, coming third overall. It was a British result not to be repeated. The medals – one gold, one silver and two bronzes – were not for skiing, but curling, four-man bob and figure skating, in that order. There were British entrants for the skiing disciplines, but they scratched, every single one. The jumping alone, with a length of around 50 m, was beyond them. The Nordic events were not really to their taste. They were incipient Alpine skiers. Their presence and their sport can be traced back to a singular Edwardian.

# 32

# Mass Winter Tourism

It was at Chamonix, in the winter of 1898–9, that a certain Dr Henry Lunn organized a party of English skiers. This was the first known package skiing holiday. Among the English, skiing was then still sparse and individualistic. Henry Lunn foresaw its mass appeal. He was an unlikely harbinger of pleasure. He once personally removed what he called 'outrageous pictures' by a French artist illustrating Rabelais from a public exhibition in London and nearly persuaded the courts to have them burned.

Henry Lunn came from the evangelical middle class that was typical of Victorian enterprise. He was a latter-day Puritan. Born in 1859 in the Lincolnshire town of Horncastle, he was also a precocious entrepreneur. He found a highly profitable opening in equipment by mail order for what was still the infant sport of tennis. By the time he was 20 he had become financially independent, whereupon he sold out to his father so that he could pursue his vocation.

An ardent scion of a Methodist family, Henry Lunn had decided that he was meant to be a missionary, so he qualified as a doctor and was ordained a minister before going out to India in 1887. A mysterious breakdown, physical or otherwise, quickly sent him home. He abandoned medicine and mission work, believing now that he had been chosen to reunify a divided Christendom. Between 1892 and 1895, Dr Lunn invited English divines to confer on the neutral soil of Switzerland at Grindelwald. His quixotic proceedings ebbed out in theological discord. He resigned the ministry in 1893, although his Methodist calling was undimmed. His sad, stony face, weighed down by the mass of a moustache, reflected these and other contradictions.

'In competition with [an] active interest in church affairs', as Henry Lunn himself put it, he had preserved an 'instinctive grasp of business possibilities in unusual directions.'[1] In other words, like many Puritans, he had a facility for reconciling God and Mammon.[2] He had organized the conferences, and so impressed some delegates by his efficiency, that they asked him to arrange a visit to Rome. He had failed to reunite Christendom, but found his *métier*. He launched the travel agency named after himself (traces of which survived for more than a hundred years, notably in the travel firm Lunn Poly).

One of its innovations was the *fin de siècle* group at Chamonix. It was the forerunner of the all-inclusive winter break, providing skis and an instructor, both from Switzerland as it happened. It was another unlikely twist. Henry Lunn never skied himself but he had sensed one more business opportunity.

He probably discovered skiing at Grindelwald. There, in 1891, an Englishman called Gerald Fox was the first to ski, having already learned a little in Norway. As a matter of fact, the ski proved to be Dr Lunn's salvation.

Queen Victoria had died in 1901, and the coronation of King Edward VII was announced for the 26 June 1902. Dr Lunn saw money in it. He acquired seats along the route of the procession through London and ships for spectators at the Coronation naval review off Portsmouth, charging optimistically inflated prices for both. At the last moment, the King had to have an operation for appendicitis – one of the first of its kind – and the whole affair was postponed. Dr Lunn had to refund the tickets and still cover his expenses. He had blithely neglected his insurance. The coronation eventually did take place on 9 August but, for Dr Lunn, it was too late and financially disastrous. 'Mammon', as he put it, 'is a jealous god.' With memories of Chamonix, winter, thought Dr Lunn, might come to the rescue.

Where his rival, Thomas Cook, worked with small groups, personally conducted, Dr Lunn had always believed in numbers and low prices. He had discovered the economies of scale. He was the original budget tour operator. His selling point was community of interest. He ushered Free Churchmen round the Holy Land. Classicists he took on cruises to Salamis and Thermopylae. He now turned to affinities of class.

A grammar-school boy himself, he wanted his sons to go to public school and therefore moved to Harrow for their education. In the autumn of 1902, he persuaded a Harrow schoolmaster called John Stogdon to circularize Harrovians, and Etonians too on his behalf, proposing a visit to the Swiss resort of Adelboden, where the hotels were as yet open only in summer, but the winter potential of which he, Dr Henry Lunn had allegedly discovered. The hoteliers of Adelboden, like true Swiss, at first had misgivings over anything new and needed some persuasion to keep open. Dr Lunn sent out more than four hundred guests over Christmas and the New Year. The hoteliers were persuaded.

Over the next few years, numbers burgeoned. For the winter of 1904–5, Dr Lunn shepherded a thousand visitors by train and Channel ferry to the Alps. Dr Lunn found his fortunes on the mend, initiating mass winter tourism into the bargain. He was the first to discover the white gold that was snow.

He concentrated on Switzerland, the English Alpine playground. Hitherto, English skiing had belonged to the rarefied expatriates of Davos and St Moritz. Dr Lunn saw the opportunity for expansion. He developed new resorts. Most of his promotions were in western Switzerland; Wengen for one, Mürren for another. Both, like Adelboden, lay in the Bernese Oberland, still confined to summer; both under his aegis first opened in winter, to become the twin citadels of English skiing. Circumstances played into his hands. For one thing, rising expectations broadened the desire to flee the damp greyness of an English winter. For another, after a decade of miserable Alpine seasons the climatic cycle was offering plenty of snow, which in turn produced a skiing renaissance.

Because skiing was alien to England, Dr Lunn had to create a demand. Discreet advertising properly channelled was one means. This emphasized the thrills of skiing downhill, probably the first advertising to do so. A pioneer of marketing, Dr Lunn targeted his audience. Moving customers economically en masse over the English Channel and across northern France to the Alps required intricate organization but potential skiers were acutely class-conscious and shrank from the plebeian taint of party travel. There Dr Lunn had become a byword, as many a luggage label blazed. At Adelboden, he had hidden behind Mr Stogdon, but now he had to broaden his appeal. He formed a club.

He called it the 'Public Schools Alpine Sports Club'. The object, to quote its prospectus, was to provide 'all the elective advantages of an English club'[3] and 'secure the presence at ... Swiss resorts ... of a congenial society of people'. Each member had to be 'a Public School or a University man', or an officer in the Army and Navy; also, by courtesy, their daughters, their sisters or their wives. The President was the headmaster of Eton. The vice-presidents included three peers of the Realm. It was all a front for Lunn's business. It kept the taint of trade at one remove.

The son of a chemist, Dr Lunn was a self-made man and, like many of his kind, he had a profound understanding of the English class system. Given that the public schools were the pioneers of modern sport that was logically where the market lay. This made English skiing unique in its blend of social hierarchy and rank commercialism.

Dr Lunn's clientele went by appearances. They were interested not in people but in places. They wanted to take their own milieu wherever they went. Dr. Henry Lunn found it natural to oblige. Although internationalist in theory, he spoke no language but his own and shared with his customers an invincible prejudice against all things foreign.

He booked entire Swiss hotels and bought them if necessary to guarantee his customers their homely exclusiveness. Social lepers need not apply and certainly no foreigners. Even Swiss were barred; as guests, that is. It left them unperturbed. They had two centuries' experience of pandering to English travellers. In his heyday, Henry Lunn sent 5,000 like-minded English skiers to the Alps every year. He opened a string of Swiss resorts in winter for the first time. He thus eliminated the dead months of the year. He popularized the Swiss international winter season. He brought money into many a languishing mountain village. He was a pioneer of the movement that prevented depopulation of the Alpine valleys. Exclusion from this or that hotel was a small price to pay.

More irksome were the ukases of Dr Lunn. His customers paid him to take them to the Alps; he included solicitude for their virtue in the price. He censored what came to be known as après-ski. Sympathetic Alpine dives still being rare, he had a captive audience, with his hotel ballrooms often the sole recourse. In 1913, on grounds of immorality, he banned the bunny-hug, an American dance of the jazz age. 'Everyone in consequence felt highly respectable', as one victim put it. 'Foreigners [were] laughing at our hypocrisy.'[4]

It was at any rate Lunn who made skiing newsworthy in England, even to the eminence of a third leader in *The Times*. His 'enterprising firm of tourist agents', to quote the inimitable column:

> even, we believe, organizes challenge competitions for ... ski-running ... a pastime which the Roman satirist JUVENAL would surely have stigmatized in the uncomplimentary language which he used about HANNIBAL, *I, demens, curre ... per Alpes* ['Go madman and run over the ... Alps']. But for those who are young and strong enough to enjoy it, this new craze (shall we call it?) makes a sensible addition to the possibilities of winter amusement.[5]

A journalist, as usual, had caught the spirit of the age. This was after all the Edwardian era, with its frantic hunger for pleasure. Lunn was indeed exploiting a craze. The visitors' race was absolutely a part of his winter holidays. Lunn wanted to entertain his customers to keep them coming back and, as a by-product, he became a pioneer of Alpine ski racing. Early in January 1903, he had arranged the first British ski race in Adelboden.

Lunn's races spread to all his Swiss resorts. In 1912, at Lenzerheide, in the Grisons, one of the competitors was a Royal Naval officer, Engineer Commander Reginald Skelton. Skelton had been with Robert Falcon Scott on his first Antarctic expedition ten years before. 'Although English people are supposed to be bad skiers,'[6] Skelton was writing to Scott on the 21 February, 'I was much struck with how good they are.' By a neat coincidence, the same day in the Antarctic Scott, on the last homeward stage of his rout by Amundsen at the South Pole, recorded 'heavy toiling'[7] – mostly explained by incompetence on skis, which was in turn the result of Scott's unaccountable failure to recruit experienced skiers. Skelton was not to know this for another year. Meanwhile, 'in the big race', he went on conversationally, 'I came in 4th, having done very well up hill – but I rolled a good part of the distance down hill.' This was an artless characterization of the events, which were quasi-Nordic, with a preliminary climb, before letting gravity do its worst.

In 1911, Lunn broke the mould. He was now Sir Henry Lunn, knighted in 1910 for no very clear reason except that, under a Liberal government, he was Liberal in politics as well as liberal in opinion. Nor did a title come amiss in business promotion. Sir Henry sponsored a pure downhill race, for which he presented a trophy.

How it was named is a story of its own. It starts with the privilege accorded to British peers of choosing their territorial title. Soldiers liked to commemorate their victories. Now in the age of empire there was a British Field Marshal, born (in 1832) Frederick Roberts. When he was ennobled, it was as Earl Roberts of Kandahar. This commemorated a famous march of his from Kabul to Kandahar, in 1880, during one of the Afghan wars. The Earl was a vice-president of the Public Schools Alpine Sports Club and Sir Henry Lunn exploited his standing as a national hero by persuading him to lend the new trophy his name. The

Roberts of Kandahar Challenge Cup was the exact form. This was how the echo of an uncouth Afghan city, founded by Alexander the Great, entered the folklore of Alpine skiing. It was how Guido Reuge found the name for his Kandahar binding.

The Roberts of Kandahar Cup was first decided at Montana, above Sierre, in the Valais, on 7 January 1911. There were 10 competitors. On the eve, there being no lifts at all, they had to climb up to the start at the Wildstrubel Alpine Hut, 3,300 m above sea level, where they spent the night. The course, in natural snow, untracked, was 11½ kilometres long, with a vertical drop of nearly 2,000 metres. For the record, the winner was Cecil Hopkinson, of St Paul's, in just over an hour. This was the first British downhill race.

It was the echo of an earlier event. During January 1903, there had been a contest in Austria, at St Anton on the Arlberg Pass, the frontier of the eastern and the western Alps. It was run on the Galzig slopes that overhang the village. The vertical drop was some 1,800 metres. Unlike the Roberts of Kandahar, with the perils of a massed start, here the competitors were sent off one by one, in the now familiar safer, ordered style. This was the first true modern downhill race. It had been organized by the Arlberg Ski club, still a name to conjure with, and founded on 3 January 1901 by a few pioneers in an alcoholic haze after a day of powder snow, 'entranced by Nature, and enthused by sport', to quote the minutes of the meeting.[8] That race at St Anton was historic in another way as well. The runner-up was a certain teenager called Johann – later Hannes – Schneider. He and Sir Henry Lunn became the twin architects of modern Alpine skiing.

Schneider, aquiline-nosed and irascible, was an Austrian mountain peasant. Born in 1890 in Stuben, a village at the western end of the Arlberg Pass, he left the local village school at the regulation age of 14. He was introduced to skiing as a small boy when the pioneers came to the Arlberg at the turn of the century. Something set him apart from the other village boys. He attracted patronage. To begin with, he made an impression on one of those early winter visitors, a man called Viktor Sohm. From Bregenz, in the Vorarlberg, near the Swiss border, Sohm had briefly tried skiing in 1887, but now, after a decade, having resumed the sport – thanks to a Norwegian friend, so it was said – belonged to the generation of pioneers. Sohm genially taught Schneider how to turn, starting with the stem.

A natural athlete, Schneider found himself winning races in the Arlberg and its environs. Someone with Swiss connections took note. The upshot was an offer to Schneider in 1907 as resident ski teacher at Les Avants, above Montreux. That showed his true worth, and triggered a campaign to keep the prodigy at home.

Les Avants had offered Schneider two Swiss francs a day all found, about £3.50 in present terms. The owner of the Gasthof Post in St Anton, Walter Schuler, was prepared to match the board and lodging but, in his own words, 'could not risk the pay'. Then the Arlberg ski club would give a guarantee, so the Chairman said. He was an engineer called Rudolf Gomperz, who had settled in St Anton to recover from malaria contracted while working on the Berlin to Baghdad Railway. When

Schuler objected that the Arlberg Ski Club had no money, Gomperz personally took over the guarantee, with the rider that 'We will employ [Schneider] as the Club ski teacher.' Schuler happily agreed. On 25 October 1907, a contract was signed and Schneider had been saved for St Anton. On 7 December he moved into the Gasthof Post to begin his first season as a ski instructor. At the age of seventeen-and-a-half, he had found his *métier*. The timing was impeccable.

When the Arlberg railway tunnel opened in 1884, St Anton lost its historic function as a staging post on the road across the Arlberg pass. The tunnel avoided the pass and carried traffic through the rock underneath instead. St Anton had been reduced to the railway station at the eastern end of the tunnel; an obscure stop on the line between Paris and Vienna. Ever since, in a quest for survival, the village had been looking for a new rôle to replace the old one. It was Gomperz who saw the answer in the nascent business of winter sports, and in Schneider, the man. Although Schneider usually won when he raced, he was not temperamentally a racer. He was a natural teacher who taught without appearing to do so. He also had ideas and the strength of character to impose them. It was a lethal combination.

Gomperz took Schneider under his wing. So did Bernhard Trier, another St Anton habitué. Both born in 1878, Gomperz was a Viennese; Trier came from Darmstadt, in southern Germany. Together with a mysterious Austrian Baron Beess, they completed Schneider's education. They showed him how to analyse his thoughts so that he could explain to his pupils what he wanted them to do, instead of simply telling them to copy what he did. They also refined his patois, to make him intelligible to outsiders, and able to cope with a varied clientele, high-born or not. Gomperz and Trier were moulding him into the first modern ski teacher, based on the cult of personality.

Schneider quickly outgrew his original deal with the Gasthof Post. The steam-drawn trains were decanting visitors in such numbers that, from about 1910, he was running his own, eponymous ski school at St Anton. Under the tutelage of his mentors, or otherwise, he divided his pupils into classes, according to ability. Obvious as it seems, this was an innovation at the time. It was a precursor of the ski school as we know it.

One result was that, in the winter of 1911–12, Schneider took on his first assistant, a local skier primed to teach in his way. Schneider charged what the market would bear, which made his classes a paying proposition. That completed his invention of the modern ski school as a commercial enterprise, purveying formalized instruction.

Gomperz and Trier were Schneider's constant companions but malleable he was not. They and other patrons drawn to him by his personal magnetism were ski tourers, to whom the proper aim of skiing was the exploration of the winter mountains, with safety their concern. Schneider was grateful for their support, but unimpressed. He was a bit of a revolutionary. In the last days of the Habsburgs, and the twilight reign of the emperor Franz-Josef, with its sense of collapsing order, this was somehow appropriate. On the Arlberg, Schneider's bare open native slopes above the treeline persuaded him that speed was the only proper goal of skiing. Unconsciously he sensed, perhaps, that fear of boredom was in the air and thrills were the attraction. At least it brought in the customers. That was the origin of what came to be called the Arlberg school, from which all modern downhill skiing is derived.

In search of speed, Schneider developed a very personal, specialized technique. He based it on the stem-Christiania turn. This was a variation of the Christiania, in which the turn began with the skis at an angle, in the stem position, before being moved parallel to each other in the normal way. (It also happened to suit the teaching of beginners, because the stem position simplified entry to the turn.) Schneider combined this with a low, cramped, more or less aerodynamic running posture, eventually dubbed the Arlberg Crouch. They were, he said, his own invention. Unsurprisingly, they had Norwegian roots. Both had been elaborated 40 years earlier in Christiania by the newspaper article that pioneered the analysis of the dynamics of skiing (see Chapter 11).

The stem-Christiania actually came to Schneider from an itinerant Norwegian instructor called Jacob Schappel-Jacobsen – appropriately enough another member of the Verdande ski club in Christiania. Schappel-Jacobsen was working at Kitzbühel in 1910. His first pupil was the aforementioned Baron Beess, a regular visitor. As a matter of course, he taught Beess the turn, which the Baron then demonstrated to Schneider at St Anton.

Schneider's own story of the crouch in an unguarded moment is equally revealing. In 1912, he ran by invitation at Bödele, in the Vorarlberg, in the Austrian national ski championships – still Nordic – albeit only as a forerunner. Since 1908 ski teachers had been barred from racing on grounds of professionalism. The amateur still ruled. At any rate, the course at Bödele included a fierce descent complete with bumps. In Schneider's own words:

> As I shot down [someone] yelled 'ooh … how can you ski so horribly!' I was running in a low crouch with skis wide apart. [Afterwards] the famous Norwegian ski king [Lauritz] Bergendahl … came down in exactly the same posture. Nor did the other Norwegian [participants] ski any differently. After that race … nobody laughed at me any more.[9]

Using the stem-Christiania and his crouch, Schneider had developed a skiing technique adapted to long steep slopes. He was following in the wake of Zdarsky, but without Zdarsky's limitations. Schneider not only spurned the everlasting snowplough of Zdarsky but also his short Lilienfeld ski and fearsome single stick, in favour of the longer Telemark ski and two sticks of the Norwegian school. Schneider had devised the first coherent system flexible enough to cope with all Alpine terrain and with unrestricted speed. In that sense, he opened up the Alps.

From another point of view, he exerted a baleful influence. Like Zdarsky, he espoused a rigid regimented style, which had to be copied slavishly in every detail. He abolished individual variation. He turned the slopes into repetitive processions of army ants. The crouch replaced the upright, supple stance in all circumstances, to become mannered at best and a subject of lampoon. He precipitated the schism between Alpine and Nordic skiing.

By 1912, after a few hectic years, Schneider had completed his method. He was the pioneer of prescriptive form, hence the dominance of the ski schools and the resultant commercialization, based on exploiting slavery to fashion. To him is ultimately due the modern winter sports industry.

In February 1912, by another odd coincidence, with Skelton at Lenzerheide, the Arlberg saw a figure from the past. Fridtjof Nansen had come with two companions to sample Alpine skiing. One day he climbed the Valluga, the pointed landmark ridge above St Anton. With his long single staff, to which he clung fanatically against the advance of two sticks, his massive upright form slowly wound its way down the long mountain flanks like something from another age, to remind any passing skiers of their roots. Afterwards, Nansen wrote lyrically to one of his companions: 'My thoughts drift back to the mountains, to the golden clouds over pointed peaks … to the lovely peaceful Stuben in the middle of the snowbound isolation, with silent falling snow.'[10]

Nansen also sent the recipient – Greta Gulbransson, the wife of a friend – a copy of *The First Crossing of Greenland*, this event being now more than 20 years in the past. 'It is [nothing] to be proud of', he wrote; 'it is in all respects … puerile.'[11] He was yet another forerunner to suffer disillusion.

There was a link between Nansen and Schneider in that Schneider had helped to build the Ulmer hut where Nansen stayed. They did not meet, however. Schneider was caught up by the outbreak of war in 1914. He joined the Austro-Hungarian mountain troops and fought against the Italians in the Alps. On both sides, avalanches killed more than the enemy.

Schneider survived, which is more than Austria-Hungary managed to do. Three years after the end of the war in 1918, in the winter of 1921–2, with Austria reduced to the German-speaking rump of the old Habsburg empire, he recommenced teaching at St Anton in what he now called the Arlberg Ski School. It bore the stamp of his wartime service.

Like Zdarsky (from whom perhaps he had learned more than he cared to admit), Schneider had been a military ski instructor. That taught him above all how to manage large heterogeneous groups and quickly turn absolute beginners into passable skiers, which had been Zdarsky's original aim, after all. One result was that Schneider now divided his pupils into three classes instead of two. He refined his method on systematic pedagogic principles. Employing more assistants, he applied the mass production in teaching that he had used during the war. He depended on rigid uniformity and, in that sense, proved himself the philosophical heir of Zdarsky. Schneider pioneered the modern ski school and paved the way for mass winter tourism.

# 33

# The International Recognition of Downhill Skiing

In Switzerland, meanwhile, in the sober Bernese Alpine citadel of Mürren, Sir Henry Lunn's eldest son, Arnold Henry Moore, had been pursuing his own crusade for Alpine skiing, coupled with a vendetta against Hannes Schneider. To Schneider technique was an end in itself but Lunn saw it as a means to an end. His origins lay in ski mountaineering, and technique was required for the descent from the summit.

Moon-faced, bespectacled and politely arrogant, Arnold Lunn went to Harrow and then Balliol, but left Oxford without taking his degree. He had a way with words, inherited perhaps from an Anglo-Irish mother. Despite vastly different backgrounds, he and Schneider had much in common. Each was a crusader disinclined to give credit to his forerunners. They were of the same generation, Arnold Lunn having been born in 1888 in Madras, during his father's abortive Indian stay.

Each owed success to an understanding parent. Schneider *père* was a small farmer, liberal enough to abandon plans for a conventional trade and let his son concentrate on skiing. Sir Henry Lunn quite frankly subsidized young Arnold's predilection. Sympathy played a part. Arnold Lunn had grown up with a passion for snow and mountains but, in 1909, narrowly escaped being killed while – foolishly – descending alone from a climb on Cadr Idris in Wales. His right leg was shattered and was left inches shorter, with an open wound that took long to heal and his racing career was prematurely finished. Somehow he overcame this disaster to continue skiing for pleasure. But, in constant pain, he was marked for life. Sir Henry Lunn might have ruefully considered that it was all his fault. His son had first skied at the age of ten on the party that he had organized at Chamonix in 1898.

As a 'by-product', of his ski mountaineering so Lunn declared, he developed a passion for downhill skiing; not as a competitor, because of his injured leg, but as an organizer.[1] His accident had driven him into sporting politics. In a bizarre twist, he fronted a campaign for the recognition of downhill racing. England was hardly a skiing power but Arnold Lunn outweighed this with an addiction to controversy, which he practised like a boxer in the ring, being no mean exponent of the strategic jab below the belt.

He nursed a violent antagonism to Nordic skiing. In 1925, he published an article called 'The revolt against the long-distance race.' It was a philippic of which the main points were that *langlauf* – he used the German term – was a 'severer strain on the heart than any other form of sport. [It] is a poor test of technique.'[2] This is disingenuous, but it did articulate a looming conflict. The rulers of skiing in the Alps still believed that the Nordic disciplines, by cultivating the all-rounder, were the true test of a champion. Hannes Schneider and Arnold Lunn, in their different ways, represented an opposing downhill faction.

Lunn thought that 'to ski downhill is normal and to race uphill is abnormal'. He was among the most vociferous of the downhill advocates. His chief argument against Nordic skiing was that 'races are often won by sturdy mountain peasants [while] the town dweller has little chance of winning'. It also held for a straight downhill race. This revealed his true intentions. He was using Alpine ski racing as a cover for an event that would favour the British. He was experimenting with a tightly controlled turning race, where acrobatic skill alone would count and stamina not at all. For this, oddly enough, he borrowed the Norwegian term 'slalom' – an echo perhaps of a visit to Norway in 1909. In any case, slaloms, so-called, had been run in the Alps since the turn of the century. Zdarsky's *torlauf* from 1905 was an obvious precursor.

Lunn changed this to a sprint of a few hundred yards, crowded with gates formed by pairs of flags closely spaced in contorted figures. This meant slithering through a maze. It was specialized and artificial, with its roots in the grandiose complexities of figure skating. In this case, however, style did not count and the result depended on time alone. At Mürren on 6 January 1922, the first such race was run. It was a purely British affair. Thus the modern slalom was born out of chauvinistic machination.

Thereafter, Arnold Lunn began making converts to the cause. It was part of a highly personal campaign to recognize his new event. This took place while skiing was being internationally organized which, unfortunately for Lunn, was a Norwegian initiative. It began at the French races at Morez, in the Jura on 1 February 1909. At a farewell banquet, Harald Durban-Hansen proposed the formation of an international governing body. He was speaking not as the apostle of skiing in France but as the representative of the newly founded Norwegian skiing federation – Norges Skiforbund (NSF), The upshot was the establishment at a meeting in Christiania, on 18 February 1910, of the Commission Internationale de Ski. Ten nations were represented, Spain, Bohemia and Switzerland being represented by Norwegian skiing missionaries. The first President was a Norwegian, Johannes Dahl, as was the second, Hasse Horn, Zdarsky's discomfiter.

Horn was still president when, on 2 February 1924, the CIS met at Chamonix during the first Winter Olympics to transform itself into a more comprehensive international governing body. Seeing a dilution of their power, the Norwegians first objected but then bowed to a compact majority. 'Much of the meeting was taken up discussing … the name', to quote the British delegate, a cheerful Tory of the old school called Sir Harry Brittain.[3]

I [suggested] that as we were meeting in France the title 'Fédération Internationale de

Ski' would not only be a compliment to our hosts but would, of course, be [widely] understandable ... This was hotly contested by ... representatives from Central Europe [but my] supporters eventually had their way.

So the Comission Internationale de Ski turned into the Fédération Internationale de Ski, with the universal initials FIS. It remains the governing body of international ski racing; both the handmaiden and rival of the IOC, holding world championships of its own. It changed the whole complexion of competitive skiing. The founding of the FIS presaged global formalization.

Anticipating the Security Council of the United Nations by a quarter of a century, Sweden, Norway and Finland as the skiing powers, originally had permanent seats on the governing Council of the FIS. The FIS went one better. The offices of President, Vice President and Secretary-General were also reserved for the same three countries.

The first President was a Swede, Colonel (later General) Ivar Holmquist. So was the Secretary-General Carl Nordenson and the headquarters followed him to Stockholm. In other words, the Nordic countries had kept their domination.

Sir Harry Brittain, a notable philo-Norwegian, regarded this with equanimity. He had little sympathy for Arnold Lunn, who preferred any domination to be his. Lunn had other grounds for annoyance. Although E.C. Richardson, the English skiing pioneer, had attended the constituent assembly of the CIS in 1910, somehow Great Britain never actually joined, and had to be admitted to the FIS in 1924. Also by a historical quirk, the Ski Club of Great Britain, founded in May 1903 was almost the oldest national ruling body, preceded only by Russia in 1896.

The Nordic countries saw in Alpine skiing a threat to their own, original form of the sport. Going up and down some slope like a yo-yo was an insult to the spirit of the snows. They resented any further encroachment on their preserves. In self-defence, they used their hegemony to banish the infant Alpine events from all international competition. They had extra power because Finland, having finally wrested itself from Russian rule, wished to assert its new-found independence. The Alpine countries, meanwhile, were growing restive.

There Arnold Lunn saw his chance. British ski racers were a negligible quantity. However, they formed a clique that, in the way of cliques, was open to political manipulation. Lunn manipulated, finally appointing himself British delegate to the FIS. That gave him the platform he desired. The Swiss half-jokingly dubbed him *der skipapst* – 'the ski pope' – and indeed Lunn converted to Catholicism in 1933. A prolific author, with more than a touch of the casuist, he thrived on controversy in his oddly juxtaposed fields of skiing and Christian apologetics. With his arrogant public persona – which actually hid great personal kindness – he combined the wily zealot and the proselytizer.

In January 1924, Lunn engineered the formation of a British club to promote downhill racing. It was called, ringingly, the Kandahar, after the trophy of that name. It was domiciled at Mürren. This was Arnold Lunn's adopted winter home.

It was also the Swiss headquarters of his father's travel agency, which, with or without conflict of interest, he cheerfully continued to represent. A year later, across the valley in Wengen, the Kandahar spawned a rival offshoot, with the self-explanatory title of the Downhill Only Club. Together they encapsulated British skiing and the germination of the Alpine events. It was at Mürren that Arnold Lunn lorded over his little clubby fiefdom, developing his slalom. He stumped over the snow among fashionable English skiers in wide billowing trousers, an adaptation of the 'Oxford bags' as then worn by young blades. On the slopes, women wore them too, without skirts now, jettisoned with other conventions after the war. Both sexes combined the trousers with short jackets, presenting the contemporary lopsided figure that was all legs and shrunken torso.

Lunn periodically emerged from his lair to propagate the slalom. In February 1927, he found himself at St Anton. This was strange, because his hostility to Schneider was notorious. His presence in the lion's den was due to an intermediary. An ulterior motive lurked behind the deed. To promote the nascent sport of Alpine skiing, there was a move afoot to reconcile the antagonists.

Lunn's dislike had several strands. Schneider's influence was spreading. There was a veritable pilgrimage to him at St Anton; he sent emissaries to help organize ski schools abroad, notably in France. Schneider was shaping Alpine skiing in his image, where Lunn would have preferred it to have been in his. Also Schneider was doing more than anyone else to popularize the sport. Like Zdarsky – still living sadly in semi-eclipse – he had the dangerous gift of making fanatically devoted followers.

The cinema turned out to be Schneider's medium. He owed this to a producer called Arnold Fanck. In 1920, Fanck shot a silent instructional film with Schneider called *Wunder des Schneeschuhs* – *The Wonders of Skiing*, as it was translated – the first of its kind, as it happened. Fanck discovered that the camera liked Schneider. There followed a succession of 'B' movies with titles like *The Mountain of Fate*, starring Schneider who, with his trademarks of jaunty white peaked cap, cheroot in the corner of his mouth, and a squint in the sunlight, created the image of the Alpine skier. One of his leading ladies was Leni Riefenstahl, later the equivocal director of a brilliant film glorifying the Nazis.

Lunn's opinions might have been tinged with envy. Schneider exuded star quality and good looks, neither of which Lunn possessed. What really damned Schneider in his eyes was the fact that Schneider had banned the telemark. This was in the interests of speed but also to simplify teaching. The telemark, requiring delicate lateral balance, is more difficult than the Christiania. However, as Lunn discerned, it was a brilliant soft snow turn. By neglecting it, Schneider had removed a whole section of the skier's repertoire, and paved the way for the artificialities of piste skiing.

Faced with his opponent, Lunn found Schneider as charming and magnetic in the flesh as on the silver screen. He duly succumbed and, in the interests of expediency, condoned the murder of the telemark. It was the price to pay for using the Austrian as an ally or, perhaps a tool. Lunn arranged a little demonstration of his slalom among the local schoolboys. The upshot was an agreement to organize a race at St Anton in 1928, to be decided on a combination of a straight downhill race and Lunn's slalom. A floating trophy was promised by the Kandahar Club – in the person of Arnold Lunn – to be given the ringing name of the Arlberg Kandahar. Such was the breakthrough of the modern slalom and the origin of the first Apine classic. It was another calculated step in Lunn's campaign.

Mysteriously, the IOC simultaneously asked the FIS to include Lunn's slalom as a demonstration event at the next Olympic Winter Games. These were to be held at St Moritz, also in 1928. The FIS categorically declined.[4] So when the Games opened a year later, the skiing events were still purely Nordic. Against that background the FIS biennial congress met, also at St Moritz, once more to discuss the recognition of the Alpine events. The auguries had not been good. To begin with, the Norwegian skiing authorities had at first decided to boycott the winter Olympics. Despite the victory of 1924, they saw in it a rising threat to the Norwegian method: 'Olympic humbug and nothing else', as Einar Lindboe, chairman of the NSF put it.[5] St Moritz was exclusive and commercialized and had little in common with genuine skiing. True skiers were not going to help foreign tourist trade.

At home this distressed the leading racers. They wanted their Olympic medals; they shuddered at the prospect of Swedes and Finns, especially Swedes, walking off with all the gold, for *they* were going, whether the Norwegians did or not. What is more the Norwegian skiers were trying to shake off the tyranny of the Nordic combination, which Lindboe proclaimed as 'the best foundation for all-round skiers, and best secures us against … perversion in the form of record-making'. There was a move to separate jumping and cross-country for those who wished and the Olympics offered hope. Petitions were circulated and the outcome, in February 1927, was a palace revolution. The purists directing the NSF were replaced by a more tolerant regime. The new chairman was an army captain (later Colonel), Nicolai Ramm Østgaard. Himself a distinguished skier – ninth in both the 50 km and the Nordic combination at Holmenkollen in 1913 – Østgaard was notably open-minded. At the eleventh hour, the Norwegians agreed to go to St Moritz after all. Moreover, Østgaard became ex officio vice president of the FIS. When it met, on 14 February 1928, the situation therefore had changed.

Downhill races were now commonplace, but still internationally unrecognized. The Alpine countries resented the Nordic hegemony. They did not mind the Nordic disciplines but they were aggrieved by the dismissal of their own events. A not-so-quiet threat to form a breakaway association influenced the proceedings. The shadow of schism loomed. Arnold Lunn, whose first FIS congress as British delegate this was, lobbied unrestrainedly. He could use the incipient first Arlberg-Kandahar, as an embryonic Alpine world championship, to make his point.

With or without him, however, the matter was resolving itself. Neither Holmquist, Østgaard, nor the Swedish Secretary-General, Count Hamilton, wanted a split, because that would deprive the Nordic countries of their influence.

They invoked the usual device of a committee and a compromise. The outcome was provisional approval of the Alpine events, with trials outside the Alps.

Austrians, meanwhile, passed another milestone. 'As so often in Austria', someone ironically remarked, 'a new occupation needs a new law.'[6] That same year of 1928, State authorization of Austrian ski instructors was introduced, complete with a centrally prescribed syllabus and an obligatory test. This was the first of its kind in the world.

Then the FIS duly reconsidered the Alpine events at its next conference, on 24 February 1930 in Oslo. This was no talking shop; the FIS had the power to act. Since 1925, they had been holding their own international races; world championships in all but name. They took place annually in different venues. During the 1929 fixture at Zakopane, a gloomy and scattered resort in the Polish Tatra mountains, the FIS had run a downhill race as a demonstration event. In another trial, the first known women's international cross-country race – over 6 km – was also run. Nordic women racers however, had to wait over 30 years for international recognition. Alpine skiers were luckier. As a result of the Zakopane experiment, when the FIS met in 1930, opposition to the straight downhill race had subsided. The slalom remained the issue.

The first two Arlberg-Kandahar races, in 1928 and 1929, were used as evidence for the defence. The Norwegians, at least were unimpressed. One of them, an army officer called Kristian Krefting had actually been to Mürren as a spy, so to say. In the 'weird thing they called the Slalom', as he put it, 'they scurried round some small flags as fast as they could … altogether looking quite comical'.[7]

Østgaard was more measured and far-seeing. He agreed that this slalom was contrived, perverted and threatened to make a fetish of technique. Things by now, however, had gone too far. Holmquist, Østgaard and Hamilton were, after all, men of the world. Since the turn of the century, they had been in the Alps and recognized that different terrain bred different styles not to mention different personalities. No doubt they rued the spread of skiing and would have preferred to keep it under control as a private badge of national identity. Now that it had escaped, it had taken on a life of its own. They decided to live and let live. If the British and the Alpine countries wished to rumba down the slalom to perdition, that was their concern. The Norwegians, Swedes and Finns, having privately agreed, washed their hands of the affair. Both Alpine events were recognized without dissent.

From start to finish, Arnold Lunn had not spoken a word, on the floor that is. He had been muzzled by a Swiss called Walter Amstutz, the power behind the throne. Amstutz was the son of a Mürren hotelier. Eventually tourist director at St Moritz, he was one of the original exponents of product branding before becoming a publisher, and a pioneer of modern poster design. He also happened to be an early aficionado of Alpine racing and, in 1924 founded the Swiss Academic ski club. He was one of the first converts to the Lunn or modern slalom. He saw it as a test of skill to balance the courage of the straight event. Quietly, behind the scenes, like the Swiss he was, he exerted more influence than the combative Lunn himself. In Oslo, it was their jointly conceived rules that the FIS accepted. These included a ban on stick riding, and the necessity of running in the downhill race to qualify for the slalom, the results of the one deciding the starting order of the other. To even things out, the slalom had to be run in two legs, over separate courses, the starting order of the second, being the inverse of the first. Also, thanks to Lunn, seeding – copied from tennis – was adopted with the field sorted into groups.

The fundamentals still hold today. Thus the Alpine events achieved international recognition – at least partly by British intrigue, as some would say. It was the inevitable break with the Nordic disciplines, each going their own way under the same aegis. It was the final division of skiing into two branches. In one way, it was merely codifying a fundamental distinction with psychological consequences. The Nordic events implied fighting the force of gravity. Alpine skiing *exploits* it. Ski-jumping is a hybrid: on the approach run you use gravity for the take-off but once in the air you fight it to keep aloft as long as possible.

The Oslo accord was too late for the third Winter Olympics – and the first in America – at Lake Placid in 1932. The Olympic debut of the Alpine events would have to wait for the next Games in 1936. The FIS was another matter. They had held their first international Alpine races already in the winter of 1931. These were run at Mürren but organized by the Ski Club of Great Britain. Walter Prager won the men's downhill race, David Zogg the slalom. Each was Swiss. Esmé MacKinnon won both women's events and she was English. Thus by a neat twist of Fate, both organization and results were Anglo-Swiss, doing historical justice for once.

British racers proceeded to excel for a time during the 1930s, the women in particular. This may have been due to the aftermath of the suffragette movement. Also in the upper middle classes from whom most British skiers still came, the women had the leisure to spend all season in the Alps, while their menfolk had to stay at home and work. Nonetheless, both had had a head start in the Alpine disciplines and reaped their share of glory. This was not only true of World Championships. The Arlberg Kandahar – now held alternately at Mürren and St Anton – had spawned two emulations. One was the Lauberhorn, at Wengen, first held in 1930; the other, in Austria, the Hahnenkamm at Kitzbühel, which began the following year, both named after local mountains. These three, Arlberg-Kandahar, Lauberhorn, Hahnenkamm, became the Alpine classics, with a mystique that, though battered, survives to this day. At any rate it was an Englishman, Gordon Cleaver, who won the Alpine Combination (Downhill and slalom) at the first Hahnenkamm. Then an RAF officer, H.R.D. Waghorn was runner-up in the straight downhill at the Lauberhorn in 1931. He was, incidentally, the winner of the Schneider Trophy, given for an air speed record in a seaplane. Waghorn flew a British model, which led to the design of the Spitfire, with all that was to mean in the war that was to come.

Indeed, aviators were noticeable among British skiers of the time. Perhaps this was because flying and skiing were still matters of trailblazing. Also the sensations of downhill racing were connected with those of flying the primitive aircraft of the period 'by the seat of the pants', as the saying has it. Among the most extraordinary of these characters was the wraith-like figure of Audrey Sale-Barker (later the Countess of Selkirk). She drifted through the Alps, from winning the women's downhill and Alpine combination at the 1929 Arlberg-Kandahar via a fourth place in the combination at the FIS world Championships at St Moritz in 1934, to being runner-up in the Arlberg Kandahar downhill the following year. Meanwhile, in 1933, she became one of the first women to fly from England down the length of Africa to the Cape, narrowly escaping being killed in a crash on the return – due to her own dreamy incaution, be it said – perhaps garnered on the pistes.

Within a few years, British skiers had faded. 'In the mechanics of skiing they were not far behind', said *The Times*.[8] 'It was only in the intuitive skill resulting from lifelong practice that their rivals outdistanced them.' The phraseology hinted at the national trait of explaining uncomfortable facts away but nonetheless revealed the underlying truth. The British epoch petered out, with the modern slalom as its questionable lasting imprint.

The Alpine countries proceeded to dominate the Alpine events. The contours of the modern sport were beginning to emerge. In 1937, the first Americans appeared in an Alpine prize list. Marian McKean was fourth in the Arlberg-Kandahar combined. Clarita Heath came fourth in the straight downhill at Chamonix in the FIS world Championships. These were the first to be so dignified; and retroactively also the previous events back to their inception in 1925.

Those same FIS championships of 1937 saw the triumph of Emile Allais. Born in Megève in 1912, he won a winter grand slam, as it were; downhill, slalom and combined. Arguably the greatest Alpine skier of the age, he had the rare gift of choosing the right line to shave off seconds while avoiding disaster. He was the first French international champion. He was something more. He started one of the first French ski schools. In fact he launched the French school of skiing; the first rival of Schneider and the Arlberg. Allais had devised his own technique, based on the parallel Christiania. That, he claimed, was his secret of success. He used his victories to advertise his system – the first to do so. He pioneered the exploitation of international racing to promote a national style, and hence advance the tourist trade. He was the forerunner of commercializing World Championships and Olympic Games.

# 34

# Skiing Mechanized and Politicized

Downhill skiing, like so much else, grew out of technical innovation. The Kandahar binding was one such innovation; the Lettner steel edge another. Everything, however, paled before the question of reaching the top of the run. Unlike their Nordic rivals, downhill skiers were not enamoured of the preparatory climb. They were thirsting for mechanical aids.

Mountain transport as we know it, dates from the mid-nineteenth century. It was an exuberant by-product of the railway age. It was then that the three basic systems arose: the funicular, the rack railway and the cableway.

Oldest in order of invention is the funicular. This consists of two counterbalancing carriages, moving up and down on rails, linked by a cable running over some pivot at the top. The first one in the world opened on 3 June 1862 in Lyon. About 400 m long, it connected the city centre with the plateau of Croix Rousse, up a steep slope, saving untold drudgery and acquiring its enduring French nickname of *La ficelle* – 'The String'. It was followed by other cities, like Budapest and Vienna. The first electric *ficelle* opened in Lausanne, in French-speaking Switzerland, in 1888.

Meanwhile in 1863, a French-born Swiss engineer called Niklaus Riggenbach first patented the rack railway. This works by means of a cogwheel on the locomotive engaging with a toothed rack between the rails to secure adhesion on steep gradients. Riggenbach had to take out his patent in France, because the Swiss authorities declined it. This may have been due to various precursors, notably an English patent of 1811, before the adhesion of ordinary railway wheels had been proven. In any case, as a copy of Riggenbach's patent or not, the first rack railway in the world appeared in America, on Mount Washington, New Hampshire, in 1869. Urgent reports from America led to the opening, a mere two years later, of the line up the Rigi in Switzerland. Designed by Riggenbach, this was the first rack railway in Europe.

Another Swiss invention, the aerial cableway, first appeared in 1866. It was driven by hand and used to ferry workmen across the Rhine at Schaffhausen to a water turbine station. This system of cabins, buckets, seats or other carriers suspended from a steel cable running over pylons, was to prove the most versatile of all. Nonetheless it was not until 1908 that the first public passenger version appeared. It ran up the Wetterhorn at Grindelwald. This was the first mountain cableway in the world.

In the patent application for his rack system, Riggenbach declared that he wanted 'to carry everyone up to the mountains, so that they can enjoy our magnificent country'.[1] This neatly defines the aim of the early lifts. They were either utilitarian or scenic conveyances. That holds even for the first lifts built in the original ski resorts; the Schatzalp at Davos in 1899 and the Chantarella Bahn at St Moritz in 1913. Both were funiculars.

The first conveyance specifically designed for skiing was a funicular up to the Corviglia terrace at St Moritz. It opened in 1928, the same year as the second winter Olympics there. It was the herald of an era.

The trouble with all these devices was that although they opened up this or that mountain flank, by definition they catered only to the practised skier. The less adept easily passed the point of no return and found themselves marooned. What is more, there was always a wait for the next departure. Some contrivance was needed for the practice slopes. That is a story in itself.

It begins in the last century with a technically minded German called Robert Winterhalder. He owned the Kurhaus Schneckenhof, a hotel at Schollach in the Black Forest. It lay at the foot of a slope, which was a haunt of early skiers. Winterhalder saw a commercial opportunity in saving them the uphill trudge to concentrate on running down. He happened to own a small water mill which, since 1900, he had used to hoist loads up to his loft by a continuous rope. That was the germ of the idea. He diverted the water by an underground pipe to a new mill at the foot of the nearby slope. An endless steel wire, looped over a flywheel driven by the mill, ran parallel to the slope. It was supported by five wooden posts with pulleys, and at intervals were attached a piece of rope to which the skier (or tobogganer) clung by main force.

It was, in other words, a primitive drag lift. It was the first ski lift in the world. It opened on 14 February 1908. The length was 280 m, with a difference of height of 28 m.

Winterhalder took out a patent, and wanted to build more. In the bureaucratic German state, he needed a permit. His invention, however, breaking new ground, he first had to find an authority to which he could apply. The state railway was eventually deemed appropriate. 'The concept is good', a very senior official is supposed to have told Winterhalder:

> but you have no background. You must be a [PhD], a trained engineer, or at the very least a mechanic. You see, my dear … fellow, we live in a *Doktor* age, and nothing good can be expected of anyone who is not a *Doktor*. God-given intelligence or experience count for nothing. The 'Title' makes blind people see.[2]

It is a moral tale for our times too. Winterhalder did not get his permit. He made no money out of his invention. His lift closed for good at the outbreak of war in 1914. After the war, the patent lapsed, he himself was all but forgotten and his idea was sporadically copied; mostly substituting electric power for the original hydraulic drive. It offered what other uphill transport did not – continuous operation – but it never caught on, because of a fundamental fault of design.

Whatever the variation, the skier still had to cling to the cable.

The critical advance came in 1934 with the opening at Davos of a new drag lift. Instead of holding on, the passenger was supported by a bar attached at one end to the moving cable by a spring-loaded wire, and bent at the other into a crook that went round the upper thighs. That single-seater was the first modern ski lift. By removing the strain on hands and arms, the length of the lift was no longer restricted, nor the customers discouraged. This was the progenitor of all modern drag lifts and is the most common hardware festooning mountainsides the world over today. It was designed by a local Davos ski teacher called Jack Ettinger. He deserves to be remembered. He it was who opened the floodgates to the slopes.

Thus by the mid-1930s, the principles of uphill transport had been established. Without it, Alpine skiing would have stagnated, and competition would certainly have done so. To trudge upwards for several hours in order to race down for as many minutes was not an enticing prospect. The mechanization of the slopes prepared the industrialization of skiing and, as a consequence, the rise of the professional ski teacher.

As it happened, uphill technology was ready for the fourth Olympic Winter Games at Garmisch-Partenkirchen, in Bavaria in 1936. A cableway to a mountain called the Kreuzeck made the straight downhill event a practical possibility and fortunately so. This was the Olympic debut of the Alpine skiing events.

Those Games were historic in other ways as well. When they were awarded to Germany, in 1931, the Weimar Republic still ruled. In the meantime, the Nazis had come to power. After some hesitation, they saw the propaganda potential. The Winter Games at Garmisch, followed by the summer Olympics in Berlin, were used to blazon out their ideology, replete with icons and symbolism. In yoking sport so spectacularly to political ends, they were pioneers.

The Olympics had hitherto been a muted event. It was the Nazis who, exploiting radio and cinema for the first time, gave it the bombastic televisuality that we know, decades before its time. They invented the semi-comical opening and closing ceremonies, with their paramilitary overtones, organized by an army officer. They also started the custom of carrying the Olympic flame from Greece. At the Winter Games, the Olympic flame was also lit for the first time, but without that preliminary. It flickered over the snow atop a wooden tower, fed by cylinders of propane gas. With hindsight, it was redolent not so much of Olympus as the Wagnerian fires of Götterdämmerung. The invention of tradition!

Under the flapping of the swastika, there was something of the menace of the age at Garmisch. Hitler himself opened and closed the Games, besides being present at the ski-jumping. This was at the dawn of the photo opportunity; also a Nazi invention. Another one was the *Reichssportführer* – 'state sports leader' – a certain Hans von Tschammer und Osten, also present, and the forerunner of all Ministers of Sport that we now know.

Luckily for their propaganda, Germans took the first Alpine gold medals; Franz Pfnür for the men and an extraordinary skier called Christel Cranz for the women. Germans won both silver medals too. Among the men, Emile Allais took bronze; the first French Olympic skiing medal.

In another innovation, Garmisch had seen the first women's Olympic ski races. That it happened through the Alpine disciplines seemed no more than right. This was also the year of the Norsemens' revenge. Third in the women's Alpine combination was an all-round Norwegian athlete called Laila Schou-Nilsen. Fourth among the men was another Norwegian, Birger Ruud, and thereby hangs a tale.

No Alpine specialist he, Ruud was probably the finest ski-jumper of his generation. He was one of three legendary ski-jumping brothers; Sigmund and Asbjørn were the others. They came from Kongsberg, the centre of a new style of ski-jumping, which involved bending sharply from the waist – together with absolutely close and parallel skis as specified by the standards of the age. It was a precursor of the later aerodynamic style. In any case, at Garmisch, Birger Ruud won his second Olympic gold medal for ski-jumping. He also won the straight downhill race, more in the air than on the ground, or so it seemed, as if still on the jumping hill, which proved that Nordic skiers could master Alpine events as an inherent fraction of their own technique.

At the time, Olympic Alpine skiing medals – unlike the FIS – were not given on individual races, but only on the combination; no doubt the residual effect of Nordic attitudes. Nonetheless, Birger Ruud remains the only skier to have won both an Olympic Nordic and an Alpine event. Laila Schou-Nilsen, won the women's' straight downhill event. She and Birger Ruud each swooped down nonchalantly like Vikings on a raid, before disappearing back into northern mists. Both failed comically in the slalom; watched with fathomless eyes by Walter Amstutz and Arnold Lunn, now on the Alpine jury.

One way or another, Garmisch signalled the breakthrough of Alpine ski racing. It had begun filtering back to Scandinavia. Embryonic downhill clubs appeared here and there. The Olympic movement also affected Nordic skiing. For one thing, from the start the Winter Olympics recognized both the ski-jump on its own – the special jump, so-called, in which Birger Ruud, incidentally won his medals – and the Nordic combination. For the Scandinavians and especially the Norwegians this was a breath of fresh air. Finally in 1933, Holmenkollen followed suit. The same year, as a result of the Olympics, the 18 km cross-country race (15 km from 1954) was approved both as part of the combination and as an event in its own right. All this set the pattern as we know it. Garmisch brought competitive skiing out into a wider world and indirectly encouraged skiing as a recreation.

In Norway itself, the rise of Olympic skiing caused a reaction. There was unease over the spectre of a growing gap between the ordinary skier and the elite. As a kind of remedy, the *Birkebeinerrenn* was founded. It was first run in 1932. Based on the Swedish *Vasalopp*, it was also open to ordinary skiers, allowing them to compete with the champions. It also has historical associations rooted in national identity. The *Birkebeinerrenn* commemorates the exploit of two skiers who, during the medieval Norwegian civil wars, saved Håkon Håkonson, the infant heir to the throne. At New Year 1206, they carried him on skis out of the mortal danger of a disputed royal succession across a mountain range to safety in the valley of Østerdalen, and changed the course of history. They were called *Birkebeiner*, or 'birch legs', because they belonged to a faction that was once poor, reduced to wearing shoes of birch bark and that is what gave the modern race its name. It is actually run in the opposite direction, from east to west, starting in Østerdalen and finishing at Lillehammer. It is only 54 km to the *Vasalopp*'s 85 km. However, each competitor has to carry a rucksack weighing 3.5 kg to symbolize the infant Håkon. What is more, there is a vertical climb of 600 m to reach the summit at 900 m and, unlike the *Vasalopp*, much of the track is above the treeline. In the first race, the two leaders are supposed to have stopped briefly to enjoy the view. This is plausible, given the massed start. The *Birkebeinerrenn* became an institution and is still run every year. It was the first of a new kind of mountain touring race, which let an average skier identify with the elite. For the health of the sport, this was thought to be vital. It was a counterbalance to passive Olympic mania.

In other ways, the winter Olympics affected Nordic skiers. The acceptance of the Alpine events forced them seriously to consider downhill technique. When preparing for Garmisch the Norwegian authorities, for example, had told their cross-country racers to 'use the Easter holidays' – by now the traditional mountain skiing festival: 'to practise running downhill. You will know how much a mistake in a downhill section during a cross-country race means in lost time.'[3]

In the end, this did not much help the cross-country skiers. Since the second Winter Olympics at St Moritz in 1928, they had faltered, to be in eclipse for a generation. There were no Norwegian cross-country gold medals at Garmisch. Swedes and Finns had taken over. The Finns won the 4 × 10 km relay. This was a memorable victory as it was the first time that the relay was an Olympic event. It had made its international debut at the FIS Nordic world championships at Sollefteå in Sweden in 1934; appropriately enough since it was a Swedish invention from around the turn of the century.

All round, Garmisch was bloated with records. There were more countries (28) and competitors (756) than ever before. What is more, with 21 countries against 22, the Alpine disciplines had almost equalled the Nordic ones from the start. The great absentee was Soviet Russia, immured in its Stalinist isolation, its Gulags and the bloodbath of the purges; the model of what was growing in Germany.

By contrast, there were Japanese in the Alpine events. This was largely due to Hannes Schneider, and that is a story in itself. In 1930, he had visited Japan as the guest of the Japanese government. Ignoring the Ainu of Hokkaido, skiing had been introduced by resident Norwegians about 1902. It was still the era of Europeanization. When the moment came, the authorities wanted to copy Alpine skiing too. In 1919, they had invited an Austrian officer, a certain Major Lerch, but he taught the Zdarsky style, very much obsolescent. So the Japanese seized on Schneider because his was the celebrated name. He owed this to Fanck's instructional film; more perhaps to the spin-off book, probably the first of its kind. Also called *The Wonders of Skiing*, it was an instructional manual, illustrated by frames from the film. That too was a piece of pioneering. It first appeared in 1925. When Schneider landed in Japan (after a fortnight's travel via the Trans-Siberian railway) he found a pirated edition in Japanese. At any rate, there were legions of skiers practising the Arlberg style as well as they could from the book.

Schneider had been called in to give a final polish by personal example. In the mountains of Hokkaido and Honshu, Schneider was politely exploited, hour after hour, sometimes teaching classes of five hundred and more, using interpreters and a public address system. In the middle of April, after a month of hard work, Schneider set sail for home via Suez. He teased his hosts by giving them his skis and bindings as a parting present, knowing that they been photographed and minutely examined – a common experience of the age. It also transpired that the Japanese military had been behind his invitation. Some general told him that downhill skiing was a good preparation for flying; the reverse of the British attitude, as it were. So perhaps the Japanese kamikaze pilots of the Second World War first issued from the slopes. The behaviour of the modern Alpine skier makes this wholly credible.

Japan was not alone. The 1930s brought the spread of Alpine skiing overseas. Sometimes with the help of Schneider's pupils, it came to Australia and South America, notably in Chile, at Portillo in the Andes. It appeared both in Canada and the United States, with its bland but emblematic resort of Sun Valley, Idaho.

Sun Valley has a particular claim to distinction. The first chair lift in the world opened there in 1936. That completed the repertoire of uphill transport systems. It arose from a drawback of the drag lift. This required some skill to use. Inherent in the device were periodical stoppages due to entanglement of customers in the machinery. The chair lift obviated most trouble. This early model had fixed seats, so difficulty was confined to getting on and getting off. All this was happening in the Depression. However, the years of want also favoured skiing. Especially in the Alps, it meant new pleasures for those with money; for those without, new jobs and, for mountain peasants, escape from the serfdom of rural poverty.

Meanwhile one casualty of the Depression had been Sir Henry Lunn's travel agency. In September 1931, following an economic crisis, England abandoned the Gold Standard. Philip Snowden, a more than usually hapless Chancellor of the Exchequer, asked all Englishmen to save the pound and stay at home. Without reserves, Sir Henry's firm naturally collapsed. It was taken over by his son Arnold as Chairman, with his intimate friend Charles Mackintosh, a leading British ski racer and Scottish rugby international, as managing director. On the one hand, this gave Arnold Lunn a Swiss financial base. On the other, those Swiss hotels that had depended on the British faced financial ruin. In future they would spread the risks. One by-product of the whole affair was the end of British domination in the Swiss Alps. A shrunken enclave survived in Mürren and Wengen. Refugees from their atmosphere of RAF officers' mess and suburban tennis club found sympathetic asylum elsewhere, notably at the original resorts of Davos and St Moritz, where a cosmopolitan beau monde set the tone.

Between the wars, in fact, Switzerland remained pre-eminent as the Alpine goal of skiers. Partly this was due to its long history as the home of mountaineering, which followed from its position along the crest of the Alps, with the symbolic Matterhorn ruling the imagination. It also followed from the peculiar nature of the Swiss resorts. For reasons of culture and topography, they seemed cut off from the world, a refuge from the troubles of the times, a metaphor of Shangri-La. Other resorts, whether in France, Italy, Austria or elsewhere, were anchored in the outside, often like suburbs of the capital cities.

This partly explains the attraction of Switzerland for British skiers of the age. They were middle-class, exclusive and snobbish. They in turn were looked down upon by English mountaineers. Mostly belonging to the Alpine Club, *they* considered themselves socially superior. Their ambience was that of a cross between an Oxford or Cambridge High Table and a London club. Skiers were considered irritating and laughable intruders in the holy mountain fastness.

This hierarchical complexity was unique to the English. Among others, skiing prospered as a universal sport, although it still had a touch of the elite. From the early nineteen-thirties, ski mountaineering was popularized in the Alps, notably in Switzerland and France. The Haute Route, the classic high-altitude route along the crest of the Alps between Chamonix and Saas Fee in the Swiss Canton of the Valais, became a rite of passage.

Philosophically, in Germany and Austria, ski touring was infused by the *kampf am Berg* – 'the battle on the mountain'. This was defined as the inner struggle against personal weakness and the outer one against rock and ice. It had questionable antecedents in mountaineering. All the major peaks had been climbed and this was the age of new routes and record-breaking. It culminated in 1938 with the conquest of the North Face of the Eiger, 2,000 m of uninterrupted precipice: so-called 'the last Alpine problem'. Seven climbers had already perished in the attempt. The victors were a mixed party of two Germans and two Austrians, led by a German, Anderl Heckmair.

With or without such influence, skiing as a recreation spread among all classes, not only in the Alpine countries, including Italy and what was then Yugoslavia, but in the Jura, Tatras, Carpathians and other lesser European ranges. Although it was gradually being popularized, it still paled before the mass participation in the Nordic countries. It surpassed all other sports combined. Norway, of course, led the way, with its iconic Easter exodus to the mountains of a horde of Nordic ski tourers approaching 100,000. In Sweden, skiing for pleasure was still predominantly middle-class. One went to the mountains with a unique mixture of patriotism and Nature worship. Curiously, the Swedes looked for untouched snow, while the Norwegians wanted marked and prepared tracks so that they could race along the valleys and over the plateau. Another difference: Swedes carried equipment to face the elements; the Norwegians put their trust in mobility and light equipment, sometimes with dire consequences. In both cases, hut to hut touring was now in vogue. The difference from Alpine touring was this. Whereas in the Alps, civilization was never far away and often all too visible down in the valley, in the Nordic countries, ski touring meant the flight into the wilderness leaving habitation far away, out of sight and probably out of mind.

In Norway, Jotunheimen and the Hardangervidda plateau became the classic playgrounds of the ski tourer. In Sweden, the characteristic route was *Kungsleden*, 'The Royal Trail'. This ran for several hundred kilometres from Swedish Lapland, through the mountain wilderness of the Scandinavian watershed. It neatly symbolized the distinction between Nordic and Alpine skiing. The track was marked by wooden posts surmounted by diagonal crosses. In the summer, they fit into rocks and vegetation as naturally as they do among the winter snows. On Alpine slopes, when the ground is bared, the ski lifts remain derelict and intrusive.

Meanwhile during the 1930s, ski racing lurked as a growing spectator sport, appropriated by the Olympic movement. That was replete with stiff-necked principle. It clung to the amateur ideal. Like most ideals, it was pregnant with hypocrisy. The FIS, being ruled by military men and practising skiers, was less idealistic. The Olympic games banned ski teachers as professionals; not so the

56. Norwegian soldier, c. 1814. *The National Library of Norway*

FIS. Immediately after the Garmisch Olympics, therefore, to include ski teachers, the FIS held their own races at Innsbruck for the Alpine disciplines. The Nordic events were untouched because there the instructor was absent from the active elite. Emile Allais was the only Garmisch medallist to appear at Innsbruck but there he was unplaced. The upshot was that Rudi Rominger, a Swiss ski teacher, won the downhill and the Alpine Combined.

All this was happening against a backdrop of unease. In 1938, came the *Anschluss*: the annexation of Austria by Germany and the installation of a Nazi regime. Arnold Lunn, brave and uncompromising in a cause, made his own characteristic gesture. He took the Arlberg-Kandahar away from St Anton, telling the local Nazis that it would not return until they and their ilk had disappeared.

Meanwhile, the Olympic movement and the FIS had come to an impasse over amateurism. The schism of 1936 at Innsbruck seemed set to last. The FIS decided to boycott the next winter Olympics, at Sapporo, in Japan, in 1940, holding their own World Championships that year instead. There would be no official ski events at Sapporo, so the games would be a rump. With hindsight, this heralded open competition. It was all academic anyway. The FIS held its usual championships at Zakopane in February 1939 but it was to be the last for nearly a decade. In September the Germans attacked Poland and started the Second World War.

# 35

# Military Skiing

In the bitter years that followed, men on skis played their part in battle. The protagonists were Finns and Norwegians, but Finns above all, 'a people of uncertain parentage', to quote a Finnish writer, 'orphans of history, who for centuries have clung with almost perverse devotion to the bleak corner of Europe where their ancestors chose to halt their trek from Central Asia'.[1] Be that as it may, Finnish skiers had an unsung but decisive rôle in the vast drama of the Second World War.

At first sight this seems odd, because skiing nowadays is synonymous with peace and pleasure. At the other end of the scale however, the ski, like most devices, was inevitably used in war. This has deep historical roots. It goes far back, long before the Norwegian ski regiments of the eighteenth century. It is older than firearms in fact.

Thus in China around AD900, the Mu-Ma Turks were said to ski so fast that 'they ... can rapidly muster their forces. By night they rob, and by day they hide.'[2]

57.  Ski-jumping, military style Norway, 18th century. Grüner, 1765.
*The Norwegian Armed Forces Museum*

Over to the West, about the same time, a Danish Viking king, Ragnar Lodbrog, found himself at war with the Finns. In the words of Saxo Grammaticus, the medieval Danish chronicler, they

> attacked Ragnar's army with impunity where it was encamped for the winter in Bjarmeland [Northern Finland]. The fact is that the Finns glide rapidly on slippery planks, and move as quickly as they wish, so that … in a twinkling they can be upon you, and then as quickly far away.[3]

This is the earliest record of Finnish ski-borne warriors. It might have been written a thousand years later. In other words, the ski gave speed, manoeuvrability, tactical surprise; all the benefits of cavalry without the upkeep of the horse. Ragnar, however, was a victim of guerrillas. The first known use of the ski in regular warfare was at the battle of Oslo on 6 March 1200. It was during one of the various medieval uprisings. Sverre, generally accepted at the time as the rightful Norwegian king, faced a rebel force the size and position of which were unknown. So he ordered a patrol of skiers up onto a mountain to reconnoitre. 'A great deal of snow had fallen', says the Saga

> and the skiing was good … When [they] reached the heights they looked down, and the country was glittering with people … Northwards … as far as the eye could see. [They] rushed back as fast as they could to tell the King.[4]

Sverre duly (with some trouble) triumphed. The medieval Norsemen, however, preferred to fight in summer. By contrast, the Russians, at an early stage, took to winter warfare. They lived in a harsh climate and their sprawling domains, with steppe and taiga on the eastern marches, were ideal for the predator on skis. Their earliest documented use of ski in battle took place in 1444. That was in a raid against the Tartars of Riazan, to the south-east of Moscow. Organized by the Grand Duke Basil II of Moscow, it was part of the protracted struggle against the historic foe from central Asia. Slowly Russia recovered the lost lands and then moved further on.

In December 1582, an ambiguous Cossack called Yermak, having ravaged the land beyond the Urals, sent skiers with the good news back to the Tsar, Ivan the Terrible, in Moscow. Yermak is generally credited with opening the Russian conquest of Siberia. This was mostly a succession of winter campaigns. The crisp sweep of skis on endless snow was infinitely preferable to the soggy plod of summer, not to mention gnats. Russia's eastern march of empire depended on the ski.

Despite the skiing mastery of the Siberian tribes, the Russians had the upper hand, chiefly through firearms and sheer weight of numbers. Also, the Russians showed technical finesse. Their bindings, for example, consisted of toestraps made of thin strips of wood, which, unlike leather, would not become wet and freeze up. In another refinement, their boots – with turned-up tips to hook on to the toestrap – had extra pieces of leather sewn across the front to protect against blistering.

The Russians did not have everything their own way, however. Various tribes, notably the Buryats, started winter insurrections. One eighteenth-century Russian officer complained to the Tsar that he had been reduced to eating his 'leather boots … and also the fur lining of [my] skis'.[5]

While in Siberia, Russia was building an empire almost unnoticed by the outside world, to the West, she was indulging in more obvious expansion. There, her opponents were not primitive tribes but civilized kingdoms. Since the battlegrounds were in northern Europe, and the Little Ice Age was in full spate, winter warfare was a strategic necessity. At a critical juncture the Lithuanians, an obstacle to the Russian advance, were overcome because they, for some reason, lacked the ski.

In the Swedes, meanwhile, Russia faced an enemy of a different stamp, for they definitely did have the ski, and they were then a power to be reckoned with. During March 1610, a Swedish General, Jakob de la Gardie entered Moscow, one of the few Western invaders to do so. De la Gardie attacked in winter because *he* knew that the hostile seasons were really summer and autumn, with their dust, heat, mud and rain. Winter, then, with its snow, frost and frozen ground gave him a sweeping highway to the east. He took advantage of this with ski troops, thanks to whom he not only marched on Moscow but marched safely back again. As a result, he helped the Swedish King, the formidable Gustavus Adolphus, secure the highly advantageous Peace of Stolbova. Gustavus acquired all the land round the Gulf of Finland, making it a Swedish mare nostrum and cutting Russia off from the open sea.

The Swedes allowed themselves the luxury of fighting on two fronts. In the east, they clashed with Russia for mastery of the Baltic; to the west they aspired to conquer the whole of Scandinavia. Denmark bore the brunt of fighting in the south but Norway was the northern front. There, too, winter was the campaigning season, if only because an invader found military transport easier, with sledges preferable to creaking carts listing on rutted roads.

In 1644, orders went out to capture two central Norwegian parishes, Idre and Särna, bordering on Dalecarlia, traditionally the province of Swedish skiers. No soldiers being near, a party was raised from the local Dalecarlians. They rejected the official commander, calling instead for 'our Daniel'.[6] This Daniel, surnamed Buscovius was their much loved (Lutheran) priest. At first he protested that bearing arms was unseemly for a man of the cloth. His bishop persuaded him otherwise. So on 18 March Buscovius led a company of some 200 skiers with motley weapons from his church at a village called Älvdalen.

Buscovius himself skied out in front. Next to him, also on skis, he had his deacon bearing the bible and chalice. After four days, they arrived at the church in Särna. Buscovius, suitably menacing with a monstrous blunderbuss, in working order or not, issued his ultimatum: submit to Swedish rule or suffer fire and sword. The astonished inhabitants could not see the point of suffering. They were all good Protestants; they understood each others' dialects. Queen Christina of Sweden and King Cristian IV of Denmark-Norway were equally remote. They chose submission. Daniel preached a sermon, gave communion, carried out baptism with his usual amiability and then stumped home on skis again at the head of his flock. What the local clergy were doing history does not reveal but the two parishes remained Swedish for evermore.

This was a whimsical episode in an ancestral feud. Swedes and Norwegians had been at loggerheads since the Viking age. Between the sixteenth and the early nineteenth centuries, they fought 12 winter campaigns. For long, neither had regular ski troops, but local peasantry were simply pressed into service as required.

In Norway, a letter from 1612 makes the point. 'I sent out some local skiers on a reconnaissance [some 200 kilometres] into … Sweden', the Governor of Trondheim wrote on 17 March to the Royal Chancellor in Copenhagen, 'and … they brought back a prisoner.'[7] This tantalizingly brief remark was in fact the first known record of Norwegian military skiing since the Middle Ages.

Norwegian soldiers were then part of the Danish Army, under the direct command of the headquarters in Copenhagen, where skiing was virtually unknown, much less understood. In 1628, Norway was given its own national army, having its own commander in chief, within the Danish-Norwegian forces.

Finally, in 1676, three companies of Norwegian ski troops were raised, each of 140 men. They were the first regular ski units, anywhere. They were also the first military skiers considered an elite. Mounted in summer, they turned to skis in winter. They were used for highly mobile border operations.

All this was on the periphery of the convoluted power struggles of the seventeenth century. The Little Ice Age was still flourishing and continued to have a hand in events. Snow and frost secured the Norwegian border. Then after 30 years' quiescence the Swedish threat once more erupted. Charles XII, the legendary warrior king of Sweden, after a string of classic victories against Russia in the Great Northern War, was defeated by Peter the Great at the battle of Poltava in the Ukraine in June 1709. That same year, foiled in the East, the Swedes once more turned west to attack Norway.

With usual political myopia, the Norwegian ski companies had been disbanded. Now at the outbreak of yet another war, they were revived. When winter came, the Swedes sent their own skiing levies over the mountains. They were confined to skirmishing and a little mutual plundering. At least their clashes made colourful pageants in the snow: the Swedes in sombre dark blue; Norwegians in their green and white.

Nature is not always on the side of the big battalions. In the late winter of 1716, Charles decided to break the stalemate and invaded southern Norway in full force. Although a military genius in the open country of continental Europe, with large formations and set-piece battles, Charles was less certain of himself in the very different conditions of Norway. He did not understand winter warfare. He neglected his ski troops, and put his trust in cavalry. He took Christiania, but the Norwegian commander, General Lützow, had slipped out with all his troops west of the city to fight another day.

Meanwhile, at Hakadal, to the north of Christiania, someone had discovered the Swedish battle plan. A local skier was sent off to warn Lützow of a surprise attack. With orders 'to go day and night', he had to make a wide detour to avoid Swedish patrols. He had plenty of snow with some hard crust but it was broken upland, untracked with the vagaries of early spring. He had to cover 90 km, across Nordmarka, passing landmarks familiar to modern skiers, like the Kikut plateau where the eponymous hut now stands. He skied for 26 hours at a stretch and reached General Lützow at midday on 28 March. This was just in time for Lützow to make his dispositions. He sent a cavalry detachment north and stopped the Swedes at a place called Norderhov, famous both in Swedish and Norwegian history. It was only a skirmish, but it was enough to upset Charles's plans and he thereupon withdrew. The name of the courier went unrecorded. So an unknown skier sent the mighty Charles XII home again. (This has been commemorated since 1969 by a popular touring race over the same route. It is called *Grenader-løpet* – 'The Grenadier's Race'. The winning time is about five hours.)

In 1718, Charles returned to the attack. This time he did so in autumn and, again, the winter that followed was a skier's dream. The weather was fair with deep early frost and snow. Now the Swedes had a few hundred ski troops as well. They fought a few skirmishes, the dull plop of the musket or the crack of the sharpshooter's rifle mingling with the sough of skis over snow-blanketed forest and field. The Norwegians were on familiar ground entirely suited to their taste. Dodging between the trees and the snowbanks lining the roads, they gave another lesson in skill offsetting sheer numbers. The invading army was more than 40,000 strong.

Charles had attacked on two fronts. In the north, an ill-starred Finnish general called Carl Gustav Armfelt was investing Trondheim. Charles himself, sombre, single-minded, aloof as ever, lay far to the south directing the siege of Frederiksten, a strategic Norwegian frontier fortress. There he fell to a sniper's bullet on 30 November 1718.

The loss of their King shocked the Swedes beyond redemption. They raised the siege of Frederiksten and marched home again. Armfelt gave up and set off homewards too. Unfortunately for him, he had to cross the frontier mountains swathed in the deep early snows of winter. Very few of his men had skis – and he inevitably paid the price. Norwegian ski troops harried the cumbersome procession of men and horses. On the heights, on New Year's Day 1719, the Swedes were overtaken by a blizzard. Of the 8,000 who started out, at least half froze to death. 'Whole companies', in the words of one Norwegian officer, 'lay stiff upon each other, after having burned gun stocks and ... anything else that would burn to keep out the cold.'[8] Armfelt – frostbitten in the face – was among the survivors who straggled back to a village called Handöl on the Swedish side of the mountains; to this day a melancholy landmark.

The lasting impression that the Norwegians brought away was how they had skied effortlessly around in the same snow where a whole doomed army had floundered and frozen to death. In other words, one more proof that there is no bad weather, only bad equipment.

With familiar pusillanimity, the Government in Copenhagen then pared down the Norwegian ski troops, before eventually grasping that the frontier still had to be defended. In 1747, the skiing units were permanently established as an independent corps that expanded in the end to more than 2,000 all told. The Swedes, by contrast, still had no standing ski units and, on their own admission, the Norwegian ski corps was an effective deterrent. In its dual rôle as guardian of skiing technique and the use of skis on the battlefield, it was ahead. Since the original version in 1733, it was alone in having up-to-date training manuals.

For almost a century after the fall of Charles XII, Norway was more or less at peace along its eastern border. That changed with the shifting sands of the Napoleonic Wars. At the end of March 1808, the Swedes invaded yet again, and again history obligingly repeated itself. Once more, it was a good skiing season.

58. Attack on Tartars by Russians and Mordvins 1444. Russian manuscript, fifteenth century, after Artsikhovskii, 1944. *Cambridge University Library*

Once more, with the curious limping gait of ski and andor, the Norwegians used their superiority on skis to counter a stronger but cumbrous foe, winning some minor local victories, the psychological effect of which was out of all proportion to their military significance.

The Swedes understood that, floundering in the soft, coarse-grained spring snow, they faced an unprofitable military entanglement and yet again withdrew. They had what they wanted in the end when, in 1814, the Great Powers let them annexe Norway at last. By an ironical twist of fate, the Norwegians then enjoyed the longest period of peace they had ever known, with independence along the way. It all came to an end after more than a century on 9 April 1940 when the Germans invaded. After a short campaign, the Norwegians, having neglected their defence and a British expeditionary force, victims of the same malaise, were ingloriously defeated. Norway was left to its own devices and the country was under Nazi occupation for the rest of the Second World War.

A resistance movement sprang up. Winter was its friend, because the symbiosis of the skier and the snow allowed the Norwegians to exploit the landscape, creating a mystical sense of superiority. The British Special Operations Executive (SOE) used some of them. They organized sabotage against the Germans in occupied Europe, and in 1941 started planning to destroy a Norwegian factory at Rjukan. It was the start of the nuclear arms race.

The plant at Rjukan produced heavy water, which was being shipped to Germany. Heavy water was used in experimenting with nuclear fission, and the Allied High Command feared that the Germans were developing an atom bomb. This had to be stopped at all costs. Heavy water seemed the key, hence SOE's interest in Rjukan. The Manhattan Project was under way and the question was who would be the first to get the bomb.

59. Finnish ski troops moving up to the firing line, northern front, Russo-Finnish Winter War, December 1939–January 1940.

The Rjukan plant was made for sabotage. It lay in a deep narrow valley on the edge of Hardangervidda. It was there because the drainage system of the plateau offered unlimited hydroelectric power. This was needed for making fertilizer, which was the real purpose of the plant. Heavy water was a by-product. It arose from the fact that in producing the fertilizer, water was first electrolysed to give off hydrogen, which in turn was made into ammonia, its vital component. Rjukan was the only source of heavy water in commercial quantities under the control of the Germans. The SOE proposed to cut off the supply.

They trained specialized Norwegian saboteurs who had escaped to England and parachuted them on to Hardangervidda in midwinter. They were somehow glad to be on skis again, even although it meant exchanging the relative comfort of wartime England, embattled but unoccupied, for the rigours of midwinter on the plateau. It was like coming home, for this was Telemark, with all its historical significance. They felt less like soldiers; more as if they were on a ski tour with certain complications. In peacetime they were fleeing the cities; now it was a foreign invader but the principle was the same. In the words of their second in command, Knud Haukelid, who came from the district and knew the terrain intimately, 'we soon came to realize that civilization was a mass of superfluities'.[9]

Haukelid and his companions melted into the wintry, storm-swept plateau, living in small huts belonging to local sympathizers or out in some snowdrift. The terrain was exposed, with no tree cover, but they understood its intricacies. They had Nature on their side. Knowing how to mask their tell-tale ski tracks by merging them with those of hunters or other local inhabitants and helped by white overclothes, they were invisible to their enemies. Led by Haukelid, they blew up the heavy water installation on the night of 27–28 February 1943.

This only delayed production by a few months. The US Air Force bombed the plant in November, without destroying the heavy water installation. The Nazis now decided to take the apparatus back to Germany and start production there. The SOE asked Haukelid to stop them. With a few companions, he spent a second successive winter on the snowbound uplands of Hardangervidda, exposed to the force of Nature, but safe from the Germans. 'We learned that one cannot defy nature, but must adapt to her', he wrote. He and his companions were forced to live off the land. That was complicated by deep cold and hateful drift snow on which skis refused to move, as if in an icy Sahara. For a time they survived by hunting wild reindeer.

> Not only did we live in the same surroundings as the reindeer [in Haukelid's words], but we came to live in approximately the same way. We followed the reindeer on its wanderings, and could do without a house – and without sleeping-bags.[10]

They needed skis to keep up with the herds. They might have been prehistoric tribesmen. It was an atavistic life that, arguably, gave them the self-possession to carry out their orders. Finally on 19 February 1944, Haukelid together with one of his group called Rolf Sørlie descended from the plateau to Rjukan down a hair-raising icy slope and went into action. The production apparatus and a stock of heavy water had been loaded onto a train, which would be carried by a ferry across the neighbouring lake of Tinnsjø the next day on the first stage of its journey. Haukelid and his companion crept on board and, in the bilges, placed an explosive charge with a delayed action detonator improvised out of two alarm clocks. It worked. Next morning, the ferry with all its cargo sank to the bottom of the lake at its deepest point. Haukelid and Sørlie got away to Sweden, which was a neutral haven. A few men on ski had stopped the German nuclear programme, with all that might have meant.

This was the emblematic operation of the Norwegian underground. Otherwise, in the universal conflict, ski were of lesser military importance – with one exception. The ski played a momentous rôle in the Russo-Finnish Winter War of 1939–40. The outcome of the whole Second World War arguably hinged on this half-forgotten campaign. It began with the invasion of Finland by the then Soviet Union under Stalin, its unspeakable Georgian-born tyrant.

The result seemed a foregone conclusion. After all a country of 170,000,000 had attacked one of less than 4,000,000. Nonetheless, even after the collapse of the Soviet Union, the Winter War remained 'one of the least studied events in the history of our Fatherland', as a latter-day Russian author tellingly put it: '105 days of the most brutal, bloody battles'.[11]

It was nothing new, as the Soviet rulers pretended. It was merely the latest chapter in a long historical saga. Since time immemorial Finnish tribes had skirmished with the advancing Slavs. The Russians, prisoners of their own Soviet propaganda, had forgotten their history but the Finns had not. In the Tartar raid of 1444, for example, the skiers were not Russians, but Mordvins, a Finnish tribe from the Volga. The Russian chronicle recording the event uses a word for ski, *rta* of Finnish derivation, instead of the native Russian *lyzhi*.[12]

Another age, another war and another lesson ignored by the Soviet *apparatchiks* in 1939. When De la Gardie entered Moscow in 1610, his ski troops were mostly Finnish. This was understandable. Finland was after all the Swedish border province with Russia, and De la Gardie was not exactly the first Swedish general to confront Russia. The two countries had been squabbling since the Middle Ages. Back and forth the winter fighting swayed and the Finns, being the people of the frontier, bore the brunt. Knowing however that they were vastly better skiers; quicker, more adroit and decidedly more at home in the terrain over which they fought, they dismissed the behemoth from the steppes.

In 1573, under their own general, Claes Fleming, the Finns sent more than a thousand skiers to invade the province of Ingria, where St Petersburg now stands. Then in 1590, the Russians returned the compliment by attacking over the Karelian Isthmus, only to be stopped by 600 skiing farmers; not hard to believe, given their ferocious reputation.

And so it went on until, in 1703, Peter the Great at last broke through the Swedish barrier round the eastern Baltic to give Russia an outlet to the open sea, and his much-sought window on the West. He captured a Swedish town called Nyen, where the River Neva flows into the Gulf of Finland and founded St Petersburg in its stead.

Despite their victory, 'the Russians have absolutely no order in waging war', as one Swede had put it. They had 'no order of battle ... They usually had infantry ... which they used in a very undisciplined fashion [including] those that run over the snow on [ski].'[13] This accurately mirrored the tactics of Peter the Great. In the Baltic campaign, which led to the founding of St Petersburg, he released hordes of cavalry flanked by swarms of skirmishers on skis.

Still the Swedish rulers of Finland eschewed standing ski regiments, but raised units by conscription as required. This was not as irresponsible as it first appears. Although the Norwegians founded skiing as a sport, it is fair to say that the ski meant more to Finland as a whole. Because the country is flat or gently undulating, pure Nordic skiing was the rule and there was none of the specialization demanded by running downhill, as in the ubiquitous Norwegian mountainous terrain. On that account, the Finns did not face technical decay. They needed the ski in their everyday life. Virtually everyone of military age could ski and instruction was therefore as superfluous as teaching the infantry to walk. So from a certain point of view, wartime conscription made sense. With its endless forests and lakes, the whole countryside was a friendly winter battlefield.

Skis loomed large again in the fateful Russian war of 1808–9. Part of the Napoleonic conflict, this was the other half of the campaign in which Sweden was repulsed by the Norwegians. The Russians attacked Finland with overwhelming force. Finnish skiers stemmed the onslaught here and there. It was to no avail. Count Buxhoevden, the general commanding the Russian army in Finland understood the circumstances all too well. He used Russian ski troops in undisciplined swarms, as usual, sometimes as advance guards, mostly as traditional skirmishers on the flanks of massed cavalry. Helped by poor generalship on the other side, Buxhoevden won the war. Thus the ski did much to defeat the Swedes and finally conquer Finland for the empire of the Tsars.

For Finland, mirroring Norway, the change of masters brought unaccustomed peace. That came to an end in 1917, with the Bolshevik revolution in Russia and the independence of Finland for the first time in recorded history. The Finns paid for this the following year with a civil war to crush their own communist insurrection and save their independence. Thereafter the Soviet Union reverted to the giant uncomfortable neighbour familiar from Russia of the *ancien régime*. There was a touch of the inevitable when the Soviet Union's Red Army invaded Finland on 30 November 1939 to begin the Winter War. Stalin's pretext was that from St Petersburg, or Leningrad as it was then known, the border was too close for comfort. For the safety of the city, he wanted it moved back; the concern of all Russian rulers since Peter the Great. The Finns begged to differ. The whole question had become urgent after the outbreak of the Second World War in September, accentuating Soviet fears of an attack via the Baltic by Germany or the Western Powers.

The Red Army began with a diffuse traditional offensive along the whole frontier of Finland – 900 km from the Baltic to the Arctic coast. In the south, a frontal attack on the Karelian Isthmus, the historic highway of invasion, would overrun southern Finland with the capital, Helsinki. The whole operation was supposed to take 10 or 12 days. As Stalin had unleashed 600,000 troops against a Finnish field army of 150,000, the estimate was not inherently unreasonable.

In the central front, where the country was narrowest, the Red Army launched a westwards push to Oulu, on the Gulf of Bothnia, in order to cut Finland in two at the waist. Out of this came the Battle of Suomussalmi. It was a typical piece of winter warfare, which, in the end, decided the outcome of the whole campaign.

Suomussalmi was a strategic village near the frontier on the road to Oulu. On 7 December it fell. The way to the Bothnian shore seemed open. The Red Army had attacked with two divisions in a pincer movement. Including specialist units, they numbered nearly 40,000 men. Opposing them were 7,000 Finns. The Soviet forces had abundant armour and air power at their disposal; the Finns had neither. Nor did the Finns have much artillery; their attackers had all they needed. Whether the Finns' true enemy was the Red Army or their own mediocre politicians who had starved them of equipment was a moot point. The officer corps worked out a strategy to offset both, with more success against the Soviet divisions, be it said. Mobility was all and it depended on the ski.

Luckily for the Finns, this particular winter was made for Nordic skiers. It was one of the coldest on record. More to the point, the early snow around Suomussalmi not only covered the landscape but also bore a certain weight, so that the whole terrain was skiable, and the going was good. When war broke out this played into the defenders' hands. Somehow two battalions of Finnish ski troops, about 800 men, stopped the Soviet advance outside the village.

The Finnish commander at Suomussalmi was a gifted field officer, Colonel Hjalmar Siilasvuo. To him, morale and adaptability were most of the game. On that principle, the bizarre disparity of strength was more apparent than real. The Finns also had another moral advantage: They concentrated on a single aim; survival, where the Soviet Union was distracted by the multiple objectives of a great Power.

Suomussalmi lay in a flat northern semi-wilderness, which to a Russian, in the graphic words of one Red Army soldier, was 'dark, empty and antagonistic … Its countless ridges and hills [are] covered with forest, its lakes and marshes make it grim and gloomy'.[14]

To the highly adapted inhabitants, with their different culture and language, it means home. This gave them the psychological mastery. They are children of the forest, and winter with its eerie, frosted silence, broken only by the muffled sough of skis is their natural season of the year. What is more, the maze of lakes and waterways interweaving their sombre pine-clad woodland ensured a tactical advantage by channelling a conventional attack along predictable paths.

Most of the troops at Suomussalmi came from such a landscape. They were connected with forestry, used to working in deep cold and moving in small groups. They were also hunters and marksmen. To these Finns, the ski was still an instrument of daily life. There was something atavistic about them. Particularly in the north they might use special long, broad, soft-tipped forest skis of old-fashioned solid wood to cope with the temperamental snow among the tree-roots and undergrowth. Like a throwback to another age, their bindings were often simple toestraps, into which they hooked the turned-up toes of *pieksu*, traditional high boots of cowhide marde by local cobblers. The purpose was ease of getting on and off their skis; necessary because they skied to move around but the ski was an encumbrance at work. Also when skiing across frozen lakes, it might be a matter of life and death instantly to kick off your skis if you broke through a weak patch of ice. The same applied to winter fighting, when seconds counted in slipping into your skis to speed away through the comforting prepared forest tracks after a raid. In other words, when they were mobilized, the Finnish soldiers were ready-trained. From a certain point of view, the war they faced was merely an extension of their daily life. It was just one more hunt on skis, with men instead of animals now the prey. They had long ancestral memories to guide them.

In 1555 the Swedish King Gustav Vasa – he of the Vasalopp – found himself at war with the Tsar Ivan the Terrible. As usual in the flat forests and swampy borderlands round Lake Ladoga and the Gulf of Finland, winter was the season for campaigning. 'Since there is much … brittle snow, not strong enough to bear [undistributed] weight', Gustav wrote knowledgeably late in January 1556 to his commanders in Satakunta, the border provinces of Finland, 'it is advisable that you conscript all skiers … that you can lay your hands on.'[15] And again, on 4 March, he enunciated the principles of winter warfare, the first to do so in fact:

> because of the deep snow everywhere, it is reasonable to assume that the Russians will mostly use skiers … in attack … Therefore we wish to make it clear that you recruit as many skiers as you can manage [so that] the enemy does not take you by surprise … And as it is to be assumed that the enemy will be in great force, we do not think it advisable to give battle on open land, but exploit your advantage in narrow [forest] paths, where the enemy cannot operate on a broad front.[16]

Four centuries on, at Suomussalmi, history repeated itself. The Red Army did stick in columns to the roads. The Finns used the whole terrain. As skiers, they worked instinctively in flying columns. They did not need specialized ski troops; theirs was a whole army on skis. Nonetheless there was an elite. Siilasvuo called this euphemistically 'reconnaissance units'.[17] The units consisted of 'about 50 men each … composed of unafraid, first-class skiers' and, he went on with quiet menace, 'they … never [came] back from their excursions with their mission unaccomplished. They were a terror to the enemy.' Or, to quote a captured Russian diary, 'the butchers', as the writer called the Finns, using typical Soviet invective, 'the butchers take full advantage of their great skill in skiing. They secretly approach our marching columns and with their knives stab to death all those leaving the road.'[18] Indeed a Russian epithet for white-clad Finns on skis was *belaya smert*, 'the white death'. One Soviet officer ruefully confessed that 'we had problems overcoming the Finnophobia among the troops'.[19]

Siilasvuo applied this psychological advantage to move his forces around and concentrate their strength at will. 'It was a matter of using flank attacks to carve up the column in separate pieces', as he put it, 'and encircle and destroy each one in turn.'[20] This was eventually dubbed the *motti*, a Finnish word meaning a pile of logs waiting to be sawn up. It was a journalistic contrivance. It became the slogan of the whole winter war, with the implication, good for propaganda, that the system had been lately improvised. It concealed the fact that Siilasvuo had learned from history.

In another winter war, the Finns had discovered how to deal with a numerically superior foe. Lieutenant-Colonel Count Karl Johan Stjernstedt, was a Swedish officer who had fought the Russians under Charles XII.[21] In 1741, he found himself in command of the Finnish border districts. He exploited a Russian weakness. Since the end of the seventeenth century, the Russians had standing regiments of skiers; but they did not really understand the ski. Nor did they show tactical initiative. They stuck to predictable routes in rigid formation like infantry on parade. Stjernstedt devised a method by which Finnish ski troops, with their greater mobility, would encircle part of a hostile column, and destroy it. They would repeat the process, gnawing a stronger force bit by bit, as it were, until it finally succumbed. The Swedes were defeated but Stjernstedt did win local victories. His tactics entered military lore. They were waiting for Siilasvuo in his hour of need. It was a kind of exalted guerrilla warfare. After many years, the Finns had lost none of their flair for this kind of fighting.

At Suomussalmi, Siilasvuo faced a tactical conundrum. To the north lay the 163rd Russian division; to the south, the 44th division. He only had the forces to deal with one at a time. He began with the 163rd, because it seemed the more aggressive. First, he drove a wedge between them by blocking a road. Then he proceeded to devour the 163rd *motti* by *motti*. The skiing was good, so he could switch his forces quickly over the terrain and creep up on the enemy unawares. He ploughed winter roads parallel to the Russian column, iced like a bob run here and there to speed the skiing as if it were a race. It also allowed him to move his few, obsolete pieces of artillery about for maximum effect. Even there, his disadvantage was not all it seemed. Although the Russians had much more artillery, this was mostly the flat-trajectory field gun, of little use against the shield of tree trunks in thick forest because that calls for the high-trajectory howitzer, which drops projectiles overhead.

Siilasvuo began his counter-offensive on 12 December. The cold was his ally. During the battle, the temperature dropped to −40°C but the Finns were unperturbed. They knew all about it, and dressed on the layer principle, all in woollen underclothes. Since they mostly skied fast, overheating was their trouble. Also they knew how to keep warm when at rest. Behind the lines, they had big specialized bell-tents ingeniously pitched round a small, portable wood-burning stove using the flue as the central pole. Outside, skis and sticks were stuck in the snow; inside the tent, with aromatic pine branches strewn on the floor and dimly lit like some tribal dwelling, with 10 or 15 men draped radially round the stove, crackling from the sap of fresh-cut conifer, it was as hot as a sauna – genuine examples of which, incidentally, were to be found in shallow dugouts near the front. After a raid the Finns were back in the warmth with something hot to drink, in as long as it took to ski a kilometre or two – say a quarter of an hour. The wounded were hauled back in *pulkas*, or boat-like sledges by reindeer, dogs or men on the prepared tracks, to reach a forward dressing station within an hour.

The contrast with the Russians was grotesque. They mostly had no proper winter clothes or shelter. The Finns would space attacks, so that the cold could have time do its work and spread depression and demoralization. The Russians often froze to death in droves where they stood; yet another, grisly proof that there is no bad weather, only bad clothing. This was the outcome of a rigid timetable that had gone awry – the triumph of policy over tactics!

Prisoner of his own propaganda, Stalin believed that the attack on Finland would be an armed parade, with happy workers welcoming the Red Army as the liberator from their wicked capitalist bosses. From another point of view: 'We could fire one shot, and the Finns would put up their hands and surrender', Khrushchev, the original de-Stalinizer, but then one of Stalin's closest henchmen reputedly said with hindsight – 'or so we thought'.[22]

Either way, the Soviet leaders had bungled the affair. They had never expected to fight a winter war. Inconceivably, despite all historical precedent, the Red Army had no ski troops. They tried improvising in the field, but 'this meant little', as Marshal Gustav Mannerheim, the Finnish commander-in-chief, blandly put it, 'because ... skiing, especially as practised in war, cannot be mastered in a few weeks'.[23] What is more, without time to copy models from the West, a command economy was incapable of supplying the right kind of skis and bindings. The upshot was that, throughout the war, the Finns had a virtual monopoly of the ski. This gave them a unique technical supremacy. There was also something else. Khadzhen-Umar Mamsurov, a Soviet regimental commander who improvised the one major skiing unit of the Red Army described how he did acquire some skiing volunteers from Leningrad, but 'they could not even read a compass or a map properly'.[24] The Finns, however, in part because of the recondite sport of orienteering, were adept at both, which reinforced their crushing individual superiority.

The Russians also faced demoralization in a different quarter. A Soviet officer put it this way: 'My whole division was dressed in [dark] jackets ... the black spots on the snow were good targets.'[25] For their part the Finns were camouflaged in white overclothes – improvised from sheets brought from home where necessary – to blend in with the snow. In the few hours of daylight, and especially at dawn and dusk, they were like ghostly shapes on ski; misty shadows flitting across the subtle green and blue tints of snow under a northern winter sky. A few elite Russian soldiers followed their lead but most passively remained in the ordinary brown uniform of the Red Army. They were helpless victims of unseen Finnish snipers dodging among the trees, the fading hiss of skis on snow the only sign of their presence as they disappeared.

With hardly any anti-tank weapons, the Finns fought back in close combat with hand grenades, dynamite, or the primitive incendiary devices they dubbed 'Molotov cocktails' after the Soviet Foreign Minister. In Siilasvuo's envelopment of the Russian 163rd division at Suomussalmi, immobilized enemy tanks were part of the barricades that demarcated the *mottis*, and stopped the one from rescuing the other. The overwhelming Russian air power was all but useless because the canopy of forest and snow effectively hid the Finns. The whole 163rd division, meanwhile was helplessly strung out in a stranded column 40 km long on the road to the border. The eerie misty shapes of white-clad Finnish skiing soldiers, with their characteristic powerful heaving style, rifles slung across their backs, roamed up and down in silence broken only by the creak of ski sticks in cold packed snow, blended with rifle shots and the staccato bursts of automatic weapons that hinted at the destruction of each *motti*, one by one. On their side, the Finns had the Suomi sub-machine gun, a rare domestic product, said then to be the most advanced weapon of its kind.

At a certain point, the Soviet onslaught cracked. Defeat, as usual, began not at the front, but at the rear, in the minds of the commanders. From generals down to lieutenants in charge of platoons, there was a paralysis of will. 'Contrary to his Finnish adversary', so Mannerheim explained, 'the Russian infantryman ... was a mass fighter ... incapable of independent action.'[26]

True to a certain degree, this hardly does justice to Mannerheim's rôle. He embodied not only Finnish resistance but the source of Soviet shortcomings. Like other ambitious Finns, Mannerheim had served in the Russian Army under the Tsars. A Swedish-speaking Finn, he was born in 1867, attaining the rank of Major-General before fleeing the Bolshevik revolution in 1917 for his native land. There he commanded the forces that defeated the communist uprising, and became Regent for a time. He was the architect of an independent Finland; in the absence of a great political leader, he *was* Finland.

Mannerheim knew the mind of the Russian soldier intimately. More to the point, he was a Baron in the nobility of Sweden and, tall, imposing, elegant, looked every inch the part. That was *his* secret weapon. The drab despots in the Kremlin respected a strong leader. At heart they were also dreadful snobs. Having destroyed their own nobility, they grovelled before a title. Confronted with a true aristocrat like Mannerheim, they nursed an inferiority complex. That was compounded by the prominence of Finns in Russia before the Revolution; the last two Russian governors of Alaska, for instance, happened to be Finnish. Whatever his technical failings Mannerheim had the fire of leadership. His was the unseen presence that held his own army together, and disconcerted the enemy.

It filtered down to the soldiers in the field – on both sides of the front. At Suomussalmi the Russians, broken in spirit, plodded gloomily back towards the border. They stumbled through the snow leaving all their vehicles behind. The

Finns pursued them, like primitive hunters on skis slaughtering their hapless prey. Their own records say that they killed 5,000 men. Nobody knows how many thousands more perished by cold in their confusion. By 28 December, the Finns had retaken the village of Suommusalmi. Two days later, the Soviet 163rd Division had ceased to exist.

After a continuous battle of three weeks, fighting against the odds, Colonel Siilasvuo might have been mentally exhausted. However, with his granite face and hooded eyes hinting at some force within, he was the personification of *sisu*; the great attribute in which Finns see themselves – with its shadow side of perverseness and obstinacy. It underpinned the great Finnish long-distance runners between the wars and now their skiers, transformed into troops.

After the Soviet 163rd Division, it was the turn of the 44th, and for Siilasvuo and his little army there was no rest. In skiing alone, always moving in endless frost, they had already done more than their share. Beyond that they had the strain of battle, having fought hard and taken casualties, yet perversely almost seemed to have enjoyed themselves.

Again the explanation was the ski. The ordinary Finnish junior officer was not so much a military personage as a citizen leader on ski. A confirmed individualist, he was a brilliant tactical improviser. From long peacetime contact, he understood the limitations of his men. Going into battle he skied fast, but at a pace that did not exhaust them, so that they arrived in full vigour with strength for the fight and enough in reserve for the swift withdrawal that was an essential part of their style. It almost seemed an amalgam of ski racing and orienteering. The distinction between sport and war was blurred. On the other side, a Russian officer made the point:

> Tens of thousands ... go to watch soccer matches. But I think that soccer is of little use for national defence ... You have [twenty-two] people playing and thousands merely standing and applauding. We must build up skiing and devote our ... attention to the defensive aspects of sport.[27]

The Finns had long since grasped the connection. It underpinned the morale of the troops at Suomussalmi. Having disposed of the 163rd Russian division, as if moving to another race, they skied over to the Raate road, the southern route to the border, where the 44th Division was waiting passively, the commander transfixed. The Finns continued their work, skiing up and down along their tracks, slicing the column in Stjernstedt's *mottis* as before and within a week, at little cost to themselves, the 44th division had shared the fate of the 163rd. Once more a forest road with bloodstained snow was packed for miles with mounds of enemy dead and abandoned ordnance strewn like a junk heap. By 8 January 1940, the Battle of Suomussalmi was over. The Finns had *naturally* won, as they might have said. In London, 'Finnish Mastery in the Art of War', was the headline in *The Times*; 'like a page from an epic poem', it went on, consumed by the spirit of the age.[28]

There were other like encounters, but Suomussalmi was the turning point of the war. It was a classic of its kind. The Red Army did not try to cut Finland in two again. The Finns could not know at the time that they had won the battle for national survival. After Suomussalmi, the Russians decided to cut their losses. They had other, pressing international concerns and time was not on their side. They abandoned all thought of conquest, which was their real intention, to the point of jettisoning a puppet government they had installed on Finnish soil under a renegade Finnish Communist called Otto Kuusinen. They settled for a negotiated peace. When the fighting stopped, on 13 March 1940, the Soviet Union achieved its original stated objectives. It moved the border back from Leningrad, annexed a swathe of Finnish territory, and acquired a naval base on the coast of Finland. Even the Kremlin, however, saw this as a pyrrhic victory. The Red Army had lost some 250,000 killed, against 25,000 Finns. Little Finland, albeit at a terrible cost, had fought the mighty Soviet Union to a standstill and humiliated it before the world. It was a strange fate for a country that had pioneered winter warfare but was only used to set-piece battles on the plains and could not adapt to the very different circumstances of a Nordic forest.

Four hundred thousand Finns spontaneously left the occupied territories under Soviet control, and were quietly resettled in the rest of the country. Defeated but unconquered, Finland had kept her independence, which has lasted to this day. Or as Mannerheim put it, 'Such a nation has earned the right to live.'[29] The ramifications, however, went far beyond the fate of Finland or the security of Leningrad. For one thing, the Germans had been watching events with the closest attention. The apparent weakness of the Red Army, especially in leadership, undoubtedly had a hand in persuading Hitler to oblige the Allies and attack Russia the following year.

Just as fateful was the effect on the Red Army itself. Khrushchev told a story about Voroshilov, the Soviet Minister of Defence, and Stalin, in the aftermath of Suomussalmi: '"You have only yourself to blame for all this", shouted Voroshilov. "You're the one who annihilated the Old Guard of the army, you had our best generals killed!"'[30] This alluded to the Stalinist purges of the 1930s, with their show trials, the model for today's international tribunals. 'Stalin rebuffed him [so Khrushchev went on] and at that, Voroshilov picked up a platter with a roast suckling pig on it and smashed it on the table.'

Voroshilov survived but the commander of the 44th Division, a certain A. I. Vinogradov, was not so lucky. An order of the Soviet General Staff dated 19 January tersely announced that he had been court-martialled and shot before the remnants of his own troops, *pour encourager les autres*. The document was baldly headed 'the reasons for the defeat of the 44th infantry division, and the punishment of the culprits'.[31]

On that account, even more interesting was the simultaneous execution of one I. T. Pakhomenko. He was the chief political commissar of the 44th Division. At the time, the Red Army had a dual chain of command; military and political. Each unit had its so-called *politruk*, or political representative of the Communist

Party. He had to countersign every order issued by an officer down to platoon level. The officer corps was bitterly opposed to this dilution of their authority. They were not displeased with the imbroglio of the Winter War. It enabled them to rid themselves of the political interference in operational matters to which the setbacks in Finland were largely due. It also enabled them to right a minor grudge. The Communist Party had abolished the old military titles, imposing horrible acronyms on the rank of colonel or above; now generals could be generals again.

Stalin was so chastened by the Winter War that he allowed the high command to start reforming the Soviet armed forces and rectifying the deficiencies exposed in the forests and snowdrifts of Finland. The work was not finished by the time Hitler attacked in June 1941 but it had gone far enough to save the Red Army from total collapse and secure victory in the end. The Germans guaranteed their own defeat by being unprepared for winter warfare – but that's another story. Without the Winter War, history might well have taken another turn.

So the outcome of the last War may be said to have flowed from the Battle of Suomussalmi. A few thousand Finnish skiers who happened to be soldiers probably decided the fate of the world as we know it. In a romantic sidelight there were the foreign idealists who wanted to help gallant little Finland defend democracy and freedom. 'Many a modern Byron on skis volunteered', to quote one gently ironic Finn, 'and, though few got as far as the firing line … there are men who think of Finland, a little wistfully perhaps, as the country they almost died for.'[32]

# 36

# Skiing Since 1945

By the outbreak of war in September 1939, skiing had found its modern form. What followed since peace returned in 1945 has been popularization and technical refinement. Much was due to Marshall Aid, under which the United States poured money into post-war Europe to revive a bankrupt continent. Austria, a vanquished enemy, used some of her share to build cableways and ski lifts. This was part of a far-sighted plan to foster tourism and hence promote national recovery. It also shaped events elsewhere.

From 1945 to 1955, Austria was occupied by Britain, America, Russia and France. The French zone was in the Tyrol, centred at Innsbruck, which meant that the slopes were at the barrack gates. Since France had a conscript army, the upshot was that tens of thousands of men from all over the country, of all classes of society, were introduced to skiing.

When General de Gaulle became President in 1958, he saw in all this an aspect of his grand design for France. He wanted to produce Olympic ski champions as a way of regenerating national pride. By judicious state finance and through an extraordinary national coach called Honoré Bonnet, the General had his way. There had been isolated gold medallists; Henri Oreiller in the straight downhill at St Moritz in 1948 for one – the first French Olympic champion, at the first post-war Winter Olympics where, for the first time, medals were awarded for the separate Alpine events. De Gaulle's breakthrough, however, came in the ninth Olympic Winter Games at Innsbruck in 1964 with three gold medals: François Bonlieu in the giant slalom, Christine Goitschel in the womens' slalom, and her sister, Marielle in the giant slalom.

The giant slalom was a relatively new event, its first Olympic appearance being at the Oslo games of 1952. It was a kind of halfway house between the slalom, which required skill, and the straight downhill, a test of courage. It was in all but name a tightly controlled downhill course, with wide gates. In the tenth Winter Olympics at Grenoble in 1968, Jean-Claude Killy – most elegant and self-contained of skiers – won that event, and the slalom and straight downhill too. He thereby repeated the Austrian Toni Sailer's performance at the Cortina Winter Olympics of 1956 in winning all the Alpine medals. Marielle Goitschel – an engaging down to earth character whose motto was that of *Madame Mère*, Napoleon's mother, 'Just so long as it lasts' – won the womens' slalom. She and Killy had between them broken the Swiss and Austrian hegemony. Since they had won on French soil, they were doubly heroic, and the nation basked in their reflected glory. De Gaulle had achieved his aim, although 1968 was also the year of the students' revolt – but that's another story.

To De Gaulle, the French medallists were simply the apex of the so-called Olympic pyramid; that is, mass participation. That was his real goal: to improve the health of the nation and enhance political stability. It was all very well giving citizens a winter holiday, but ignoring an outlet for pent-up urban frustration was, in French terms, politically unwise and skiing was a safety valve. De Gaulle, far-seeing, also wished to provide work and avoid depopulation of the Alpine valleys, with a resultant drift to the cities and an injection of yet more urban discontent, which would have been just as bad. On all counts, he ordained a quick expansion of winter sports. He even enlisted the help of the Church, and priests in flapping cassocks were to be seen swooping down on skis with local schoolchildren to implant the idea that there was a future in their native slopes after all.

With state subsidies, and supervised planning, a bumper crop of shining new artificial ski resorts sprang up to develop the French Alps during the 1960s. Beautiful most of them were not; all concrete and high rise in a Le Corbusier lampoon, like the epitome of its kind, Les Menuires in Savoy. Others tried to mimic the old village at the heart of Swiss and Austrian resorts with a nostalgic chalet style. There the forerunner was Meribel, also in Savoy.

Meribel was unexpectedly the creation of a Scots entrepreneur called Peter Lindsay. As the story goes, during the last war, Lindsay was an officer in a British regiment, which, at the end of hostilities in 1945, found itself in the French Alps. Passing through Paris on his way – unenthusiastically – back to Scotland for demobilization, he visited Baron Elie de Rothschild, who had been in the same regiment. Baron Elie asked what Lindsay really wanted to do. Lindsay, a pre-war skier and climber, wanted to develop a marvellous little valley called Meribel into a new kind of ski resort that preserved local architecture. In that case the Baron – without a moment's thought – would finance him. So Lindsay had himself demobilized in Paris, turned back and settled down happily in Meribel to realize his idea. He may have set the scene for what came later.

Whatever their style, all these resorts were indisputably functional. They had urbanized holiday accommodation, ski terrain, groomed pistes on the doorstep and a rational layout so that each ski run finished at the start of the next lift. It was all designed by official experts from Paris under the aegis of the Minister of Sports, Maurice Herzog, wartime resistance leader and, conqueror of Annapurna in the Himalayas, a popular hero and mountaineering legend. Thus mass skiing as we know it was hatched out of Gaullist political calculation.

Naturally all this had its prelude. The first artificial resort was Sestriere in the Italian Savoy Alps. Founded in 1930 as a forlorn hotel in the shape of a squat cylindrical tower, it had a futuristic air. It belonged to the Agnelli family, of the Fiat automotive concern in Turin, an image of their singular private ambition.

Sestriere, however, was an eccentric forerunner. The first true purpose-built resort as planned property development to colonize untenanted land was in

America, at Sun Valley, Idaho. It was the brainchild of Averell Harriman. A future United States Secretary of Commerce, Harriman also happened to be Chairman of the Board of the Union Pacific Railroad. To sustain passenger traffic he wanted to build a ski resort along the line. Sun Valley opened in 1936. It was not only the first modern purpose-built Alpine ski resort but the first in America to be conceived as a destination in its own right.

Harriman moulded American Alpine skiing in its formative years. To choose the site of Sun Valley, Harriman had called in a certain Count Felix Schaafgotsche, who was Austrian. On that account or otherwise, Sun Valley used Austrian instructors for its ski school from the start. American downhill skiing began as an Austrian import. It became a branch of the Arlberg school.

Schaafgotsche was the brother of a ski instructor under Hannes Schneider at St Anton and in 1939 Schneider himself moved to America. He came as a refugee from the Nazis after the *Anschluss* – Hitler's annexation of Austria – the previous year. Schneider largely owed his escape to Harvey Gibson, an influential American banker with German connections. Gibson owned a rising ski resort in New Hampshire called North Conway, to which he appointed Schneider as skiing director. Schneider settled there for the rest of his life. He put his stamp on Alpine skiing in America. Authoritative as always, he laid down the rules of preparing runs from the kind of grass needed for the underlayer, to the removal of natural obstacles. His pupils, émigrés like himself, dominated the ski schools from coast to coast. He could fulfil himself because, unlike the Alps of his homeland, in America it was a question of private enterprise and building up from scratch.

In the 1930s and 1940s, however, American skiing was somewhat exclusive. Popularization, there as elsewhere, came with the post-war years. In the United States, one impulse was the return of the Tenth Mountain Division. It had fought well in Italy, and traced its origins to the embryonic American ski patrols, privately organized to keep order on the slopes and the first of their kind in the world. Another influence was the ex-servicemen from the army of occupation in Germany or Austria and those who had studied – or loafed around – in Europe under the GI Bill of Rights. Good propaganda came from the American Olympic breakthrough; Gretchen Frazer taking the first medal for the country by winning the slalom at St Moritz in 1948, followed by Andrea Mead Lawrence, double winner in slalom and giant slalom at Oslo in 1952.

All this was marginal at best. At least General de Gaulle saw that populist skiing belonged to mass tourism which, in its turn, was to depend on cheap air travel, which he did not foresee. Sooner than most, however, he did grasp the rôle of television. That was what would bring in the crowds. Modern downhill skiing is a creation of the little screen. The first Olympic Winter Games to be televised were those at Cortina d'Ampezzo, in Italy, in 1956. The impact was modest because it was only in black and white. Glorious colour finally made its Olympic debut at the tenth Winter Games in Grenoble in 1968.

That was a watershed of sorts. These were not only the first games to be televised in colour: they were the first to be conceived for the little screen, from the opening and closing ceremonies as chauvinistic television spectaculars – another Gaullist innovation – to the scheduling of events for live coverage. Henceforth the masters were the television networks and their audience strewn about the globe. This is as it should be, since downhill skiing is no spectator sport. By contrast, it is televisual to a degree. Only an aficionado will stand by the side of a track for a fleeting glimpse of skis topped by some figure flashing by at ever-increasing speed; or sustain the repetitive waddling of the special slalom. The television camera can zoom in to give individuality to some anonymous shape and pick out technical finesse. As in other sports, the advent of electronic timing, measuring to within a hundredth of a second, or a thousandth if you wish, somehow deadens the excitement on the piste itself. It all makes for good television, however, and many a slope has turned into an outside broadcast location, strewn with cameras cables and satellite dishes, like an aliens' landing site.

The World Cup thrived on television too, although it was a creation of the press. Mooted in at least one article during the 1960s, it was invented by a journalist called Serge Lang, of the French sporting newspaper *L'Équipe*. With all its editorial verve, *L'Équipe* promoted Lang's idea. The reputation of *L'Equipe* is such that, within a year, the Cup had become a reality. It was first run in the winter of 1966–7. For the record, the winner was the Jean-Claude Killy, one of the greatest downhill skiers, while the women's cup went to Nancy Greene, of Canada.

The origins of the World Cup lay in what the participants themselves laughingly called the ski-circus. A caravan of racers, journalists, trainers, attendants and hangers-on roamed the Alps in an aimless succession of unconnected races. It was difficult to bolster interest over a whole winter. Inspired by the football World Cup, the skiing version was designed as a cure. By linking the different disciplines in a single contest it could, with luck, keep tension going until the last fixture of the season. Also, as an annual event, the cup dissipated the flatness of an off season, when there were neither World Championships nor Olympic Winter Games. The Cup started as an independent competition (with Lang as its Secretary-General) but was quickly absorbed by the FIS. In a discreet feud with the International Olympic Committee one purpose of the Cup was to be a counterweight to the Winter Olympics. Indeed, the races for the Cup spread from Europe to North America, and yet further still, so that it became truly international. From a certain point of view, winning the World Cup became the equivalent of an Olympic gold medal. It certainly opened up competition. The prime example was Ingemar Stenmark, the white-clad Swede from Southern Lapland, who broke the hegemony of the Alpine countries by winning the cup in three successive seasons from 1976.

This was all to the good. The ski-circus was a freemasonry. Nationality meant little; personality was all. That was what made good copy for the journalists and they and the stars lived in symbiosis. The same held for manufacturers of skiing equipment. They, too, belonged to the ski-circus because placing their products with the champions – they hoped – meant sales among an ever-burgeoning public. Given that equipment dominated skiing, the market was great and so, too, the competition. Companies even-handedly sponsored skiers; all they wanted were winners, irrespective of flag. Also in the days of the amateur illusion, the ski circus was a refreshing island of frank professionalism; suitably doctored, with more or less success, not to offend the Olympic movement.

The World Cup as television spectacle was also a showcase for the winter tourist industry. The resorts where the events were run had what amounted to extended free (we suppose) commercials throughout the season. One side effect of televised races was to promote leisure skiing and, more than any other single cause, generate mass participation.

Although the World Cup began as a purely Alpine trophy, it was only a matter of time before the Nordic disciplines were drawn in too. Ski-jumping began in 1980, followed by cross-country in 1982, and the Nordic Combined in 1984. That too helped to open competition. Thus Stefania Belmondo of Italy won the women's cross-country World Cup in 1999, upsetting the domination of the Nordic countries and Russia. By contrast, Bjørn Dæhlie, of Norway set a record, as yet unbroken, by winning the mens' Cup for cross-country six times between 1989 and 1999, besides six Olympic gold medals during the same decade. He became, naturally, a national hero because, for all its globalization, skiing still occupies a place in the Norwegian psyche.

In ski-jumping, the arrival of the World Cup coincided with a quantum shift in performance. The critical point of standard jumping hills exceeded 100 m and the so-called ski-flying around 150 m. Luckily all this was in the dawn of the IT era. The complexity of the various systems of points to decide standings added to the sheer number of participants and keeping track of Winter Olympics and World Championships into the bargain cried out for computerization. In fact, computers had first been used at the eighth Winter Olympics at Squaw Valley in 1960. It was still the age of the mainframe, with links to distant installations, and press rooms battered by the staccato hammering of high-speed teleprinters.

Proliferation of events added to the information overload. The original Alpine events of downhill and slalom were first awarded separate medals at the 1948 Winter Olympics at St Moritz; the first post-war games and the first since Garmisch-Partenkirchen in 1936. Then came the giant slalom, followed, after a decent interval, by the super-giant slalom, or Super G, more loosely controlled and approaching even more closely a straight downhill course. It first appeared in the World Cup of 1986, with its Olympic debut at Calgary in 1988. That year, the Alpine Combination was revived, having lapsed since the St Moritz Games of 1948. The new version required separate downhill and slalom races. So in the half-century since the first Alpine Olympic events at Garmisch, the programme had swollen from four to 14. This was all part of a drive to specialization on the one hand and opening competition on the other.

It was in the Nordic disciplines, however, that proliferation ran riot. It began innocently enough with a women's 10 km cross-country race at the Oslo Winter Olympics in 1952. That was the start of women's Olympic participation and simply evened out what had been a male preserve. It was followed in all fairness at the Cortina winter games of 1956 by a womens' 3 × 5 km relay. As on the downhill *piste*, however, specialization was beginning to raise its head. The Cortina Olympics added a mens' 30 km race. The winner was the imperturbable Finn Verkko Hakulinen, but Pavel Koltchin from the then Soviet Union was third.

Indeed, those games of 1956 saw the Olympic breakthrough of the Soviet Union and an end to the domination of the Nordic countries. There had been a prelude at the 1954 World Championships at Falun, in Sweden. They included the first recognized international 30 km race and the winner was a Russian called Vladimir Kutsin. Running at Cortina in the Winter Olympics for the first time, the Soviet Union took home a clutch of silver and bronze medals in cross-country, besides winning the men's relay and the women's 10 km events. This was during the Cold War, so Soviet behaviour had a political undertone. The Kremlin was now using international sport to fortify national self-esteem, and promote communist ideology. It was in fact confined to an artificially generated elite with little of the mass participation that propaganda claimed. Before that pious sham ended with the fall of the Berlin Wall and the collapse of communism in the early 1990s, the Soviet system had had two lasting effects on the Winter Olympics, beneficial or not. For one thing, masking State subsidy of competitors by bogus employment unconnected with sport ironically showed the capitalist world how to circumvent the amateur rules and, by the 1990s, introduce open Olympic Games. For another, the Soviets saw propaganda in the sheer number of medals, whatever they stood for and this consequently favoured the proliferation of events.

At the Innsbruck Winter Olympics of 1964, a women's 5 km cross-country race was added – won by a Soviet – and a second ski-jumping competition for the men. Jumps of 90 m were now usual among the elite so there was another hill with a critical point of around 75 m for the less venturesome. Because there was also a Nordic combination and, since the Squaw Valley Games of 1960, a biathlon, or combined cross-country race and target shooting with a rifle carried over the whole course, the programme was becoming unwieldy. In the end, it was exacerbated by the skating technique.

This arose because it proved faster. Its essence was pure sliding without the need for a wax that gripped. Adhesion for the kick-off, exactly as on the ice with skates, came from the inside edge of the rear ski, and sliding from that of the other. However, it aroused fierce opposition, particularly from the Norwegians, because it was so specialized that it threatened to divorce elite racers from the ordinary skier. After a Norwegian rearguard action, the traditional technique was preserved under the name of 'classic'. This led to official recognition on the one hand of classic and on the other, skating events; the latter now dubbed 'free style'. The distinction first appeared internationally in 1982 at the World Ski Championships in Oslo. Among the men, the 15 and 30 km races were free-style, but the 50 km remained classic. After much controversy and experimentation, this took yet another form. By the twentieth Winter Olympics in Turin, in 2006, the 15 km race (10 km for the women) had reverted to classic. There was also a classic revival in the 30 km event, 15 km for the women. Each was run in two equal sections; one classic, and free-style in the other. Technically, it was called the pursuit. This tacitly recognized the monotony of skating for the public, against the artistic variation of the classic technique, with its ballet-like repertoire of different steps. To complete the picture, duplicate sprints were established; one for each technique, not to mention team jumping and Nordic combined, with a sprint for the latter.

The upshot was that from the first to the twentieth Winter Olympics, Chamonix to Turin, 1924 to 2006, the traditional skiing disciplines multiplied from 3 to 18; 28 including the variations of the biathlon. This means an annual inflation of 10 per cent. Nor does that include new Alpine events like snowboarding, with its roots in surfing; the confusingly named free style – bearing no relation to its Nordic namesake – which, with its aerial contortions, belongs to acrobatics, or even moguls, running through the mini-seismic hummocks of that name caused by ruthless downhill skiers, all of which lie outside the mainstream.

The skating revolution led to the massed start, and for much the same reason. New machines enabled the preparation of wide tracks needed by both. The massed start had always belonged to the relay race, besides the Vasalopp and kindred mass events. Its Olympic debut in an individual discipline, however, was at Albertville in 1992. By the Turin Olympics of 2006 it had appeared in the 50 km event, and the corresponding women's 30 km race; both now free-style events. (The winner of the 50 km, Giorgio di Centa, of Italy, took 2 hours 6 minutes 11.8 seconds, against the 4 hours 26 minutes 30 seconds of Torjus Hemmestveit in the world's first 50 km race at Huseby in 1888.) It was another impact of television. For one thing the massed start shortened the proceedings. Also the sensational, underhand confusion of the start and the simplicity of the finish, with the winner being the first to arrive, made for good viewing. By the same token, it degraded the sport by making the contestants part of a crowd fighting each other instead of the individual racing against the clock in the sequential start.

The older system had its own subtleties. The Scandinavian ski racer was often a hunter at home. 'Now he himself is a hunted animal', as one Norwegian author graphically put it, 'and minutes and seconds are the spear with which he will be slain.'[1] The hunting metaphor encapsulated one of the great duels of modern cross-country ski racing. This was beween Sixten Jernberg and the equally great little Finn, Veikko Hakulinen in the 50 km event at the 1958 World Ski Championships at Lahti, in Finland. It was played out before an audience of 60,000. Hakulinen started 30 seconds after Jernberg, and after 20 km was only 17 seconds behind, the rasp of his ski and sticks all too audible in the winter air. Jernberg bided his time, and then instinctively pulled ahead. In his own words:

Hakulinen … had made desperate attempts to overtake me … Now I had my great chance … He would be forced to fall behind and … lose contact with me, and he would not be able to overcome that. I know [when hunting] how this sort of thing affects dogs that have been running for a long time and following a scent.[2]

Having broken Hakulinen mentally, Jernberg won by over a minute. It was grim psychology, a product of the true lone wolf fighting on a single track. The fact that they were using the classic style also affected their behaviour. Mass starts and skating have produced another cast of mind, more akin to the athlete on his running track than the skier in the snow.

To be fair, the modern skating style was an outgrowth of technology and landscape. It comes naturally on the flat. Between the wars, Swedes and Finns used it to break long-distance records on frozen lakes and rivers. The technique flourished, however, during the 1960s in the recondite sport of ski orienteering. This is the winter version of normal orienteering or racing between checkpoints given as map references, with a compass to show the way. To cope with crust on untracked snow, orienteering skis had a partial steel edge along the inside edge of each ski. This was ideal for skating, which uses the inside edge, because it gave the proper grip. Swedish ski orienteerers became masters of the style, because they gained thereby on forest roads or frozen lakes and peat bogs that littered the terrain. This was however a little world of its own, closed off from ordinary ski racing.

Someone had to bridge the gap, and the key figure here was a Finn called Pauli Siitonen. During the early 1960s, he perfected skating in ski orienteering. Unusually, he was also a cross-country racer. He ran in the 50 km event at the Grenoble Winter Olympics in 1968, coming nineteenth. Thereafter he concentrated on international touring races. These are long-distance mass events that, inspired by the Swedish Vasalopp, have proliferated since the 1960s. Away from official interference, Siitonen evolved his skating technique.

Somehow he came in contact with Bill Koch, an extraordinary American from Vermont. Koch was the first American cross-country skier of the first rank. Sensationally, he came second in the 30 km race at the Innsbruck Olympics of 1976. He owed this to an intermittent use of skating. Influenced by Siitonen, Koch proceeded to skate all through subsequent events. Thanks to this technique, he won the first World Cup in 1982. The same season, he came third in the 30 km at the World Championships. That established skating technique for good. By virtue of his medals, Koch had the kudos, but Siitonen was the pioneer. In fact, among central European skiers, skating was long called the 'Siitonen step'.

As usual, technique followed equipment. Competitive skating needed good glide in all conditions, and a sharp edge without artificial reinforcement. This came with the advent of synthetic materials. Their great advantage over wood was that they did not absorb moisture, so they ran fast even in wet snow. In a repetition of the Splitkein era, Peter Østbye was once more the pioneer. In 1951, he patented a bonded, composite ski of plastic, the purpose of which was to develop a strong, waterproof design.[3] He made a few experimental pairs but they never went into production. Østbye had been a collaborator during the wartime Nazi occupation, which meant forced sale of his Splitkein concern and, in the bitter post-war recrimination, great personal antagonism. That reinforced the prejudice of traditional ski manufacturers against new technology. They stuck to wood and duly paid the price.

The use of new materials originated in Alpine skiing. The first model to be put into production was the Gomme ski. It appeared in 1946. Oddly enough, it was English, and that is a story of its own. It begins in the 1920s at the Cavendish Laboratory in Cambridge. A physicist called Norman Adrian de Bruyne – of Trinity College, Isaac Newton's old college – was working at the Cavendish on atomic structure but, with the soul of an entrepeneur, he switched to aeronautical engineering and founded his own research company in Cambridge. To improve aircraft construction, he developed high-performance synthetic resin adhesives based on Kaurit. He called them 'Aerolite'. They were extensively used to build the all-wood de Havilland Mosquito fighter bomber during the Second World War. One of the companies involved in its production was Gomme, a family firm at High Wycombe, near London, which normally made furniture. Among de Bruyne's techniques used in the Mosquito was stressed and moulded plywood. Meanwhile, in 1942, de Bruyne produced 'Redux', the first modern synthetic structural adhesive for metals. After the war, Donald Gomme, a grandson of the founder, guided the firm back to peacetime use. He had skied since 1922 and saw the potential of de Bruyne's work in a new generation of skis.

So to diversify the boredom of mass-producing furniture, Donald Gomme manufactured his eponymous ski. It consisted of a thin steel core bonded to a plastic layer above and finished with laminated wood as the upper surface. The sole was a thin layer of hard wood bonded directly to the steel. Furthermore, the steel projected a few millimetres to form an edge. From several points of view, this was an innovative construction. It was the first composite metal ski on the market, the first steel one and the first with a one-piece integrated steel edge. Also this was the first ski built to a specification, so that one pair was exactly like the other. The first models had too great a camber and tips so soft and thin that they broke in soft snow. These drawbacks rectified, the British team at the 1948 Winter Olympics in St Moritz used the ski. Since they finished in the lower depths of the results, it was no advertisement and the Gomme ski quickly disappeared from the market. Donald Gomme himself, perhaps in expiation for the hideous furniture he had perpetrated, eventually became a patron of the arts. Nonetheless his creation was the precursor of modern technology in making skis.

The breakthrough was another by-product of wartime aircraft production. An American aeronautical engineer called Howard Head, a skier himself, also began designing composite metal and plastic skis; aluminium in this case. With a technical and marketing bent, besides the kind of public that escaped Gomme, Head set up a dedicated ski factory, releasing his first model in 1950. Thereafter the Head ski, as it was called, achieved an almost iconic status. With modifications, Head introduced Gomme's integrated steel edge, which did much for flexibility. At first, Head cornered the market but of course other companies, notably in France, Switzerland and Austria were soon aggressively competing with new designs and new materials, fibreglass for one. The upshot was that by the late 1960s, the bonded synthetic ski monopolized Alpine skiing and, in the process, wiped out the Scandinavian manufacture of downhill wooden skis.

Alpine skiing had pioneered synthetic products because of its simplicity. After all, it merely demands speed downhill. In the first place this implies a slippery running surface. Secondly the ski must have rigid torsion to keep the whole edge in contact with the snow, and hold turns on steep, hard slopes. That explained the use of metal. It made skis as rigid laterally as you like.

All this was unspeakably crude when compared with Nordic skiing. Scandinavian ski makers thought that no synthetic product could ever cope with the subtleties of the cross-country track. They reckoned without technological advances, unfettered thought, the subtlety of the algorithm and the power of marketing. They had forgotten the prophetic experimentation of Peter Østbye. Continental manufacturers, however, eyed the potential of the Nordic market, with its boundless reservoir of cross-country skiers. Regardless of cost, they had hordes of engineers, chemists and so on, designing cross-country skis with glass fibre structure and advanced plastic soles. These new devices had their international breakthrough at the FIS World Ski Championships of 1974 at Falun, in Sweden. This happened in the 30 km race, the opening event on 17 February. Although they did not realize it, for the Scandinavian ski makers this was their day of doom.

Snow and air temperatures oscillated around freezing point. With their sticky going, these are about the worst conceivable circumstances for wooden skis. Conversely they were an ideal test for the new synthetic generation. The upshot was that Thomas Magnusson, a Swede, won on Kneissl plastic skis from Austria.[4] Runner-up was the great bear of a Finn, Juha Mieto, forcing wooden skis along by brute force. Third was an unknown Pole on synthetic skis. 'Thomas Magnusson … ran down on gentle slopes drinking juice', as someone put it, while Ivar Formo, a Norwegian on wooden skis 'poled along like one possessed'. Four of the top six skiers raced on plastic skis. Three days later, another Norwegian, Magne Myrmo, won the 15 km race. That too was historic in its way. This was the last international cross-country race to be won on wooden skis. Within a few years the Nordic ski industry paid the price of retrogression. It virtually disappeared, overcome by imports from Austria, mostly Fischer, and Rossignol from France, with their unassailable technical lead. They even solved the problem of porous synthetic soles to hold wax – again anticipated by Peter Østbye in the 1950s.

In any case, the new hard, plastic soles were only half the technology needed for the skating technique. The other half was the binding. There the Scandinavians, in the shape of the Norwegian Rottefella concern, held their own. For some reason, Rottefella understood the interplay of innovation, design and marketing. From the skating point of view, the drawback of the classical Rottefella binding was the clamped toe and resistance of a flexing sole. Between 1983 and 1985, the company logically invented a device that would allow the boot to rotate freely round a point so as to approximate to the natural movement of the foot. The outcome was the NNN – New Nordic Norm – binding. New synthetic materials allowed a system in which the boot soles had an axle moulded into the toe and this meshed with a bearing fitted with an opening and closing device. The system

60. The modern heirs of Amundsen. Erling Kagge being dropped off in Antarctica,
18 November 1992, at the start of the first solo unsupported ski tour to the South Pole.
His sledge is modelled on the ancient boat-like pulka of the Samoyeds and Lapps. Food
and materials owe much to space travel. *Erling Kagge*

was standardized, so no adjustment was needed and it was a case of one device
fitting all sizes of boots. Because it was not patented in time, other maufacturers
copied the pattern. To be fair, the NNN, like most inventions, had a precursor;
in this case a Swiss product called Long-Step. In any case, the upshot was that
the NNN principle, combined with plastic soles on skis, favoured the advance
of the skating technique.

In Alpine skiing, meanwhile, bindings underwent a parallel evolution. Here
preservation of life and limb was the goal. Because running downhill needed
rigid attachment, the Kandahar type of cable binding, together with defective
boot construction, put intolerable strain on bones. In the 1950s and 1960s
the procession of what was cheerfully called the 'blood wagon', or red-painted
accident sledge, manned by placid ski instructors or piste auxiliaries, was a feature
of most resorts. Half a dozen fractures were a common daily toll. Clinics made
fortunes from insurance money. Orthopaedic surgery, however, was promoted,
with advances in screwing bones together instead of the traditional splint. At
one Swiss resort, in the Valais, there was a surgeon who ran a production line for

broken legs, with final-year German medical students to make the incisions and sew them up afterwards. He built a substantial hotel with the proceeds.

He and others like him had to make money while they could. The pandemic of splintered bones speeded the emergence of a quick-release mechanism. The first safety binding was actually Norwegian, and dated from 1892. It consisted simply of a thick rubber heelstrap so that, in the words of the inventor, 'you never risk wrenching your foot … in a fall … because it is held rigidly in the … toestrap … since the rubber always stretches during strong twisting'.[5] That was all every well at the time but modern downhill skiing needed something more sophisticated. Eventually, after perhaps a decade of evolution, proper safety bindings appeared. These hold the foot rigid on the ski at toe and heel but when the strain approaches the breaking point of bones, as in a fall, it opens, to decant the victim in relative safety. Because of the complex stresses of the rotation, flexing and twisting involved, sophisticated mathematics were needed for the various designs. The appearance of plastic boots to support the leg at its weakest point and with standardized soles, completed the system. By the 1980s leg fractures were almost a thing of the past, although rarer, more complicated knee injuries remained.

This helped the pressured popularization of skiing. Subliminal TV images also played a rôle. An integral part of Alpine skiing was fashion-driven clothing. In this case it was a potent mélange of sex-and-power fantasy, Formula One motor racing and the great outdoors. The compulsory helmets in racing enhanced the illusion. They originated in safety, after the death of racers by collision with trees and rocks in the 1950s and early 1960s. Their design turned them into a fashion accessory.

Backdoor television advertising also generated the lurid decorations peppering most skis in all disciplines today. These originated in the simple colours and patterns of an earlier generation to stimulate brand recognition when at rest directly through the human eye. The little screen exploited subliminal flashes at speed through the medium of a lens. Dazzling motifs on the tops and soles of skis are designed to be shot from every conceivable angle, or flourished by the happy victors before the cameras during the obligatory journalistic interview at the finish.

Another vital development was the appearance of so-called carving skis, exaggerated waisted skis, short in length to ease turning. These were billed as the latest advance, although in fact they had their origin in Norwegian skis at least 300 years old.

The outcome has been intense mechanization. That has led to mass skiing, indifferent to place, complete with crowded pistes regulated by traffic codes. From the Alps to the Rockies, the Caucasus and the Carpathians, lifts and cablecars of ever greater sophistication and capacity festoon the slopes. This has drawn ever more visitors, which is economically beneficent, saving whole valleys from depopulation.

It has naturally come at a price. Skiers with their grinding turns compress the snow, which then transmits their pounding to the soil beneath. This affects the delicate balance of the mountain world. In Switzerland, at Fiesch in the Canton of Valais, for example, a new lift and attendant piste caused the disappearance of a small Alpine lake: 'The effect of … numberless [skiers] and … occasionally … motorised vehicles … makes the recolonisation of the soil by Alpine plants even more difficult', in the words of one report. So the piste machines manicuring the runs as demanded by the customers have their drawbacks. In the groundwork for new pistes: 'bulldozers and explosives in the Alpine zone are particularly destructive'.[6]

All this is compounded of course by climate change. The contour lines along upland valleys mark the retreat of winter snow up into the heights. In low-lying resorts silent lifts stand like derelict remains of a moribund industry. Snow structure registers the subtle influence of rising temperature, atmospheric variability and obscure shifts in solar radiation. There are also the far-reaching consequences of a little advertised effect of constant climatic shift. The jet stream has moved, and snowfalls with it. This has sent Alpine skiers overseas in search of reliable conditons; some as far as Hokkaido, the north island of Japan, but more to America.

In the vanguard of this movement was Stein Eriksen, the charismatic Norwegian, the first Scandinavian downhill skier to break the hegemony of the skiers from the Alpine countries by winning the giant slalom and coming second in the slalom at the Oslo Winter Olympics of 1952. He decided to exploit his medals and his personality by moving to the Americas. In the 1950s he was to be found as an instructor at Portillo in the Andes, before moving to Montana and Aspen and Vail in Colorado. Then he discovered Deer Valley, Utah, near Salt Lake City, developing it as a resort, becoming its director of skiing and a luxury hotelier into the bargain. It is American skiing in a nutshell; the saga of the entrepreneur.

The attraction of American skiing is billed as skiing in powder snow; loose, dry, air-filled and knee deep. Elsewhere it is potentially lethal because it forms the deadliest kind of avalanche. Under the right conditions, however it is a desirable sensation, caressing the skis, as it were. This is turning history on its head because it was this kind of snow that generated the snowshoe and kept the ski out of America until modern times. Eriksen's Aspen and Vail, together with Jackson Hole in Wyoming, well promoted, have diverted skiers from the Alps to the mountain states. As elsewhere, this derives from cheap air travel.

Because of mass participation, a blanket of artificiality descended on Alpine skiing, symbolized by snow machines to counteract the weather, and regimented ski instruction. Reaction inevitably set in. It took various forms. One of the earliest appeared in Switzerland as antagonism to the Winter Olympics. In 1969, popular referenda quashed an official proposal to apply for the 1976 Games. The issue was the cost to the taxpayer – anathema to any good Swiss. To organize the Olympics now meant squandering money on a bloated symbol of national prestige. The experience of Innsbruck in 1964 and Grenoble in 1968 suggested a bill of £20,000,000 or more. Also the Winter Olympics damaged the tourist trade by frightening off regular visitors. In America, for similar reasons, a referendum in the state of Colorado also rejected the 1976 Winter Olympics, which Denver had by then secured, and which the Austrians none too enthusiastically saved by bringing them back to Innsbruck for a second time. The Olympic aura, however sullied, proved too enticing in the end. America was forgiven to the extent of acquiring the Winter Olympics in 1980 at Lake Placid, and 2002, Salt Lake City; New York State and Utah. A black mark no doubt still clings to Colorado.

Another form of reaction was the revival of cross-country skiing. Despite a negligible effect on even a delicate biosphere, it was once considered a laughable aberration in downhill centres; now no Alpine resort is complete without its Nordic tracks, including the Norwegian loan-word *loipe*, to distinguish them from the downhill pistes. Luckily for the ski schools, skating had taken hold. It is easier to teach than the classical style, because there is fundamentally only one step, against variations of the other, and waxing is irrelevant – for beginners anyway.

By the same token, in Scandinavia, Nordic ski touring was popularized even more. In Norway, the Easter exodus to the mountains kept its momentum. The movement spread to America, notably in the Rockies, the Sierras and New England. One curious aspect of the reaction to formalization was the appearance of the 'V' style in ski-jumping, where parallel skis were rigidly demanded for good style points. In 1985, a red-headed Swede called Jan Boklöv discovered by accident that skis kept in a 'V' formation were aerodynamically more efficient. He sailed so far down the slope that points for length outweighed penalties for style. After much troubled experimentation, he won the World Cup in 1989. At that, outraged traditionalists, particularly Norwegians, were confounded and, in a minor revolution the heretical 'V' became received orthodoxy. A touching side to this story is that Boklöv is an epileptic, who suffered a childhood speech defect.

Another reaction to the industrialized ski run was thrill-seeking downhill in extreme skiing on suicidal couloirs from Patagonia to the Himalayas. Since that usually needed helicopters – 'heli-skiing' – it was still mechanized. More typical was a tiny, niche renaissance of the wooden cross-country ski, followed by the rise of wood in the core of downhill skis. This is connected with the appearance of small, specialized ski-makers slipping in between the globalized behemoths. Madshus and Åsnes in Norway; Karhu in Finland and Tegsnäs in Sweden spring to mind. A more than usually instructive example comes from Stöckli, of the canton of Luzern, the last remaining Swiss ski manufacturer. A Swiss newspaper arranged a meeting between Stöckli's chief designer, Ruedi Arnet, and a violinmaker from Zürich called Felix Rast. They discovered that their *métiers* had much in common. 'Wood is a natural high-tech product', so Arnet said. 'In elasticity, precision … flexibility it is unsurpassed by an synthetic material.'[7] It was in the control of vibration that the violin and the ski most closely resembled each other. In each case it was necessary to eliminate undesirable frequencies. Vibration affects the tone of a violin and the speed of a ski. 'It is … vital … to remove the heavy and unwanted vibrations from a ski', in Arnet's words, 'but to preserve the light ones.'

That was a return to the past. So too was the telemark revival, arguably the most far-reaching reaction to the artificiality of the piste. For decades, the lone practioners of this soft-snow turn, especially in the Alps, among the stylized waddling of the approved method, had to bear derision or admiring shouts of 'telemark!' – each disturbing in its way. Then Norwegian students brought the telemark turn to America, where it developed into a cult, was re-exported back to Norway and, in an ambiguous development, has finally been recognized internationally as a competitive discipline of its own.

All this is a far cry from the original form of skiing as a kind of Nature-worship and its kindred use in polar exploration. So it is entirely appropriate that the ultimate reaction to mechanized skiing has been the return to the polar regions. Latter-day adventurers wanted to follow in the tracks of the classic explorers and go one better if they could. Thus in 1968–9, Sir Wally Herbert led a British expedition with dogs and skis on the first crossing of the Arctic from Alaska to Spitsbergen and, given the controversy to this day dogging Cook's and Peary's original claims, also becoming the first *incontestably* to reach the North Pole by surface travel. Then in 1990 the American, Will Steger, made the first crossing of Antarctica using dogs and skis, thereby fulfilling the failed ambition of Ernest Shackleton on the *Endurance* expedition in 1914–17.

However, the ski was incidental to Herbert and Steger. Born into a culture that was different from that of the skiing heartland, they had other motives. For an expedition of which skiing was the essence, it is necessary to turn to the pioneer of repeating the classic polar journeys. He is a Norwegian, Bjørn Staib. In 1962, together with a compatriot, Bjørn Reese, he crossed Greenland on skis, following Nansen's original route in 1888 from Umivik to Godthaab. He was the first to do so, albeit with improvements. Unlike Nansen, he had a dog team. His intention, as he baldly explained, 'was far from … scientific [research]. The tour was first and foremost of a sporting kind … its 600 km … rather like a large-scale Easter [ski] tour [at home].'[8]

That is a succinct definition of the school that Staib founded. Its leading exponents have been Norwegian. Like him, their journeys have simply been extensions of their customary environment. To make sense, new challenges had to be invented. The logical conclusion was unsupported travel, by main force, without dogs, solo in the end. It had to wait on technology. One invention was waxless touring skis, originally conceived for lazy skiers. A kind of fishscale pattern in the centre of the sole provided adhesion for the kick-off, while new plastics gave unimpeded glide in nearly all conditions. The sledge, however, was the key. The classic model with ski-like runners had been heavy, sluggish and a drag. A reversion to the *pulka*, the ancient boat-like pattern of Samoyed and Lapp, allied to modern synthetic materials, produced something that was light, strong and easy to haul. The same advances reduced the weight of equipment all round to a manageable load.

The Antarctic, with its firm ground and endless snowfields, became the natural playground of ambitious skiers. The opening of the continent to tourism made all things possible. It culminated in the southern summer of 2005–6 with the longest crossing yet of the Antarctic Continent from Queen Maud Land to Terra Nova Bay in Victoria Land, via the South Pole, and the Pole of Inaccessibility, a small matter of 4,800 km solo, unsupported and all on skis. The skier who did this was another Norwegian, Rune Gjeldnes, one of a new breed of professional polar adventurers. They trace their lineage back to Roald Amundsen, the first modern professional polar explorer.

Gjeldnes was a little off the beaten track. Most ski trips start in West Antarctica, at Patriot Hills, on the coast of the Weddell Sea. Tour operators maintain base camps, local air transport and, as a legal obligation, rescue services too. The main reason for this route is the gentle slope up to the South Pole, with following winds, instead of the mountain crossing up to the polar plateau from the Ross Ice Shelf, with headwinds all the way.

Here too Norwegians made the running. In the southern summer of 1996–7, Børge Ousland made the first solo unsupported crossing of Antarctica from the Weddell Sea to McMurdo Sound, 2,845 km in 64 days. The climb that perplexed the classic explorers became a downhill run. Ousland had no adventures. Nor did Liv Arnesen, the first woman to ski solo and unsupported to the South Pole in 1994, taking 50 days. It was the hallmark of this school of polar adventurers. They took their lead from Roald Amundsen, with his meticulous planning and complete lack of a sick desire for heroic suffering. Consciously or not, they were going back in time to re-enact his triumph in the race to be first at the South Pole all those years ago. It was certainly the case with Erling Kagge, an Oslo lawyer who, in 1993, had become the first ever to ski solo and unsupported to the South Pole – he too in 50 days. In fact, at the corresponding point, on the eve of arrival, Kagge quoted from the diary of one of Amundsen's companions, that idiosyncratic skiing champion, Olav Bjaaland, running in his longest race: 'I hear the [Earth's] axle creaking, but tomorrow it will be oiled.'[9]

The wheel had come full circle. Bjaaland lived long enough to span the age of the old explorers, with skis and dogs, and their mechanized successors. In 1959, he was visited by Sir Vivian Fuchs who, the year before, had led a British expedition to make the first crossing of Antarctica. They met, nostalgically for Bjaaland, on the deck of *Fram*, in its museum by the waters of the fjord in Oslo. Sir Vivian explained how, he too, with the aid of aircraft and tractors, had been to the South Pole, nearly 50 years after Bjaaland on his skis. 'Oh well', said the old skier drily, 'not much has changed there, I'm sure of that!'[10]

# Notes

*Abbreviations*: DBD: Dokumentationsbibliothek Davos. IOC: International Olympic Committee, Lausanne, archives. MZ: Winter Sport Museum Mürzzuschlag, Austria. NBA: National Board of Antiquities, Helsinki. NBO: Norwegian National Library in Oslo. RAK: Danish State Archives in Copenhagen. RA: Norwegian State Archives in Oslo. SH: Ski museum, Holmenkollen, Oslo. SPRI: Scott Polar Research Institute, Cambridge. TLG: Thesaurus Linguae Graecae, Digital Library, University of California, Irvine.

*Notes to Chapter 1: Skiing Necesse Est*

1 Amundsen, diary, 15 December 1911. NBO Ms.8°1249.
2 Ibid., 6 January 1912.
3 Mason (1894, p. 384).

*Notes to Chapter 2: Ski Tracks in the Milky Way*

1 Patkanov (1897, pp. 118–19).
2 Thevet (1575, vol. 11, p. 1011).
3 Burov (1985, p. 391, *et seq.*).
4 Ravdonikas (1936); Savvateev (1970, 1990).
5 Luho (1951); NBA personal communication.
6 Berg (1933b, pp. 143–6; 1950, p. 114.); Clark (1952 p. 299).
7 Jacobsen (1994), Torgersen (1999), Sørensen (1993).
8 Naskali (1989); NBA personal communication.
9 Vilkuna (1984, p. 36.)
10 Burov (1996, p. 8.); Clark (1954, p. 177).
11 Manker (1971, p. 79).
12 Vilkuna (1998, p. 72).
13 Pryakhin (1970).
14 Chernykh (1992 pp. 200–10); Pryakhin (1970).
15 Åström and Norberg (1984, p. 84.); Modin (1928).
16 Rosander (1964, p. 8).

17 Lid (1938).
18 Manker (1971, p. 80).
19 Åström and Norberg (1984, p. 84.), Berg (1950, p. 153).
20 Sørensen (1996, pp. 14–15).
21 Berg (1950, p. 123.), Åström and Norberg (1984. p. 84).
22 Åström and Norberg (1984, p. 85).
23 Øverland (1888, pp. 5–8).

*Notes to Chapter 3: The Earliest Written Sources*

1 Xenophon (1968, p. 312).
2 Aall, 1959.
3 *Suidae Lexicon* (1853, ii, p. 626).
4 Strabo (1969, p. 240).
5 Iamblihi (1715, p. 286).
6 Virgil (1967, p. 180).
7 TLG Berosus Fragmenta, Fragment 1a, line 59.
8 Mathieu (1983, p. 643).
9 Chavannes (1905, p. 561).
10 Solini (1864, p. 105).
11 Mathieu (1983, p. 75).
12 Pomponius Mela (1968, p. 68).
13 *Bei Shi*, 1974, p. 3130 (personal communication Charles Aylmer).
14 Schott (1864, p. 448).
15 Huan-ju ki, quoted in Schott (1864, p. 448).
16 *Xin Tang Shu*, quoted in Needham (1971, p. 14.)

17 *Xin Tang Shu.* 1975, p. 6148. (personal communication Charles Aylmer).
18 Eberhard (1942, p. 50.); Schott (1864, p. 446).
19 Erman (1838, p. 325).
20 Schott (1864, p. 433).
21 Markwart (1930, p. 86).
22 *Da Ming yi tong zhi*, 89/8A-9B (personal communication Charles Aylmer).
23 Ibid.
24 D'Ohsson (1852, p. 421.); Erdmann (1841, p. 124.); Khetagurov (1952, p. 124.); Meuli (1960, p. 183.); Schott (1864, p. 448).
25 Markwart (1924, pp. 289–90).
26 Dubler (1953, pp. 57–8).
27 Virgil (1967, p. 100.)
28 Procopius (1961, p. 418.)
29 Paulus Diaconus (1878, pp. 54–5).
30 Jordanes (1915, pp. 55–6).
31 Tacitus (1970, p. 212.)
32 Adami (1595, p. 142).
33 Bureus (1631, p. 43).
34 Adami (1595, p. 142).

*Notes to Chapter 4: Old Norse Sagas and the Finnish National Epic:* Kalevala

1 *Snorres Konge Sagaer* (1944, p. 60).
2 *Grágás* (1867, p. 406).
3 Jónsson (1912, vol. A1, p. 357).
4 *Flateyarbók* (1862, vol. iii, 'Hemings þáttr Aslakssonar', pp. 400–10.), Vigfússon (1887, vol. i, 'Hemings þáttr', pp. 347–87).
5 *Flateyarbók* (1862, vol. i, p. 579).
6 Petersen (1862, p. 97).
7 Snorri Sturluson (1944, p. 191).
8 Ibid., p. 331.
9 *Regis Magni legum reformatoris leges Gula-thingenses* (1817 p. 449).
10 Citizens of Jämtland to King Frederik I, 20 March 1530, *Diplomatarium Norvegicum* (1847, vol. xiv, p. 691).
11 Brøgger (1947, p. 21).
12 Snorri Sturluson (1944, p. 92).
13 Snorri Sturluson (1926, pp. 31, 84).
14 *Flateyarbók* (1862, vol. i, p. 21).
15 Collinder (1960, p. 92, *passim*); Wiklund (1931b, p. 64, *passim*).
16 Wiklund (1926, p. 17).

*Notes to Chapter 5: The First Printed Sources*

1 Nansen (1911, pp. 70, 120).
2 Saxo Grammaticus (1644, p. 173).
3 Olaus, Magnus (1539).
4 Ibid.
5 Herberstein (1571, p. 85).
6 Artsikhovsky (1947, p. 59).
7 Likhachev (1907).
8 Cornell (1981, p. 9).
9 Guagnini (1578, fol. 12).
10 Olaus, Magnus (1555, book I, Chapter 22).
11 Ibid., Chapter 4.
12 Negri (1700, p. 35 *passim*).
13 *Diplomatarium Norvegicum* (1847, vol. xii, p. 687).
14 Bureus (1631, p. 43).
15 Saxo Grammaticus (1644 notae uberiores 8, p. 126).
16 Ibid.
17 Olearius (1647, p. 190).
18 Bureus (1631, p. 43).
19 Schefferus (1674, p. 99).
20 Tornæus (1900, p. 56 *passim*).
21 Linné (1913, p. 158).
22 Stenström (1932, p. 20).
23 Lappi (1905, p. 13).
24 Körningh (1956, p. 28).
25 Cervantes (1969, p. 255 *passim*).

*Notes to Chapter 6: Norway – The Cradle of Skiing as a Sport*

1 Schröder (1900, p. 34 *passim*).
2 Sandberg (1893, p. 29), Wiklund (1931b, p. 64).
3 Studiosus Barhows, 1754–67.
4 Emahusen (1733, No. 14.3).
5 Ibid., No. 26.
6 Allerunderdanigst Udkast (1762, pp. 76–7.)
7 Ibid., p. 1.
8 Nordberg (1994, p. 44).
9 Smith (1797, p. 6).
10 Allerunderdanigst Udkast (1762, p. 2).
11 Holm (1965, p. 10)
12 Ibid., p. 30.
13 Ibid.
14 Ibid., p. 32.
15 De Jong (1802, vol. ii, p. 286 *passim*).
16 James (1966, p. 215 *passim*).
17 Brooke (1827, p. 327).

## Notes to Chapter 7: The Influence of Rousseau

1 Platou (1812, p. 137)
2 Riksforsamlings Forhandlinger (1914, vol. i, pp. 230–1).
3 Schøning (1771, vol. ii, introduction b).
4 Ibid., vol. i, p. 20.
5 Montesquieu (1955, p. 190).
6 Voltaire (1917, p. 26).
7 Brun (1818, p. 274).
8 Zetlitz (1789, p. 11).
9 Ibid.
10 Wille (1786, p. 229).
11 Ryd (2001, p. 240 passim).
12 Leem (1767, p. 57).
13 Hauch (1867, p. 120).
14 GutsMuths (1804, p. 387).
15 Wergeland (1918, vol. i, Blaamyra, p. 279).
16 Moe (1914, vol. i, p. 58 Knud og Birgit).
17 Christensen (1993, p. 119).
18 Asbjørnsen (1934, p. 34).
19 Asbjørnsen (1839, p. 98).

## Notes to Chapter 8: The Ski in Foreign Literature

1 Balzac (1927, p. 186).
2 Pushkin (1976, vol. vii, p. 55).
3 Högström (1748).
4 Grosses vollständige Universallexikon (1737, p. 811).
5 Pallas (1776, vol. iii, p. 39).
6 Middendorff (1848, vol. iv, part 2, p. 1349 et seq.).
7 Rockhill (1900, p. 198).
8 Middendorff (1848, vol. iv, part 2, p. 1349 et seq.).
9 Schrenck (1858, vol. iii, p. 472 et seq.).
10 Lloyd (1830, p. 219).
11 Jonge (1779, p. 125).
12 Laing (1836, p. 143).
13 Thomson (1981, p. 242).

## Notes to Chapter 9: Evolution of Skiing as a Sport

1 Tromsø-Tidende, 19 March 1843.
2 Skirenden 1843.
3 Lie (1886–87), p. 263.
4 Tromsø-Tidende, 31 December 1843.

5 Morgenbladet, 1 April 1866.
6 Adresseavisen, 24 February 1849.
7 Throndhjems Stiftsavis, 2 April 1863.
8 Ibid., 9 April 1863.
9 Morgenbladet, 4 February 1860.
10 Ibid., 12 February 1862.
11 Illustreret Nyhedsblad, 30 March 1862, passim.
12 Aftenposten, 18 February 1862.
13 Illustreret Nyhedsblad, 30 March 1862, passim.
14 Turnskue i Trysil 1862.
15 Morgenbladet, 3 February 1863.
16 Hedemarkens Amtstidende, 11 March 1863.
17 Kristianssands-Stiftsavis, 8 March 1862.
18 Lillehagen (n.d., p. 106).
19 Addresseavisen, 4 February 1863.

## Notes to Chapter 10: The Men of Telemark

1 Aftenbladet, 16 March 1866.
2 Munch (1954, p. 112).
3 Ringeriges Ugeblad, 1 March 1866.
4 Aftenbladet, 16 March 1866.
5 Ibid.
6 Finmarksposten, 15 February 1867.
7 Indherredsposten, 7 March 1866.
8 Morgenbladet, 15 February 1867.
9 Aftenbladet, No. 4, 10 February 1868.
10 Ibsen (1962, vol. ii p. 176).
11 Vinje (1916, p. 154 passim).
12 Aftenbladet, 13 March 1866.
13 Loupedalen (SH p. 30).
14 Vinje (1916, p. 154 passim).
15 Skirend i Hvitesejd 1868.
16 Kiærland (1964, p. 19).
17 Berge (1904, p. 84).
18 Morgenbladet, 19 February 1870.
19 Aftenbladet, 12 February 1877.
20 Bjerknes (1933, p. 16).
21 Aftenbladet, 14 April 1868.
22 Nydalens Spirderei 1872.
23 Weibull (1971, p. 61).
24 Nydalens Compagnie 100 år (1945, p. 30).
25 Morgenbladet, 29 February 1876.
26 Quoted in Meinich and Petersen (1941, p. 74).
27 Quoted in Rode (1952, p. 102).
28 Aftenbladet, 14 April 1868.
29 Egeberg (1919, p. 2).
30 Praemieskirendet Huseby 1879.
31 Torjus Bjørgulfsen, letter to Christiania Ski Club, 12 April 1879. SH.

32   Skirendet ved Huseby 1879.
33   Aubert (1879).


Notes to Chapter 11: Development of
Technique and Equipment

1   Morgenbladet, 22 March 1867.
2   Thoresen 1868.
3   Morgenbladet, 18 February 1868.
4   Meinich and Petersen (1941, p. 77).
5   Morgenbladet, 24 March 1867.
6   Morgenbladet, 8 March 1868.
7   Morgenbladet, 11 February 1868.
8   Aall et al. (1903).
9   Adresseavisen, 5 April 1863
10  Vaage (1972, p. 144)
11  Adresseavisen, 28 February 1863.
12  Morgenbladet, 28 February 1868.
13  Morgenbladet, 7 March 1868.
14  Reichert (1958, p. 231).
15  Morgenbladet, 7 March 1868.
16  Dagbladet, No. 48, 1879.
17  Aftenbladet, 13 February 1879.
18  Worm (1655, p. 373).
19  Adresseavisen, 19 March 1863.
20  Adresseavisen, 4 February 1863.
21  Adresseavisen, 21 March 1865.
22  GutsMuths (1804, p. 389).
23  Balduinus (1667, p. 39).
24  Adresseavisen (28 February 1863).


Notes to Chapter 12: The First Nordic
Marathon

1   Daily News, 20 January 1881.
2   Norsk Idrætsblad (1881, p. 42).
3   Ibid.
4   Ibid., p. 60.
5   Adresseavisen, 27 March 1866.
6   Norsk Idrætsblad (1881, p. 43).
7   Ibid., p. 54.
8   Ibid., p. 78.
9   Norsk Idrætsblad (1885, p. 22).
10  Ibid., p. 21 passim.
11  Ibid. (1883, p. 40).
12  Adresseavisen, 13 February 1884.
13  Norsk Idrætsblad (1885, p. 21).
14  Ibid.
15  Bjerknes (1933, p. 29 passim.)
16  Norsk Idrætsblad (1885, p. 215).
17  Ibid. (1886, p. 54).

18  Ibid.
19  Lillehagen (n.d., p. 115).
20  Aftenposten, 25 February 1890.
21  Wulfsberg (1886, p. 31).
22  Norsk Idrætsblad (1886, p. 31).
23  Morgenbladet, 6 February 1881.
24  Foreningen (1888, p. 21).
25  Ibid.


Notes to Chapter 13: The Conquest of the
Mountain World

1   Bø (1966, p. 59).
2   Bergens Stiftstidende, 3 January 1850.
3   Berge (1908, p. 64).
4   Prahl (1946, p. 76 passim).
5   I Snestorm paa Tydalsfjeldene.
6   Keilhau (1820, p. 385).
7   Vinje (1862).
8   Hansteen (1823, p. 247).
9   L. S. (1883 passim).
10  Aftenposten, 14 January 1887.
11  Ibid., 7 January 1888.
12  Dagsposten, 25 January 1887.
13  Ibsen (1962, vol. i, p. 371).
14  Tønseth (n.d.), p. 30 passim.


Notes to Chapter 14: Fridtjof Nansen and
the first crossing of Greenland

1   Nordenskiöld (1880, vol. ii, p. 107).
2   Ibid., p. 232.
3   Nordenskiöld (1883, p. 240).
4   Orstadius (1897–8, p. 244).
5   Ibid., p. 241.
6   Grundström (1934, p. 38).
7   Orstadius (1897–8, p. 244).
8   Grundström (1934, p. 40).
9   Loupedalen (1947, p. 259).
10  Nansen (1893, p. 7)
11  Norsk Idrætsblad (1881, p. 42).
12  Nansen (1886-87, p. 87).
13  Nansen, Om Hurtigløb på Ski, passim.
14  Angell 1884 passim.
15  Fridtjof Nansen (1884, 1 April.)
16  Ibid., 9 April.
17  Henrik Angell, letter to Fridtjof Nansen,
     24 November 1887. (NBO Ms.fol.1923
     1a(2)).
18  E. Isachsen, letter to Fridtjof Nansen, 28
     January 1888 (NBO Ms.fol.1924 1a(2)).

19  Aasheim (1989, p. 78).
20  Ibid., p. 9.
21  Ibid., p. 134.
22  Nansen (1890, p. 127).
23  Balto (1980, p. 95).
24  Hamsun (1889b).
25  *Aftenposten*, 5 June 1889.
26  *Geografisk Tidskrift*, vol. x, 1889–90, p. 61;
    Nansen (1890b, p. 477).
27  The *Spectator*, 2 May 1891, p. 631.
28  Nansen (1890, p. 78).


*Notes to Chapter 15: The Nordic Olympia*

1  *Aftenposten*, 13 June 1889.
2  *Norski Idrætsblad* (1892, pp. 25–6 *passim*).
3  *Aftenposten*, 1 February 1892.
4  Balck (1892a)
5  Balck (1892b).
6  Balck (1892a).
7  Quoted in Wolcker (1925, p. 79).
8  *Aftonbladet*, 25 February 1879.
9  Balck (1892c).
10  *Aftenposten*, 2 March 1892.


*Notes to Chapter 16: The Waisted Telemark Ski*

1  *Norsk Idrætsblad* (1892, p. 27).
2  *Norsk Idrætsblad* (1881, p. 46).
3  Huitfeldt (1922, p. 80 *passim*).
4  Vaage (1968, p. 44).
5  Huitfeldt (1922, p. 84).
6  Huitfeldt (1896, p. 17).
7  *Norsk Idrætsblad* (1896), p. 49.


*Notes to Chapter 17: The rise of ski touring and the Misadventures of Roald Amundsen*

1  Bjerknes (1933, p. 84)
2  Urdahl (1902–3, p. 95).
3  Urdahl (1896, p. 99).
4  Urdahl (1902–3, p. 97).
5  *Aftenposten*, 13 December 1890.
6  *Norsk Idrætsblad*, vol. x, 1892, p. 357.
7  Ibid., p. 358.
8  Ibid., p. 281 *passim*.
9  Ibid., 1893, p. 42.
10  Ibid., 1892, p. 358.
11  *Morgenbladet*, 9 January 1890.

12  Urdahl (1912, p. 21).
13  Urdahl (1894, 13 January.)
14  Ibid.
15  Ibid., 17 January.
16  Urdahl (1912, p. 21).
17  Urdahl (1894, 10 January).
18  Amundsen (1896 *passim*).
19  Sandberg (1893, p. 118).
20  Urdahl (1893a, p. v).


*Notes to Chapter 18: As Important as the Plays of Ibsen*

1  Aars (1929, p. 16).
2  *Aftonbladet*, 26 February 1879.
3  Urdahl (1893a, p. 81).
4  Ibid.
5  Løchen (1887, p. 147).
6  *Norske Skiløpere, Møre og Romsdal*, p. 97.
7  Ibid.
8  Huitfeldt (1889b, p. 341).
9  Urdahl (1893a, p. 75).
10  *Morgenbladet*, 8 February 1893.
11  *Morgenbladet*, 13 January 1893.
12  *Morgenbladet*, 19 February 1893.
13  *Morgenbladet*, 12 February 1893.
14  *Morgenbladet*, 17 February 1893.
15  Lossius (1937), p. 58.
16  Eva to Fridtjof Nansen 18 February 1892.
    (NBO Brevs. 48.)
17  Nansen, Eva (1893).
18  Gulbransson (1894).
19  *Christiania Nyheds-og Avertissements-Blad*,
    10 February 1896 *passim*.


*Notes to Chapter 19: The Spread of Skiing on the Continent*

1  *Die Kunst Tialfs*, Klopstock (1798).
2  Wasmannsdorf (1884, p. 405).
3  Rieck (1867, p. 74 *passim*).
4  *Norsk Idrætsblad*, 7 March 1884, p. 44.
5  A.S. (1885).
6  Nansen (1890, p. 78).
7  Naumann (1822, p. 648).
8  Neumayr (1893, p. 26).
9  *Norsk Idrætsblad*, No. 7 (1900, p. 77).
10  Vaage (1952, p. 41).
11  Ibid., p. 53.
12  Isachsen (1949 *passim*).

13   Vaage (1952, p. 64).
14   Vorwerg (1893–4a).
15   Vorwerg (1893–4 *passim*.)


*Notes to Chapter 20:  Norwegians bring
Skiing to Austria-Hungary and Montenegro*

1    Valvasor (1689, vol. iv, p. 584 *passim*).
2    Angell (1893a, p. 3).
3    Ibid.
4    Angell (1895, p. 33).
5    Ibid., p. 53.
6    Quoted in Hochholdinger (1992, p. 26).
7    Wangenheim (1892, p. 11).
8    Fischer (1985, p. 13).
9    *Norske skipionerer* (1943, vol. I, p. 13).
10   Max Kleinoscheg, undated letter to Toni
     Schruf, MZ.
11   Ibid., Hüttenegger and Pfliger (1968,
     p. 13).
12   Nicolay Noodt, letter to Max Kleinoscheg,
     11 December 1890, MZ.
13   Max Kleinoscheg, undated letter to Toni
     Schruf, MZ.
14   Hüttenegger and Pfliger (1968, p. 19).
15   Max Kleinoscheg, undated letter to Toni
     Schruf, MZ.
16   Leblanc (1898, pp. 31, 51).
17   Trævarefabrikken Ydal to Nansen, 13
     October 1892, NBO Ms.fol.1924:2a9.
18   Advertisement for Josef Bachmann, 1892,
     MZ.
19   Quoted in Hüttenegger and Pfliger (1968,
     p. 28), MZ.
20   Ibid., p. 34.
21   *Norsk Idrætsblad*, 24 January 1893, p. 30.
22   Quoted in Hüttenegger and Pfliger (1968,
     p. 35), MZ.
23   Unidentified cutting MZ
24   Reisch (1893, p. 4).
25   Vaage (1952, p. 77).
26   Schmal (1912, p. 29).


*Notes to Chapter 21:  Skiing Comes to
Switzerland*

1    Saas-Fee Tourism, personal
     communication.
2    Senger (1941, p. 33).
3    Mercier (1928, p. 7).
4    Iselin (1929, p. 43).

5    Quoted in Mercier (1928, p. 9 *passim*).
6    Iselin (1929, p. 43).
7    Ibid.
8    Quoted in Mercier (1928, p. 15).
9    Vaage (1952, p. 100 *passim*).
10   Thudichum (1896, p. 89).
11   Weber-Bauler (1935, p. 30).
12   Thudichum (1896, p. 51.
13   Roeder (1923, p. 56).
14   Rousseau (1782, p. 69).


*Notes to Chapter 22:  Davos: The cradle of
the Ski Resort*

1    Hans Hold to Alexander Spengler, 25
     March 1865, quoted in Ferdmann (1990,
     p. 17).
2    *Davoser Blätter*, vol. xii, 24 November
     1883.
3    Ibid., 23 January 1875.
4    Quoted in Ferdmann (1990, p. 60).
5    Brevkasse (1884).
6    Schneeschuhlaufen (3 January 1891).


*Notes to Chapter 23:  The English Skiing at
Davos*

1    J. A. Symonds (1878, p. 78).
2    Stevenson (1905, p. 219 *et seq.*).
3    Ibid., pp. 207, 209.
4    Ibid., p. 217.
5    *Davoser Blätter*, 17 January 1891.
6    Ibid., 10 December 1892.
7    Ibid., 7 January 1893.
8    Branger (1960, p. 21).
9    Mann (2004, p. 372).
10   Doyle (1894, p. 68 *passim*).
11   Snow-skate race in Norway (1879).
12   Doyle (1894, p. 58 *passim*).
13   Ibid.
14   Paulcke (1896, p. 27).
15   Beauclerk (1868, pp. 123, 127).
16   Branger (1960, p. 65).
17   Quoted in Lockett (1928–9, p. 99).
18   Baddeley (1921, p. 254).


*Notes to Chapter 24:  Mathias Zdarsky*

1    Zdarsky (1911, p. 4 *passim*).
2    Quoted in Polednik (1969, p. 73).

3   Zdarsky (1911, p. 6).
4   Quoted Mehl (1949, p. 55).
5   Zdarsky (1911, p. 3).
6   Zdarsky (1897) quoted in Mehl (1949, p. 57).
7   Horn (1905, p. 50 *passim*).
8   Wallner (1950).
9   Zdarsky (1911, p. 95).

*Notes to Chapter 25:  St Moritz*

1   Iselin (1929, p. 46.)
2   Ibid.
3   *Gazette de Lausanne* 28 January 1903 quoted Mercier (1928, p. 59).
4   Ski-ing at St. Moritz (1904).
5   Iselin (1929, p. 50.)
6   Berg (1905, p. 11.)
7   Iselin.(1929, p. 51.)
8   Nilssen ['B. N.'] (1906, p. 83)
9   Nilssen (1905, p. 113 *et seq.*).
10  Nilssen ['B. N.'] (1906, p. 84).
11  Ibid., p. 87.
12  Rucki (1989, p. 162).

*Notes to Chapter 26:  Skiing in France*

1   Clerc (1902, p. 3).
2   Ibid., p. 59.
3   Quale (1903, p. 57).
4   Angell (1904, p. 105).
5   *Norske skipionerer* (1943, vol. i, p. 19).
6   Quale (1903, p. 3 *passim*).
7   Quale (1903, p. 53).
8   Clerc (1903, p. 94 *passim*).
9   Rougier (1907, p. 105).
10  *Concours international de Ski* (1907, p. 138).
11  Amundsen (1908, p. 67).
12  Rivas (1907, p. 6).
13  Leudet (1908).
14  Amundsen 23 January 1908.
15  Gérard de Beauregard, *L'Illustration* February 1908, quoted in Ballu (1991, p. 62).
16  Leudet (1908)
17  Durban-Hansen (1908, p. 401).
18  *Le Figaro*, 1 February 1909.
19  Olav Bjaalands Museum (1970, p. 17 *passim*.)

*Notes to Chapter 27:  Polar Exploration*

1   Munk (1624).
2   Parry (1828, p. 5).
3   Sigurd Scott Hansen, diary 18 February 1894 (NBO Ms.8°3423:1).
4   Astrup (1898, p. 9).
5   Weems (1967, p. 123).
6   R. E. Peary to Eivind Astrup, 25 January 1893. (Astrup papers, in private ownership.)
7   Quoted in Blossom (1932, p. 295).
8   Sverdrup (1903, vol. i, p. 19).
9   Ibid., vol. ii, p. 228.
10  Ibid., p. 493.
11  R. Amundsen, diary, 6 June 1904 (Amundsen family).
12  Ibid., 13 November 1905.
13  R. Amundsen, diary, 10 February 1904 (NBO Ms.4°1550).
14  R. Amundsen, diary, 14 August 1898 (NBO Ms.8°1196 XVI).
15  Ibid.
16  R. Amundsen, diary, 26 January 1898 (NBO Ms.8°1196 X).
17  Larsen (1893–4, pp. 126–7).
18  Conway (1898, p. 90).
19  Ibid. p. 49.
20  Ibid., p. 17.
21  A. B. Armitage, *Discovery*, diary 25 February 1902. (In private ownership.)
22  Amundsen (1912a, p. 57).
23  Scott (1905, vol. i, p. 334).
24  Amundsen (1912b, vol. i, p. 238).
25  Amundsen (1912a, p. 62).
26  Ibid.
27  Amundsen (1912b, vol. i, p. 180).
28  Nansen (1912b, p. 95).
29  Bjaaland (15 December 1911).
30  Amundsen (1912a, p. 66).
31  Bjaaland (15 December 1911).
32  Ibid., (22 January 1912).

*Notes to Chapter 28:  The Inventions that Founded Modern Skiing*

1   Brødr Næsheim, letter to Fridtjof Nansen, 26 December 1887 (NBO Ms.fol.1924.1.a(2)).
2   Amundsen (1912a, p. 66).
3   *Aftenposten*, 11 December 1891.
4   Norwegian patent no. 57126.

## Notes to Chapter 29: The New World

1   Davydov (1977, p. 200).
2   Teben'kov (1981, pp. 21–2).
3   *Indherreds-Posten*, 10 March 1866.
4   Hamilton (1919, p. 174).
5   Vaage (1952, p. 191).
6   Quoted in Vaage (1940, p. 83).
7   *Odes of Pindar* (1978, Olympian I, p. 4)
8   Dan de Quille, *Territorial Enterprise*, 13 February 1876, quoted in Berry (1991, p. 82).
9   Quoted Berry (1991, p. 55).
10  *Downieville Mountain Messenger*, quoted in Berry (1991, p. 71).
11  Quoted in Berry (1991, p. 40).


## Notes to Chapter 30: The Study of Snow Structure

1   Needham and Gwei-Djen (1961 p. 320).
2   Ibid., p. 321.
3   Olaus Magnus (1555, Book I, Chapter 22)
4   Kepler (1966, p. 7).
5   Martens (1675, p. 40).
6   Rossetti (1681, p. 1).
7   Just (1930, p. 136).
8   Tornæus (1900, p. 57).
9   Schefferus (1673, p. 247).
10  Jonge (1779, pp. 125–6).
11  Smith (1797, pp. 10–11).
12  *Vinter-Exerceer-Reglement* (1804, p. 1).
13  *Morgenbladet*, 24 December 1890.
14  *Norsk Idrætsblad* (1884, p. 28).
15  *Morgenbladet*, 24 December 1890.
16  Vaage, *Ski-smøringens historie* (n.d., p. 44).
17  Peter Østbye, Norwegian patent, 20 December 1913.


## Notes to Chapter 31: The First Winter Olympics at Chamonix

1   Coubertin (1914, p. 39).
2   Coubertin (1901, p. 17).
3   Coubertin (1909, p. 90).
4   *The Times*, 18 June 1894.
5   MacAloon (1981, p. 171.)
6   *Odes of Pindar* (1978, Olympian v, p. 48)
7   Ibid., Olympian i, p. 4.
8   Balck (1901, p. 73).

9   Lindroth (1974, p. 190).
10  Balck (1901, p. 73).
11  *Idun*, vol. xiv (1901, p. 145).
12  *Ny Tidning för Idrott*, vol. iv (1901, p. 105).
13  *Les Jeux d'Hiver de Chamonix* (1924, p. 721)
14  Johan Grøttumsbråten, letter to Maggi Hansen, 31 January 1924. (NBO Brevs.776.)
15  Tegnér (1924, p. 125).


## Notes to Chapter 32: Mass Winter Tourism

1   Henry Lunn (1934, p. 6).
2   Ibid., p. 75.
3   Watkins (1909, p. v, *passim*).
4   H.R. Wakefield, letter to *The Times*, 21 May 1913.
5   *The Times*, 5 January 1905.
6   R.W. Skelton to R.F. Scott, 21 February 1912 (SPRI).
7   *Scott's Last Expedition* (1913 vol.1, p. 576)
8   Hauser (1990–1, p. 6).
9   Schneider (1935, p. 16).
10  Fridjof Nansen, letter to Greta Gulbransson, 23 February 1912 (NBO Brevs.610).
11  Ibid., 30 March 1912.


## Notes to Chapter 33: The International Recognition of Downhill Skiing

1   Lunn (1952, p. 72).
2   Lunn (1925, p. 20 *passim*).
3   Brittain (1949, p. 253).
4   FIS *Procès-verbal*, 4 February 1927 (IOC, catalogue no. FI SKI FIS OU Notice: 0087403 FIS 1927-1981).
5   Gotaas (2003, p. 115 *passim*).
6   Hauser (1990–1, p. 10).
7   Krefting (1930, p. 566).
8   *The Times*, 10 February 1936, p. 14.


## Notes to Chapter 34: Skiing Mechanized and Politicized

1   Riggenbach, Niklaus, www.swissrails.ch, 2 June 2005.
2   Winterhalder, Robert, www.eisenbach.de, 2 May 2004.
3   Quoted in Gotaas (2003, p. 160).

*Notes to Chapter 35: Military Skiing*

1   Jakobson (1961, p. 6.)
2   *Xin Tang Shu* (1975, p. 6148)
     (personal communication, Charles
     Aylmer).
3   Saxo Grammaticus (1644, p. 173).
4   *Sverris Saga* (1920, p. 174).
5   Ovsyannikov (1989, p. 31).
6   Quoted in Zettersten (1940, p. 19)
7   Lange (1860, p. 69)
8   Ibid., p. 538.
9   Haukelid (1954, p. 132).
10  Ibid., p. 143.
11  Volkovski'i (2000, p. 3).
12  Artsikhovskii (1947, p. 60).
13  Jansonium (1619, p. 101).
14  *Dnevnik politruka Oreshina* (1941, p. 127).
15  Almquist (1911, p. 55).
16  Ibid., p. 144.
17  Siilasvuo (1940, p. 115).
18  *Dnevnik politruka Oreshina* (1941, p. 129).
19  Shukman (2002, p. 59).
20  Siilasvuo (1940, p. 142).
21  Zettersten (1901–2, p. 2).
22  Talbott (1971, p. 152).
23  Lewenhaupt (1953, p. 368.)
24  Shukman (2002, p. 236).
25  Ibid., p. 107.
26  Lewenhaupt (1953, p. 367.)
27  Shukman (2002, p. 237.)
28  *The Times*, 27 December 1939.
29  Lewenhaupt (1953, p. 373.)
30  Talbott (1971, p. 154.)
31  Volkovski'i (2000, p. 285.)
32  Jakobson (1961, p. 4.)


*Notes to Chapter 36: Skiing Since 1945*

1   Fønhus (1981, p. 24).
2   Jernberg (1960, p. 103).
3   Gotaas (2003, p. 251).
4   Ibid., p. 345.
5   Birger Pedersen, letter to Fridjof
     Nansen, 11 December 1892 (NBO
     Ms.fol.1924.2C2B).
6   Béguin and Theurillat (1981, p. 171).
7   Schlatter (2005).
8   Staib (1962, p. 7).
9   Bjaaland (14 December 1911).
10  Quoted in Lunde (1961, p. 100).

# Bibliography

*Abbreviations:* DBD: Dokumentationsbibliothek Davos. IOC: International Olympic Committee, Lausanne, archives. MZ: Winter Sport Museum Mürzzuschlag, Austria. NBA: National Board of Antiquities, Helsinki. NBO: Norwegian National Library in Oslo. RA: Norwegian State Archives in Oslo. RAK Danish State Archives in Copenhagen. SH: Ski museum, Holmenkollen, Oslo. SPRI: Scott Polar Research Institute, Cambridge. TLG: Thesaurus Linguae Graecae, Digital Library, University of California, Irvine.

101 Ans de Ski à Chamonix, *Ski Francais,* brochure for exhibition, Chamonix 1994.

*75 Jahre Schweizerische Ski-Verband,* jubiläums-Jahrbuch, 1979.

Aa, Pieter van der, *Voyages faites principalement en Asie dans les XII, XIII, XIV et XV siècles,* The Hague, Jean Neaulme, 1735.

Aall, C., Skiminner 1881–1900, *Foreningen til Ski-Idrettens Fremme Årbok,* 1943, pp. 15–26.

Aall, C., Veiledning i hoprend, *På Skidor,* 1901–2, pp. 155–8.

Aall, C., Tandberg, K. and Tandberg, O., Skiidrætten. Veiledning ved instruction i hoprend, *Centralforeningen for udbredelse af idræt Aarsberetning for 1902,* 1903, p. 167.

Aall, Lily Weisser, Ethnographical Survey, Norsk, Folkmuseum, 1959.

Aars, Hanna, Beretning om dameskirennet i Fjelbakken 1891, *Asker skiklub 1889–1929, 40 års jubileumsfestskrift,* 1929, p. 16.

Aasheim, Stein, *Veskysten eller døden,* Oslo, Scanbook, 1989.

*Abashevskaia kul'tura b srednem povolzh'e,* Moscow, Izdatel'stvo akademii nauk SSSR, 1961.

Acerbi, Joseph. *Travels through Sweden, Finland and Lapland to the North Cape in 1798 and 1799,* London, Joseph Mawman, 1802.

Adami, M. [Adam of Bremen], *Historia Ecclesiastica,* Leyden, Ex officina Plantiniana, 1595.

Adelung, Friedrich von. *Kritisch-literärische Uebersicht der Reisende in Russland bis 1700,* St Petersburg, Eggers & Comp. 1846.

A. G. G., Snow Skating in Scandinavia, *The Field,* 23 December 1882, p. 890.

A. H., Om brugen af to skistave, *Foreningen til Ski-Idrettens Fremme Årbok,* 1895–6, pp. 111–13.

Allerunderdanigst Udkast Til Et Exercitie Reglement For Ski Löberne i Norge, RA Militærarkiv K. G. ID pk.99, 13 October 1762.

Allerunderdanigst Udkast til Et Winter-Exercitie-Reglement For Skielöberne udi Norge, RA Militærarkiv K. G. IIC.nr.468, 3 November 1774.

Almquist, Helge, *Sverge och Ryssland 1595–1611,* Uppsala, Almquist & Wiksells Boktryckeri A. B., 1907.

Almquist, J. (ed.), *Konung Gustaf den Förstes Registratur xxvi 1556,* Stockholm p. A.Norstedt & Söner, 1911.

Alsvik, Elling, En helt annen verden? Om skihistorie i Sovjetunionen, *Trøndelag Folkemuseum Sverresborg Årbok,* 1991, pp. 41–58.

Altai-skidorna, *På Skidor,* 1940, pp. 343–6; 1941, pp. 282–3.

Amundsen, K. V., De norske Skiløbere i Chamonix, *Aftenposten* 17, 18, 23 January 1908.

Amundsen, K. V., Norske skiløbere i Frankrige, *Centralforeningen for udbredelse af idræt Aarsberetning for 1907,* 1908, pp. 66–9.

Amundsen, K. V., *Skiløpning,* Christiania, H.Aschehoug & Co., 1924.

Amundsen, Petter, Med grønne skiluer fra Skjenningen til Schweiz, *Snø og Ski, Foreningen til Ski-Idrettens Fremme Årbok,* No. 1, February 1995, pp. 72–3.

Amundsen, Roald, Brødrene Amundsens eventyrlige Færd over Hardangervidden, *Frederikstad Blad,* 8 February–5 March 1896.

Amundsen, Roald, *Belgica* diaries 1898. NBO Ms.8° 1196:X, XVI. Ms.fol.1210.

Amundsen, Roald, North West Passage sledging diaries, 16 March 1904–25 November 1905 in private ownership, 26 November 1905–10 March 1906 NBO Ms.8°1196:III.

Amundsen, Roald, *Nordvestpassagen*, Christiania, H. Aschehoug & Co., 1907.

Amundsen, Roald, South Pole sledging diaries 1911–12. NBO Ms.8°1196:IV, Ms.8°1249.

Amundsen, Roald, Litt om vore Ski, Bindinger og Fotbeklædning samt deres betydning for Sydpolsfærden, *Foreningen til Ski-Idrettens Fremme Årbok*, 1912a, pp. 57–66.

Amundsen, Roald, *Sydpolen*, Christiania, Jacob Dybwads Forlag, 1912b.

Andersen, Bjørn G., *The Ice Age World*, Stockholm, Scandinavian University Press, 1994.

Andersen, Roy, *Henrik Angell*, Oslo, Forum-Aschehoug, 2000.

Andresen, Harald, Norsk ski-litteratur, på grunnlag av Universitetsbibliotekets samlinger, *Foreningen til Ski-Idrettens Fremme Årbok*, 1937.

A New International Ski Association? *British Ski Year Book*, 1929, pp. 113–15.

A New Method of Skiing, *The Alpine Post and Engadin Express*, xxxix, No. 2, 1903, pp. 6–7.

An alle Freunde des Schneeschuhsports, *Deutscher Wintersport* xi, No. 1, 1901–2, pp. 1–2.

An English Glimpse of Old Davos Sixty-Seven Years Ago, *The Courier Davos*, lvii, No. 18, 1928, pp. 3–4.

Angell, H., En Skitur fra Hardanger til Kongsberg, *Morgenbladet*, No. 69, 10 March 1884.

Angell, H., Fra en skitur i Montenegro *Norsk Idrætsblad*, xi, 28 February 1893a.

Angell, H. A., Skiclub i Montenegro, *Norsk Idrætsblad*, xi, No. 12, 21 March 1893b, p. 95.

Angell, H., *Gjennem Montenegro paa ski*, Christiania, H. Aschehoug & Co.s Forlag, 1895.

Angell, H., Over Hardangervidda, *Foreningen til Ski-Idrettens Fremme Årbok* 1895–6, pp. 94–7.

Angell, H., Norske skiløberafdelinger, *Centralforeningen for udbredelse af idræt Aarsberetning for 1903*, 1903, pp. 116–24.

Angell, H., *Kjække Gutter og Jenter*, Christiania, H. Aschehoug & Co., 1904.

Angell, H., *Norsk Skilauparsoga Øystredølarne*, Christiania, H. Aschehoug & Co., 1908.

Angell, H., Norske ski paa Mourmansk-fronten 1918–19, *Foreningen til Ski-Idrettens Fremme Årbok*, 1920, pp. 97–103.

Anglo-Swiss Race, *British Ski Year Book*, 1927, pp. 138–9.

Antropova, V. V., Lyzhi narodov Sibiri, *Sbornik Muzeia antropologii i etnografii*, xiv, 1953, pp. 5–36.

APEX, Ski-ing, *The Alpine Post and Engadin Express*, xxxix, No. 7, 1903, p. 30.

Appelgren-Kivalo, Hjalmar, Muinaisajan suksista, *Suomen Museo*, xviii, 1911, pp. 7–16.

Arentz, Premierløitnant, Skiløpning i Rusland, *Foreningen til Ski-Idrettens Fremme Årbok*, 1911, pp. 68–78.

Arlberg-Kandahar results 1929, *British Ski Year Book*, 1929, pp. 248–51.

Arlt, Stefanie, Von den Nordischen Spielen über die olympischen Wintersportwettbewerbe (1908–1920) zu den ersten Olympischen Winterspielen in Chamonix, Mainz, Johannes Gutenberg-Universität, 2000 [Unpublished thesis] MZ.

Armstrong, Terence (ed.), *Yermak's Campaign in Siberia*, London, The Hakluyt Society, 1975.

Arnesen, Liv, *Snille piker går ikke til Sydpolen*, Oslo, Damm, 1995

Arnstorp, Odd, Da hjemmelagede ski var vanligst, Foreningen til Ski-Idrettens Fremme Årbok, 1997, pp. 65–78.

Artsikhovskii, A. V., *Drevnerusskie Miniatyury kak istoricheskii istochnik*, Moscow, Izdanie MGY, 1944.

Artsikhovskii, A. V., Lyzhi na Rusi, *Trudy instituta etnografii Akademiya Nauk Soyuza SSR*, Novaya Seriya I, 1947, pp. 55–64.

A. S., En skitur i Harzen, *Norsk Idrætsblad*, 10 April 1885, pp. 61–2.

Asbjørnsen, P. C., Norske Skiløbere, *Billed-Magazin for Børn*, ii, 1839, pp. 97–100.

Asbjørnsen, P. C., I Rumhelgen, *Juletræet for 1851*, pp. 61–3.

Asbjørnsen, P. C., *Norske huldreeventyr og folkesagn*, Oslo, H. Aschehoug & Co., 1934.

Asker Skiklubs Præmierend, *Aftenposten*, 2 March 1891.

Åström, Kenneth and Norberg, Ove, Förhistoriska och medeltida skidor, *Västerbotten*, 2, 1984, pp. 82–90.

Astrup, Eivind, Løitnant Peary's Groenlandsekspedition 1891–2, *Det Norske Geografiske Selskabs Aarbog*, v, (1891–2), pp. 25–44.

Astrup, Eivind, *With Peary near the Pole*, London, C. Arthur Pearson, 1898.

Attribution des Jeux de la XIème Olympiade, *Bulletin Officiel du Comité International Olympique*, July 1931, p. 10.

Aubert, Andreas, Om Skiløbningen i Øvre Telemarken, *Fædrelandet*, No. 20, 8 March 1879.

Auf Schneeschuhen, *Davoser Blätter*, Nos 1 and 9, 7 January and 4 March 1893.

Auf Schneeschuhen von der Brucker Hochalpe bis zur Gleinalpe, *Deutscher Eis-Sport*, i, No. 25, 1892, p. 196.

Auf Skiern zum Feldberg, *Deutscher Wintersport*, xi, No. 2, 1901–2, pp. 11–14; No. 3, pp. 19–21; No. 4, pp. 30–3; No. 5, pp. 42–4.

Austbø, Johan, *Olav Bjåland*, Oslo, Fonna Forlag, 1945.

Avezac, Marie Armand Pascal d' (ed.), Ioannis de Plano Carpini, Historia Mongalorum, *Recueil de Voyages et de Memoires*, published by the Societé de Geographie, iv, 1839, pp. 399–868.

Bååth, Johan, Några drag ur skidlöpningens historia, *På Skidor*, 1900–1, pp. 81–117.

Bååth, Johan, Fornsvenska Idrottsbilder, *På Skidor*, 1908–9, pp. 1–14.

Baddeley, John F., *Russia in the 'Eighties'*, London, Longman, Green & Co., 1921.

Bakke, Ranveig, Skiløyping og skiløyparar i gamal tid, *Tinn Skilag 1893–1993*, pp. 39–51, Skien, 1993.

Balck, Viktor (ed.), *Illustrerad Idrottsbok*, Stockholm, C. E. Fritze's K. Hofbokhandel, 1888.

Balck, Viktor, Skidtäflingarna vid Kristiania, *Stockholms Dagblad Extranummer*, 7 February 1892a.

Balck, Viktor ['V. G. B.'], Täflingarne i skidlöpning vid Christiania, *Tidningen för Idrott*, 1892b, p. 43.

Balck, Viktor ['V. G. B.'] [Täflingarne i skidlöpning vid Stockholm den 28 och 29 februari, *Tidning för Idrott*, No. 9, 1892c, pp. 72–4.

Balck, Viktor, Nordiska Spelen i Stockholm, *Ny Tidning för Idrott* Nos 7,8, 1901, p. 73.

Balck, Viktor, Olympiska Spelen i Stockholm, *Svenska Turistforeningens Årsskrift 1913*, 1912, pp. 168–78.

Balck, Viktor to Baron Coubertin 16 May 1921. IOC CIO MBR Balck Corr.M Against Winter Olympics.

Balduinus, Benedictus, *De calceo antiquo*, Amsterdam, Andreæ Frisi, 1667.

Ballu, Yves, *L'épopée du ski*, Paris, Arthaud, 1981.

Ballu, Yves, *L'hiver de glisse et de glace*, Découvertes Gallimard Sports et Jeux, 1991.

Balto, Samuel J., *Med Nansen over Grønlandsisen i 1888*, Oslo, Universitetsforlaget, 1980.

Balzac, Honoré de, *Séraphîta*, Paris, Louis Conard, 1927.

Bandi, Hans-Georg, *Die Schweiz zur Rentierzeit*, Frauenfeld, Verlag Huber & Co., 1947.

Bartholini, Erasmi, *De Figura Nivis*, Copenhagen, P. Hauboldi, 1661.

Basberg, Bjørn L., Telemarksvingen-refleksjoner om en renessanse, *Foreningen til Ski-Idrettens Fremme Årbok*, 1994, pp. 42–56.

Beauclerk, D., *A Summer & Winter in Norway*, London, John Murray, 1868.

Bégouën, H. and Breuil, H., *Les Cavernes du Volp*, Paris, Arts et Métiers Graphiques, 1958.

Béguin, Claude and Theurillat, Jean-Paul, Impacte des pistes de ski sur les lacs alpins, *Les Alpes*, lvii, 1981, pp. 171–5.

*Bei Shi (Northern History)*, Peking, 1974.

Belov, M.I, Ovsiannikov, O. V. and Starkov, V. F., *Mangazeia. Material'naia Kul'tura Russkikh Poliarnykh morekhodov i zemleprokhodtsev XVI–XVII BB.*, Moscow, Izdatel'stvo Nauka, 1981.

Berckenmeyern, P. L., *Vermehrter Curieuser Antiquarius*, Hamburg, Benjamin Schiller und Johann Christoph Kitzner, 1720.

Beretning om Norges deltagelse i de olympiske leker sommeren 1924 og Vinteridrettsstevnet i Chamonix, Oslo, B. Bentzens Boktrykkeri, 1925.

Berg, Gösta, *Artur Hazelius, Mannen och hans verk*, Stockholm, Bokförlaget Natur och Kultur, 1933a.

Berg, Gösta, Förhistoriska skidor i Sverige, *På Skidor*, 1933b, pp. 142–69.

Berg, Gösta, Hällristningar med skidlöpare, *På Skidor*, 1940, pp. 346–9.

Berg, Gösta, De båda stavarna och våra skidtyper än en gång, *På Skidor*, 1944, pp. 89–94.

Berg, Gösta, Den botniska skidtypen och dateringen av ett finskt myrfynd, *På Skidor*, 1946, pp. 276–8.

Berg, Gösta, *Finds of skis from Prehistoric Time in Swedish Bogs and Marshes*, Stockholm, Generalstabens Litografiska Anstalts Förlag, 1950.

Berg, Gösta, Nya Fynd av förhistoriska skidor i Sverige, *På Skidor*, 1951, pp. 181–6.

Berg, Gösta, Ett ryskt bidrag til skidforskningen, *På Skidor*, 1952, pp. 229–32.

Berg, Karin, Skihistorisk i Grenoble, *Foreningen til Ski-Idrettens Fremme Årbok Snø og Ski*, No. 1, February 1995, p. 49.

Berg, Karin, *Ski i Norge*, Oslo, Aventura, 1993.

Berg, Leif, En vinter I Schweiz, *Norsk Idrætsblads Julenummer*, 1905, pp. 10–15.

Berge, Rikard, *Norsk Visefugg*, Christiania, Olaf Norlis Forlag, 1904.

Berge, Rikard, *Myllarguten*, Christiania, H. Aschehoug & Co., 1908.

Bergeron, T., Fries, M., Moberg, C.-A., Ström, F., Fimbulvinter, *Fornvännen*, li, 1956, pp. 1–18.

Berggren, Elof, Med ryssar på skidor, *På Skidor,* 1902–3, pp. 64–73.

Bergman, C. O., Anteckningar vid skidlöpningstäflan i Jokkmokk den 3 och 4 April 1884, *Den anda Dicksonska expeditionen til Grönland,* pp. 244–9.

Berry, William Banks, *Lost Sierra*, Soda Springs, CA, Western America Ski Sport Museum, 1991.

Besheim, Asbjørn, Samiske transport-og fremkomstmidler, *Norsk Folkemuseums samlinger,* 2, 1976, pp. 1–32.

Bilgeri, Georg, *Der Alpine Skilauf,* Munich, Verlag der Deutschen Alpenzeitung, 1911.

Bilgeri, Georg, Erfahrungen mit Ski im Hochgebirge, *Les Alpes* (1928), pp. 1–12.

Bistrup, Rie, I motesporet – før og nå, *Foreningen til Ski-Idrettens Fremme Årbok,* 1974, pp. 33–8.

Bjaaland, Vlav, Antarctic diary, copy in the possession of the author.

Bjarnason, Bjørn, *Nordboernes legemlige uddannelse i oldtiden,* Copenhagen, Vilhelm Priors Hofboghandel, 1905.

Bjerknes, Ernst, Paa Iversløkken, 1933. Unpublished manuscript, SH.

Bjerknes, Ernst, *Med ski, velosiped og skissebok,* Oslo, Jacob Dybwads forlag, 1943.

Bjerknes, Ernst, Skiløping i Gudbrandsdalen i 1890-aarene, *Norsk Skiløpere, Østlandet Nord,* 1955, pp. 220–2.

Bjerregaard, H. A., *Digtninger,* Christiania, Feilberg & Landmarks Forlag, 1848.

Blackmore, R. D., *Lorna Doone,* London, Mammoth, 1990.

Blossom, F. A., *Told at the Explorers' Club,* London, G. G. Harrap & Co., 1932.

Bø, Olav, *Norsk skitradisjon,* Oslo, Det norske Samlaget, 1966.

Bobé, Louis, *Hans Egede,* Copenhagen, C. A. Reitzels Forlag, 1944.

Bodenhoff, E., *Et lykkeligt Hjem,* Copenhagen Gyldendalske Boghandel Nordisk Forlag, 1909.

*Bol'shaia sovetskaia entsiklopediia,* Moscow, Gosudarstvennoe nauchnoe izdatel'stvo, 1949.

Bondidier, L. Le, Concours de ski des Pyrénées, *La Montagne,* iv(a), 1908, pp. 123–35.

Bonsall, Clive (ed.), *The Mesolithic in Europe,* Edinburgh, John Donald, 1985.

Borchgrevink, Carsten E., *Nærmest Sydpolen aaret, 1900,* Copenhagen and Christiania, Gyldendalske Boghandel nordisk Forlag, 1905.

Bosley, Keith (tr.), *The Kalevala,* Oxford, Oxford University Press, 1989.

Branger, Johannes, Ueberschreitung der Mayenfelder Furka am 23/24 März 1893, *Schweizerischer Skiverband Jubiläums Jahrbuch 1929,* n.d., pp. 40–2.

Branger, Johannes, Aus der Frühzeit des Skilaufs in Davos, *Davoser Revue,* xxxv, 1960, pp. 20–3, 60–7, 92–7.

Brann, David, Russian Skiers The First to Make Tracks in North America, *Proceedings, Ski History Congress,* Utah, 2002.

Brask, Christofer, and Karlsson, Petter, *Ur Spår!* Rimbo, Fischer & Co., 2005.

Brekke, Aasmund, Fra Aasmund Brekke, *Foreningen til Ski-Idrettens Fremme Årbok,* 1924, pp. 98–101.

Breuil, H., *Les Peintures Rupestres Schématiques de la Péninsule Ibérique,* Imprimerie de Lagny, 1933.

Breuil, H., *Les hommes de la pierre ancienne,* Paris, Payot, 1959.

Brevkasse A. Davos, Schweiz, *Norsk Idrætsblad,* No. 1, 18 January 1884, p. 11.

Brittain, Sir Harry, *Happy Pilgrimage,* London, Hutchinson & Co., 1949.

Broch, Leif, Den norske Skiløpertrop i Utlandet 1910, *Foreningen til Ski-Idrettens Fremme Årbok,* 1910, pp. 80–7.

Broche, Gaston-E., *Pythéas le Massaliote,* Paris, Société Francaise d'Imprimerie et de Librairie, 1935.

Brøgger, A. W. (tr.), *Kongespeilet,* Oslo, H. Aschehoug & Co., 1947.

Brooke, A. de Capell, *Travels through Sweden, Norway and Finmark,* London, Rodwell & Martin, 1823.

Brooke, A. de Capell, *A Winter in Lapland and Sweden,* London, John Murray, 1827.

Brosset, M., *Collection D'Historiens Arméniens,* St Petersburg, Imprimerie de l'Académie Impériale des Sciences, 1874.

Brun, Johan Nordahl, *Johan Nordahl Bruns mindre Digte,* Christiania, Jacob Lehmann, 1818.

Bugge, Astrid, Bydamer kledd til vintersport, *By og bygd,* xi, 1956–7, pp. 19–62.

Bull, Edvard, *Det norske Folks Liv og Historie*, Oslo, Aschehoug, 1929.

Bunbury, E. H., *A History of Ancient Geography*, London, John Murray, 1879.

Bureus, Andrea, *Svecia, sive de Suecorum Regis Dominiis et opibus*, Leyden, Ex officina Elzeviriana, 1631.

Burman, O. A., Om skidlöpare, *På Skidor*, 1927, pp. 309–16.

Burov, Grigoriy M., Fragmenty sanei s poseleniï Vis I (mezolit) i Vis II(I tysyacheletie n.e.), *Sovetskaia arkheologiia*, 2, 1981, pp. 117–31.

Burov, Grigoriy M., Some Mesolithic Wooden Artefacts from the Site of Vis I, *The Mesolithic in Europe. Symposium*, Edinburgh, Bonsall, 1985, pp. 391–401.

Burov, Grigoriy M., On Mesolithic means of water transportation in northeastern Europe, *Mesolithic Miscellany*, xvii, No. 1, 1996, pp. 5–15.

Burtscher, August and Rhomberg, Ingo, *Künstliche Skikanten*, Munich, Bergverlag Rudolf Rother, [n.d.].

Buryat ski, *På Skidor*, 1938, p. 381.

Bydamer i Touristinde-Dragt, *By og bygd*, xii, 1957–8, pp. 1–42.

Caminada, Paul, *Wintersport. Entstehung und Entwicklung: St.Moritz, Davos, Arosa, Klosters, Lenzerheide, Flims Disentis/Mustér*, Disentis, Desertina Verlag, 1986.

Campbell, Victor, Ski in the Antarctic, *British Ski Year Book*, 1910.

Carl von Linné som skidforskare, *På Skidor*, 1950, pp. 249–51.

Carlsen, Dagfinn, *Der Skilauf*, Vienna, Kommissionsverlag J. Rubinstein, 1925.

Castell, Alexandre (ed.), *Les Jeux sur les Cimes*, Paris, Les Éditions C. Crés & Cie. [n.d.].

Castrén, M.Alexander, *Kalevala*, Helsinki, J. Simelii enka, 1841.

Castrén, M.Alexander, *Nordische Reisen und Forschungen*, St Petersburg, Kaiserliche Akademie der Wissenschaften, 1853.

Catlin, Geo., *Letters and Notes on the Manners, Customs and Conditions of the North American Indians*, London, published by the author, 1841.

Caulfeild, Vivian, *How to Ski and How Not To*, London, James Nisbet, 1913.

Cederberg, Sven J., En gammal skogslöpares funderingar och erfarenheter om skidforskning och tjurvirke, *På Skidor*, 1938, pp. 21–39.

Cederhjelm, Carl Wilhelm, Lapparnas skidor, *På Skidor*, 1938 p. 379.

Cereghini, Mario, Le ski dans la litterature et l'iconographie italiennes du 16 sc, *Les Alpes* xxvi, 1950, p. 114.

Cervantes, Miguel de, *Los Trabajos de Persiles y Sigismunda*, Madrid, Clásicos Castalia, 1969.

Chavannes, E., *Les mémoires historiques de Se-Ma Ts'ien*, Paris, E. Leroux, 1895.

Chavannes, E., Les Pays d'Occident d'après le Wei lio, *T'oung Pao*, II series, vi, No. 5, 1905, pp. 519–71.

Chernykh, E. N., *Ancient Metallurgy in the USSR*, Cambridge, Cambridge University Press, 1992.

Chew, Allen F., *The White Death: The Epic of the Soviet–Finnish Winter War*, Michigan State University Press, 1971.

Christensen, Olav, *Skiidrett før Sondre*. Ad Notem Gyldendal, 1993a.

Christensen, Olav, Skiidrett før Sondre, *Foreningen til Ski-Idrettens Fremme Årbok*, 1993b, pp. 34–7.

*Christiania Skiklubb 125 år*, Oslo, 2002.

*Christiania Skiklubb 1877–1977*, Oslo, Emil Mostue, 1977.

Christophersen, H. O., Jørgen Moe og Krokskogen, *Foreningen til Ski-Idrettens Fremme Årbok*, 1963, pp. 33–42.

Christophersen, H. O., Ett historisk skiløp for 250 år siden, *Foreningen til Ski-Idrettens Fremme Årbok*, 1968, pp. 18–27.

Clark, J. G. D., *Excavations at Star Carr*, Cambridge, Cambridge University Press, 1954.

Clark, J. G. D., *Prehistoric Europe: the Economic Basis*, London, Methuen, 1965.

Clark, J. G. D., *The Earlier Stone Age Settlement of Scandinavia*, Cambridge, Cambridge University Press, 1975.

Claudii Ptolemæi, *Geographia*, Paris, Editore Alfredo Firmin Didot, 1883.

Clerc, Capitaine, Rapport sur les Expériences de Skis Exécutées dans les Environs de Briançon par le 159me Reg'ent d'Inf'rie au Cours des Hivers 1900–1901 et 1901–1902, unpublished manuscript, SH, 1902.

Clerc, Capitaine, Rapport sur les expériences de matches en skis exécutées à Briançon durant l'hiver 1902–03, unpublished manuscript, SH, 1903.

CN, 'Skididrottens framsteg å kontinenten', *På Skidor*, 1910–11, pp. 64–72.

Colbeck, Samuel C., A Review of the Processes that Control Snow Friction, *US Army Corps of Engineers*,

*Cold Regions Research & Engineering Laboratory,* Monograph 92-2, 1992.

Collinder, Björn, Der älteste überlieferte germanische Name, *Namn och Bygd,* xxiv, 1936, pp. 92–7.

Collinder, Björn (tr.), *Kalevala,* Stockholm, Forum, 1960.

Comité Olympique Français, Les Jeux d'Hiver de Chamonix, *Les Jeux de la VIIIe Olympiade, Paris 1924* Rapport Officiel Paris, Librairie de France, 1924, pp. 643–777.

Concours International de Ski, 9/13 Février 1907, *La Montagne,* iii, 1907, pp. 136–41.

Condé, Marie-Anne, Det bästa hos människan är skidorna Budskap som blir perspektiv 1880–1950, *Svensk Idrottsforskning,* No. 1, 2000, pp. 13–17.

Condé, Marie-Anne, Folkets skidor och herrskapets, *Folkets historia,* xxii, 1994, pp. 18–36.

Condé, Marie-Anne, Öfva den svingande rörelsen! Svensk skidåkning under femtio år, *Svensk idrottsforskning,* No. 2, 2000, pp. 11–15.

Condé, Marie-Anne, *Skidåkning i Sverige. Från Hedenhös til Heijkenskiöld.,* Stockholm, Institutet for Folklivsforskning, Stockolms Universitet, 1991.

Condé, Marie-Anne, *Skidan i friluftslivet 1890–1960,* Stockholm, Etnologiska Institutionen, Stockholms Universitet, 1999.

Constitution and Rules, *The Public Schools Alpine Sports Club Year Book,* 1910, pp. xv–xviii.

Conway, Martin, *The First Crossing of Spitsbergen,* London, J. M. Dent & Co., 1897.

Conway, Martin, *With Ski and Sledge over Arctic Glaciers,* London, J. M. Dent, 1898.

Cornell, Henrik, *Albertus Pictor,* Stockholm, Kungl. Vitterhets Historie och Antikvitets Akademien, 1981.

Coubertin, Pierre de, *Olympie,* Geneva, Imprimerie Burgi, [n.d.].

[Coubertin, Pierre de], Olympiades Boréales, *Revue Olympique,* April 1901, pp. 17–24.

Coubertin, Pierre de, *Une Campagne de vingt-et-un Ans,* Paris, Librairie de L'Éducation Physique, 1909.

[Coubertin, Pierre de] La décadence des sports d'hiver, *Revue Olympique,* March 1914, pp. 39–40.

CY, Ski Competition at Christiania, *The Field,* 25 February, 1888, p. 255.

Czant, Hermann, Militära vinteröfningar i fjällen, *På Skidor,* 1907–8, pp. 42–58.

Dalbäk, Sigurd, Skidorna och Torne-Kalix'folk, *På Skidor,* 1926, pp. 19–32.

Dalen, Arnold, Scandinavian Ski Terminology, *History of Skiing Conference Holmenkollen, Oslo 16–18 September 1998,* Oslo, Skiforeningen, 1998, pp. 49–57.

Damer af den paa Stenkjær netop stiftede Dameskiklub 'Skade', *Indherreds-Posten,* 23 March 1889.

Damernes skiddräkt, *På Skidor,* 1908–9, pp. 120–3.

Dancing at Swiss Resorts. Public Schools Alpine Sports Club, *The Times,* 11 June 1913.

Das Schneeschuhlaufen, *Davoser Blätter,* 1892, Nos 46–47, 10 and 17 December 1892.

Dass, Petter, *Nordlands Trompet,* Oslo, H. Aschehoug & Co., 1958.

Davidson, Daniel Sutherland, Snowshoes, *Memoirs of the American Philosophical Society,* vi, 1937.

Davos English Ski Club, *The Courier Davos,* xxxix, No. 4, 1920, p. 2.

*Davos-Platz: A New Alpine Resort for Sick and Sound . . . By One Who Knows it Well,* London, Edward Stanford, 1878.

Davydov, Gavriil Ivanovich, *Two Voyages to Russian America 1802–1807,* Kingston, Ontario, Limestone Press, 1977.

De Jong, Cornelius, *Reizen naar de Goede Hoop, Ierland en Noorwegen,* Haarlem, François Bohn, 1802.

De Kinesiska sumpskidorna, *På Skidor,* 1936, pp. 348–9.

De la Brunière, M., Excursion en Mandchourie en 1845, *Nouvelles Annales des Voyages,* Nouvelle Série, iv, 1848, pp. 82–115.

Delaquis, Gaston, *75 Jahre Pferderennen in St Moritz 1906 bis 1980* St Moritz, Rennverein, [n.d.].

Den första avbildningen av en svensk arméskida, *På Skidor,* 1943, pp. 305–7.

Den internationella skidutställningen i Stockholm, *På Skidor,* 1902–3, pp. 234–84.

Den internationella sportutställning i Berlin 1907, *På Skidor,* 1907–8, pp. 135–44.

Den södra skidtypens urform, *På Skidor,* 1938, p. 375.

Descartes, René, *Discours de la Méthode,* Leyden, Ian Maire, 1637.

Dickson, Oscar, A Race on Snow Skates in Lapland, *The Times,* 21 May 1884.

Die Einführung der Schneeschuhe in der nord-europäischen Armeer, *Deutscher Eis-Sport* ii (1893), No. 6, p. 45.

Die erste oesterreichische Wintersportausstellung, *Deutscher Eissport,* iii (1893–94) No. 3, pp. 16–17.

Die nordischen Spiele in Mürzzuschlag, *Illustriertes Wiener Extrablatt*, 4 February 1904.

Die nordischen Spielen in Mürzzuschlag, *Österreische Touristen-Zeitung*, xxiv, 1904 No. 5, pp. 89–91.

Dillon, Arthur, *A Winter in Iceland and Lapland*, London, Henry Colburn, 1840.

*Diplomatarium Danicum* 1 række 2 bind, Copenhagen, Ejnar Munksgaards Forlag, 1963.

*Diplomatarium Norvegicum*, Christiania, P. T. Mallings Boghandels Forlag, 1847.

*Dnevnik politruka Oreshina*, Helsinki, privately printed, 1941.

Døbler, Hermann, Kristianiateknikken før og nå, *Foreningen til Ski-Idrettens Fremme Årbok*, 1967, pp. 80–3.

Døderlein, Doctor, Skiløbning sett fra et hygienisk standpunkt med specielt hensyn paa kvinden, *Centralforeningen for udbredelse af idræt Aarsberetning for 1896*, pp. 70–3.

D'Ohsson, M. le Baron C., *Histoire des Mongols*, Amsterdam, Frederik Muller, 1852.

Donner, Kai, Über die Jenissei-ostjaken und ihre sprache, *Journal de la Société Finno–Ougrienne*, xliv, No. 2, 1930.

Dowitsch, Emil, *Der Ski und seine Behandlung*, Vienna, H. Kapri & Co., 1934.

Doyle, A. Conan, An Alpine Pass on Ski, *The Strand Magazine*, viii, 1894, December, pp. 657–61.

Doyle, A. Conan, *Memories and Adventures*, London, Hodder & Stoughton, 1924.

Düben, Gustaf von, *Om Lappland och Lapparne*, Stockholm, p. A. Norstedt & Söners förlag, 1873.

Dubler, César E., *Abu Hamid el Granadino*, Madrid, Imprenta y Editorial Maestre, 1953.

Durban-Hansen, H., Fra Frankrigs første internationale Skiløb, *Foreningen til Ski-Idrettens Fremme Årbok*, 1907, pp. 106–8.

Durban-Hansen, H., Quelques notes sur le ski en France et l'usage du batôn, *La Montagne*, iv(a) (1908), pp. 400–3.

Dybdahl, Audun, *Fra stav til stasvogn*, Steinkjer, Steinkjer Museum, 1990.

Dyhlén, Gunnar, Med björnspjut och annare, *På Skidor*, 1929, pp. 212–17.

Eberhard, W., Kultur und Siedlung der Randvölker Chinas, *T'oung Pao*, xxxvi, 1942, supplement.

Edelman, Robert, *Serious Fun*, A History of Spectator Sports in the USSR, Oxford, Oxford University Prress, 1993.

Edgren, J. S., *Catalogue of the Nordenskiöld Collection of Japanese Books in the Royal Library*, Stockholm, Norstedts Tryckeri, 1980.

Edman, Gunnar, Naturen och poeterna, *På Skidor*, 1963, pp. 7–20.

Edström, J. S. to Count Clary 26 April 1922 IOC JO-1924W-CORR Against Winter Olympics.

Egeberg, F., Lidt gammelt nyt fra Christiania Skiklub. Unpublished manuscript, 6 November 1919, SH.

Egger, Carl, Geschichtliches, Ski, *Jahrbuch des Schweiz. Ski-Verbandes*, v, 1909, pp. 76–94.

Egger, Carl, Ein Rückblick auf die ersten 10 Jahre des Schweizerischen Skiverbands, *Ski*, x, 1914, pp. 4–29.

Egger, Carl, Etwas von der Entdeckung des Winters, *Schweizerischer Skiverband Jubiläums Jahrbuch 1929*, [n.d.], pp. 34–40.

Eggset, A. and Sandnes, J., *På Trønderski*, Trondheim, Tapir Forlag, 1988.

*Egils saga Skallagrímssonar*, Reykjavík, Sigurdur Kristjánsson, 1910.

Ein Skitour im nördlichen Schwarzwald, *Deutscher Wintersport*, xii, 1902–3, No. 20, pp. 203–5.

Elling Bækkens Skirend, *Morgenbladet*, 17 March 1866.

Emahusen, J. A., *Exercises von Eine Compagnie Schieleuffers auf denen Schiihen*, 26 March 1733. RAO militærarkiv, KGIC, No. 467.

Engle, Eloise and Paananen, Lauri, *The Winter War*, London, Sidgwick & Jackson, 1973.

En Skiløbermøde i Næsseby, *Finmarksposten*, 15 February 1867.

En vinterdag på Saltsjöbaden, *Idun*, xiv, 1901, pp. 156–7.

Erb, Fritz, Erste Durchquerung der Bernalpen auf Ski, *Schweizerischer Skiverband Jubiläums Jahrbuch 1929*, n.d., pp. 59–62.

Erdmann, F. von, *Vollstaendige Uebersicht der Voelkerstaemme nach Raschid-ud-din's Vorgange*, Kazan, In der Universitäts-Typographie, 1841.

Erdmann, F. von, *Temudschin der Unerschütterliche*, Leipzig, F. A. Brockhaus, 1862.

Erman, Adolph, *Reise um die Erde durch Nord-Asien und die beiden Oceane*. Berlin, G. Reimer, 1838.

Erster Ski-Curs für patentierte Führer, *Deutscher Wintersport*, xi, No. 16, 1901–2, pp. 153–4.

Erstes schweizerisches Ski-Rennen auf dem Gurten bei Bern, *Deutscher Wintersport*, xi, No. 17, 1901–2, pp. 165–6.

Eskimå-skidor från Alaska, *På Skidor*, 1937, pp. 398–400.

Et 60 aar gammelt brev om å lage ski, *Foreningen til Ski-Idrettens Fremme Årbok*, 1949, p. 135.

Exercice-Reglement for Skielöber-Compagnierne udi Norge, 6 November 1748, RA Militærarkiv K.G.IC, no.11.

Exercices von Eine Compagnie Schielauffers auf denen Schiihen, 2 May 1733. RA Militærarkiv K.G.IC, no. 467.

Fagan, B.M., *The Great Journey: The Peopling of Ancient America*, London, Thames & Hudson, 1987.

Fairlie, Gerard, *Flight without Wings, the Biography of Hannes Schneider*, London, Hodder & Stoughton, 1957.

Fanck, Arnold and Schneider, Hannes, *Wunder des Schneeschuhs*, Hamburg, Gebrüder Enoch Verl., 1925.

Fendrich, A., *Der Skiläufer*, Stuttgart, Franckh'sche Verlagshandlung, 1908.

Ferdmann, Jules, *Die Anfänge des Kurortes Davos*, Davos, Verlag der Davoser Revue, Davos, 1938.

Ferdmann, Jules, Alte Skiänliche Geräte in Davos und andernorts in Graubunden, *Davoser Revue*, xvi, 1941, pp. 113–18, 151.

Ferdmann, Jules, *Der Aufstieg von Davos*, Davos, Verlag Genossenschaft Davoser Revue, 1990.

Finnish Mastery in the Art of War, *The Times*, 27 December 1939.

Finsterlin, A., Weitere Mittheilungen über das Skilaufen, *Deutscher Eis-Sport,* i, No. 10, 1892, p. 75.

Fischer, Manfred, Die Geschichte des Alpinen Schisports in Wien, Universität Wien, 1985. Unpublished thesis. MZ.

FIS Procès-verbal 3–4 February 1927, IOC: CIO FI SKI FIS OU. FIS refuse CIO request for slalom as demonstration at St Moritz, 1928.

Flaten, Rune, Hvem var skiguden Ull? *Foreningen til Ski-Idrettens Fremme Årbok*, 1999, pp. 38–53.

*Flateyarbók*, Christiania, P. T. Mallings Forlagsboghandel, 1862.

Fleischmann, W. and Steinbrüchel, E., *Lilienfelder oder Norweger?* Diessen near München, Verlagsanstalt Jos. C. Huber, 1910.

Flückiger-Seiler, Roland, *Hotel Paläste*, Baden, Hier+Jetzt, Verlag für Kultur und Geschichte, 2003.

Fønhus, Mikkjel, *Skiløperen*, Oslo, H. Aschehoug & Co., 1981.

Fontannaz, Félix, Souvenirs d'un vieux guide, *Les Alpes*, xiii, 1937, pp. 192–4.

Foreningen til Ski-Idrettens Fremme rend den 5, 6 og 7 februar, 50 Kilometerrendet, *Norsk Idrætsblad,* 11 February 1888, No. 4, p. 21.

Forfrysning, *Sundhedsbladet,* xiii, February 1895, pp. 20–3.

Fox, Gerald, Early Memories, *British Ski Year Book,* xi, 1942–5, pp. 135–7.

Fra Huseby til Holmenkollen, *Foreningen til Ski-Idrettens Fremme Årbok*, 1992, pp. 18–19.

Freeman, Harold, The Beginnings of Winter Sport, *The Courier Davos,* xxxvi, 1913, pp. 7–8.

Friesen, Otto von, Vår första skidlöparbild, *På Skidor*, 1925, pp. v–xi.

Friis, Hans, *De Norske Findlappers Beskrivelse*, Copenhagen, Niels Hansen Møller, 1740.

Frognerseteren for 80 år siden, *Foreningen til Ski-Idrettens Fremme Årbok*, 1971, pp. 65–6.

Furse, Katherine, Some Early Ski-runners, *British Ski Year Book,* 1921, pp. 269–70.

Furse, Katherine, *Ski Running*, London, Longman, Green & Co., 1924.

Furse, Katherine, *Hearts and Pomegranates*, London, Peter Davies, 1940.

G., Skisport i Thüringen, *Norsk Idrætsblad,* 7 March 1884, p. 44.

Gadow, H., *In Northern Spain*, London, Adam & Charles Black, 1897.

Gallaz, Christophe, *Sculpteur de Musiques,* Fribourg (Suisse), Editions La Sarine, 1999.

Gamla skidor i Ostpreussen, *På Skidor*, 1948, p. 239.

Gartmann, Joos, *Die Pferdepost in Graubünden*, Disentis, Desertina Verlag, 1985.

Geete, Erik, Med ski och andur i Särna, *På Skidor*, 1931, pp. 293–9.

Geete, Erik, Gustaf Vasas flykt, *På Skidor*, 1948, pp. 239–43.

Geete, Erik, Skidans sång, *På Skidor*, 1950, pp. 246–8.

Georgi, J. G., *Bemerkungen einer Reise im Russischen Reich*, St Petersburg, Kayserl. Academie der Wissenschaften, 1775.

Gesner, Conrad, *De Raris et Admirandis Herbis, Eusdem Descriptio Montis Fracti, Siue Montis Pilati*, Zurich, Apud Andream Gesnerum F. & Iacobum Gesnerum, fratres, 1555.

Gillquist, Hilmer, Fjällens erövring, *På Skidor*, 1931, pp. 51–8.

Giraud, Etienne, Le pays des skieurs, *Foreningen til Ski-Idrettens Fremme Årbok*, 1912, pp. 97–100.

Gjessing, Guttorm, *Nordenfjeldske Ristninger og Malinger av den arktiske Gruppe*, Oslo, H. Aschehoug & Co., 1936.

Gløersen, Kristian, Ski-idraet og Huseby-rendet, *Illustreret Tidende for Børn*, 6te Aargang, 1890–1, pp. 121–3, 133–5.

Goeteeris, Anthonis, *Journal Der Legatie ghedaen inde jaren 1616 ende 1616*, The Hague, Aert Meuris, 1619.

Gotaas, Thor, *Først i løypa*, Oslo, Andresen & Butenschøn forlag, 2003.

Gotaas, Thor, *Skimakerne*, Oslo, Gyldendal, 2007.

*Grágás, Stadarhólsbók*, Copenhagen, Gyldendalske Boghandel, 1879.

Granlund, John, Svensk skidornamentikk, *På Skidor*, 1941, pp. 117–34.

*Grosses vollständige Universallexikon*, Halle, Johann Heinrich Zedler, 1737.

Grosskurth, Phyllis, *John Addington Symonds*, London, Longmans, 1964.

Grøttumsbråten, Johan, Corrrespondence, 1924–8 NBO Brevs.776.

Grove, Jean M., *The Little Ice Age*, London, Methuen, 1988.

Grundström, H., Den store skidtävlingen Purkijaur-Kvikkjokk, *På Skidor*, 1934, pp. 32–52.

Grüner, *Gezeichnete Figuren und Maneuvres von des Königl. Nordischen Schiläuffer-Corps pro Anno 1765*. Manuscript in Norwegian Armed Forces Museum, Oslo.

Guagnini Veronensis, Alexandri, *Sarmatiae Europeæ Descriptio*, Cracow, Typis Matthiæ Wirzbietæ, 1578.

Guberti, Vincenzo, Le ski et sa technique au 17e siecle, *Les Alpes*, xxvi, 1950, pp. 129–31.

Gudmundur fra Mosdal, Skidor och skidlöpning på Island, *På Skidor*, 1937, pp. 114–21.

Guillamo, Marcel, *Historique du 159e Régiment d'infanterie alpine*, Briançon, 159e RIA, 1988.

Gulbransson, Olaf, En hævet forlovelse, *Tyrihans*, 1894, p. 112.

Gulowsen, J. Premieskirenn i Norge 1767, *Foreningen til Ski-Idrettens Fremme Årbok*, 1932, pp. 74–80.

Gunda, Béla, Snöskorna hos Karpaternes Folk, *På Skidor*, 1940, pp. 229–37.

GutsMuths, J. C. F., *Gymnastik für die Jugend*, Schnepfenthal, in der Buchhandlung der Erziehungsanstalt, 1804.

Gyger, W. J., *Wintersport in der Schweiz*, Samedan, Verlag Engadin Press Co., 1925.

Haarstad, Kjell, *Skisportens oppkomst i Norge*, Trondheim, Tapir Forlag, 1993.

Hade Skandinaviens första inbyggarre snöskor eller skidor, *På Skidor*, 1936, p. 348.

Haller, Albrecht Von, *Gedichte*, Frauenfeld, Verlag von J. Huber, 1882.

Halter, Ernst (ed.), *Davos, Profil eines Phänomens*, Davos, Offizin, 1997.

Halvorsen, Ivar, *Fra Ullevoldsæter til Blå-skia*, Nittedal, Nittedal Historielag, Skriftserie, no. 3, 2000.

Hamberg, Axel, Til skidans femtioårsjubileum såsom Redskap v. Arktisk Forskning, *På Skidor*, 1933, pp. 5–19.

Hamilton, C. G. D., A Defence of the Langlauf, *British Ski Year Book*, 1926, pp. 354–61.

Hamilton, C. G. D., De nya brittiska skidtävlingsformerna, *På Skidor*, 1928, pp. 313–31.

Hamilton, Lord Frederic, *The Vanished Pomps of Yesterday*, London, Hodder & Stoughton, 1919.

Hammarstedt, E., Skidorna och deras utvecklingsformer, *Ljus*, Nos 26 and 27, 31 March and 8 April 1899.

Hammarstedt, E., Om skidor, snöskor och skarbåger och deres utvecklingsformer, *På Skidor*, 1929, pp. 16–33.

Hamsun, Knut, Nansen-Betragtninger, *Dagbladet*, 20 June 1889a.

Hamsun, Knut, Damer paa Ski, *Dagbladet*, 23 December 1889b.

Hansen, C. Bloch, and Houge, Nils, Litt om våre eldre skibindinger og den utviking de har gjennemgått, *Foreningen til Ski-Idrettens Fremme Årbok*, 1933, pp. 106–16.

Hansteen, C., Efterskrift, *Magazin for Naturvidenskabnerne*, i, 1823, pp. 239–50.

Hantverksmässig skidtillverkning, *Västerbotten*, ii, 1984, pp. 90–4.

Harva, Uno, *Die Religiösen Vorstellungen der Altaischen Völker*, Helsinki, Werner Söderström Osakeyhtiö, 1938.

Hatt, Gudmund, *Arktiske Skinddragter i Eurasien og Amerika*, Copenhagen, J. H. Schultz forlagsboghandel, 1914.

Hatt, Gudmund, Kyst-og Indlandskultur i det arktiske, *Geografisk Tidskrift*, xxiii, 1915–16, pp. 284–90.

Hatt, Gudmund, Moccasins and Their Relation to Arctic Footwear, *Memoirs of the American Anthropological Association*, iii, 1916, pp. 151–250.

Hauch, C., *Minner fra min Barndom og min Ungdom*, Copenhagen, C. M. Reitzels Forlag, 1867.

Haukelid, Knut, *Skis against the Atom*, London, William Kimber, 1954.

Hauser, Andreas, St Anton, *Tirol*, Heimatwerbung-Tirol, 1990–1.

Helbling, Robert, Une Partie de ski au Mont-Rose, *L'Écho des Alpes*, No. 12, 1898, pp. 377–91.

Helleve, Lars, Ski-og skibruk i Vossbygdene i eldre tid, *Gamalt frå Voss*, ix, 1977, pp. 30–42.

Hellmann, G., *Schneekrystalle Beobachtungen und Studien*, Berlin, Verlag von Rudolf Mückenberber, 1893.

Helskog, Knut, *Helleristningene i Alta*, Alta, Alta Museum, 1988.

Hemmestveit, Mikkel, Nokre Minneord, *Foreningen til Ski-Idrettens Fremme Årbok*, 1922, pp. 69–78.

Hemmestveit, Torjus, Mine Skiløperminder, *Foreningen til Ski-Idrettens Fremme Årbok*, 1924, pp. 88–97.

Henrikson, Alf, *Svensk Historia*, Stockholm, Bonnier, 1964.

Herberstein, Sigismund von, *Rerum Moscoviticarum Commentarii*, Basle, Ex officinia Oporiniana, 1571.

*Herodotus*, Loeb Classical Library, London, William Heinemann, 1971.

Herr Bjarne Nilssen and Swiss Ski-Running, *The Alpine Post and Engadin Express*, xlv, 1906, No. 6, pp. 21–2.

Hess, J.-J., Zur Geschichte des Skis, *Vox Romanica*, ii, 1937, pp. 170–2, 477.

H. H., Skiklubb Ulls 25-aars Jubilæum 1883–1908, *Foreningen til Ski-Idrettens Fremme Årbok*, 1908, pp. 39–44.

Hochholdinger, Barbara, Vergleichende Skigeschichte Mitteleuropas, Vienna, Institut für Sportswissenschaften der Universität, 1992. [Unpublished thesis] MZ.

Hodge, F. W., Handbook of American Indians North of Mexico, *Bureau of American Ethnography, Bulletin*, 30, 1907–10.

Hoeeg, Ove Arbo, Vidjer og viuspenniler, *Norveg, Folkelivsgransking*, 20, 1977, pp. 7–107.

Hoek, H. and Schottelius, Ernst, Theoretisches vom Skilauf, *Deutscher Wintersport*, xi, No. 6, 1901–2, pp. 53–4.

Hoek, H., Von alten Ski in Graubünden, *Der Schneehase*, ii, No. 6, 1932, pp. 156–63.

Högström, Peter, *Beschreibung der zu Schweden gehoerenden Lappmark*, Copenhagen, Gabriel Christian Rothe, 1748.

Hohle, Per, Nordmarkas historie, *Foreningen til Ski-Idrettens Fremme Årbok*, 1966, pp. 22–30.

Holberg, Ludvig, *Danmarks og Norges Beskrivelse*, Copenhagen, Johan Jørgen Høpffner, 1729.

Hollander, Lee M., *The Skalds*, Princeton, Princeton University Press, 1945.

Holm, Oberst Tor, En Hærordningsforandring, offentlig premiering av Skiløping, *Hærmuseet Årbok*, 1965, pp. 9–48.

Holmberg, Arne, 'P.J.Bergius' Anteckningar från en resa til Dalarna år 1751, *Svenska Linné-Sällskapets Årsskrift*, xxxv, 1952, pp. 71–85.

Holmenkolrendene, *Foreningen til Ski-Idrettens Fremme Årbok* 1895–6, p. 55.

Holmenkol-Rendet, *Morgenbladet*, 1 February 1892.

Holm-Olsen, Ludvig (tr.), *Edda-Dikt*, Oslo, J. W. Cappelens forlag, 1975.

Holmquist, Ivar, 50 km längdlöpningen, *På Skidor*, 1925, pp. 222–31.

Holmquist, Ivar, La Coupe de France, Tävlingarna i Briancon 1925, *På Skidor*, 1926, pp. 102–31.

Holmquist, Ivar, När seklet var ungt, *På Skidor*, 1950, pp. 41–3.

Holmström, Arne, *Frontrapport*, Hallstavik, Svenskt Militärhistoriskt Bibliotek, 2005.

Holst, Axel and Frölich, Theodor, Experimental Studies relating to Ship-Beri-Beri and Scurvy II on the Etiology of Scurvy, *Journal of Hygiene*, vii, 1907, pp. 634–71.

Holt, Richard, *Sport and Society in Modern France*, London, Macmillan, 1981.

Honkanan, P., Kankainnen, T., Taavitsainen, J.-P., and Vilkuna, J., *The C14-dated Prehistoric Skis in the Collections of the Sports Museum of Finland*, manuscript of unidentified conference paper, SH.

Hooke, Robert, *Micrographia*, London, Martyn and J. Allentry, 1665.

Horber, Ruedi, L'équipement des Alpes en téléphériques: faits et problèmes, *Les Alpes*, No. l, 1974, pp. 149–56.

Horn, H., Nogle indtryk fra en skitur i de østerrigske Alper, *Foreningen til Ski-Idrettens Fremme Årbok*, 1905, pp. 47–63.

Høygaard, Arne, og Mehren, Martin, '*Ajungilak*' eller Grønland på Tvers, Oslo, Gyldendal norsk Forlag, 1931.

H. S., Momenter til eftertanker betræffende reformturistdragten for damer, *Nylænde*, i, 1887, pp. 89–92.

Huitfeldt, A., Ski og Skiløbning I, *Nylænde* 1889a iii, pp. 161–63.

Huitfeldt, A., Ski og Skiløbning II, *Nylænde* 1889b iii, pp. 341–43.

Huitfeldt, Fritz, *Lærebog i Skiløbning*, Christiania, Haffner & Hille, 1896.

Huitfeldt, Fritz, *Das Skilaufen*, Berlin, Verlag von F. Manning, 1907a.

Huitfeldt, Fritz, Telemarksstil, *Centralforeningen for udbredelse af idræt Aarsberetning for 1906*, 1907b, pp. 125–9.

Huitfeldt, Fritz, *Skiløbning i Text og Billeder*, Christiania, Jacob Dybwads forlag, 1908.

Huitfeldt, Fritz, Fritz Huitfeldts Skibinding, *Foreningen til Ski-Idrettens Fremme Årbok*, 1922, pp. 79–86.

Hundene paa Kamtschatka, *Billed-Magazin for Børn*, i, 1838, pp. 209–12.

Huntford, Roland, A World Cup boost to skiing, *Observer*, 5 February 1967.

Huntford, Roland, Swiss Thumbs Down, *Observer*, 9 November 1969.

Huntford, Roland, *Scott and Amundsen*, London, Hodder & Stoughton, 1979.

Huntford, Roland, *Nansen*, London, Abacus, 2001.

Huntford, Roland, *Shackleton*, London, Abacus, 2002.

Hurrungerne, *Magazin for Naturvidenskaberne*, i, 1823, pp. v–viii.

Hüttenegger, Theodor and Pfliger, Max, *Steirische Skigeschichte*, Graz, Im Selbstverlag des Steirischen Skiverbandes, 1968.

Iamblichi, Chalcidensis, *De Vita Pythagorica*, Leipzig, F. C. E. Vogelii, 1715.

Ibsen, Henrik, *Samlede verker*, Oslo, Gyldendal norsk forlag, 1962.

Ides, E.Ysbrants, *Dreijaarige reize naar China*, Amsterdam, Pieter de Coup, 1710.

IIIe Concours international de ski, à Morez du Jura, *La Montagne*, v, 1909, pp. 41–7.

*Il était une fois Megève*, Paris, Editions Champs Elysées, 2000.

Imbrie, John, *Ice Ages*, London, Macmillan, 1979.

Ingstad, Helge, Skispor fra Telemark, *Polarboken*, 1957, pp. 7–18.

Insulander, Ragnar, Tjurved fick skidan gå av sig själv, *Skogseko*, 4, 1998.

*International Olympic Committee – One Hundred Years*, Vol. I, Lausanne, International Olympic Committee, 1994.

International Racing Rules, *British Ski Year Book*, 1926, pp. 349–54.

Internationalt Skirend i Frankrige, *Morgenbladet*, No. 111, 26 February 1907.

Iordanis [Jordanes] (ed. Theodor Mommsen), *Romana et Getica*, Berlin, Apud Weidmannos (facsimile original edition 1882), 1961.

Isachsen, Einar, Et 60 år gammelt brev om å lage ski, *Foreningen til Ski-Idrettens Fremme Årbok*, 1949, pp.135–43.

Isbrand, Evert, *Relation du voyage*, Amsterdam, Jean-Luis de Lorme, 1699.

Iselin, Christof, Praktische Ergebnisse des Schneeschuhlaufens in den Glarnerbergen im Winter 1892/3 Alpina i (1893), 1 December, pp. 60–3.

Iselin, Christof, Unsere Freunde, die Norweger, in der Schweiz, *Schweizerischer Skiverband Jubiläums Jahrbuch*, 1929, pp. 43–52.

I Skirennen in St Anton am Arlberg, *Deutscher Wintersport*, xiii, No. 11, 1903–4, p. 140.

I Snestorm paa Tydalsfjeldene, *Skilling-Magazin*, 1876, pp. 107–10.

Itkonen, T. I., Fennoskandia-skienes oprinnelse, *Festskrift til Rektor J. Qvigstad*, pp. 77–87, Tromsø Museums Skrifter, Vol. II, 1928.

Itkonen, T. I., Til frågan om Fennoskandia-skidornas uppkomst, *Finskt Museum*, xxxvi, 1929, pp. 94–100; xxxvii, 1930, pp. 20–30.

Itkonen, T. I., Muinaissuksia ja -jalaksia, *Suomen Museo*, xxvii, 1930, pp. 82–90; xl, 1934, pp. 1–21, xliii, 1936, pp. 68–83, xlv, 1938, pp. 13–34; xlviii, 1941, pp. 31–43; liii (1946), pp. 47–56; lvi (1949), pp. 27–40.

Itkonen, T. I., Finlands Fornskidor, *På Skidor*, 1937, pp. 71–89.

Itkonen, T. I., Temmeksen muinaisjalas, *Suomen Museo*, xlix, 1942, pp. 28–30.

Itkonen, T. I., Suomen kielen suksisanastoa, Finnische Skiterminologie, *Suomalaisen kirjallisuuden seura*, No. 254, 1957.

*IV Olympische Winterspiele 1936, Amtlicher Bericht*, Berlin, Reichssport Verlag, 1936.

Jackson, Frederick, *A Thousand Days in the Arctic*, London, Harper Brothers, 1899.

Jacob, Christian, *La Description de la terre habitée de Denys d'Alexandrie ou la leçon de géographie*, Paris, Albin Michel, 1990.

Jacobsen, Kjell, Norges eldste ski funnet i Vefsn, *Årbok for Helgeland*, 1994, pp. 14–17.

Jaeger, Jens A., Skisporten i Tyskland vinteren 1922, *Foreningen til Ski-Idrettens Fremme Årbok*, 1922, pp. 121–48.

Jakobson, Max, *The Diplomacy of the Winter War*, Cambridge, MA, Harvard University Press, 1961.

James, Patricia (ed.), *The Travel Diaries of Thomas Robert Malthus*, Cambridge, Cambridge University Press, 1966.

Janner, Ernst, *Arlbergschule Lehrgang des Skilaufes*, Munich, Bergverlag Rudolf Nother, 1930.

Jansonium, Petrum (ed.), *Itinerarium oder Außführlicher Bericht*, Hamburg, Michael Hering, 1619.

J. D., Concours international de ski à Chamonix, *La Montagne* iv(a) (1908), pp. 77–82.

Jennissejsk skidlöpare, *På Skidor*, 1936, pp. 346–7.

Jernberg, Sixten, *I vilda spår*, Stockholm, Bonniers folkbibliotek, 1960.

Jilli, Rudolf, *Geschichte des Skiclub Alpina St Moritz 1903–1924*, St Moritz, Skiclub Alpina, 1924.

Jirlow, Ragnar, Gamle dagars vinteridrott, *På Skidor*, 1935, pp. 27–46.

Jirlow, Ragnar, Ur skidlöpningens hävder i Särna, *På Skidor*, 1942, pp. 139–50.

Johansen, Hjalmar, *Fram* diaries, 1893–96. NBO Ms.8° 2775.

John, Brian S., *The Ice Age, Past and Present*, London, Collins, 1977.

Johnsen, Ragnvald, Fridtjof Nansen og norsk ski-idrett, *Naturen*, No. 85, 1961, pp. 487–94.

Jones, Gwynn, *A History of the Vikings*, Oxford, Oxford University Press, 1968.

Jonge, Nikolay (ed.), *Baron Ludvig Holbergs Geographie eller Jordbeskrivelse*, Copenhagen. J. R. Thiele, 1779.

Jónsson, Finnur, *Sæmundar-Edda*, Reykjavík, Sigurdur Kristiánsson, 1905.

Jónsson, Finnur (ed.), *Den norsk-islandske skjaldedigtningen*, Copenhagen, Gyldendalske Boghandel, 1912.

Jónsson, Finnur, *Edda Snorra Sturlusonar*, Copenhagen, Gyldendalske Boghandel – Nordisk forlag, 1931.

Jordanes (ed. C. C. Mierow), *The Gothic History of Jordanes*, London, Oxford University Press, 1915.

Jussila, Pentti, *Suomen Hiihto*, Helsinki, Otava, 1998.

Just, Gunnar, Fridtjof Nansen i Infanteriets Vinterskole, om tresorters glidning på sne, *Foreningen til Ski-Idrettens Fremme Årbok*, 1930, pp. 135–40.

Juve, Jørgen, På norske Ski i Schweiz, *Foreningen til Ski-Idrettens Fremme Årbok*, 1931, pp. 92–100.

Kagge, Erling, *Alone to the South Pole*, Oslo, J.W. Cappelens forlag, 1993

Kamper, Erich, *Lexikon der Olympischen Winterspiele*, Stuttgart, Union Verlag, 1964.

Karl Knutssons skyrännare, *På Skidor*, 1939, p. 400.

Keilhau, Baltazar, Nogle Efterretninger om et hidtil ubekjendte Stykke af det søndenfjeldske Norge, *Budstikken*, (Anden række) II, 1820–1, No. 49–50.

Kepler, Johannes, *The Six-Cornered Snowflake*, Oxford, Clarendon Press, 1966.

Kerguelen Trémarec, *Relation d'un Voyage dans la Mer du Nord*, Amsterdam, Arkstée & Merkus, 1772.

Kern, Stephen, *The Culture of Time and Space 1880–1918*, London, Weidenfeld & Nicolson, 1983.

Khetagurov, L. A. (tr.), *Rashid al-Din: Sbornik letopisei vol.i pt.1*, Moscow-Leningrad Izdatelstvo Akademii Nauk USSR, 1952.

Kiærland, Lars, Ski og skiløpning i gamle dager, *Foreningen til Ski-Idrettens Fremme Årbok*, 1934, pp. 138–49; 1935, pp. 125–33; 1936, pp. 141–9; 1938, pp. 97–103.

Kiærland, Lars, Skiløperavdelingene og 1814, *Foreningen til Ski-Idrettens Fremme Årbok*, 1964, pp. 10–19.

Kiparsky, V., Die Narte als Skischlitten, *Suomen Museo*, lxiv, 1957, pp. 56–67.

Kirchmeyer, Hans, Abnehmbare Seehundfell-Skibespannung, *Deutscher Wintersport*, xi, No. 13, 1901–2, pp. 119–22.

Kittle, C. Frederick, Down the Slopes with Conan Doyle at Davos, *The Journal of the Conan Doyle Society*, iv, 1993, pp. 88–103.

Kjærheim, Steinar (ed.), *Fridtjof Nansen Brev*, Oslo, Universitetsforlaget, 1961.

Kjersem, Jakob, *På ski fra fjell til fjord*, Molde, 1996.

Kleinoscheg, Max, to Schruf, Toni. nd. Origin of skiing in Austria. Manuscript MZ.

Klepp, Asbjørn, Ski og truger, Magisteravhandling i etnologi, Universitetet i Oslo, 1976, unpublished thesis.

Klepp, Asbjørn, Leksvik ville ikke fungert uten skiene, *Foreningen til Ski-Idrettens Fremme Årbok*, 1977a, pp. 27–35.

Klepp, Asbjørn, Skis – Problems of Form and Adaptation, *Ethnologia Scandinavia*, 1977b, pp. 46–74.

Klepp, Asbjørn, Skimaking. Fra allmenn ferdighet til 'kjøpski, *Trøndelag Folkemuseums Årbok*, 1979–80, pp. 7–46.

Klingenberg, O. T., Om skiløbning, *Centralforeningen for udbredelse af idræt Aarsberetning*, 1902, pp. 168–74.

Klopstock, Friedrich Gottlieb, *Klopstocks Werke*, Leipzig, bey Joachim Göschen, 1798.

Klüver, Kaptejn L. W., Et Øienvidnes Beskrivelse over den svenske Armees Tog under General-Lieutenant Armfelts Commando, *Ny Minerva*, 1806, pp. 19–81.

Köchl, Greta, Die Entwicklung des Skilaufs, Vienna, Institut für Sportwissenschaften der Universität, 1997, unpublished thesis MZ.

Kock, Ernst A. (ed.), *Den Norsk-Isländska Skaldediktningen*, Lund, C. W. K. Gleerup's förlag, 1946.

Koht, Halfdan (trans.), *Sverre-Soga*, Oslo, Det Norske Samlaget, 1913.

Kolchin, B. A., Novgorodskie drevnosti. Dereviann'ie izdeliia, *Svod Arkheologicheskikh Istochnikov*, EI-55, 1968, p. 57.

Komroff, Manuel (ed.), *Contemporaries of Marco Polo*, London, Jonathan Cape, 1928.

Kopylov, A. N., *Russkie na Enisee v XVII v*, Novosibirsk, Redaktsionno-Izdatel'sky Otdel Sibirskogo Otdeleniya AN SSSR, 1965.

Körningh, Johan Ferdinand, *Berättelse om en missionsresa til Lappland 1659–60*, Uppsala, Gebers, 1956.

Krag, pr.løitnant Hj., Skiløbet i Wien winteren 1897, *Foreningen til Ski-Idrettens Fremme Årbok*, 1897, pp. 73–81.

Krefting, Captain Kristian, A Norwegian Impression of British Ski-ing, *British Ski Year Book*, 1930, pp. 563–6.

*Kulturhistorisk lexikon för nordisk medeltid*, Malmö, Allhems förlag, 1970–4.

Kunde Gustav Vasa löpa skida? *På Skidor*, 1945, pp. 284–5.

La grande Semaine d'Hiver, *Le Figaro*, 1 February 1909.

Laing, Samuel, *Journal of a Residence in Norway during The Years 1834, 1835 and 1836*, London, Longman, Rees, Orme, Brown, Green & Longman, 1836.

Lange, Christian C. A. (ed.), *Norske samlinger ii*, Christiania, Feilberg & Landmarks Forlag 1860.

Lange, Ove L., *Nordmarka og Nordmarksgods historie*, Oslo Dreyers Forlag, 1966.

Lappernes Skifærd paa Grønland 1883, *Geografisk Tidskrift*, vii, 1883–4, p. 116.

Lappi, Nicolai Lundii, Descriptio Lapponiæ, *Svenska Landsmålen*, xvii, No. 5, 1905.

Lappskatten, *På Skidor*, 1943, p. 309.

Larsen, C. A., Nogle optegnelser af sæl-og hvalfanger Jasons reise i Sydishavet 1893 og 94, *Det Norske Geografiske Selskabs Aarbog*, v, 1893–4, pp. 115–31.

Latham, Robert Gordon, *Native Races of the Russian Empire, 1854*, London, Hippolyte Bailliere, 1854.

Laufer, Berthold, The Reindeer and its Domestication, *Memoirs of the American Anthropological Association*, iv, 1917, No. 2, pp. 91–147.

Leblanc, Maurice, *Voici des ailes*, Paris, P. Ollendorff, 1898.

Leem, Knud, *Beskrivelse over Finmarkens Lapper*, Copenhagen, G. G. Salikath, 1767.

Lehtovaara, Arto, Kinetic Friction between Ski and Snow, *Acta Polytechnica Scandinavica*, Mechanical Engineering Series No. 93.

Le Ski et l'Olympisme, *Revue Olympique*, Nos 194–196, January–February 1984, pp. 51–98.

Les jeux du Nord a Kristiania, *Revue Olympique*, February 1903, pp. 13–14.

*Les Jeux d'Hiver de Chamonix, Les Jeux de la VIIIe Olympiade*, Rapport Officiel p. 643 et seq. Paris, Comité Olympique Français, 1924.

Les Sports de Neige II Le Ski, *Revue Olympique*, February 1908, pp. 23–8.

Les Sports d'Hiver des VIIIes Jeux Olympiques, *Le Figaro*, 6 February 1924.

Leudet, Maurice, Sports d'Hiver a Chamonix, *Le Figaro*, 6 January 1908.

Lewenhaupt, E. (tr.), *The Memoirs of Marshal Mannerheim*, London, Cassell, 1953.

*L'Histoire des Jeux Olympiques d'Hiver*, Morzine, Editions Jean Vuarnet, 1979.

Lid, Nils, Skifundet frå Øvrebø, *Universitetets Oldsakssamlings Aarbok*, 1930, pp. 152–78.

Lid, Nils, Til Norsk Skihistorie, *Foreningen til Ski-Idrettens Fremme Årbok*, 1931, pp. 71–9.

Lid, Nils, *Skifundet frå Øvrebø*, Oslo, A. W. Brøggers Boktrykkeri A/S, 1932.

Lid, Nils, Gamle norske skiformer, *Syn og Segn*, xl, 1934, pp. 410–19.

Lid, Nils, Gamle norske skiformer, *Foreningen til Ski-Idrettens Fremme Årbok*, 1937a, pp. 139–55.

Lid, Nils, *On the History of Norwegian Skis*, Oslo, Foreningen til Skiidrættens Fremme, 1937b.

Lid, Nils, Skifundet frå Furnes *Ord og Sed*, 1938, pp. 1–44.

Lid, Nils, Norsk skifunn VI: Steinhaugmo i Hemnes, *Foreningen til Ski-Idrettens Fremme Årbok*, 1939, pp. 95–7.

Lie, Erik, *Jonas Lie*, Oslo, Gyldendal Norsk Forlag, 1933.

Lie, Jonas, Lidt fra Gutteaarene, *Illustreret Tidende for Børn* (1886–87), pp. 259–64.

Lie, Michael, Litt av hvert om Skiløpning og annet i Spanien og Syd-Frankrike, *Foreningen til Ski-Idrettens Fremme Årbok*, 1927, pp. 85–92.

Lie, Michael, Et par skiturer på Høifjellet for 35–40 år Siden, *Turistforenings Årbok*, 1928.

Lie, Michael, Litt om Skiløpning før og nu, *Foreningen til Ski-Idrettens Fremme Årbok*, 1929, pp. 67–72.

Likhachev, N. P., *Borisa i Gleba*, St Petersburg, Typografiia M. A. Aleksandrova, 1907.

Lillehagen, E., *Skiløbning, praktiske Vink og Erfaringer*, Christiania, Alb. Cammermeyers Forlag, 1896.

Lillehagen, E., Småstubber av Edvard Lillehagens optegnelser, *Baerums Skiklubb gjennem 50 år 1885–1935*, Oslo, Nikolai Olsens Boktrykkeri, n.d., pp. 105–16.

Lilliehöök, Lennart, Några idrottsminnen från Grenoble vintern 1896, *På Skidor*, 1950, pp. 66–73.

Lindbæk, Sofie Aubert, *Årgang 1875*, Oslo, Tiden Norsk Forlag, 1948.

Lindboe, Gustave E., Norge Ski Club Chicago, *Foreningen til Ski-Idrettens Fremme Årbok*, 1949, pp. 81–7.

Lindquist, Ivar, Gudar På Skidor, *På Skidor*, 1929, pp. 8–15.

Lindroth, J., *Idrottens väg til folkrörelse*, Uppsala, Acta Universitatis Upsaliensis, 1974.

Liniger, Max, Alpes périlleuses du Moyen Age, *Les Alpes*, lviii, 1982, pp. 35–40.

Linné, Carl von, *Iter Lapponicum*, Skrifter v Uppsala, Almquist & Wiksells Boktryckeri, 1913.

Linné, Carl von, *Iter Dalekarlicum*, Ungdomsresor ii, Stockholm, P. A. Norstedt & Söners Förlag, 1929.

Ljunggren, Jens, Tradition eller tävling? Nordiska spelen och kampen om vad idrott är, *Historisk tidskrift*, cxvii, 1997, pp. 351–74.

Lloyd, L., *Field Sports of the North of Europe*, London, Henry Colburn and Richard Bentley, 1830.

Løchen, Fru Antonie, Om kvindelighed, *Nylænde*, 1887, i, pp. 145–51, 161–9.

Løchen, Ingeborg Motzfeldt, *To unge i en svunnen tid*, Oslo, H. Aschehoug , 1945.

Lockett, W. G., An English-Davos Picture Gallery, *Davoser Revue*, iv, 1928–9, pp. 26–8, 99–102, 125–9, 160–3, 279–82, 308–13, 335–9; v, 1929, pp. 8–14, 49–54, 114–21, 161–7; vi 1930–1, 14–21.

Lockett, W. G., *Robert Louis Stevenson at Davos*, London, Hurst & Blackett, 1934.

Lossius, Fredrikke, De første Fjellskiturer for Damer, *Trondhjems Skiklub Årbok*, 1937, pp. 58–9.

Loupedalen, Torjus, *Morgedal Skisportens vogge*, Oslo, H. Aschehoug, 1947.

Loupedalen, Torjus, Skiidrettens renessanseår. Unpublished manuscript, SH.

L. S., En Julevisit paa Ski til Jotunfjeldene, *Morgenbladet*, 25 February 1883, 4 March 1883.

Luho, Ville, Lapinlahden jättiläisjalas, *Suomen Museo*, lviii, 1951, pp. 108–16.

Lund, Niels (ed.), *Two Voyagers at the Court of King Alfred*, York, William Sessions, 1984.

Lunde, Reidar, Olav Bjaaland, *Foreningen til Ski-Idrettens Fremme Årbok*, 1961, pp. 99–101.

Lunn, Arnold, *Ski-ing*, London, Eveleigh Nash, 1913.

Lunn, Arnold, The Revolt Against the Long-distance Race, *British Ski Year Book*, 1925, pp. 19–24.

Lunn, Arnold, The Fifth Arlberg-Kandahar Meeting, *British Ski Year Book*, 1932, pp. 535–8.

Lunn, Arnold, *Come What May*, London, Eyre & Spottiswoode, 1940.

Lunn, Arnold, *Switzerland and the English*, London, Eyre & Spottiswoode, 1944.

Lunn, Arnold, *The Story of Skiing*, London, Eyre & Spottiswoode, 1952.

Lunn, Henry S., *Nearing Harbour*, London, Ivor Nicholson & Watson, 1934.

Luther, Carl J., Die Anfänge des Skilaufes in Mitteleuropa, *Ski-Chronik*, ii, 1909/10, pp. 1–20.

Luther, Carl J., Skitouristik und Skisport, *Foreningen til Ski-Idrettens Fremme Årbok*, 1913, pp. 76–87.

Luther, Carl J., *Schneelauf-Ausbildung*, Munich, Bergverlag Rother, 1921.

Luther, Carl J., Skandinavische Kriegsereignisse, *Der Winter*, xvii, 1923/24, pp. 59–60, 113–14.

Luther, Carl J., Auf der Spur des älteste alpinen Ski, *Der Winter* xxiv, 1930–1, pp. 129–32.

Luther, Carl J., Versuch einer Geschichte der Skibindung, *Der Winter*, xxxi, 1937/38, pp. 7–16.

Luther, Carl J., En besök i Krains skidområde, *På Skidor*, 1938, pp. 136–46.

Luther, Carl J., *Das Bilderbuch der alten Schneeläufer*, Erfurt, Gebr. Richters Verelagsanstalt, 1942.

Luther, Carl J., Hippopodes (Horse-footed men), *British Ski Year Book*, 1952, pp. 57–68.

Luther, Carl J., Geschichte des Schnee-und Eissports, *Geschichte des Sports alle Völker und Zeiten*, 1926, ii, pp. 497–557.

Lutter, Otto, Ski-Bindung, *Deutscher Wintersport,* xiv, 1904–5, No. 11, p. 125.

MacAloon, John J., *This Great Symbol,* Chicago, University of Chicago Press, 1981.

Madlener, Dr Paulcke, Wilhelm, Der Skilauf, *Deutscher Wintersport,* xii, No. 8, 1902–3, p. 85.

Maigaard, C., Beretning om den af Civilingeniør Robert E. Peary ledede Expedition paa den grønlandske Indlandsis, *Geografisk Tidskrift,* ix, 1887–8, Hefte V–VI, pp. 86–93.

Mallory, J. P., *In Search of the Indo-Europeans,* London, Thames & Hudson, 1989.

Mamiya, Rinzo, *Kita Ezo zusetso,* Edo, Harimaya Katsugoro, 1855.

Manker, Ernst, Trerännade Lapska Vargrännarskidor, *På Skidor,* 1940, pp. 222–8.

Manker, Ernst, Ett förhistorisk skidfynd, *Nordiska museets och Skansens årsbok Fataburen,* 1946.

Manker, Ernst, Lomsjökulleskidan, *På Skidor,* 1947, pp. 167–73.

Manker, Ernst, En norrbottenslapp som skidmakare, *På Skidor,* 1948, pp. 188–95.

Manker, Ernst, Lapptrummornas skidlöpar figurer, *På Skidor,* 1952, pp. 137–40.

Manker, Ernst, Den bottniska skidtypen i nya myrfynd, *På Skidor,* 1957, pp. 167–82.

Manker, Ernst, Fynd och Forskningen i Lappmarken, *Fataburen,* 1958, pp. 136–57.

Manker, Ernst, Fennoskandias fornskidor, *Fornvännen* lxvi, 1971, pp. 77–91.

Mann, Thomas, *Der Zauberberg,* Frankfurt am Main, Fischer Taschenbuch Verlag, 2004.

Margadant, Silvio and Maier, Marcella, *St Moritz, Streiflichter auf eine auusergewöhnliche Entwicklung,* St Moritz, Verlag Walter Gammeter, 1993.

Marillier, Bernard, *Jeux Olympiques,* Puiseaux, Pardès, 2000.

Markwart, J., Ein arabischer Bericht über die arktischen (uralischen) Länder aus dem 10. Jahrhundert, *Ungarische Jahrbücher,* Berlin, iv, 1924, pp. 261–334.

Markwart, J., *Südarmenien und die Tigrisquellen nach griechischen und arabischen Geographen,* Vienna, Mechitharisten-Buchdruckerei, 1930.

Martens, Friderich, *Spitzbergische oder Groenlandische Reise Beschreibung gethan im Jahr 1671,* Hamburg, Auff Gottfried Schultzens Kosten gedruckt, 1675.

Martin, Thomas (ed.), *Faraday's Diary,* iv, London, G. Bell & Sons, 1933.

Martinière, Sieur de la, *Voyage des Païs Septentrionaux,* Paris, Louis Vendosme, 1671.

Mason, O. T., Primitive travel and transportation, *Annual Report of the Smithsonian Institution,* 1894, pp. 237–593.

Mathieu, Rémi, *Étude sur la Mythologie et l'Ethnologie de la Chine Ancienne.* Traduction annotée du Shanhai jing, Paris, De Boccard, 1983.

Maurer, K., Das Schneeschuhlaufen in Norwegen, *Zeitschrift des Vereins für Volkskunde,* 1892, pp. 301–13.

Mehl, Erwin, Die Älteste Deutsche Anleitung zum Schneelauf, *Der Winter* xix (1925–6), pp. 230–2.

Mehl, Erwin, *Zdarsky: Festschrift zum 80. Geburtsdage,* Vienna, Jugend und Volk, 1936.

Mehl, Erwin, Ein halbes Jahrhundert Alpine Schifahrtechnik, *Österreichische Alpenzeitung* No. 1244 (1949), pp. 49–62.

Mehl, Erwin, Der erste Schifahrer in der Weltliteratur war ein Deutscher, *Der Bergsteiger* [Munich] ii (1954), pp. 188–93.

Mehl, Erwin, Ein neues Bild der Weltgeschichte des Schifahren, *Jahrbuch des Österreiches Alpenvereins,* 1957.

Mehl, Erwin, *Grundriss der Weltgeschichte des Schifahrens,* Schorndorf bei Stuttgart Verlag Karl Hofmann, 1964.

Meinich, Jens, Major Peter Munch Petersen *Foreningen til Ski-Idrettens Fremme Årbok,* 1941, pp. 73–79.

Mercier, Joachim, *Aus der Urgeschichte des Schweiz. Skilaufes,* Glarus, Verlag Skiclub Glarus, 1928.

Mere om Keilhaus og Bowecks opdagelse af Jotunfjeldene, *Den norske Turistforenings Årbog for 1873,* pp. 109–12.

Merle, Roger, *Histoire du ski dans le Briançonnais,* Gap, Ophrys, 1989.

Meuli, Karl, Scythica Vergiliana, *Schweizerisches Arkiv für Volkskunde* 56 band (1960), pp. 88–200.

Meuli, Richard, *Le Tourisme Grison,* Geneva, Imprimerie de La Tribune de Genève, 1940.

Mexmontan, Mauritz, Om skidsporten i Finland och det finska löpsättet, *På Skidor,* 1901–2, pp. 281–92.

Middendorff, A. T. von, *Reise in den äussersten Norden und Osten Sibiriens während der Jahre 1843 und 1844,* St Petersburg, Kaiserlichen Akademie der Wissenschaften, 1848.

Minelle, Pierre, Harald Durban-Hansen, *La Revue du Ski* (1937) January, pp. 23–6.

Minns, E. H., *Scythians and Greeks*, Cambridge, Cambridge University Press, 1913.

Minorsky, V. (tr.), *Sharaf al-Zaman Tahir Marvazi on China, the Turks and India*, London, Royal Asiatic Society, 1942.

Modin, Erik, Den gamla ångermanländska skidan, *På Skidor*, 1927, pp. 99–118.

Modin, Erik, En förhistorisk skida, *På Skidor*, 1928, pp. 266–75.

Moe, Jørgen, *Samlede Skrifter*, Christiania, H. Aschehoug, 1914.

Møller, Arvid, *Jo Gjende*, Oslo, J. W. Cappelens Forlag, 1979.

Montesquieu, Charles de Secondat, *De l'Esprit des loix*, vol. ii, Paris, Société les belles lettres, 1955.

*Morkinskinna*, Christiania, Det forr.B. M. Bentzen's Bogtrykkeri, 1867.

Mortensson-Egnund, Ivar (tr.), *Edda-Kvede*, Oslo, Det norske Samlaget, 1964.

Mossige, Erling, Christiania Skiklub 90 år, *Foreningen til Ski-Idrettens Fremme Årbok*, 1967, pp. 86–91.

M. P., Recettes utiles: Un fart, *La Montagne*, v, 1909, pp. 185–6.

Mückenbrünn, H. and Hallberg, Fredrik, *Le Ski Grenoble*, B. Arthaud, 1930.

Müllerus, Carolus (ed.), *Geographi Græci Minores [Dionysius periegetes]*, Paris, Editore Ambrosio Firmin Didot, 1861.

Munch, Anna E., *Et Nordisk Digterhjem*, Copenhagen, Sischers Forlag, 1954.

Münchener Ski-Club, Schneeschuh und Alpinistik, *Deutscher Eis-Sport*, ii, No. 1, 1893, pp. 5–6.

Munk, Jens, *Navigatio Septentrionalis*, Copenhagen, Henrich Waldkirch, 1624.

Nachwort zu der Zdarsky'schen herausforderung an die Norwegeger, *Deutscher Wintersport*, xiv, No. 20, 1904–5, pp. 244–5.

Nansen, Baldur. Correspondence 1883–84. NBO Ms.8° 2329. About Nansen's early mountain ski tours.

Nansen, Eva, Skiløbningen, *Verdens Gang*, 3 March 1893, No. 53.

Nansen, E., Til Cortina d'Ampezzo, *Foreningen til Ski-Idrettens Fremme Årbok*, 1928, pp. 119–28.

Nansen, Fridtjof, En Skitur fra Voss til Kristiania, *Aftenposten*, 29 March, 1, 9 and 16 April 1884.

Nansen, Fridtjof, Skiløb i Thelemarken, *Illustreret Tidende for Børn*, Anden Aargang, 1886–7, pp. 87–9.

Nansen, Fridtjof, Peder Næsheim to Nansen, 26 December 1887, MS fol. 1924.1a(2). About steel edges.

Nansen, Fridtjof, E. Isachsen to Nansen 28 January 1888. MS fol.1924 1a(2) About waxless ski using inlaid sealskins.

Nansen, Fridtjof, Greenland diaries 1888–9 NBO MS.8° 2224 and in private ownership.

Nansen, Fridtjof, Fra Grønlandsfærden, *Det Norske Geografiske Selskabs Aarbog*, No. 1 (1889–90), pp. 1–18.

Nansen, Fridtjof, Chr. Jacobsen to Nansen 24 January 1890a. Ms.fol.1924:2a(3). Names for the ski in various Fenno-Ugric, Siberian and Asiatic languages.

Nansen, Fridtjof, *Paa Ski over Grønland*, Christiania, H. Aschehoug Forlag, 1890b.

Nansen, Fridtjof, Birger Pedersen to Nansen 11 December 1892 Ms.fol.1924 2c2 B. An early safety binding.

Nansen, Fridtjof, Eva to Fridtjof Nansen 21 February 1892. Brevs. 48. About skiing across Hardangervidda.

Nansen, Fridtjof, *A travers le Grönland*, Paris, Hachette, 1893.

Nansen, Fridtjof, Fra barneaarene, *Illustreret Tidende for Børn*, Ottende aargang (1893a), pp. 6–7.

Nansen, Fridtjof, *Fram* diaries, 1893–6. NBO Ms.8°2201; MS fol.1924:2e.

Nansen, Fridtjof, *Fram over Polhavet*, Christiania, H. Aschehoug Forlag, 1897.

Nansen, Fridtjof, Tale for idretten, *Foreningen til Ski-Idrettens Fremme Årbok*, 1903, pp. 20–6.

Nansen, Fridtjof, Theodor Caspari to Nansen 21 January 1907. Brevs. 48. About writing to defend Norwegian skiing in Austria.

Nansen, Fridtjof, *Nord i Tåkeheimen*, Christiania, Jacob Dybwads Forlag, 1911.

Nansen, Fridtjof, correspondence with Grete Gulbransson, Brevs. 610, 1912a.

Nansen, Fridtjof, The Equipment of Polar Expeditions, *The Field*, cxix, pp. 39, 95, of 6 and 13 January 1912b.

Nansen, Fridtjof, *Frilufts-Liv*, Christiania, Jacon Dybwads Forlag, 1916.

Nansen, Fridtjof, Correspondence and papers, NBO mostly Brevs. 48, Ms.8° 2201-30, Ms.fol.1924, Ms.fol. 2260-70, 2273-5, 2381, 3920.

Nansen, Fridtjof, Correspondence with Christiansen, Ydal and others, preparations for *Fram* expedition. RA Priv.ark.61 Arb.Kom.

Nansen, Fridtjof, Om Hurtigløb på Ski. Unpublished MS. NBO MS fol.2269.

Naskali, E., Suksi muinaislöytöjen valossa, *Latua! Hiihtomuseon julkaisuja*, No. 1, 1989.

Naumann, Carl, Einige Bemerkungen auf Asflügen in die norwegischen Schneegefilde, *Isis von Oken* (1822) erster Band heft VI, pp. 642–63.

Needham, Joseph, *Science and Civilisation in China*, iv, Part 3, Cambridge, Cambridge University Press, 1971.

Needham, Joseph and Gwei-Djen, Lu, The Earliest Snow Crystal Observations, *Weather*, xvi, No. 10, 1961, pp. 319–25.

Negri, Francesco, *Viaggio settentrionale*, Padua, Stamperia del Seminario, 1700.

Neumayr, Theodor, *Praktische Anleitung zur Erlernung des Schneeschuh-(Ski-) Laufens*, Hamburg, Verlags und Druckerei A.-G., 1893.

Nilsen, Knut A., *Nordmarksboka*, Oslo, Grøndahl & Søn Forlag, 1988.

Nilssen, Bjarne, Einiges über Dauerläufe in Norwegen, *Deutscher Wintersport*, xii, 1902–3, No. 20, pp. 205–6.

Nilssen, Bjarne, Skiløbning i Schweiz, *Centralforeningen for udbredelse af idræt Aarsberetning for 1905*, pp. 112–15.

Nilssen, Bjarne, Fra Schweiz og Schwarzwald, *Foreningen til Ski-Idrettens Fremme Årbok*, 1906, pp. 82–92.

Nilssen, Kristian, Samer i Polarforskningen, *Sameliv*, 1961–3, pp. 48–80.

Nilssen, Leon, En skitur i Alperne, *Norsk Idrætsblad*, xxii, 19 May 1904, p. 168.

Niurenius, Olaus Petri, Lappland, *Svenska Landsmålen*, xvii, No. 4, 1905.

Noodt, Nicolay, to Max Kleinoscheg 11 December 1890 MZ Personen A-L.

Nordal, Sigurdur (ed.), *Egils Saga Skalla-Grímssonar*, Reykjavik, Hid Islenzka Fornritafélag, 1933.

Nordberg, Hans (ed.), *Idrettens historie i Nord-Trøndelag*, Steinkjer, Nord-Trøndelag Idrettskrets, 1994.

Nordenskiöld, A. E., *Vegas färd kring Asien och Europa*, Stockholm, F. & G. Beijers förlag, 1880.

Nordenskiöld, A. E., Den svenska expeditionen til Grönland, år 1883, rapporter . . ., *Ymer*, 1883, pp. 211–60.

Nordenskiöld, A. E., *Den Andra Dicksonska Expeditionen till Grönland*, Stockholm, F. & G. Beijers Förlag, 1885.

Nordenson, Carl, De nationella och internationella Skidtäflingarna år 1901, *På Skidor*, 1901–2, pp. 122–54.

Nordenson, Carl, Den VII internationella skidkongressen, *På Skidor*, 1924, pp. 235–45.

Nordenson, Carl, Internationella skidkongressen i Chamonix, *På Skidor*, 1925, pp. 231–5.

Nordiska Spelen och deres Ledande Män, *Idun* xiv, 16 February 1901.

Norrman, Olof, Striden om Lappland, *På Skidor*, 1935, pp. 5–26.

*Norsk Biografisk Leksikon*, Oslo, Aschehoug, 1986.

Norska gardets skidlöpning, *Stockholms Dagblad*, 22 February 1881.

*Norske Skiløpere*, Oslo, Skiforlaget Erling Ranheim, 1955.

*Norske skipionerer*, unpublished manuscript notes of interviews, 1943, SH.

North, George, *The Description of Swedland, Gotland and Finland*, London, John Awdely, 1561.

Nya Skidbindingar, *På Skidor*, 1909–10, pp. 236–8; 1910–11, pp. 201–4; 1916, pp. 137–9.

*Nydalens Compagnie 100 år*, Oslo, 1945.

Nydalens Spinderi og Væveri et Skirend, *Morgenbladet*, 6 March 1872.

Obholzer, S., Gamla skidor i utländska museer, *På Skidor*, 1974, pp. 101–8.

*Odes of Pindar, The*, London, The Loeb Classical Library, William Heinemann, 1978.

Olaus Magnus, *Opera Breve*, Venice, Giouan Thomaso, 1539.

Olaus Magnus, *Historia de Gentibus Septentrionalibus*, Rome, Apud Joannem Mariam, 1555.

Olaus Magnus, *Carta Marina* [facsimile edition], Uppsala, Bokgillet, 1964.

Olav Bjaalands Museum Morgedal, *Ski og Sudpol*, Skien, Erik Tanche Nilssen, 1970.

*Oldnordiske Sagaer*, Copenhagen, Poppske Bogtrykkerie, 1826.

Olearius, Adam, *Beschreibung der Moscovitischen und Persischen Reise*, Schleswig, Jacob zur Glocken, 1647.

Olearius, Adam, *Gottorffische Kunst-Kammer*, Schleswig, Johan Holwein, 1666.

Olsen-Nauen, Marie, Da ski-kvinnen erobret mannsbuksen, *Foreningen til Ski-Idrettens Fremme Årbok*, 1975, pp. 31–4.

Olympic Winter Games. The Opening Ceremony, *The Times*, 7 February 1936.

Olympic Winter Games, *The Times*, 26 and 31 January 1948.

Om skidlöpningen i Jockmock, *Norrbottens-Kuriren*, 15 April 1884.

Orel, Boris, *Bloske Smuci*, Ljubljana, Institut za Slovensko Narodopisje, 1964.

Orre, Sigurd, Blandt tyske franske og italienske skiløpere, nd. SH. Reminiscences of skiing, 1907–9.

Orre, Sigurd, Norske militære skiløberes færd til Frankrige 1909, *Centralforeningen for udbredelse af idræt Aarsberetning for 1908, pp.* 70–5.

Orre, Sigurd, Skiløpning i Pyrenæerne, *Foreningen til Ski-Idrettens Fremme Årbok*, 1909, pp. 95–103.

Örsan, Karl, Huru verkligt stilig är ej denne bild af täflan, *Studier i idrott, historia och samhälle, festschrift for Professor Jan Lindroth*, 2000.

Orstadius, Axel, Skilda drag från det s.k. 'Nordenskjöldstäflingen' å skidor i Jockmock, *På Skidor*, 1897–8, pp. 237–48.

Ostjakernas skidor, *På Skidor*, 1941, pp. 286–7.

Outhier, M., *Journal d'un voyage au Nord en 1736 et 1737*, Paris, Piget, Durand, 1744.

Øverland, O. A., *Fra en svunden tid. Sagn og optegnelser*, Christiania, Alb. Cammermeyer, 1888.

Ovsyannikov, Oleg V., Medieval Skis in Northern Russia, MS paper for unidentified conference, 1989a.

Ovsyannikov, Oleg, V., On old Russian skis, *Fennoscandia Archaeologica*, vi, 1989b, pp. 29–50.

P. Å., Fastskruede støvler istedetfor paabindinger, *Norsk Idrætsblad*, No. 50, 20 December 1892, p. 358.

Pallas, Peter Simon, *Reise durch verschiedene Provinsen des Russischen Reichs*, St Petersburg, Kayserlichen Academie der Wissenschaften, 1776.

Pallière, Johannes, Les Premiers Jeux d'Hiver de 1924, *L' Histoire en Savoie*, xxvi, No. 103, 1991.

Palmarès du 1er Concours International de skis, *La Montagne*, iii, 1907, pp. 172–7.

Palmer-Tomkinson, J., Gomme Ski, *British Ski Year Book*, 1948, pp. 48–50.

Parienté, Robert and Lagorce, Guy, *La Fabuleuse Histoire des Jeux Olympiques*, Geneva, Minerva, 2000.

Parry, W. E., *Narrative of an Attempt to Reach the North Pole*, London, John Murray, 1828.

Patkanov, S., *Die Irtysch-Ostjaken und ihre Volkspoesie*, St Petersburg, L'Académie Impériale des Sciences, 1897.

Paulaharju, S., Vähäisen entisajan hiitoneuvoista Perä-Pohjolassa, *Suomen Museo*, xxi, 1914, pp. 9–11.

Paulcke, W., Eine Besteigung des Oberalpstock (3330m.) mit norwegischen Schneeschuhen, *Alpina*, iv, 15 February 1896, pp. 25–7.

Paulcke, W., Eine Winterfahrt auf Schneeschuhen quer durch das Berner Oberland (18 bis 23 Jänner 1897), *Oestereischische Alpen-Zeitung*, xix, 1897, pp. 117–23, 129–35, 141–6.

Paulcke, W., *Der Skilauf*, Freiburg i.Br., Fr.Wagner'sche Universitäts-Buchhandlung, 1899.

Paulcke, W., Skilauf einst und jetzt, *Davoser Zeitung*, lvi, No. 4, 6 January 1936a, p. 2.

Paulcke, W., *Berge als Schicksal*, Munich, F. Burckmann, 1936b.

Paulsen, Gunder, *Minder fra Tiden omkring aaret 1830 til 1848*, Oslo, Halvorsens Bokhandel, 1944.

Paulus Diaconus, *Historia Langobardorum*, Hannover, Hahn, 1878.

Pauly, August Friedrich von, *Paulys Realenzyklopädie der klassischen Altertumswissenschaft*, Stuttgart, J. B. Metzlersche Buchhandlung, 1913.

Peary, R. E., A Reconnaissance of the Greenland Inland Ice, *Bulletin of the American Gegraphical Society*, xix, 1887, pp. 261–89.

Peary, R. E., *Northward over the Great Ice*, London, Methuen, 1898.

Pedersen, J. W., *Steinkjer 100 År*, Steinkjer, Steinkjer Kommune, 1957.

Petersen, N. M. (trans.), *Egils Saga*, Copenhagen, Fr Wøldikes forlagsbokhandel, 1862.

Petersson, Sven Plex, *50 Vasalopp*, Sveriges Radios förlag, 1972.

Planitz, Edler von der, 'Skisport i Tyskland', *Foreningen til Ski-Idrettens Fremme Årbok* 1913, pp. 74–5.

Planta, Albert von, *75 Jahre Skiclub Alpina St Moritz*, St Moritz, Skiclub Alpina, n.d.

Plantning av hickory i Norge, *Foreningen til Ski-Idrettens Fremme Årbok*, 1932, pp. 126–49.

Platou, Over det Udsatte Priis-Spørgsmaal, *Budstikken*, 181.2, No.17–18, p.1

Pliny, *Natural History [Naturalis Historia]*, London, The Loeb Classical Library, William Heinemann, 1961.

Polednik, Heinz, *Weltwunder Skisport*, Wels, Verlag Welsermühl, 1969.

Polednik, Heinz, *Das Glück im Schnee*, Vienna, Amalthea Verlag, 1991.

Polska och ryska skidor i Etnografiska museet i Warschau, *På Skidor*, 1936, pp. 350–3.

Pomponius Mela, *De Chorographia*, Stuttgart, B. G. Teubner, 1968.

Pontoppidan, Erich, *Det første Forsøg paa Norges Naturlige Historie*, Copenhagen, Gottmann Friderich Risel, 1753.

Powys, Llewelyn, *Swiss Essays*, London, John Lane the Bodley Head, 1947.

Præmie Skirendet i Skedsmo, *Aftenbladet*, 1 March 1870.

Præmieskirendet Huseby, *Aftenbladet*, 13 February 1879.

Prag, *Deutscher Eissport*, iii, No. 7, 1893–94, p. 45.

Prahl, G. C. C. W., En Skitur paa 35 Mile i 1824, *Foreningen til Ski-Idrettens Fremme Årbok*, 1946, pp. 76–83.

Pram, Christen, *Christen Prams udvalgte digteriske Arbeider*, Copenhagen, J. Softerup Schultz, 1828.

Premieopvisningen i bakke, *Foreningen til Ski-Idrettens Fremme Årbok*, 1894–5, p. 21.

Premieskirendet i Stockholm, *Norsk Idrætsblad*, No. 10, 12 March 1892, p. 56.

Prévost, Abbé, *Histoire générale des voyages*, Amsterdam, Chez E.van Harrevelt et D. J. Changuinon, 1777.

Procopius, *History of the Wars*, London, Loeb Classical Library, William Heinemann, 1961.

Profiler af skibakker, *Centralforeningen for udbredelse af idræt Aarsberetning for 1899*, pp. 227–32.

Pryakhin, A. D., Novye svedeniya ob abashevskoï kul'ture, *Arkheologicheskie otkrytiya*, 1970, pp. 62–4.

Pushkin, A. S., *Sobranie Sochineny*, vii, pp. 7–153, 'Istoriya Pugacheva', Moscow, Khudozhestvennaya Literatura, 1976.

Quale, Finn, Fra skiskolen i Briançon, *Foreningen til Ski-Idrettens Fremme Årbok*, 1903, pp. 51–60.

Quale, Finn, Fra Skirendene i Grenoble, Albertville, Chamonix og Morez 1909, *Foreningen til Ski-Idrettens Fremme Årbok*, 1909, pp. 33–53.

Quale, Finn, Skiløpning i Italien, *Foreningen til Ski-Idrettens Fremme Årbok*, 1910, pp. 74–6.

Quale, Finn, Skistøvelen, *Foreningen til Ski-Idrettens Fremme Årbok*, 1920, pp. 137–41.

Quale, Finn, Standardisering av skistøvlesåler og bindinger, *Foreningen til Ski-Idrettens Fremme Årbok*, 1934, pp. 150–1.

Qvigstad, J., *Lappiske Eventyr og Sagn*, Oslo, H. Aschehoug, 1928.

*Rapport Général, IImes Jeux Olympiques d'Hiver, St Moritz 1928*, Lausanne, Comité Olympique Suisse, 1928.

*Rapport Général sur les Ves Jeux Olympiques d'Hiver, St Moritz 1948*, Lausanne, Comité Olympique Suisse Sécretariat Général, 1948.

Ravdonikas, V. I., *Naskal'nye izobrazheniya Onezhskogo ozera i Belogo morya*, Moscow, Izdatel'stvo Akademiya nauk SSSR, 1936.

Ravennas Anonymus, (tr.) Joseph Schnetz, *Cosmographia: Eine Erdbeschreibung um das Jahr 700*, Uppsala, Nomina Germanica 10, Almquist & Wiksells Boktryckeri, 1951.

Ravenstein, E. G., *The Russians on the Amur*, London, Trübner, 1861.

*Recueil de lettres, Proclamations et Discours de Charles Jean*, Stockholm, de l'imprimerie de C. Deleen, 1825.

Refsum, Helge, Skityper paa Romerike, *Romerike*, 18 September 1930.

Refsum, Helge, De gamle ski paa Romerike, *Romerike*, 2 February 1934.

Refsum, Helge, Småplukk fra skihistorien, *Foreningen til Ski-Idrettens Fremme Årbok*, 1952, pp. 116–21.

*Regis Magni legum reformatoris leges Gulathingenses [Gulaþingslög hin yngri]*, Copenhagen, Ex Typographeo Thorstani Enaris Rangelii, 1817.

Regnard, J.-F., *Voyage de Laponie*, Oeuvres complètes i, Paris, Haut-Coeur, 1820, pp. 96–250.

Reichborn-Kjennerud, I., *Skiernes Brug i Felt*, Christiania, Grøndahl & Søns bogtrykkeri, 1905.

Reichborn-Kjennerud, I., Træk av vor skiløpnings Historie, *Foreningen til Ski-Idrettens Fremme Årbok*, 1907, pp. 67–80.

Reichert, F., Hur skidans form inverkar på riktningsförändringer i utförslöpor, *På Skidor*, 1958, pp. 225–40.

Rein, Jonas, *Jonas Reins Samlede Digte*, Kiöbenhavn Arntzen & Hartier, 1802.

Reisch, Franz, Mit dem Ski auf das Kitzbühler Horn, *Der Schneeschuh*, i, No. 1, 1 December 1893, pp. 3–4.

Reutenfels, Jacobus, *De Rebus Moschoviticus*, Padua, Typis Petri Mariæ Frambotti, 1680.

Review of the Year, The International Rules for Downhill Racing, *British Ski Year Book*, 1930, pp. 818–19.

Rheen, Samuele [1671], En kortt Relation om Lapparnes Lefwarne och Sedher, *Svenska Landsmålen*, xvii, No. 1, 1905.

Ribi, Adolf, Die Französische Skifahrer-Sprache, *Davoser Revue*, xvi, 1941, pp. 118–22.

Richardson, E. C., English Ski-running, *Foreningen til Ski-Idrettens Fremme Årbok*, 1907, pp. 119–23.

Richardson, E. C., Early Days, *British Ski Year Book*, 1920, pp. 10–14.

Richardson, E. C., *The Ski Runner*, London, Cecil Palmer, 1924.

Richardson, E. C. and Richardson, C. W., Davos as the Ski-er's Paradise, *The Courier Davos*, xvi, No. 25, 1902.

Richardson, John, *Arctic Searching Expeditions*, London, Longman, Brown, Green & Longman, 1851.

Richardson, Rickmers, Crighton Somerville, *Ski-running*, London, Horace Cox, 1904.

Rickmers, W. Rickmer, The Ski in St Moritz, *The Alpine Post and Engadin Express*, xli, No. 8, 1904, pp. 29–32.

Rieck, C. W., *Fra Fjeld og Hav*, Christiania, A. Cammermeyer, 1867.

Riese, Alexander (ed.), *Geographi Latini Minores*, Hildesheim, Georg Olms Verlagsbuchhandlung, 1964.

*Riksforsamlingens Forhandlinger*, Christiania, Grøndahl & Søns Boktrykkeri, 1914.

Risch, Friedrich (tr.), *Johann de Plano Carpini*, Leipzig, Verlag von Eduard Pfeiffer, 1930.

Risting, Sigurd, *Kaptein C. A. Larsen*, Oslo, J. W. Cappelens Forlag, 1929.

Rivas, M., Petit Manuel du Skieur, *La Montagne*, iii, 1907, pp. 6–8.

Rockhill, William Woodville, *The Journey of William of Rubruck*, London, The Hackluyt Society, 1900.

Rode, Leif S., Christiania skiklub – 75 år, *Foreningen til Ski-Idrettens Fremme Årbok*, 1952, pp. 101–5.

Roeder, Günther, *Urkunden zur Religion des alten Ägypten*, Jena, Eugen Diedrichs, 1923.

Roll, Karl, Norske skiløbere i Wien og skirendene der 5. og 6. januar 1896, *Foreningen til Ski-Idrettens Fremme Årbok*, 1895, pp. 126–38.

Roos, A. G. (ed.), *Flavii Arriani quae exstant omnia*. Leipzig, B. G. Teubner, 1928.

Roosen, Carl B., *Om Skiløbningen*, Trondheim, J. L. Sundts Bogtrykkeri, 1865.

Røraas-Ski, *Morgenbladet*, 5 January 1840.

Rosander, Göran, Ur skidans och snöskons historia, *Västerbotten* (1964), pp. 2–32.

Ross, Immanuel, *Kaptein Georg Prahl 1798–1883*, Bergen, Giertsen, 1896.

Rossetti, Donato, *La Figura della Neve*, Turin, Vedova Gianelli e Domenico Paulino, 1681.

Rougier, Mme M., Silhouettes d'Hiver, *La Montagne*, iii, 1907, pp. 101–5.

Rousseau, J. J., *La nouvelle Héloïse*, Geneva, 1782.

Rubin, Robert (ed.), *Final Report, VIII Olympic Winter Games, Squaw Valley, California 1960*, California Olympic Commission, 1960.

Rucki, Isabelle, *Das Hotel in den Alpen. Die Geschichte der Oberengadiner Hotelarkitektur von 1860 bis 1914*, Zürich, Institut für Geschichte und Theorie der Architektur, 1989.

Rüttimann, B., Dr Alexander Spengler als Kurazt, *Davoser Revue*, März 2001, pp. 29–35.

Ryd, Yngve, Varför hittar man skidor i myrar? *Samefolket*, No. 4, 1994.

Ryd, Yngve, Bo Östergren skidmakare, *Hemslöjden*, 1, 1998a, pp. 8–9.

Ryd, Yngve, Sommarförvaring i myren, *Hemslöjden*, 1, 1998b, pp. 10–11.

Ryd, Yngve, *Snö*, Stockholm, Ordfront, 2001.

Rydgren, Harald, Litt av Hvert fra Finnland, *Foreningen til Ski-Idrettens Fremme Årbok*, 1930, pp. 80–6.

Sabro, G. N., Skiløpningen før og nu i Østerdalene, *Foreningen til Ski-Idrettens Fremme Årbok*, 1934, pp. 119–28.

Sandaker, Bjarne, Sondre Nordheim, *Foreningen til Ski-Idrettens Fremme Årbok*, 1924, pp. 80–7.

Sandars, N. K. (ed.), *The Epic of Gilgamesh*, London, Penguin Books, 1979.

Sandberg, Hugo Rich, *Hiihtourheilu Suomessa*, Omalla Kustannuksella, 1891.

Sandberg, Hugo Rich, *Den finska Skidan*, Helsinki, Söderström, 1893.

Sandblad, Henrik, *Olympia och Valhalla*, Stockholm, Almqvist & Wiksell International, 1985.

Sario, Niilo N., *Revue Internationale d'Histoire Militaire* xxiii Edition Finlandaise Helsinki, Uudenmaan Kirjapaino, 1961.

Sars, E., Keilhaus opdagelse af Jotunheimen, *Den Norske Turistforeningens Aarbog*, 1872, pp. 54–65.

Savvateev, Yu. A., *Zalavruga*, Leningrad, Izdatel'stvo Nauka, 1970.

Saxo Grammaticus, *Historiae Danicae*, Soræ, Joachimi Moltkenii, 1644.

Saxvik, Kjell, *Skiidrett i Steinkjer gjennom 300 år*, Steinkjer, Steinkjer Skiklubb, 1985.

Schefferus, Joannis, *Lapponia*, Frankfurt am Main, Christiani Wolffii, 1673.

Schefferus, Joannis, *The History of Lapland*, Oxford, 1674.

Scheller, Johann Gerhard, *Reise-Beschreibung nach Lappland und Bothnien*, Jena, Johann Rudolph Stückers, 1748.

Schilling, Hj., Strøbemærkninger fra en militær skifærd, *Centralforeningen for udbredelse af idræt Aarsberetning for 1899*, pp. 215–27.

Schiøtt, Nils, Litt fra en fjelltur Julen 1890, *Foreningen til Ski-Idrettens Fremme Årbok*, 1934, pp. 153–4.

Schiötz, Eiler H., *Utlendingers reiser i Norge [Itineraria Norvegica]*, Oslo, Universitetsforlaget, 1970.

Schlatter, Corinne, Zwischen Hightech und Intuition, *Neue Zürcher Zeitung (Internationale Ausgabe)*, 31 December 2005.

Schmal, Felix, Die Ersten Wiener Skirennen, *Zwanzig Jahre Österrichischer Ski-Verein*, Vienna, Im Verlage des Österreichischen Ski-Verein, 1912, pp. 29–32.

Schmid, Yvonne, Davos-Platz: A New Alpine Resort for Sick and Sound, Licentiatsarbeid der Philosophischen Fakultät I an der Universität Zürich, 1998. Unpublished thesis. DBD.

Schneeschuhlaufen, *Davoser Blätter* 1891 Nos 1 and 2, 3 and 10 January 1891.

Schneeschuhlaufen, *Mittheilungen des Steirischen Radfahrer-Gauverbandes*, 15 October 1892.

Schneeschuh und Schlitten für Sport, Jagd und Vekehr. Von Max Schneider, *Deutscher Wintersport*, xiv, 1904–5, No. 10, pp. 117–18.

Schneeschuhsport, *Deutscher Eis-Sport*, ii, No. 9, 1893, pp. 67–8.

Schneider, Hannes, *Auf Schi in Japan*, Innsbruck, Tyrolia Verlag, 1935.

Schøning, Gerhard, *Norges Riiges Historie*, Sorøe, Heineck Mumme og Faber paa Børsen i Kiøbenhavn, 1771.

Schøning, Gerhard, *Reise gjennem en Deel af Norge i de Aar 1773, 1774, 1775*, Trondheim, A/S Adresseavisens Bogtrykkeri, 1910.

Schott, W., Über die ächten Kirgisen, *Abhandlungen der Königlichen Akademie der Wissenchaften zu Berlin* 1864, pp. 429–74.

Schottelius, E., Eine Besteigung des Dammastockes (3633 m), *Deutscher Wintersport*, xi, No. 5, 1901–2, pp. 39–42.

Schrenck, Leopold von, *Reisen und Forschungen im Amur-Lande*, St Petersburg, Kaiserlichen Akademie der Wissenschaften, 1858.

Schröder, Gustaf, *Om skidor och skidlöpning för jägare och turister*, Stockholm Alf. Samuelssons Förlag, 1900.

Schwach, Conrad N., *Samlede Digte*, i and ii, Christiania, R. Hoiids Enkes Bogtrykkerie, 1837.

Scott, Robert F., *The Voyage of the Discovery*, London, Macmillan, 1905.

*Scott's Last Expedition*, London, Smith, Elder, 1913

Scott-Hansen, Sigurd, *Fram diaries 1893-96* NBO Ms.8° 3423.

Seeberg, F. G., *Centralforeningen for utbredelse av Idræt 1861–1911*, Christiania, Emil Moestues Boktrykkeri, n.d.

Seeberg, F. G., *Centralforeningen for udbredelse af idræt 1893–1901*, Christiania, Steen'ske bogtrykkeri, 1901.

Sejersted, F. C., Fra de internationale skirend i Pyrenæerne, Auvergne, Schwartzwald og Vogeserne 1910, *Centralforeningen for udbredelse af idræt Aarsberetning for 1909*, 1910, pp. 76–85.

Seligman, G., *Snow Structure and Ski Fields*, London, Macmillan, 1936.

Senger, Max, *Wie die Schweiz zum Skiland wurde*, Zürich, M. S. Metz, 1941.

Senger, Max, *Wie die Schweizer Alpen erobert wurden*, Zürich, Büchergilde Gutenberg, 1945.

Setterberg, Karl, Från 1924 års Chamonixfärd, *På Skidor*, 1925, pp. 209–22.

Shukman, H.(ed.), *Stalin and the Soviet-Finnish War 1939–1940*, London, Frank Cass, 2002.

Siilasvuo, H., *Striderna i Suomussalmi*, Stockholm, Medéns Förlags Aktiebolag, 1940.

Simmler, Josias, *De Alpibus commentarius*, Zurich, Froschouerus, 1574.

Sinding-Larsen, Kaptein, Meldingsløp paa Ski, *Foreningen til Ski-Idrettens Fremme Årbok*, 1910, pp. 77–9.

Sirelius, U. T., Ueber einige Prototype des Schlittens, *Journal de la société Finno-Ougrienne*, xxx, No. 32, 1913–18, pp. 1–26.

Sirelius, U. T., Kourupälkäälliset sukset, *Suomen Museo*, xxxv, 1928, pp. 80–5.

Sirelius, U. T., Lumikengät ja sukset, *Suomen Kanssanomaista kulttuuria*, i, 1919, pp. 366–78.

Skelton, R. W. to Scott, R. F., 21 February 1912. SPRI MS 342/14/10. Skiing in Lenzerheide.

*Ski-Club Alpina St Moritz, Statuten*, St Moritz, Ski-Club Alpina, 1903.

Ski-Club Todtnau er Mellem-Europas eldste skiklubb, unidentified newspaper cutting, 10 January 1933.

Skidans brättning, *På Skidor*, 1941, pp. 285–6.

Skidforskningarna, *På Skidor*, 1930, pp. 391–2.

Skidlöparekåren på Karlberg, *På Skidor*, 1939, p. 405.

Skidlöpning i Australien, *På Skidor*, 1937, p. 400.

Skidmakare, *På Skidor*, 1940, pp. 349–52.

Skidor i Ostpreussen, *På Skidor*, 1936, pp. 349–50.

Skidslöiden hos dolganerne i Jenisejska provinsen, *På Skidor*, 1940, pp. 341–3.

Skidstavar, *Västerbotten*, No. 2, 1984, pp. 108–11.

Skidtäflan i Uleåborg, *Nya Pressen*, 2 March 1887.

Skidtyper, *Västerbotten*, No. 2, 1984, pp. 95–101.

Skifahrten in den Dolomiten, *Deutscher Wintersport*, xiv, 1904–5, No. 18, pp. 221–3.

Ski-ing at St Moritz, *The Alpine Post and Engadin Express*, 23 January 1904, p. 52.

Skiing International Races at Murren, *The Times*, 24 February 1931.

Skikart over Nordmarken, *Morgenbladet*, No. 583, 3 November 1889.

Skilaufen in Norwegen, *Deutscher Eis-Sport*, i, No. 18, 1892, pp. 135–6.

Skiløbene i Chamonix, *Aftenposten*, 29 January 1909.

Skiløbermøde, *Morgenbladet*, 14 December 1892.

Skiløbermødet, *Norsk Idrætsblad*, 20 December 1892, No. 50, p. 357.

Skiløbermødet paa Grorud, *Illustreret Nyhedsblad*, No. 13, 30 Marts 1862, pp. 54–6.

Skiløbningen omkring aar 1870, *Foreningen til Ski-Idrettens Fremme Årbok*, 1898, pp. 45–65.

Skiløber-Vise [Trysil-Knud], *På Skidor*, 1900–1, pp. 140–5.

Skiløbning i Frankrige, *Morgenbladet*, Morgen No. 739, 13 December 1902.

Skiløpning i 1860-aarene, *Norsk Skytter-Tidende*, 1 aargang, 1862–3.

Skirend i Amerika, *Norsk Idrætsblad*, 11 February 1888, p. 23.

Skirend i Hvitesejd i Thelemarken, *Aftenbladet*, 7 April 1868.

Skirenden, *Tromsø-Tidende*, 6 April 1843.

Skirendet ved Huseby, *Morgenbladet*, 14 February 1879.

Ski-running at the Crystal Palace, *The Times*, 1 October 1907.

Skis, *L'Écho des Alpes*, No. 3, 1895, p. 107.

Skisport auf dem Arlberg, *Deutscher Wintersport*, xi, No. 9, 1901–2, p. 86.

Ski-Sport in Davos, *Deutscher Wintersport*, xiv, No. 18, 1904–5, pp. 223–4.

Skitouren im Harz, *Deutscher Wintersport*, xiv, No. 11, 1904–5, pp. 124–5.

Skiudstillingen, *Foreningen til Ski-Idrettens Fremme Årbok*, 1895–6, pp. 16–48.

Skiutstyret gjennom tidene, *Tinn Skilag 1893–1993*, 1993, pp. 21–37.

Ski-Wettlaufen in Mürzzuschlag am 18 Januar 1903, *Deutscher Wintersport*, xii, No. 14, 1902–3, p. 143.

Ski-Wettrennen in St Moritz, *Engadin Express*, viii, 1904, No. 12, pp. 51–3.

Skjeldsø, Lars T., Skiløpningen i Gjerstad i gamle dager, *Foreningen til Ski-Idrettens Fremme Årbok*, 1922, pp. 160–2.

Sletsjöe, L., Cervantes, Torquemada y Olao Magno, *Anales Cervantinos*, viii, 1959–1960, pp. 139–50.

Slingsby, W. Cecil, Round the Horungtinder in Winter, *Den Norske Turistforeningens Aarbog for 1880*, pp. 87–107.

Slingsby, W. Cecil, *Norway the Northern Playground*, Oxford, Basil Blackwell, 1941.

Smith, Axel Christian, Beskrivelse over Trysild Præstegjeld i Aggershus Stift i Norge, *Topographisk Journal for Norge*, vi, 21 Hefte 1797, pp. 1–18.

Smith, Bernt Thomas, Mestertyven Gjest Bårdsen på ski i sørlandsheiene i 1820-årene, *Foreningen til Ski-Idrettens Fremme Årbok*, 1944, pp. 109–11.

Smith, Georg, Norwegische Skiläufer als Gäste im Riesengebirge, *Deutscher Wintersport*, xii, No. 11, 1902–3, pp. 108–9.

Smythe, F. S., The Popular Ski. British Prowess Abroad, *The Times*, 23 December 1933.

Snorri Sturluson (tr. P. A. Munch), *Norges Konge-Sagaer*, Christiania, Feilberg & Landmarks Forlag, 1871.

Snorri Sturluson, *Heimskringla*, (ed.) Finnur Jónsson, Copenhagen, S. L. Møllers Bogtrykkeri (Møller & Thomsen), 1896.

Snorri Sturluson, *Edda*, Copenhagen, G. E. C. Gads Forlag, 1926.

Snorri Sturluson, *Gylfaginning*, translated by Finnur Jónsson, Copenhagen, G. E. C. Gads Forlag, 1929.

Snorri Sturluson, *Snorres Konge Sagaer*, Oslo, Gyldendal norsk Forlag, 1944.

Snow-shoe Contest at Christiania, *The Field*, 22 March 1884, p. 421.

Snow-skate Race in Norway, *The Field,* 8 March 1879, p. 252.

Sognness, Kalle, Verdens største skiløper? *Foreningen til Ski-Idrettens Fremme Årbok,* 2001, pp. 89–91.

Solini, C. Iulii (ed. Theodor Mommsen), *Collectanea Rerum Memorabilium,* Berlin, G. Parthey, 1864.

Sommarström, Bo, Skidor och Spjut, *Fataburen,* 1964, pp. 224–8.

Sondre Nordheim, Et skiløp 15 mars 1866 *Foreningen til Ski-Idrettens Fremme Årbok,* 1924, p. 156.

Sørensen, Steinar, Ski og skibruk i Østerdalen, *Glomdalmuseet Årbok,* 1982, pp. 62–94.

Sørensen, Steinar, Den eldste skitradisjonen i Østerdalen, *Årbok for Trysil,* 1987a, pp. 87–104.

Sørensen, Steinar, Paa øjnnar, tænaski og tryer, *Alfarheim Årbok for Elverum,* No. 2, 1987b, pp. 176–203.

Sørensen, Steinar, Skifunnet fra Steinhaugmo og de skinnkledde skiene i Fennoskandias fortid, *Viking,* lvi, 1993, pp. 87–111.

Sørensen, Steinar, Skifunnet fra Utrovatn og den eldste skitradisjonen i Valdres, *Årbok for Valdres,* 1995a, pp. 155–66.

Sørensen, Steinar, Skihistorie i tusen år, *Foreningen til Ski-Idrettens Fremme Årbok,* 1995b, pp. 46–64.

Sørensen, Steinar, Daterte skifunn fra middelalderen, *Collegium Medievale,* ix, 1996, pp. 7–55.

Sørensen, Steinar, Helleristninger som skihistorisk kilde, *Adoranten,* 1997a, pp. 25–32.

Sørensen, Steinar, Langski og andor, *Foreningen til Ski-Idrettens Fremme Årbok,* 1998, pp. 23–45.

*Sport aus drei Jahrtausenden,* Basle, Friedrich Reinhardt Verlag, 1998.

Stadler, Herta, Die Skikante, Universität Innsbruck, 1936. Unpublished thesis, MZ.

Staib, Bjørn O., *Nanok,* Oslo, Ernst G. Mortensens forlag, 1962.

Steen, Tryggve B., *Det var en annen tid-,* Oslo, Johan Grundt Tanum, 1943.

Steiger, Alexander von, Pragel und Schild im Winter 1892/93, *Schweizerischer Skiverband Jubiläums Jahrbuch 1929,* 1929, pp. 53–8.

Steinsholt, Kjetil and Høihelle, Knut, *Sondre Nordheim fra Morgedal,* Trondheim, Tapir Forlag, 1993.

Steller, Georg Wilhelm, *Beschreibung von den Lande Kamtschatka,* Frankfurt und Leipzig, Johann Georg Fleischer, 1774.

Stenström. Fritz, En glömd Linnélärjunge i Alströmers Stad, *Svenska Linnésällskaps årsskrift* xv, 1932, pp. 13–40.

Stephanius, Stephen Hansen, *Notae uberiores in Historiam Danicam Saxonis Grammatici,* Copenhagen, Museum Tusculanum Press, 1978.

Sterba, Otto, Die Entwicklung der Fahr-und Lehrweise des schilaufes von 1900 bis 1945, Vienna, 1964. Unpublished thesis, MZ.

Stevenson, Robert Louis, *Essays of Travel,* London, Chatto & Windus, 1905.

Stockholms skidlöpareklubbs prisåkning, *Nya Dagligt Allehanda,* 25 February 1879.

Stoltenberg, Einar, Um skivyrket i gamal tid, *Syn og segn,* xli, 1935, pp. 413–20.

Stoltenberg, Einar, Dei gamle telemarkskiene, *Den Norske Turistforeningens Årbok 1937,* pp. 116–21.

Stoltenberg, Einar, Ski og skiløiping i Telemark i gamal tid, *Skien-Telemark Turistforeningens Årbok,* 1938–9, pp. 1–23.

Stoltenberg, Einar, Det norske skikorpset. Et 200 års minne, *Foreningen til Ski-Idrettens Fremme Årbok,* 1947, pp. 83–9.

Stoltenberg, Einar, Det norske skiløperkorpset 1747–1826, *By og Bygd* 6 aargang 1948–9, pp. 21–40.

Strabo, *The Geography,* London, The Loeb Classical Library, William Heinemann, 1969.

Studiosus Barhows Manuskripter RAK Danske Kancelli d 150: 1754–67.

Stunz, Hans, Skilauf, hochwertigste körperliche Betätigung Warnung vor seiner 'Denaturierung', *Les Alpes,* xl, 1964, pp. 262–7.

*Suidae Lexicon,* Halle & Brunswick, Sumptibus Schwetschkiorum, 1853.

Sund, Tore, Litt om skisportens geografi i Norge, *Foreningen til Ski-Idrettens Fremme Årbok,* 1941, pp. 68–72.

Svennung, J., *Skandinavien bei Plinius und Ptolemaios,* Uppsala, Almquist & Wiksell, 1974.

Svensson, Sigfrid, *Introduction till Folklivsforskningen,* Bokförlaget Natur & Kultur, 1966.

Sverdrup, Otto, *Nyt Land,* Christiania, H. Aschehoug, 1903.

*Sverris Saga,* Christiania, Den Norske Historiske Kildeskriftkommission, 1920.

Sviggum, Jens, *Skiløping i Grong i Historiens Lys,* Grong, Eget forlag, 1967.

Sydow, H., Zum Schneeshuhsport, *Deutscher Eis-Sport,* i, No. 8, 1892, 59–60.

*Symbole ad Historiam Antiquiorum Rerum Norvegicarum*, Christiania, Carl C. Werner, 1850.

Symonds, J. Addington, Davos in Winter, *The Fortnightly Review*, xxiv, New Series, May 1878, pp. 74–87.

Symonds, J. A. and Vaughan, M., *Our Life in the Swiss Highlands*, London, Adam & Charles Black, 1907.

Tacitus, *Germania*, London, The Loeb Classical Library, William Heinemann, 1970.

Talbott, Strobe (tr.), *Krushchev Remembers*, London, André Deutsch, 1971.

Teben'kov, M. D., *Atlas of the Northwest Coasts of America from Bering Strait to Cape Correientes*, Kingston, Ontario, Limestone Press, 1981.

Tegnér, Torsten, *Paris-Antwerpen-Chamonix*, Stockholm, Albert Bonniers Förlag, 1924.

The Arlberg-Kandahar Cup. Rules, *British Ski Year Book*, 1929, pp. 251–2.

The British at Davos III, *The Courier Davos*, xxxix, 1920, No. 5, pp. 3–4; No. 8, pp. 3–4; No. 9, pp. 3–4; No. 10, pp. 2–3; No. 11, pp. 2–3; No. 12, p. 3; No. 13, pp. 3–4; No. 14, p. 4; No. 15, pp. 3–4; No. 16, pp. 3–4; No. 17, pp. 3–4.

The Great Battle in Finland, *The Times*, 12 January 1940.

Theophanes, *Chronographia* (ed.) De Boor, Carolus, Leipzig, B. G. Teubneri, 1883.

The 'Roberts of Kandahar' Challenge Cup, *The Times*, 7 January 1911.

*Thesaurus Linguae Graecae*, Digital Library, University of California, Irvine.

Thevet, André, *Les singularitez de la France Antarctique, autrement nommée Amerique*, Antwerp, De l'imprimerie de Christophe Plantin, 1558.

Thevet, André, *Cosmographie Universelle*, Paris, Pierre l'Huillier, 1575.

Thomson, James, *The Seasons*, Oxford, Clarendon Press, 1981.

Thöni, Hans, *Hannes Schneider*, Innsbruck, Verlagsanstalt Tyrolia, 1990.

Thoresen, Distriktslaege, Nogle Bemærkningr. i Anledning af Sidste Premieskirend ved Huseby, *Morgenbladet*, 17 February 1881.

Thoresen, Skiløbningen i Christiania, *Morgenbladet* 14 February 1868.

Thörn, Folke, Räcker Skidvirket i våre skogar? *På Skidor*, 1942, pp. 134–8.

Thorp, Tyskerne og skisporten, *Norsk Idrætsblad*, xi, No. 44, 7 November 1893, p. 355.

Thudichum, G., Les skis Norvegiens et nos Montagnes, *L'Écho des Alpes*, Nos 2–3, 1896, pp. 47–64, 89–96.

Thudichum, G., Faut-il grogner ou se réjouir? *Schweizerischer Skiverband Jubiläums Jahrbuch*, 1929, p. 138.

Thudichum, G., Les origines du ski à Genève, *Association Suisse des clubs du Ski Annuaire*, 1935, pp. 101–4.

Thv., Skisport i Schweiz, *Norsk Idrætsblad*, xxi, 26 February 1903, pp. 94–5.

Tidemand-Johannesen, Øistein, Den norske Skiambulance i Frankrike, *Foreningen til Ski-Idrettens Fremme Årbok*, 1916, pp. 78–94.

Till skidans historia, *På Skidor*, 1945, pp. 288–90.

Tjerneld, Håkan, Cervantes och skidlöpningen, *På Skidor*, 1943, pp. 313–14.

Toftedahl, Hanne, Kjerringer mot strømmen, *Foreningen til Ski-Idrettens Fremme Årbok*, 1994, pp. 71–88.

Togan, A. Zeki Validi, Ibn Fadlan's Reisebericht, *Abhandlungen für die kunde des Morgenlandes*, xxiv, No. 3, 1939.

Tomaschek, Wilhelm, Kritik der älteste Nachrichten über den skythischen Norden. *Sitzungsberichte (der Kaiserlichen) Akademie der Wissenschaften (in Vienna)*. Philosophisch-historische Classe, cxvi, 1888, pp. 715–80 and cxvii, 1889, pp. 1–67.

Tomasson, Torkel, Några tanker om skidrännans och de oliklånga skidornas uppkomst, *Samefolkets Egen Tidning*, 1928, No. 3, pp. 21–4.

Tønseth, E. A., Fjellskiturenes 40 års jubileum, *Trondhjems Skiklubb Årbok*, 1984–6, pp. 30–3.

Torgersen, Leif, 50 km rennets historie, *Foreningen til Ski-Idrettens Fremme Årbok*, 1988, pp. 69–76.

Torgersen, Leif, A Tribological Approach to Problems of the Glide of Skis on Snow, *Senter for Industriforskning Report no. 870112-1*, 1989.

Torgersen, Leif, Bindingens-ideen som revolusjionerte skisporten, *Foreningen til Ski-Idrettens Fremme Årbok*, 1994a, pp. 38–41.

Torgersen, Leif, Fra kjellerkokerier til industri, *Foreningen til Ski-Idrettens Fremme Årbok*, 1994b, pp. 57–67.

Torgersen, Leif, Fra den antikke slalåm til den moderne alpinidrett, *Foreningen til Ski-Idrettens Fremme Årbok*, 1996, pp. 21–42.

Torgersen, Leif, De første Husebyrennene, *Foreningen til Ski-Idrettens Fremme Årbok*, 1997, pp. 28–47.

Torgersen, Leif, Hva myrene skjulte, *Foreningen til Ski-Idrettens Fremme Årbok*, 1999, pp. 24–37.

Tornæus, Johannis, Berättelse om Lapmarckerna och Deras Tillstånd, *Svenska Landsmålen*, xvii, No. 3,

1900, pp. 1–64.

Torres, R. Peyronnet de, A la Veille des Jeux Olympiques allons-nous réagir? *Le Miroir des Sports*, 7 February 1924.

Træffen, Aage, Et minneverdig blad fra historiens bok, *Foreningen til Ski-Idrettens Fremme Årbok*, 1949, pp. 13–26, 114–17.

Trotter, William R., *The Winter War*, London, Aurum Press, 2002.

Turnskue i Trysil, *Morgenbladet*, 2 February 1862.

Två gamla bilder med skidor och skidlöpare, *På Skidor*, 1939, p. 403.

Två hjältinnor vid de nordiska Spelen, *Idun*, xiv, 1901, p. 145.

Två par lapska skidor med stavar, *På Skidor*, 1938, pp. 377–9.

Tvinnereim, Jon, *Ski-idrett i Sogn og Fjordane*, Volda, 1998.

Twenty years ago. Davos winter sports in 1888/1889, *The Courier Davos*, xxx, 1909, No. 2, pp. 1–3.

Ueber Schneeschuhlauf i Böhmen, Skifahrten in Gaustad, *Deutscher Eis-Sport*, ii, 1892–3, No. 8, 7 December 1892, p. 60.

Ueber Skier, Bindungen und Skilauf, Für die Beibehaltung des Norweger Skis, *Deutscher Wintersport*, xii, No. 22, 1902–3, pp. 227–34.

Undset, Sigrid, *Elleve Aar*, Oslo, H. Aschehoug, 1934.

Unverzagt, Georg Johann, *Gesandschafft Ihrer Käyserl.Majest. von Groß-Rußland an den Sinesischen Käyser*, Lübeck, bey Johann Christian Schmidt, 1727.

Urdahl, Laurentius, Skilaufen, *Deutscher Eis-Sport*, ii, 1892–93, No. 24, pp. 174–7 and Nos 25/26, pp. 183–4.

Urdahl, Laurentius, *Haandbog i Skiløbning*, Christiania, Hjalmar Biglers Forlag, 1893a.

Urdahl, Laurentius, Paa ski over Hardangervidda, *Norsk Idrætsblad*, 7 February 1893b.

Urdahl, Laurentius, *Vom Skilaufen und Schlittenrutschen*, Christiania, Alb. Cammermeyers Forlag, 1893c.

Urdahl, Laurentius, I Styggeveir paa Fjeldet Midtvinters, *Aalesunds Handels og Søfartstidende*, 10 January–7 February 1894.

Urdahl, Laurentius, *Vinterliv paa Fjeldet*, Christiania, P. T. Mallings Boghandels Forlag, 1896.

Urdahl, Laurentius, 4 Uger paa Ski i de norske Höifjelde, *På Skidor*, 1902–3, pp. 93–117.

Urdahl, Laurentius, Roald Amundsens første høifjeldstur paa ski, *Norsk Idrætsblad* Julenummer, 1912, pp. 20–4.

Urdahl, Laurentius, Et Skirend paa Holmenkollen 1893, *Foreningen til Ski-Idrettens Fremme Årbok*, 1993, pp. 38–41.

Vaage, Jakob, *Ski-smøringens historie*, Skårer, Swix Sport International [n.d.].

Vaage, Jakob, Nordmenn innførte skisporten i Amerika, *Foreningen til Ski-Idrettens Fremme Årbok*, 1940, pp. 75–87.

Vaage, Jakob, Ishpeming er hoppløperbyen i Amerika, *Foreningen til Ski-Idrettens Fremme Årbok*, 1948, pp. 78–83.

Vaage, Jakob, Hvordan skiløperne i hovedstaden skaffet seg ski i det forrige århundre, *Foreningen til Ski-Idrettens Fremme Årbok*, 1949, pp. 118–24.

Vaage, Jakob, *Norske ski erobre verden*, Oslo, Gyldendal norsk Forlag, 1952.

Vaage, Jakob, De limte skis historie, *Foreningen til Ski-Idrettens Fremme Årbok*, 1962, pp. 10–20.

Vaage, Jakob, Skismørning gjennom tidene, *Foreningen til Ski-Idrettens Fremme Årbok*, 1963, pp. 19–32.

Vaage, Jakob, Skismøring i tiden 1914–20, *Foreningen til Ski-Idrettens Fremme Årbok*, 1964, pp. 95–110.

Vaage, Jakob, Skihopping gjennom 200 år, *Foreningen til Ski-Idrettens Fremme Årbok*, 1965, pp. 16–19.

Vaage, Jakob, Skibindingene gjennom 4000 år, *Foreningen til Ski-Idrettens Fremme Årbok*, 1966, pp. 42–53 and 1968, pp. 36-47.

Vaage, Jakob, Sportsforretninger i det forrige aarhundre, *Byminner*, No. 4, 1971, pp. 31–42.

Vaage, Jakob, Skimakerkunsten i det 19 aarhundre, *Norveg*, xv, 1972, pp. 139–74.

Vaage, Jakob, Da Nordmenn innførte skiene i Japan, *Foreningen til Ski-Idrettens Fremme Årbok*, 1974, pp. 95–8.

Vaage, Jakob, Skistavernes Historie, *Foreningen til Ski-Idrettens Fremme Årbok*, 1975, pp. 84–94 and 1977, pp. 16–23.

Vaage, Jakob, *Skienes Verden*, Oslo, Hjemmenes Forlag, 1979.

Vaage, Jakob, Det første landsrenn i Trondhjem for 100 år siden, *Foreningen til Ski-Idrettens Fremme Årbok*,

1989a, pp. 50–2.

Vaage, Jakob, Skade – Verdens første Dame skiklubb er 100 år, *Foreningen til Ski-Idrettens Fremme Årbok,* 1989b, pp. 66–7.

Vaage, Jakob, Skikongen Lauritz Bergendahl, *Foreningen til Ski-Idrettens Fremme Årbok,* 1990, pp. 65–71.

Vaage, Jakob and Kristensen, Tom, *Holmenkollen,* Oslo, De Norske Bokklubbene, 1992.

Validi, A. Zeki, Die Nordvölker bei Biruni, *Zeitschrift der deutschen morgenländischen Gesellschaft,* xc, 1936, pp. 38–51.

Valonen, Niilo, Den finska folkkulturen i Nordskandinavien, särskilt skidans historia, *Umeå Studies in the Humanities,* xxiv, 1980, pp. 207–33.

Valvasor, J. W., *Die Ehre des Herzogthums Crain,* Ljubljana, Wolfgang Moritz Endter, 1689.

Vecellio, Cesare, *Vecellio's Renaissance Costume Book,* New York, Dover Publications, 1977.

Veer, Gerrit de, *Tre Navigazione fatti dagli Olandesi e Zeelanesi al settentrione della Norvegia, Moscovia et Tartaria, etc.,* Venice, Apresso Gio. Battista Ciotti, 1599.

Veiledning ved arrangement af større skirend, *Centralforeningen for udbredelse af idræt Aarsberetning for 1905,* pp. 166–8.

Vereinigung Steirischer Skiläufer, *Deutscher Eissport,* iii, No. 3, 1893–4, p. 31.

*Verhandlung des Siebenten Internationalen Geographen-Kongresses,* Berlin, W. H. Kühl, 1901.

Verne, Rudolf J. and Hellström, Uno, Skidsporten i Canada, *På Skidor,* 1925, pp. 236–41.

Vesterlund, Otto, En skidlöperveteran, *På Skidor,* 1904–5, pp. 45–52.

Vieth, Gerhard Ulrich Anton, *Versuch einer Encyklopädie der Leibesübungen,* Halle, beym Kunsthändler Dreyssig, 1794.

Vigfússon, G. (ed.), *Icelandic Sagas,* Vol. I, Orkneyinga Saga and Magnus Saga, London, Her Majesty's Stationery Office, 1887.

*VII Giochi Olimpici Invernali Corina d'Ampezzo,* Comitato Olympico Nazionale Italiano, 1956.

VIII Internationaler Skikongress in Chamonix, *Amtliches Jahrbuch des Wintersports,* vii, 1926, pp. 50–3.

Vilkuna, Janne, Ancient Skis of Central Finland, *Fennoscandia Archaeologica,* i, 1984, pp. 31–40.

Vilkuna, Janne, The binding of the prehistoric ski from Mänttä, Finland, *History of Skiing Conference Holmenkollen,* Oslo 16–18 September 1998, pp. 70–4.

Vinje, A. O., Fjøllstaven min, *Illustreret Nyhedsblads Nytaarsgave 1862,* pp. 181–99.

Vinje, A. O., *Skrifter i Samling,* Christiania, J. W. Cappelens Forlag, 1916.

*Vinter-Exerceer-Reglement for Skiløberne i Norge,* Copenhagen, Johan Frederik Schultz, 1804.

Urdahl, Laurentius, *Vinterliv paa Fjeldet,* Christiania, P. T. Mallings Boghandels Forlag, 1896.

Virgil, *Eclogues, Georgics, Aeneid,* London, Loeb Classical Library, William Heinemann, 1967.

Volkovski'i, N.L. (ed.), *Tain'i i Uroki Zimnei Voin'i 1939–40,* St Petersburg, Poligon, 2000.

Voltaire, *Histoire de Charles XII Roi de Suéde,* Paris, Ernest Flammarion, 1917.

Urdahl, Laurentius, *Vom Skilaufen und Schlittenrutschen,* Christiania, Alb. Cammermeyers Forlag, 1893.

Vore Skiløbende Damer, *Morgenbladet,* No. 23, 13 January 1892.

Vorren, Ørnulv, Ski og skiløping hos samene, *Norske Skiløpere, Namdal og Nord-Norge,* 1960, pp. 159–65.

Vorren, Ørnulv, Med Samer paa Ski over Groenland, *Ottar,* No. 88, 1976, pp. 36–41.

Vorren, Ørnulv, Paa Ski i Nordkalottens Fortid, *Ottar,* No. 115, 1979, pp. 11–17.

Vorwerg, O., Der Schneeschuh-oder Skisport, *Deutscher Eissport,* ii, No. 11, 1893–4a, pp. 81–3.

Vorwerg, O., Die erste Schneeschuhfahrt über die Schneekoppe, *Deutscher Eissport* iii, No. 15, 1893–4b, p. 106; No. 16, pp. 112–13; No. 17, pp. 118–19; No. 20, pp. 137–8.

*Voyages de Corneille le Brun par la Moscovie, en Perse, et aux Indes Orientales,* Amsterdam, Les Frères Wetstein, 1718.

Wallner, Josef, Aufzeichnungen. Reminiscences of Conflict with Zdarsky, MZ, 1950.

Walter, F. W. von, En skidfärd för 200 år sedan, *På Skidor,* 1902–3, pp. 80–6.

Wancke, Folke, Några ord om skidlöpning i Stockholm under 1870–1880 talen, *På Skidor,* 1901–2, pp. 266–80.

Wangenheim, Wilhelm freiherr von, *Die Norwegischen Schneeschuhe (Ski),* Hamburg, Verlagsanstalt und Druckerei, 1892.

Wanner, Kurt, *Spiel und Sport in Graubünden,* Chur, Verlag Bündner Monatsblatt, 1991.

Was wir wollen, *Der Schneeschuh* i, No. 1, 1 December 1893, pp. 1–2.

Wassmannsdorff, Karl, Aus dem Turn-und Jugendleben in Schnepfanthal unter GutsMuths, von 1787–1839, *Jahrbücher der deutschen Turnkunst*, Neue Folge Band III, 1884, pp. 392–404.

Wasteson, Reidar G., Paa Skitur i Nordspanien, *Foreningen til Ski-Idrettens Fremme Årbok*, 1917, pp. 78–84.

Watkins, Watkin, Preface, *The Public Schools Alpine Sports Club Year Book*, 1909, pp.v–vi.

Weber-Bauler, Léon, Le ski, sa physiologie et ses débuts à Genève, *Les Alpes*, xi, 1935, pp. 29–33.

Weems, John Edward, *Peary*, London, Eyre & Spottiswoode, 1967.

Weibull, Jörgen, *Bernadotterna på Sveriges tron*, Stockholm, Bonniers, 1971.

Welhaven, Hjalmar, Skityper og modelski, *Centralforeningen for udbredelse af legemsøvelser Aarsberetning for 1893*, pp. 93–6.

Welhaven, Hjalmar, Skitypen, *Deutscher Eis-Sport*, ii, No. 18, 1893, pp. 144–5 and Nos 21/22, pp. 164–5., Welhaven, Hjalmar, Skipaabindingsspørgsmaalet, *Centralforeningen for udbredelse af idræt Aarsberetning for 1901*, 1894a, pp. 112–16.

Welhaven, Hjalmar, Om skiture i høifjeldet, *Centralforeningen for udbredelse af idræt Aarsberetning for 1902*, 1894b, pp. 198–202.

Welhaven, Hjalmar, Strøbemerkninger vedrørende skiidrætten, *Centralforeningen for udbredelse af idræt Aarsberetning for 1903*, 1894, pp. 162–5.

Wergeland, Henrik, *Samlede Skrifter I. Digte 1ste Bind 1825–33*, Christiania, Steenske Forlag, 1918.

Wergeland, O., *Skiløbning, dens historie og Krigsanvendelse*, Christiania, Trykt hos Chr. Schibsted, 1865.

Westerlund, G., Om skidlöpning i Frankrike, *På Skidor*, 1910–11, pp. 83–99.

Wettlaufer, John S., and Dash, J.Greg, Melting below Zero, *Scientific American*, February 2000, pp. 34–7.

Weyergang, Helge, På jakt etter en pioner, *Foreningen til Ski-Idrettens Fremme Årbok*, 1946, pp. 91–6.

Whitaker, Ian, Tacitus Fenni and Ptolemy's Phinnoi, *Classical Journal*, lxxv, No. 3, February–March 1980, pp. 215–24.

Whitaker, Ian, Othere's Account Reconsidered, *Arctic Anthropology*, xviii–1, 1981, pp. 1–10.

Whitaker, Ian, The Hyperboreans of the Ancient World, *Inter-Nord*, No. 16, 1982, pp. 139–57.

Whitaker, Ian, Skridefinnas in Widsid, *Neophilologus*, lxvi, 1982, pp. 602–8.

Whitaker, Ian, Late Classical and Early Mediaeval Accounts of the Lapps (Sami), *Classica et Mediaevalia*, Vol. xxxiv, 1983, pp. 283–303.

Wiklund, K. B., Några tankar om snöskors och skidors upprinnelse, *På Skidor*, 1926, pp. 1–18.

Wiklund, K. B., Ur skidans och snöskons historia, *På Skidor*, 1928, pp. 5–56.

Wiklund, K. B., Mera om skidans historia, *På Skidor*, 1929, pp. 252–79.

Wiklund, K. B., Den nordiska skidan, den södra och den arktiska, *På Skidor*, 1931a, pp. 5–50.

Wiklund, K. B., Kalevalas trettonde runa och balladen om den gottländske köpmannens älgjakt, *På Skidor*, 1931b, pp. 59–69.

Wiklund, K. B., Den Södra skidtypens källa, *På Skidor*, 1933, pp. 20–6.

Wiklund, K. B., Untersuchungen über die älteste Geschichte der Lappen und die entstehung der Renntierzucht, *Folk-Liv*, 1938, pp. 12–15, 16–47, 362–70, 371–404.

Wille, Hans Jacob, *Beskrivelse over Sillejords Præstegield i Øvre-Tellemarken i Norge*, Copenhagen, Gyldendals Forlag, 1786.

Willis, Göran, Traditioner i trä, *Turist*, No. 5, 2003, pp. 66–72.

Willoch, Jan, Om snø, ski og gli, *Foreningen til Ski-Idrettens Fremme Årbok*, 1973, pp. 71–81.

Wirth, M. H., *Davoser Fliegende Blätter 1872–73*, Davos-Platz, Buchdruckerei Hugo Richter, [n.d.]

Witsen, Nicolaas, *Noord en Oost Tartaryen*, Amsterdam, M. Schalekamp, 1785.

Wochenschau, *Davoser Blätter*, 1875, No. 3, 23 January 1875.

Wolcker, Erik von, Anteckningar om skididrott i Sverige f.Skidlöpningsf.tillkomst, *På Skidor*, 1925, pp. 66–103.

Wolf, Karl, Lesefrüchte aus einem Kriegsbuch des 17 Jahrhunderts, *Zeitschrift für Volkskunde*, Neue Folge Band 6, 1934, pp. 286–7.

Wolfgang, Friedl and Neumann, Bertl, *Offizieller Bericht der IX Olympischen Winterspiele Innsbruck 1964*, Innsbruck, Organisationskomitee der IX Olympischen Winterspiele, 1964.

Worm, Ole, *Danica Literatura Antiquissima*, Copenhagen, Melch. Martzan & Georg Holst, 1651.

Worm, Ole, *Museum Wormianum*, Leyden, Elseviriorum, 1655.

W. R. H., The Winter Sports of Norway, *The Field*, 17 January 1885, p. 73.

Wroughton, E., Memories of Ski-ing at Davos, *The Courier Davos*, xxxi, No. 14, 1909, pp. 17–19.

Wulfsberg, N., Lægens beretning fra Husebyrendet 1886, *Norsk Idrætsblad,* 17 February 1886, p. 31.

W. W., Schneeschuwettlauf des Ski-clubs Vogesen, *Deutscher Wintersport,* xiv, No. 18, 1904–5, pp. 224–5.

Wyder, Margrit, *Kräuter, Kröpfe Höhenkuren,* Zürich, Verlag Neue Zürcher Zeitung, 2003.

Wyler, Theo, *Als die Echos noch gepachtet wurden,* Zürich, NZZ Verlag, 2000.

Xenophon, *Anabasis,* London, The Loeb Classical Library, William Heinmann, 1968.

*X^{es} Jeux Olympiques d'Hiver, Rapport Officiel,* Grenoble, Comité d'organisation des X^e jeux olympiques d'hiver, 1968.

*Xin Tang Shu (New Tang History),* Peking, 1975.

Ytreberg, N. A., *Det gamle Tromsø,* Oslo, J. W. Cappelens Forlag, 1936.

Ytreberg, N. A., *Tromsø bys Historia,* Oslo, Tell Forlag, 1946.

Zagoskin, Lavr.Al., *Lieutenant Zagoskin's travels in Russian America 1842–1844,* Toronto, University of Toronto Press, 1967.

Zakhoder, B. N., *Kaspyiski svod svedenii o Vostochnoi Europe,* ii, Moscow, Glavnaya redaktsiya vostochnoi literaturi, 1967.

Zdarsky, Mathias, *Alpine (Lilienfelder) Skifahr-Technik,* Berlin, Konrad W. Mecklenburg, 1911.

Zeiller, Martin, *Regnorum Suecia, Gothiae, Magnique Ducatus Finlandiæ,* Amsterdam, Aegidium Janssonium Valckenier, 1656.

Zetlitz, Jens, *Poesier af Jens Zetlitz, Første Samling,* Copenhagen, Gyldendals Forlag, 1789.

Zettersten, Artur, Skidlöpare på ryska gränsen 1742, *På Skidor,* 1901–2, pp. 2–14.

Zettersten, Artur, Huru begagnades skidan under vårt sista vinterkrig på sv. botten? *På Skidor,* 1903–4, pp. 1–18.

Zettersten, Artur, Den södra skidtypen, *På Skidor,* 1932, pp. 7–27.

Zettersten, Artur, Jugoslaviska skidor, *På Skidor,* 1933, pp. 96-103.

Zettersten, Artur, Svenska skidtyper, *På Skidor,* 1934, p. 5.

Zettersten, Artur, Om militär Skidlöpning, *På Skidor,* 1940, pp. 14–28.

Zettersten, Artur, Den Skandiska Skidtypens ursprung, *På Skidor,* 1942, pp. 13–22.

Zettersten, Artur, Lapparnes Pilbåge som skidstav, *På Skidor,* 1944, pp. 83–9.

Zettersten, Artur, Vetenskapen och skidan, *På Skidor,* 1946, pp. 257–8.

Zost, A. I. (ed.), *Kratkaya sibirskaya letopis' (Kungurskaya),* St Petersburg, Tipografiya F. G. Yeleonskago, 1880.

Zur Ski-Ausrüstung, *Deutscher Wintersport,* xii, No. 8, 1902–3, pp. 81–2.

*Zwantzig Jahre Österrichischer Ski-Verein,* Vienna, Verlage des Österreichischen Ski-Verein, 1912.

Zweiter Schneeshuhwettlauf des Akademischen Ski-Clubs München in Garmisch-Partenkirchen, *Deutscher Wintersport,* xii, No. 14, 1902–3, pp. 142–3.

# Index